BATMAN

THE DARK KNIGHT

ARCHIVES ▾ VOLUME 1

BOB KANE

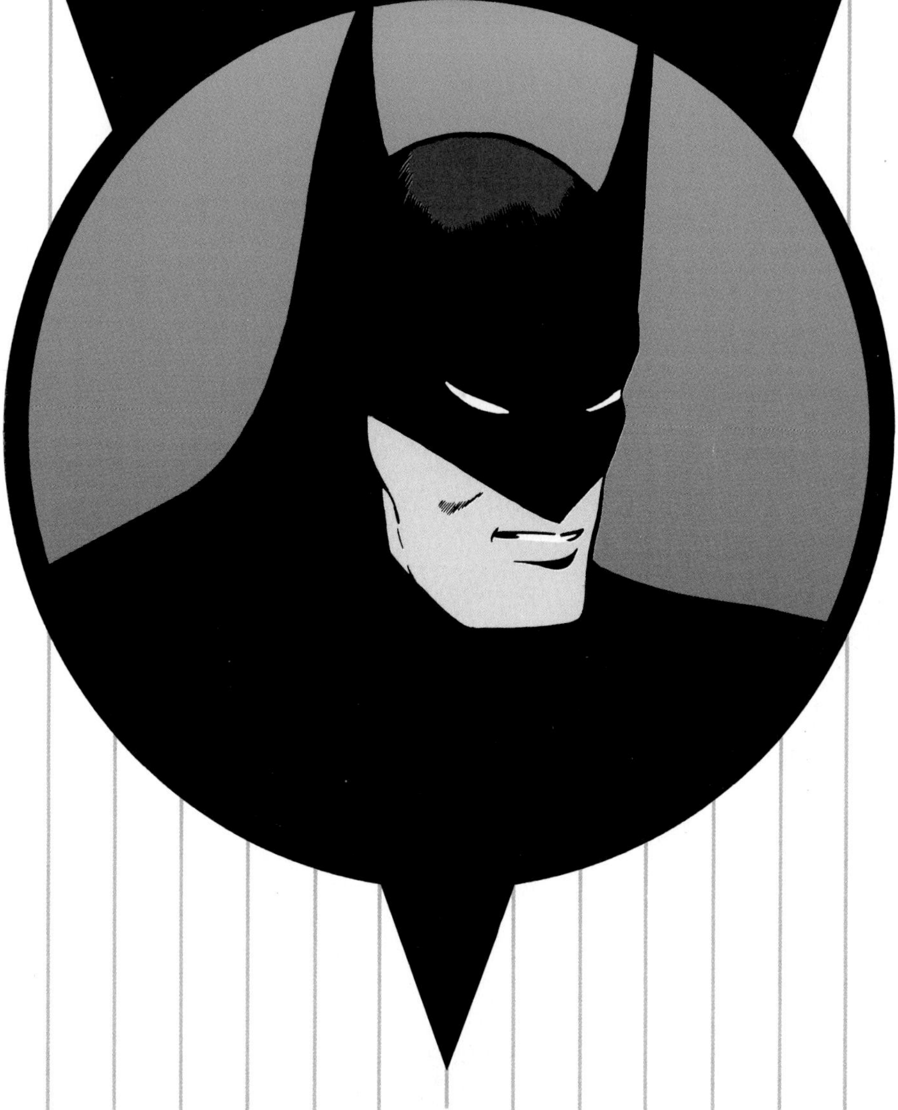

ARCHIVE DC EDITIONS

DC COMICS

DAN DIDIO
VP-EDITORIAL

DALE CRAIN
SENIOR EDITOR-COLLECTED EDITIONS

ROBBIN BROSTERMAN
SENIOR ART DIRECTOR

PAUL LEVITZ
PRESIDENT & PUBLISHER

GEORG BREWER
VP-DESIGN & RETAIL PRODUCT
DEVELOPMENT

RICHARD BRUNING
SENIOR VP-CREATIVE DIRECTOR

PATRICK CALDON
SENIOR VP-FINANCE & OPERATIONS

CHRIS CARAMALIS
VP-FINANCE

TERRI CUNNINGHAM
VP-MANAGING EDITOR

ALISON GILL
VP-MANUFACTURING

RICH JOHNSON
VP-BOOK TRADE SALES

HANK KANALZ
VP-GENERAL MANAGER, WILDSTORM

LILLIAN LASERSON
SENIOR VP & GENERAL COUNSEL

JIM LEE
EDITORIAL DIRECTOR-WILDSTORM

DAVID MCKILLIPS
VP-ADVERTISING &
CUSTOM PUBLISHING

JOHN NEE
VP-BUSINESS DEVELOPMENT

GREGORY NOVECK
SENIOR VP-CREATIVE AFFAIRS

CHERYL RUBIN
SENIOR VP-
BRAND MANAGEMENT

BOB WAYNE
VP-SALES & MARKETING

BATMAN CREATED BY BOB KANE

BATMAN: THE DARK KNIGHT ARCHIVES
VOLUME ONE

ISBN 1-4012-0375-2

DC COMICS
1700 BROADWAY
NEW YORK, NY 10019

A WARNER BROS. ENTERTAINMENT COMPANY
PRINTED IN HONG KONG.
THIRD PRINTING.

THE DC ARCHIVE EDITIONS

DUST JACKET ART RECONSTRUCTION
BY RICK ARTHUR

SERIES DESIGN BY ALEX JAY/STUDIO J

PUBLICATION DESIGN BY BRIAN PEARCE

BLACK-AND-WHITE RECONSTRUCTION ON
INTERIOR COVERS AND SELECTED STORIES BY
RICK KEENE

COLOR RECONSTRUCTION
BY BOB LE ROSE

TABLE OF CONTENTS

TABLE OF CONTENTS

*THESE STORIES WERE ORIGINALLY UNTITLED. THEY ARE TITLED HERE
FOR READER CONVENIENCE.

*Special thanks to Joe Desris, Martin O'Hearne, and Richard Morrissey for
their invaluable assistance in assembling this information.*

FOREWORD

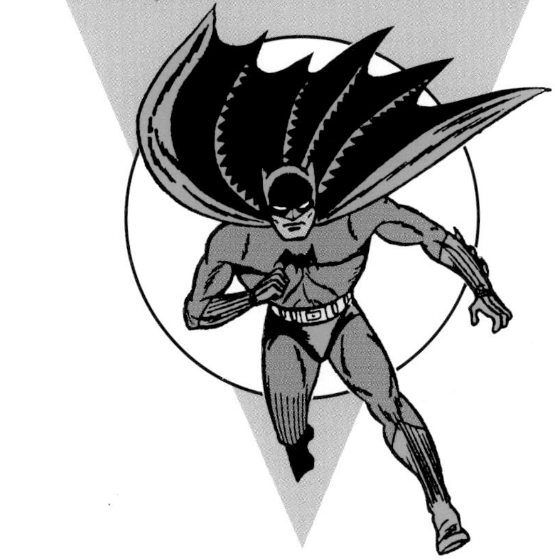

Batman was born in 1939. I followed a year later in 1940 and began following his adventures when I was five. My parents, like those of most children, would have preferred comic books with ducks in sailor suits to one about a millionaire in a bat suit.

Not me. What may have been unreal to parents was very real to a youngster growing up in the forties and fifties. Bad things happened in the night, but we saw The Batman as one who could protect us from forces we couldn't control—but *he* could. He had been seared by an unspeakable tragedy when his parents were murdered before his very eyes. His war against evil would protect others from that tragedy, and when young Dick Grayson's parents were murdered, Bruce Wayne adopted him as his ward.

I never remember anyone envying Dick Grayson's access to Wayne Manor and the wealthy life. Instead we all envied his association with Batman as his partner, Robin. Everyone knew Batman had superior intellect, detective training and wealth, but the youthful Robin got the use of the Batcave and even got to drive the Batmobile. When you are years from a driver's license it was obvious Batman's creator, Bob Kane, had held out the greatest treasure.

During childhood years it was not unusual to have long arguments over who was the better hero—Superman or Batman. For some of us the answer was easy. We all knew Superman, but who could *really* identify with him?

Batman had vulnerabilities but Superman did not. Sure, Superman's x-ray vision could be foiled by a clever criminal with lead shields and some archfiend would occasionally render him powerless with Kryptonite. But these were only temporary setbacks to one invulnerable to bombs and bullets and able to fly anywhere at any speed.

Batman we could identify with. He could be injured, imprisoned, foiled, or overpowered. A villain could escape from The Batman's clutches. In a later generation, the Dark Knight series shows a badly injured Bruce Wayne in a hospital after being machine-gunned along with his Gordon Liddy look-alike lawyer. The doctors ask him about the x-rays which reveal earlier bone fractures. Bruce replies that he fell from a tree as a child, and the incredulous doctor notes that he is talking about more than thirty fractures. Replies Bruce: "It was a very *tall* tree."

Every follower of Batman knows where each broken rib, bullet, stab wound, or consciousness-robbing concussion comes from! These are problems Superman could never understand.

The early Batman stories were written for youngsters. Only later were attempts made to bridge generations, especially through Frank Miller's Dark Knight series.

We all knew The Batman was a vigilante. In the early days the police were always trying to arrest him. Only later did he become "politically correct" as a regular officer of the law and then, eventually, became a vigilante "acceptable" to the police. He did what others could not. Search warrants were not an issue when Batman crashed through a door.

As one goes back to the early stories, Bob Kane's genius is apparent in laying the groundwork for characters that would exist, in various forms, for a half century. As notable is the collective genius of the writers, editors, pencillers and inkers of today's BATMAN, DETECTIVE, and DARK KNIGHT series who bring these early characters into the nineties.

The early editors showed an edition-by-edition evolution of both Bruce Wayne and The Batman. With today's emphasis on fitness, it is hard to remember the early Bruce Wayne with a constantly lighted pipe in his mouth. We also forget that before there was a Batcave there was an "abandoned" barn on the Wayne Estate which was connected, through a hidden trap door, to Wayne Manor. Today the Batmobile doesn't even slow down as it enters the cave through a hologram of a solid wall.

The Batmobile also changed. Originally, it was a nondescript car that evolved into a "powerful roadster," heralding an entire series of Batmobiles. I remember a distinctly early fifties vintage Batmobile skidding off the road, being wrecked, and being replaced by a car which still appears periodically in the background of the Batcave today. Certainly the early Batman didn't envision a car containing computer links, sophisticated communications, an alarm system with an ejection seat, a silent running mode and air bags.

One mainstay as important as The Batman's cowl is the Bat Signal. This floodlit signal in the night has survived satellite communication, two-way radios, cellular phones and, mercifully, beepers. Nothing has become more symbolic of the mystery of The Batman than the projected Bat Signal. Nothing reminds us more that Batman really exists in the night.

Batman's costume, car, home, cave, and other items have evolved while keeping the same basic foundations they had in the forties. The same can be said of his primary antagonists, who are some of the most recognized villains in the comics.

In the forties we met a woman burglar referred to as the Cat. Later we knew her as Catwoman, a.k.a. Selina Kyle. Catwoman's background and sexual orientation have shifted over the years, but both in the forties and in the nineties there is an obvious attraction between her and Batman. This character, more than any other, goes back and forth. She is both an opponent of Batman and the law, and an aide to Batman, if not the law.

The tragedy of Two-Face develops. A talented District Attorney named Harvey Dent (after an earlier, similar name was changed) becomes a schizophrenic good-evil person. Many see this as an obvious, but different, reflection of Bruce Wayne-Batman.

Dr. Hugo Strange is another who evolves from the mad scientist of the forties to a sexually perverted egoist nearly fifty years later.

The Penguin seems to bounce from the humorous—typified by Burgess Meredith in the television series—to the murderous psychotic Cobblepot, an evolution of fifty years. Whenever he appears The Batman recognizes a familiar, if not friendly, face.

No villain facing The Batman has been so consistently evil a vision as the Joker. No enemy in comic book literature is as well known and recognizable as the Joker. None so constant.

Bob Kane, and all who have followed him, have known the importance of the Joker. If the archangel Michael needs a Lucifer, then the Batman needs a Joker.

Probably no one has been "killed" more than the Joker. He has plummeted off cliffs, been stabbed by his own knife, drowned, crashed in airplanes, been shot, and otherwise destroyed. Everyone knows he will be back. No villain this well drawn disappears.

Joker, himself, has evolved in the Batman series until he has become evil incarnate. He has murdered legions. The Joker paralyzed Commissioner Gordon's daughter, and it follows that the Joker would commit the worst of all crimes, killing Batman's surrogate son, the second Robin, Jason Todd. The Joker would remain as the symbol of evil and lawlessness throughout BATMAN (which leaves Commissioner Gordon as a symbol of good and adherence to the law) until he finally commits a grotesque suicide in front of a fifty-year-old Batman in THE DARK KNIGHT RETURNS.

Some characters were added, expanded on, and remain. Vicki Vale has remained as one of Bruce Wayne's most important love interests, but she faces constant revisions based on the times.

Another relatively stable character is Alfred Pennyworth, the Wayne butler. Alfred did not exist in the earliest Batman series. With the exception of a period of strange behavior, Alfred has remained the only person who has been the one constant strong figure in both Bruce Wayne's and Batman's life. Unlike Commissioner Gordon, he is a part of both lives and identities.

And lastly we have Robin. While Robin appealed to youngsters who really want to help the Batman father figure, he hasn't proven as enduring as Bruce Wayne-Batman. For many reasons, some not really defensible, the first Robin was dispensed with and Dick Grayson went, like a tv series, to his own character in the comics as Nightwing.

Later it was decided that The Batman needed another Robin, and he took on a streetwise kid he caught stealing the wheels off the Batmobile. This Robin had a lot less appeal than the first one and was, after a Roman gladiator-like readers vote, killed by the Joker.

His death had the effect of establishing the Joker as the primary villain of the Batman series. It also established the Dark Knight as a man driven by a dark soul. Where the forties refer to him as a Dark Knight occasionally (and even had him intentionally shooting people to death before renouncing the taking of human life forever), it wasn't until the death of Jason Todd that The Batman descended into his own personal hell. It wasn't until two generations after the first Batman series that we were to learn how dark the soul and the struggle of the Dark Knight would be.

Throughout the years Batman has really spanned the generations. Today he tackles everything from drug abuse to intolerance. In a simpler time what were seen as America's virtues was emphasized. There was even a dream sequence where a grown-up Robin realizes why he wants to teach his son to obey as his guardian, Bruce Wayne, taught him (and ends up mowing the lawn as punishment for not obeying—a scene that every young person can identify with).

In writing these pages, the questions occur how the Batman kept my and others' attention for all these years—from my days as a youngster in a small city in Vermont to the U.S. Senate.

I have a specially drawn Batman edition provided by the brilliant folks at DC Comics. In it Batman and I discuss bedtime reading. I tell him I read Batman late at night—he says he curls up in the Batcave with the Congressional Record.

Having read both, there are days when I think I made the better choice.

—PATRICK LEAHY
United States Senator

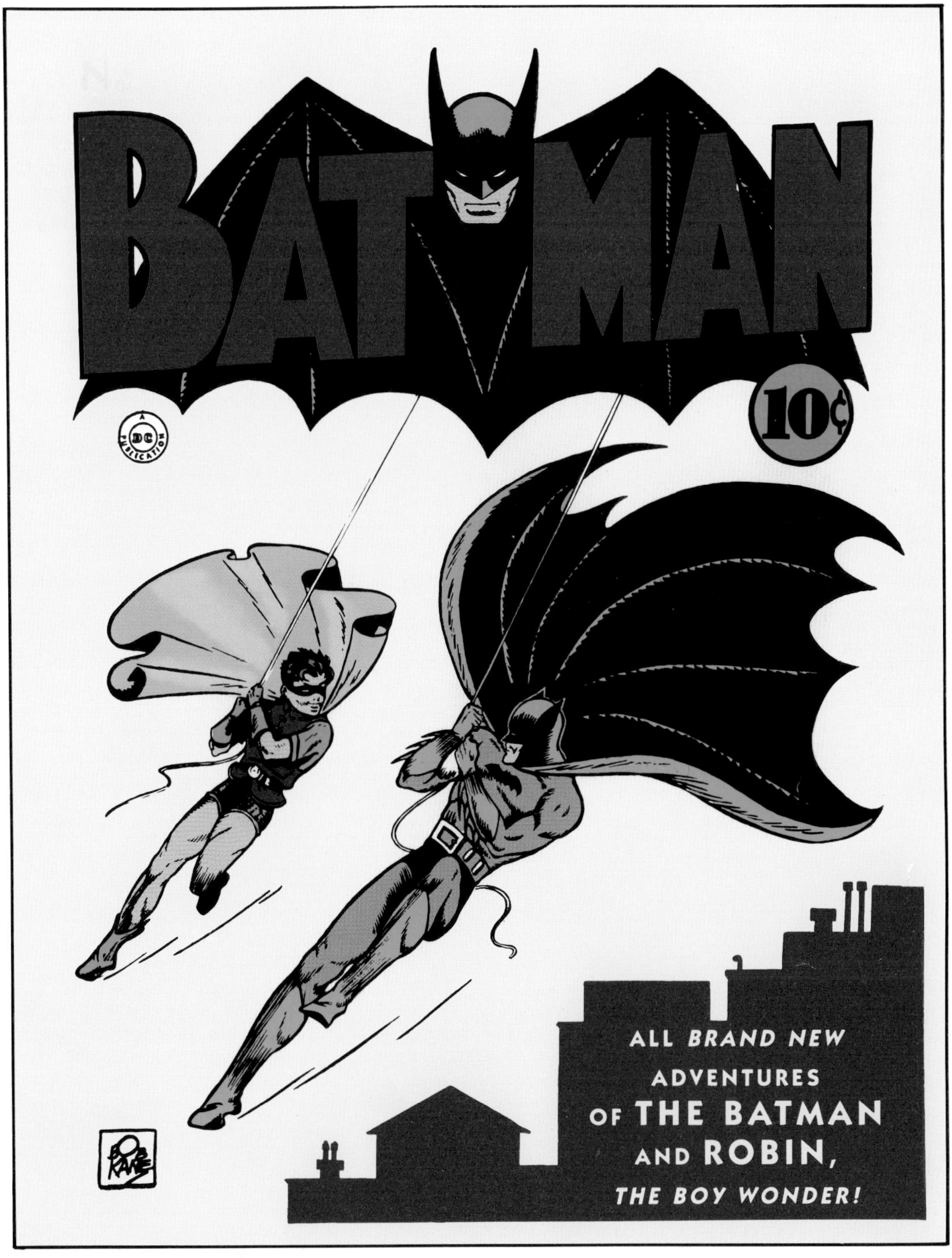
BATMAN
10¢
A DC PUBLICATION
ALL BRAND NEW
ADVENTURES
OF THE BATMAN
AND ROBIN,
THE BOY WONDER!
BOB KANE

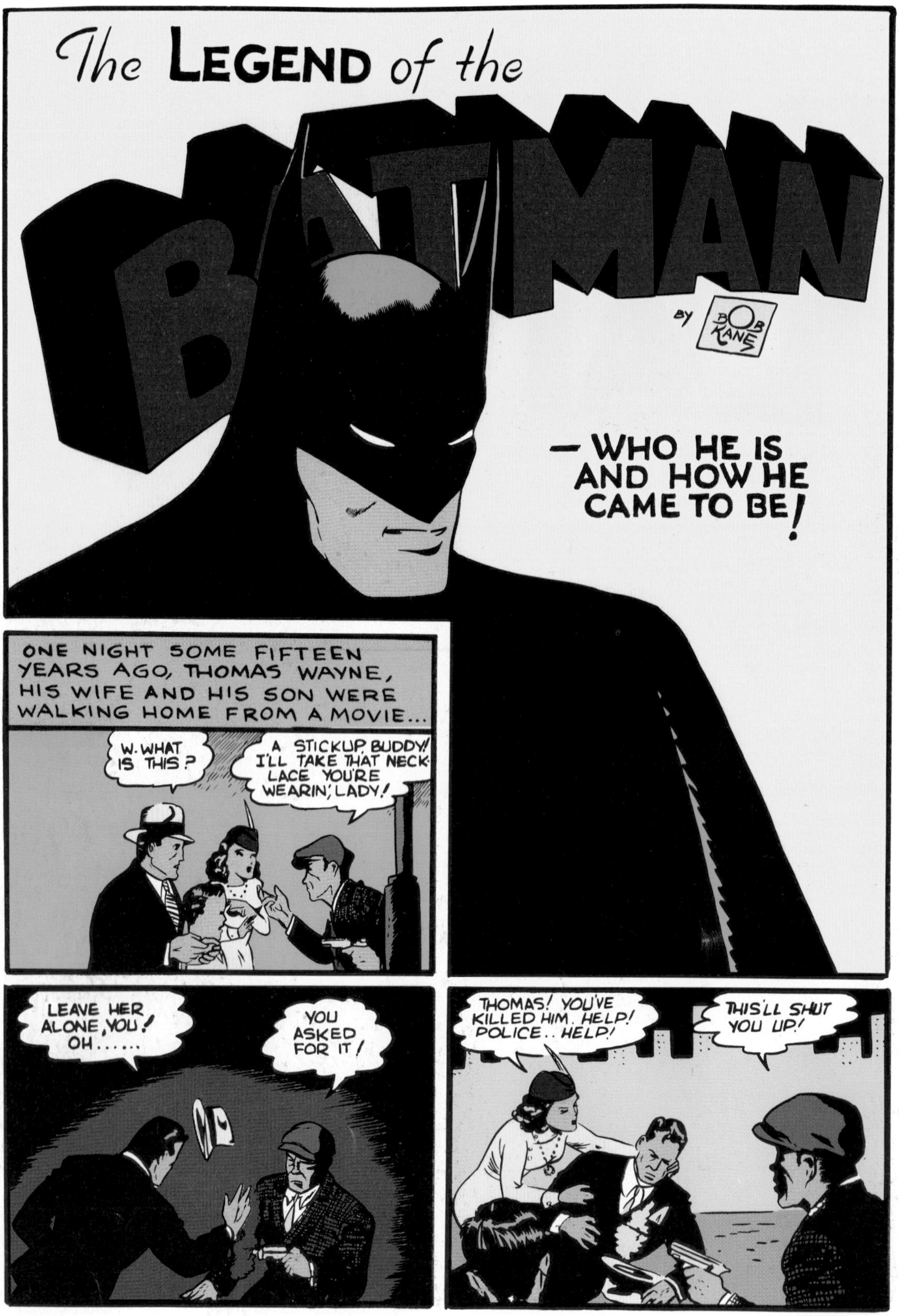
The LEGEND of the
BATMAN
BY BOB KANE
— WHO HE IS AND HOW HE CAME TO BE!
ONE NIGHT SOME FIFTEEN YEARS AGO, THOMAS WAYNE, HIS WIFE AND HIS SON WERE WALKING HOME FROM A MOVIE...
W. WHAT IS THIS?
A STICKUP, BUDDY! I'LL TAKE THAT NECKLACE YOU'RE WEARIN', LADY!
LEAVE HER ALONE, YOU! OH......
YOU ASKED FOR IT!
THOMAS! YOU'VE KILLED HIM. HELP! POLICE.. HELP!
THIS'LL SHUT YOU UP!

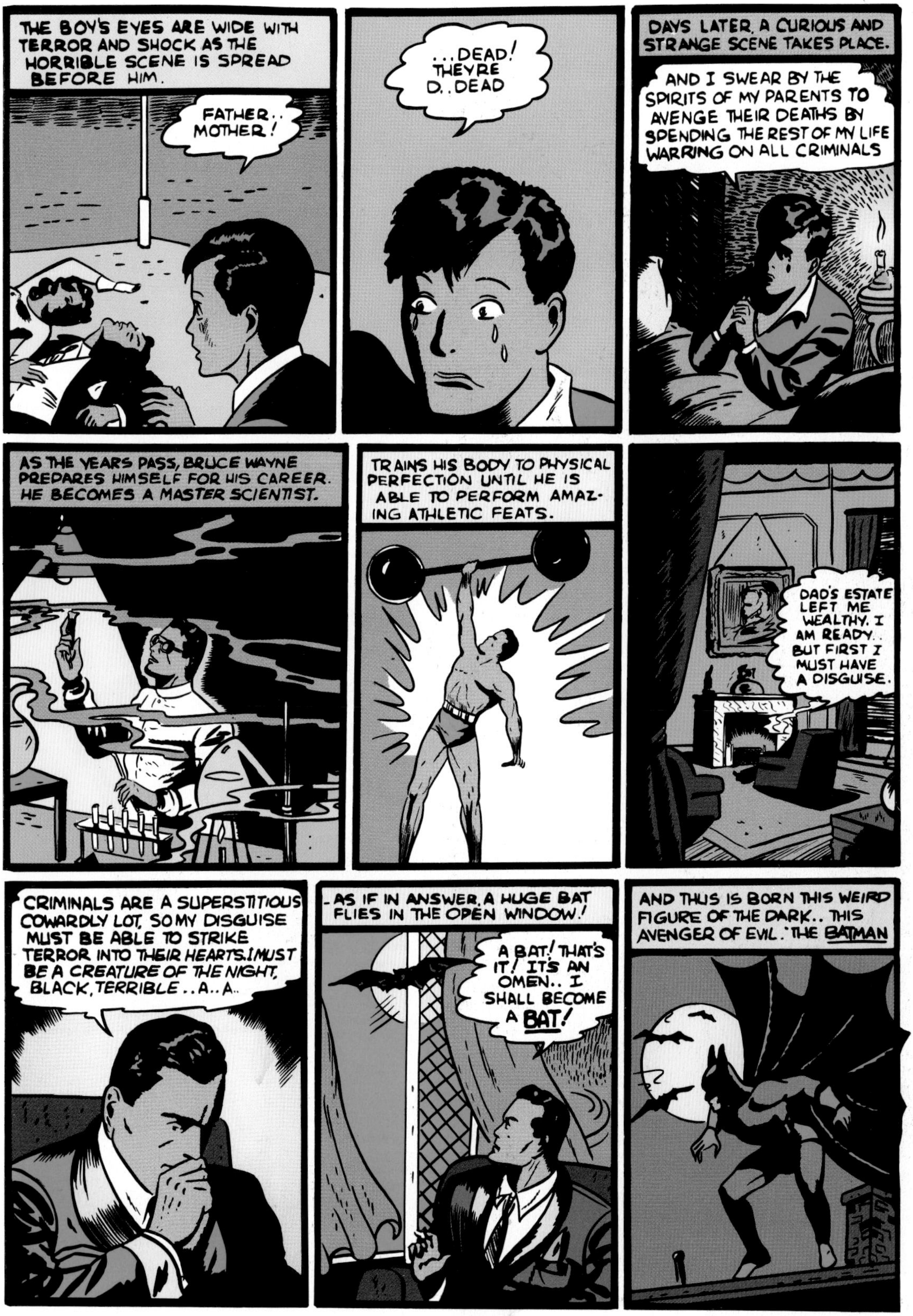
THE BOY'S EYES ARE WIDE WITH TERROR AND SHOCK AS THE HORRIBLE SCENE IS SPREAD BEFORE HIM.
FATHER.. MOTHER!
...DEAD! THEYRE D..DEAD
DAYS LATER, A CURIOUS AND STRANGE SCENE TAKES PLACE.
AND I SWEAR BY THE SPIRITS OF MY PARENTS TO AVENGE THEIR DEATHS BY SPENDING THE REST OF MY LIFE WARRING ON ALL CRIMINALS
AS THE YEARS PASS, BRUCE WAYNE PREPARES HIMSELF FOR HIS CAREER. HE BECOMES A MASTER SCIENTIST.
TRAINS HIS BODY TO PHYSICAL PERFECTION UNTIL HE IS ABLE TO PERFORM AMAZING ATHLETIC FEATS.
DAD'S ESTATE LEFT ME WEALTHY. I AM READY.. BUT FIRST I MUST HAVE A DISGUISE.
CRIMINALS ARE A SUPERSTITIOUS COWARDLY LOT, SO MY DISGUISE MUST BE ABLE TO STRIKE TERROR INTO THEIR HEARTS. I MUST BE A CREATURE OF THE NIGHT, BLACK, TERRIBLE..A..A..
-AS IF IN ANSWER, A HUGE BAT FLIES IN THE OPEN WINDOW!
A BAT! THAT'S IT! IT'S AN OMEN.. I SHALL BECOME A BAT!
AND THUS IS BORN THIS WEIRD FIGURE OF THE DARK.. THIS AVENGER OF EVIL, "THE BATMAN"

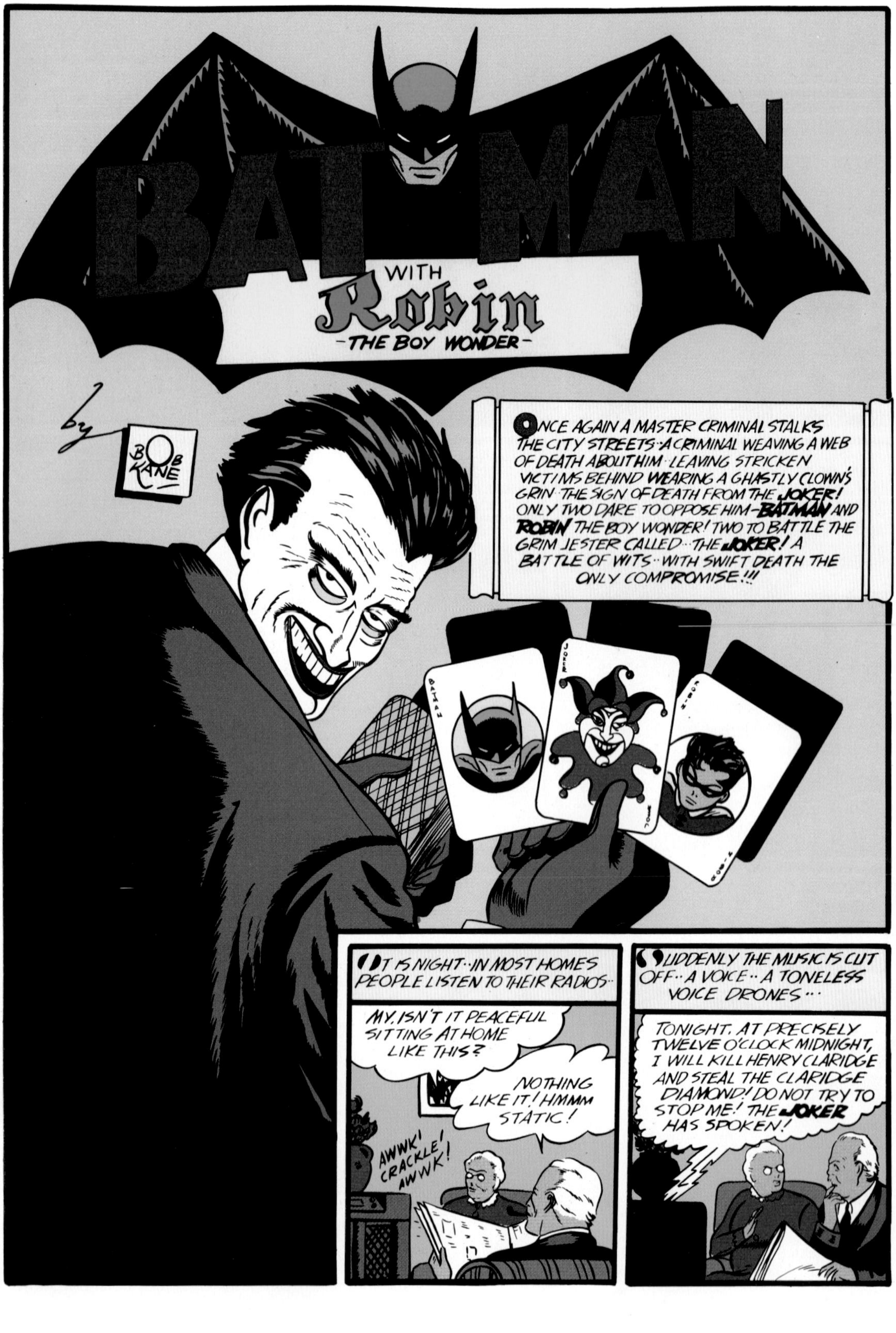
BATMAN
WITH
Robin
-THE BOY WONDER-
by BOB KANE
ONCE AGAIN A MASTER CRIMINAL STALKS THE CITY STREETS··A CRIMINAL WEAVING A WEB OF DEATH ABOUT HIM··LEAVING STRICKEN VICTIMS BEHIND WEARING A GHASTLY CLOWN'S GRIN··THE SIGN OF DEATH FROM THE JOKER! ONLY TWO DARE TO OPPOSE HIM-BATMAN AND ROBIN THE BOY WONDER! TWO TO BATTLE THE GRIM JESTER CALLED··THE JOKER! A BATTLE OF WITS··WITH SWIFT DEATH THE ONLY COMPROMISE!!!
BATMAN
JOKER
ROBIN
IT IS NIGHT··IN MOST HOMES PEOPLE LISTEN TO THEIR RADIOS··
MY, ISN'T IT PEACEFUL SITTING AT HOME LIKE THIS?
NOTHING LIKE IT! HMMM STATIC!
AWWK! CRACKLE! AWWK!
SUDDENLY THE MUSIC IS CUT OFF··A VOICE··A TONELESS VOICE DRONES···
TONIGHT, AT PRECISELY TWELVE O'CLOCK MIDNIGHT, I WILL KILL HENRY CLARIDGE AND STEAL THE CLARIDGE DIAMOND! DO NOT TRY TO STOP ME! THE JOKER HAS SPOKEN!

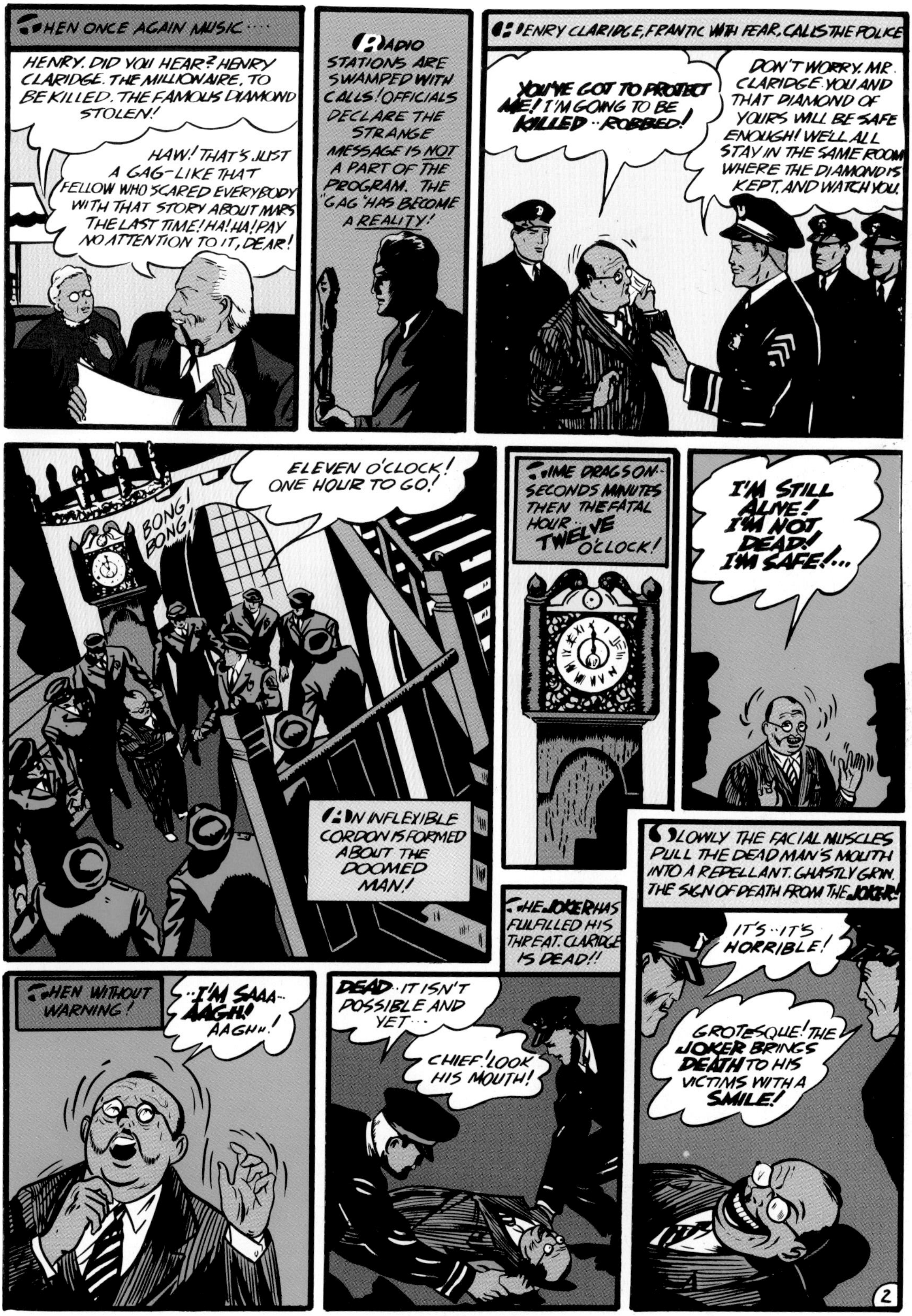
THEN ONCE AGAIN MUSIC....
HENRY. DID YOU HEAR? HENRY CLARIDGE, THE MILLIONAIRE, TO BE KILLED. THE FAMOUS DIAMOND STOLEN!
HAW! THAT'S JUST A GAG-LIKE THAT FELLOW WHO SCARED EVERYBODY WITH THAT STORY ABOUT MARS THE LAST TIME! HA! HA! PAY NO ATTENTION TO IT, DEAR!
RADIO STATIONS ARE SWAMPED WITH CALLS! OFFICIALS DECLARE THE STRANGE MESSAGE IS NOT A PART OF THE PROGRAM. THE "GAG" HAS BECOME A REALITY!
HENRY CLARIDGE, FRANTIC WITH FEAR, CALLS THE POLICE
YOU'VE GOT TO PROTECT ME! I'M GOING TO BE KILLED..ROBBED!
DON'T WORRY, MR. CLARIDGE. YOU AND THAT DIAMOND OF YOURS WILL BE SAFE ENOUGH! WE'LL ALL STAY IN THE SAME ROOM WHERE THE DIAMOND IS KEPT, AND WATCH YOU.
BONG! BONG!
ELEVEN O'CLOCK! ONE HOUR TO GO!
AN INFLEXIBLE CORDON IS FORMED ABOUT THE DOOMED MAN!
TIME DRAGS ON-- SECONDS MINUTES THEN THE FATAL HOUR... TWELVE O'CLOCK!
I'M STILL ALIVE! I'M NOT DEAD! I'M SAFE!...
THEN WITHOUT WARNING!
..I'M SAAA-- AAGH! AAGH..!
THE JOKER HAS FULFILLED HIS THREAT. CLARIDGE IS DEAD!!
DEAD.. IT ISN'T POSSIBLE AND YET...
CHIEF! LOOK HIS MOUTH!
SLOWLY THE FACIAL MUSCLES PULL THE DEAD MAN'S MOUTH INTO A REPELLANT, GHASTLY GRIN. THE SIGN OF DEATH FROM THE JOKER!
IT'S.. IT'S HORRIBLE!
GROTESQUE! THE JOKER BRINGS DEATH TO HIS VICTIMS WITH A SMILE!
2

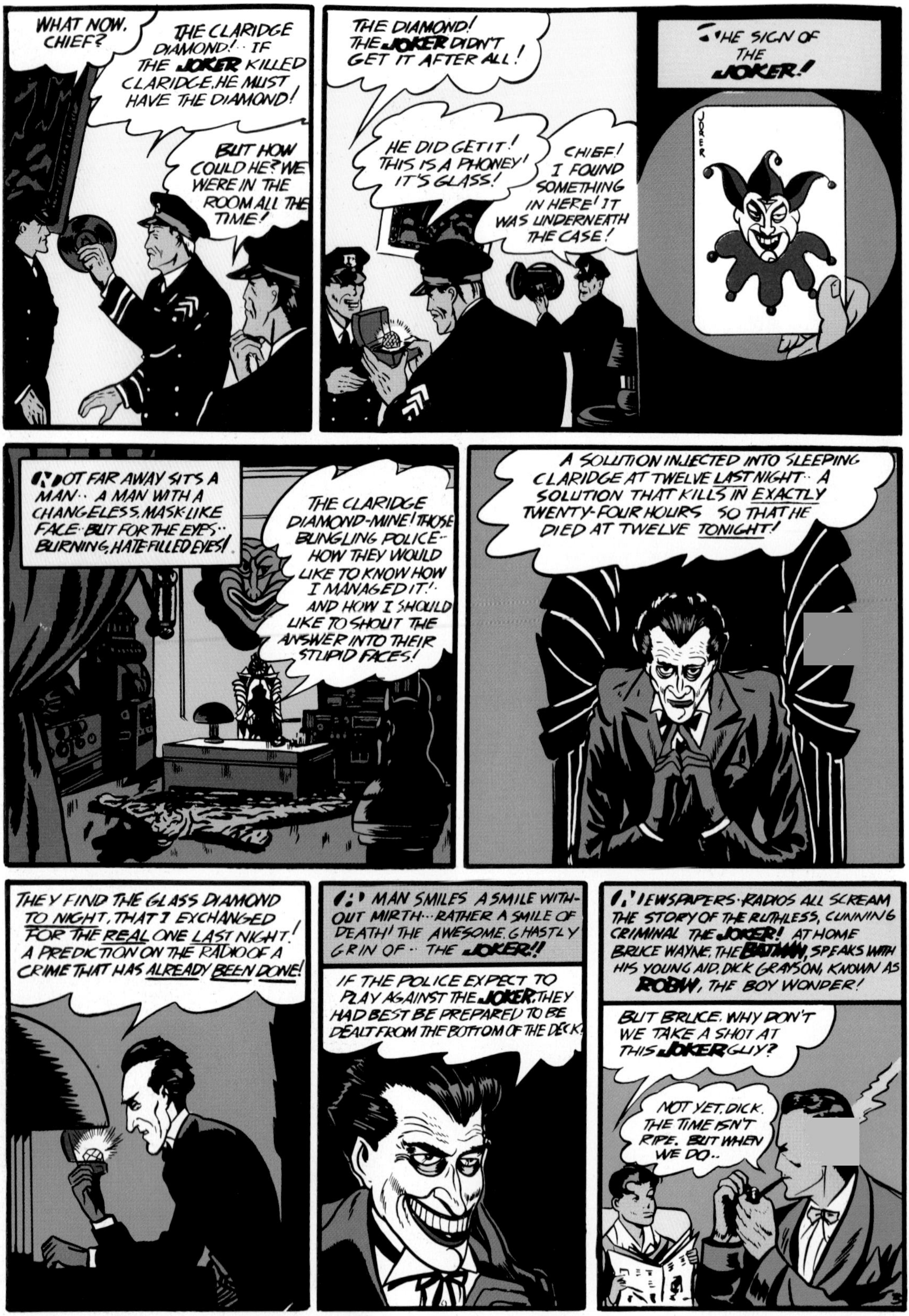
WHAT NOW, CHIEF?
THE CLARIDGE DIAMOND!.. IF THE JOKER KILLED CLARIDGE, HE MUST HAVE THE DIAMOND!
BUT HOW COULD HE? WE WERE IN THE ROOM ALL THE TIME!
THE DIAMOND! THE JOKER DIDN'T GET IT AFTER ALL!
HE DID GET IT! THIS IS A PHONEY! IT'S GLASS!
CHIEF! I FOUND SOMETHING IN HERE! IT WAS UNDERNEATH THE CASE!
THE SIGN OF THE JOKER!
JOKER
NOT FAR AWAY SITS A MAN.. A MAN WITH A CHANGELESS, MASK-LIKE FACE.. BUT FOR THE EYES.. BURNING, HATE-FILLED EYES!
THE CLARIDGE DIAMOND-MINE! THOSE BUNGLING POLICE.. HOW THEY WOULD LIKE TO KNOW HOW I MANAGED IT!.. AND HOW I SHOULD LIKE TO SHOUT THE ANSWER INTO THEIR STUPID FACES!
A SOLUTION INJECTED INTO SLEEPING CLARIDGE AT TWELVE LAST NIGHT.. A SOLUTION THAT KILLS IN EXACTLY TWENTY-FOUR HOURS SO THAT HE DIED AT TWELVE TONIGHT!
THEY FIND THE GLASS DIAMOND TO NIGHT, THAT I EXCHANGED FOR THE REAL ONE LAST NIGHT! A PREDICTION ON THE RADIO OF A CRIME THAT HAS ALREADY BEEN DONE!
A MAN SMILES A SMILE WITHOUT MIRTH.. RATHER A SMILE OF DEATH! THE AWESOME, GHASTLY GRIN OF.. THE JOKER!!
IF THE POLICE EXPECT TO PLAY AGAINST THE JOKER, THEY HAD BEST BE PREPARED TO BE DEALT FROM THE BOTTOM OF THE DECK!
NEWSPAPERS.. RADIOS ALL SCREAM THE STORY OF THE RUTHLESS, CUNNING CRIMINAL THE JOKER! AT HOME BRUCE WAYNE, THE BATMAN, SPEAKS WITH HIS YOUNG AID, DICK GRAYSON, KNOWN AS ROBIN, THE BOY WONDER!
BUT BRUCE, WHY DON'T WE TAKE A SHOT AT THIS JOKER GUY?
NOT YET, DICK. THE TIME ISN'T RIPE. BUT WHEN WE DO..

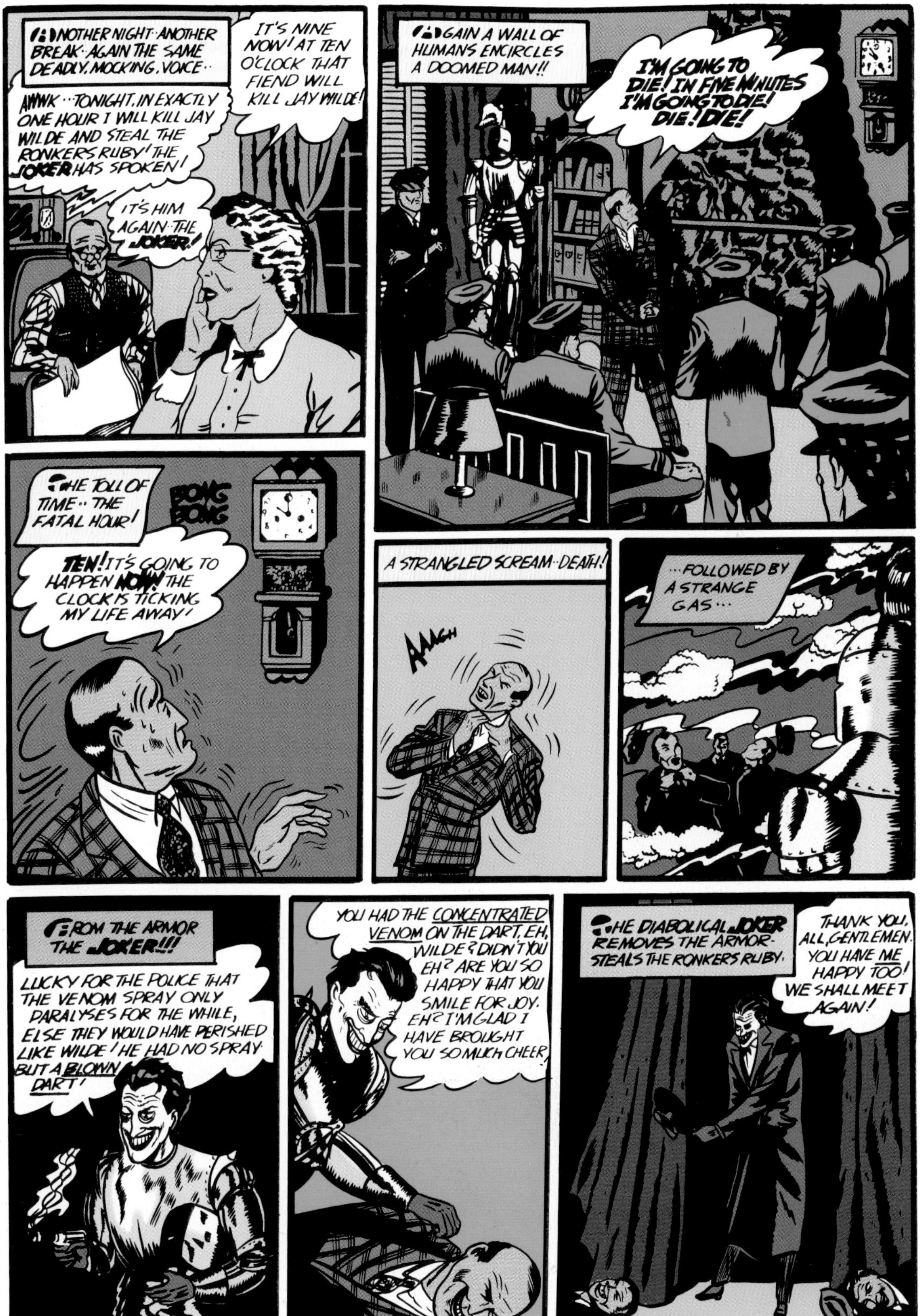
ANOTHER NIGHT - ANOTHER BREAK - AGAIN THE SAME DEADLY, MOCKING, VOICE --
AWWK -- TONIGHT, IN EXACTLY ONE HOUR I WILL KILL JAY WILDE AND STEAL THE RONKERS RUBY! THE JOKER HAS SPOKEN!
IT'S NINE NOW! AT TEN O'CLOCK THAT FIEND WILL KILL JAY WILDE!
IT'S HIM AGAIN - THE JOKER!
AGAIN A WALL OF HUMANS ENCIRCLES A DOOMED MAN!!
I'M GOING TO DIE! IN FIVE MINUTES I'M GOING TO DIE! DIE! DIE!
THE TOLL OF TIME -- THE FATAL HOUR!
BONG BONG
TEN! IT'S GOING TO HAPPEN NOW! THE CLOCK IS TICKING MY LIFE AWAY!
A STRANGLED SCREAM - DEATH!
AAAGH
...FOLLOWED BY A STRANGE GAS...
FROM THE ARMOR THE JOKER!!!
LUCKY FOR THE POLICE THAT THE VENOM SPRAY ONLY PARALYSES FOR THE WHILE, ELSE THEY WOULD HAVE PERISHED LIKE WILDE! HE HAD NO SPRAY - BUT A BLOWN DART!
YOU HAD THE CONCENTRATED VENOM ON THE DART, EH, WILDE? DIDN'T YOU EH? ARE YOU SO HAPPY THAT YOU SMILE FOR JOY. EH? I'M GLAD I HAVE BROUGHT YOU SO MUCH CHEER!
THE DIABOLICAL JOKER REMOVES THE ARMOR - STEALS THE RONKERS RUBY.
THANK YOU, ALL, GENTLEMEN. YOU HAVE ME HAPPY TOO! WE SHALL MEET AGAIN!

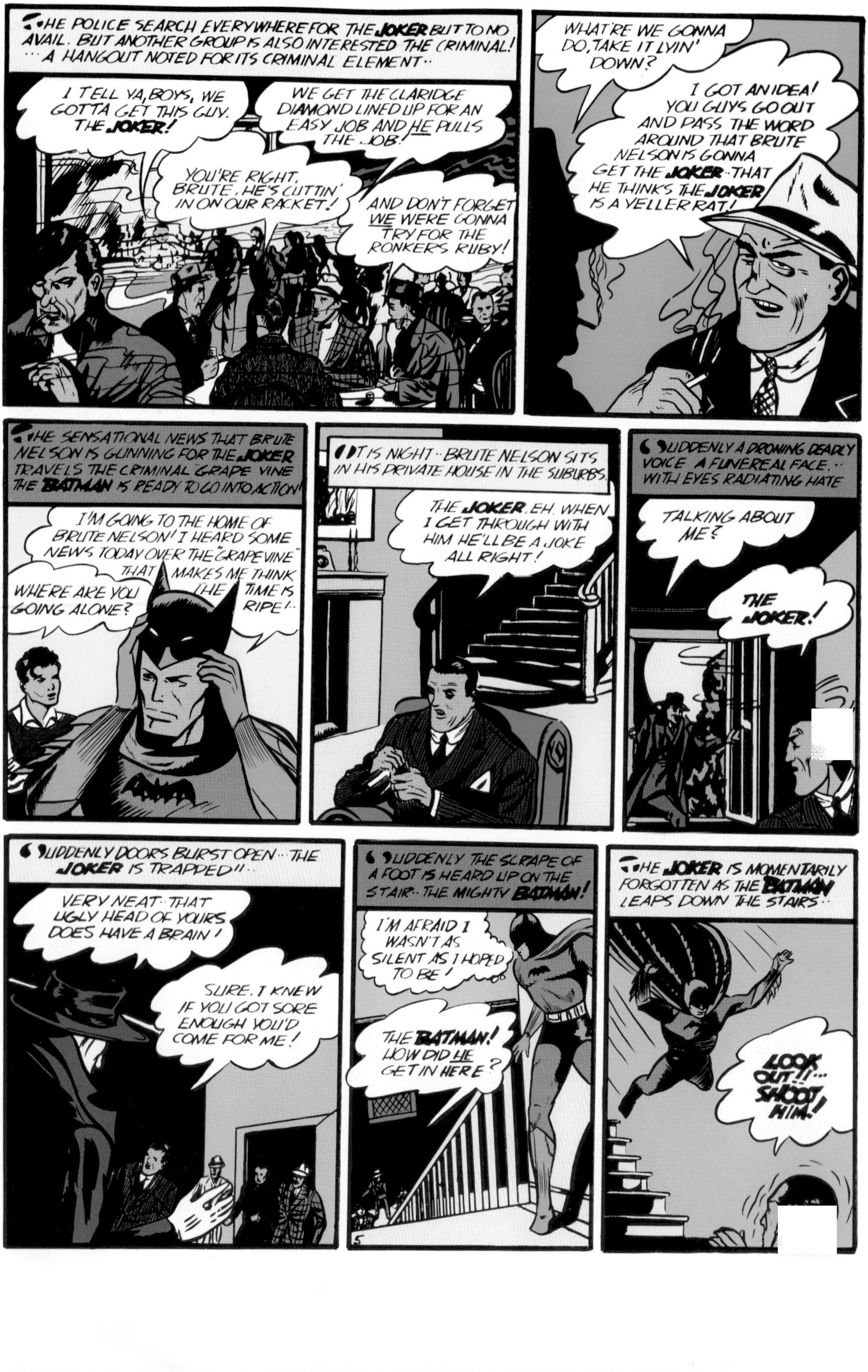
THE POLICE SEARCH EVERYWHERE FOR THE JOKER BUT TO NO AVAIL. BUT ANOTHER GROUP IS ALSO INTERESTED THE CRIMINAL! ... A HANGOUT NOTED FOR ITS CRIMINAL ELEMENT..
I TELL YA, BOYS, WE GOTTA GET THIS GUY. THE JOKER!
WE GET THE CLARIDGE DIAMOND LINED UP FOR AN EASY JOB AND HE PULLS THE JOB!
YOU'RE RIGHT, BRUTE, HE'S CUTTIN' IN ON OUR RACKET!
AND DON'T FORGET WE WERE GONNA TRY FOR THE RONKERS RUBY!
WHAT'RE WE GONNA DO, TAKE IT LYIN' DOWN?
I GOT AN IDEA! YOU GUYS GO OUT AND PASS THE WORD AROUND THAT BRUTE NELSON IS GONNA GET THE JOKER.. THAT HE THINKS THE JOKER IS A YELLER RAT!
THE SENSATIONAL NEWS THAT BRUTE NELSON IS GUNNING FOR THE JOKER TRAVELS THE CRIMINAL 'GRAPE VINE' THE BATMAN IS READY TO GO INTO ACTION!
WHERE ARE YOU GOING ALONE?
I'M GOING TO THE HOME OF BRUTE NELSON! I HEARD SOME NEWS TODAY OVER THE "GRAPEVINE" THAT MAKES ME THINK THE TIME IS RIPE!..
IT IS NIGHT.. BRUTE NELSON SITS IN HIS PRIVATE HOUSE IN THE SUBURBS.
THE JOKER, EH. WHEN I GET THROUGH WITH HIM HE'LL BE A JOKE ALL RIGHT!
SUDDENLY A DRONING DEADLY VOICE A FUNEREAL FACE.. WITH EYES RADIATING HATE
TALKING ABOUT ME?
THE JOKER!
SUDDENLY DOORS BURST OPEN... THE JOKER IS TRAPPED!!..
VERY NEAT.. THAT UGLY HEAD OF YOURS DOES HAVE A BRAIN!
SURE. I KNEW IF YOU GOT SORE ENOUGH YOU'D COME FOR ME!
SUDDENLY THE SCRAPE OF A FOOT IS HEARD UP ON THE STAIR.. THE MIGHTY BATMAN!
I'M AFRAID I WASN'T AS SILENT AS I HOPED TO BE!
THE BATMAN! HOW DID HE GET IN HERE?
THE JOKER IS MOMENTARILY FORGOTTEN AS THE BATMAN LEAPS DOWN THE STAIRS..
LOOK OUT!!... SHOOT HIM!

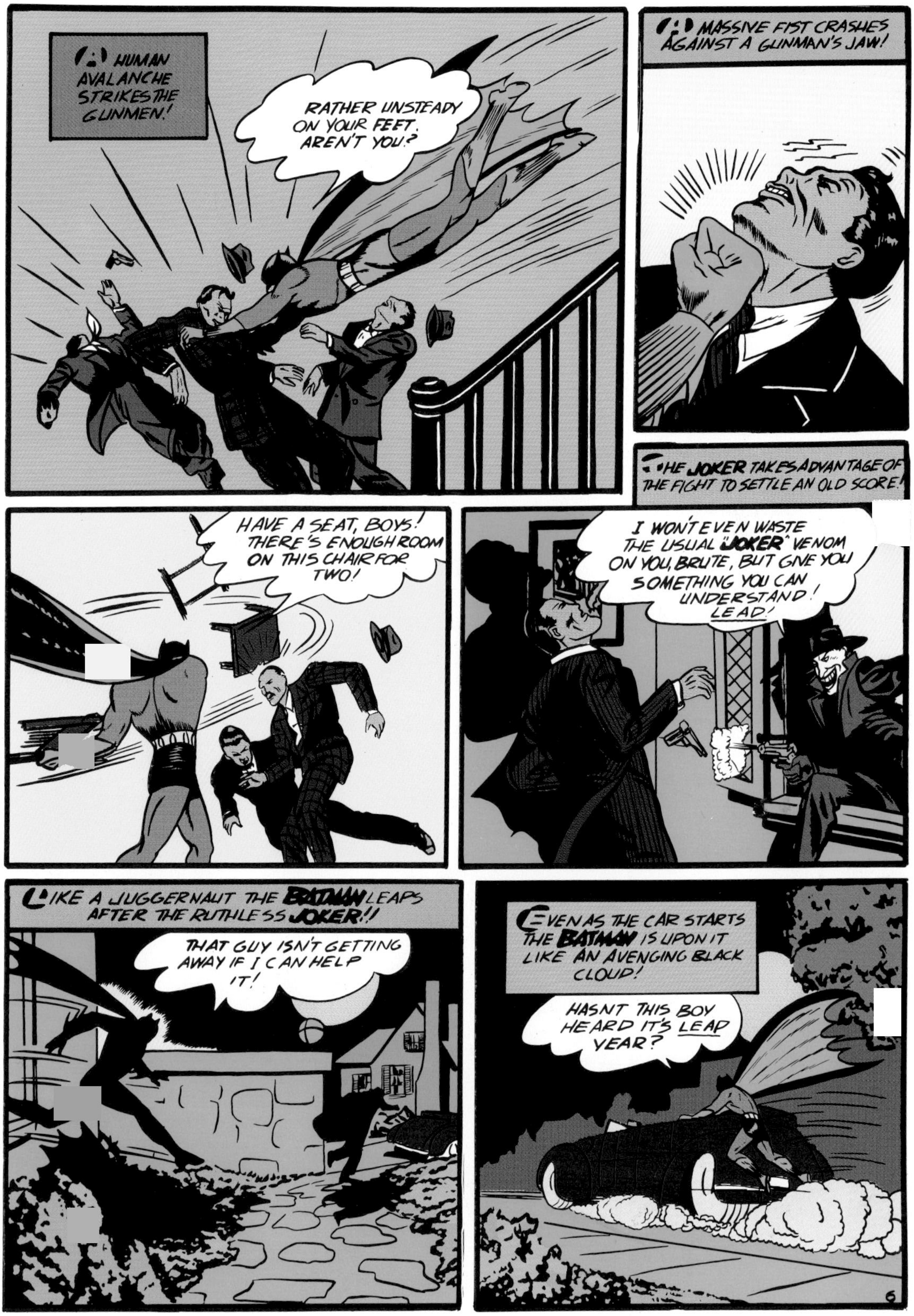
A HUMAN AVALANCHE STRIKES THE GUNMEN!
RATHER UNSTEADY ON YOUR FEET. AREN'T YOU?
A MASSIVE FIST CRASHES AGAINST A GUNMAN'S JAW!
HAVE A SEAT, BOYS! THERE'S ENOUGH ROOM ON THIS CHAIR FOR TWO!
THE JOKER TAKES ADVANTAGE OF THE FIGHT TO SETTLE AN OLD SCORE!
I WON'T EVEN WASTE THE USUAL "JOKER" VENOM ON YOU, BRUTE, BUT GIVE YOU SOMETHING YOU CAN UNDERSTAND! LEAD!
LIKE A JUGGERNAUT THE BATMAN LEAPS AFTER THE RUTHLESS JOKER!!
THAT GUY ISN'T GETTING AWAY IF I CAN HELP IT!
EVEN AS THE CAR STARTS THE BATMAN IS UPON IT LIKE AN AVENGING BLACK CLOUD!
HASNT THIS BOY HEARD IT'S LEAP YEAR?
6

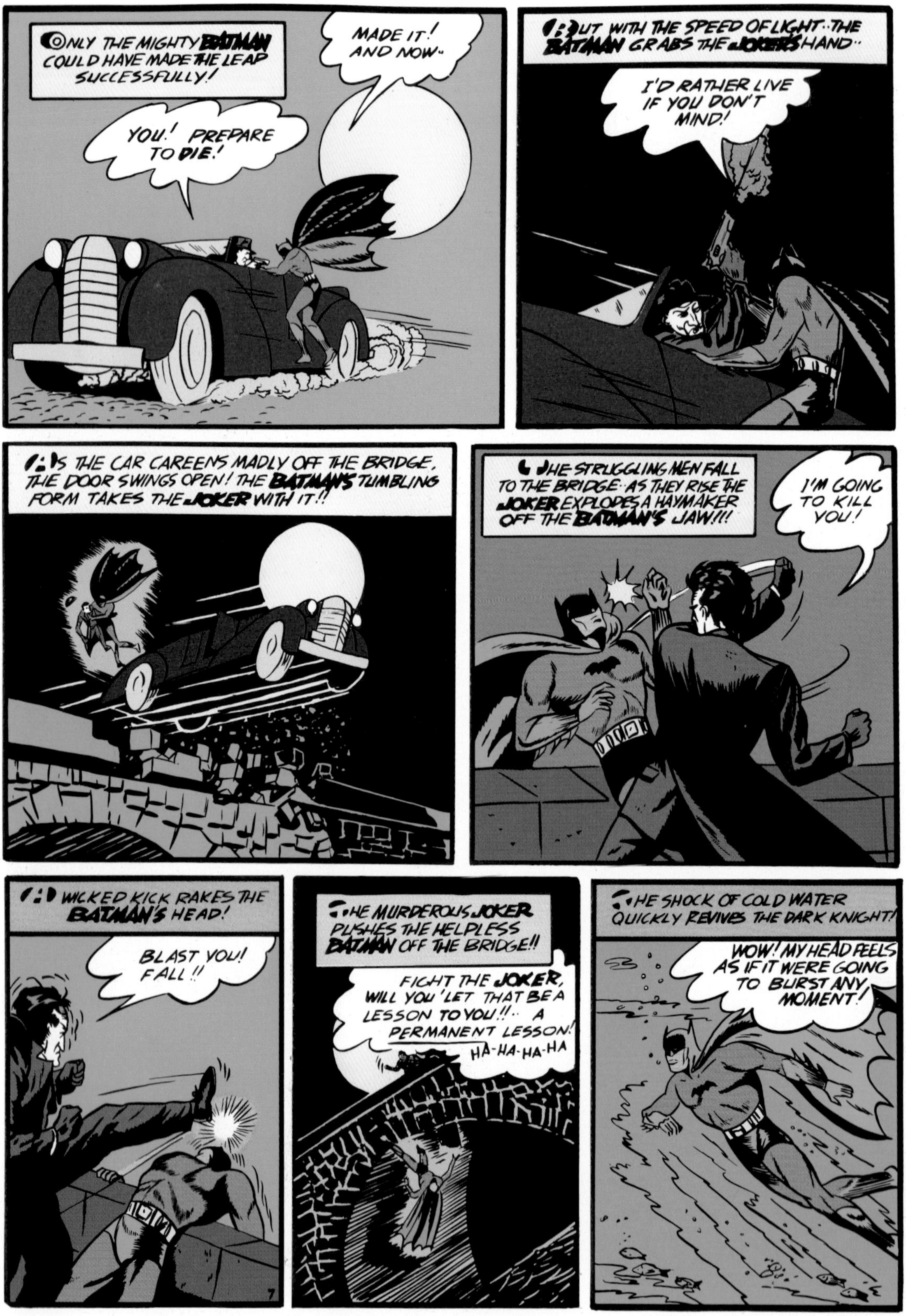
ONLY THE MIGHTY BATMAN COULD HAVE MADE THE LEAP SUCCESSFULLY!
MADE IT! AND NOW--
YOU! PREPARE TO DIE!
BUT WITH THE SPEED OF LIGHT.. THE BATMAN GRABS THE JOKER'S HAND--
I'D RATHER LIVE IF YOU DON'T MIND!
AS THE CAR CAREENS MADLY OFF THE BRIDGE, THE DOOR SWINGS OPEN! THE BATMAN'S TUMBLING FORM TAKES THE JOKER WITH IT!!
THE STRUGGLING MEN FALL TO THE BRIDGE.. AS THEY RISE THE JOKER EXPLODES A HAYMAKER OFF THE BATMAN'S JAW!!!
I'M GOING TO KILL YOU!
A WICKED KICK RAKES THE BATMAN'S HEAD!
BLAST YOU! FALL!!
THE MURDEROUS JOKER PUSHES THE HELPLESS BATMAN OFF THE BRIDGE!!
FIGHT THE JOKER, WILL YOU! LET THAT BE A LESSON TO YOU!!.. A PERMANENT LESSON!
HA-HA-HA-HA
THE SHOCK OF COLD WATER QUICKLY REVIVES THE DARK KNIGHT!
WOW! MY HEAD FEELS AS IF IT WERE GOING TO BURST ANY MOMENT!

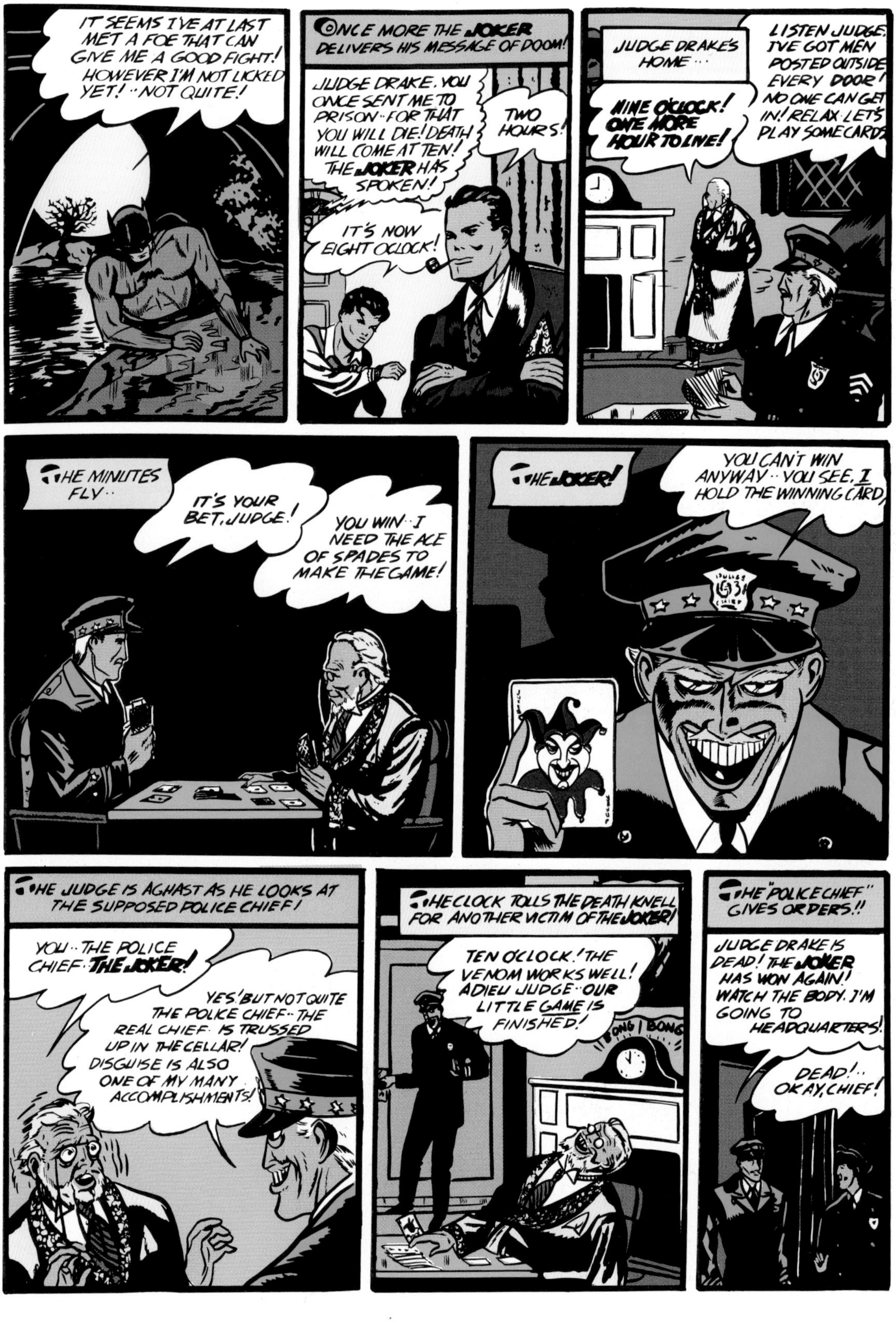
IT SEEMS I'VE AT LAST MET A FOE THAT CAN GIVE ME A GOOD FIGHT! HOWEVER I'M NOT LICKED YET! .. NOT QUITE!
ONCE MORE THE JOKER DELIVERS HIS MESSAGE OF DOOM!
JUDGE DRAKE. YOU ONCE SENT ME TO PRISON .. FOR THAT YOU WILL DIE! DEATH WILL COME AT TEN! THE JOKER HAS SPOKEN!
TWO HOURS!
IT'S NOW EIGHT O'CLOCK!
JUDGE DRAKE'S HOME ...
NINE O'CLOCK! ONE MORE HOUR TO LIVE!
LISTEN JUDGE. I'VE GOT MEN POSTED OUTSIDE EVERY DOOR! NO ONE CAN GET IN! RELAX. LET'S PLAY SOME CARDS!
THE MINUTES FLY ..
IT'S YOUR BET, JUDGE!
YOU WIN .. I NEED THE ACE OF SPADES TO MAKE THE GAME!
THE JOKER!
YOU CAN'T WIN ANYWAY .. YOU SEE, I HOLD THE WINNING CARD!
THE JUDGE IS AGHAST AS HE LOOKS AT THE SUPPOSED POLICE CHIEF!
YOU .. THE POLICE CHIEF .. THE JOKER!
YES! BUT NOT QUITE THE POLICE CHIEF .. THE REAL CHIEF IS TRUSSED UP IN THE CELLAR! DISGUISE IS ALSO ONE OF MY MANY ACCOMPLISHMENTS!
THE CLOCK TOLLS THE DEATH KNELL FOR ANOTHER VICTIM OF THE JOKER!
TEN O'CLOCK! THE VENOM WORKS WELL! ADIEU JUDGE .. OUR LITTLE GAME IS FINISHED!
BONG! BONG
THE "POLICE CHIEF" GIVES ORDERS!!
JUDGE DRAKE IS DEAD! THE JOKER HAS WON AGAIN! WATCH THE BODY. I'M GOING TO HEADQUARTERS!
DEAD! .. OKAY, CHIEF!

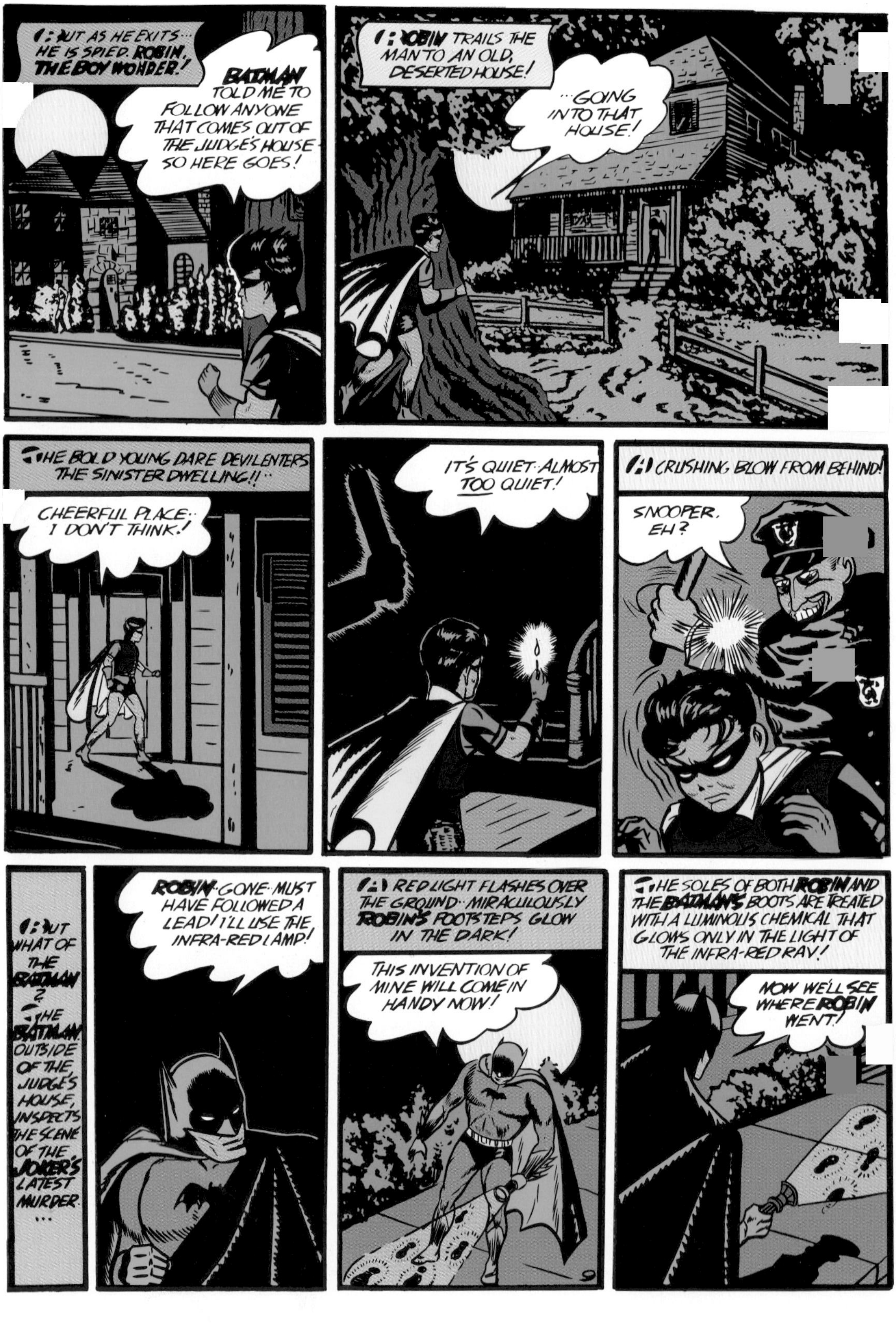
BUT AS HE EXITS... HE IS SPIED. ROBIN, THE BOY WONDER!
BATMAN TOLD ME TO FOLLOW ANYONE THAT COMES OUT OF THE JUDGE'S HOUSE-- SO HERE GOES!
ROBIN TRAILS THE MAN TO AN OLD, DESERTED HOUSE!
...GOING INTO THAT HOUSE!
THE BOLD YOUNG DARE DEVIL ENTERS THE SINISTER DWELLING!!..
CHEERFUL PLACE.. I DON'T THINK!
IT'S QUIET. ALMOST TOO QUIET!
A CRUSHING BLOW FROM BEHIND!
SNOOPER, EH?
BUT WHAT OF THE BATMAN? THE BATMAN, OUTSIDE OF THE JUDGE'S HOUSE, INSPECTS THE SCENE OF THE JOKER'S LATEST MURDER...
ROBIN-GONE-MUST HAVE FOLLOWED A LEAD! I'LL USE THE INFRA-RED LAMP!
A RED LIGHT FLASHES OVER THE GROUND.. MIRACULOUSLY ROBIN'S FOOTSTEPS GLOW IN THE DARK!
THIS INVENTION OF MINE WILL COME IN HANDY NOW!
THE SOLES OF BOTH ROBIN AND THE BATMAN'S BOOTS ARE TREATED WITH A LUMINOUS CHEMICAL THAT GLOWS ONLY IN THE LIGHT OF THE INFRA-RED RAY!
NOW WE'LL SEE WHERE ROBIN WENT!

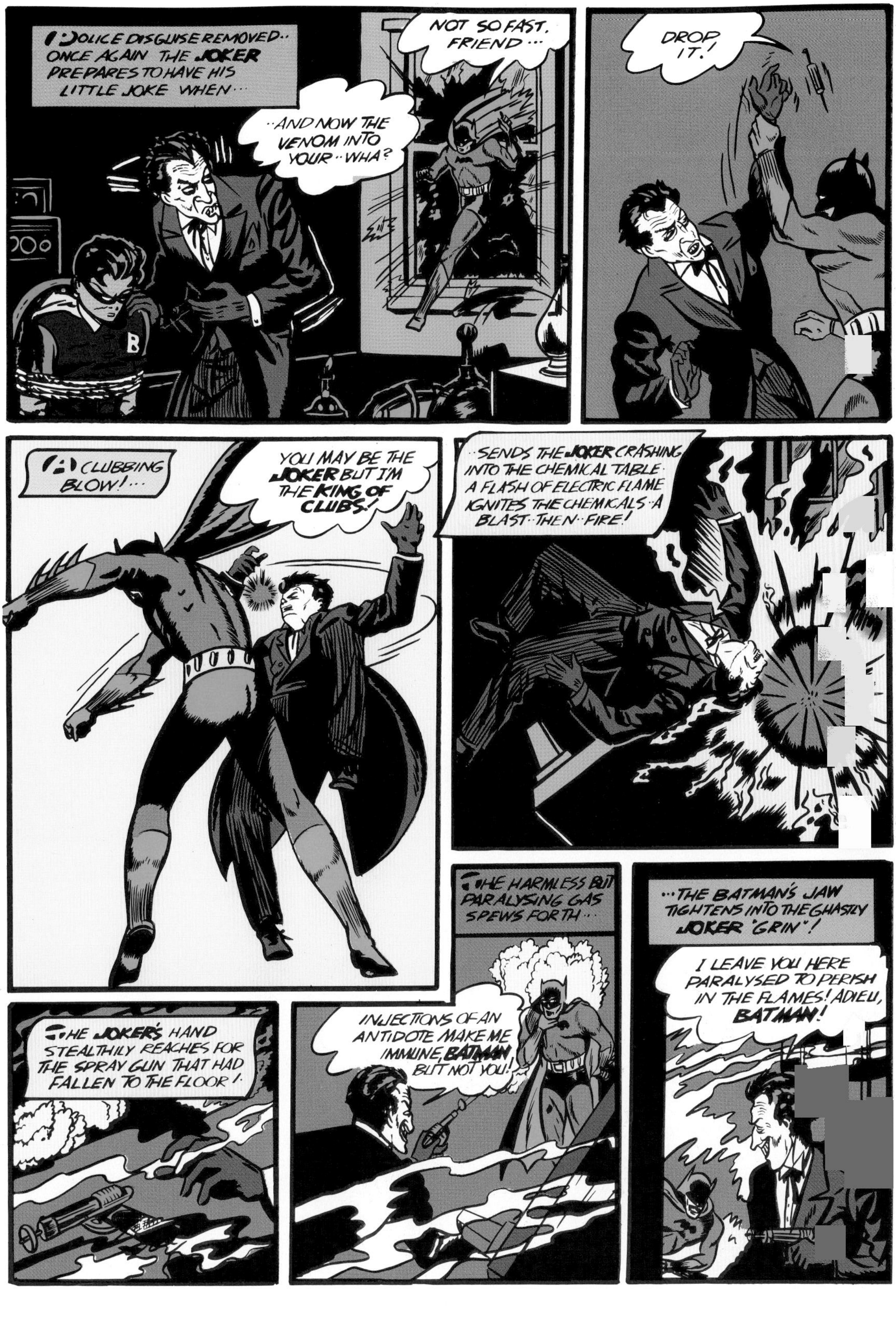
POLICE DISGUISE REMOVED.. ONCE AGAIN THE JOKER PREPARES TO HAVE HIS LITTLE JOKE WHEN...
NOT SO FAST, FRIEND...
..AND NOW THE VENOM INTO YOUR.. WHA?
DROP IT!
A CLUBBING BLOW!...
YOU MAY BE THE JOKER BUT I'M THE KING OF CLUBS!
..SENDS THE JOKER CRASHING INTO THE CHEMICAL TABLE. A FLASH OF ELECTRIC FLAME IGNITES THE CHEMICALS. A BLAST.. THEN.. FIRE!
THE HARMLESS BUT PARALYSING GAS SPEWS FORTH...
...THE BATMAN'S JAW TIGHTENS INTO THE GHASTLY JOKER "GRIN"!
I LEAVE YOU HERE PARALYSED TO PERISH IN THE FLAMES! ADIEU, BATMAN!
THE JOKER'S HAND STEALTHILY REACHES FOR THE SPRAY GUN THAT HAD FALLEN TO THE FLOOR!
INJECTIONS OF AN ANTIDOTE MAKE ME IMMUNE, BATMAN BUT NOT YOU!

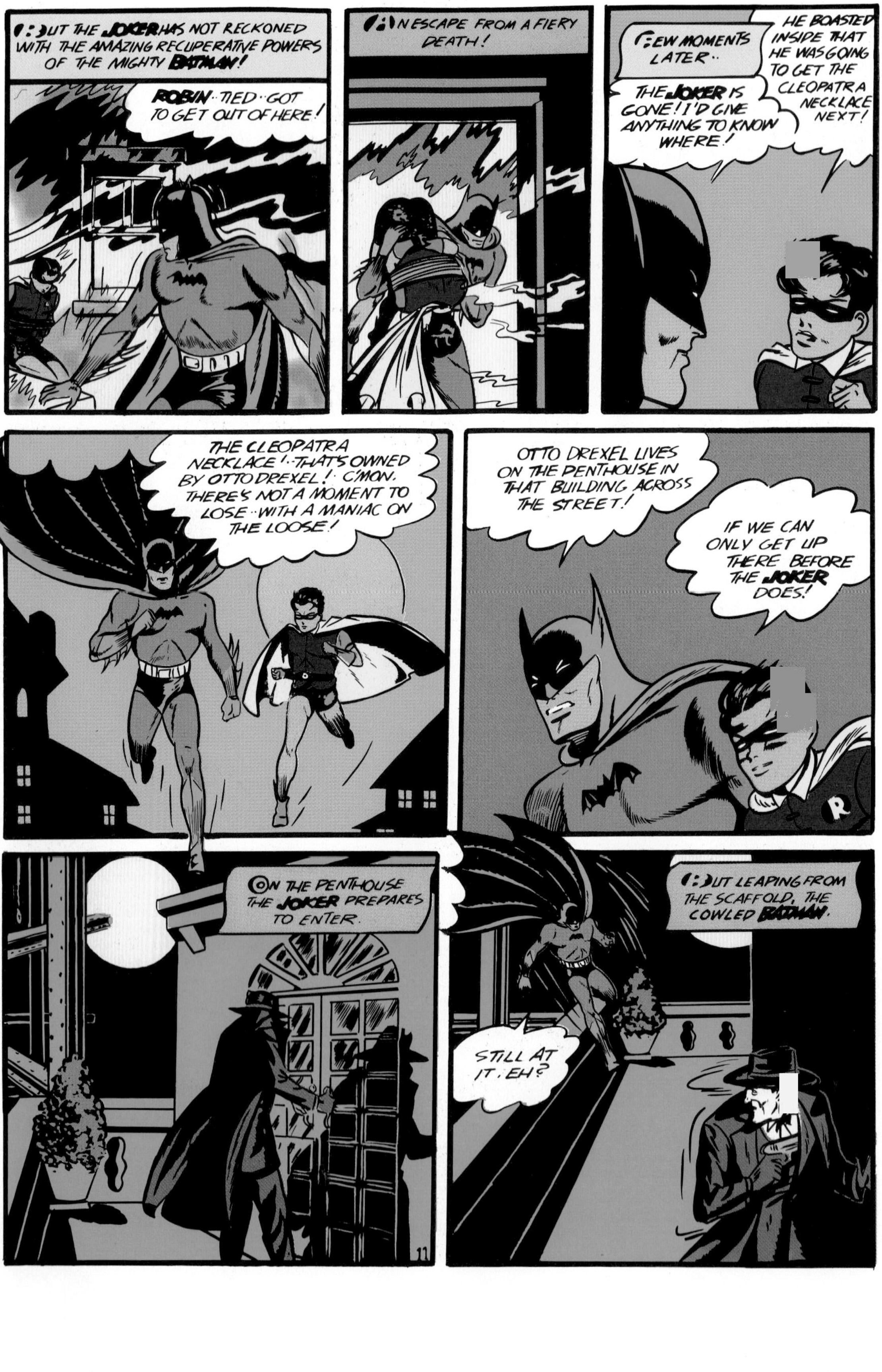
BUT THE JOKER HAS NOT RECKONED WITH THE AMAZING RECUPERATIVE POWERS OF THE MIGHTY BATMAN!
ROBIN.. TIED.. GOT TO GET OUT OF HERE!
AN ESCAPE FROM A FIERY DEATH!
FEW MOMENTS LATER..
THE JOKER IS GONE! I'D GIVE ANYTHING TO KNOW WHERE!
HE BOASTED INSIDE THAT HE WAS GOING TO GET THE CLEOPATRA NECKLACE NEXT!
THE CLEOPATRA NECKLACE!..THAT'S OWNED BY OTTO DREXEL! C'MON. THERE'S NOT A MOMENT TO LOSE..WITH A MANIAC ON THE LOOSE!
OTTO DREXEL LIVES ON THE PENTHOUSE IN THAT BUILDING ACROSS THE STREET!
IF WE CAN ONLY GET UP THERE BEFORE THE JOKER DOES!
ON THE PENTHOUSE THE JOKER PREPARES TO ENTER.
11
BUT LEAPING FROM THE SCAFFOLD, THE COWLED BATMAN.
STILL AT IT, EH?

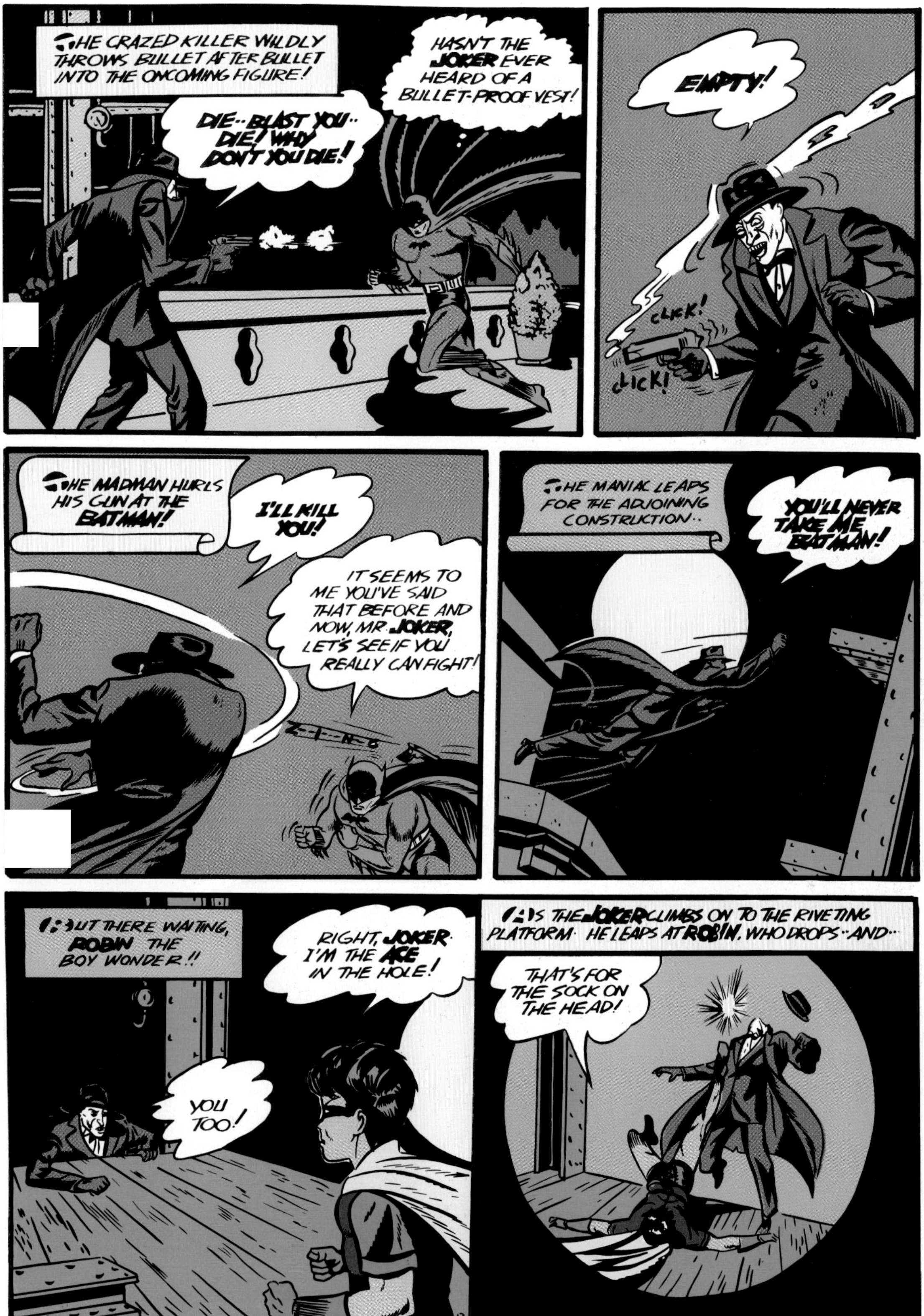
THE CRAZED KILLER WILDLY THROWS BULLET AFTER BULLET INTO THE ONCOMING FIGURE!
HASN'T THE JOKER EVER HEARD OF A BULLET-PROOF VEST!
DIE.. BLAST YOU.. DIE! WHY DON'T YOU DIE!
EMPTY!
CLICK!
CLICK!
THE MADMAN HURLS HIS GUN AT THE BATMAN!
I'LL KILL YOU!
IT SEEMS TO ME YOU'VE SAID THAT BEFORE AND NOW, MR. JOKER, LET'S SEE IF YOU REALLY CAN FIGHT!
Z-I-N-G
THE MANIAC LEAPS FOR THE ADJOINING CONSTRUCTION..
YOU'LL NEVER TAKE ME, BATMAN!
BUT THERE WAITING, ROBIN THE BOY WONDER!!
RIGHT, JOKER. I'M THE ACE IN THE HOLE!
YOU TOO!
AS THE JOKER CLIMBS ON TO THE RIVETING PLATFORM. HE LEAPS AT ROBIN, WHO DROPS.. AND...
THAT'S FOR THE SOCK ON THE HEAD!
12

THE SMASHING KICK SENDS THE JOKER FLYING OFF THE SCAFFOLDING!
AS THE FRANTIC MAN FALLS PAST THE PENTHOUSE BALUSTRADE, A HAND REACHES OUT...
AAGH! I'M FALLING!
OH NO YOU'RE NOT!
THE STRONG ARM OF THE BATMAN HAULS HIM BACK TO SAFETY!
YOU'RE TOO VALUABLE A PRIZE TO LOSE!
YOU PLAYED YOUR LAST HAND, JOKER!
A FINAL BLOW WITH ALL THE STRENGTH OF THE BATMAN BEHIND IT!!
NEXT DAY
DAILY STAR
2¢
FINAL
BATMAN CAPTURES JOKER
LEAVES JOKER I
FRONT OF POLIC
STATION. DRIVES A
BUT WHAT I'D LIKE TO KNOW IS HOW HIS VICTIMS' MOUTHS TURNED UP IN THAT TERRIBLE GRIN!!
SOME SORT OF DRUG THAT PULLED THE MUSCLES OF THE FACE! THE JOKER WAS A CLEVER BUT DIABOLICAL KILLER! TOO CLEVER AND TOO DEADLY TO BE FREE!
BUT EVEN AS BRUCE SPEAKS, AT THE STATE PRISON, THE JOKER IS PLANNING, PLOTTING FOR HIS ESCAPE!
THEY CAN'T KEEP ME HERE! I KNOW OF A WAY OUT—THE JOKER WILL YET HAVE THE LAST LAUGH!
BOB KANE
THE Amazing BATMAN
AMERICA'S MOST FAMOUS ADVENTURE-STRIP CHARACTER... WITH THAT SENSATIONAL NEW DISCOVERY, THAT LAUGHING YOUNG DARE-DEVIL
Robin THE BOY WONDER
WILL THRILL YOU EVERY MONTH WITH THEIR ASTOUNDING EXPLOITS IN DETECTIVE COMICS

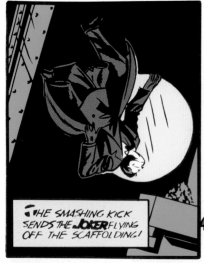

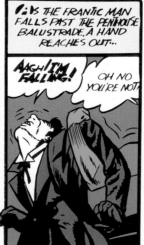

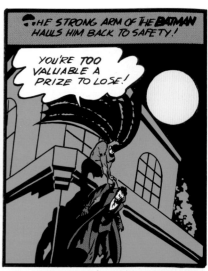

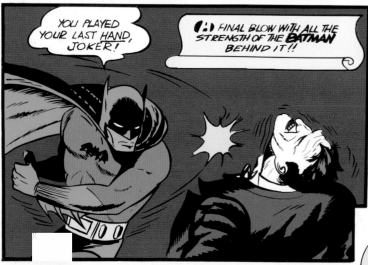

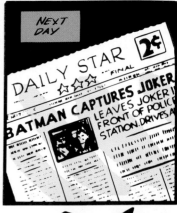

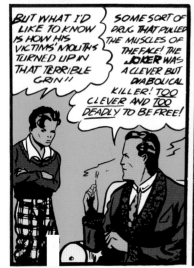

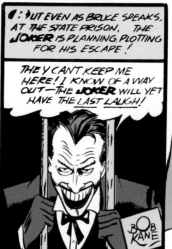

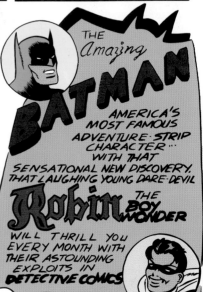

BATMAN
BY BOB KANE
ALREADY AN ALMOST LEGENDARY FIGURE, THE COWLED SHADOW OF THE BATMAN PROWLS THROUGH THE NIGHT PREYING UPON THE CRIMINAL PARASITE, LIKE THE WINGED CREATURE WHOSE NAME HE HAD ADOPTED
WHILE AN INNOCENT METROPOLIS SLEEPS, LITTLE DOES IT REALIZE THAT HUGE, TERRIFYING MAN-MONSTERS SHALL SOON STALK THE STREETS AND BRING TO THEM HAVOC AND DESTRUCTION: AND LITTLE DOES BRUCE WAYNE SUSPECT THAT FATE SHALL TOUCH HIS SHOULDER AND SINGLE HIM OUT AS THE ONE TO DO BATTLE WITH THESE MONSTERS, AS HE GOES FORTH CLAD IN THE GARB OF THE WEIRD AND MENACING.... BATMAN!
STRAND
NOT LONG AGO THE BATMAN HAD SEEN THE ARCH-CRIMINAL, PROFESSOR HUGO STRANGE IMPRISONED...AND YET...
ONE OF YOU MEN GET THE WARDEN. WE'LL USE HIM AS A SHIELD!
OKAY STRANGE!
ONCE MORE PROFESSOR HUGO STRANGE IS FREE TO CARRY OUT THE NEXT OF HIS DIABOLICAL SCHEMES.
WUXTRY! PROFESSOR STRANGE ESCAPES IN PRISON BREAK!
THE NEXT NIGHT.... THE METROPOLIS INSANE ASYLUM.
GET THEM OUT QUICKLY!
C'MON, NUTS!
GOODY! GOODY!
OH GOO!

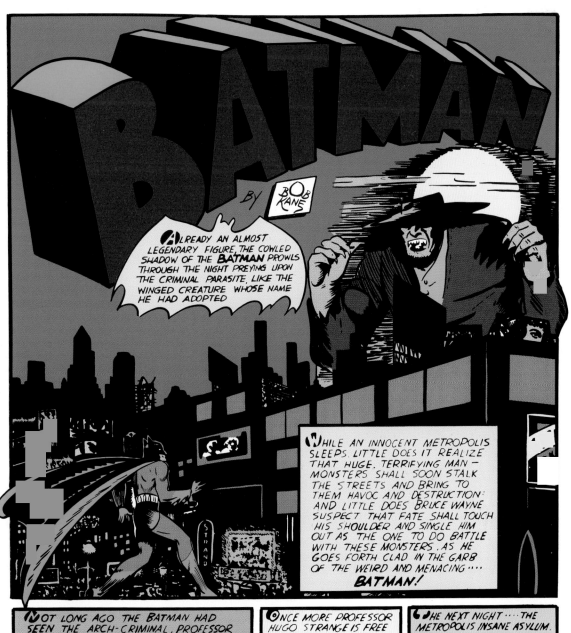

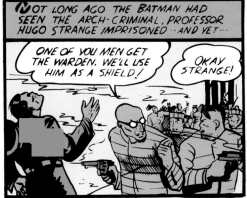

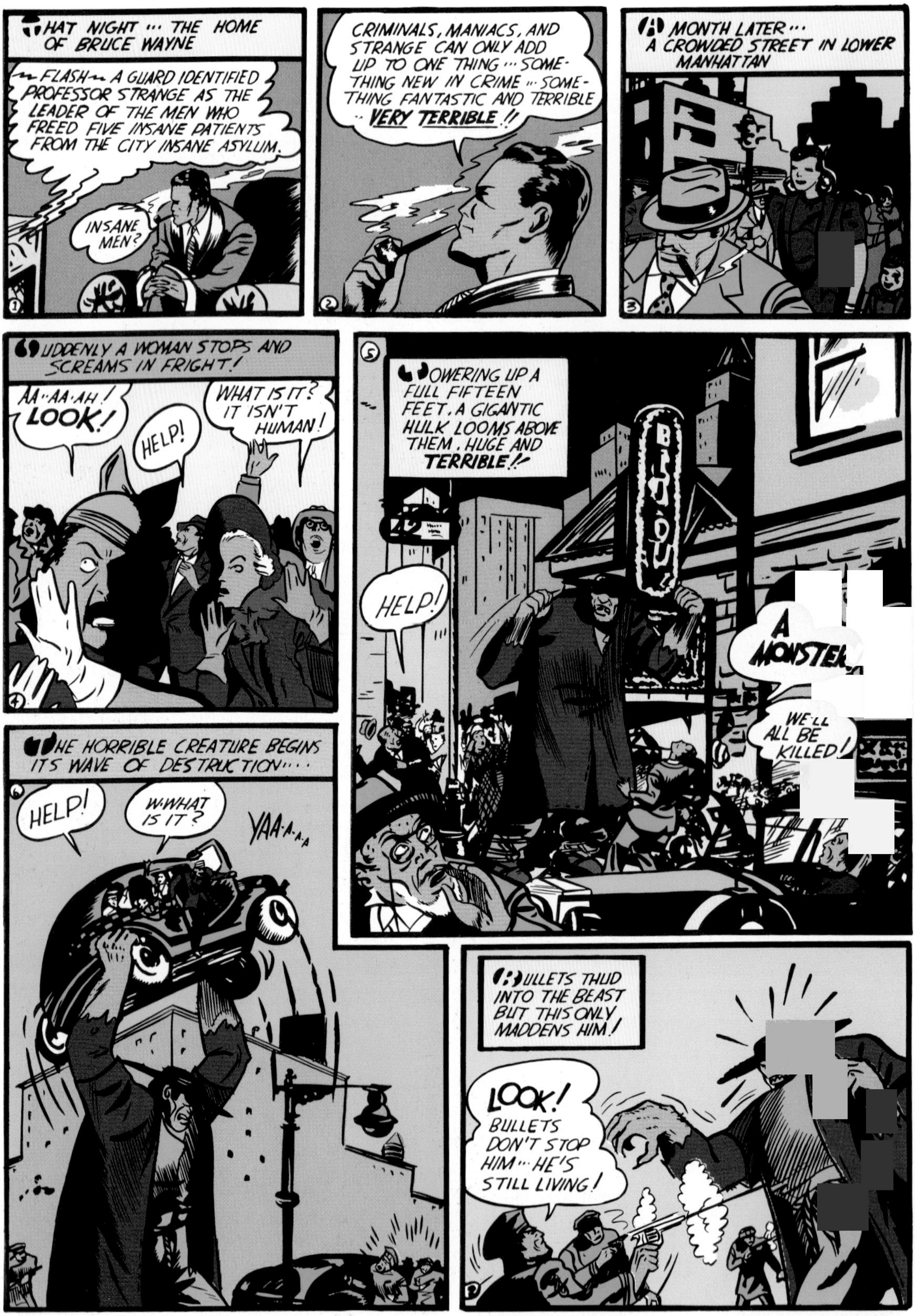
THAT NIGHT ... THE HOME OF BRUCE WAYNE
FLASH -- A GUARD IDENTIFIED PROFESSOR STRANGE AS THE LEADER OF THE MEN WHO FREED FIVE INSANE PATIENTS FROM THE CITY INSANE ASYLUM.
INSANE MEN?
CRIMINALS, MANIACS, AND STRANGE CAN ONLY ADD UP TO ONE THING ... SOMETHING NEW IN CRIME ... SOMETHING FANTASTIC AND TERRIBLE .. VERY TERRIBLE !!
A MONTH LATER ... A CROWDED STREET IN LOWER MANHATTAN
SUDDENLY A WOMAN STOPS AND SCREAMS IN FRIGHT!
AA..AA-AH! LOOK!
HELP!
WHAT IS IT? IT ISN'T HUMAN!
TOWERING UP A FULL FIFTEEN FEET, A GIGANTIC HULK LOOMS ABOVE THEM. HUGE AND TERRIBLE!!
BIJOU
HELP!
A MONSTER
WE-LL ALL BE KILLED!
THE HORRIBLE CREATURE BEGINS ITS WAVE OF DESTRUCTION...
HELP!
W-WHAT IS IT?
YAA-A-A-A
BULLETS THUD INTO THE BEAST BUT THIS ONLY MADDENS HIM!
LOOK! BULLETS DON'T STOP HIM ... HE'S STILL LIVING!

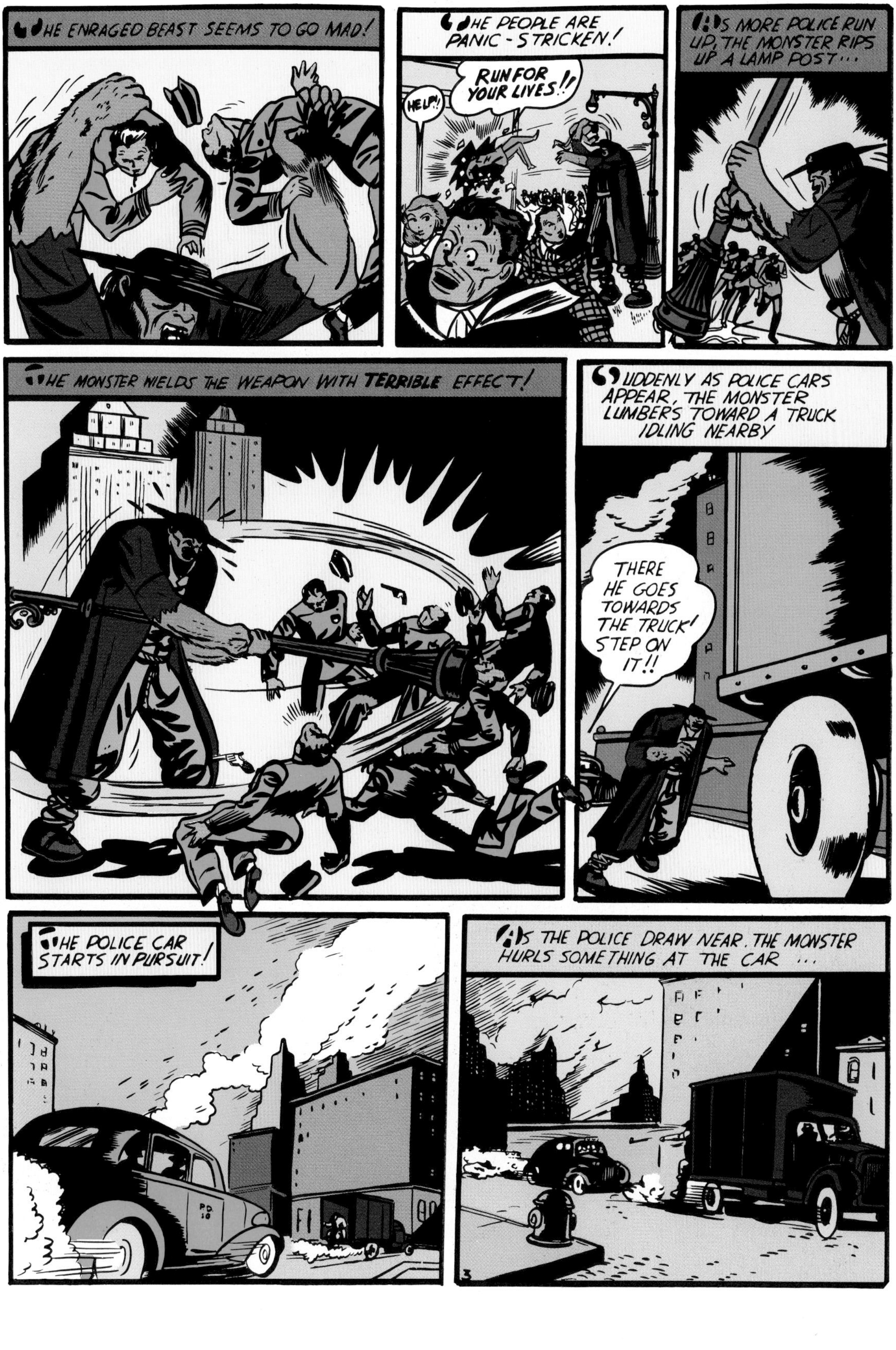
THE ENRAGED BEAST SEEMS TO GO MAD!
THE PEOPLE ARE PANIC-STRICKEN!
HELP!
RUN FOR YOUR LIVES!!
AS MORE POLICE RUN UP, THE MONSTER RIPS UP A LAMP POST...
THE MONSTER WIELDS THE WEAPON WITH TERRIBLE EFFECT!
SUDDENLY AS POLICE CARS APPEAR, THE MONSTER LUMBERS TOWARD A TRUCK IDLING NEARBY
THERE HE GOES TOWARDS THE TRUCK! STEP ON IT!!
THE POLICE CAR STARTS IN PURSUIT!
AS THE POLICE DRAW NEAR, THE MONSTER HURLS SOMETHING AT THE CAR ...
PD 10
3

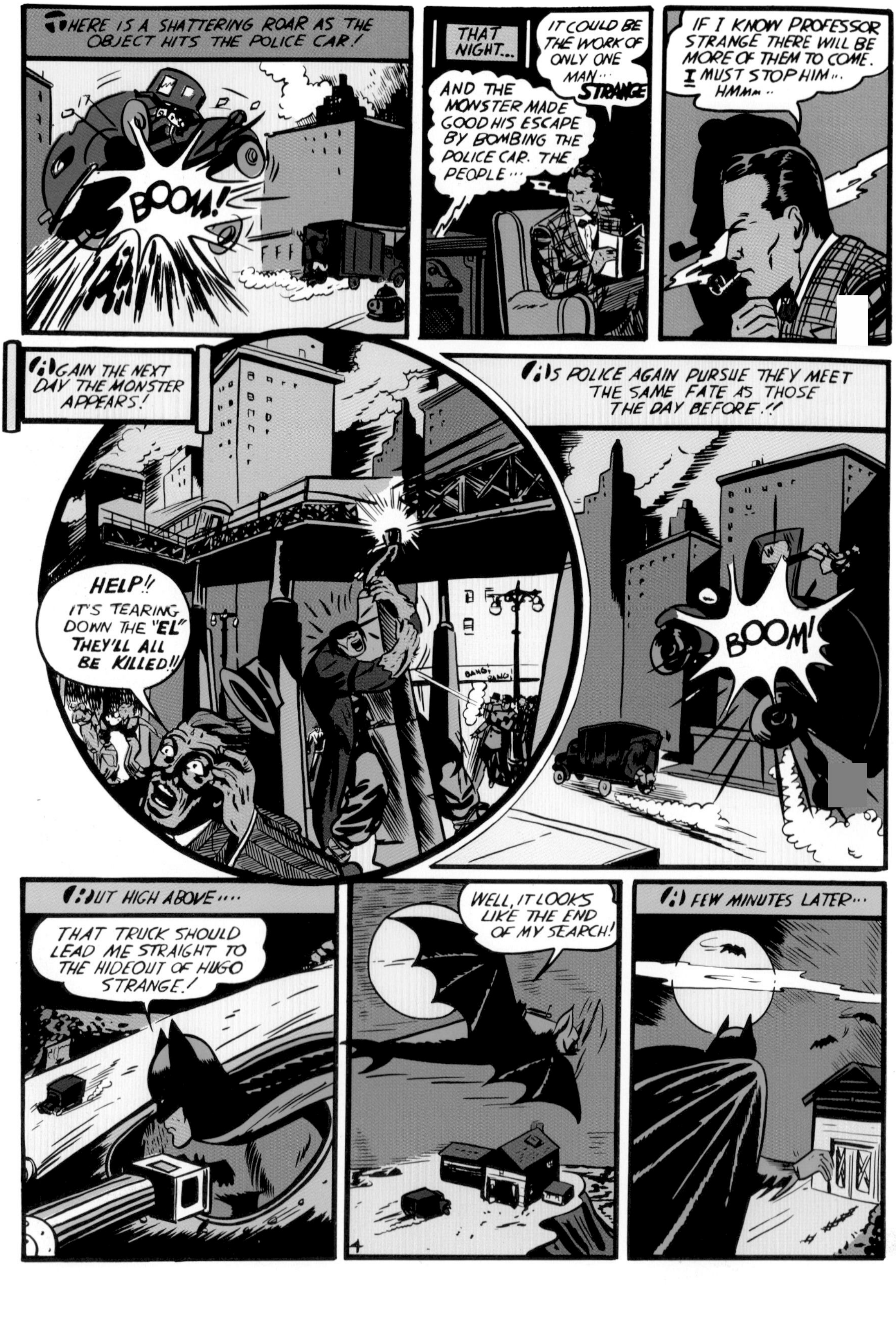
THERE IS A SHATTERING ROAR AS THE OBJECT HITS THE POLICE CAR!
BOOM!
THAT NIGHT...
IT COULD BE THE WORK OF ONLY ONE MAN... STRANGE
AND THE MONSTER MADE GOOD HIS ESCAPE BY BOMBING THE POLICE CAR. THE PEOPLE...
IF I KNOW PROFESSOR STRANGE THERE WILL BE MORE OF THEM TO COME. I MUST STOP HIM... HMMM...
AGAIN THE NEXT DAY THE MONSTER APPEARS!
HELP!! IT'S TEARING DOWN THE "EL" THEY'LL ALL BE KILLED!!
BANG! BANG!
AS POLICE AGAIN PURSUE THEY MEET THE SAME FATE AS THOSE THE DAY BEFORE!!
BOOM!
BUT HIGH ABOVE....
THAT TRUCK SHOULD LEAD ME STRAIGHT TO THE HIDEOUT OF HUGO STRANGE!
WELL, IT LOOKS LIKE THE END OF MY SEARCH!
A FEW MINUTES LATER...

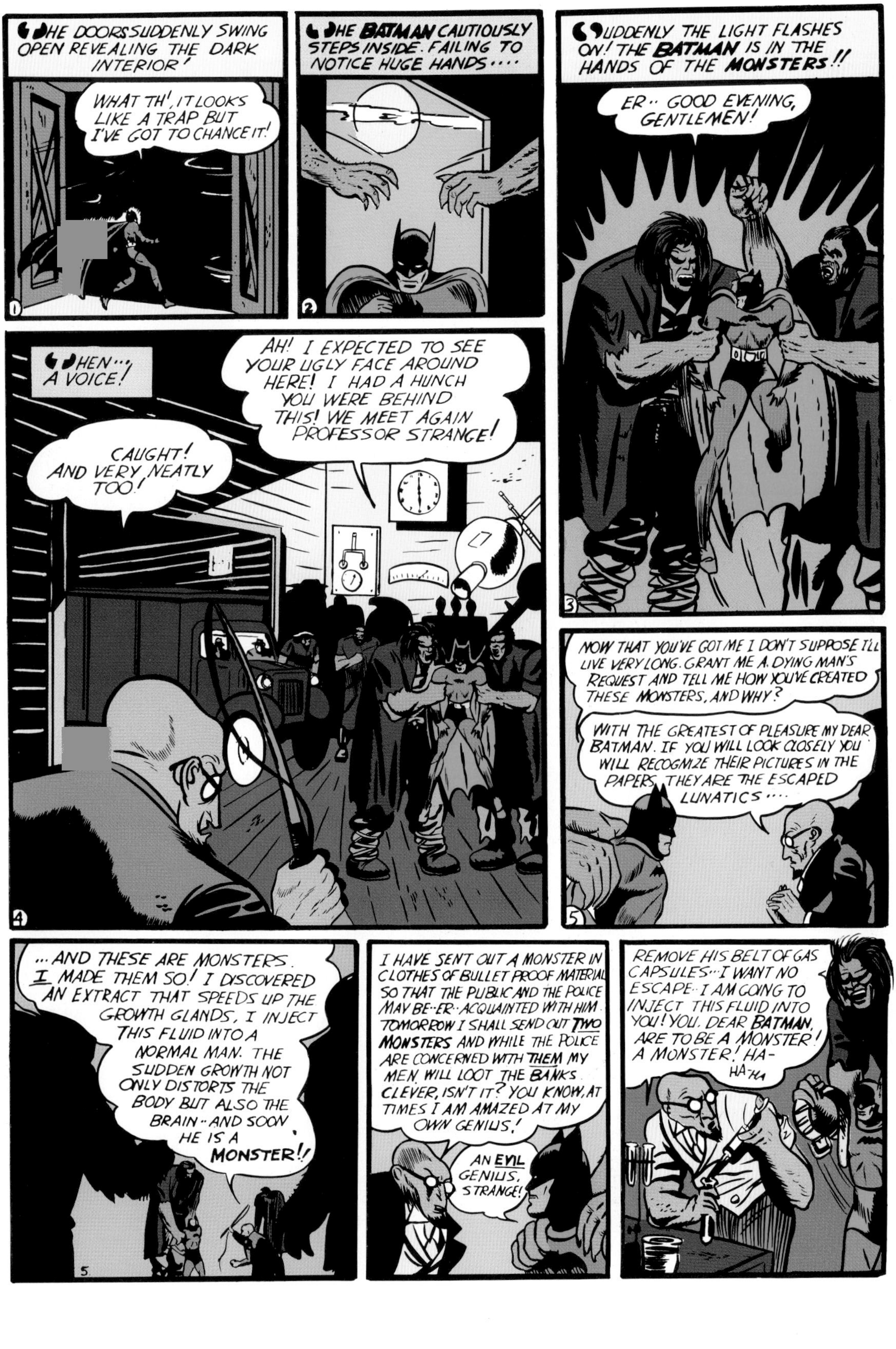
THE DOORS SUDDENLY SWING OPEN REVEALING THE DARK INTERIOR!
WHAT TH', IT LOOKS LIKE A TRAP BUT I'VE GOT TO CHANCE IT!
THE BATMAN CAUTIOUSLY STEPS INSIDE. FAILING TO NOTICE HUGE HANDS....
SUDDENLY THE LIGHT FLASHES ON! THE BATMAN IS IN THE HANDS OF THE MONSTERS!!
ER.. GOOD EVENING, GENTLEMEN!
THEN..., A VOICE!
CAUGHT! AND VERY NEATLY TOO!
AH! I EXPECTED TO SEE YOUR UGLY FACE AROUND HERE! I HAD A HUNCH YOU WERE BEHIND THIS! WE MEET AGAIN PROFESSOR STRANGE!
NOW THAT YOU'VE GOT ME I DON'T SUPPOSE I'LL LIVE VERY LONG. GRANT ME A DYING MAN'S REQUEST AND TELL ME HOW YOU'VE CREATED THESE MONSTERS, AND WHY?
WITH THE GREATEST OF PLEASURE MY DEAR BATMAN. IF YOU WILL LOOK CLOSELY YOU WILL RECOGNIZE THEIR PICTURES IN THE PAPERS. THEY ARE THE ESCAPED LUNATICS....
...AND THESE ARE MONSTERS. I MADE THEM SO! I DISCOVERED AN EXTRACT THAT SPEEDS UP THE GROWTH GLANDS. I INJECT THIS FLUID INTO A NORMAL MAN. THE SUDDEN GROWTH NOT ONLY DISTORTS THE BODY BUT ALSO THE BRAIN.. AND SOON HE IS A MONSTER!!
I HAVE SENT OUT A MONSTER IN CLOTHES OF BULLET PROOF MATERIAL SO THAT THE PUBLIC AND THE POLICE MAY BE..ER..ACQUAINTED WITH HIM. TOMORROW I SHALL SEND OUT TWO MONSTERS AND WHILE THE POLICE ARE CONCERNED WITH THEM MY MEN WILL LOOT THE BANKS. CLEVER, ISN'T IT? YOU KNOW, AT TIMES I AM AMAZED AT MY OWN GENIUS!
AN EVIL GENIUS, STRANGE!
REMOVE HIS BELT OF GAS CAPSULES...I WANT NO ESCAPE..I AM GOING TO INJECT THIS FLUID INTO YOU! YOU, DEAR BATMAN, ARE TO BE A MONSTER! A MONSTER! HA-HA-HA

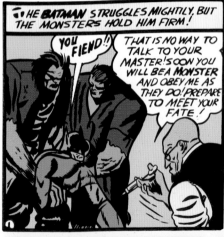

THE BATMAN STRUGGLES MIGHTILY, BUT THE MONSTERS HOLD HIM FIRM!

YOU FIEND!!

THAT IS NO WAY TO TALK TO YOUR MASTER! SOON YOU WILL BE A MONSTER AND OBEY ME AS THEY DO! PREPARE TO MEET YOUR FATE!

THE DEADLY NEEDLE PLUNGES DEEP INTO THE ARM OF THE BATMAN!

DONE!!

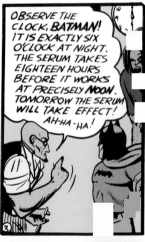

OBSERVE THE CLOCK, BATMAN! IT IS EXACTLY SIX O'CLOCK AT NIGHT. THE SERUM TAKES EIGHTEEN HOURS BEFORE IT WORKS AT PRECISELY NOON. TOMORROW THE SERUM WILL TAKE EFFECT! AH-HA-HA!

MASSIVE FIST CRASHES AGAINST THE BATMAN'S JAW... THEN BLACKNESS

THEN THE BATMAN SEES...

NOW REMEMBER! THREE MEN TAKE A MONSTER ONE TRUCK WILL GO BY DALY AVENUE AND THE OTHER BY THE POST ROAD. NOW GET GOING...AND NO SLIP UPS!

DON'T WORRY STRANGE! THOSE BANKS ARE AS GOOD AS OPENED RIGHT NOW!

HOURS LATER

WOW! WHAT HIT ME! THE CLOCK! IT SAYS ALMOST A QUARTER TO TWELVE. I'VE BEEN UNCONSCIOUS ALMOST EIGHTEEN HOURS...AND IT'S ALMOST TIME FOR THE SERUM TO WORK!!

I'VE GOT TO GET OUT OF HERE! THEY TOOK MY BELT BUT THEY DIDN'T KNOW ABOUT MY BOOT HEELS. BY MIXING SOME CHEMICALS I HAVE IN THEM I CAN MAKE AN EXPLOSIVE! THE TRUCKS HAVE GONE WITH TWO OF THE MONSTERS, SO THAT AT LEAST GIVES ME A CHANCE!

A MOMENT LATER...

THAT DOES IT!

BOOM!

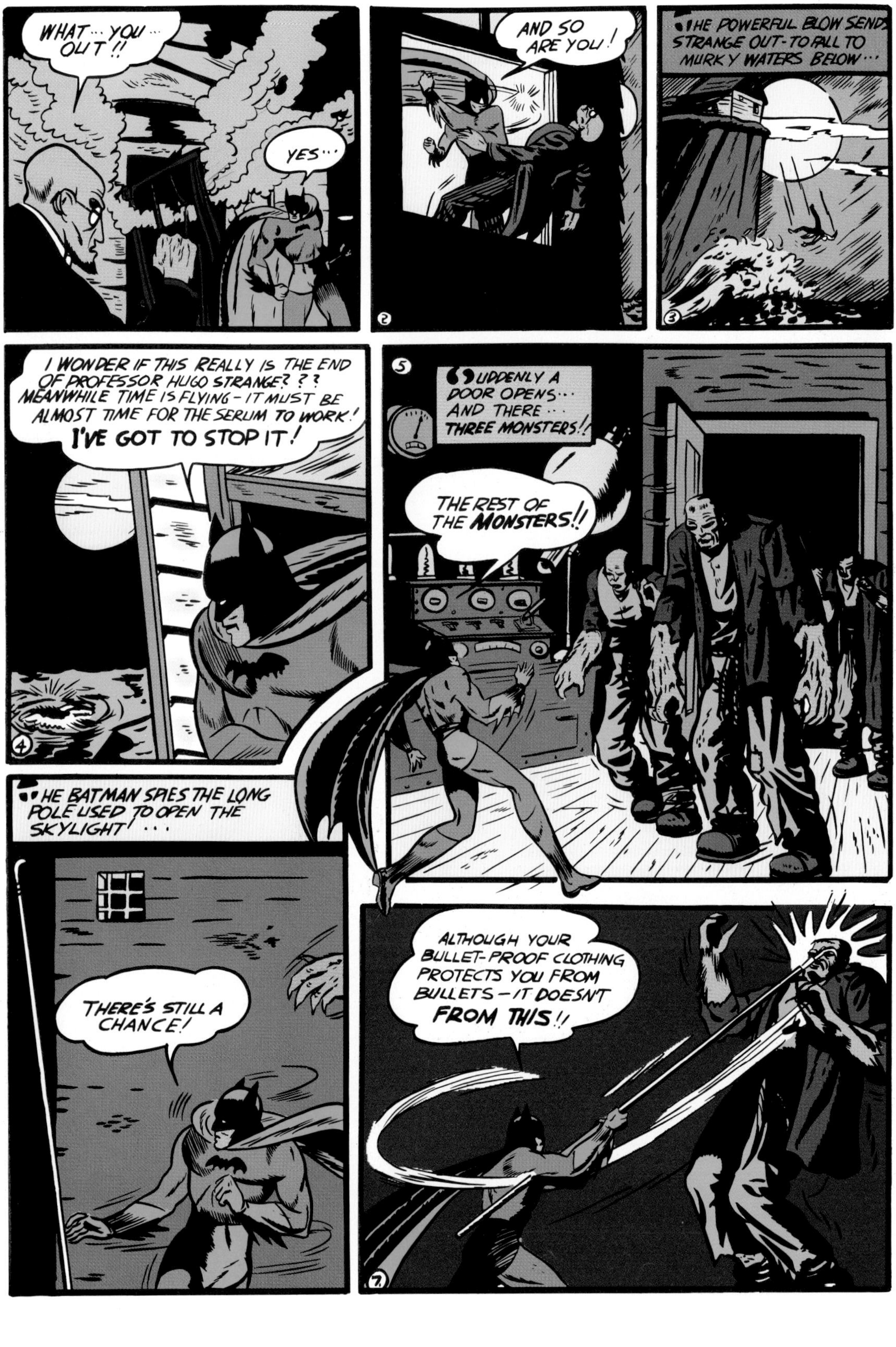
WHAT... YOU... OUT!!
YES...
AND SO ARE YOU!
THE POWERFUL BLOW SENDS STRANGE OUT-TO FALL TO MURKY WATERS BELOW...
I WONDER IF THIS REALLY IS THE END OF PROFESSOR HUGO STRANGE? ? ? MEANWHILE TIME IS FLYING - IT MUST BE ALMOST TIME FOR THE SERUM TO WORK! I'VE GOT TO STOP IT!
SUDDENLY A DOOR OPENS... AND THERE... THREE MONSTERS!!
THE REST OF THE MONSTERS!!
THE BATMAN SPIES THE LONG POLE USED TO OPEN THE SKYLIGHT...
THERE'S STILL A CHANCE!
ALTHOUGH YOUR BULLET-PROOF CLOTHING PROTECTS YOU FROM BULLETS - IT DOESN'T FROM THIS!!

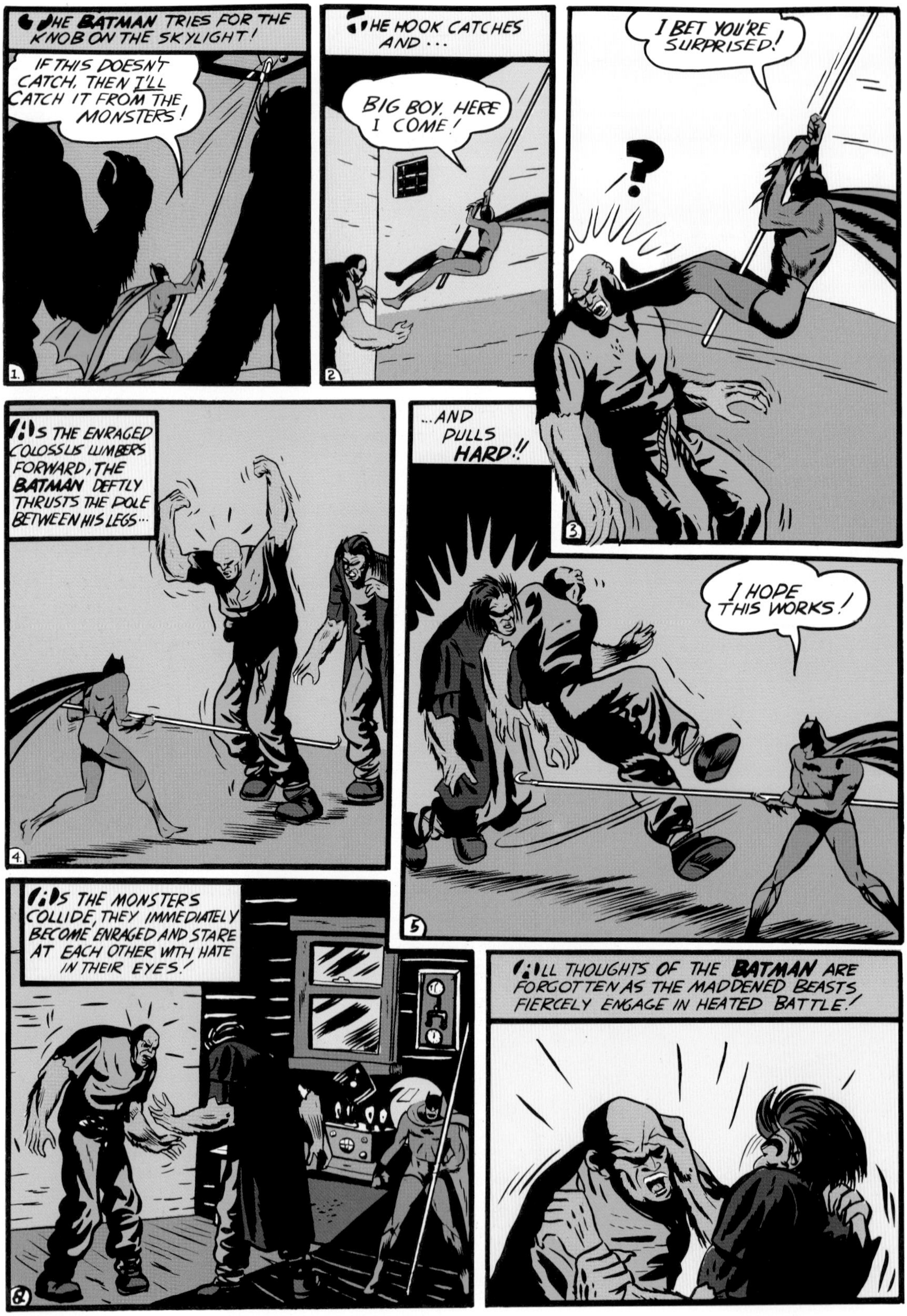
THE BATMAN TRIES FOR THE KNOB ON THE SKYLIGHT!
IF THIS DOESN'T CATCH, THEN I'LL CATCH IT FROM THE MONSTERS!
1.
THE HOOK CATCHES AND...
BIG BOY, HERE I COME!
2.
I BET YOU'RE SURPRISED!
?
3.
AS THE ENRAGED COLOSSUS LUMBERS FORWARD, THE BATMAN DEFTLY THRUSTS THE POLE BETWEEN HIS LEGS...
4.
...AND PULLS HARD!!
I HOPE THIS WORKS!
5.
AS THE MONSTERS COLLIDE, THEY IMMEDIATELY BECOME ENRAGED AND STARE AT EACH OTHER WITH HATE IN THEIR EYES!
8.
ALL THOUGHTS OF THE BATMAN ARE FORGOTTEN AS THE MADDENED BEASTS FIERCELY ENGAGE IN HEATED BATTLE!

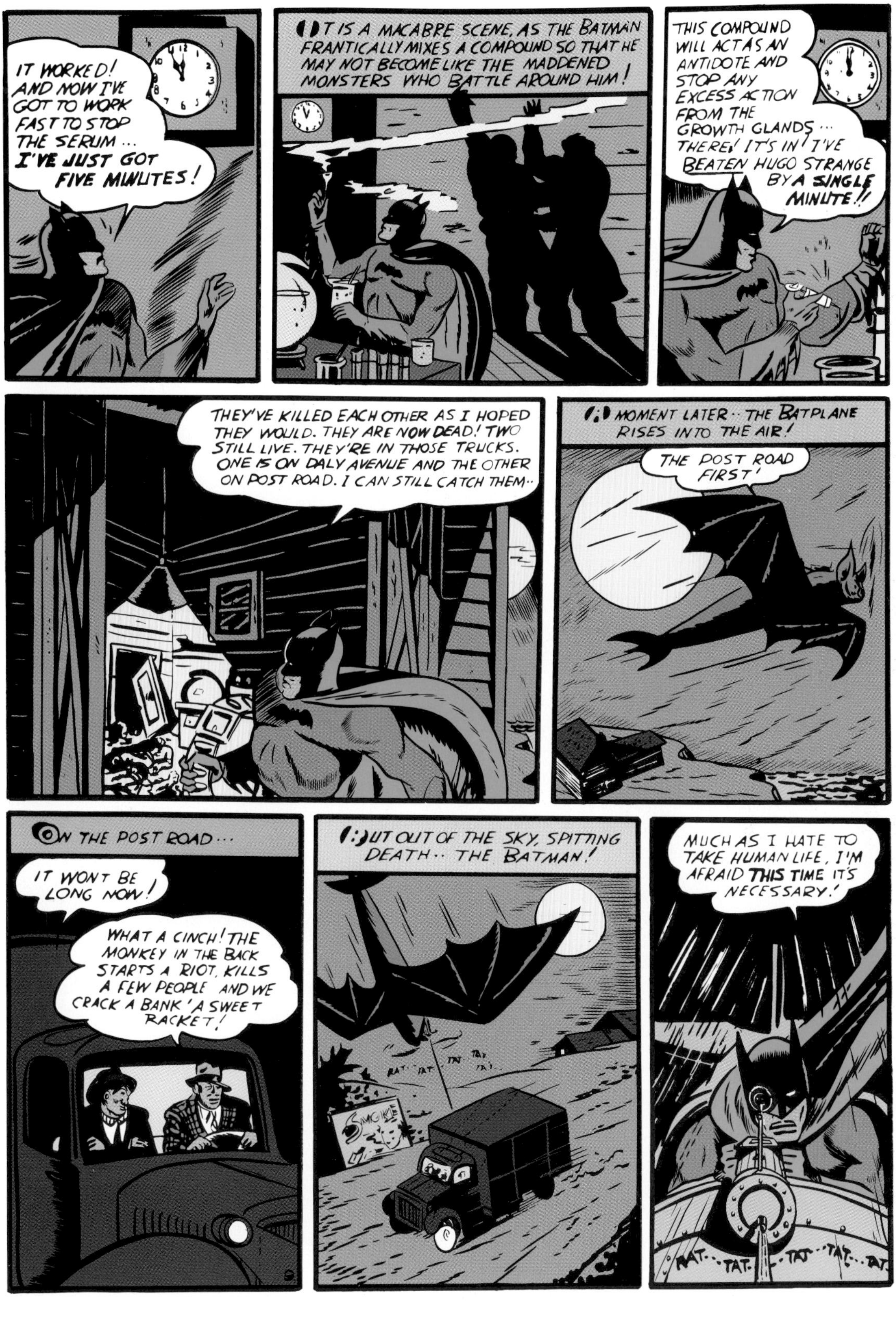
IT WORKED! AND NOW I'VE GOT TO WORK FAST TO STOP THE SERUM... I'VE JUST GOT FIVE MINUTES!
IT IS A MACABRE SCENE, AS THE BATMAN FRANTICALLY MIXES A COMPOUND SO THAT HE MAY NOT BECOME LIKE THE MADDENED MONSTERS WHO BATTLE AROUND HIM!
THIS COMPOUND WILL ACT AS AN ANTIDOTE AND STOP ANY EXCESS ACTION FROM THE GROWTH GLANDS... THERE! IT'S IN! I'VE BEATEN HUGO STRANGE BY A SINGLE MINUTE!!
THEY'VE KILLED EACH OTHER AS I HOPED THEY WOULD. THEY ARE NOW DEAD! TWO STILL LIVE. THEY'RE IN THOSE TRUCKS. ONE IS ON DALY AVENUE AND THE OTHER ON POST ROAD. I CAN STILL CATCH THEM..
A MOMENT LATER.. THE BATPLANE RISES INTO THE AIR!
THE POST ROAD FIRST!
ON THE POST ROAD...
IT WONT BE LONG NOW!
WHAT A CINCH! THE MONKEY IN THE BACK STARTS A RIOT, KILLS A FEW PEOPLE AND WE CRACK A BANK 'A SWEET RACKET!
BUT OUT OF THE SKY, SPITTING DEATH.. THE BATMAN!
RAT-TAT-TAT-TAT
MUCH AS I HATE TO TAKE HUMAN LIFE, I'M AFRAID THIS TIME IT'S NECESSARY!
RAT-TAT-TAT-TAT-TAT

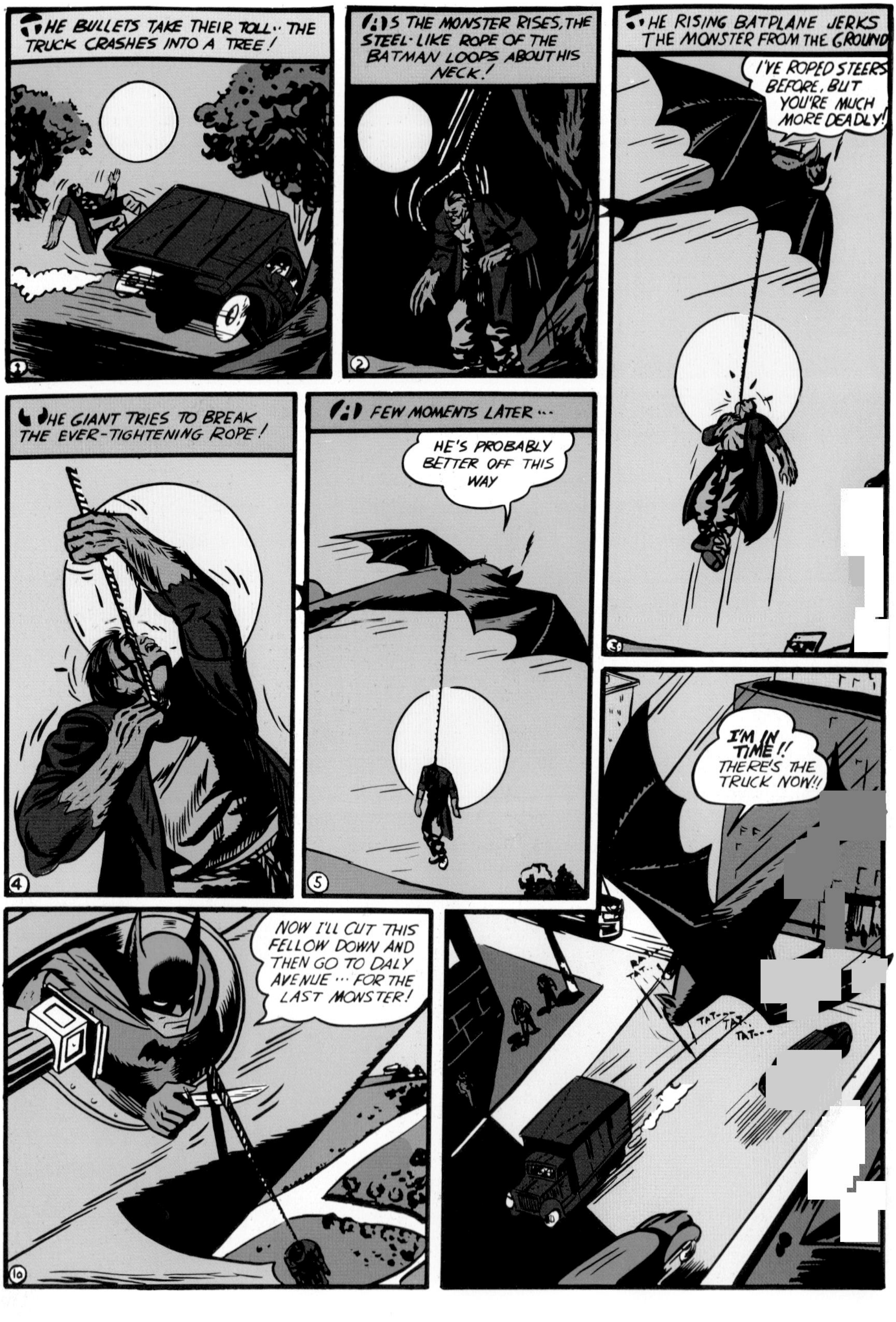
THE BULLETS TAKE THEIR TOLL.. THE TRUCK CRASHES INTO A TREE!
AS THE MONSTER RISES, THE STEEL-LIKE ROPE OF THE BATMAN LOOPS ABOUT HIS NECK!
THE RISING BATPLANE JERKS THE MONSTER FROM THE GROUND
I'VE ROPED STEERS BEFORE, BUT YOU'RE MUCH MORE DEADLY!
THE GIANT TRIES TO BREAK THE EVER-TIGHTENING ROPE!
A FEW MOMENTS LATER...
HE'S PROBABLY BETTER OFF THIS WAY
I'M IN TIME!! THERE'S THE TRUCK NOW!!
TAT-- TAT-- TAT---
NOW I'LL CUT THIS FELLOW DOWN AND THEN GO TO DALY AVENUE ... FOR THE LAST MONSTER!

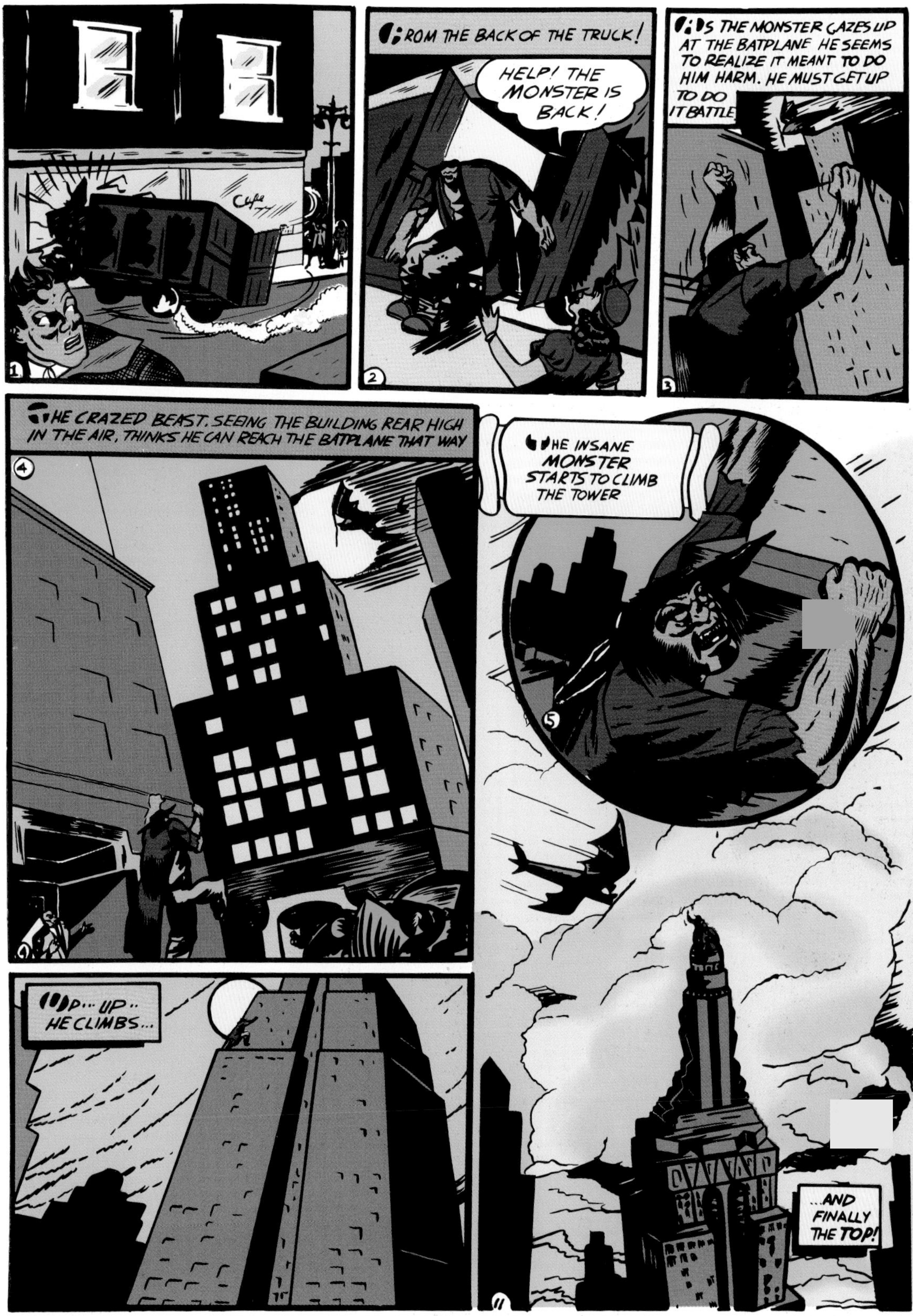
FROM THE BACK OF THE TRUCK!
HELP! THE MONSTER IS BACK!
AS THE MONSTER GAZES UP AT THE BATPLANE HE SEEMS TO REALIZE IT MEANT TO DO HIM HARM. HE MUST GET UP TO DO IT BATTLE
THE CRAZED BEAST, SEEING THE BUILDING REAR HIGH IN THE AIR, THINKS HE CAN REACH THE BATPLANE THAT WAY
THE INSANE MONSTER STARTS TO CLIMB THE TOWER
UP... UP.. HE CLIMBS...
...AND FINALLY THE TOP!

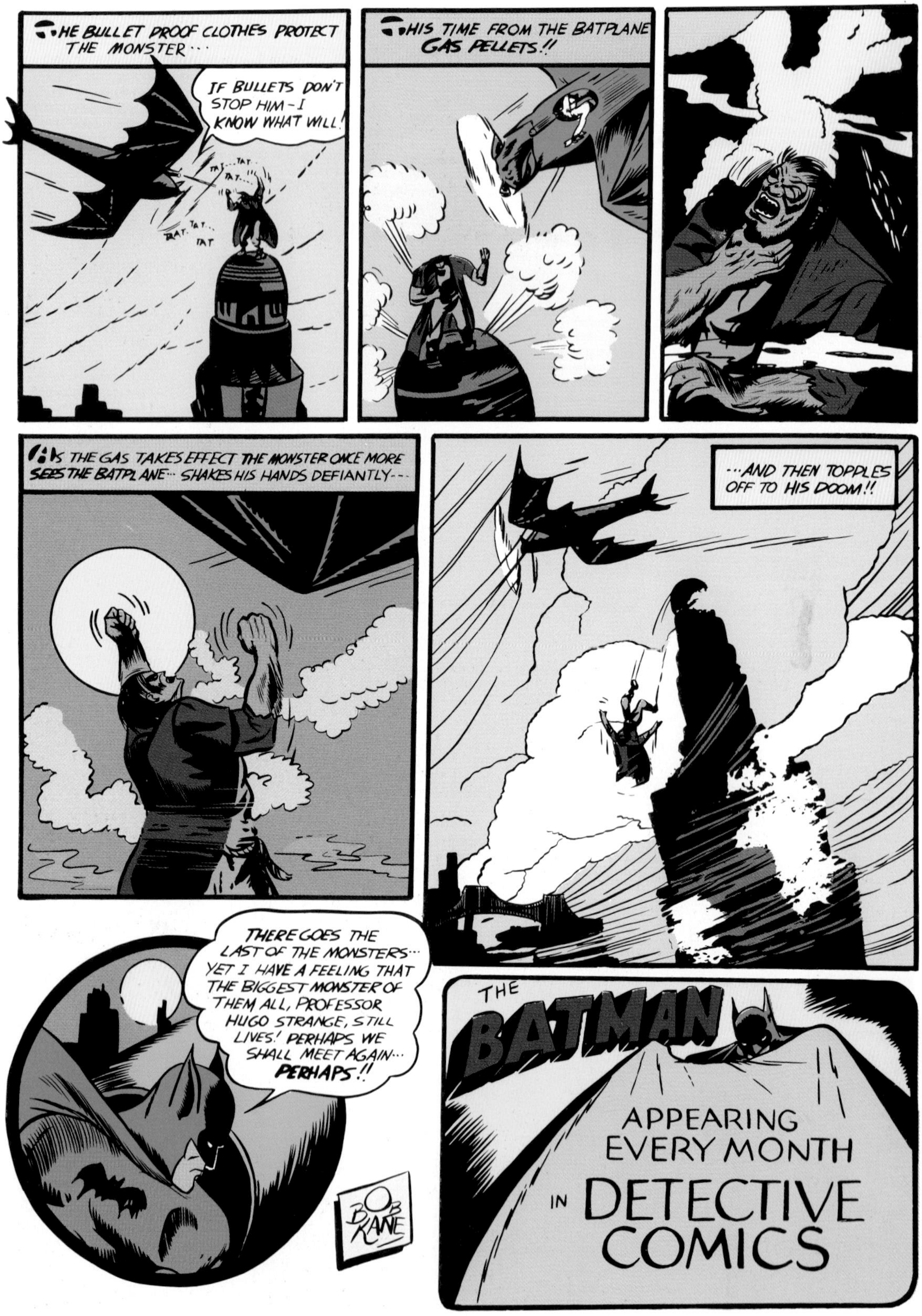
THE BULLET PROOF CLOTHES PROTECT THE MONSTER···
IF BULLETS DON'T STOP HIM - I KNOW WHAT WILL!
THIS TIME FROM THE BATPLANE GAS PELLETS!!
AS THE GAS TAKES EFFECT THE MONSTER ONCE MORE SEES THE BATPLANE··· SHAKES HIS HANDS DEFIANTLY···
···AND THEN TOPPLES OFF TO HIS DOOM!!
THERE GOES THE LAST OF THE MONSTERS··· YET I HAVE A FEELING THAT THE BIGGEST MONSTER OF THEM ALL, PROFESSOR HUGO STRANGE, STILL LIVES! PERHAPS WE SHALL MEET AGAIN··· PERHAPS!!
BOB KANE
THE BATMAN
APPEARING EVERY MONTH IN DETECTIVE COMICS

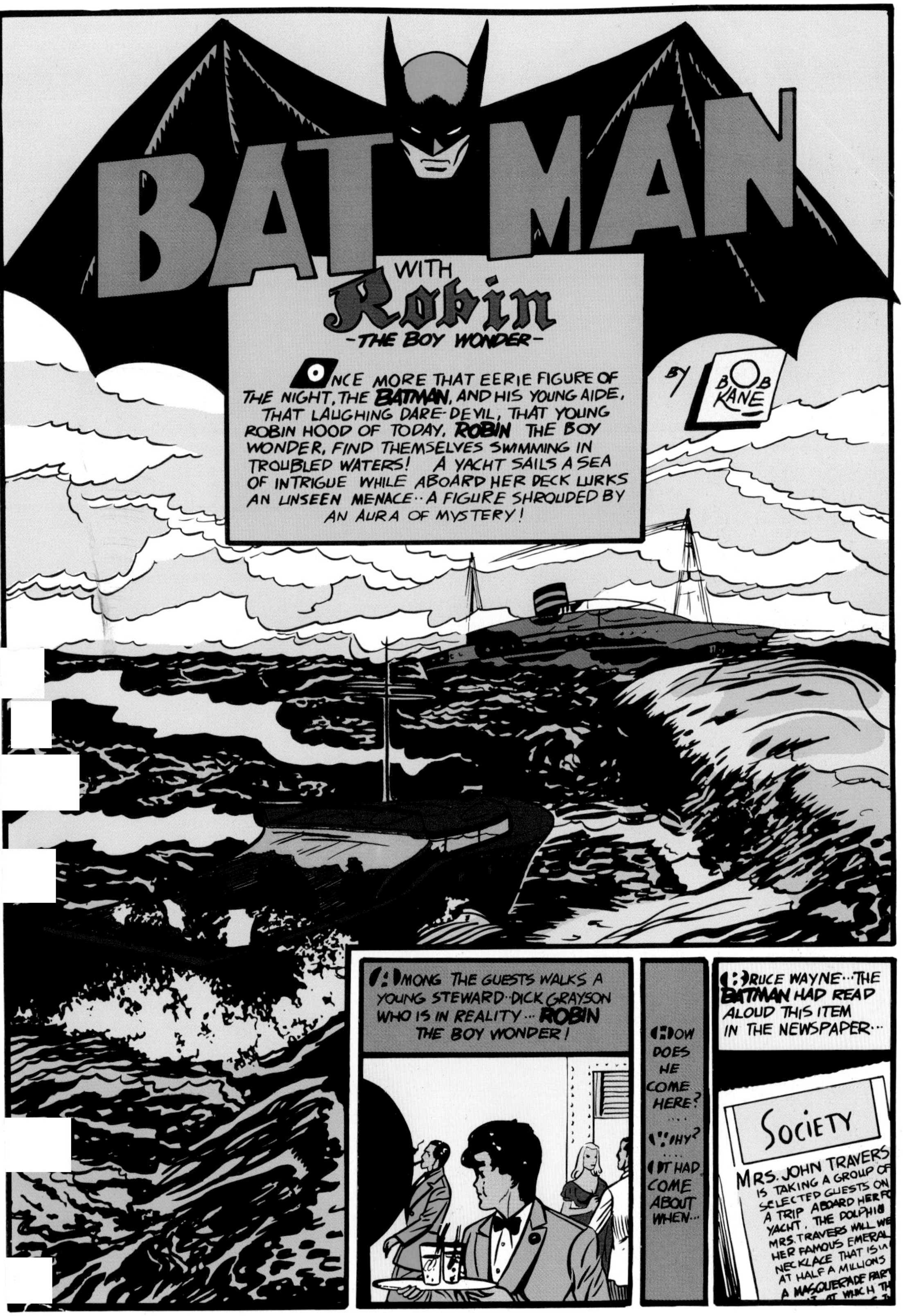
BATMAN
WITH Robin -THE BOY WONDER-
BY BOB KANE
ONCE MORE THAT EERIE FIGURE OF THE NIGHT, THE BATMAN, AND HIS YOUNG AIDE, THAT LAUGHING DARE-DEVIL, THAT YOUNG ROBIN HOOD OF TODAY, ROBIN THE BOY WONDER, FIND THEMSELVES SWIMMING IN TROUBLED WATERS! A YACHT SAILS A SEA OF INTRIGUE WHILE ABOARD HER DECK LURKS AN UNSEEN MENACE.. A FIGURE SHROUDED BY AN AURA OF MYSTERY!
AMONG THE GUESTS WALKS A YOUNG STEWARD..DICK GRAYSON WHO IS IN REALITY... ROBIN THE BOY WONDER!
HOW DOES HE COME HERE? .... WHY? .... IT HAD COME ABOUT WHEN...
BRUCE WAYNE...THE BATMAN HAD READ ALOUD THIS ITEM IN THE NEWSPAPER...
SOCIETY

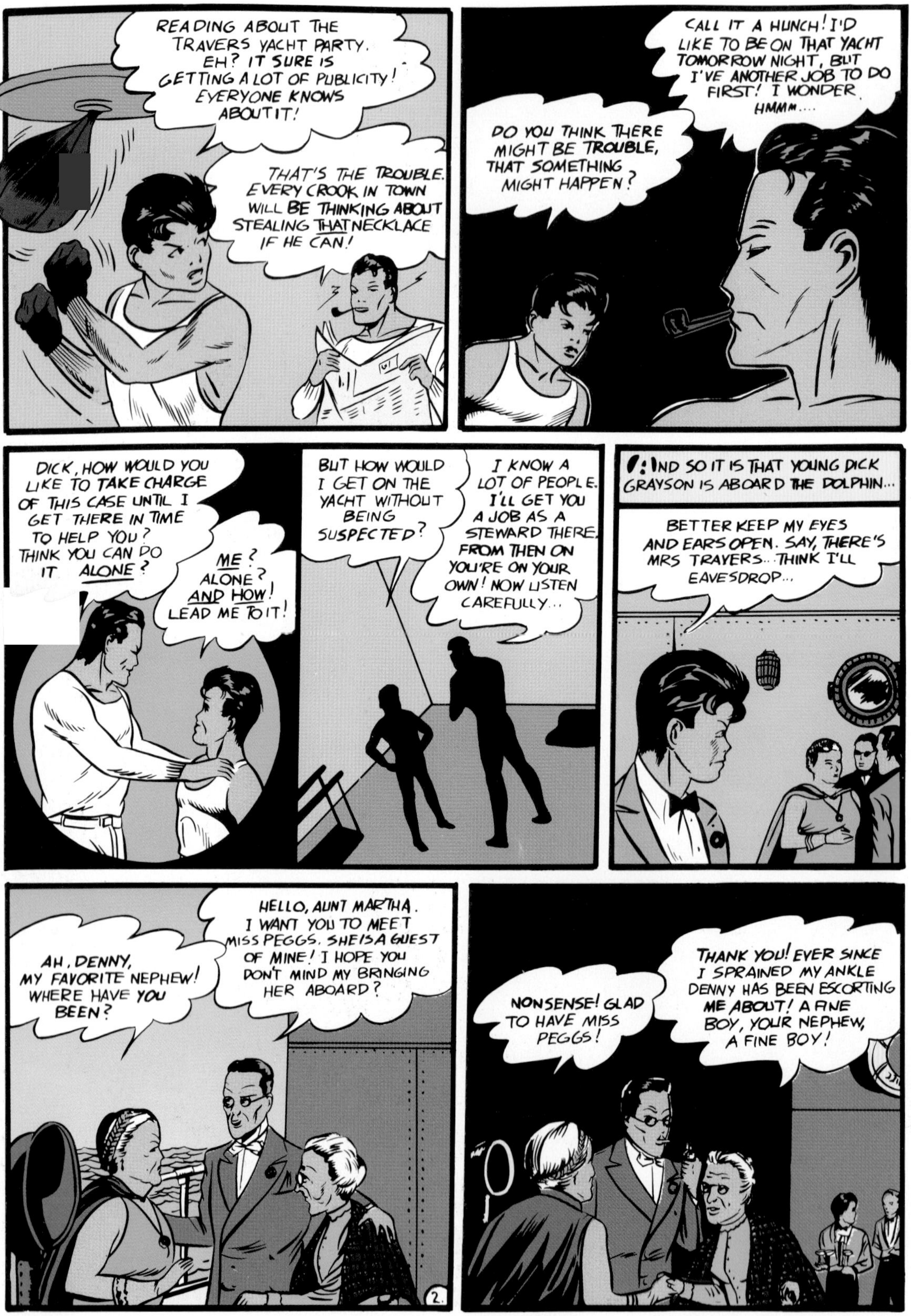
READING ABOUT THE TRAVERS YACHT PARTY. EH? IT SURE IS GETTING A LOT OF PUBLICITY! EVERYONE KNOWS ABOUT IT!
THAT'S THE TROUBLE. EVERY CROOK IN TOWN WILL BE THINKING ABOUT STEALING THAT NECKLACE IF HE CAN!
DO YOU THINK THERE MIGHT BE TROUBLE, THAT SOMETHING MIGHT HAPPEN?
CALL IT A HUNCH! I'D LIKE TO BE ON THAT YACHT TOMORROW NIGHT, BUT I'VE ANOTHER JOB TO DO FIRST! I WONDER HMMM....
DICK, HOW WOULD YOU LIKE TO TAKE CHARGE OF THIS CASE UNTIL I GET THERE IN TIME TO HELP YOU? THINK YOU CAN DO IT ALONE?
ME? ALONE? AND HOW! LEAD ME TO IT!
BUT HOW WOULD I GET ON THE YACHT WITHOUT BEING SUSPECTED?
I KNOW A LOT OF PEOPLE. I'LL GET YOU A JOB AS A STEWARD THERE. FROM THEN ON YOU'RE ON YOUR OWN! NOW LISTEN CAREFULLY...
AND SO IT IS THAT YOUNG DICK GRAYSON IS ABOARD THE DOLPHIN...
BETTER KEEP MY EYES AND EARS OPEN. SAY, THERE'S MRS TRAVERS... THINK I'LL EAVESDROP...
AH, DENNY, MY FAVORITE NEPHEW! WHERE HAVE YOU BEEN?
HELLO, AUNT MARTHA. I WANT YOU TO MEET MISS PEGGS. SHE IS A GUEST OF MINE! I HOPE YOU DON'T MIND MY BRINGING HER ABOARD?
2.
NONSENSE! GLAD TO HAVE MISS PEGGS!
THANK YOU! EVER SINCE I SPRAINED MY ANKLE DENNY HAS BEEN ESCORTING ME ABOUT! A FINE BOY, YOUR NEPHEW, A FINE BOY!

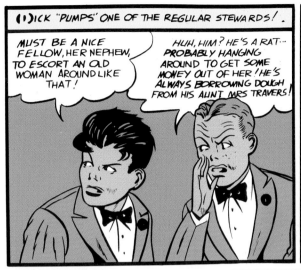

(1) DICK "PUMPS" ONE OF THE REGULAR STEWARDS!

MUST BE A NICE FELLOW, HER NEPHEW, TO ESCORT AN OLD WOMAN AROUND LIKE THAT!

HUH, HIM? HE'S A RAT... PROBABLY HANGING AROUND TO GET SOME MONEY OUT OF HER! HE'S ALWAYS BORROWING DOUGH FROM HIS AUNT MRS. TRAVERS!

THEY ALL TRY TO GET DOUGH OUT OF HER! SEE THAT GUY WHO JUST WALKED OVER? THAT'S HER DOCTOR... WALLACE... GAMBLES ALL HIS DOUGH AWAY... AND THEN HE BORROWS MONEY FROM MRS. TRAVERS! I BET HE OWES HER PLENTY!... **PLENTY!**

(?) SOMETIME LATER AS DICK PASSES A CABIN...

VOICES! SOUNDS LIKE A QUARREL!

NO! I WON'T LEND YOU A CENT, ROGER AND THAT'S **FINAL!**

BUT I NEED IT TO COVER MY STOCK LOSSES! PLEASE!

JUST BECAUSE YOU'RE MY BROTHER, DOESN'T MEAN I MUST FINANCE ALL YOUR STUPID PLUNGES IN THE STOCK MARKET!

I'LL BE RUINED! AND YOU'LL BE THE CAUSE OF IT ALL! I'LL GET THAT MONEY SOMEHOW, SOMEWAY!

WHEW! LOOKS LIKE THIS YACHT ISN'T THE SAFEST PLACE IN THE WORLD FOR A NECKLACE WORTH A HALF A MILLION DOLLARS!

(?) AS HE TURNS A CORNER HE SEES DENNY FURTIVELY THROW A PAPER OVER THE RAIL!

IF EVER A GUY LOOKED GUILTY ABOUT SOMETHING, HE DOES! WONDER WHAT'S IN THAT PAPER?

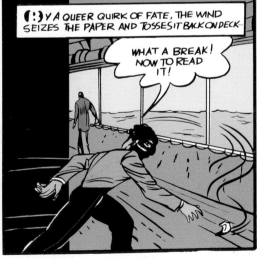

(?) BY A QUEER QUIRK OF FATE, THE WIND SEIZES THE PAPER AND TOSSES IT BACK ON DECK...

WHAT A BREAK! NOW TO READ IT!

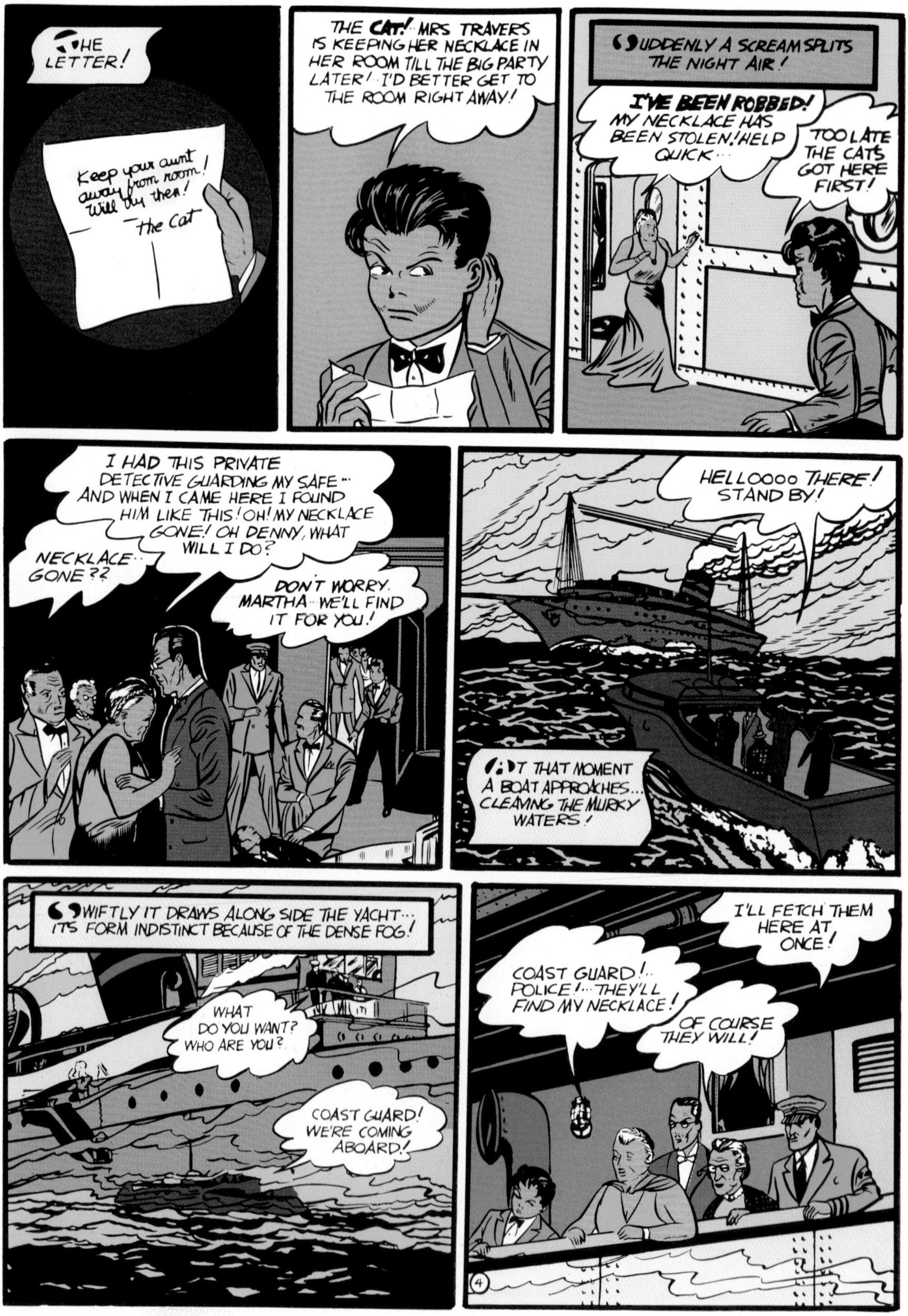
THE LETTER!
Keep your aunt away from room! Will try then! —The Cat
THE CAT! MRS TRAVERS IS KEEPING HER NECKLACE IN HER ROOM TILL THE BIG PARTY LATER! I'D BETTER GET TO THE ROOM RIGHT AWAY!
SUDDENLY A SCREAM SPLITS THE NIGHT AIR!
I'VE BEEN ROBBED! MY NECKLACE HAS BEEN STOLEN! HELP QUICK...
TOO LATE THE CAT'S GOT HERE FIRST!
I HAD THIS PRIVATE DETECTIVE GUARDING MY SAFE... AND WHEN I CAME HERE I FOUND HIM LIKE THIS! OH! MY NECKLACE GONE! OH DENNY, WHAT WILL I DO?
NECKLACE... GONE??
DON'T WORRY MARTHA... WE'LL FIND IT FOR YOU!
HELLOOOO THERE! STAND BY!
AT THAT MOMENT A BOAT APPROACHES... CLEAVING THE MURKY WATERS!
SWIFTLY IT DRAWS ALONG SIDE THE YACHT... ITS FORM INDISTINCT BECAUSE OF THE DENSE FOG!
WHAT DO YOU WANT? WHO ARE YOU?
COAST GUARD! WE'RE COMING ABOARD!
I'LL FETCH THEM HERE AT ONCE!
COAST GUARD!... POLICE!... THEY'LL FIND MY NECKLACE!
OF COURSE THEY WILL!
4

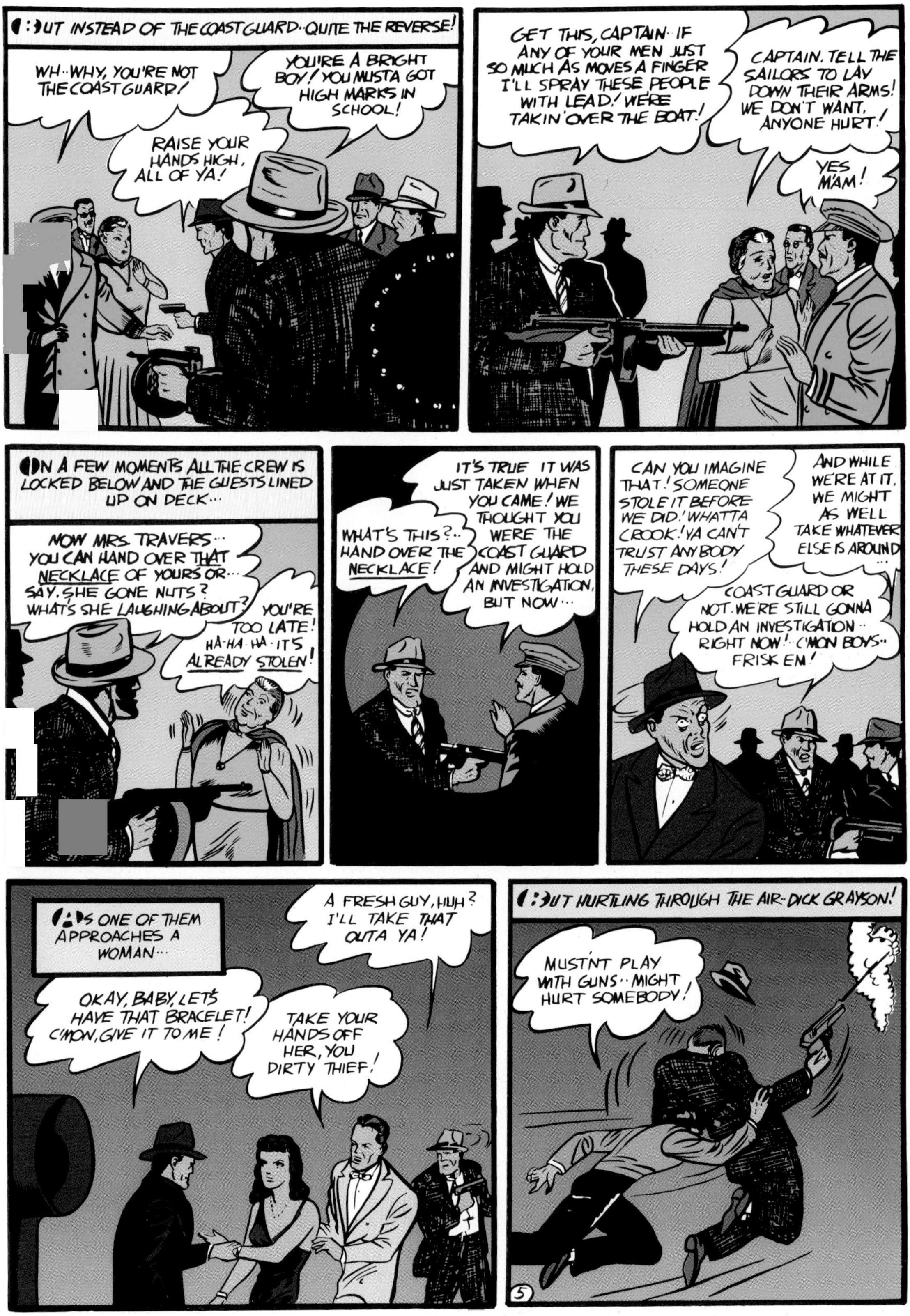
BUT INSTEAD OF THE COAST GUARD..QUITE THE REVERSE!
WH..WHY, YOU'RE NOT THE COAST GUARD!
YOU'RE A BRIGHT BOY! YOU MUSTA GOT HIGH MARKS IN SCHOOL!
RAISE YOUR HANDS HIGH, ALL OF YA!
GET THIS, CAPTAIN.. IF ANY OF YOUR MEN JUST SO MUCH AS MOVES A FINGER I'LL SPRAY THESE PEOPLE WITH LEAD! WE'RE TAKIN' OVER THE BOAT!
CAPTAIN, TELL THE SAILORS TO LAY DOWN THEIR ARMS! WE DON'T WANT ANYONE HURT!
YES M'AM!
IN A FEW MOMENTS ALL THE CREW IS LOCKED BELOW AND THE GUESTS LINED UP ON DECK...
NOW MRS. TRAVERS.. YOU CAN HAND OVER THAT NECKLACE OF YOURS OR... SAY, SHE GONE NUTS? WHAT'S SHE LAUGHING ABOUT?
YOU'RE TOO LATE! HA-HA-HA-IT'S ALREADY STOLEN!
WHAT'S THIS?.. HAND OVER THE NECKLACE!
IT'S TRUE IT WAS JUST TAKEN WHEN YOU CAME! WE THOUGHT YOU WERE THE COAST GUARD AND MIGHT HOLD AN INVESTIGATION, BUT NOW...
CAN YOU IMAGINE THAT! SOMEONE STOLE IT BEFORE WE DID! WHATTA CROOK! YA CAN'T TRUST ANYBODY THESE DAYS!
AND WHILE WE'RE AT IT, WE MIGHT AS WELL TAKE WHATEVER ELSE IS AROUND...
COAST GUARD OR NOT WE'RE STILL GONNA HOLD AN INVESTIGATION.. RIGHT NOW! C'MON BOYS.. FRISK EM!
AS ONE OF THEM APPROACHES A WOMAN...
OKAY, BABY, LET'S HAVE THAT BRACELET! C'MON, GIVE IT TO ME!
TAKE YOUR HANDS OFF HER, YOU DIRTY THIEF!
A FRESH GUY, HUH? I'LL TAKE THAT OUTA YA!
BUT HURTLING THROUGH THE AIR.. DICK GRAYSON!
MUSTN'T PLAY WITH GUNS.. MIGHT HURT SOMEBODY!
5

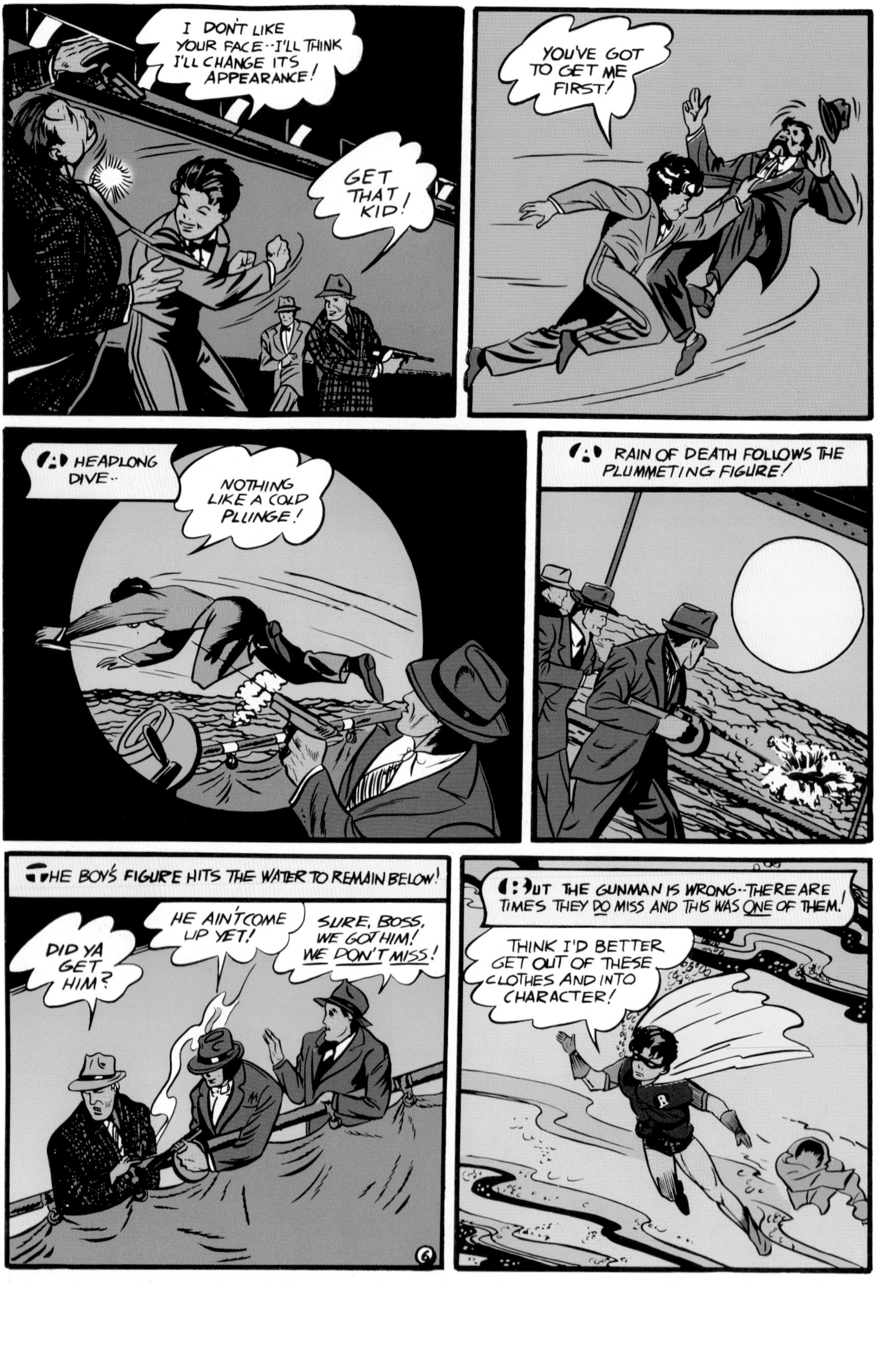
I DON'T LIKE YOUR FACE--I'LL THINK I'LL CHANGE ITS APPEARANCE!
GET THAT KID!
YOU'VE GOT TO GET ME FIRST!
A HEADLONG DIVE--
NOTHING LIKE A COLD PLUNGE!
A RAIN OF DEATH FOLLOWS THE PLUMMETING FIGURE!
THE BOY'S FIGURE HITS THE WATER TO REMAIN BELOW!
DID YA GET HIM?
HE AIN'T COME UP YET!
SURE, BOSS, WE GOT HIM! WE DON'T MISS!
6
BUT THE GUNMAN IS WRONG--THERE ARE TIMES THEY DO MISS AND THIS WAS ONE OF THEM!
THINK I'D BETTER GET OUT OF THESE CLOTHES AND INTO CHARACTER!

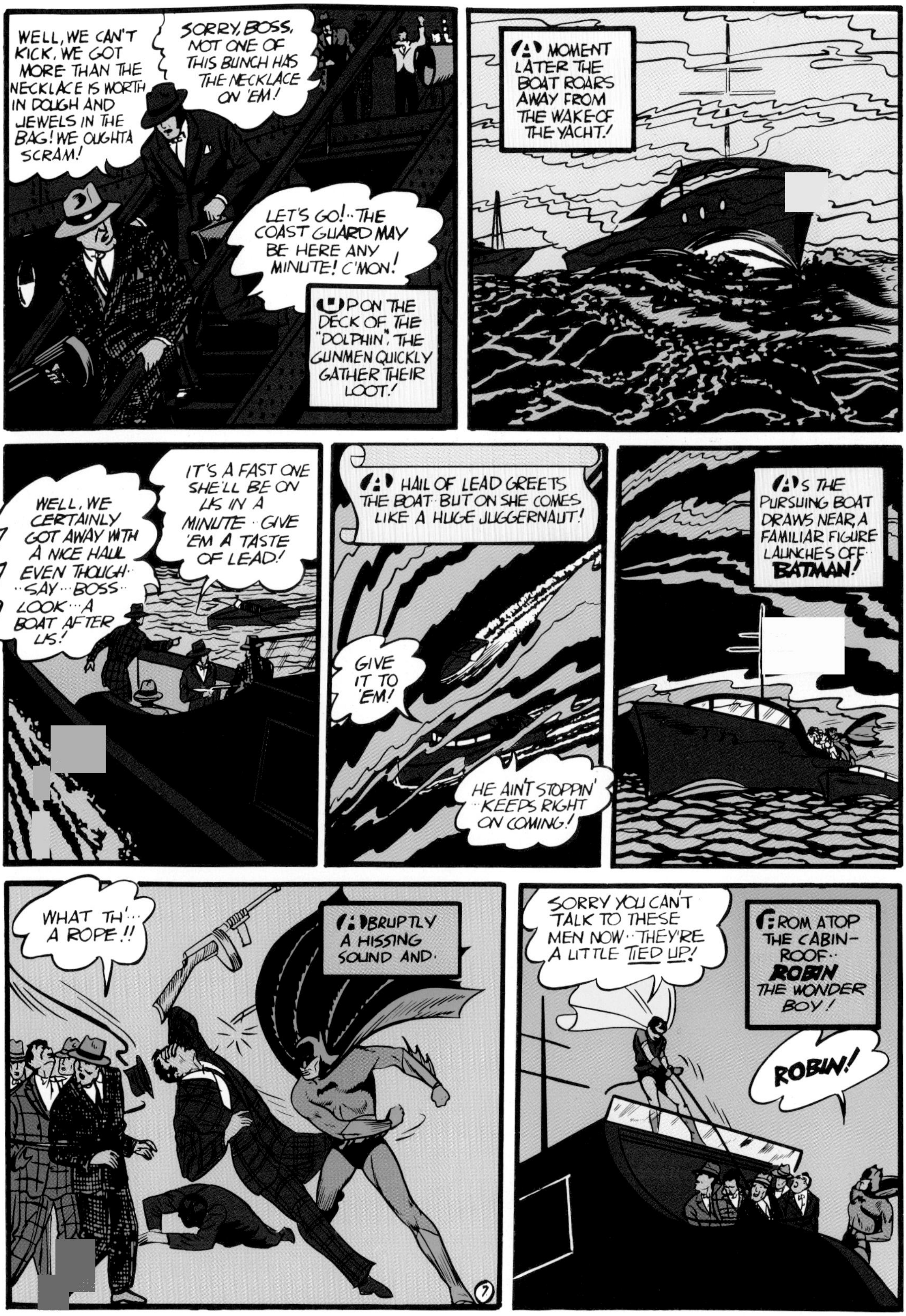
WELL, WE CAN'T KICK, WE GOT MORE THAN THE NECKLACE IS WORTH IN DOUGH AND JEWELS IN THE BAG! WE OUGHTA SCRAM!
SORRY, BOSS, NOT ONE OF THIS BUNCH HAS THE NECKLACE ON 'EM!
LET'S GO!.. THE COAST GUARD MAY BE HERE ANY MINUTE! C'MON!
UP ON THE DECK OF THE "DOLPHIN", THE GUNMEN QUICKLY GATHER THEIR LOOT!
A MOMENT LATER THE BOAT ROARS AWAY FROM THE WAKE OF THE YACHT!
WELL, WE CERTAINLY GOT AWAY WITH A NICE HAUL EVEN THOUGH.. ..SAY...BOSS.. LOOK...A BOAT AFTER US!
IT'S A FAST ONE SHE'LL BE ON US IN A MINUTE ..GIVE 'EM A TASTE OF LEAD!
A HAIL OF LEAD GREETS THE BOAT. BUT ON SHE COMES LIKE A HUGE JUGGERNAUT!
GIVE IT TO 'EM!
HE AIN'T STOPPIN' ..KEEPS RIGHT ON COMING!
AS THE PURSUING BOAT DRAWS NEAR, A FAMILIAR FIGURE LAUNCHES OFF.. BATMAN!
WHAT TH'... A ROPE!!
ABRUPTLY A HISSING SOUND AND.
SORRY YOU CAN'T TALK TO THESE MEN NOW.. THEY'RE A LITTLE TIED UP!
FROM ATOP THE CABIN-ROOF.. ROBIN THE WONDER BOY!
ROBIN!

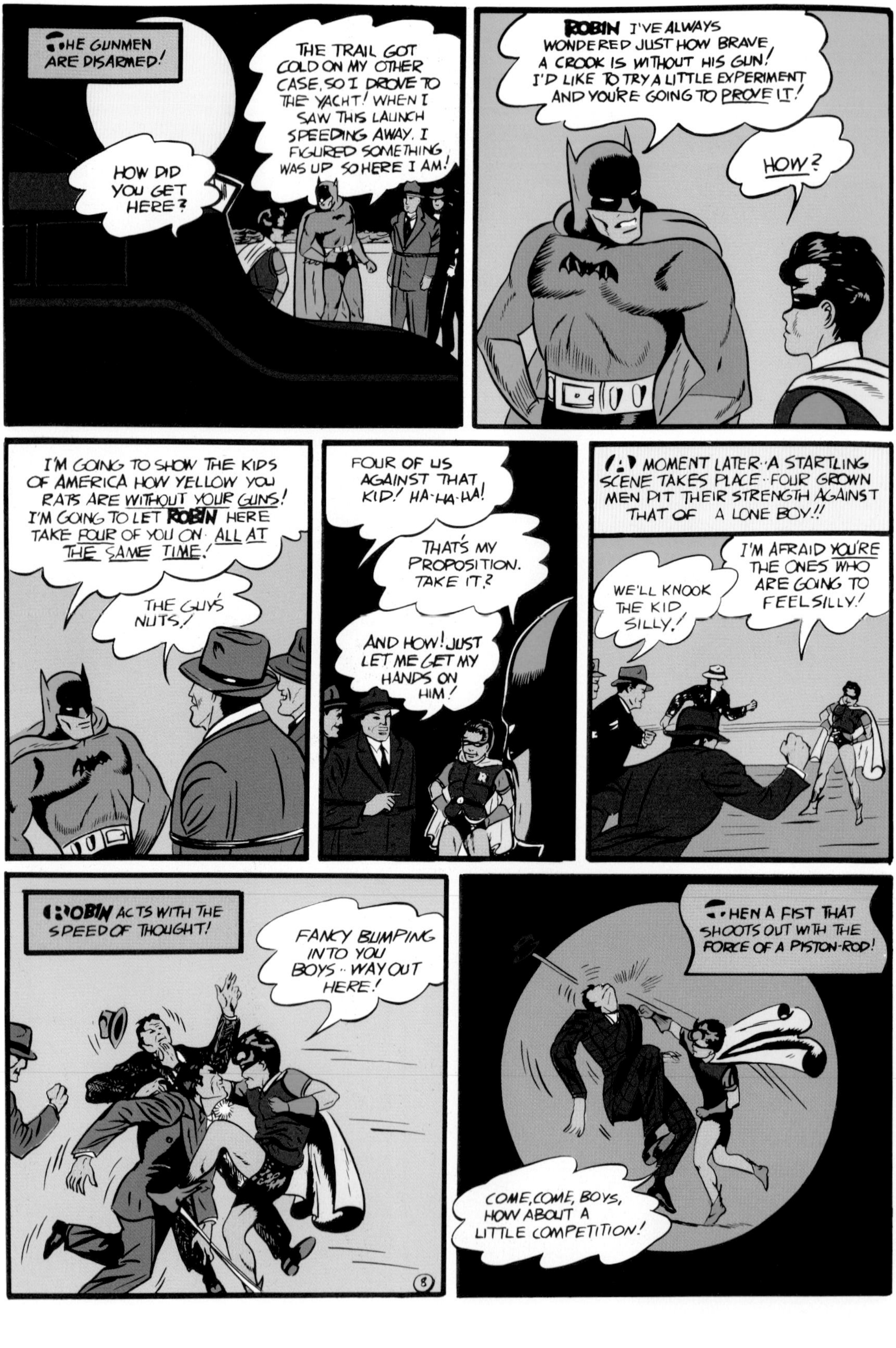
THE GUNMEN ARE DISARMED!
HOW DID YOU GET HERE?
THE TRAIL GOT COLD ON MY OTHER CASE, SO I DROVE TO THE YACHT! WHEN I SAW THIS LAUNCH SPEEDING AWAY, I FIGURED SOMETHING WAS UP SO HERE I AM!
ROBIN I'VE ALWAYS WONDERED JUST HOW BRAVE A CROOK IS WITHOUT HIS GUN! I'D LIKE TO TRY A LITTLE EXPERIMENT AND YOU'RE GOING TO PROVE IT!
HOW?
I'M GOING TO SHOW THE KIDS OF AMERICA HOW YELLOW YOU RATS ARE WITHOUT YOUR GUNS! I'M GOING TO LET ROBIN HERE TAKE FOUR OF YOU ON · ALL AT THE SAME TIME!
THE GUY'S NUTS!
FOUR OF US AGAINST THAT KID! HA-HA-HA!
THAT'S MY PROPOSITION. TAKE IT?
AND HOW! JUST LET ME GET MY HANDS ON HIM!
A MOMENT LATER · A STARTLING SCENE TAKES PLACE · FOUR GROWN MEN PIT THEIR STRENGTH AGAINST THAT OF A LONE BOY!!
WE'LL KNOOK THE KID SILLY!
I'M AFRAID YOU'RE THE ONES WHO ARE GOING TO FEEL SILLY!
ROBIN ACTS WITH THE SPEED OF THOUGHT!
FANCY BUMPING INTO YOU BOYS · WAY OUT HERE!
8
THEN A FIST THAT SHOOTS OUT WITH THE FORCE OF A PISTON-ROD!
COME, COME, BOYS, HOW ABOUT A LITTLE COMPETITION!

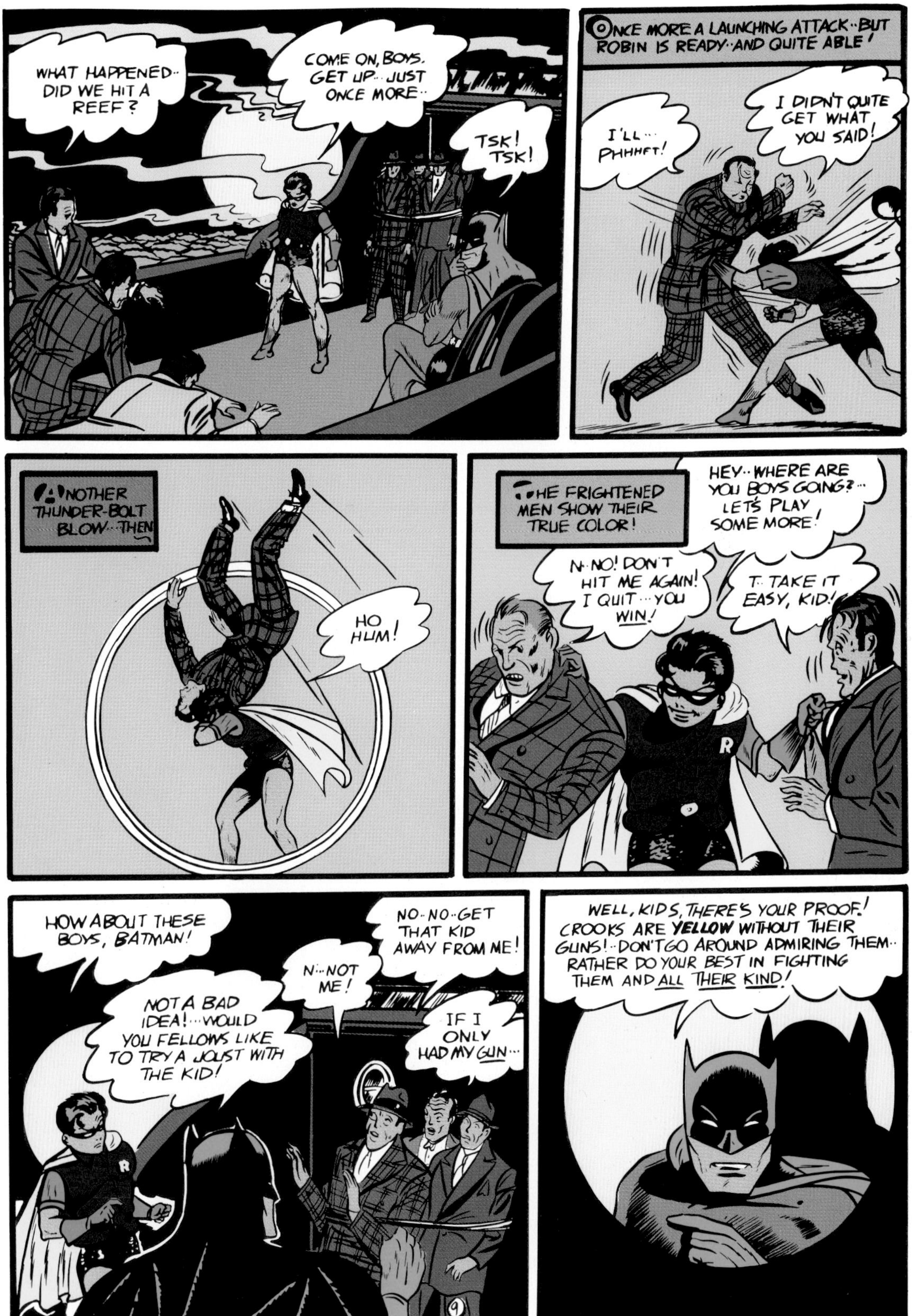
WHAT HAPPENED.. DID WE HIT A REEF?
COME ON, BOYS. GET UP.. JUST ONCE MORE..
TSK! TSK!
ONCE MORE A LAUNCHING ATTACK..BUT ROBIN IS READY..AND QUITE ABLE!
I'LL... PHHHFT!
I DIDN'T QUITE GET WHAT YOU SAID!
ANOTHER THUNDER-BOLT BLOW..THEN
HO HUM!
THE FRIGHTENED MEN SHOW THEIR TRUE COLOR!
HEY..WHERE ARE YOU BOYS GOING?.. LET'S PLAY SOME MORE!
N-NO! DON'T HIT ME AGAIN! I QUIT...YOU WIN!
T-TAKE IT EASY, KID!
HOW ABOUT THESE BOYS, BATMAN!
NOT A BAD IDEA!...WOULD YOU FELLOWS LIKE TO TRY A JOUST WITH THE KID!
N...NOT ME!
NO..NO..GET THAT KID AWAY FROM ME!
IF I ONLY HAD MY GUN...
9
WELL, KIDS, THERE'S YOUR PROOF! CROOKS ARE YELLOW WITHOUT THEIR GUNS!..DON'T GO AROUND ADMIRING THEM.. RATHER DO YOUR BEST IN FIGHTING THEM AND ALL THEIR KIND!

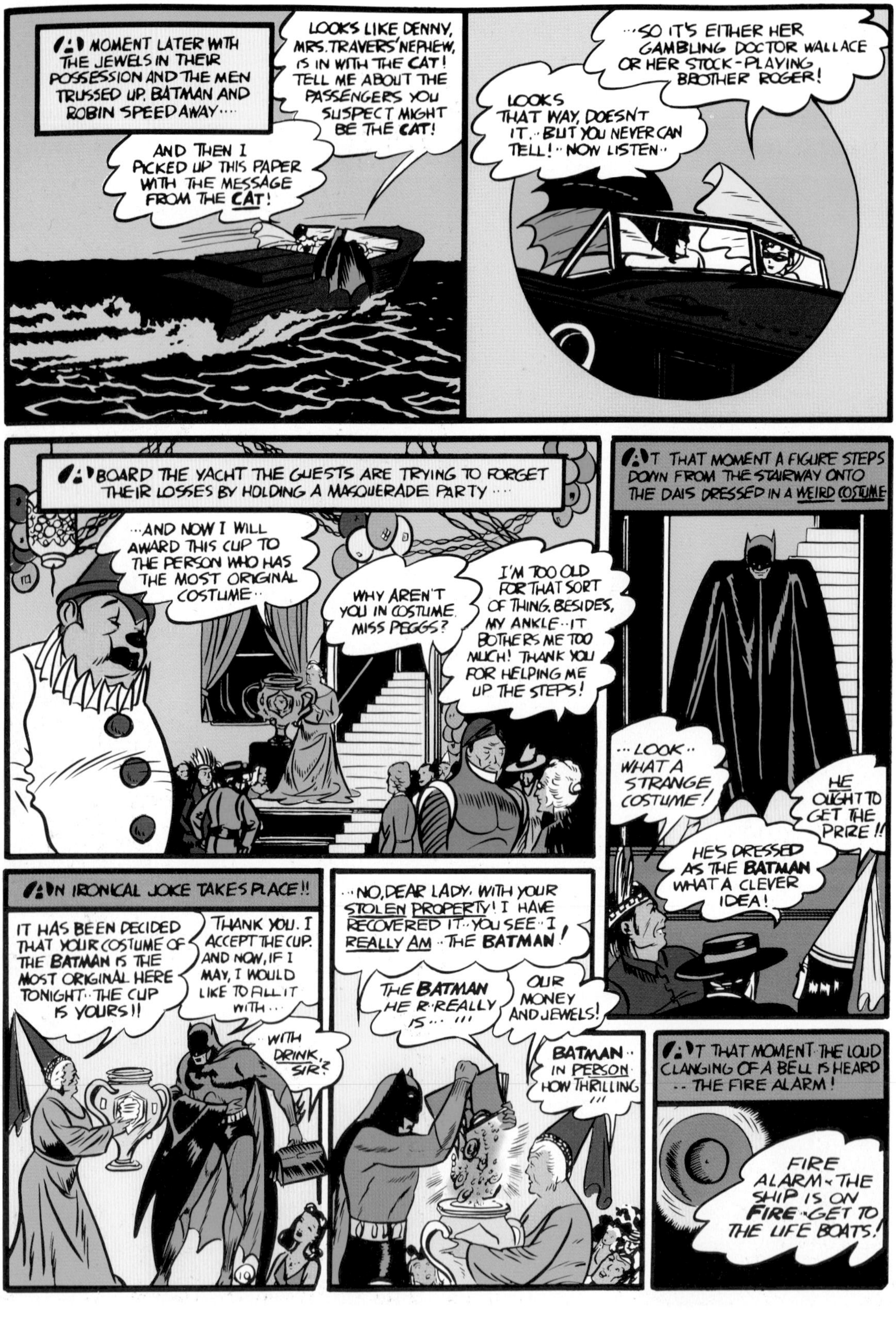
A MOMENT LATER WITH THE JEWELS IN THEIR POSSESSION AND THE MEN TRUSSED UP. BATMAN AND ROBIN SPEED AWAY....
LOOKS LIKE DENNY, MRS. TRAVERS' NEPHEW, IS IN WITH THE CAT! TELL ME ABOUT THE PASSENGERS YOU SUSPECT MIGHT BE THE CAT!
AND THEN I PICKED UP THIS PAPER WITH THE MESSAGE FROM THE CAT!
...SO IT'S EITHER HER GAMBLING DOCTOR WALLACE OR HER STOCK-PLAYING BROTHER ROGER!
LOOKS THAT WAY, DOESN'T IT..BUT YOU NEVER CAN TELL!..NOW LISTEN..
ABOARD THE YACHT THE GUESTS ARE TRYING TO FORGET THEIR LOSSES BY HOLDING A MASQUERADE PARTY....
...AND NOW I WILL AWARD THIS CUP TO THE PERSON WHO HAS THE MOST ORIGINAL COSTUME..
WHY AREN'T YOU IN COSTUME, MISS PEGGS?
I'M TOO OLD FOR THAT SORT OF THING. BESIDES, MY ANKLE..IT BOTHERS ME TOO MUCH! THANK YOU FOR HELPING ME UP THE STEPS!
AT THAT MOMENT A FIGURE STEPS DOWN FROM THE STAIRWAY ONTO THE DAIS DRESSED IN A WEIRD COSTUME
...LOOK.. WHAT A STRANGE COSTUME!
HE OUGHT TO GET THE PRIZE!!
HE'S DRESSED AS THE BATMAN. WHAT A CLEVER IDEA!
AN IRONICAL JOKE TAKES PLACE!!
IT HAS BEEN DECIDED THAT YOUR COSTUME OF THE BATMAN IS THE MOST ORIGINAL HERE TONIGHT..THE CUP IS YOURS!!
THANK YOU. I ACCEPT THE CUP. AND NOW, IF I MAY, I WOULD LIKE TO FILL IT WITH...
...WITH DRINK, SIR?
...NO, DEAR LADY. WITH YOUR STOLEN PROPERTY! I HAVE RECOVERED IT..YOU SEE..I REALLY AM..THE BATMAN!
THE BATMAN HE R-REALLY IS... !!!
OUR MONEY AND JEWELS!
BATMAN.. IN PERSON HOW THRILLING !!!
AT THAT MOMENT THE LOUD CLANGING OF A BELL IS HEARD -- THE FIRE ALARM!
FIRE ALARM - THE SHIP IS ON FIRE..GET TO THE LIFE BOATS!

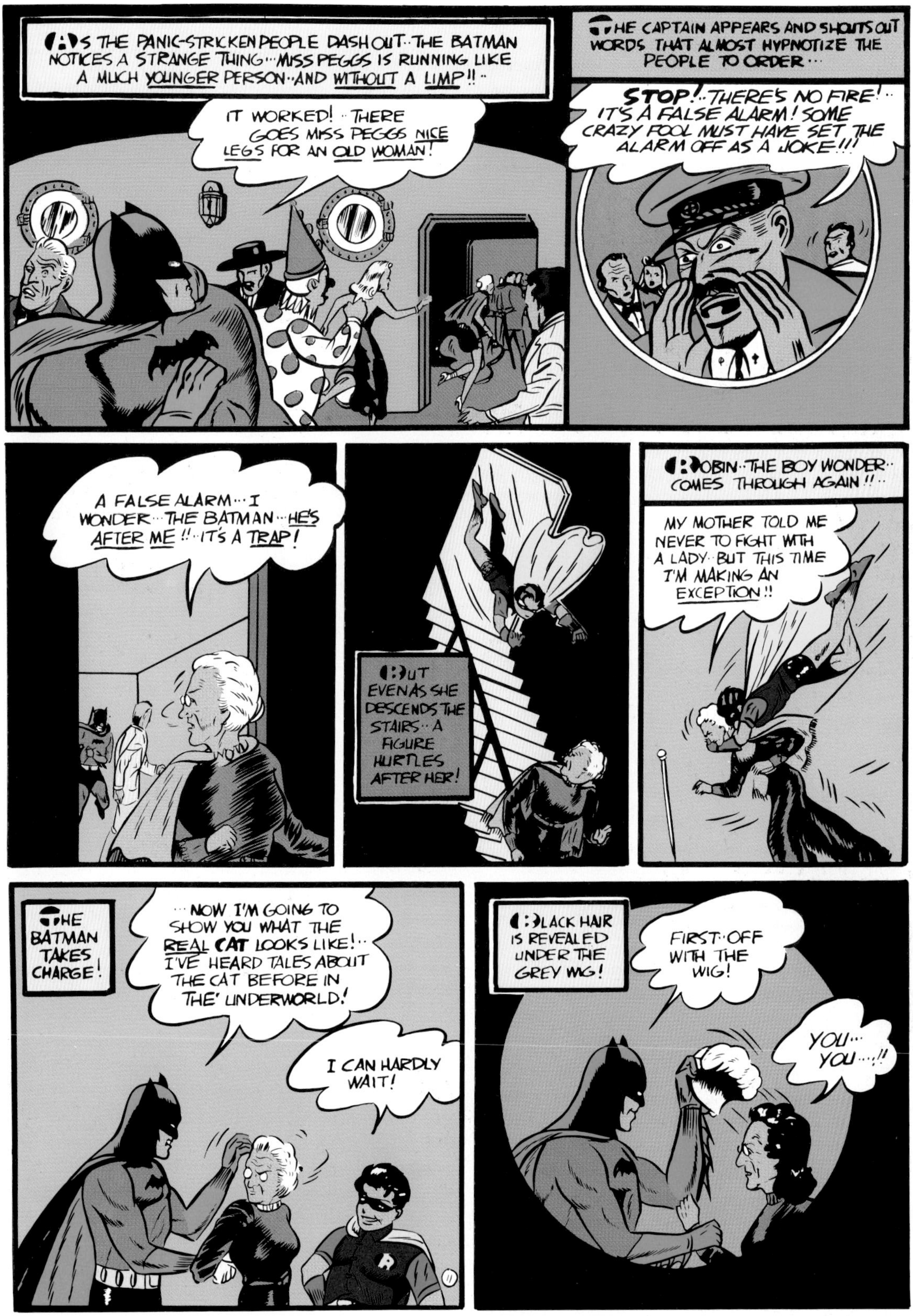
AS THE PANIC-STRICKEN PEOPLE DASH OUT..THE BATMAN NOTICES A STRANGE THING...MISS PEGGS IS RUNNING LIKE A MUCH YOUNGER PERSON..AND WITHOUT A LIMP!!..
IT WORKED! ..THERE GOES MISS PEGGS NICE LEGS FOR AN OLD WOMAN!
THE CAPTAIN APPEARS AND SHOUTS OUT WORDS THAT ALMOST HYPNOTIZE THE PEOPLE TO ORDER...
STOP!..THERE'S NO FIRE!.. IT'S A FALSE ALARM! SOME CRAZY FOOL MUST HAVE SET THE ALARM OFF AS A JOKE!!!
A FALSE ALARM... I WONDER... THE BATMAN...HE'S AFTER ME!!..IT'S A TRAP!
BUT EVEN AS SHE DESCENDS THE STAIRS.. A FIGURE HURTLES AFTER HER!
ROBIN..THE BOY WONDER.. COMES THROUGH AGAIN!!..
MY MOTHER TOLD ME NEVER TO FIGHT WITH A LADY..BUT THIS TIME I'M MAKING AN EXCEPTION!!
THE BATMAN TAKES CHARGE!
...NOW I'M GOING TO SHOW YOU WHAT THE REAL CAT LOOKS LIKE!.. I'VE HEARD TALES ABOUT THE CAT BEFORE IN THE UNDERWORLD!
I CAN HARDLY WAIT!
11
BLACK HAIR IS REVEALED UNDER THE GREY WIG!
FIRST..OFF WITH THE WIG!
YOU... YOU...!!

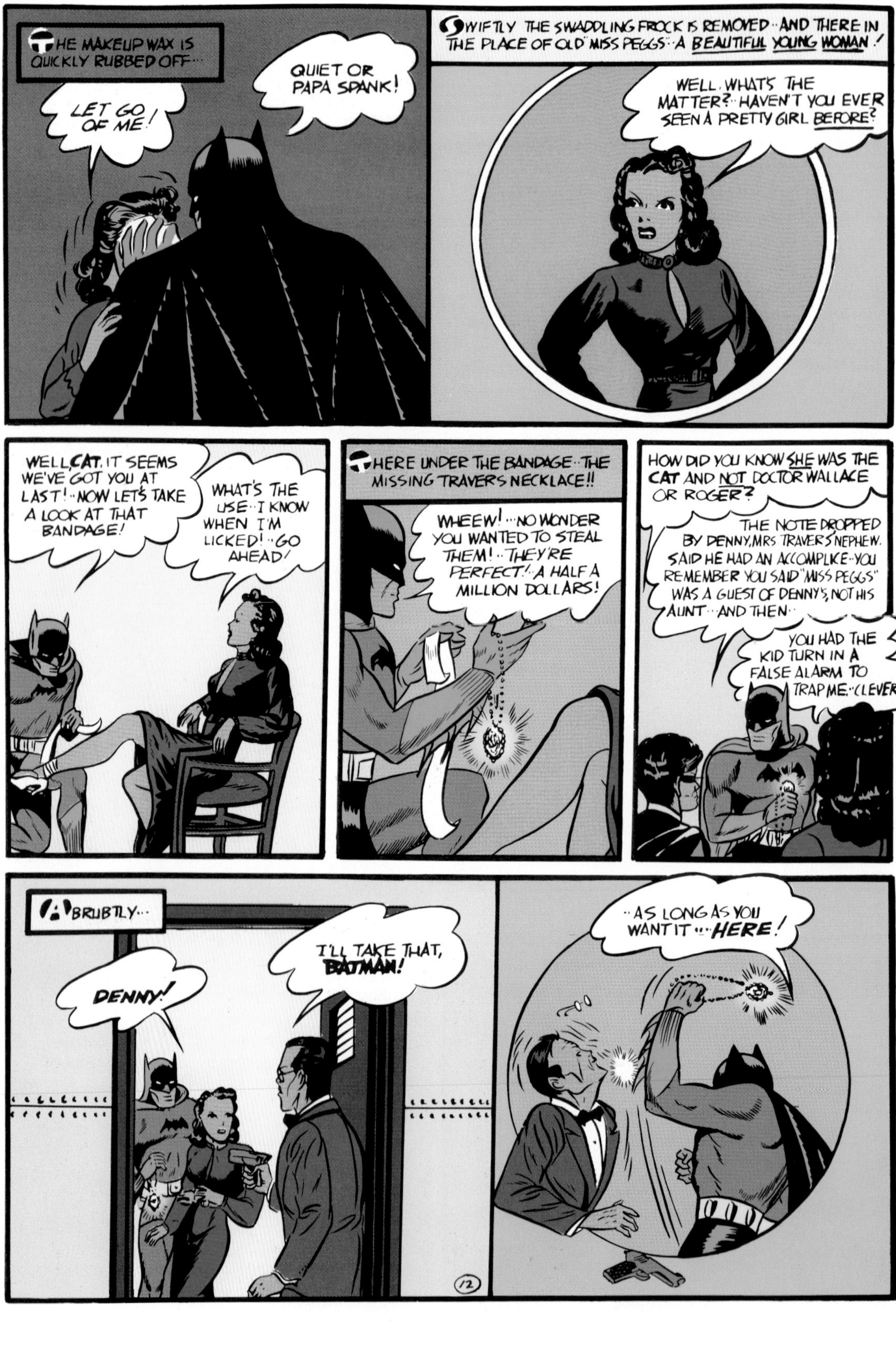
THE MAKEUP WAX IS QUICKLY RUBBED OFF...
LET GO OF ME!
QUIET OR PAPA SPANK!
SWIFTLY THE SWADDLING FROCK IS REMOVED.. AND THERE IN THE PLACE OF OLD "MISS PEGGS".. A BEAUTIFUL YOUNG WOMAN!
WELL, WHAT'S THE MATTER?.. HAVEN'T YOU EVER SEEN A PRETTY GIRL BEFORE?
WELL, CAT, IT SEEMS WE'VE GOT YOU AT LAST!.. NOW LET'S TAKE A LOOK AT THAT BANDAGE!
WHAT'S THE USE.. I KNOW WHEN I'M LICKED!.. GO AHEAD!
THERE UNDER THE BANDAGE.. THE MISSING TRAVERS NECKLACE!!
WHEEW!...NO WONDER YOU WANTED TO STEAL THEM!.. THEY'RE PERFECT!..A HALF A MILLION DOLLARS!
HOW DID YOU KNOW SHE WAS THE CAT AND NOT DOCTOR WALLACE OR ROGER?
THE NOTE DROPPED BY DENNY, MRS. TRAVERS'S NEPHEW, SAID HE HAD AN ACCOMPLICE.. YOU REMEMBER YOU SAID "MISS PEGGS" WAS A GUEST OF DENNY'S, NOT HIS AUNT... AND THEN..
YOU HAD THE KID TURN IN A FALSE ALARM TO TRAP ME.. CLEVER!
ABRUPTLY...
DENNY!
I'LL TAKE THAT, BATMAN!
..AS LONG AS YOU WANT IT... HERE!
12

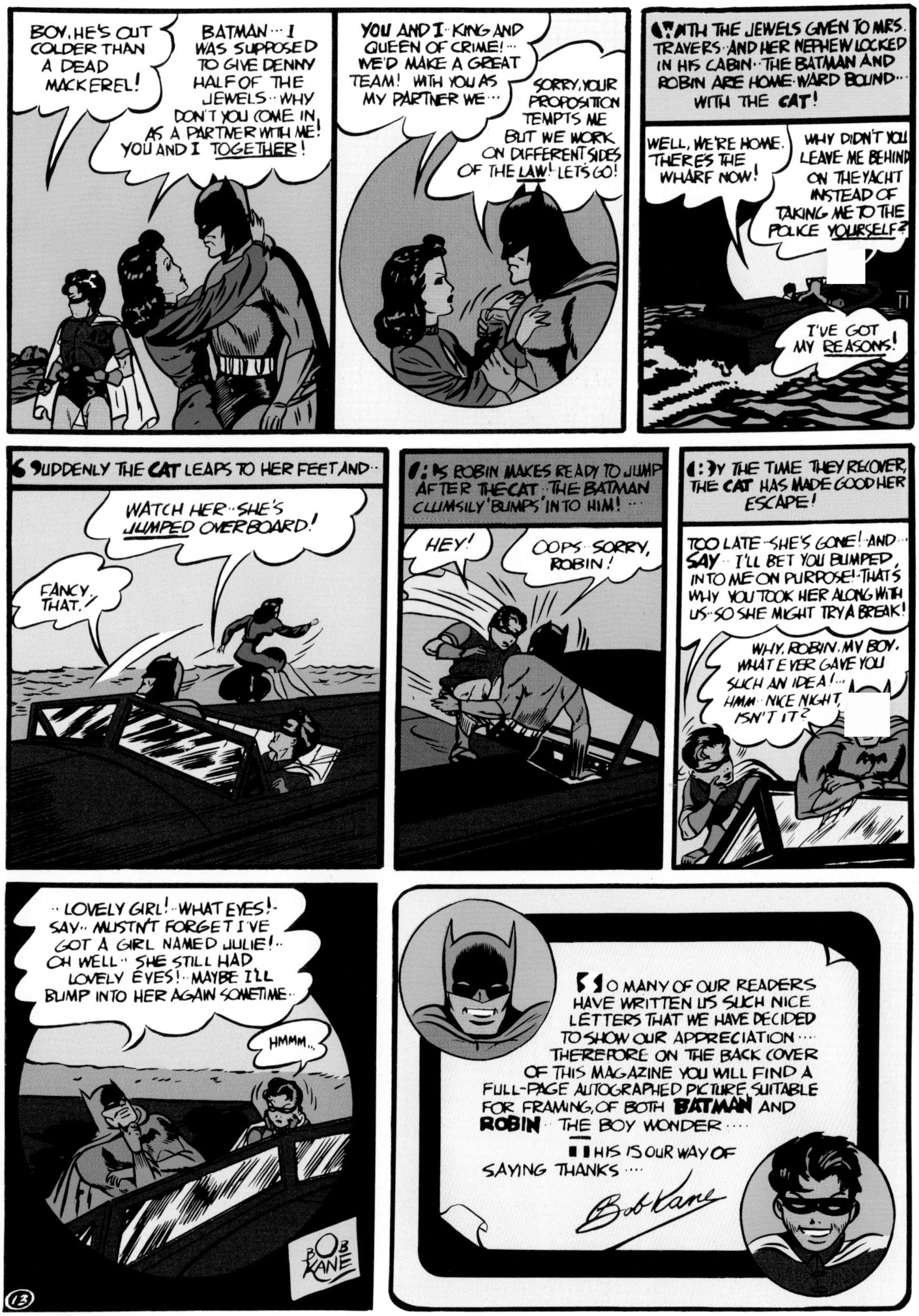
BOY, HE'S OUT COLDER THAN A DEAD MACKEREL!
BATMAN... I WAS SUPPOSED TO GIVE DENNY HALF OF THE JEWELS.. WHY DON'T YOU COME IN AS A PARTNER WITH ME! YOU AND I TOGETHER!
YOU AND I.. KING AND QUEEN OF CRIME!... WE'D MAKE A GREAT TEAM! WITH YOU AS MY PARTNER WE...
SORRY, YOUR PROPOSITION TEMPTS ME BUT WE WORK ON DIFFERENT SIDES OF THE LAW! LET'S GO!
WITH THE JEWELS GIVEN TO MRS. TRAVERS.. AND HER NEPHEW LOCKED IN HIS CABIN.. THE BATMAN AND ROBIN ARE HOME-WARD BOUND... WITH THE CAT!
WELL, WE'RE HOME. THERE'S THE WHARF NOW!
WHY DIDN'T YOU LEAVE ME BEHIND ON THE YACHT INSTEAD OF TAKING ME TO THE POLICE YOURSELF?
I'VE GOT MY REASONS!
SUDDENLY THE CAT LEAPS TO HER FEET AND..
WATCH HER.. SHE'S JUMPED OVERBOARD!
FANCY THAT.!
AS ROBIN MAKES READY TO JUMP AFTER THE CAT.. THE BATMAN CLUMSILY 'BUMPS' INTO HIM!...
HEY!
OOPS.. SORRY, ROBIN!
BY THE TIME THEY RECOVER, THE CAT HAS MADE GOOD HER ESCAPE!
TOO LATE.. SHE'S GONE!.. AND... SAY.. I'LL BET YOU BUMPED INTO ME ON PURPOSE!.. THAT'S WHY YOU TOOK HER ALONG WITH US.. SO SHE MIGHT TRY A BREAK!
WHY, ROBIN, MY BOY, WHATEVER GAVE YOU SUCH AN IDEA!... HMM.. NICE NIGHT, ISN'T IT?
..LOVELY GIRL!.. WHAT EYES!.. SAY.. MUSTN'T FORGET I'VE GOT A GIRL NAMED JULIE!.. OH WELL.. SHE STILL HAD LOVELY EYES!.. MAYBE I'LL BUMP INTO HER AGAIN SOMETIME..
HMMM...
BOB KANE
13
SO MANY OF OUR READERS HAVE WRITTEN US SUCH NICE LETTERS THAT WE HAVE DECIDED TO SHOW OUR APPRECIATION.... THEREFORE ON THE BACK COVER OF THIS MAGAZINE YOU WILL FIND A FULL-PAGE AUTOGRAPHED PICTURE SUITABLE FOR FRAMING, OF BOTH BATMAN AND ROBIN.. THE BOY WONDER....
THIS IS OUR WAY OF SAYING THANKS....
Bob Kane

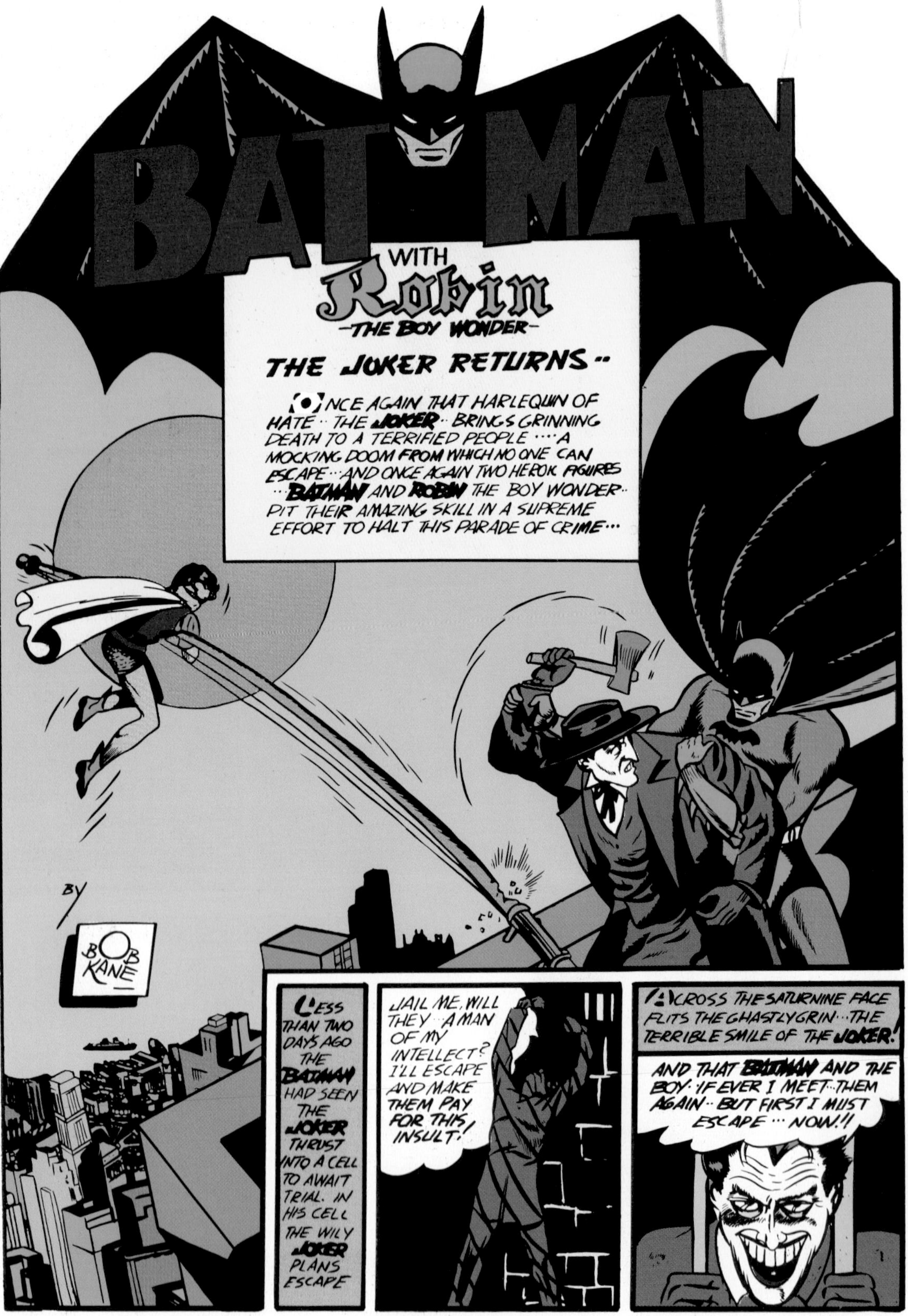
BATMAN
WITH
Robin
-THE BOY WONDER-
THE JOKER RETURNS..
ONCE AGAIN THAT HARLEQUIN OF HATE.. THE JOKER.. BRINGS GRINNING DEATH TO A TERRIFIED PEOPLE .... A MOCKING DOOM FROM WHICH NO ONE CAN ESCAPE... AND ONCE AGAIN TWO HEROIC FIGURES ... BATMAN AND ROBIN THE BOY WONDER.. PIT THEIR AMAZING SKILL IN A SUPREME EFFORT TO HALT THIS PARADE OF CRIME...
BY
BOB KANE
LESS THAN TWO DAYS AGO THE BATMAN HAD SEEN THE JOKER THRUST INTO A CELL TO AWAIT TRIAL. IN HIS CELL THE WILY JOKER PLANS ESCAPE
JAIL ME, WILL THEY.. A MAN OF MY INTELLECT? I'LL ESCAPE AND MAKE THEM PAY FOR THIS INSULT!
ACROSS THE SATURNINE FACE FLITS THE GHASTLY GRIN... THE TERRIBLE SMILE OF THE JOKER!
AND THAT BATMAN AND THE BOY.. IF EVER I MEET THEM AGAIN.. BUT FIRST I MUST ESCAPE ... NOW!!

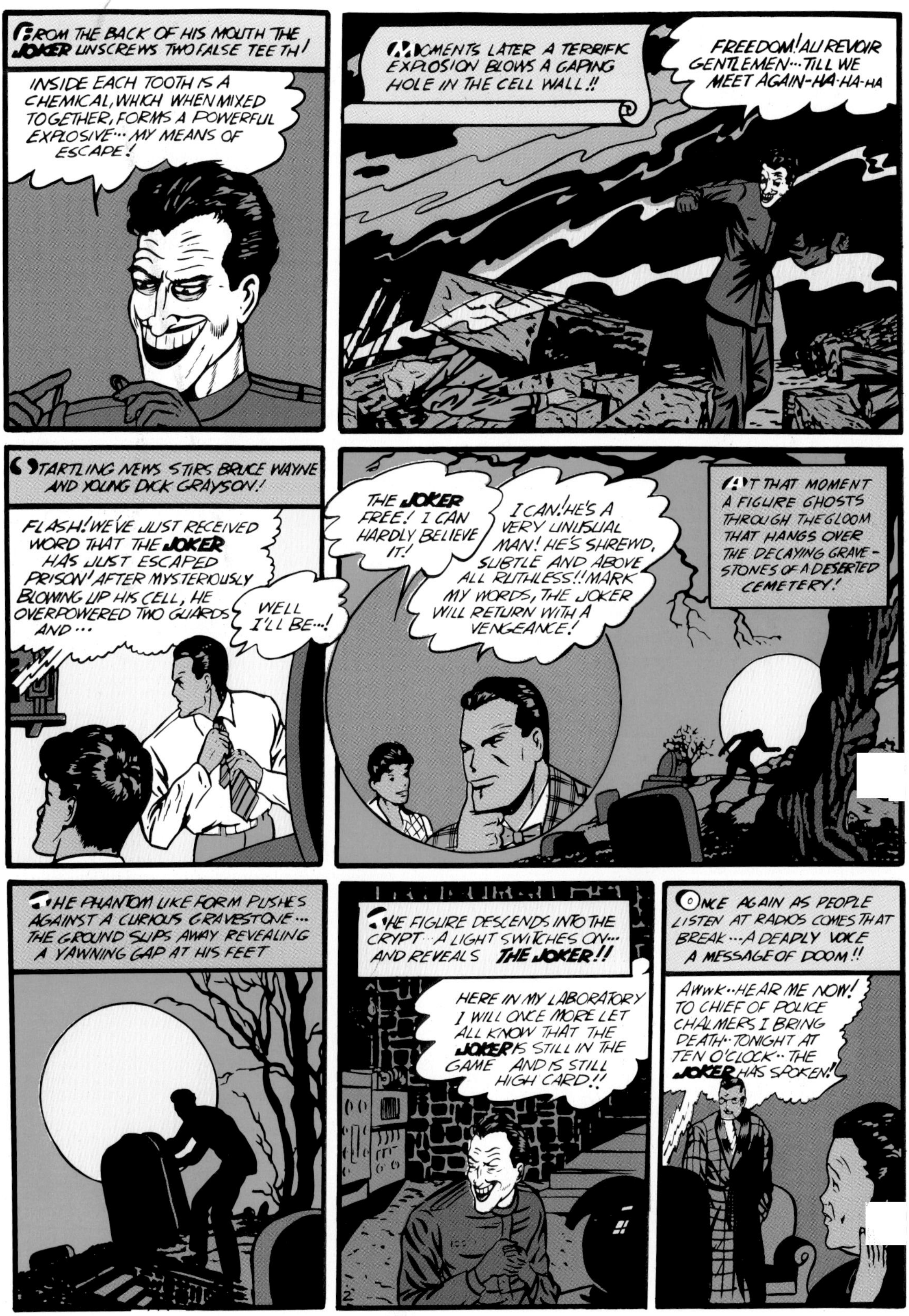
FROM THE BACK OF HIS MOUTH THE JOKER UNSCREWS TWO FALSE TEETH!
INSIDE EACH TOOTH IS A CHEMICAL, WHICH WHEN MIXED TOGETHER, FORMS A POWERFUL EXPLOSIVE... MY MEANS OF ESCAPE!
MOMENTS LATER A TERRIFIC EXPLOSION BLOWS A GAPING HOLE IN THE CELL WALL!!
FREEDOM! AU REVOIR GENTLEMEN... TILL WE MEET AGAIN-HA-HA-HA
STARTLING NEWS STIRS BRUCE WAYNE AND YOUNG DICK GRAYSON!
FLASH! WE'VE JUST RECEIVED WORD THAT THE JOKER HAS JUST ESCAPED PRISON! AFTER MYSTERIOUSLY BLOWING UP HIS CELL, HE OVERPOWERED TWO GUARDS AND...
WELL I'LL BE...!
THE JOKER FREE! I CAN HARDLY BELIEVE IT!
I CAN! HE'S A VERY UNUSUAL MAN! HE'S SHREWD, SUBTLE AND ABOVE ALL RUTHLESS!! MARK MY WORDS, THE JOKER WILL RETURN WITH A VENGEANCE!
AT THAT MOMENT A FIGURE GHOSTS THROUGH THE GLOOM THAT HANGS OVER THE DECAYING GRAVE-STONES OF A DESERTED CEMETERY!
THE PHANTOM LIKE FORM PUSHES AGAINST A CURIOUS GRAVESTONE... THE GROUND SLIPS AWAY REVEALING A YAWNING GAP AT HIS FEET
THE FIGURE DESCENDS INTO THE CRYPT... A LIGHT SWITCHES ON... AND REVEALS THE JOKER!!
HERE IN MY LABORATORY I WILL ONCE MORE LET ALL KNOW THAT THE JOKER IS STILL IN THE GAME AND IS STILL HIGH CARD!!
ONCE AGAIN AS PEOPLE LISTEN AT RADIOS COMES THAT BREAK...A DEADLY VOICE A MESSAGE OF DOOM!!
AWWK..HEAR ME NOW! TO CHIEF OF POLICE CHALMERS I BRING DEATH..TONIGHT AT TEN O'CLOCK.. THE JOKER HAS SPOKEN!

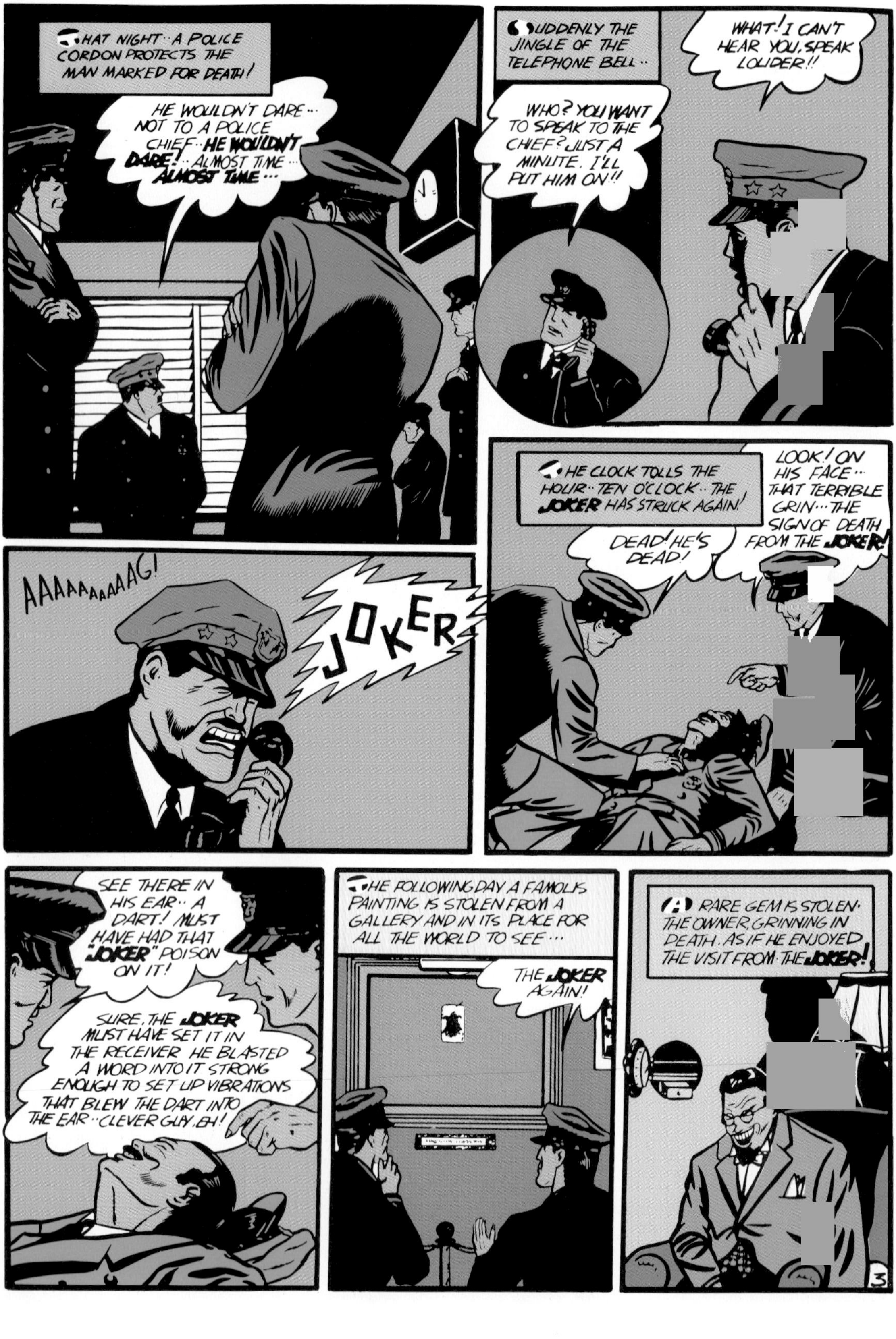
THAT NIGHT.. A POLICE CORDON PROTECTS THE MAN MARKED FOR DEATH!
HE WOULDN'T DARE... NOT TO A POLICE CHIEF.. HE WOULDN'T DARE!.. ALMOST TIME... ALMOST TIME...
SUDDENLY THE JINGLE OF THE TELEPHONE BELL..
WHO? YOU WANT TO SPEAK TO THE CHIEF? JUST A MINUTE. I'LL PUT HIM ON!!
WHAT! I CAN'T HEAR YOU, SPEAK LOUDER!!
AAAAAAAAAAG!
JOKER
THE CLOCK TOLLS THE HOUR.. TEN O'CLOCK.. THE JOKER HAS STRUCK AGAIN!
DEAD! HE'S DEAD!
LOOK! ON HIS FACE... THAT TERRIBLE GRIN... THE SIGN OF DEATH FROM THE JOKER!
SEE THERE IN HIS EAR.. A DART! MUST HAVE HAD THAT "JOKER" POISON ON IT!
SURE, THE JOKER MUST HAVE SET IT IN THE RECEIVER. HE BLASTED A WORD INTO IT STRONG ENOUGH TO SET UP VIBRATIONS THAT BLEW THE DART INTO THE EAR.. CLEVER GUY, EH!
THE FOLLOWING DAY A FAMOUS PAINTING IS STOLEN FROM A GALLERY AND IN ITS PLACE FOR ALL THE WORLD TO SEE...
THE JOKER AGAIN!
A RARE GEM IS STOLEN. THE OWNER, GRINNING IN DEATH, AS IF HE ENJOYED THE VISIT FROM THE JOKER!
3

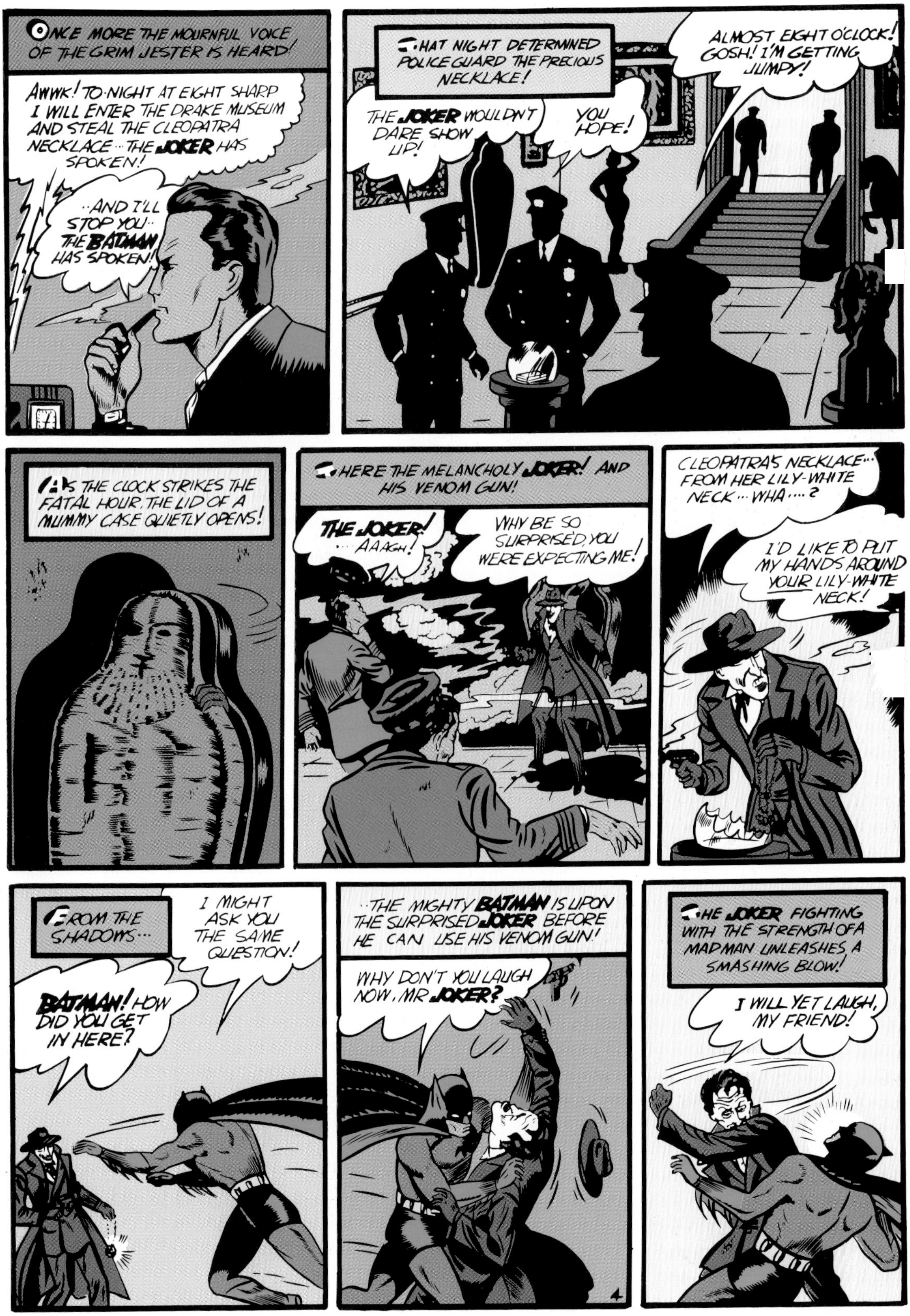
ONCE MORE THE MOURNFUL VOICE OF THE GRIM JESTER IS HEARD!
AWWK! TO-NIGHT AT EIGHT SHARP I WILL ENTER THE DRAKE MUSEUM AND STEAL THE CLEOPATRA NECKLACE... THE JOKER HAS SPOKEN!
...AND I'LL STOP YOU... THE BATMAN HAS SPOKEN!
THAT NIGHT DETERMINED POLICE GUARD THE PRECIOUS NECKLACE!
ALMOST EIGHT O'CLOCK! GOSH! I'M GETTING JUMPY!
THE JOKER WOULDN'T DARE SHOW UP!
YOU HOPE!
AS THE CLOCK STRIKES THE FATAL HOUR, THE LID OF A MUMMY CASE QUIETLY OPENS!
THERE THE MELANCHOLY JOKER! AND HIS VENOM GUN!
THE JOKER! ... AAAGH!
WHY BE SO SURPRISED, YOU WERE EXPECTING ME!
CLEOPATRA'S NECKLACE... FROM HER LILY-WHITE NECK... WHA....?
I'D LIKE TO PUT MY HANDS AROUND YOUR LILY-WHITE NECK!
FROM THE SHADOWS...
I MIGHT ASK YOU THE SAME QUESTION!
BATMAN! HOW DID YOU GET IN HERE?
...THE MIGHTY BATMAN IS UPON THE SURPRISED JOKER BEFORE HE CAN USE HIS VENOM GUN!
WHY DON'T YOU LAUGH NOW, MR JOKER?
4
THE JOKER FIGHTING WITH THE STRENGTH OF A MADMAN UNLEASHES A SMASHING BLOW!
I WILL YET LAUGH, MY FRIEND!

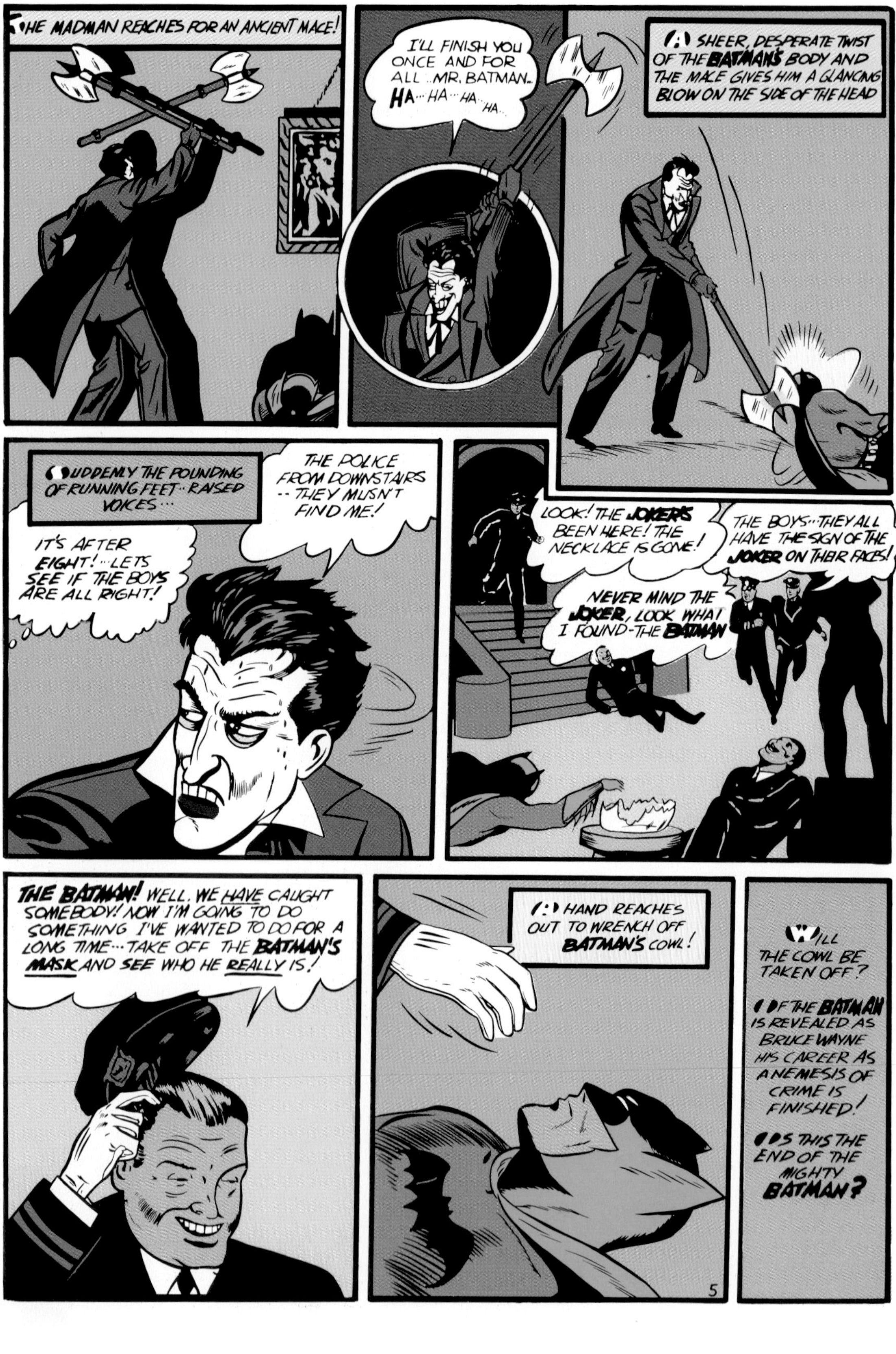
THE MADMAN REACHES FOR AN ANCIENT MACE!
I'LL FINISH YOU ONCE AND FOR ALL ..MR. BATMAN.. HA... HA... HA... HA...
A SHEER, DESPERATE TWIST OF THE BATMAN'S BODY AND THE MACE GIVES HIM A GLANCING BLOW ON THE SIDE OF THE HEAD
SUDDENLY THE POUNDING OF RUNNING FEET.. RAISED VOICES...
THE POLICE FROM DOWNSTAIRS -- THEY MUSN'T FIND ME!
IT'S AFTER EIGHT! ...LETS SEE IF THE BOYS ARE ALL RIGHT!
LOOK! THE JOKER'S BEEN HERE! THE NECKLACE IS GONE!
THE BOYS...THEY ALL HAVE THE SIGN OF THE JOKER ON THEIR FACES!
NEVER MIND THE JOKER, LOOK WHAT I FOUND-THE BATMAN
THE BATMAN! WELL, WE HAVE CAUGHT SOMEBODY! NOW I'M GOING TO DO SOMETHING I'VE WANTED TO DO FOR A LONG TIME... TAKE OFF THE BATMAN'S MASK AND SEE WHO HE REALLY IS!
A HAND REACHES OUT TO WRENCH OFF BATMAN'S COWL!
WILL THE COWL BE TAKEN OFF?
IF THE BATMAN IS REVEALED AS BRUCE WAYNE HIS CAREER AS A NEMESIS OF CRIME IS FINISHED!
IS THIS THE END OF THE MIGHTY BATMAN?
5

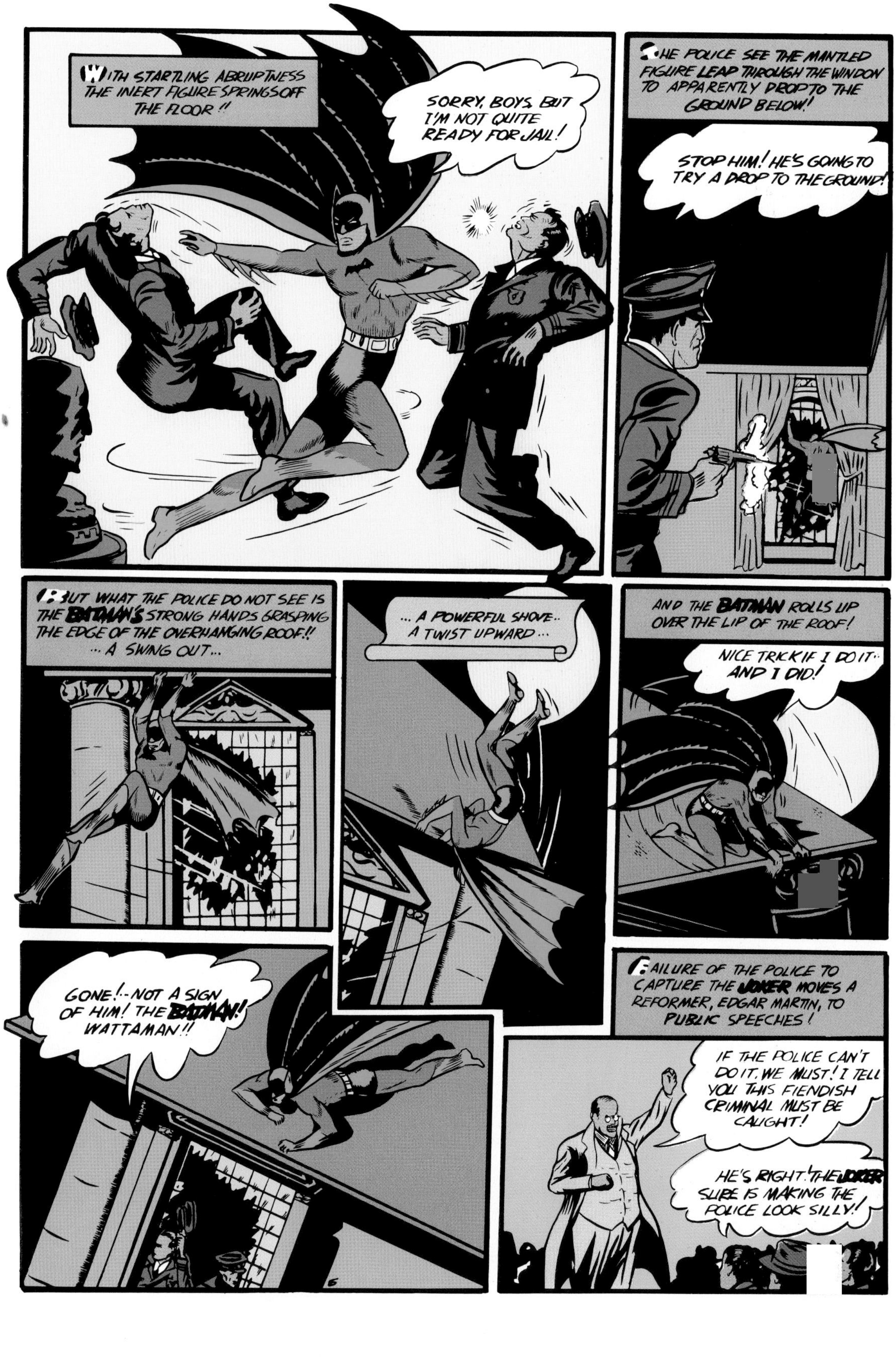
WITH STARTLING ABRUPTNESS THE INERT FIGURE SPRINGS OFF THE FLOOR!!
SORRY, BOYS, BUT I'M NOT QUITE READY FOR JAIL!
THE POLICE SEE THE MANTLED FIGURE LEAP THROUGH THE WINDOW TO APPARENTLY DROP TO THE GROUND BELOW!
STOP HIM! HE'S GOING TO TRY A DROP TO THE GROUND!
BUT WHAT THE POLICE DO NOT SEE IS THE BATMAN'S STRONG HANDS GRASPING THE EDGE OF THE OVERHANGING ROOF!! ... A SWING OUT...
... A POWERFUL SHOVE.. A TWIST UPWARD...
AND THE BATMAN ROLLS UP OVER THE LIP OF THE ROOF!
NICE TRICK IF I DO IT.. AND I DID!
GONE!--NOT A SIGN OF HIM! THE BATMAN! WATTAMAN!!
FAILURE OF THE POLICE TO CAPTURE THE JOKER MOVES A REFORMER, EDGAR MARTIN, TO PUBLIC SPEECHES!
IF THE POLICE CAN'T DO IT, WE MUST! I TELL YOU THIS FIENDISH CRIMINAL MUST BE CAUGHT!
HE'S RIGHT! THE JOKER SURE IS MAKING THE POLICE LOOK SILLY!

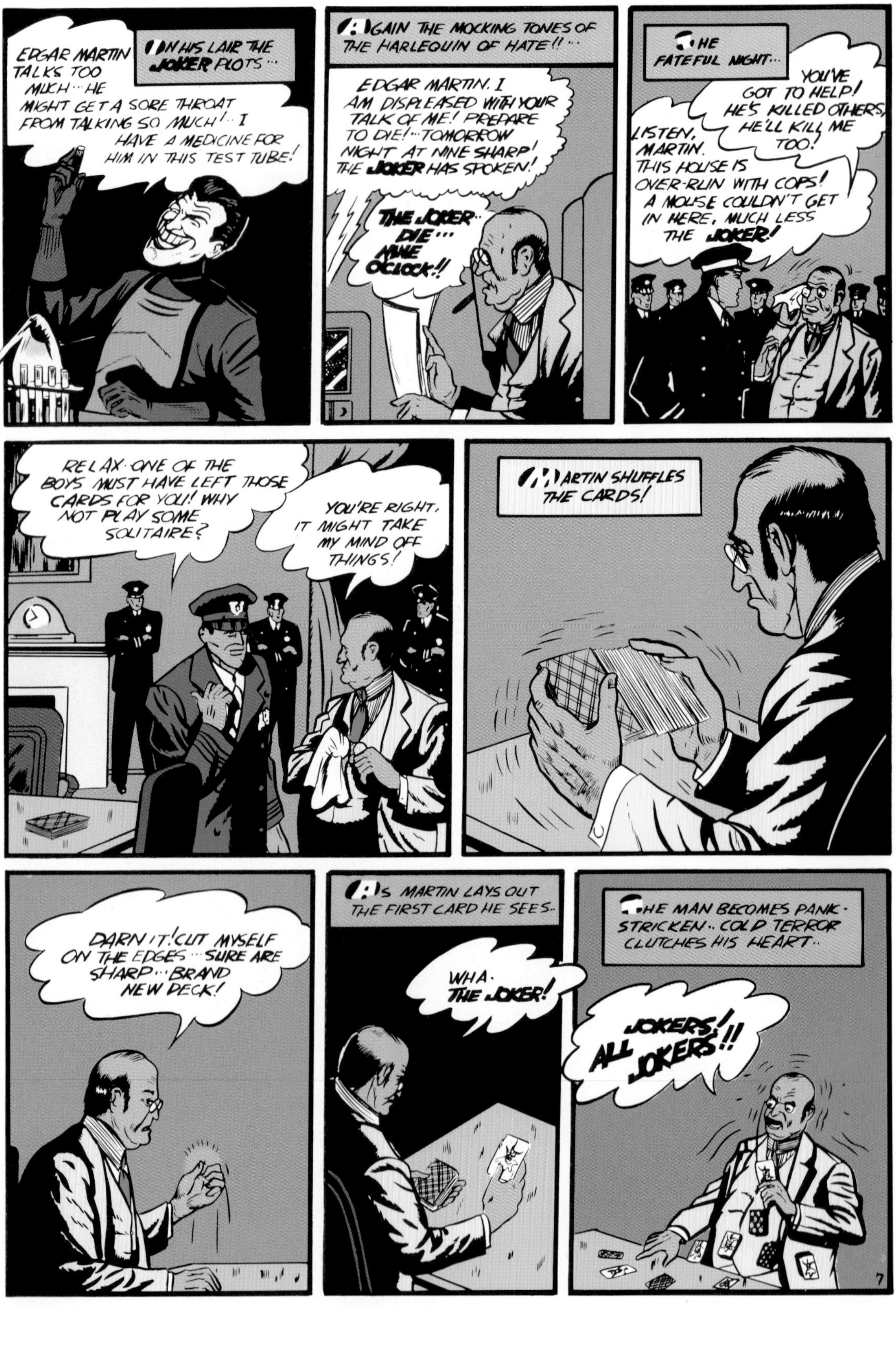
IN HIS LAIR THE JOKER PLOTS...
EDGAR MARTIN TALKS TOO MUCH... HE MIGHT GET A SORE THROAT FROM TALKING SO MUCH!.. I HAVE A MEDICINE FOR HIM IN THIS TEST TUBE!
AGAIN THE MOCKING TONES OF THE HARLEQUIN OF HATE!!...
EDGAR MARTIN, I AM DISPLEASED WITH YOUR TALK OF ME! PREPARE TO DIE!...TOMORROW NIGHT AT NINE SHARP! THE JOKER HAS SPOKEN!
THE JOKER.. DIE... NINE O'CLOCK!!
THE FATEFUL NIGHT...
YOU'VE GOT TO HELP! HE'S KILLED OTHERS, HE'LL KILL ME TOO!
LISTEN, MARTIN. THIS HOUSE IS OVER-RUN WITH COPS! A MOUSE COULDN'T GET IN HERE, MUCH LESS THE JOKER!
RELAX. ONE OF THE BOYS MUST HAVE LEFT THOSE CARDS FOR YOU! WHY NOT PLAY SOME SOLITAIRE?
YOU'RE RIGHT, IT MIGHT TAKE MY MIND OFF THINGS!
MARTIN SHUFFLES THE CARDS!
DARN IT! CUT MYSELF ON THE EDGES... SURE ARE SHARP... BRAND NEW DECK!
AS MARTIN LAYS OUT THE FIRST CARD HE SEES..
WHA. THE JOKER!
THE MAN BECOMES PANIC-STRICKEN.. COLD TERROR CLUTCHES HIS HEART..
JOKERS! ALL JOKERS!!
7

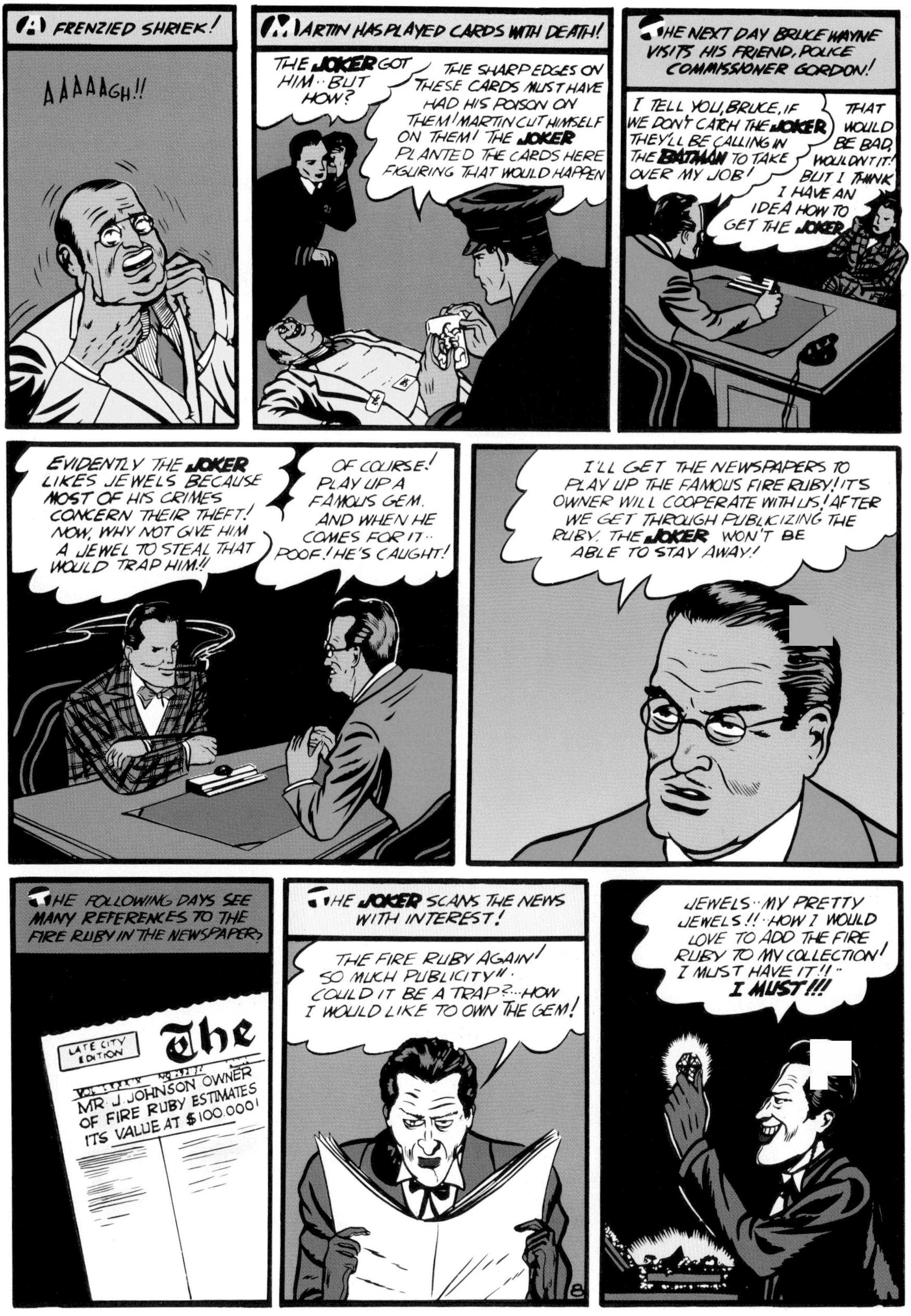
A FRENZIED SHRIEK!
AAAAAGH!!
MARTIN HAS PLAYED CARDS WITH DEATH!
THE JOKER GOT HIM.. BUT HOW?
THE SHARP EDGES ON THESE CARDS MUST HAVE HAD HIS POISON ON THEM! MARTIN CUT HIMSELF ON THEM! THE JOKER PLANTED THE CARDS HERE FIGURING THAT WOULD HAPPEN
THE NEXT DAY BRUCE WAYNE VISITS HIS FRIEND, POLICE COMMISSIONER GORDON!
I TELL YOU, BRUCE, IF WE DON'T CATCH THE JOKER THEY'LL BE CALLING IN THE BATMAN TO TAKE OVER MY JOB!
THAT WOULD BE BAD, WOULDN'T IT! BUT I THINK I HAVE AN IDEA HOW TO GET THE JOKER
EVIDENTLY THE JOKER LIKES JEWELS BECAUSE MOST OF HIS CRIMES CONCERN THEIR THEFT! NOW, WHY NOT GIVE HIM A JEWEL TO STEAL THAT WOULD TRAP HIM!!
OF COURSE! PLAY UP A FAMOUS GEM. AND WHEN HE COMES FOR IT.. POOF! HE'S CAUGHT!
I'LL GET THE NEWSPAPERS TO PLAY UP THE FAMOUS FIRE RUBY! ITS OWNER WILL COOPERATE WITH US! AFTER WE GET THROUGH PUBLICIZING THE RUBY, THE JOKER WON'T BE ABLE TO STAY AWAY!
THE FOLLOWING DAYS SEE MANY REFERENCES TO THE FIRE RUBY IN THE NEWSPAPERS
LATE CITY EDITION
The
MR. J. JOHNSON OWNER OF FIRE RUBY ESTIMATES ITS VALUE AT $100.000!
THE JOKER SCANS THE NEWS WITH INTEREST!
THE FIRE RUBY AGAIN! SO MUCH PUBLICITY!.. COULD IT BE A TRAP?...HOW I WOULD LIKE TO OWN THE GEM!
JEWELS.. MY PRETTY JEWELS!! HOW I WOULD LOVE TO ADD THE FIRE RUBY TO MY COLLECTION! I MUST HAVE IT!!..
I MUST!!!

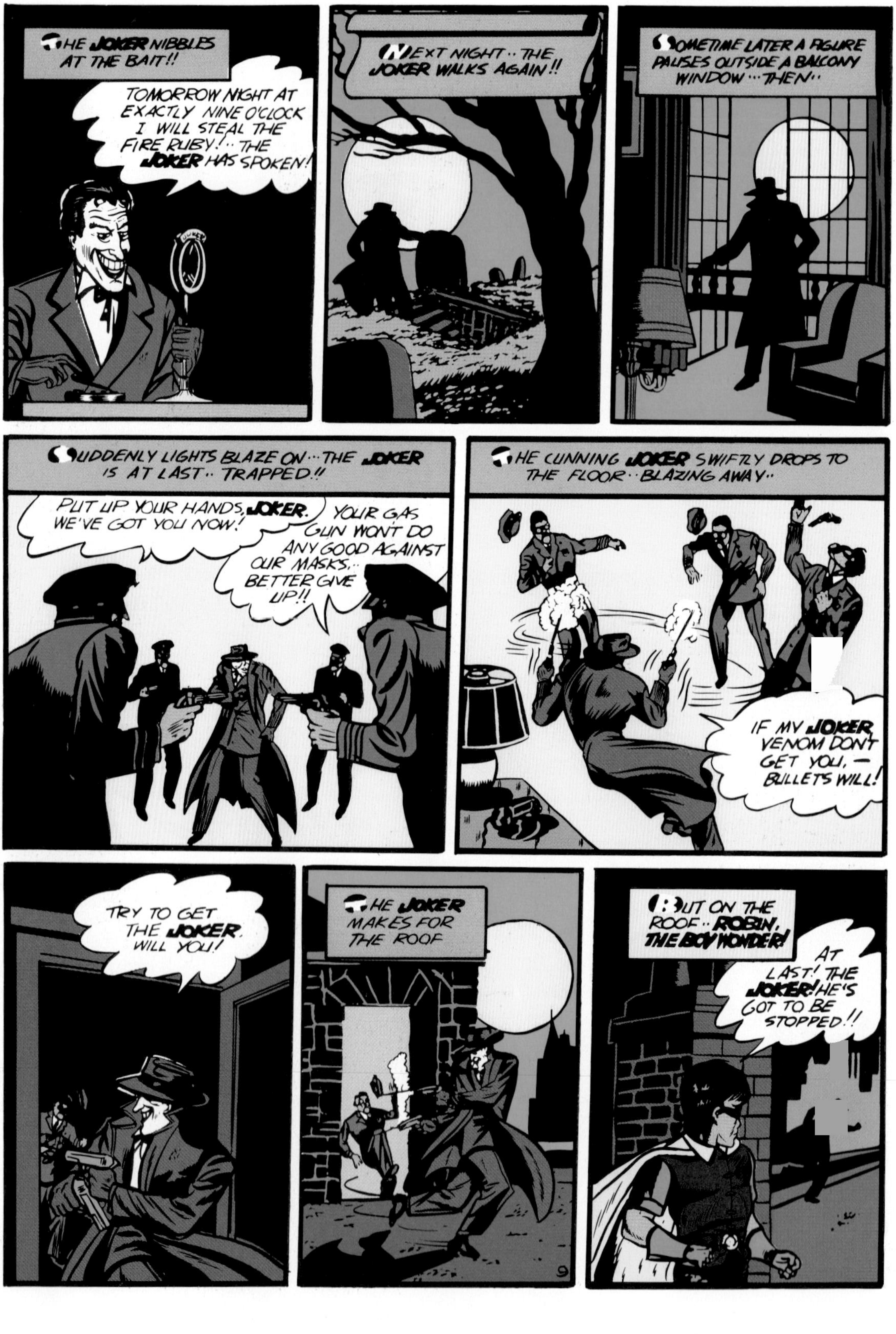
THE JOKER NIBBLES AT THE BAIT!!
TOMORROW NIGHT AT EXACTLY NINE O'CLOCK I WILL STEAL THE FIRE RUBY!.. THE JOKER HAS SPOKEN!
NEXT NIGHT.. THE JOKER WALKS AGAIN!!
SOMETIME LATER A FIGURE PAUSES OUTSIDE A BALCONY WINDOW... THEN..
SUDDENLY LIGHTS BLAZE ON... THE JOKER IS AT LAST.. TRAPPED!!
PUT UP YOUR HANDS, JOKER. WE'VE GOT YOU NOW!
YOUR GAS GUN WON'T DO ANY GOOD AGAINST OUR MASKS.. BETTER GIVE UP!!
THE CUNNING JOKER SWIFTLY DROPS TO THE FLOOR.. BLAZING AWAY..
IF MY JOKER VENOM DON'T GET YOU, — BULLETS WILL!
TRY TO GET THE JOKER, WILL YOU!
THE JOKER MAKES FOR THE ROOF
BUT ON THE ROOF.. ROBIN, THE BOY WONDER!
AT LAST! THE JOKER! HE'S GOT TO BE STOPPED!!
9

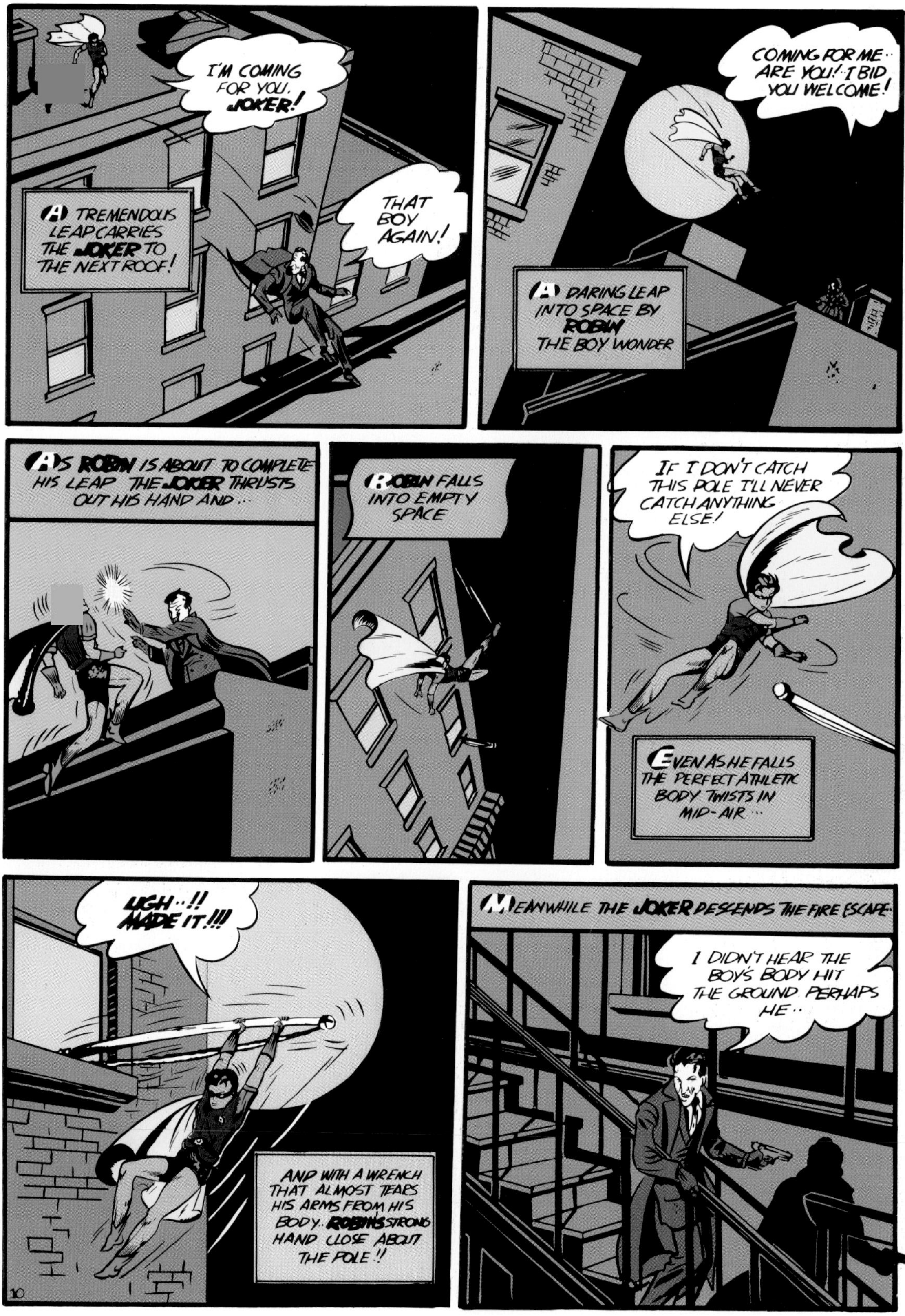
I'M COMING FOR YOU, JOKER!
A TREMENDOUS LEAP CARRIES THE JOKER TO THE NEXT ROOF!
THAT BOY AGAIN!
COMING FOR ME.. ARE YOU! I BID YOU WELCOME!
A DARING LEAP INTO SPACE BY ROBIN THE BOY WONDER
AS ROBIN IS ABOUT TO COMPLETE HIS LEAP THE JOKER THRUSTS OUT HIS HAND AND...
ROBIN FALLS INTO EMPTY SPACE
IF I DON'T CATCH THIS POLE I'LL NEVER CATCH ANYTHING ELSE!
EVEN AS HE FALLS THE PERFECT ATHLETIC BODY TWISTS IN MID-AIR...
UGH..!! MADE IT!!!
AND WITH A WRENCH THAT ALMOST TEARS HIS ARMS FROM HIS BODY.. ROBINS STRONG HAND CLOSE ABOUT THE POLE!!
10
MEANWHILE THE JOKER DESCENDS THE FIRE ESCAPE..
I DIDN'T HEAR THE BOY'S BODY HIT THE GROUND PERHAPS HE..

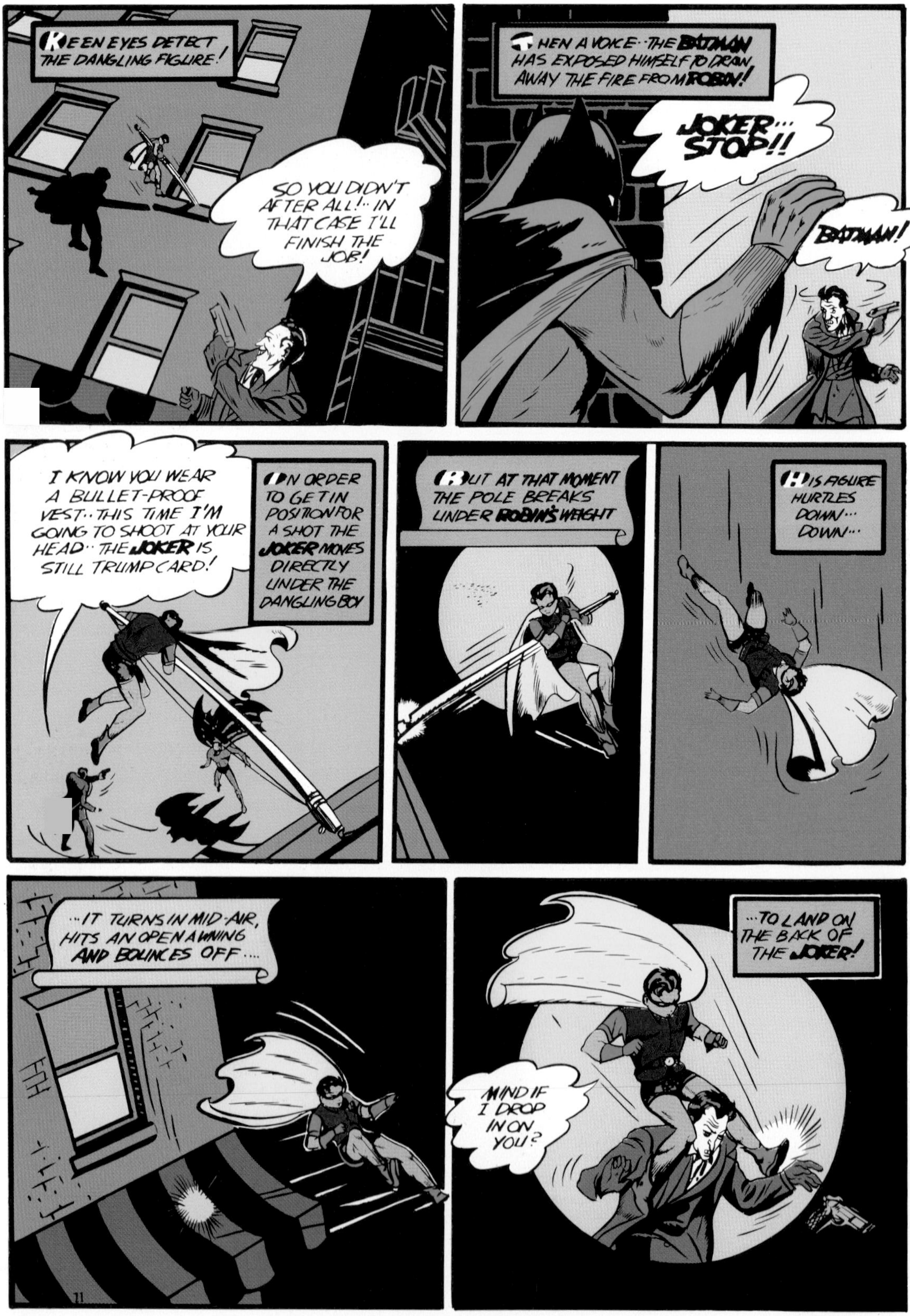
KEEN EYES DETECT THE DANGLING FIGURE!
SO YOU DIDN'T AFTER ALL!.. IN THAT CASE I'LL FINISH THE JOB!
THEN A VOICE.. THE BATMAN HAS EXPOSED HIMSELF TO DRAW AWAY THE FIRE FROM ROBIN!
JOKER... STOP!!
BATMAN!
I KNOW YOU WEAR A BULLET-PROOF VEST.. THIS TIME I'M GOING TO SHOOT AT YOUR HEAD.. THE JOKER IS STILL TRUMP CARD!
IN ORDER TO GET IN POSITION FOR A SHOT THE JOKER MOVES DIRECTLY UNDER THE DANGLING BOY
BUT AT THAT MOMENT THE POLE BREAKS UNDER ROBIN'S WEIGHT
HIS FIGURE HURTLES DOWN... DOWN...
...IT TURNS IN MID-AIR, HITS AN OPEN AWNING AND BOUNCES OFF....
11
...TO LAND ON THE BACK OF THE JOKER!
MIND IF I DROP IN ON YOU?

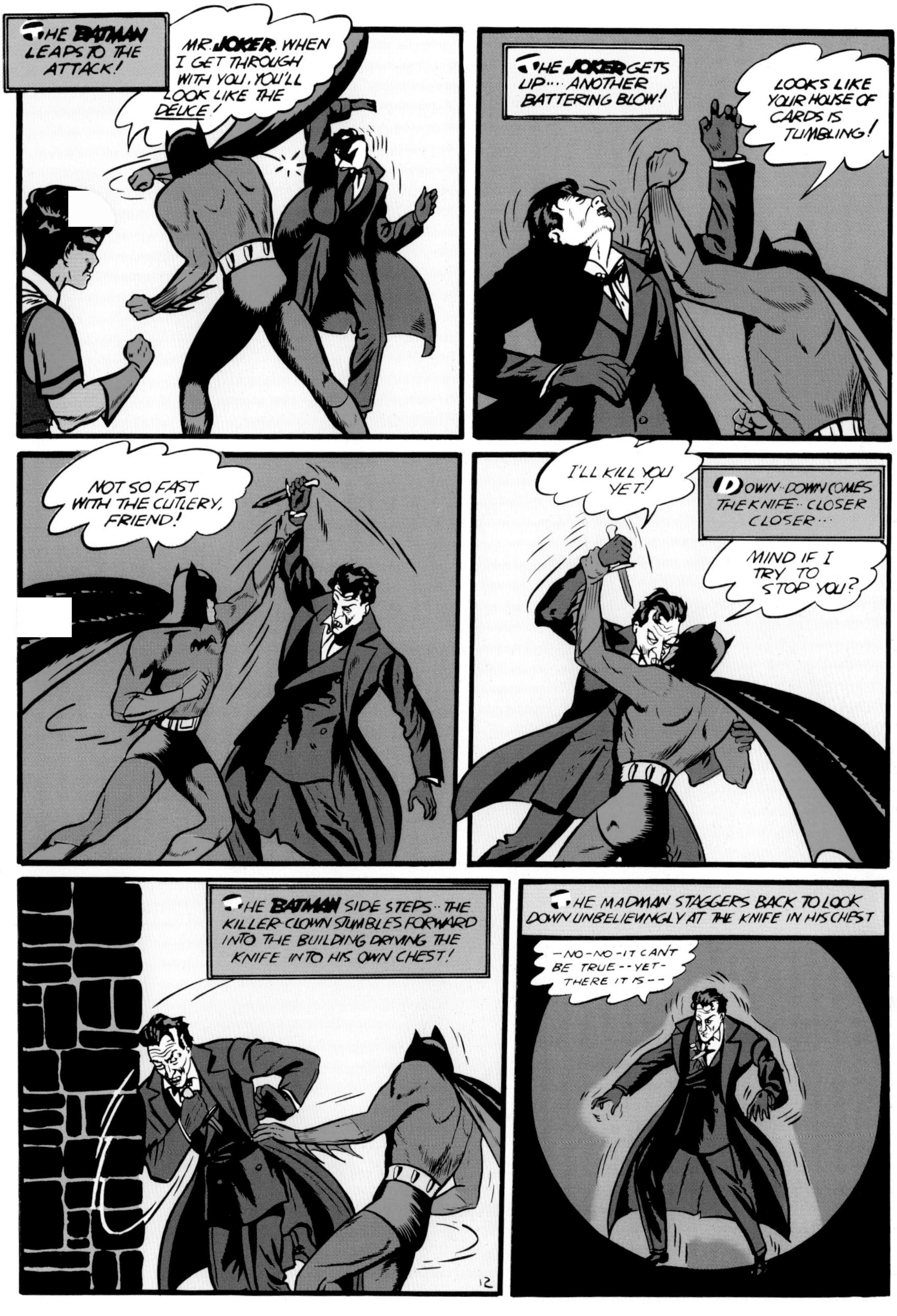
THE BATMAN LEAPS TO THE ATTACK!
MR. JOKER, WHEN I GET THROUGH WITH YOU, YOU'LL LOOK LIKE THE DEUCE!
THE JOKER GETS UP.... ANOTHER BATTERING BLOW!
LOOKS LIKE YOUR HOUSE OF CARDS IS TUMBLING!
NOT SO FAST WITH THE CUTLERY, FRIEND!
I'LL KILL YOU YET!
DOWN-DOWN COMES THE KNIFE-- CLOSER CLOSER...
MIND IF I TRY TO STOP YOU?
THE BATMAN SIDE STEPS.. THE KILLER-CLOWN STUMBLES FORWARD INTO THE BUILDING DRIVING THE KNIFE INTO HIS OWN CHEST!
12
THE MADMAN STAGGERS BACK TO LOOK DOWN UNBELIEVINGLY AT THE KNIFE IN HIS CHEST
—NO—NO—IT CAN'T BE TRUE--YET—THERE IT IS--

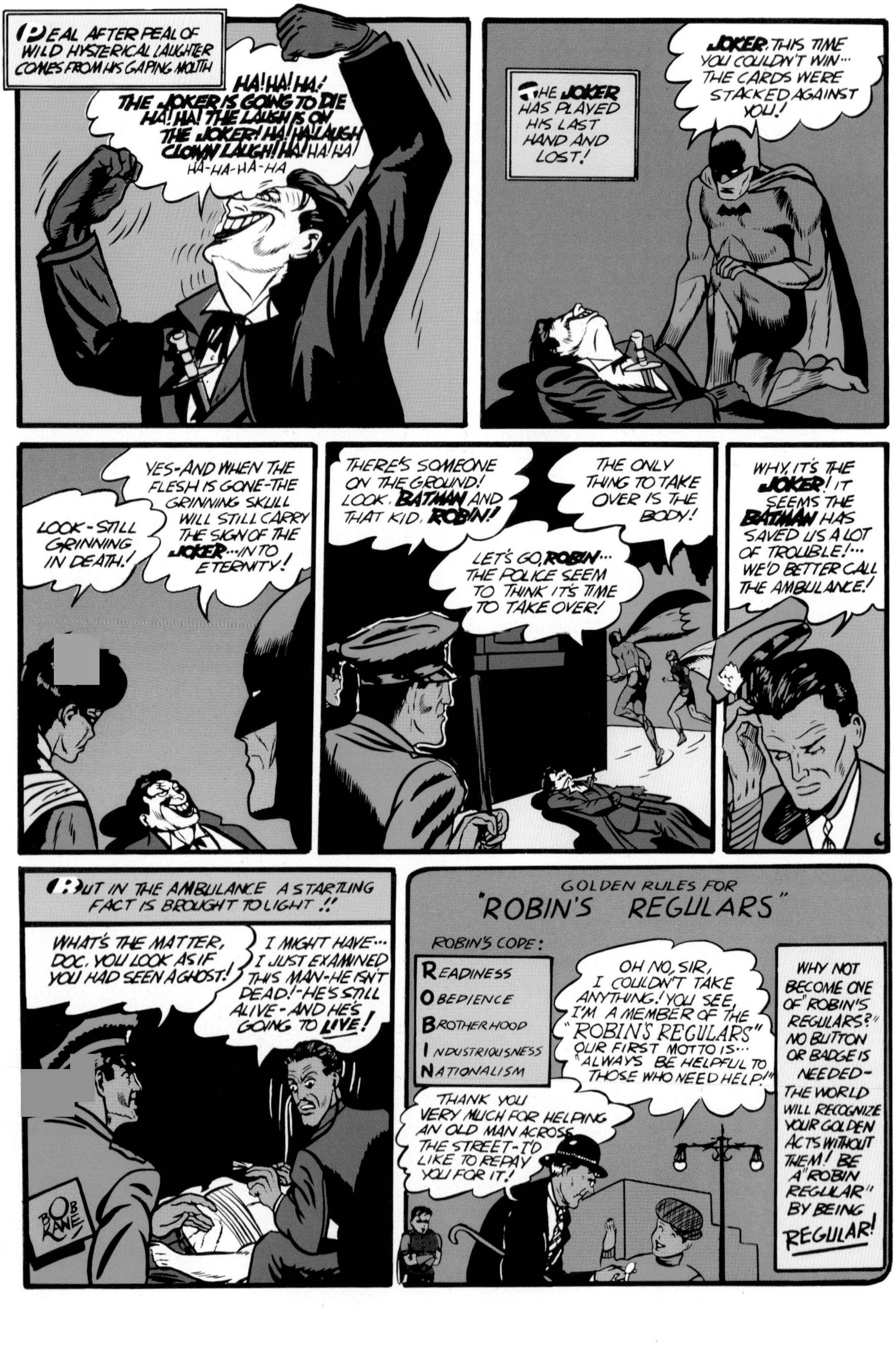
PEAL AFTER PEAL OF WILD HYSTERICAL LAUGHTER COMES FROM HIS GAPING MOUTH
HA! HA! HA! THE JOKER IS GOING TO DIE HA! HA! THE LAUGH IS ON THE JOKER! HA! HA! LAUGH CLOWN LAUGH! HA! HA! HA! HA-HA-HA-HA
THE JOKER HAS PLAYED HIS LAST HAND AND LOST!
JOKER, THIS TIME YOU COULDN'T WIN... THE CARDS WERE STACKED AGAINST YOU!
LOOK - STILL GRINNING IN DEATH!
YES-AND WHEN THE FLESH IS GONE-THE GRINNING SKULL WILL STILL CARRY THE SIGN OF THE JOKER...INTO ETERNITY!
THERE'S SOMEONE ON THE GROUND! LOOK, BATMAN AND THAT KID, ROBIN!
THE ONLY THING TO TAKE OVER IS THE BODY!
LET'S GO, ROBIN... THE POLICE SEEM TO THINK IT'S TIME TO TAKE OVER!
WHY, IT'S THE JOKER! IT SEEMS THE BATMAN HAS SAVED US A LOT OF TROUBLE!... WE'D BETTER CALL THE AMBULANCE!
BUT IN THE AMBULANCE A STARTLING FACT IS BROUGHT TO LIGHT !!
WHAT'S THE MATTER, DOC, YOU LOOK AS IF YOU HAD SEEN A GHOST!
I MIGHT HAVE... I JUST EXAMINED THIS MAN-HE ISN'T DEAD!-HE'S STILL ALIVE-AND HE'S GOING TO LIVE!
BOB KANE
GOLDEN RULES FOR "ROBIN'S REGULARS"
ROBIN'S CODE:
READINESS
OBEDIENCE
BROTHERHOOD
INDUSTRIOUSNESS
NATIONALISM
OH NO, SIR, I COULDN'T TAKE ANYTHING! YOU SEE, I'M A MEMBER OF THE "ROBIN'S REGULARS" OUR FIRST MOTTO IS... "ALWAYS BE HELPFUL TO THOSE WHO NEED HELP!"
THANK YOU VERY MUCH FOR HELPING AN OLD MAN ACROSS THE STREET-I'D LIKE TO REPAY YOU FOR IT!
WHY NOT BECOME ONE OF "ROBIN'S REGULARS?" NO BUTTON OR BADGE IS NEEDED-THE WORLD WILL RECOGNIZE YOUR GOLDEN ACTS WITHOUT THEM! BE A "ROBIN REGULAR" BY BEING REGULAR!

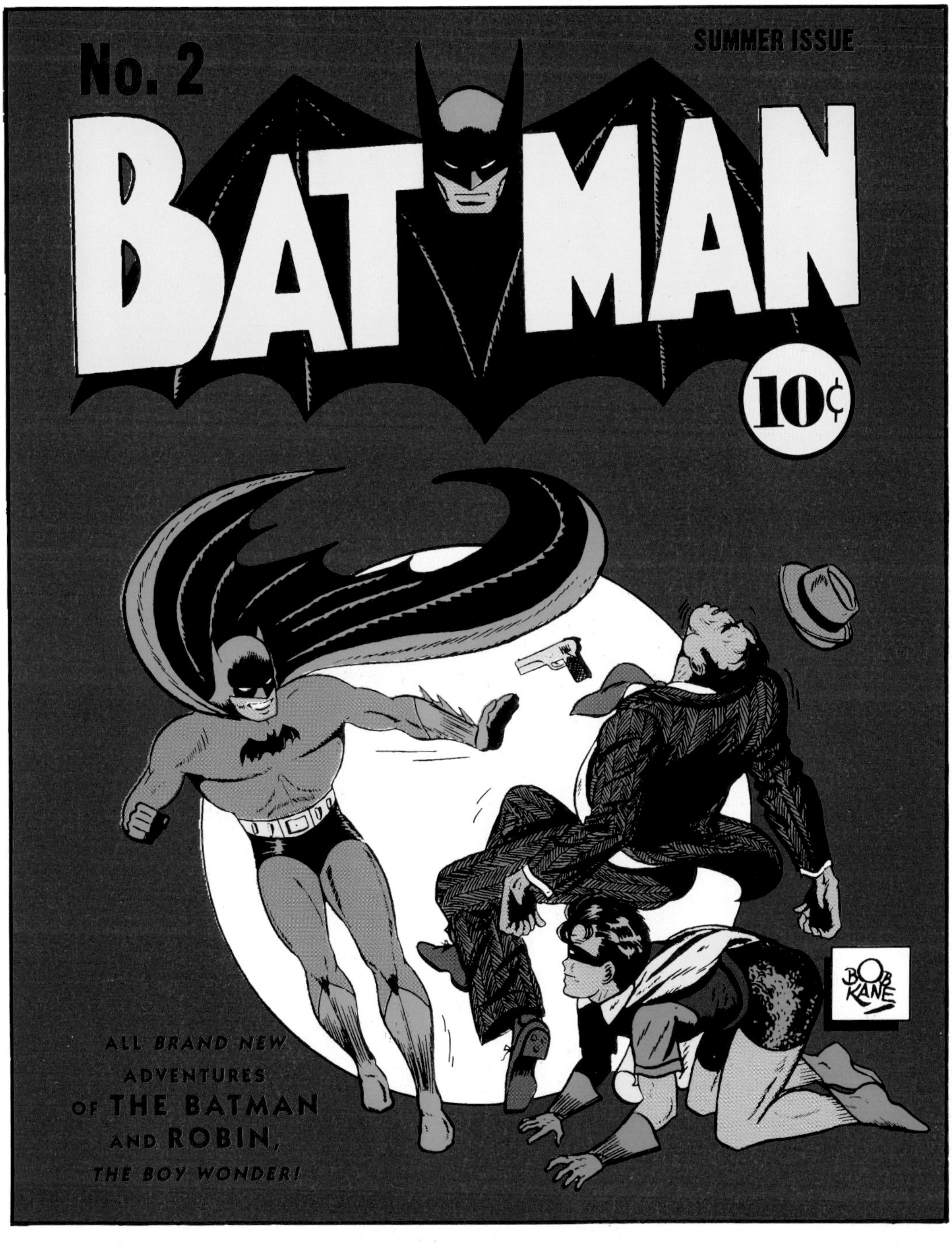
No. 2
SUMMER ISSUE
BATMAN
10¢
BOB KANE
ALL BRAND NEW ADVENTURES OF THE BATMAN AND ROBIN, THE BOY WONDER!

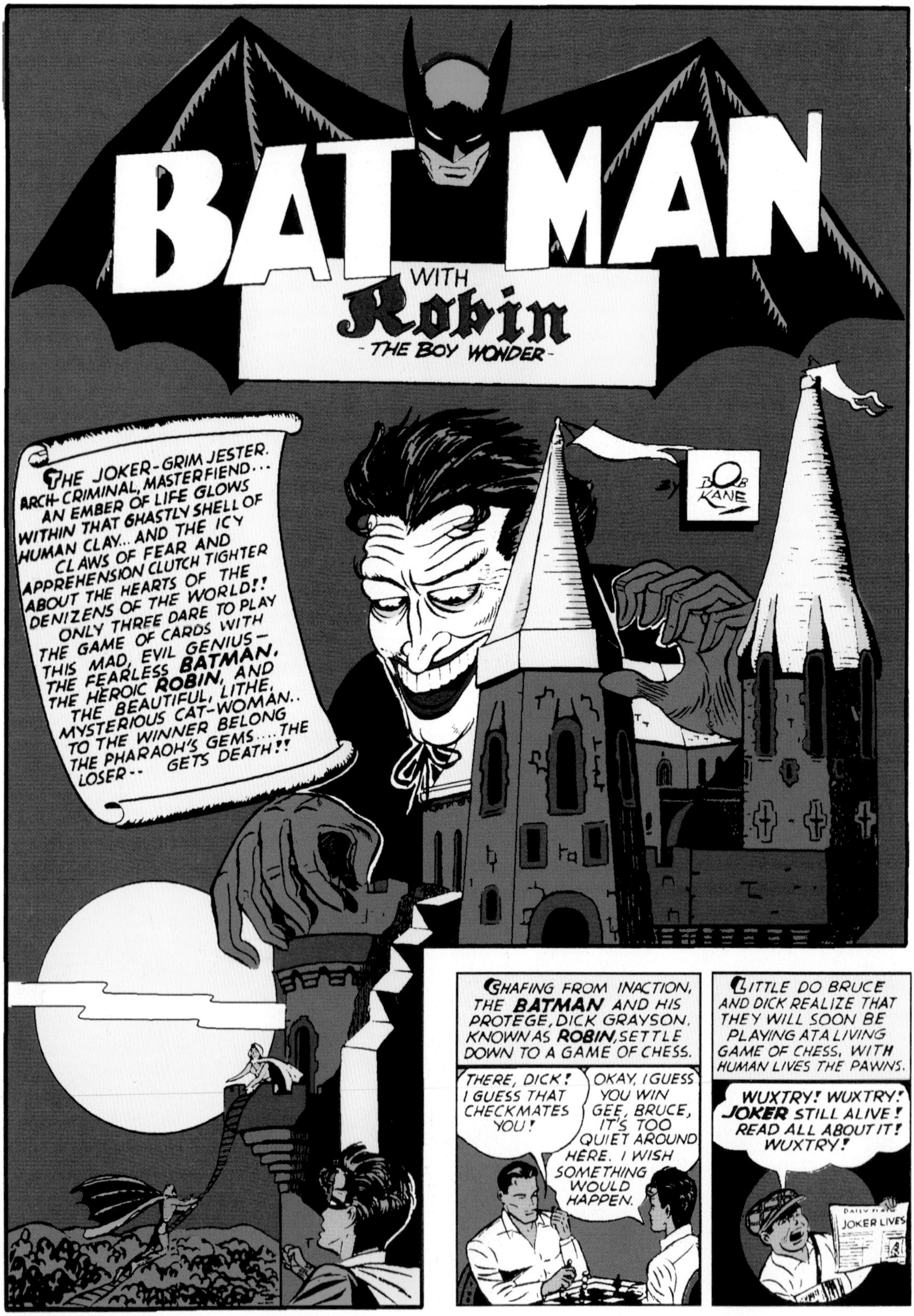
BATMAN
WITH
Robin
-THE BOY WONDER-
BY BOB KANE
THE JOKER-GRIM JESTER. ARCH-CRIMINAL, MASTERFIEND... AN EMBER OF LIFE GLOWS WITHIN THAT GHASTLY SHELL OF HUMAN CLAY... AND THE ICY CLAWS OF FEAR AND APPREHENSION CLUTCH TIGHTER ABOUT THE HEARTS OF THE DENIZENS OF THE WORLD!! ONLY THREE DARE TO PLAY THE GAME OF CARDS WITH THIS MAD, EVIL GENIUS-THE FEARLESS BATMAN, THE HEROIC ROBIN, AND THE BEAUTIFUL, LITHE, MYSTERIOUS CAT-WOMAN.. TO THE WINNER BELONG THE PHARAOH'S GEMS.... THE LOSER-- GETS DEATH!!
CHAFING FROM INACTION, THE BATMAN AND HIS PROTEGE, DICK GRAYSON, KNOWN AS ROBIN, SETTLE DOWN TO A GAME OF CHESS.
THERE, DICK! I GUESS THAT CHECKMATES YOU!
OKAY, I GUESS YOU WIN GEE, BRUCE, IT'S TOO QUIET AROUND HERE. I WISH SOMETHING WOULD HAPPEN.
LITTLE DO BRUCE AND DICK REALIZE THAT THEY WILL SOON BE PLAYING AT A LIVING GAME OF CHESS, WITH HUMAN LIVES THE PAWNS.
WUXTRY! WUXTRY! JOKER STILL ALIVE! READ ALL ABOUT IT! WUXTRY!
JOKER LIVES

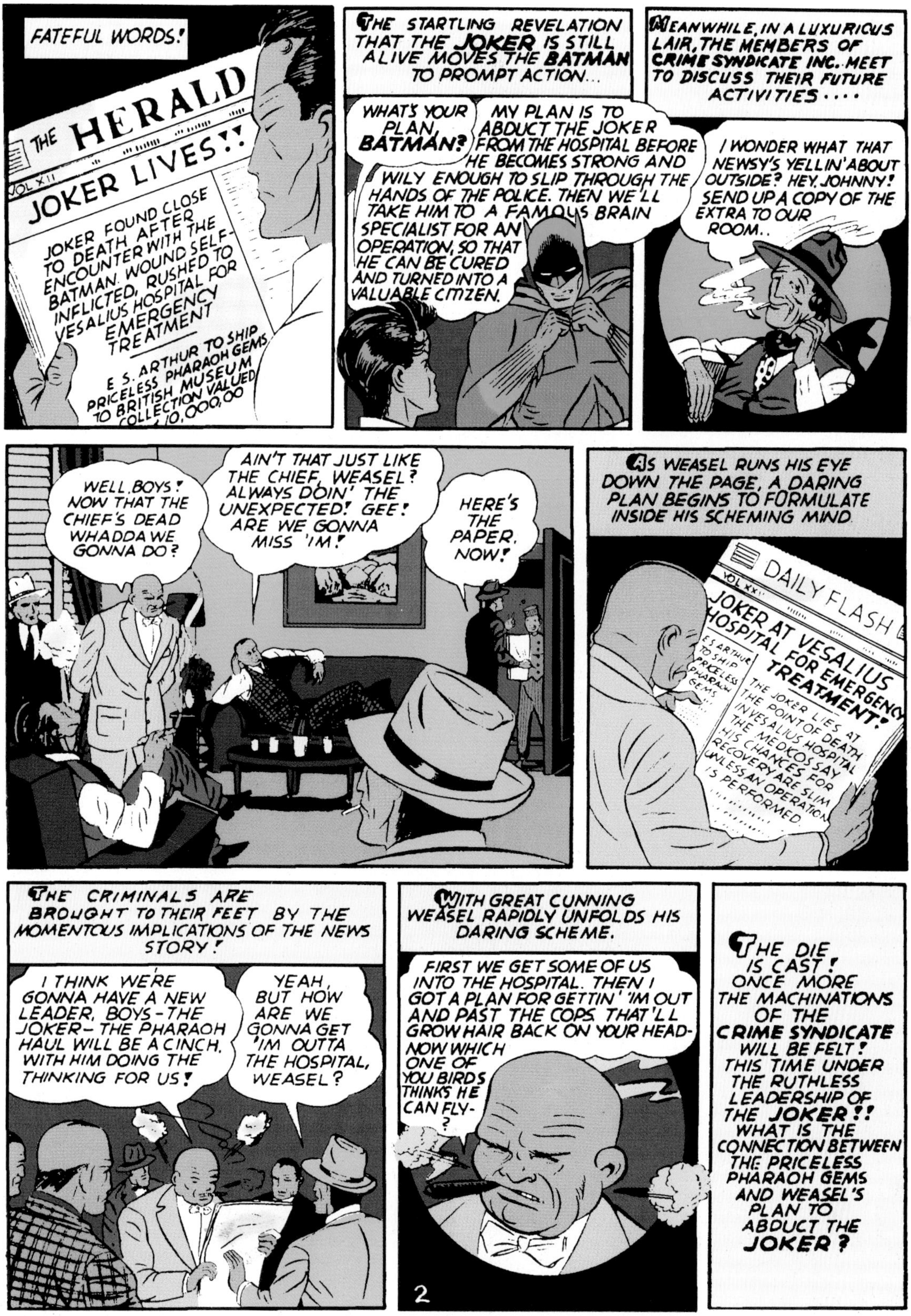
FATEFUL WORDS!
THE HERALD
VOL XII
JOKER LIVES!!
JOKER FOUND CLOSE TO DEATH AFTER ENCOUNTER WITH THE BATMAN. WOUND SELF-INFLICTED, RUSHED TO VESALIUS HOSPITAL FOR EMERGENCY TREATMENT
E. S. ARTHUR TO SHIP PRICELESS PHARAOH GEMS TO BRITISH MUSEUM COLLECTION VALUED
THE STARTLING REVELATION THAT THE JOKER IS STILL ALIVE MOVES THE BATMAN TO PROMPT ACTION...
WHAT'S YOUR PLAN, BATMAN?
MY PLAN IS TO ABDUCT THE JOKER FROM THE HOSPITAL BEFORE HE BECOMES STRONG AND WILY ENOUGH TO SLIP THROUGH THE HANDS OF THE POLICE. THEN WE'LL TAKE HIM TO A FAMOUS BRAIN SPECIALIST FOR AN OPERATION, SO THAT HE CAN BE CURED AND TURNED INTO A VALUABLE CITIZEN.
MEANWHILE, IN A LUXURIOUS LAIR, THE MEMBERS OF CRIME SYNDICATE INC. MEET TO DISCUSS THEIR FUTURE ACTIVITIES....
I WONDER WHAT THAT NEWSY'S YELLIN' ABOUT OUTSIDE? HEY, JOHNNY! SEND UP A COPY OF THE EXTRA TO OUR ROOM..
WELL, BOYS! NOW THAT THE CHIEF'S DEAD WHADDA WE GONNA DO?
AIN'T THAT JUST LIKE THE CHIEF, WEASEL? ALWAYS DOIN' THE UNEXPECTED! GEE! ARE WE GONNA MISS 'IM!
HERE'S THE PAPER, NOW!
AS WEASEL RUNS HIS EYE DOWN THE PAGE, A DARING PLAN BEGINS TO FORMULATE INSIDE HIS SCHEMING MIND.
DAILY FLASH
VOL XX
JOKER AT VESALIUS HOSPITAL FOR EMERGENCY TREATMENT!
E.S. ARTHUR TO SHIP PRICELESS PHARAOH GEMS
THE JOKER LIES AT THE POINT OF DEATH IN VESALIUS HOSPITAL. THE MEDICOS SAY HIS CHANCES FOR RECOVERY ARE SLIM UNLESS AN OPERATION IS PERFORMED.
THE CRIMINALS ARE BROUGHT TO THEIR FEET BY THE MOMENTOUS IMPLICATIONS OF THE NEWS STORY!
I THINK WE'RE GONNA HAVE A NEW LEADER, BOYS - THE JOKER - THE PHARAOH HAUL WILL BE A CINCH, WITH HIM DOING THE THINKING FOR US!
YEAH, BUT HOW ARE WE GONNA GET 'IM OUTTA THE HOSPITAL, WEASEL?
WITH GREAT CUNNING WEASEL RAPIDLY UNFOLDS HIS DARING SCHEME.
FIRST WE GET SOME OF US INTO THE HOSPITAL. THEN I GOT A PLAN FOR GETTIN' 'IM OUT AND PAST THE COPS THAT'LL GROW HAIR BACK ON YOUR HEAD - NOW WHICH ONE OF YOU BIRDS THINKS HE CAN FLY-?
2
THE DIE IS CAST! ONCE MORE THE MACHINATIONS OF THE CRIME SYNDICATE WILL BE FELT! THIS TIME UNDER THE RUTHLESS LEADERSHIP OF THE JOKER!! WHAT IS THE CONNECTION BETWEEN THE PRICELESS PHARAOH GEMS AND WEASEL'S PLAN TO ABDUCT THE JOKER?

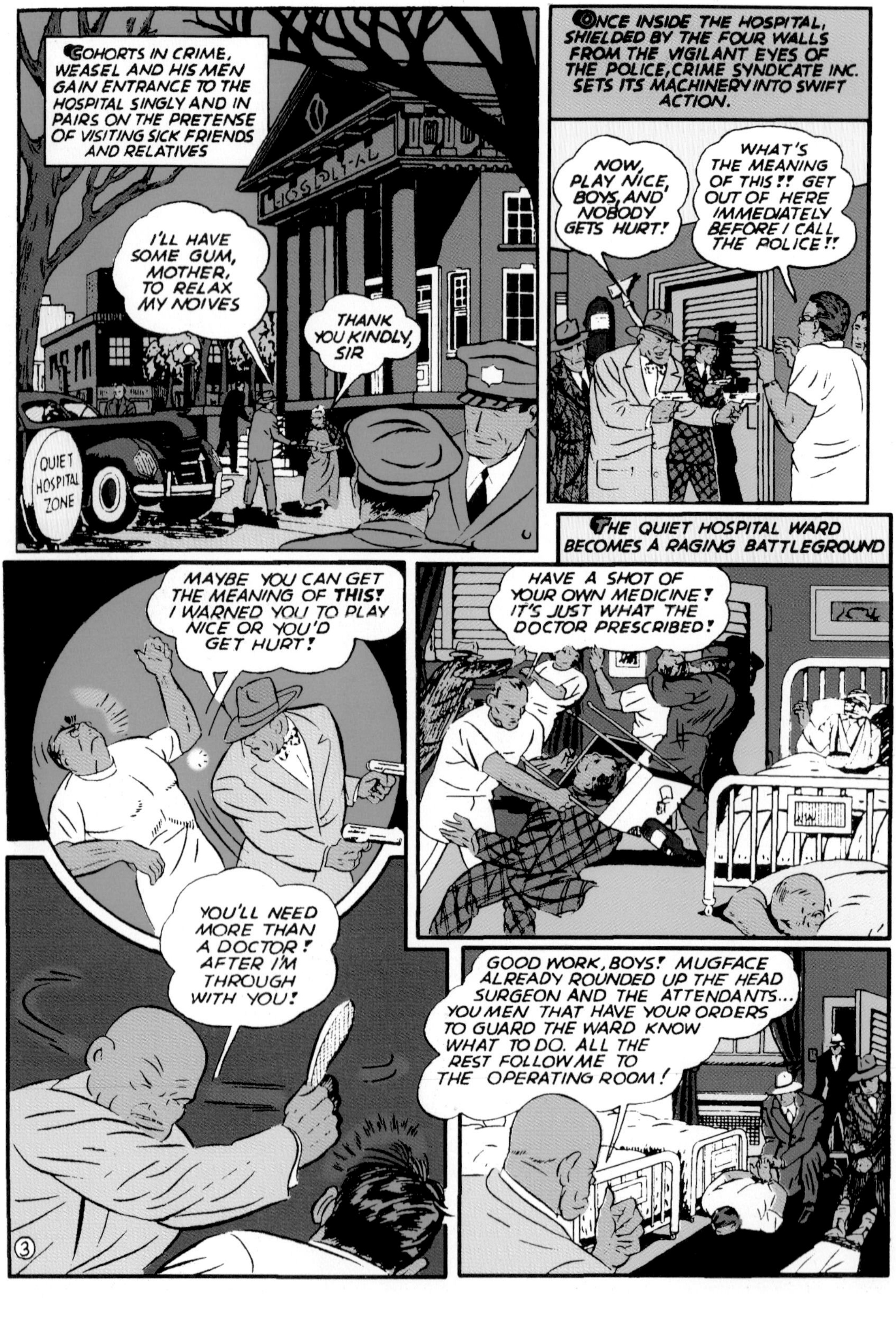
COHORTS IN CRIME, WEASEL AND HIS MEN GAIN ENTRANCE TO THE HOSPITAL SINGLY AND IN PAIRS ON THE PRETENSE OF VISITING SICK FRIENDS AND RELATIVES
I'LL HAVE SOME GUM, MOTHER, TO RELAX MY NOIVES
THANK YOU KINDLY, SIR
QUIET HOSPITAL ZONE
ONCE INSIDE THE HOSPITAL, SHIELDED BY THE FOUR WALLS FROM THE VIGILANT EYES OF THE POLICE, CRIME SYNDICATE INC. SETS ITS MACHINERY INTO SWIFT ACTION.
NOW, PLAY NICE, BOYS, AND NOBODY GETS HURT!
WHAT'S THE MEANING OF THIS!! GET OUT OF HERE IMMEDIATELY BEFORE I CALL THE POLICE!!
MAYBE YOU CAN GET THE MEANING OF THIS! I WARNED YOU TO PLAY NICE OR YOU'D GET HURT!
YOU'LL NEED MORE THAN A DOCTOR! AFTER I'M THROUGH WITH YOU!
THE QUIET HOSPITAL WARD BECOMES A RAGING BATTLEGROUND
HAVE A SHOT OF YOUR OWN MEDICINE! IT'S JUST WHAT THE DOCTOR PRESCRIBED!
GOOD WORK, BOYS! MUGFACE ALREADY ROUNDED UP THE HEAD SURGEON AND THE ATTENDANTS... YOU MEN THAT HAVE YOUR ORDERS TO GUARD THE WARD KNOW WHAT TO DO. ALL THE REST FOLLOW ME TO THE OPERATING ROOM!
3

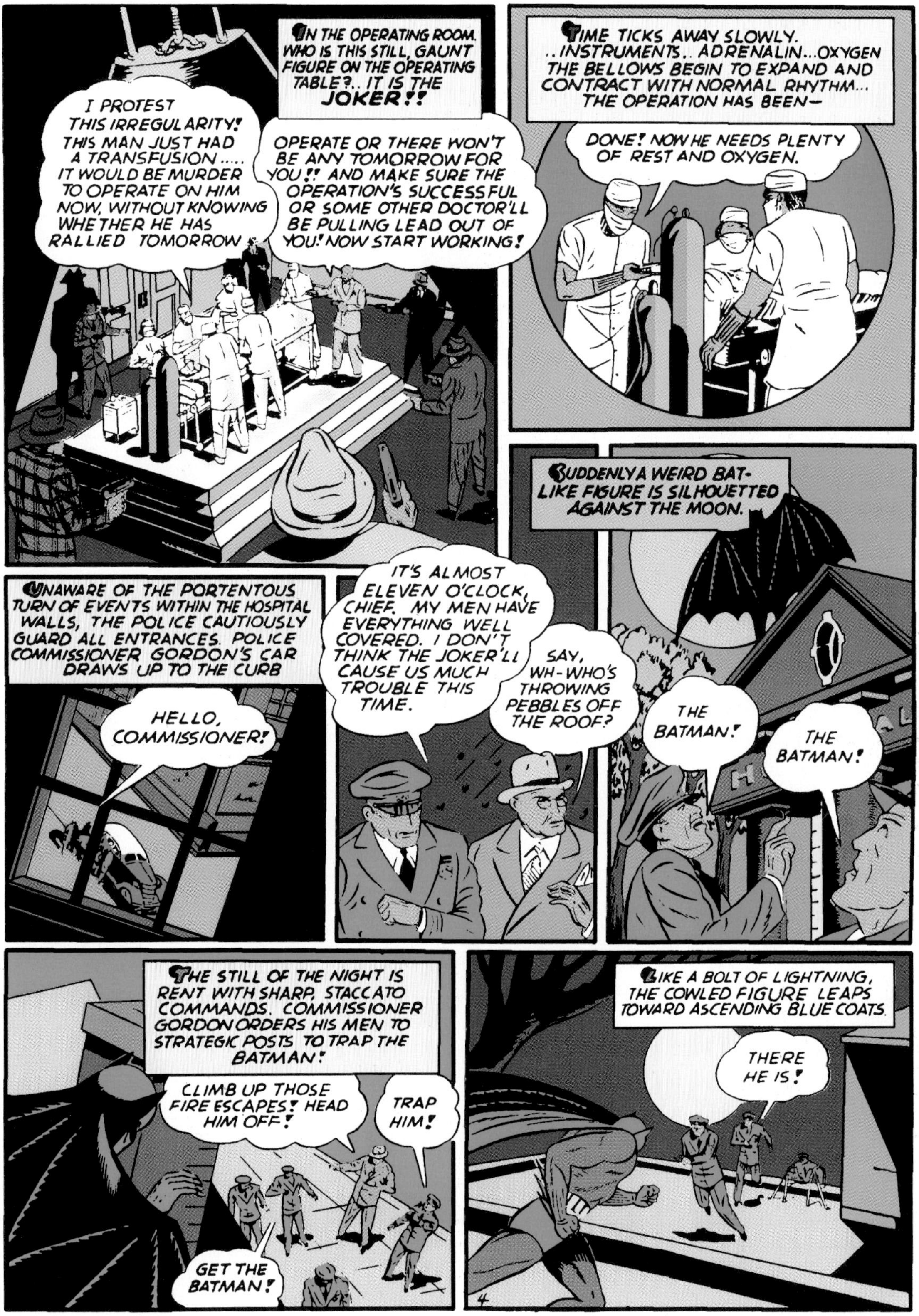
IN THE OPERATING ROOM. WHO IS THIS STILL, GAUNT FIGURE ON THE OPERATING TABLE?.. IT IS THE JOKER!!
I PROTEST THIS IRREGULARITY! THIS MAN JUST HAD A TRANSFUSION ..... IT WOULD BE MURDER TO OPERATE ON HIM NOW, WITHOUT KNOWING WHETHER HE HAS RALLIED TOMORROW
OPERATE OR THERE WON'T BE ANY TOMORROW FOR YOU!! AND MAKE SURE THE OPERATION'S SUCCESSFUL OR SOME OTHER DOCTOR'LL BE PULLING LEAD OUT OF YOU! NOW START WORKING!
TIME TICKS AWAY SLOWLY. ..INSTRUMENTS.. ADRENALIN...OXYGEN THE BELLOWS BEGIN TO EXPAND AND CONTRACT WITH NORMAL RHYTHM... THE OPERATION HAS BEEN—
DONE! NOW HE NEEDS PLENTY OF REST AND OXYGEN.
UNAWARE OF THE PORTENTOUS TURN OF EVENTS WITHIN THE HOSPITAL WALLS, THE POLICE CAUTIOUSLY GUARD ALL ENTRANCES. POLICE COMMISSIONER GORDON'S CAR DRAWS UP TO THE CURB
HELLO, COMMISSIONER!
IT'S ALMOST ELEVEN O'CLOCK, CHIEF. MY MEN HAVE EVERYTHING WELL COVERED. I DON'T THINK THE JOKER'LL CAUSE US MUCH TROUBLE THIS TIME.
SAY, WH-WHO'S THROWING PEBBLES OFF THE ROOF?
SUDDENLY A WEIRD BAT-LIKE FIGURE IS SILHOUETTED AGAINST THE MOON.
THE BATMAN!
THE BATMAN!
THE STILL OF THE NIGHT IS RENT WITH SHARP, STACCATO COMMANDS. COMMISSIONER GORDON ORDERS HIS MEN TO STRATEGIC POSTS TO TRAP THE BATMAN!
CLIMB UP THOSE FIRE ESCAPES! HEAD HIM OFF!
TRAP HIM!
GET THE BATMAN!
LIKE A BOLT OF LIGHTNING, THE COWLED FIGURE LEAPS TOWARD ASCENDING BLUE COATS.
THERE HE IS!
4

THE HOODED FIGURE EXPLODES A TERRIFIC BLOW OFF THE JAW OF THE POLICEMAN!

HERE'S A CHANCE TO CATCH UP ON LOST SLEEP, BUDDY!

HAVE A NICE TRIP...GENTLEMEN!

AAAGHHH...

BOTH POLICEMEN HURTLE TO DESTRUCTION...

I DON'T KNOW HOW I'LL BREAK THE NEWS TO THEIR FAMILIES!

THIS IS VERY STRANGE! THE BATMAN NEVER ATTACKED THE POLICE BEFORE!

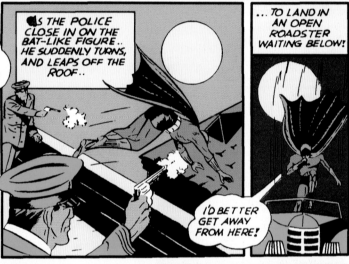

AS THE POLICE CLOSE IN ON THE BAT-LIKE FIGURE.. HE SUDDENLY TURNS, AND LEAPS OFF THE ROOF..

...TO LAND IN AN OPEN ROADSTER WAITING BELOW!

I'D BETTER GET AWAY FROM HERE!

THE POLICE START AFTER THE FLEEING AUTOMOBILE A FEW SECONDS LATER...

THE POLICE GAIN ON THE SPEEDING AUTOMOBILE ...

I'LL TURN OFF ON THAT ROAD!

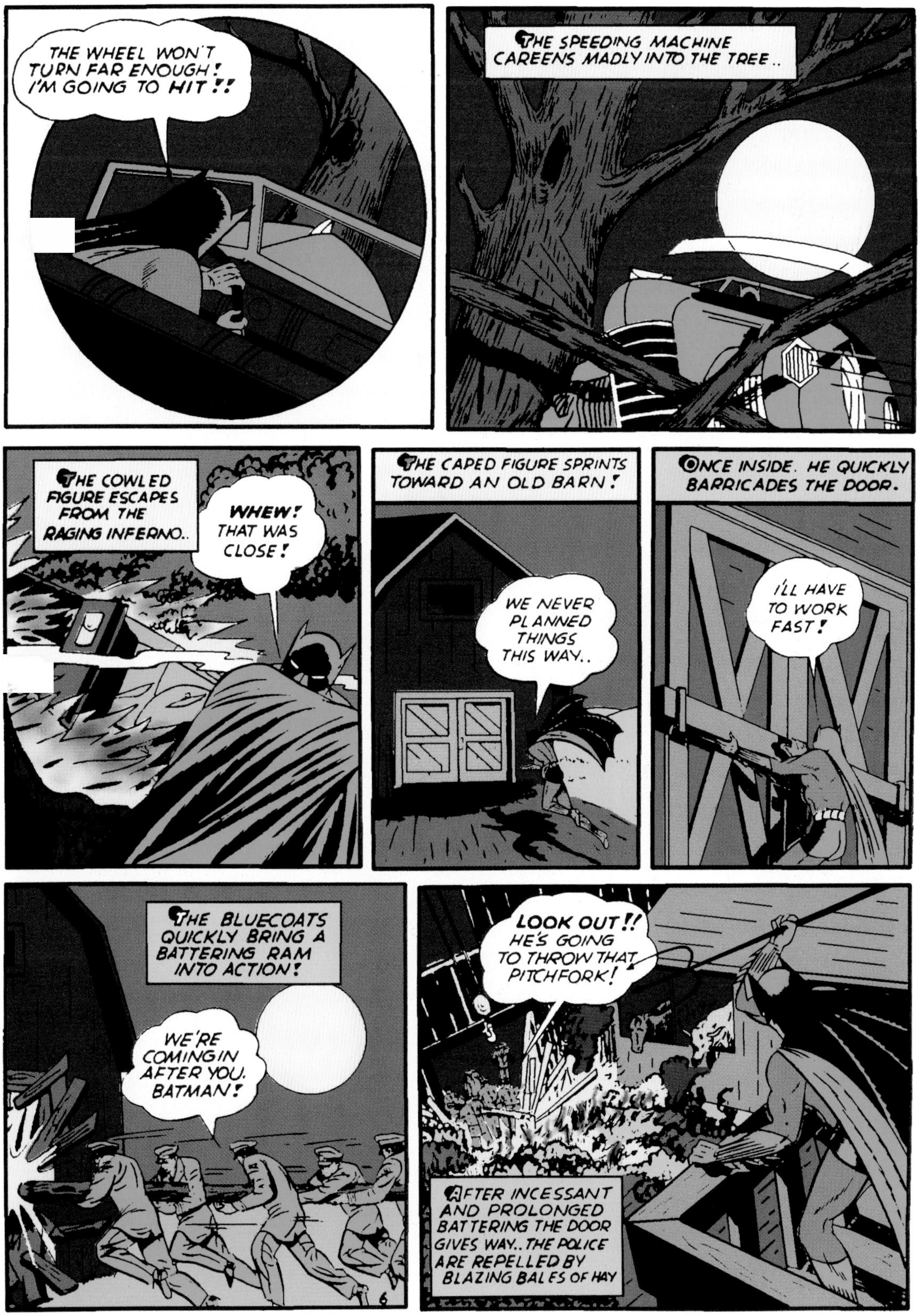
THE WHEEL WON'T TURN FAR ENOUGH! I'M GOING TO HIT!!
THE SPEEDING MACHINE CAREENS MADLY INTO THE TREE..
THE COWLED FIGURE ESCAPES FROM THE RAGING INFERNO..
WHEW! THAT WAS CLOSE!
THE CAPED FIGURE SPRINTS TOWARD AN OLD BARN!
WE NEVER PLANNED THINGS THIS WAY..
ONCE INSIDE. HE QUICKLY BARRICADES THE DOOR.
I'LL HAVE TO WORK FAST!
THE BLUECOATS QUICKLY BRING A BATTERING RAM INTO ACTION!
WE'RE COMINGIN AFTER YOU. BATMAN!
6
LOOK OUT!! HE'S GOING TO THROW THAT PITCHFORK!
AFTER INCESSANT AND PROLONGED BATTERING THE DOOR GIVES WAY..THE POLICE ARE REPELLED BY BLAZING BALES OF HAY

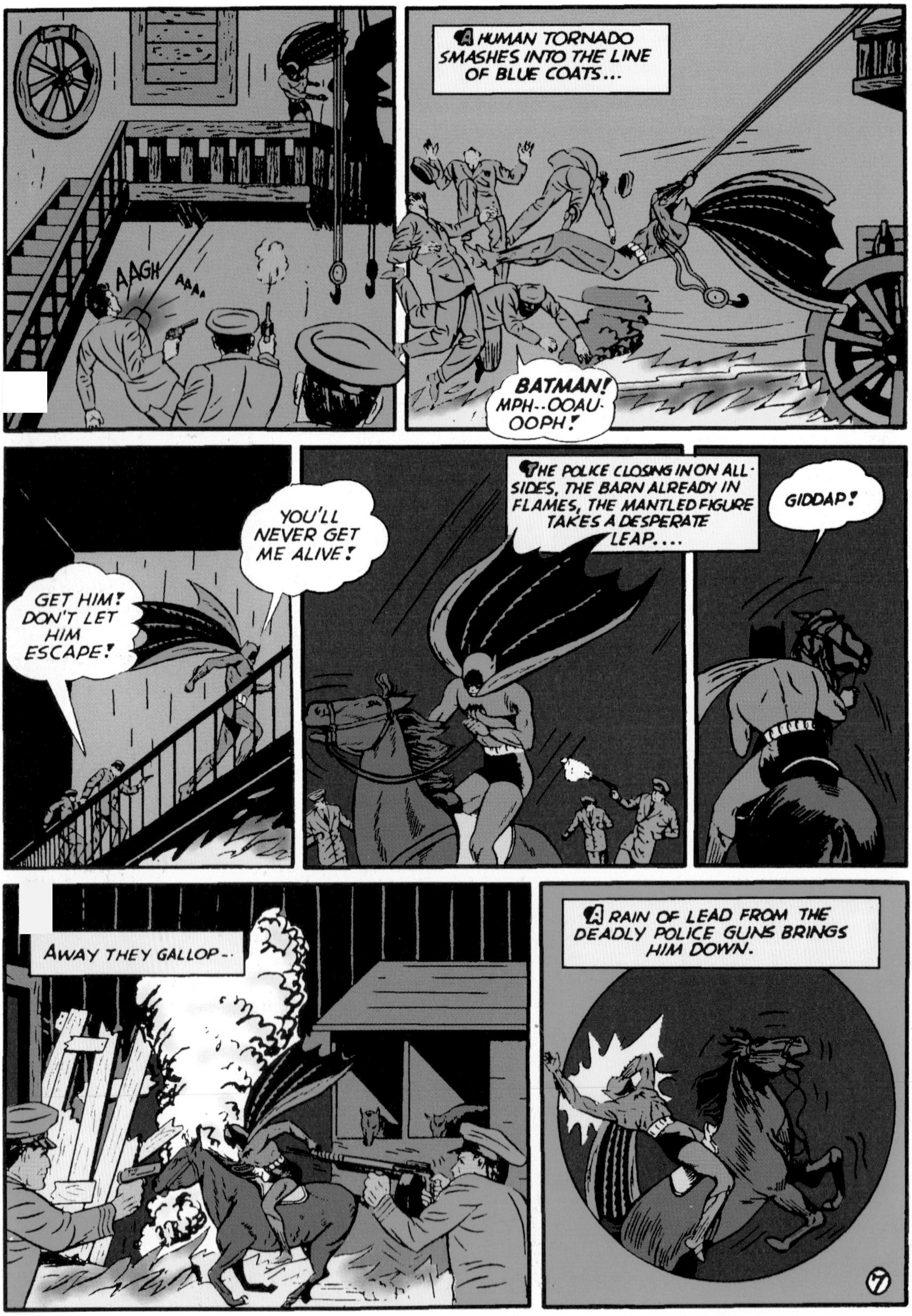
AAGH
A HUMAN TORNADO SMASHES INTO THE LINE OF BLUE COATS...
BATMAN! MPH--OOAU-OOPH!
YOU'LL NEVER GET ME ALIVE!
GET HIM! DON'T LET HIM ESCAPE!
THE POLICE CLOSING IN ON ALL-SIDES, THE BARN ALREADY IN FLAMES, THE MANTLED FIGURE TAKES A DESPERATE LEAP....
GIDDAP!
AWAY THEY GALLOP--
A RAIN OF LEAD FROM THE DEADLY POLICE GUNS BRINGS HIM DOWN.
7

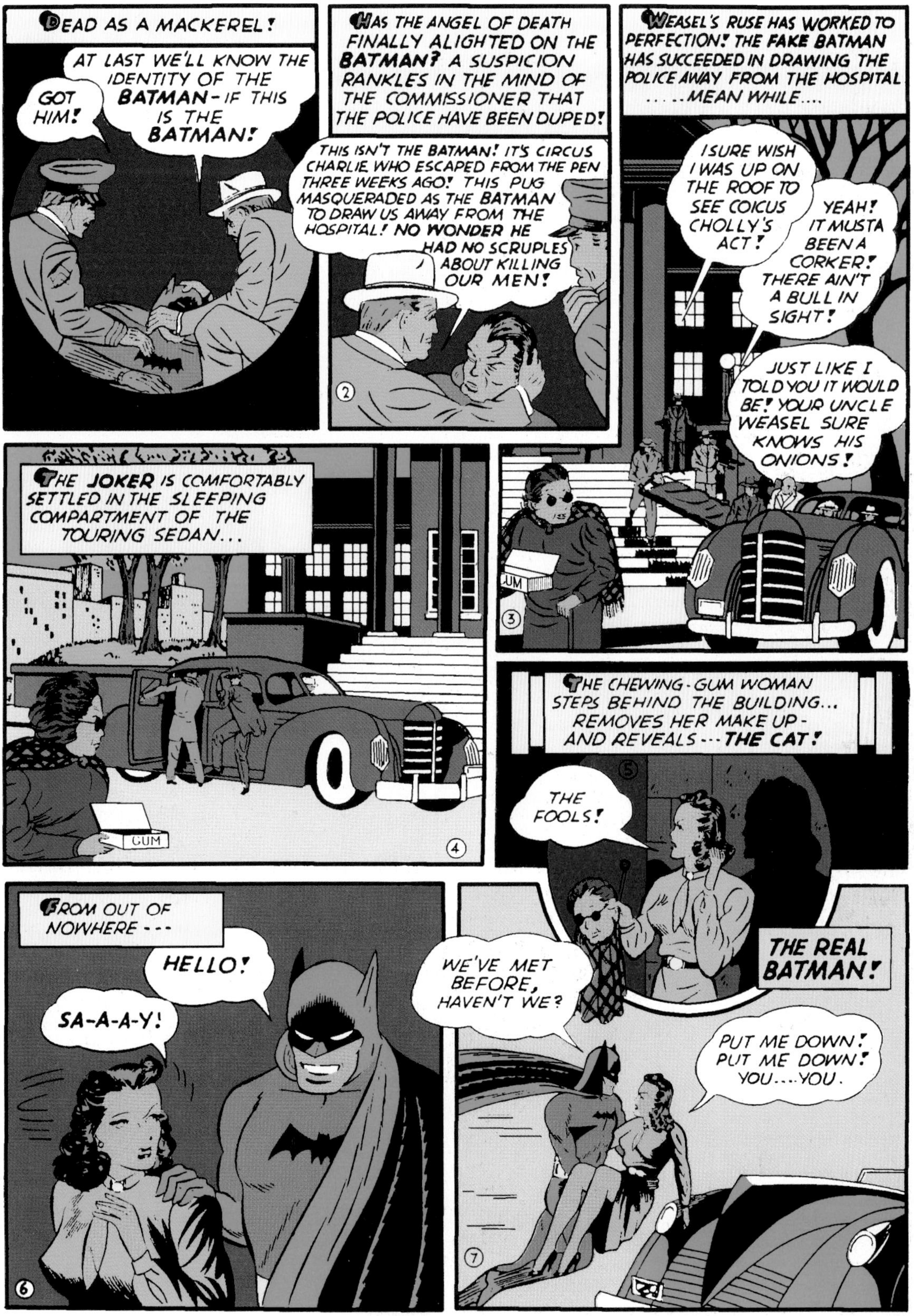
DEAD AS A MACKEREL!
AT LAST WE'LL KNOW THE IDENTITY OF THE BATMAN - IF THIS IS THE BATMAN!
GOT HIM!
HAS THE ANGEL OF DEATH FINALLY ALIGHTED ON THE BATMAN? A SUSPICION RANKLES IN THE MIND OF THE COMMISSIONER THAT THE POLICE HAVE BEEN DUPED!
THIS ISN'T THE BATMAN! IT'S CIRCUS CHARLIE WHO ESCAPED FROM THE PEN THREE WEEKS AGO! THIS PUG MASQUERADED AS THE BATMAN TO DRAW US AWAY FROM THE HOSPITAL! NO WONDER HE HAD NO SCRUPLES ABOUT KILLING OUR MEN!
WEASEL'S RUSE HAS WORKED TO PERFECTION! THE FAKE BATMAN HAS SUCCEEDED IN DRAWING THE POLICE AWAY FROM THE HOSPITAL .....MEAN WHILE....
I SURE WISH I WAS UP ON THE ROOF TO SEE COICUS CHOLLY'S ACT!
YEAH! IT MUSTA BEEN A CORKER! THERE AIN'T A BULL IN SIGHT!
JUST LIKE I TOLD YOU IT WOULD BE! YOUR UNCLE WEASEL SURE KNOWS HIS ONIONS!
GUM
THE JOKER IS COMFORTABLY SETTLED IN THE SLEEPING COMPARTMENT OF THE TOURING SEDAN...
GUM
THE CHEWING-GUM WOMAN STEPS BEHIND THE BUILDING... REMOVES HER MAKE UP - AND REVEALS --- THE CAT!
THE FOOLS!
FROM OUT OF NOWHERE ---
HELLO!
SA-A-A-Y!
THE REAL BATMAN!
WE'VE MET BEFORE, HAVEN'T WE?
PUT ME DOWN! PUT ME DOWN! YOU....YOU.

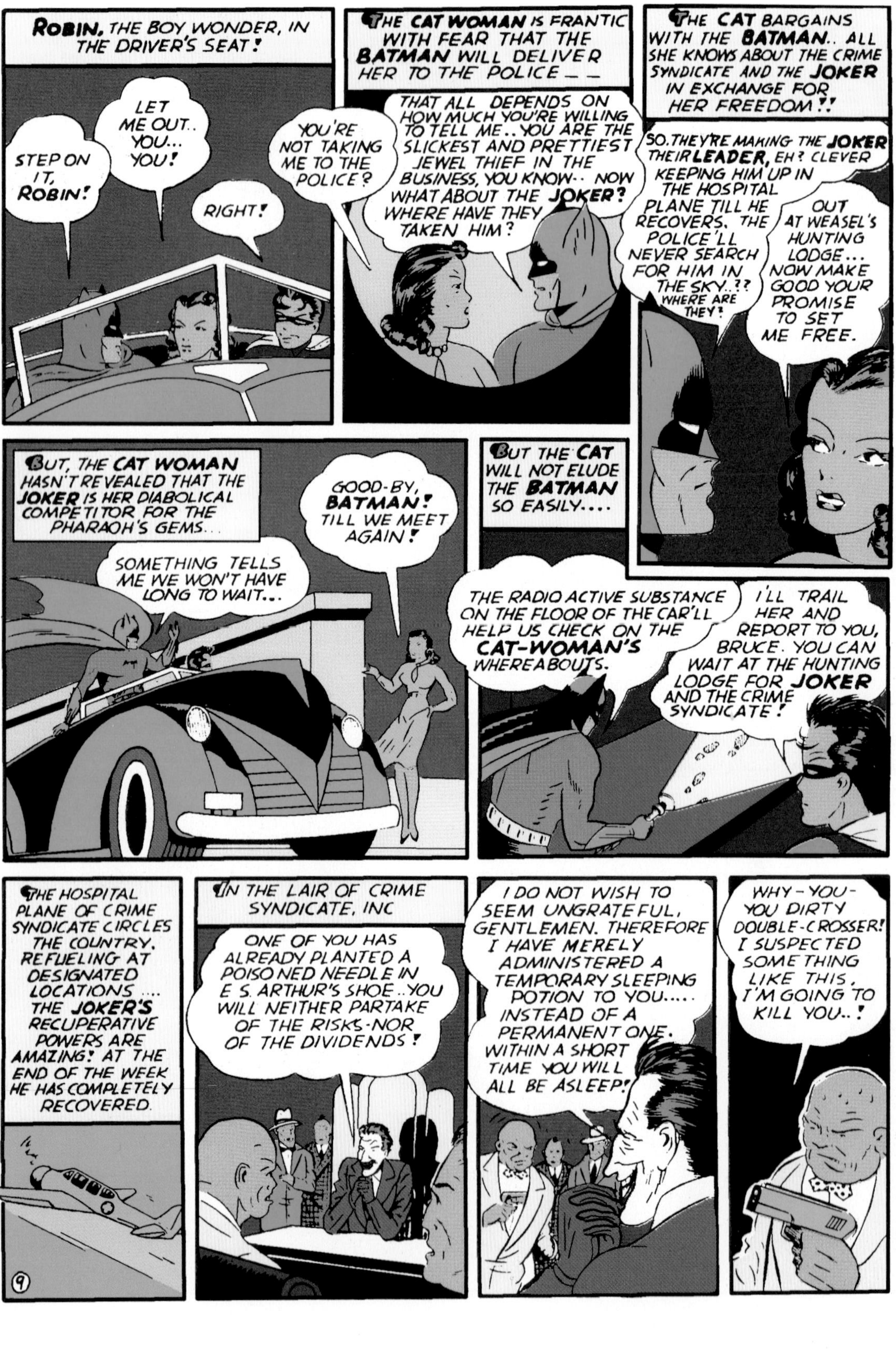
ROBIN, THE BOY WONDER, IN THE DRIVER'S SEAT!
STEP ON IT, ROBIN!
LET ME OUT.. YOU... YOU!
RIGHT!
THE CAT WOMAN IS FRANTIC WITH FEAR THAT THE BATMAN WILL DELIVER HER TO THE POLICE — —
YOU'RE NOT TAKING ME TO THE POLICE?
THAT ALL DEPENDS ON HOW MUCH YOU'RE WILLING TO TELL ME.. YOU ARE THE SLICKEST AND PRETTIEST JEWEL THIEF IN THE BUSINESS, YOU KNOW.. NOW WHAT ABOUT THE JOKER? WHERE HAVE THEY TAKEN HIM?
THE CAT BARGAINS WITH THE BATMAN.. ALL SHE KNOWS ABOUT THE CRIME SYNDICATE AND THE JOKER IN EXCHANGE FOR HER FREEDOM!!
SO, THEY'RE MAKING THE JOKER THEIR LEADER, EH? CLEVER KEEPING HIM UP IN THE HOSPITAL PLANE TILL HE RECOVERS. THE POLICE'LL NEVER SEARCH FOR HIM IN THE SKY..?? WHERE ARE THEY?
OUT AT WEASEL'S HUNTING LODGE... NOW MAKE GOOD YOUR PROMISE TO SET ME FREE.
BUT, THE CAT WOMAN HASN'T REVEALED THAT THE JOKER IS HER DIABOLICAL COMPETITOR FOR THE PHARAOH'S GEMS...
GOOD-BY, BATMAN! TILL WE MEET AGAIN!
SOMETHING TELLS ME WE WON'T HAVE LONG TO WAIT...
BUT THE CAT WILL NOT ELUDE THE BATMAN SO EASILY....
THE RADIO ACTIVE SUBSTANCE ON THE FLOOR OF THE CAR'LL HELP US CHECK ON THE CAT-WOMAN'S WHEREABOUTS.
I'LL TRAIL HER AND REPORT TO YOU, BRUCE. YOU CAN WAIT AT THE HUNTING LODGE FOR JOKER AND THE CRIME SYNDICATE!
THE HOSPITAL PLANE OF CRIME SYNDICATE CIRCLES THE COUNTRY, REFUELING AT DESIGNATED LOCATIONS .... THE JOKER'S RECUPERATIVE POWERS ARE AMAZING! AT THE END OF THE WEEK HE HAS COMPLETELY RECOVERED.
9
IN THE LAIR OF CRIME SYNDICATE, INC
ONE OF YOU HAS ALREADY PLANTED A POISONED NEEDLE IN E. S. ARTHUR'S SHOE.. YOU WILL NEITHER PARTAKE OF THE RISKS-NOR OF THE DIVIDENDS!
I DO NOT WISH TO SEEM UNGRATEFUL, GENTLEMEN. THEREFORE I HAVE MERELY ADMINISTERED A TEMPORARY SLEEPING POTION TO YOU..... INSTEAD OF A PERMANENT ONE. WITHIN A SHORT TIME YOU WILL ALL BE ASLEEP!
WHY-YOU-YOU DIRTY DOUBLE-CROSSER! I SUSPECTED SOMETHING LIKE THIS. I'M GOING TO KILL YOU..!

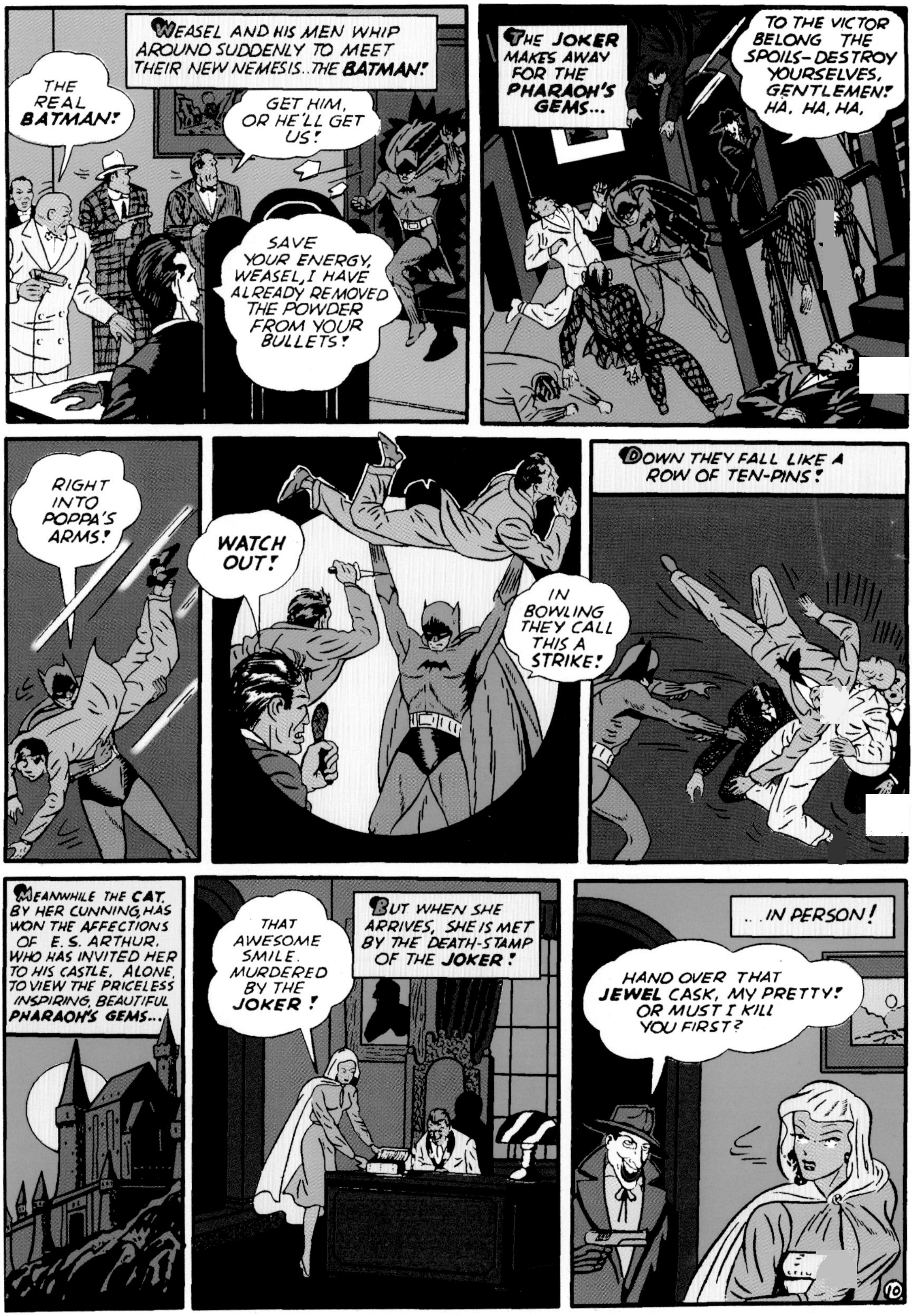
WEASEL AND HIS MEN WHIP AROUND SUDDENLY TO MEET THEIR NEW NEMESIS...THE BATMAN!
THE REAL BATMAN!
GET HIM, OR HE'LL GET US!
SAVE YOUR ENERGY, WEASEL, I HAVE ALREADY REMOVED THE POWDER FROM YOUR BULLETS!
THE JOKER MAKES AWAY FOR THE PHARAOH'S GEMS...
TO THE VICTOR BELONG THE SPOILS-DESTROY YOURSELVES, GENTLEMEN! HA, HA, HA,
RIGHT INTO POPPA'S ARMS!
WATCH OUT!
IN BOWLING THEY CALL THIS A STRIKE!
DOWN THEY FALL LIKE A ROW OF TEN-PINS!
MEANWHILE THE CAT, BY HER CUNNING, HAS WON THE AFFECTIONS OF E. S. ARTHUR, WHO HAS INVITED HER TO HIS CASTLE, ALONE, TO VIEW THE PRICELESS INSPIRING, BEAUTIFUL PHARAOH'S GEMS...
BUT WHEN SHE ARRIVES, SHE IS MET BY THE DEATH-STAMP OF THE JOKER!
THAT AWESOME SMILE. MURDERED BY THE JOKER!
...IN PERSON!
HAND OVER THAT JEWEL CASK, MY PRETTY! OR MUST I KILL YOU FIRST?
10

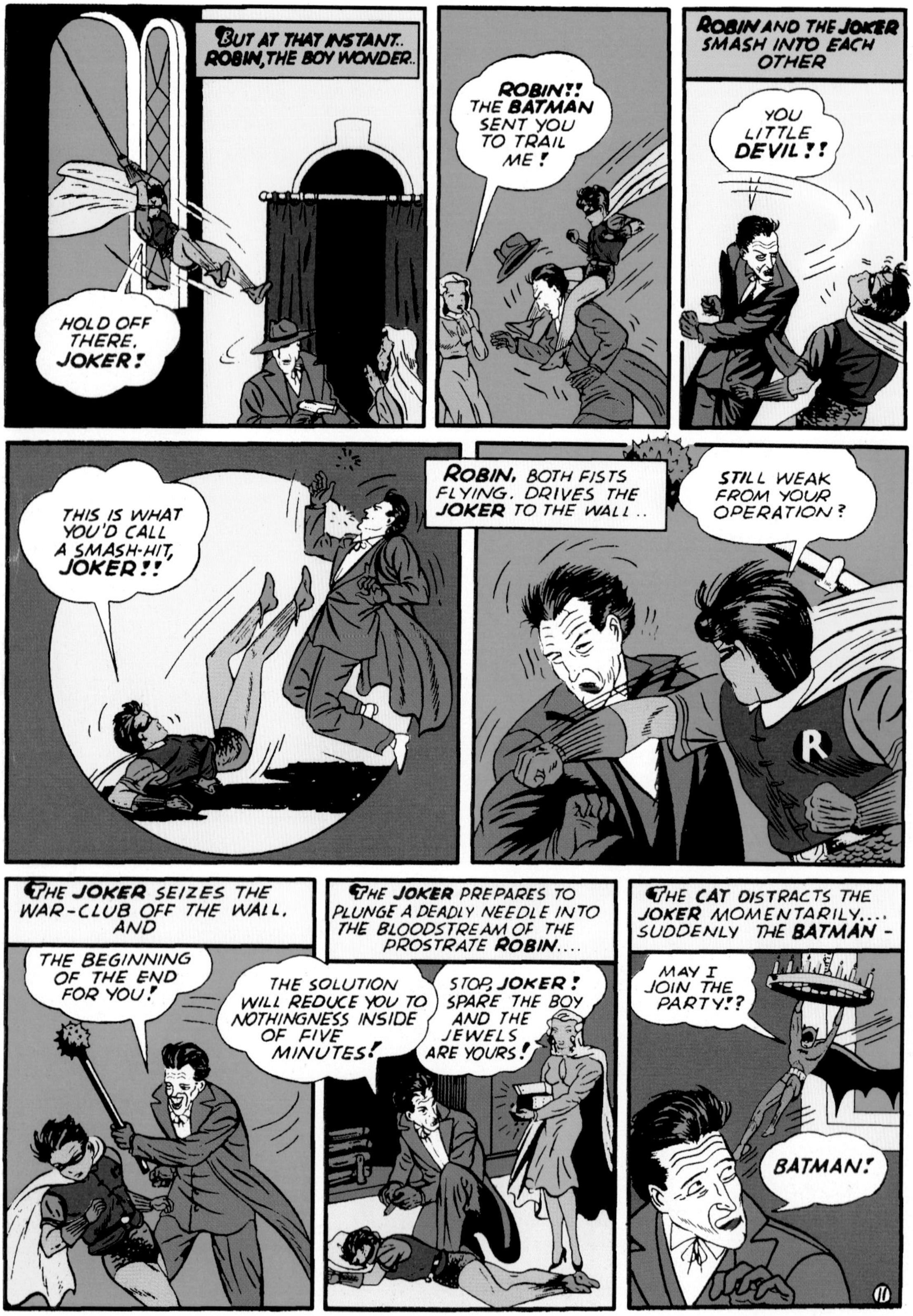
BUT AT THAT INSTANT.. ROBIN, THE BOY WONDER..
HOLD OFF THERE. JOKER!
ROBIN!! THE BATMAN SENT YOU TO TRAIL ME!
ROBIN AND THE JOKER SMASH INTO EACH OTHER
YOU LITTLE DEVIL!!
THIS IS WHAT YOU'D CALL A SMASH-HIT, JOKER!!
ROBIN, BOTH FISTS FLYING, DRIVES THE JOKER TO THE WALL..
STILL WEAK FROM YOUR OPERATION?
THE JOKER SEIZES THE WAR-CLUB OFF THE WALL, AND
THE BEGINNING OF THE END FOR YOU!
THE JOKER PREPARES TO PLUNGE A DEADLY NEEDLE INTO THE BLOODSTREAM OF THE PROSTRATE ROBIN....
THE SOLUTION WILL REDUCE YOU TO NOTHINGNESS INSIDE OF FIVE MINUTES!
STOP, JOKER! SPARE THE BOY AND THE JEWELS ARE YOURS!
THE CAT DISTRACTS THE JOKER MOMENTARILY.... SUDDENLY THE BATMAN -
MAY I JOIN THE PARTY!?
BATMAN!
11

A BIT UNSTEADY, AREN'T YOU, JOKER?

A·A·A·A· ARUMPH!

THE BATMAN CHALLENGES THE JOKER TO A DUEL --

HERE'S A CHANCE TO FIGHT FOR YOUR WORTHLESS EXISTENCE, JOKER!

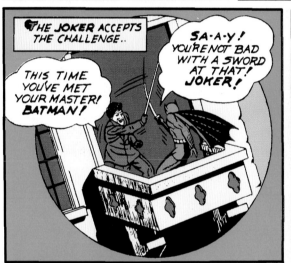

THE JOKER ACCEPTS THE CHALLENGE..

THIS TIME YOU'VE MET YOUR MASTER! BATMAN!

SA·A·Y! YOU'RE NOT BAD WITH A SWORD AT THAT! JOKER!

SLASHING FURIOUSLY, THE JOKER FORCES THE BATMAN UP ON THE LEDGE OF THE BALUSTRADE.....

A FEW MORE THRUSTS, BATMAN, AND I'LL FINISH YOU OFF!

A GOOD TRICK - IF YOU CAN DO IT!

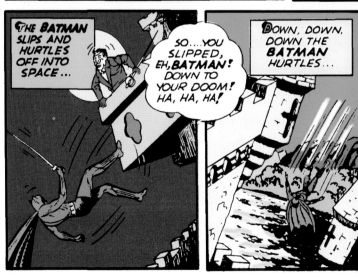

THE BATMAN SLIPS AND HURTLES OFF INTO SPACE...

SO....YOU SLIPPED, EH, BATMAN! DOWN TO YOUR DOOM! HA, HA, HA!

DOWN, DOWN, DOWN THE BATMAN HURTLES...

THE BATMAN GRASPS THE THICK, GNARLED VINES HUGGING THE WALLS OF THE CASTLE, THUS BREAKING HIS FALL...

PHEW! ALMOST PULLED MY ARM OUT- NOW TO CLIMB BACK BEFORE THAT FIEND DOES SOME SERIOUS DAMAGE.....

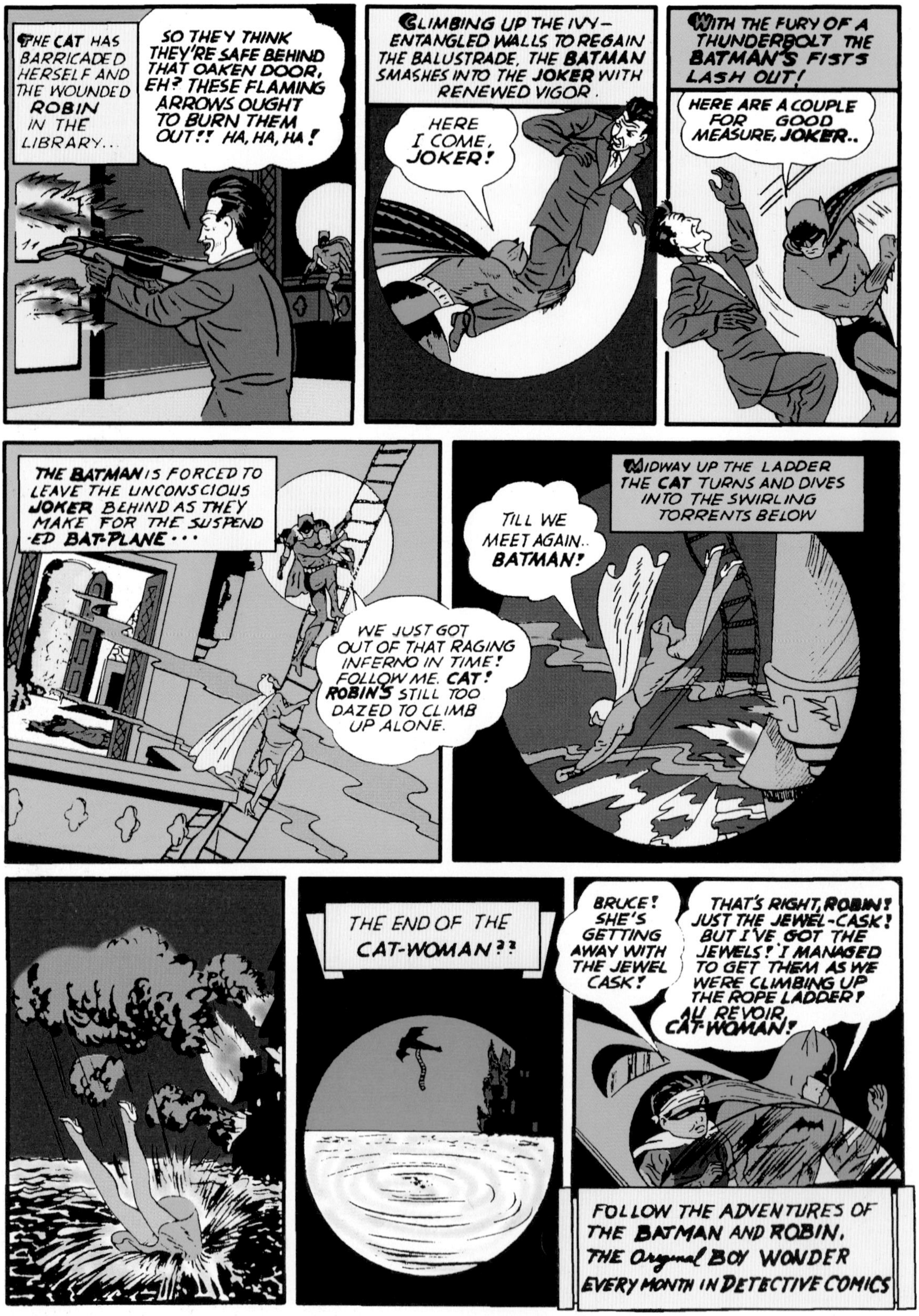
THE CAT HAS BARRICADED HERSELF AND THE WOUNDED ROBIN IN THE LIBRARY...
SO THEY THINK THEY'RE SAFE BEHIND THAT OAKEN DOOR, EH? THESE FLAMING ARROWS OUGHT TO BURN THEM OUT!! HA, HA, HA!
CLIMBING UP THE IVY-ENTANGLED WALLS TO REGAIN THE BALUSTRADE, THE BATMAN SMASHES INTO THE JOKER WITH RENEWED VIGOR.
HERE I COME, JOKER!
WITH THE FURY OF A THUNDERBOLT THE BATMAN'S FISTS LASH OUT!
HERE ARE A COUPLE FOR GOOD MEASURE, JOKER..
THE BATMAN IS FORCED TO LEAVE THE UNCONSCIOUS JOKER BEHIND AS THEY MAKE FOR THE SUSPEND-ED BAT-PLANE...
WE JUST GOT OUT OF THAT RAGING INFERNO IN TIME! FOLLOW ME. CAT! ROBIN'S STILL TOO DAZED TO CLIMB UP ALONE.
MIDWAY UP THE LADDER THE CAT TURNS AND DIVES INTO THE SWIRLING TORRENTS BELOW
TILL WE MEET AGAIN.. BATMAN!
THE END OF THE CAT-WOMAN??
BRUCE! SHE'S GETTING AWAY WITH THE JEWEL CASK!
THAT'S RIGHT, ROBIN! JUST THE JEWEL-CASK! BUT I'VE GOT THE JEWELS! I MANAGED TO GET THEM AS WE WERE CLIMBING UP THE ROPE LADDER! AU REVOIR, CAT-WOMAN!
FOLLOW THE ADVENTURES OF THE BATMAN AND ROBIN, THE Original BOY WONDER EVERY MONTH IN DETECTIVE COMICS

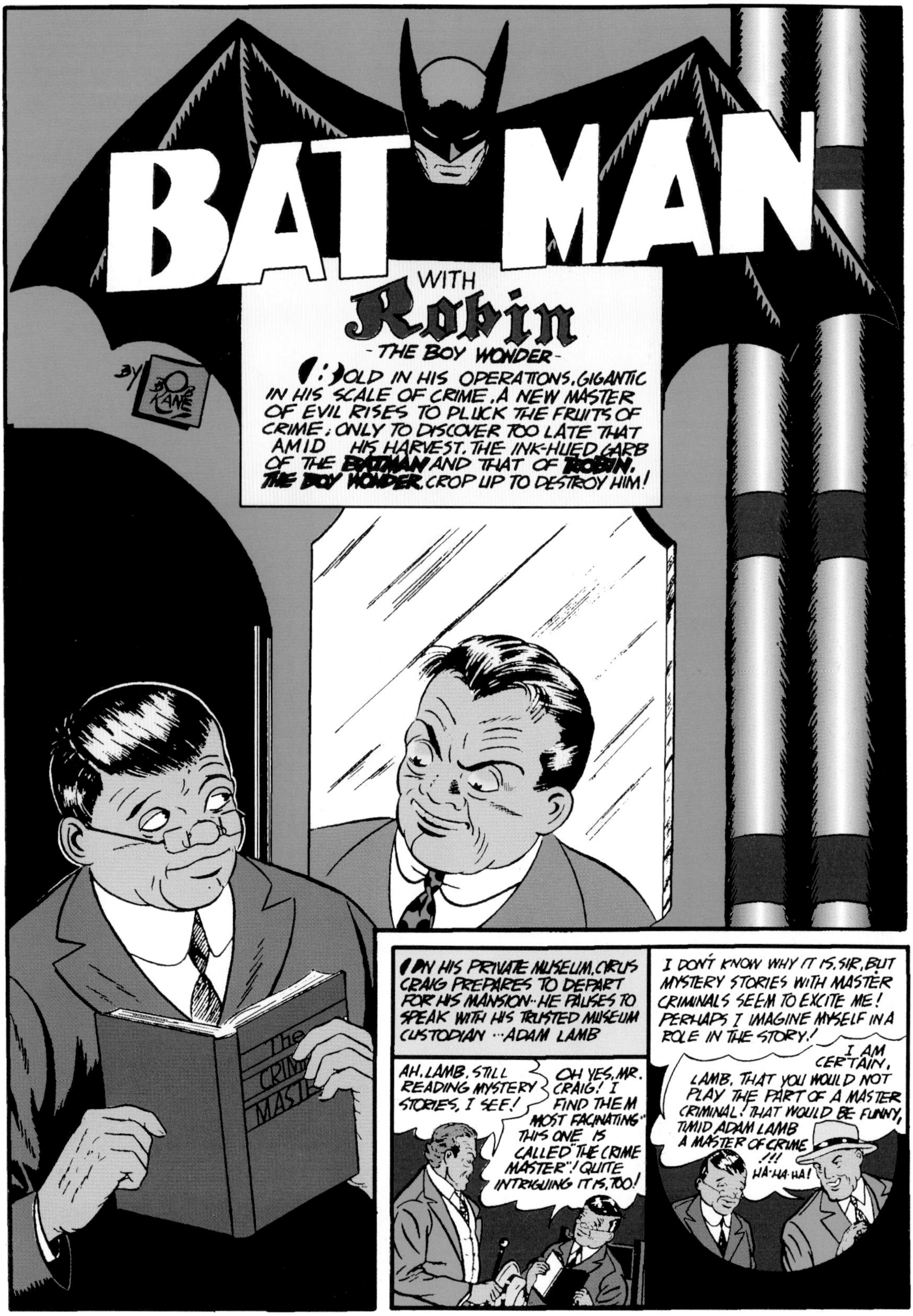
BATMAN
WITH Robin -THE BOY WONDER-
BY BOB KANE
BOLD IN HIS OPERATIONS, GIGANTIC IN HIS SCALE OF CRIME, A NEW MASTER OF EVIL RISES TO PLUCK THE FRUITS OF CRIME; ONLY TO DISCOVER TOO LATE THAT AMID HIS HARVEST, THE INK-HUED GARB OF THE BATMAN AND THAT OF ROBIN, THE BOY WONDER CROP UP TO DESTROY HIM!
The CRIME MASTER
IN HIS PRIVATE MUSEUM, CYRUS CRAIG PREPARES TO DEPART FOR HIS MANSION.. HE PAUSES TO SPEAK WITH HIS TRUSTED MUSEUM CUSTODIAN ... ADAM LAMB
AH, LAMB, STILL READING MYSTERY STORIES, I SEE!
OH YES, MR. CRAIG! I FIND THEM MOST FASCINATING-- THIS ONE IS CALLED "THE CRIME MASTER"! QUITE INTRIGUING IT IS, TOO!
I DON'T KNOW WHY IT IS, SIR, BUT MYSTERY STORIES WITH MASTER CRIMINALS SEEM TO EXCITE ME! PERHAPS I IMAGINE MYSELF IN A ROLE IN THE STORY!
I AM CERTAIN, LAMB, THAT YOU WOULD NOT PLAY THE PART OF A MASTER CRIMINAL! THAT WOULD BE FUNNY, TIMID ADAM LAMB A MASTER OF CRIME !!! HA-HA-HA!

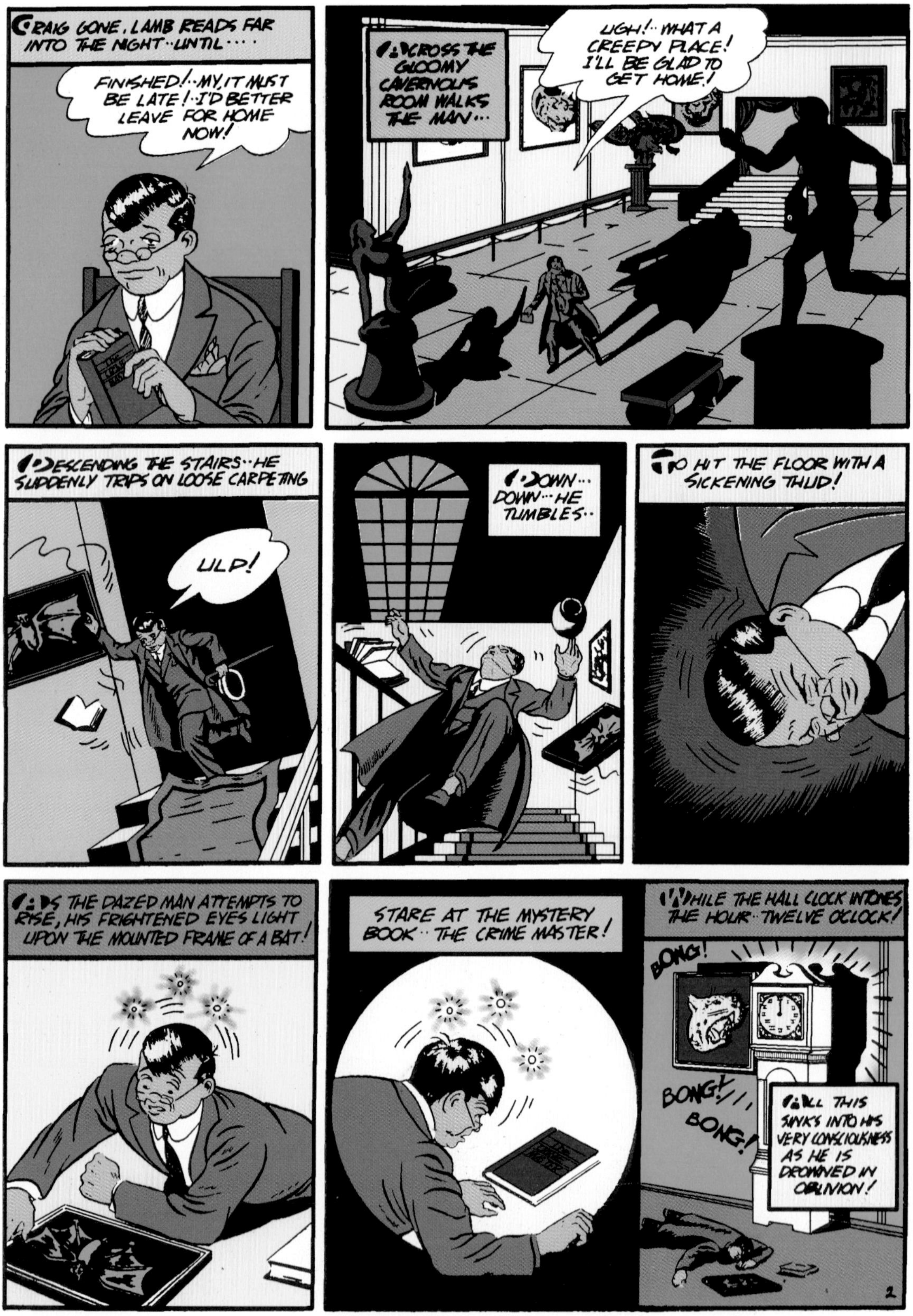
CRAIG GONE, LAMB READS FAR INTO THE NIGHT··UNTIL····
FINISHED!··MY, IT MUST BE LATE!··I'D BETTER LEAVE FOR HOME NOW!
ACROSS THE GLOOMY CAVERNOUS ROOM WALKS THE MAN···
UGH!··WHAT A CREEPY PLACE! I'LL BE GLAD TO GET HOME!
DESCENDING THE STAIRS··HE SUDDENLY TRIPS ON LOOSE CARPETING
ULP!
DOWN··· DOWN··· HE TUMBLES··
TO HIT THE FLOOR WITH A SICKENING THUD!
AS THE DAZED MAN ATTEMPTS TO RISE, HIS FRIGHTENED EYES LIGHT UPON THE MOUNTED FRAME OF A BAT!
STARE AT THE MYSTERY BOOK·· THE CRIME MASTER!
WHILE THE HALL CLOCK INTONES THE HOUR··TWELVE O'CLOCK!
BONG!
BONG!
BONG!
ALL THIS SINKS INTO HIS VERY CONSCIOUSNESS AS HE IS DROWNED IN OBLIVION!
2

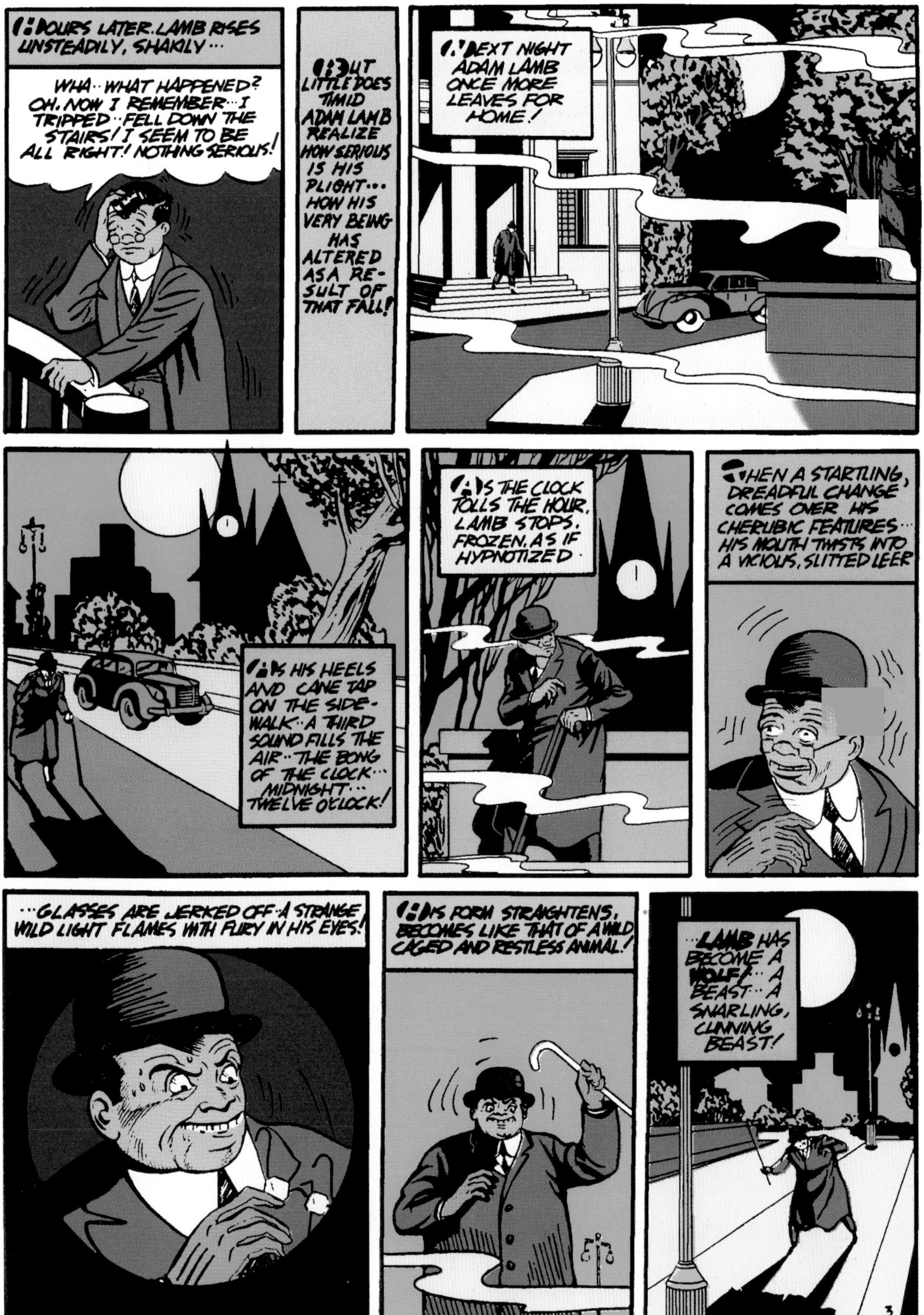
HOURS LATER. LAMB RISES UNSTEADILY, SHAKILY...
WHA.. WHAT HAPPENED? OH, NOW I REMEMBER.. I TRIPPED.. FELL DOWN THE STAIRS! I SEEM TO BE ALL RIGHT! NOTHING SERIOUS!
BUT LITTLE DOES TIMID ADAM LAMB REALIZE HOW SERIOUS IS HIS PLIGHT... HOW HIS VERY BEING HAS ALTERED AS A RESULT OF THAT FALL!
NEXT NIGHT ADAM LAMB ONCE MORE LEAVES FOR HOME!
AS HIS HEELS AND CANE TAP ON THE SIDEWALK.. A THIRD SOUND FILLS THE AIR.. THE BONG OF THE CLOCK... MIDNIGHT... TWELVE O'CLOCK!
AS THE CLOCK TOLLS THE HOUR, LAMB STOPS, FROZEN, AS IF HYPNOTIZED.
THEN A STARTLING, DREADFUL CHANGE COMES OVER HIS CHERUBIC FEATURES... HIS MOUTH TWISTS INTO A VICIOUS, SLITTED LEER
...GLASSES ARE JERKED OFF.. A STRANGE WILD LIGHT FLAMES WITH FURY IN HIS EYES!
HIS FORM STRAIGHTENS, BECOMES LIKE THAT OF A WILD, CAGED AND RESTLESS ANIMAL!
...LAMB HAS BECOME A WOLF!.. A BEAST.. A SNARLING, CUNNING BEAST!
3

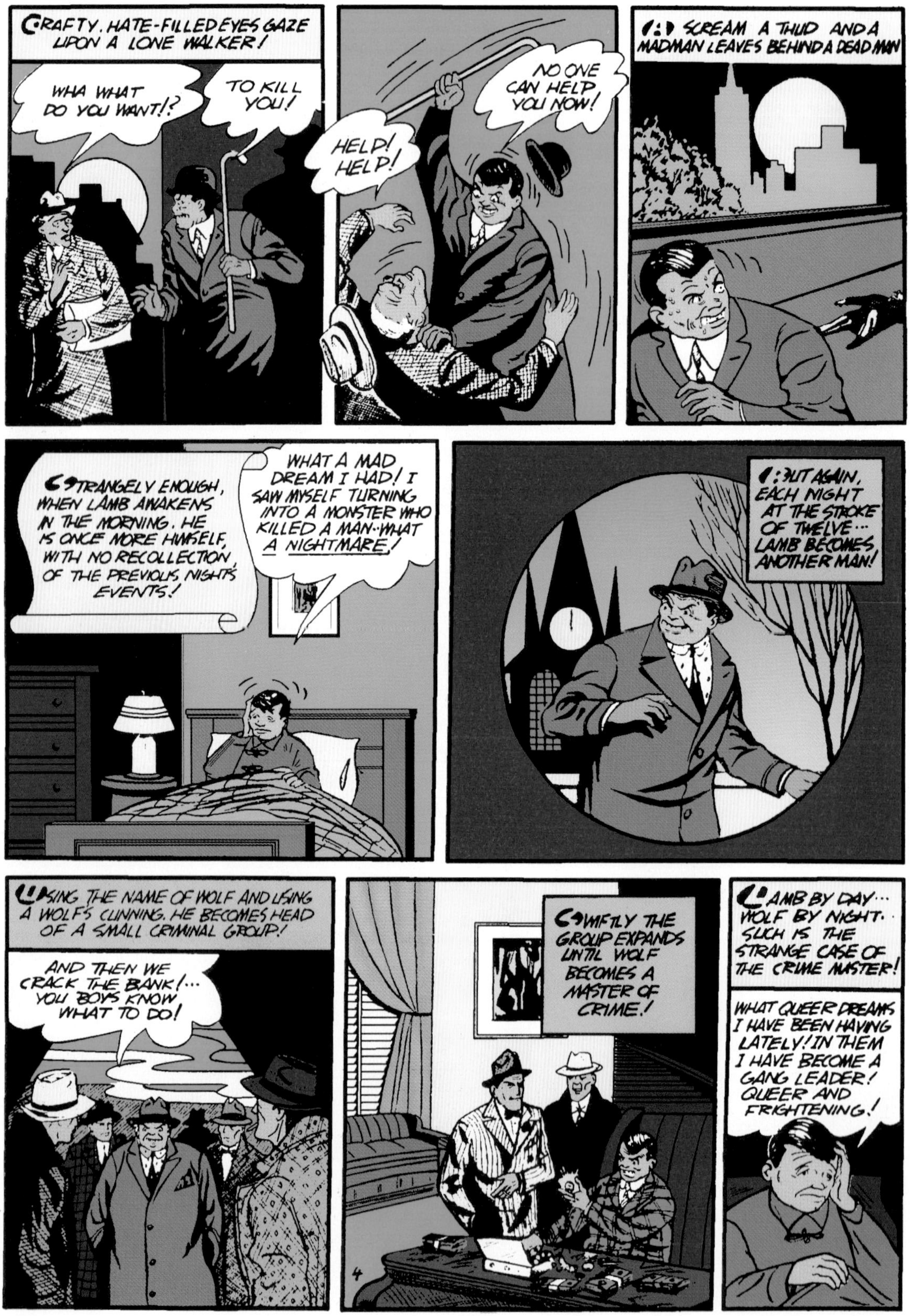
CRAFTY, HATE-FILLED EYES GAZE UPON A LONE WALKER!
WHA WHAT DO YOU WANT!?
TO KILL YOU!
NO ONE CAN HELP YOU NOW!
HELP! HELP!
A SCREAM A THUD AND A MADMAN LEAVES BEHIND A DEAD MAN
STRANGELY ENOUGH, WHEN LAMB AWAKENS IN THE MORNING, HE IS ONCE MORE HIMSELF, WITH NO RECOLLECTION OF THE PREVIOUS NIGHT'S EVENTS!
WHAT A MAD DREAM I HAD! I SAW MYSELF TURNING INTO A MONSTER WHO KILLED A MAN..WHAT A NIGHTMARE!
BUT AGAIN, EACH NIGHT AT THE STROKE OF TWELVE... LAMB BECOMES ANOTHER MAN!
USING THE NAME OF WOLF AND USING A WOLF'S CUNNING, HE BECOMES HEAD OF A SMALL CRIMINAL GROUP!
AND THEN WE CRACK THE BANK!... YOU BOYS KNOW WHAT TO DO!
SWIFTLY THE GROUP EXPANDS UNTIL WOLF BECOMES A MASTER OF CRIME!
4
LAMB BY DAY... WOLF BY NIGHT.. SUCH IS THE STRANGE CASE OF THE CRIME MASTER!
WHAT QUEER DREAMS I HAVE BEEN HAVING LATELY! IN THEM I HAVE BECOME A GANG LEADER! QUEER AND FRIGHTENING!

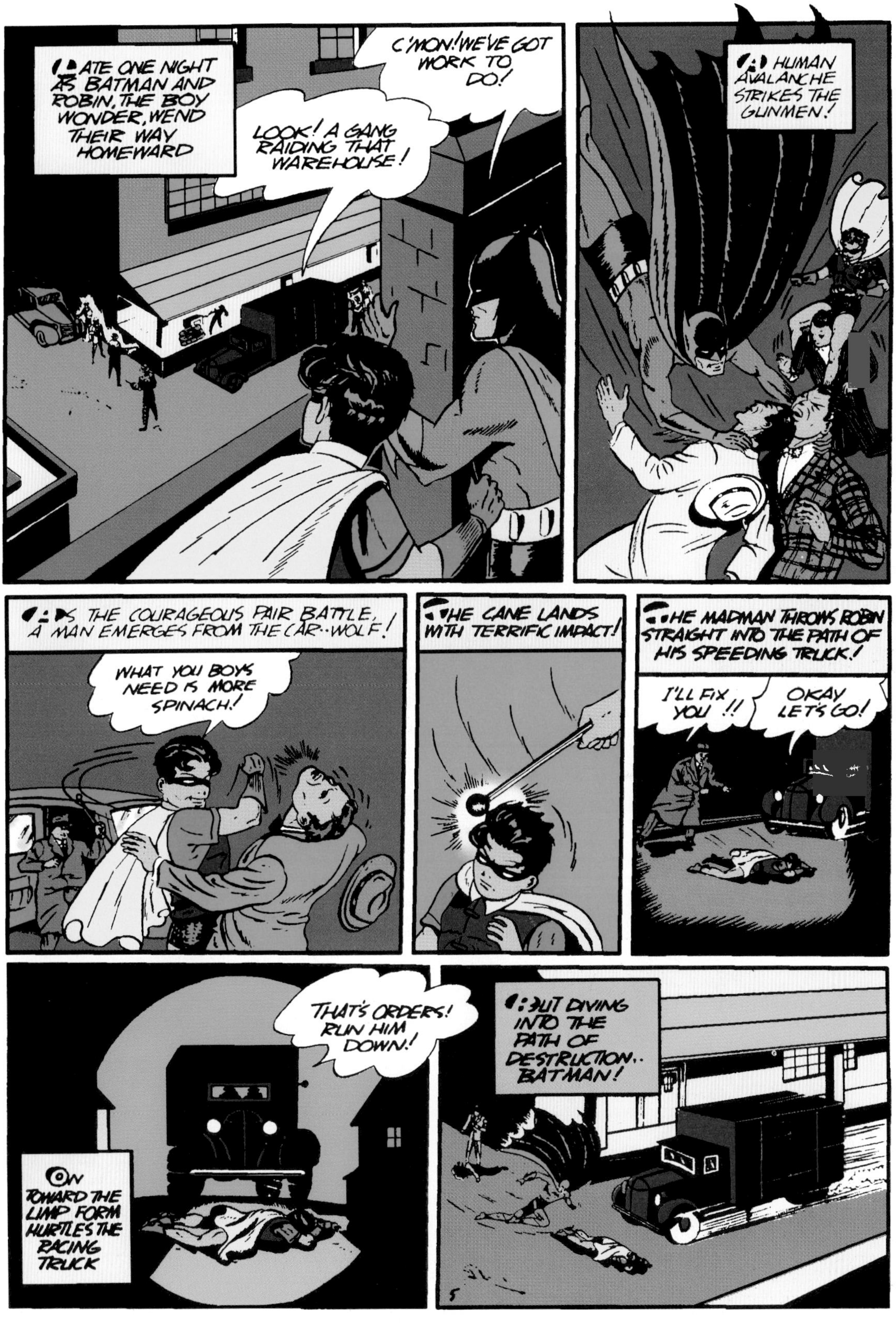
LATE ONE NIGHT AS BATMAN AND ROBIN, THE BOY WONDER, WEND THEIR WAY HOMEWARD
LOOK! A GANG RAIDING THAT WAREHOUSE!
C'MON! WE'VE GOT WORK TO DO!
A HUMAN AVALANCHE STRIKES THE GUNMEN!
AS THE COURAGEOUS PAIR BATTLE, A MAN EMERGES FROM THE CAR··WOLF!
WHAT YOU BOYS NEED IS MORE SPINACH!
THE CANE LANDS WITH TERRIFIC IMPACT!
THE MADMAN THROWS ROBIN STRAIGHT INTO THE PATH OF HIS SPEEDING TRUCK!
I'LL FIX YOU !!
OKAY LET'S GO!
ON TOWARD THE LIMP FORM HURTLES THE RACING TRUCK
THAT'S ORDERS! RUN HIM DOWN!
BUT DIVING INTO THE PATH OF DESTRUCTION.. BATMAN!

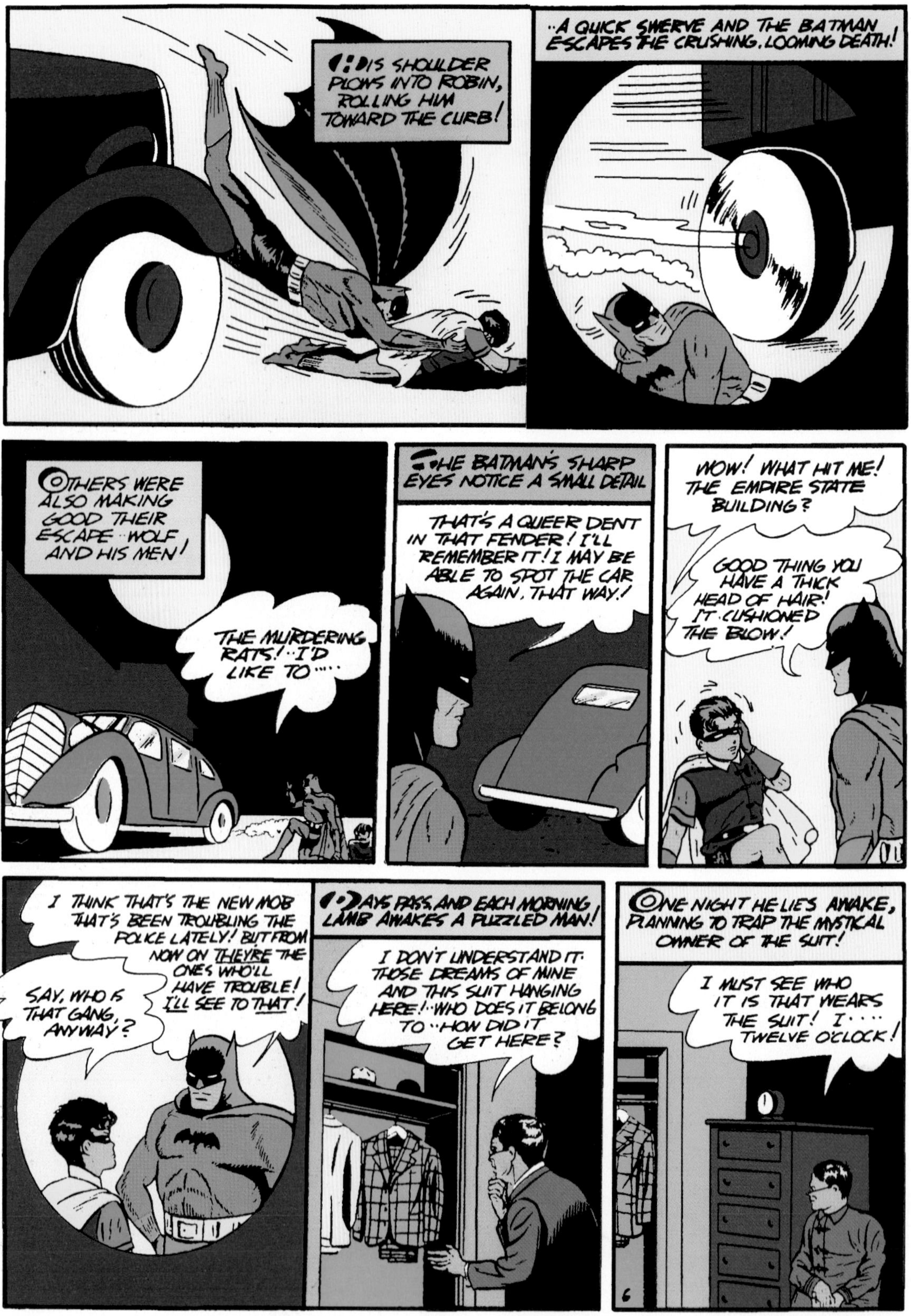
HIS SHOULDER PLOWS INTO ROBIN, ROLLING HIM TOWARD THE CURB!
..A QUICK SWERVE AND THE BATMAN ESCAPES THE CRUSHING, LOOMING DEATH!
OTHERS WERE ALSO MAKING GOOD THEIR ESCAPE..WOLF AND HIS MEN!
THE MURDERING RATS!..I'D LIKE TO.....
THE BATMAN'S SHARP EYES NOTICE A SMALL DETAIL
THAT'S A QUEER DENT IN THAT FENDER! I'LL REMEMBER IT! I MAY BE ABLE TO SPOT THE CAR AGAIN, THAT WAY!
WOW! WHAT HIT ME! THE EMPIRE STATE BUILDING?
GOOD THING YOU HAVE A THICK HEAD OF HAIR! IT CUSHIONED THE BLOW!
SAY, WHO IS THAT GANG, ANYWAY?
I THINK THAT'S THE NEW MOB THAT'S BEEN TROUBLING THE POLICE LATELY! BUT FROM NOW ON THEY'RE THE ONES WHO'LL HAVE TROUBLE! I'LL SEE TO THAT!
DAYS PASS, AND EACH MORNING LAMB AWAKES A PUZZLED MAN!
I DON'T UNDERSTAND IT.. THOSE DREAMS OF MINE AND THIS SUIT HANGING HERE!..WHO DOES IT BELONG TO..HOW DID IT GET HERE?
ONE NIGHT HE LIES AWAKE, PLANNING TO TRAP THE MYSTICAL OWNER OF THE SUIT!
I MUST SEE WHO IT IS THAT WEARS THE SUIT! I.... TWELVE O'CLOCK!
6

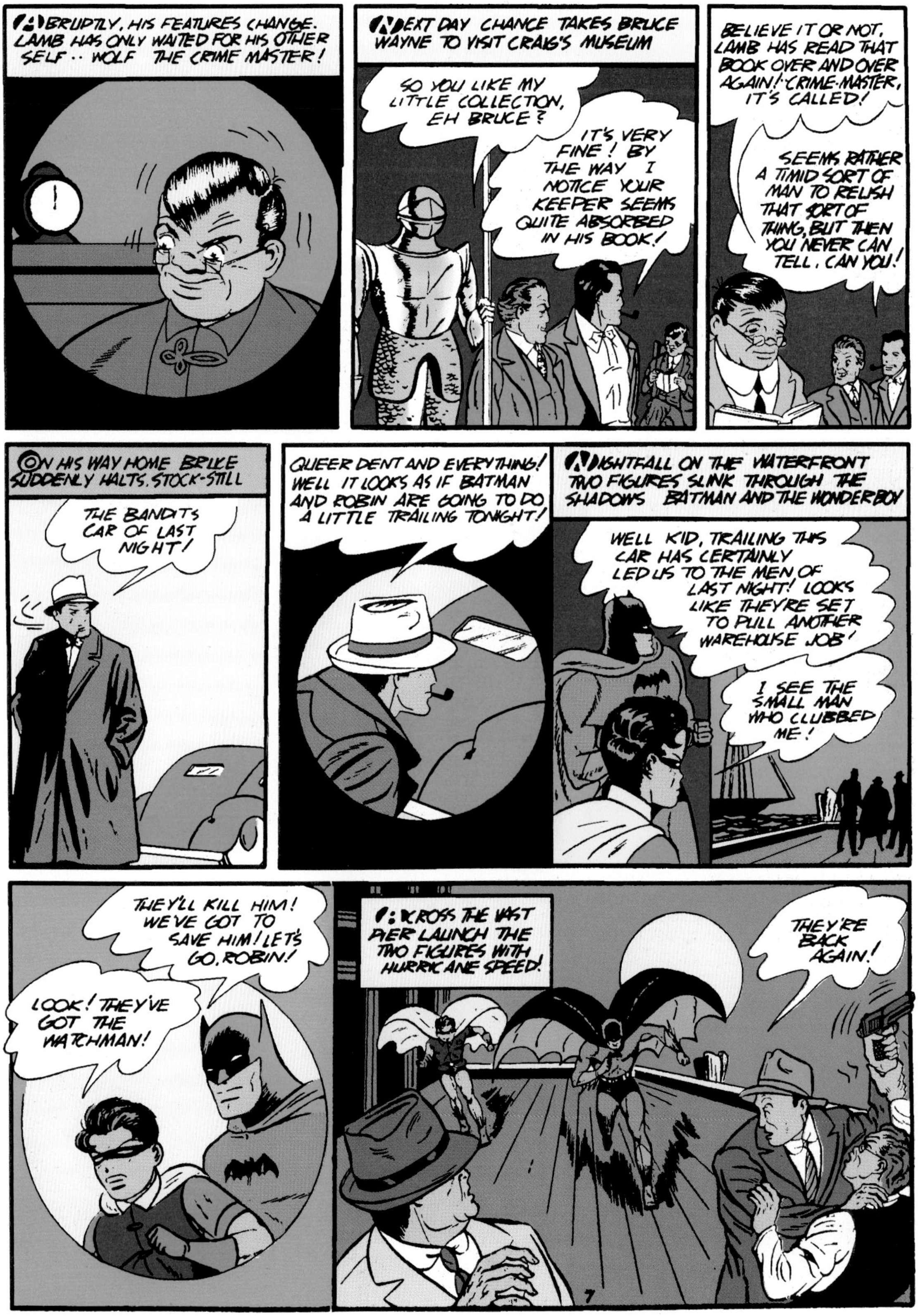
ABRUPTLY, HIS FEATURES CHANGE. LAMB HAS ONLY WAITED FOR HIS OTHER SELF .. WOLF THE CRIME MASTER!
NEXT DAY CHANCE TAKES BRUCE WAYNE TO VISIT CRAIG'S MUSEUM
SO YOU LIKE MY LITTLE COLLECTION, EH BRUCE?
IT'S VERY FINE! BY THE WAY I NOTICE YOUR KEEPER SEEMS QUITE ABSORBED IN HIS BOOK!
BELIEVE IT OR NOT, LAMB HAS READ THAT BOOK OVER AND OVER AGAIN! CRIME-MASTER, IT'S CALLED!
SEEMS RATHER A TIMID SORT OF MAN TO RELISH THAT SORT OF THING, BUT THEN YOU NEVER CAN TELL, CAN YOU!
ON HIS WAY HOME BRUCE SUDDENLY HALTS, STOCK-STILL
THE BANDITS CAR OF LAST NIGHT!
QUEER DENT AND EVERYTHING! WELL IT LOOKS AS IF BATMAN AND ROBIN ARE GOING TO DO A LITTLE TRAILING TONIGHT!
NIGHTFALL ON THE WATERFRONT TWO FIGURES SLINK THROUGH THE SHADOWS BATMAN AND THE WONDERBOY
WELL KID, TRAILING THIS CAR HAS CERTAINLY LED US TO THE MEN OF LAST NIGHT! LOOKS LIKE THEY'RE SET TO PULL ANOTHER WAREHOUSE JOB!
I SEE THE SMALL MAN WHO CLUBBED ME!
THEY'LL KILL HIM! WE'VE GOT TO SAVE HIM! LET'S GO, ROBIN!
LOOK! THEY'VE GOT THE WATCHMAN!
ACROSS THE VAST PIER LAUNCH THE TWO FIGURES WITH HURRICANE SPEED!
THEY'RE BACK AGAIN!

SMASHING UPPERCUT TO THE GUNMAN'S JAW···

DROP IT!··· OR I'LL DROP YOU!

HAIL OF LEAD IS SLUNG AT THE BATMAN!

SHOOT HIM!!

GET THAT GUY BEFORE HE GETS US!

BULLET MISSES THE STEEL VEST AND BORES INTO HIS UNPROTECTED SHOULDER!

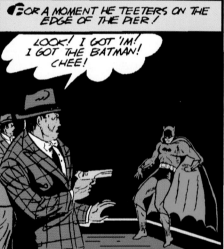

FOR A MOMENT HE TEETERS ON THE EDGE OF THE PIER!

LOOK! I GOT 'IM! I GOT THE BATMAN! CHEE!

THEN TOPPLES TO THE MURKY WATERS BELOW

AN AGONIZING SHRIEK IS TORN FROM ROBIN'S LIPS AS HE SEES HIM FALLING!

BATMAN! BATMAN!

THE BOY WONDER GOES BERSERK!

YOU MURDERERS YOU'VE KILLED HIM!··· YOU'VE KILLED HIM!

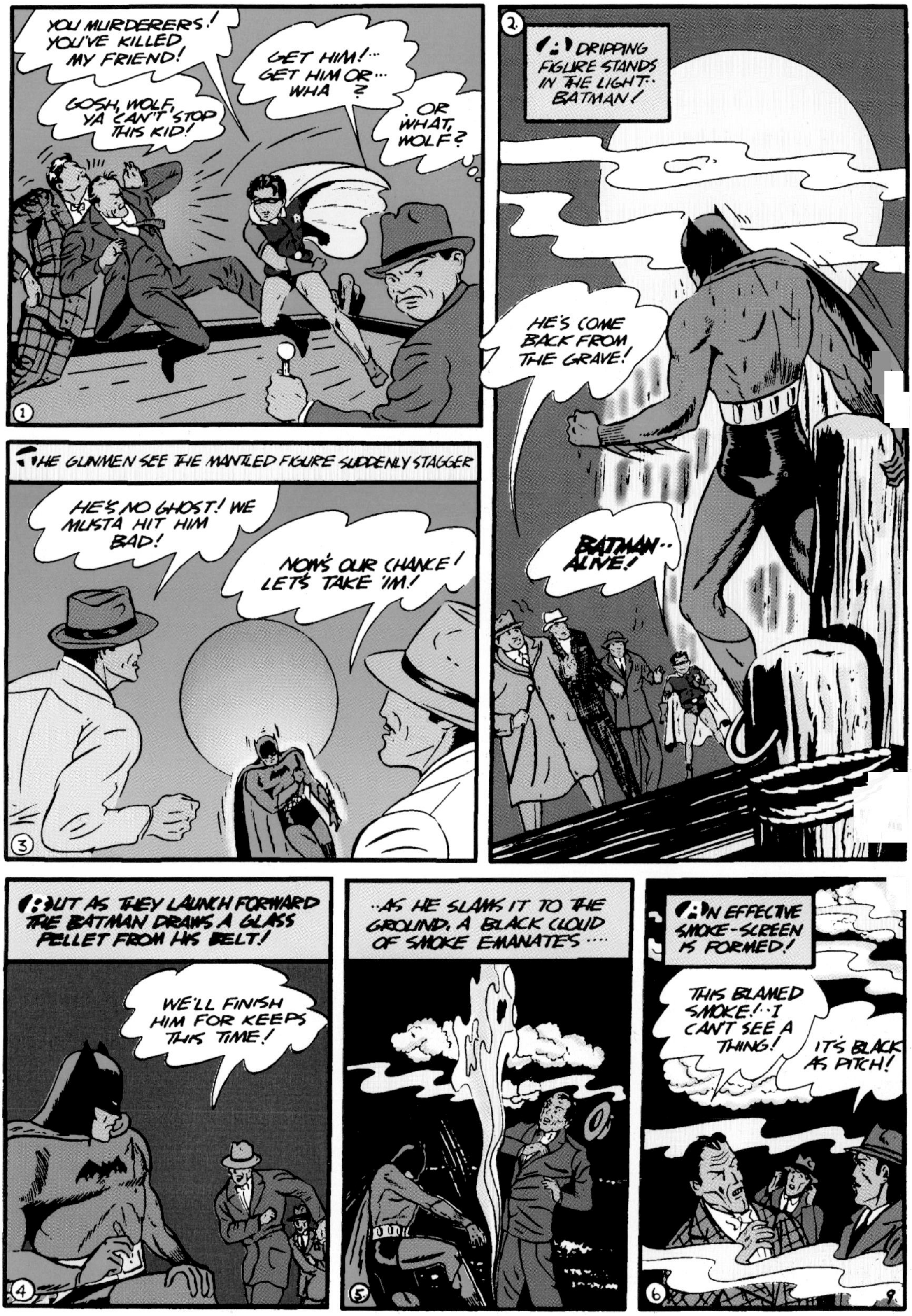
YOU MURDERERS! YOU'VE KILLED MY FRIEND!
GOSH, WOLF, YA CAN'T STOP THIS KID!
GET HIM!... GET HIM OR... WHA ?
OR WHAT, WOLF?
A DRIPPING FIGURE STANDS IN THE LIGHT. BATMAN!
HE'S COME BACK FROM THE GRAVE!
BATMAN.. ALIVE!
THE GUNMEN SEE THE MANTLED FIGURE SUDDENLY STAGGER
HE'S NO GHOST! WE MUSTA HIT HIM BAD!
NOW'S OUR CHANCE! LET'S TAKE 'IM!
BUT AS THEY LAUNCH FORWARD THE BATMAN DRAWS A GLASS PELLET FROM HIS BELT!
WE'LL FINISH HIM FOR KEEPS THIS TIME!
..AS HE SLAMS IT TO THE GROUND, A BLACK CLOUD OF SMOKE EMANATES....
AN EFFECTIVE SMOKE-SCREEN IS FORMED!
THIS BLAMED SMOKE!..I CAN'T SEE A THING!
IT'S BLACK AS PITCH!

BY AIDING THE WEAKENED BATMAN, ROBIN HELPS TO EFFECT THEIR ESCAPE!
THE DIRTY RATS! THEY TRIED TO KILL YOU!..I'D LIKE TO....
THERE'LL BE PLENTY OF TIME FOR THAT LATER! LET'S GET AWAY FROM HERE, FIRST!
OKAY BRUCE.. READY?
READY!
LATER.. IN BRUCE'S LABORATORY A NERVOUS BOY FACES A GIANT TASK!
BREATHING A SILENT PRAYER, DICK BEGINS TO PROBE FOR THE BULLET LODGED IN BRUCE'S SHOULDER!
I'VE GOT TO FIND IT!.. I'VE GOT TO!
AT LAST, AFTER WHAT SEEMS AN AGONIZING STRETCH OF TIME...
THE BULLET!.. BRUCE, I'VE GOT IT!
GOOD BOY!... GOOD BOY!
LATE THE NEXT NIGHT DICK WALKS INTO THE LIBRARY TO SEE BRUCE UP, READING...
BRUCE, IT'S NEAR TWELVE O'CLOCK! YOU SHOULD BE IN BED RESTING YOUR ARM!
DICK!-I'VE JUST FOUND OUT A STARTLING FACT!..IT'S FANTASTIC.. FANTASTIC.!!
IT ALL TIES UP WITH A MYSTERY BOOK CALLED THE CRIME MASTER! I'VE MADE A LIST OF CRIMES COMMITTED BY THE WOLF MOB, AND BELIEVE IT OR NOT..IT COINCIDES WITH THE MYTHICAL CRIMES DONE IN THIS BOOK!
The CRIME MASTER
BUT I DON'T UNDERSTAND...
FOR SOME REASON, WOLF IS FOLLOWING THE EXACT PLAN OF THE BOOK! THE CRIME MASTER!...IT'S CRAZY..CRAZY!
10

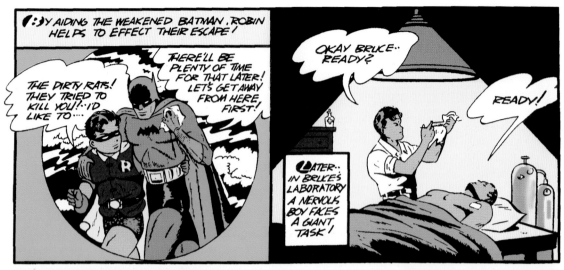

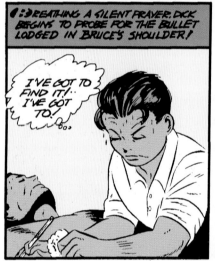

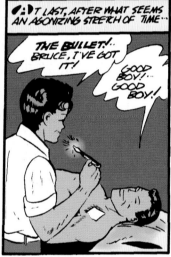

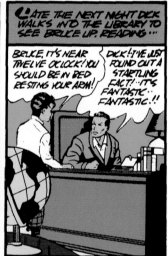

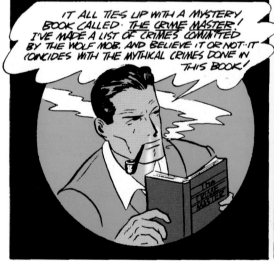

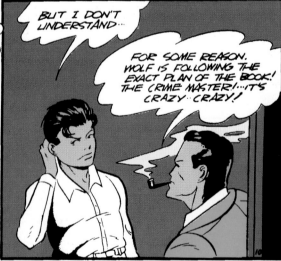

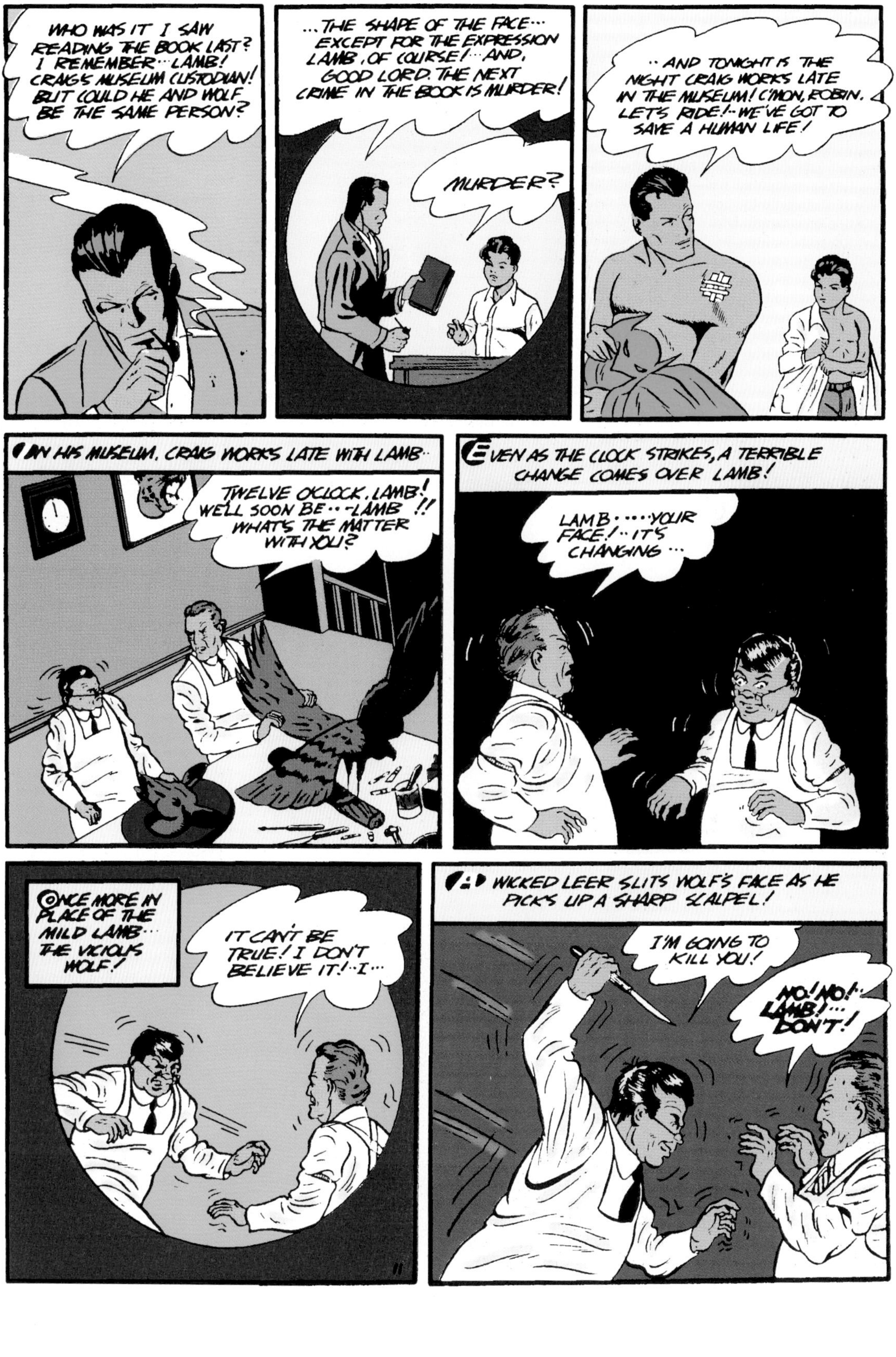

WHO WAS IT I SAW READING THE BOOK LAST? I REMEMBER··· LAMB! CRAIG'S MUSEUM CUSTODIAN! BUT COULD HE AND WOLF BE THE SAME PERSON?
...THE SHAPE OF THE FACE··· EXCEPT FOR THE EXPRESSION LAMB, OF COURSE!··· AND, GOOD LORD. THE NEXT CRIME IN THE BOOK IS MURDER!
MURDER?
·· AND TONIGHT IS THE NIGHT CRAIG WORKS LATE IN THE MUSEUM! C'MON, ROBIN. LET'S RIDE!·· WE'VE GOT TO SAVE A HUMAN LIFE!
IN HIS MUSEUM, CRAIG WORKS LATE WITH LAMB··
TWELVE O'CLOCK, LAMB! WE'LL SOON BE···-LAMB !!! WHAT'S THE MATTER WITH YOU?
EVEN AS THE CLOCK STRIKES, A TERRIBLE CHANGE COMES OVER LAMB!
LAMB·····YOUR FACE!·· IT'S CHANGING···
ONCE MORE IN PLACE OF THE MILD LAMB··· THE VICIOUS WOLF!
IT CAN'T BE TRUE! I DON'T BELIEVE IT!··I···
A WICKED LEER SLITS WOLF'S FACE AS HE PICKS UP A SHARP SCALPEL!
I'M GOING TO KILL YOU!
NO! NO!·· LAMB!··· DON'T!

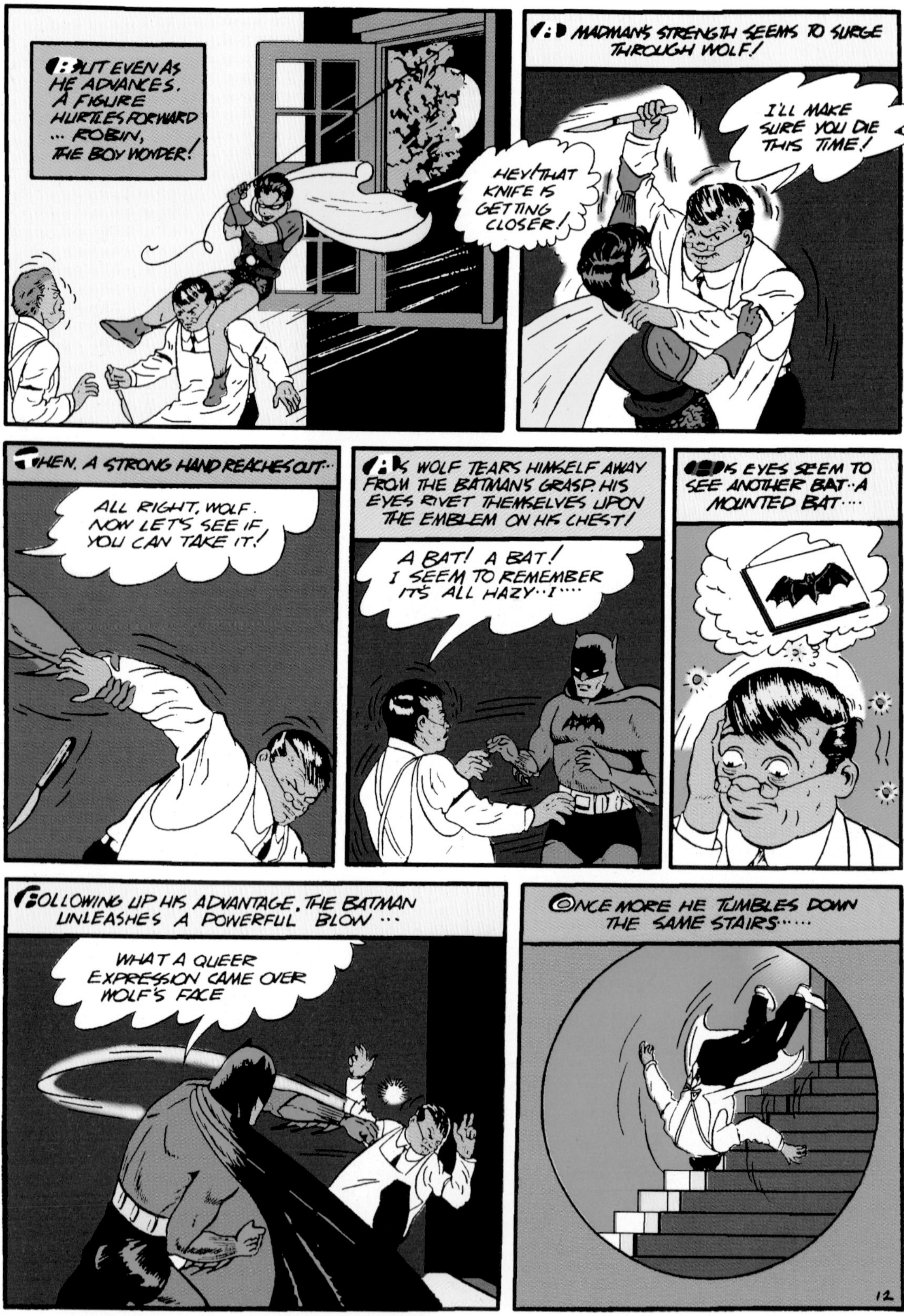
BUT EVEN AS HE ADVANCES, A FIGURE HURTLES FORWARD ... ROBIN, THE BOY WONDER!
A MADMAN'S STRENGTH SEEMS TO SURGE THROUGH WOLF!
HEY! THAT KNIFE IS GETTING CLOSER!
I'LL MAKE SURE YOU DIE THIS TIME!
THEN, A STRONG HAND REACHES OUT...
ALL RIGHT, WOLF. NOW LET'S SEE IF YOU CAN TAKE IT!
AS WOLF TEARS HIMSELF AWAY FROM THE BATMAN'S GRASP, HIS EYES RIVET THEMSELVES UPON THE EMBLEM ON HIS CHEST!
A BAT! A BAT! I SEEM TO REMEMBER IT'S ALL HAZY..I....
HIS EYES SEEM TO SEE ANOTHER BAT..A MOUNTED BAT....
FOLLOWING UP HIS ADVANTAGE, THE BATMAN UNLEASHES A POWERFUL BLOW...
WHAT A QUEER EXPRESSION CAME OVER WOLF'S FACE
ONCE MORE HE TUMBLES DOWN THE SAME STAIRS......
12

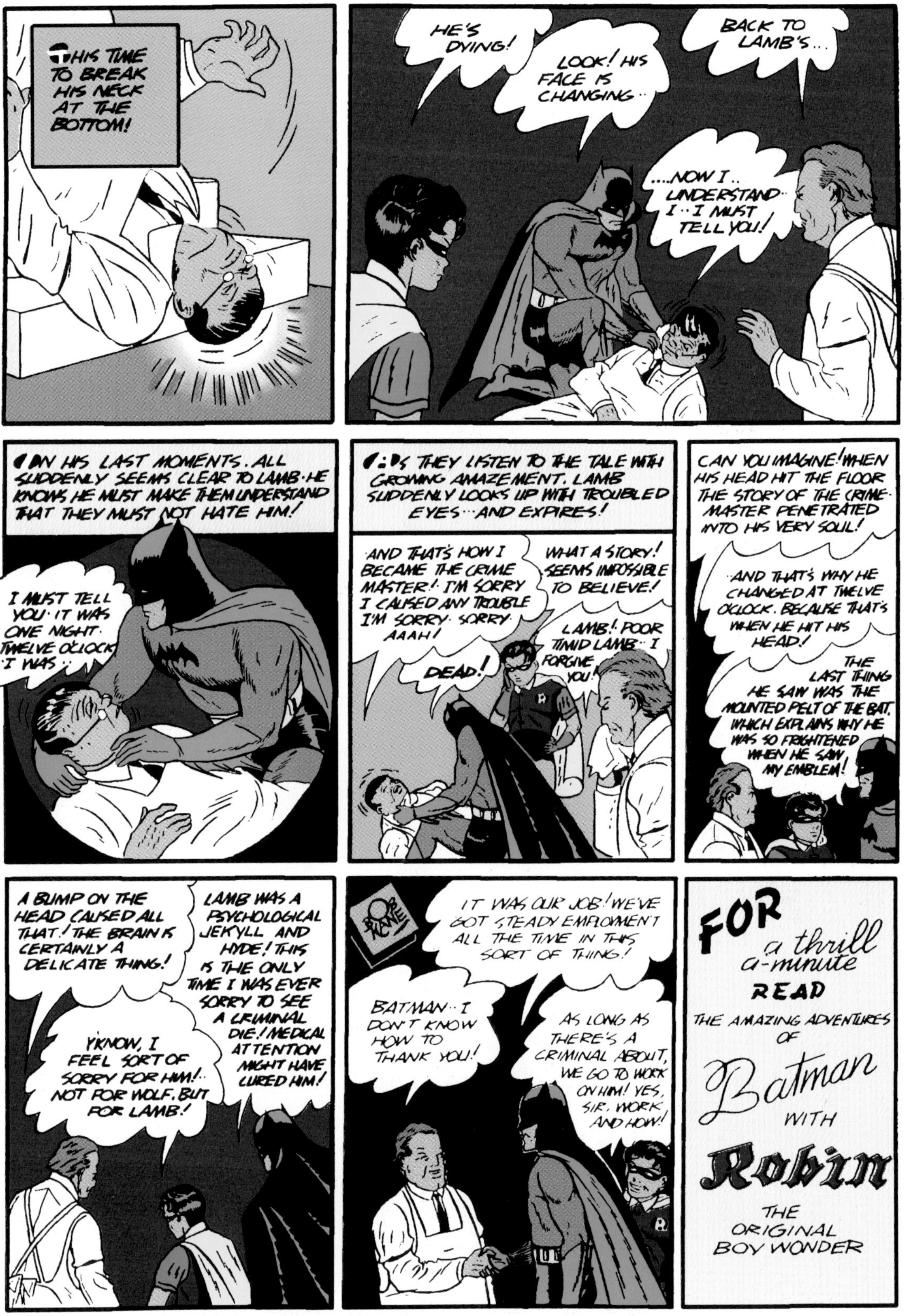
THIS TIME TO BREAK HIS NECK AT THE BOTTOM!
HE'S DYING!
LOOK! HIS FACE IS CHANGING..
BACK TO LAMB'S...
....NOW I.. UNDERSTAND.. I..I MUST TELL YOU!
IN HIS LAST MOMENTS. ALL SUDDENLY SEEMS CLEAR TO LAMB. HE KNOWS HE MUST MAKE THEM UNDERSTAND THAT THEY MUST NOT HATE HIM!
I MUST TELL YOU. IT WAS ONE NIGHT. TWELVE O'CLOCK. I WAS..
AS THEY LISTEN TO THE TALE WITH GROWING AMAZEMENT, LAMB SUDDENLY LOOKS UP WITH TROUBLED EYES...AND EXPIRES!
AND THAT'S HOW I BECAME THE CRIME MASTER! I'M SORRY I CAUSED ANY TROUBLE I'M SORRY. SORRY. AAAH!
WHAT A STORY! SEEMS IMPOSSIBLE TO BELIEVE!
DEAD!
LAMB! POOR TIMID LAMB.. I FORGIVE YOU!
CAN YOU IMAGINE! WHEN HIS HEAD HIT THE FLOOR THE STORY OF THE CRIME-MASTER PENETRATED INTO HIS VERY SOUL!
..AND THAT'S WHY HE CHANGED AT TWELVE O'CLOCK. BECAUSE THAT'S WHEN HE HIT HIS HEAD!
THE LAST THING HE SAW WAS THE MOUNTED PELT OF THE BAT, WHICH EXPLAINS WHY HE WAS SO FRIGHTENED WHEN HE SAW MY EMBLEM!
A BUMP ON THE HEAD CAUSED ALL THAT! THE BRAIN IS CERTAINLY A DELICATE THING!
LAMB WAS A PSYCHOLOGICAL JEKYLL AND HYDE! THIS IS THE ONLY TIME I WAS EVER SORRY TO SEE A CRIMINAL DIE! MEDICAL ATTENTION MIGHT HAVE CURED HIM!
Y'KNOW, I FEEL SORT OF SORRY FOR HIM!.. NOT FOR WOLF, BUT FOR LAMB!
IT WAS OUR JOB! WE'VE GOT STEADY EMPLOYMENT ALL THE TIME IN THIS SORT OF THING!
BATMAN.. I DON'T KNOW HOW TO THANK YOU!
AS LONG AS THERE'S A CRIMINAL ABOUT, WE GO TO WORK ON HIM! YES, SIR. WORK AND HOW!
FOR a thrill a-minute READ THE AMAZING ADVENTURES OF Batman WITH Robin THE ORIGINAL BOY WONDER

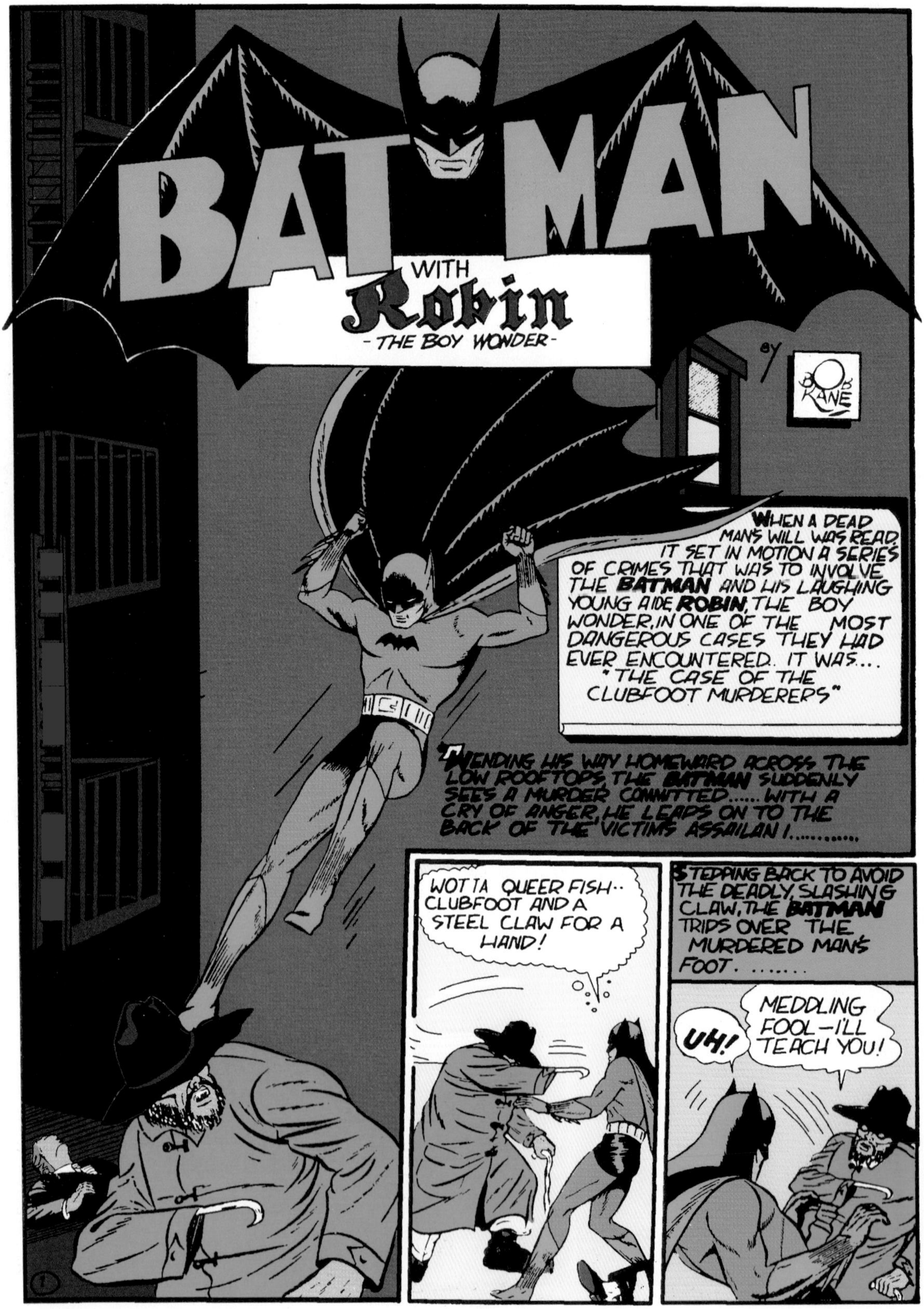
BATMAN
WITH
Robin
-THE BOY WONDER-
BY BOB KANE
WHEN A DEAD MAN'S WILL WAS READ IT SET IN MOTION A SERIES OF CRIMES THAT WAS TO INVOLVE THE BATMAN AND HIS LAUGHING YOUNG AIDE ROBIN, THE BOY WONDER, IN ONE OF THE MOST DANGEROUS CASES THEY HAD EVER ENCOUNTERED. IT WAS... "THE CASE OF THE CLUBFOOT MURDERERS"
WENDING HIS WAY HOMEWARD ACROSS THE LOW ROOFTOPS, THE BATMAN SUDDENLY SEES A MURDER COMMITTED...... WITH A CRY OF ANGER, HE LEAPS ON TO THE BACK OF THE VICTIM'S ASSAILANT...........
WOTTA QUEER FISH.. CLUBFOOT AND A STEEL CLAW FOR A HAND!
STEPPING BACK TO AVOID THE DEADLY, SLASHING CLAW, THE BATMAN TRIPS OVER THE MURDERED MAN'S FOOT. ....
UH!
MEDDLING FOOL—I'LL TEACH YOU!

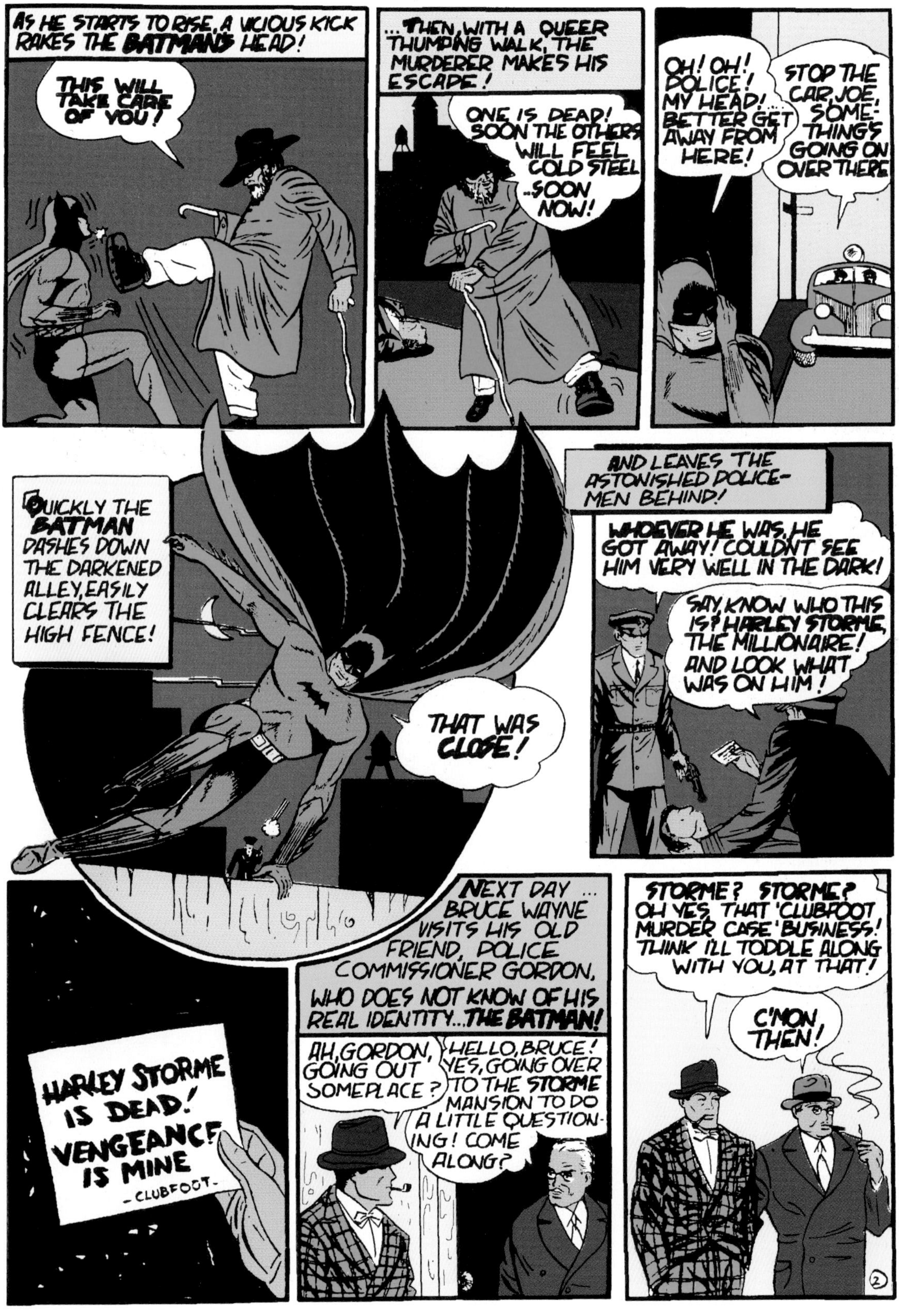
AS HE STARTS TO RISE, A VICIOUS KICK RAKES THE BATMAN'S HEAD!
THIS WILL TAKE CARE OF YOU!
...THEN, WITH A QUEER THUMPING WALK, THE MURDERER MAKES HIS ESCAPE!
ONE IS DEAD! SOON THE OTHERS WILL FEEL COLD STEEL ..SOON NOW!
OH! OH! POLICE! MY HEAD!... BETTER GET AWAY FROM HERE!
STOP THE CAR, JOE. SOMETHING'S GOING ON OVER THERE
QUICKLY THE BATMAN DASHES DOWN THE DARKENED ALLEY, EASILY CLEARS THE HIGH FENCE!
THAT WAS CLOSE!
AND LEAVES THE ASTONISHED POLICEMEN BEHIND!
WHOEVER HE WAS, HE GOT AWAY! COULDN'T SEE HIM VERY WELL IN THE DARK!
SAY, KNOW WHO THIS IS? HARLEY STORME, THE MILLIONAIRE! AND LOOK WHAT WAS ON HIM!
HARLEY STORME IS DEAD! VENGEANCE IS MINE -CLUBFOOT-
NEXT DAY ... BRUCE WAYNE VISITS HIS OLD FRIEND, POLICE COMMISSIONER GORDON, WHO DOES NOT KNOW OF HIS REAL IDENTITY...THE BATMAN!
AH, GORDON, GOING OUT SOMEPLACE?
HELLO, BRUCE! YES, GOING OVER TO THE STORME MANSION TO DO A LITTLE QUESTIONING! COME ALONG?
STORME? STORME? OH YES, THAT 'CLUBFOOT MURDER CASE' BUSINESS! THINK I'LL TODDLE ALONG WITH YOU, AT THAT!
C'MON, THEN!
2

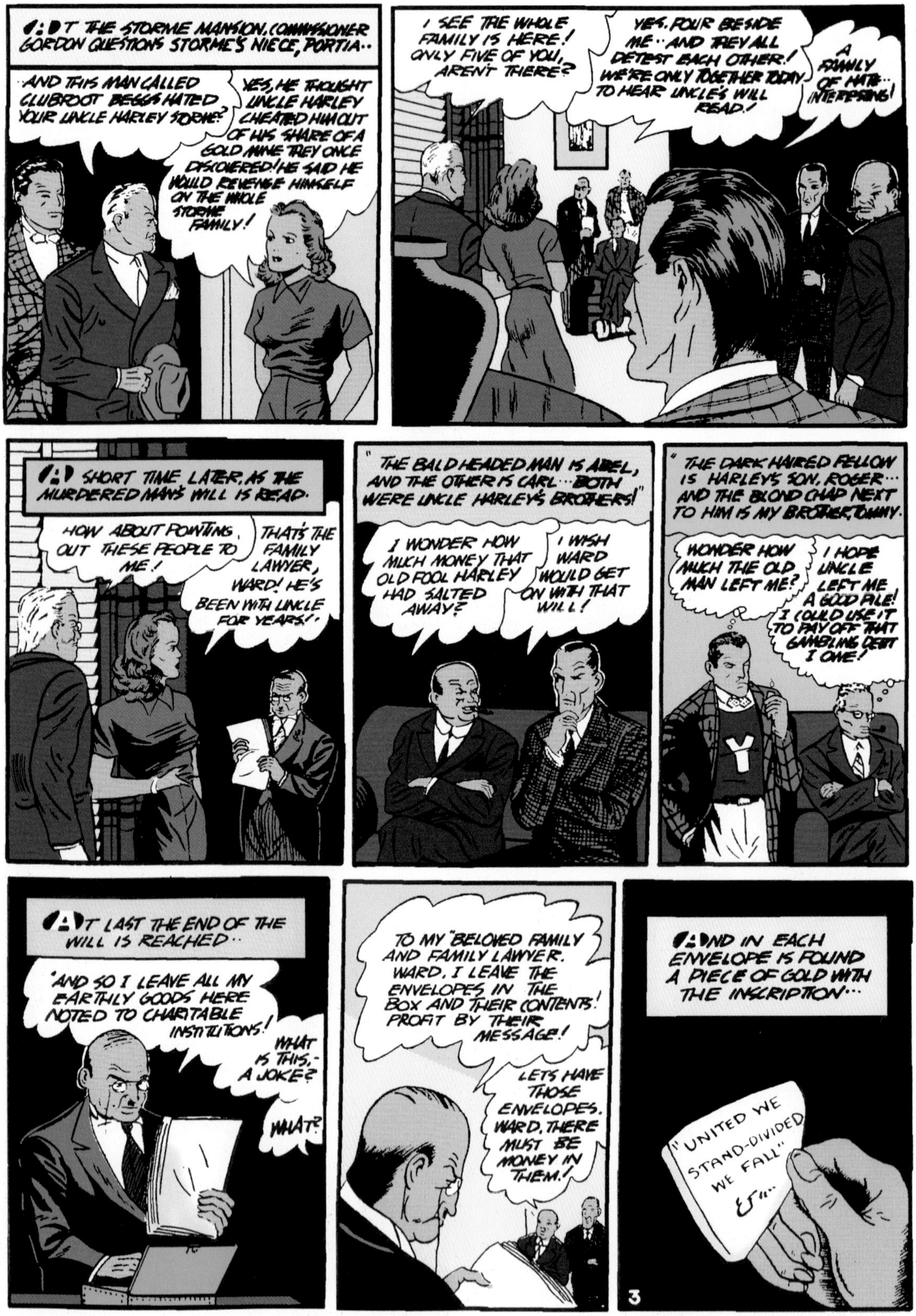
AT THE STORME MANSION, COMMISSIONER GORDON QUESTIONS STORME'S NIECE, PORTIA..
..AND THIS MAN CALLED CLUBROOT BEGGS HATED YOUR UNCLE HARLEY STORME?
YES, HE THOUGHT UNCLE HARLEY CHEATED HIM OUT OF HIS SHARE OF A GOLD MINE THEY ONCE DISCOVERED! HE SAID HE WOULD REVENGE HIMSELF ON THE WHOLE STORME FAMILY!
I SEE THE WHOLE FAMILY IS HERE! ONLY FIVE OF YOU, AREN'T THERE?
YES, FOUR BESIDE ME.. AND THEY ALL DETEST EACH OTHER! WE'RE ONLY TOGETHER TODAY TO HEAR UNCLE'S WILL READ!
A FAMILY OF HATE.. INTERESTING!
A SHORT TIME LATER, AS THE MURDERED MAN'S WILL IS READ.
HOW ABOUT POINTING OUT THESE PEOPLE TO ME!
THAT'S THE FAMILY LAWYER, WARD! HE'S BEEN WITH UNCLE FOR YEARS!
"THE BALD HEADED MAN IS ABEL, AND THE OTHER IS CARL... BOTH WERE UNCLE HARLEY'S BROTHERS!"
I WONDER HOW MUCH MONEY THAT OLD FOOL HARLEY HAD SALTED AWAY?
I WISH WARD WOULD GET ON WITH THAT WILL!
"THE DARK HAIRED FELLOW IS HARLEY'S SON, ROGER... AND THE BLOND CHAP NEXT TO HIM IS MY BROTHER, TOMMY.
WONDER HOW MUCH THE OLD MAN LEFT ME?
I HOPE UNCLE LEFT ME A GOOD PILE! I COULD USE IT TO PAY OFF THAT GAMBLING DEBT I OWE!
AT LAST THE END OF THE WILL IS REACHED..
"AND SO I LEAVE ALL MY EARTHLY GOODS HERE NOTED TO CHARITABLE INSTITUTIONS!
WHAT IS THIS,- A JOKE?
WHAT?
TO MY "BELOVED FAMILY AND FAMILY LAWYER. WARD, I LEAVE THE ENVELOPES IN THE BOX AND THEIR CONTENTS! PROFIT BY THEIR MESSAGE!
LETS HAVE THOSE ENVELOPES. WARD, THERE MUST BE MONEY IN THEM!
AND IN EACH ENVELOPE IS FOUND A PIECE OF GOLD WITH THE INSCRIPTION...
"UNITED WE STAND-DIVIDED WE FALL"
3

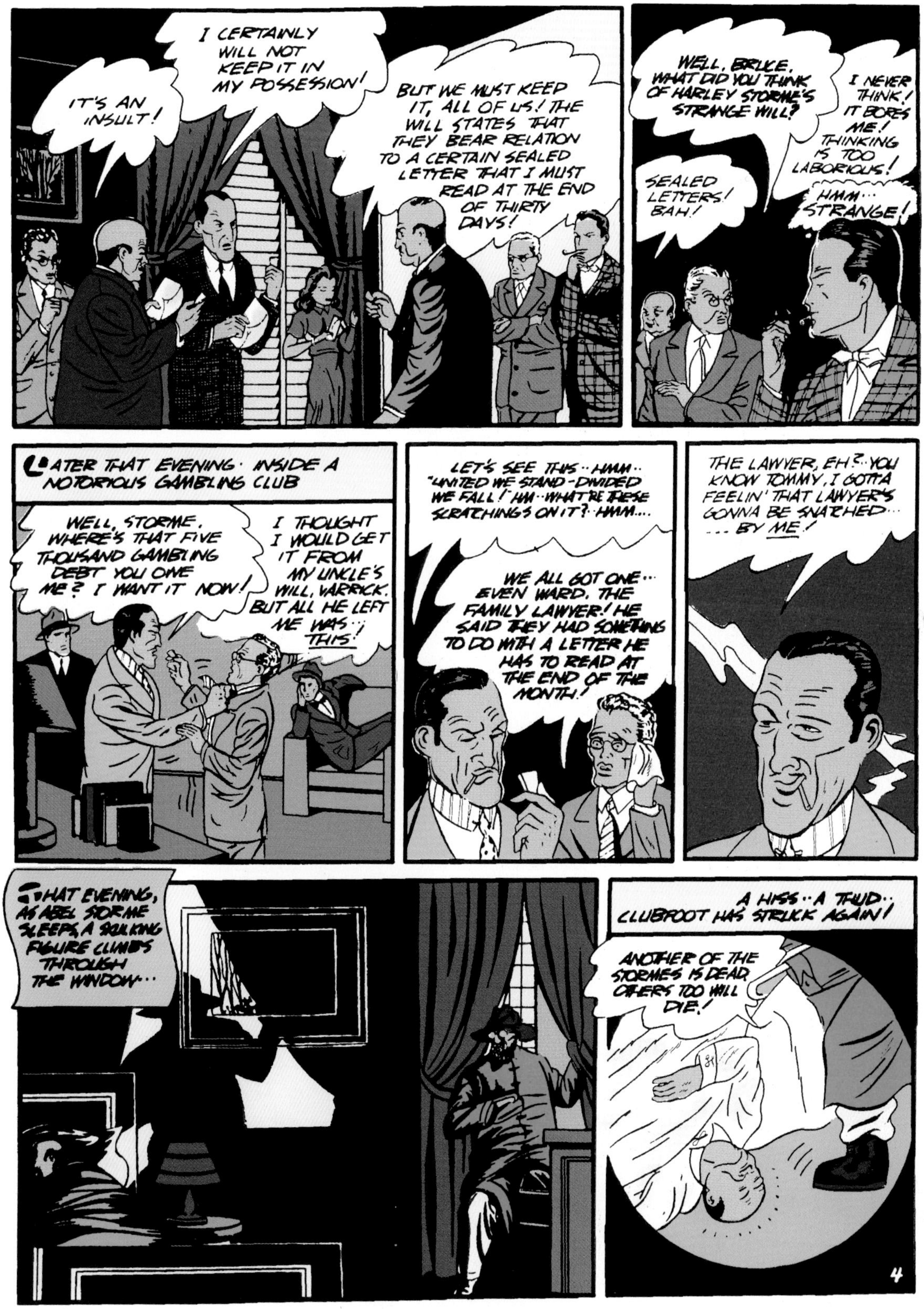
IT'S AN INSULT!
I CERTAINLY WILL NOT KEEP IT IN MY POSSESSION!
BUT WE MUST KEEP IT, ALL OF US! THE WILL STATES THAT THEY BEAR RELATION TO A CERTAIN SEALED LETTER THAT I MUST READ AT THE END OF THIRTY DAYS!
WELL, BRUCE, WHAT DID YOU THINK OF HARLEY STORME'S STRANGE WILL?
SEALED LETTERS! BAH!
I NEVER THINK! IT BORES ME! THINKING IS TOO LABORIOUS!
HMM... STRANGE!
LATER THAT EVENING · INSIDE A NOTORIOUS GAMBLING CLUB
WELL, STORME, WHERE'S THAT FIVE THOUSAND GAMBLING DEBT YOU OWE ME? I WANT IT NOW!
I THOUGHT I WOULD GET IT FROM MY UNCLE'S WILL, VARRICK. BUT ALL HE LEFT ME WAS... THIS!
LET'S SEE THIS.. HMM.. "UNITED WE STAND-DIVIDED WE FALL!" HM.. WHAT'RE THESE SCRATCHINGS ON IT?.. HMM....
WE ALL GOT ONE... EVEN WARD, THE FAMILY LAWYER! HE SAID THEY HAD SOMETHING TO DO WITH A LETTER HE HAS TO READ AT THE END OF THE MONTH!
THE LAWYER, EH? YOU KNOW TOMMY, I GOTTA FEELIN' THAT LAWYER'S GONNA BE SNATCHED... ...BY ME!
THAT EVENING, AS ABEL STORME SLEEPS, A SKULKING FIGURE CLIMBS THROUGH THE WINDOW...
A HISS.. A THUD.. CLUBFOOT HAS STRUCK AGAIN!
ANOTHER OF THE STORMES IS DEAD. OTHERS TOO WILL DIE!
4

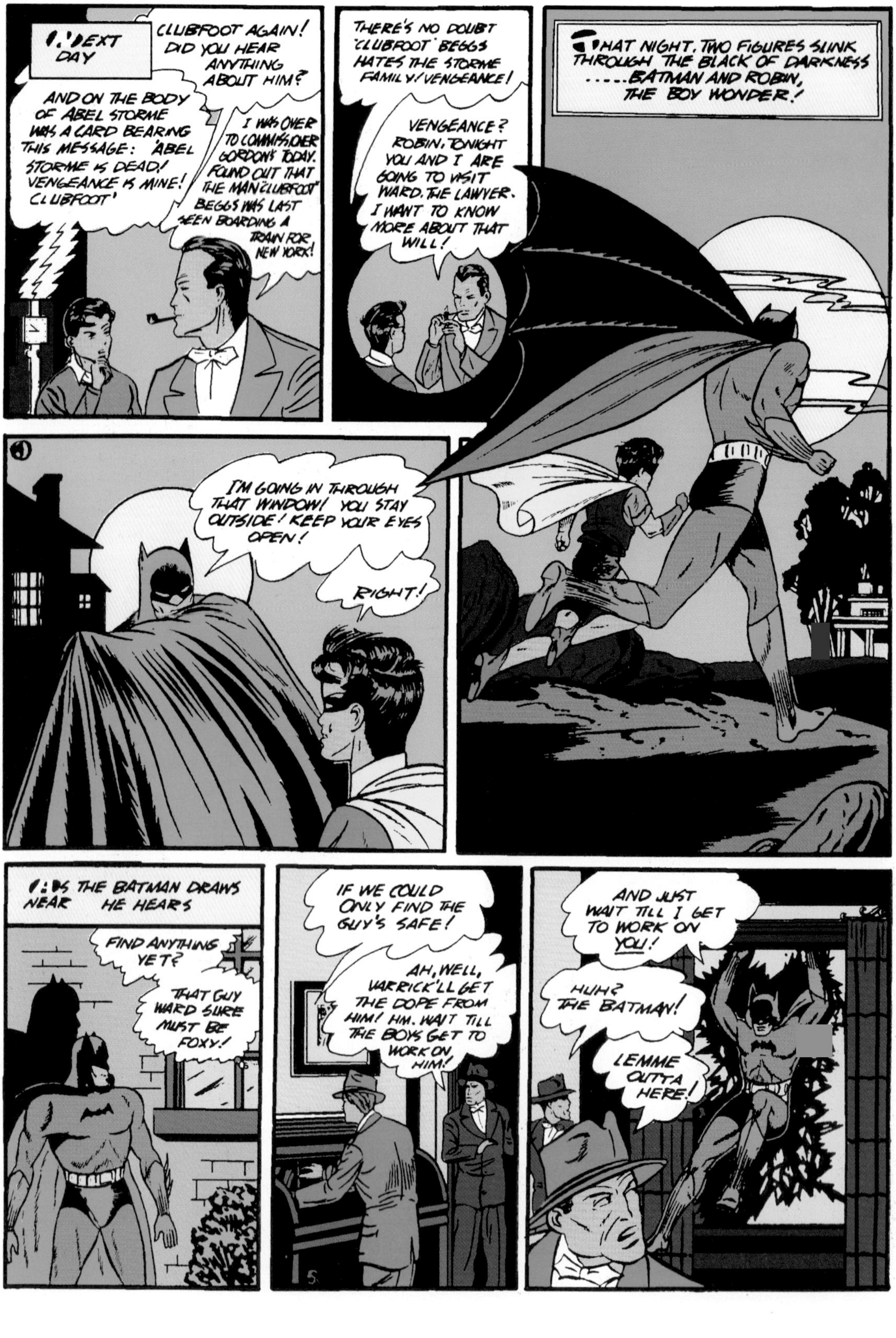
NEXT DAY
CLUBFOOT AGAIN! DID YOU HEAR ANYTHING ABOUT HIM?
AND ON THE BODY OF ABEL STORME WAS A CARD BEARING THIS MESSAGE: 'ABEL STORME IS DEAD! VENGEANCE IS MINE! CLUBFOOT'
I WAS OVER TO COMMISSIONER GORDON'S TODAY. FOUND OUT THAT THE MAN 'CLUBFOOT' BEGGS WAS LAST SEEN BOARDING A TRAIN FOR NEW YORK!
THERE'S NO DOUBT 'CLUBFOOT' BEGGS HATES THE STORME FAMILY! VENGEANCE!
VENGEANCE? ROBIN, TONIGHT YOU AND I ARE GOING TO VISIT WARD, THE LAWYER. I WANT TO KNOW MORE ABOUT THAT WILL!
THAT NIGHT, TWO FIGURES SLINK THROUGH THE BLACK OF DARKNESS .....BATMAN AND ROBIN, THE BOY WONDER!
I'M GOING IN THROUGH THAT WINDOW! YOU STAY OUTSIDE! KEEP YOUR EYES OPEN!
RIGHT!
AS THE BATMAN DRAWS NEAR HE HEARS
FIND ANYTHING YET?
THAT GUY WARD SURE MUST BE FOXY!
IF WE COULD ONLY FIND THE GUY'S SAFE!
AH, WELL, VARRICK'LL GET THE DOPE FROM HIM! HM. WAIT TILL THE BOYS GET TO WORK ON HIM!
AND JUST WAIT TILL I GET TO WORK ON YOU!
HUH? THE BATMAN!
LEMME OUTTA HERE!

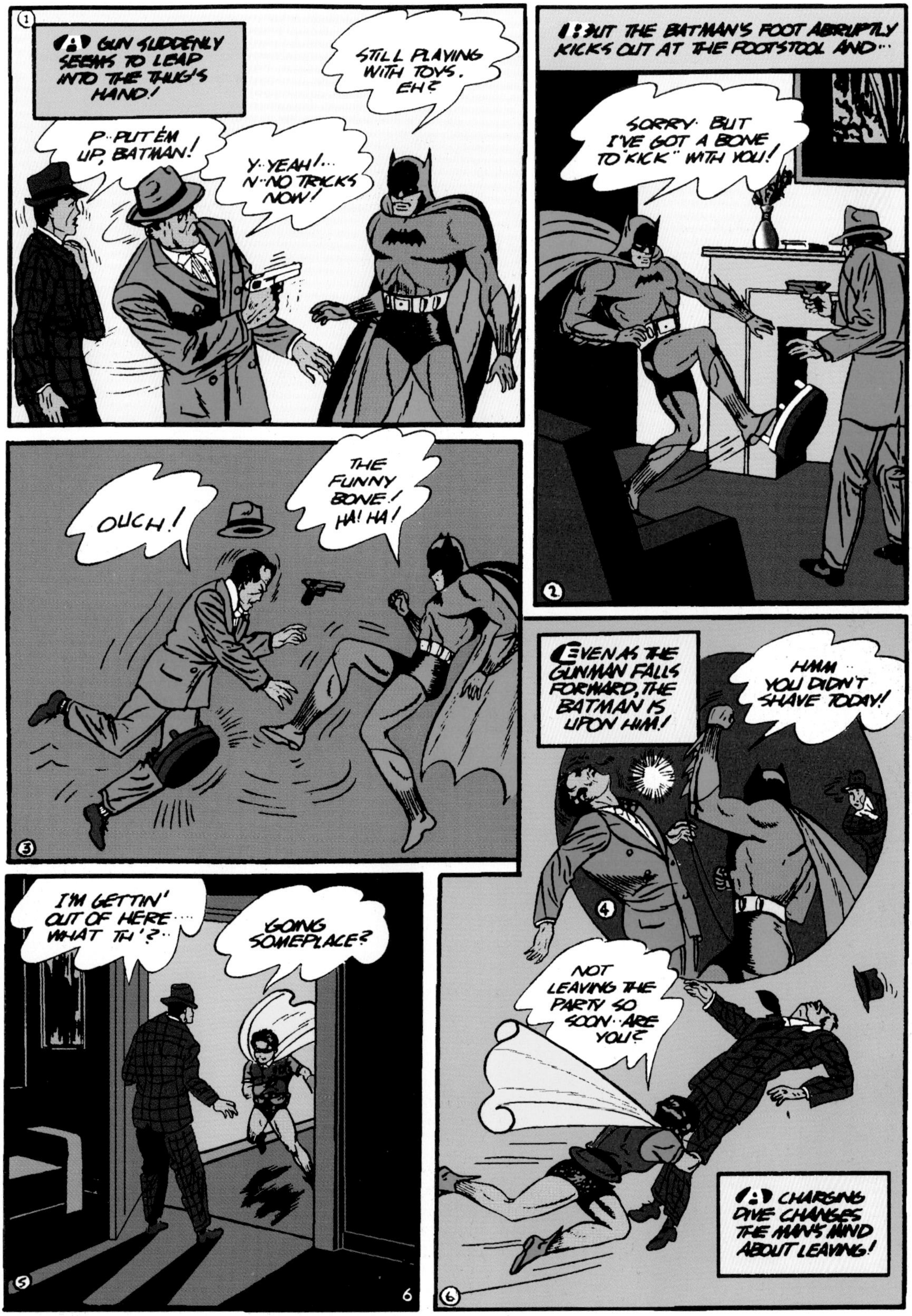
A GUN SUDDENLY SEEMS TO LEAP INTO THE THUG'S HAND!
STILL PLAYING WITH TOYS, EH?
P..PUT'EM UP, BATMAN!
Y..YEAH!.. N..NO TRICKS NOW!
BUT THE BATMAN'S FOOT ABRUPTLY KICKS OUT AT THE FOOTSTOOL AND...
SORRY.. BUT I'VE GOT A BONE TO "KICK" WITH YOU!
OUCH!
THE FUNNY BONE! HA! HA!
EVEN AS THE GUNMAN FALLS FORWARD, THE BATMAN IS UPON HIM!
HMM... YOU DIDN'T SHAVE TODAY!
I'M GETTIN' OUT OF HERE... WHAT TH'?..
GOING SOMEPLACE?
NOT LEAVING THE PARTY SO SOON.. ARE YOU?
A CHARGING DIVE CHANGES THE MAN'S MIND ABOUT LEAVING!
6

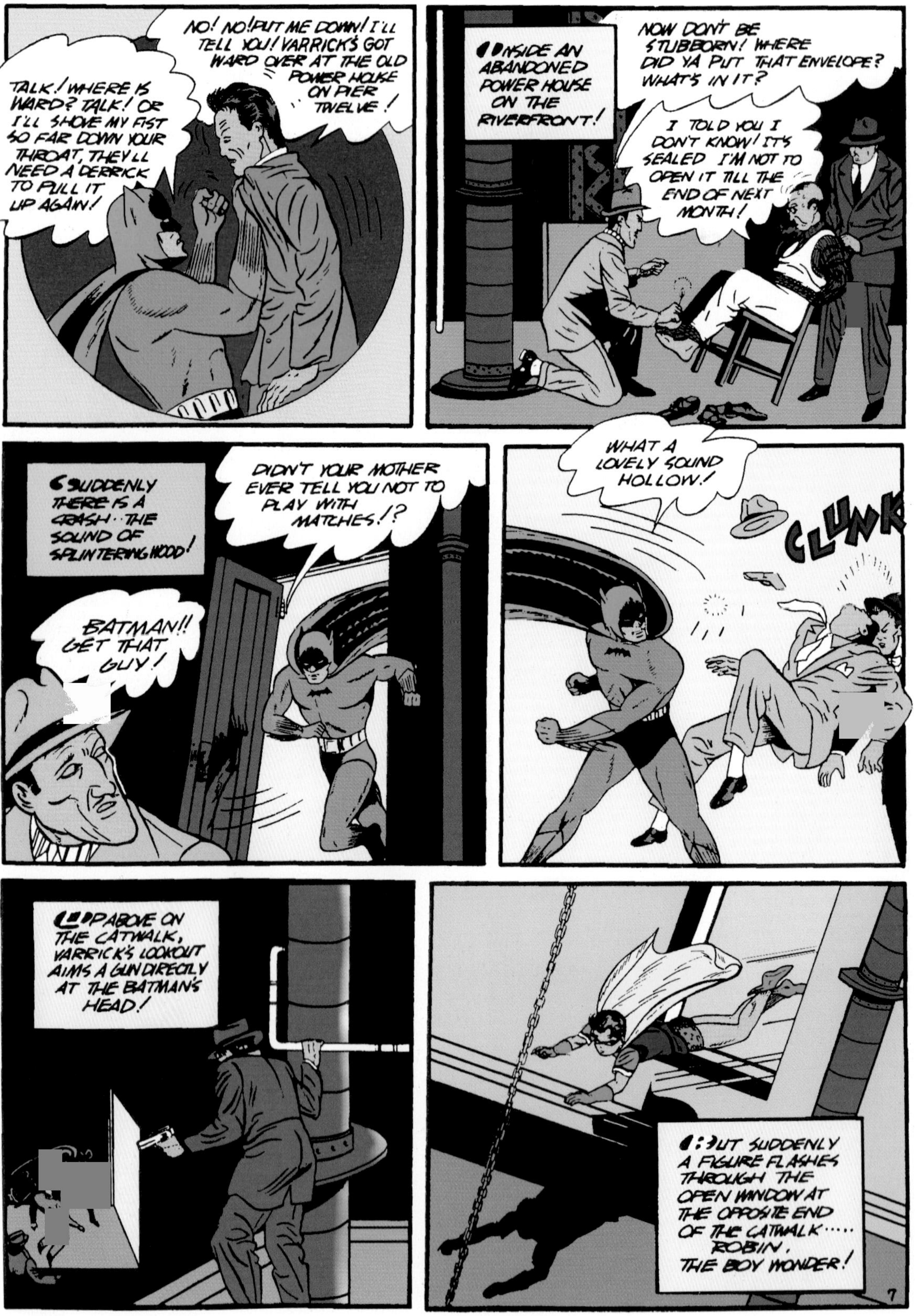
TALK! WHERE IS WARD? TALK! OR I'LL SHOVE MY FIST SO FAR DOWN YOUR THROAT, THEY'LL NEED A DERRICK TO PULL IT UP AGAIN!
NO! NO! PUT ME DOWN! I'LL TELL YOU! VARRICK'S GOT WARD OVER AT THE OLD POWER HOUSE ON PIER TWELVE!
INSIDE AN ABANDONED POWER HOUSE ON THE RIVERFRONT!
NOW DON'T BE STUBBORN! WHERE DID YA PUT THAT ENVELOPE? WHAT'S IN IT?
I TOLD YOU I DON'T KNOW! IT'S SEALED. I'M NOT TO OPEN IT TILL THE END OF NEXT MONTH!
SUDDENLY THERE IS A CRASH.. THE SOUND OF SPLINTERING WOOD!
BATMAN!! GET THAT GUY!
DIDN'T YOUR MOTHER EVER TELL YOU NOT TO PLAY WITH MATCHES!?
WHAT A LOVELY SOUND HOLLOW!
CLUNK
UP ABOVE ON THE CATWALK, VARRICK'S LOOKOUT AIMS A GUN DIRECLY AT THE BATMAN'S HEAD!
BUT SUDDENLY A FIGURE FLASHES THROUGH THE OPEN WINDOW AT THE OPPOSITE END OF THE CATWALK..... ROBIN, THE BOY WONDER!
7

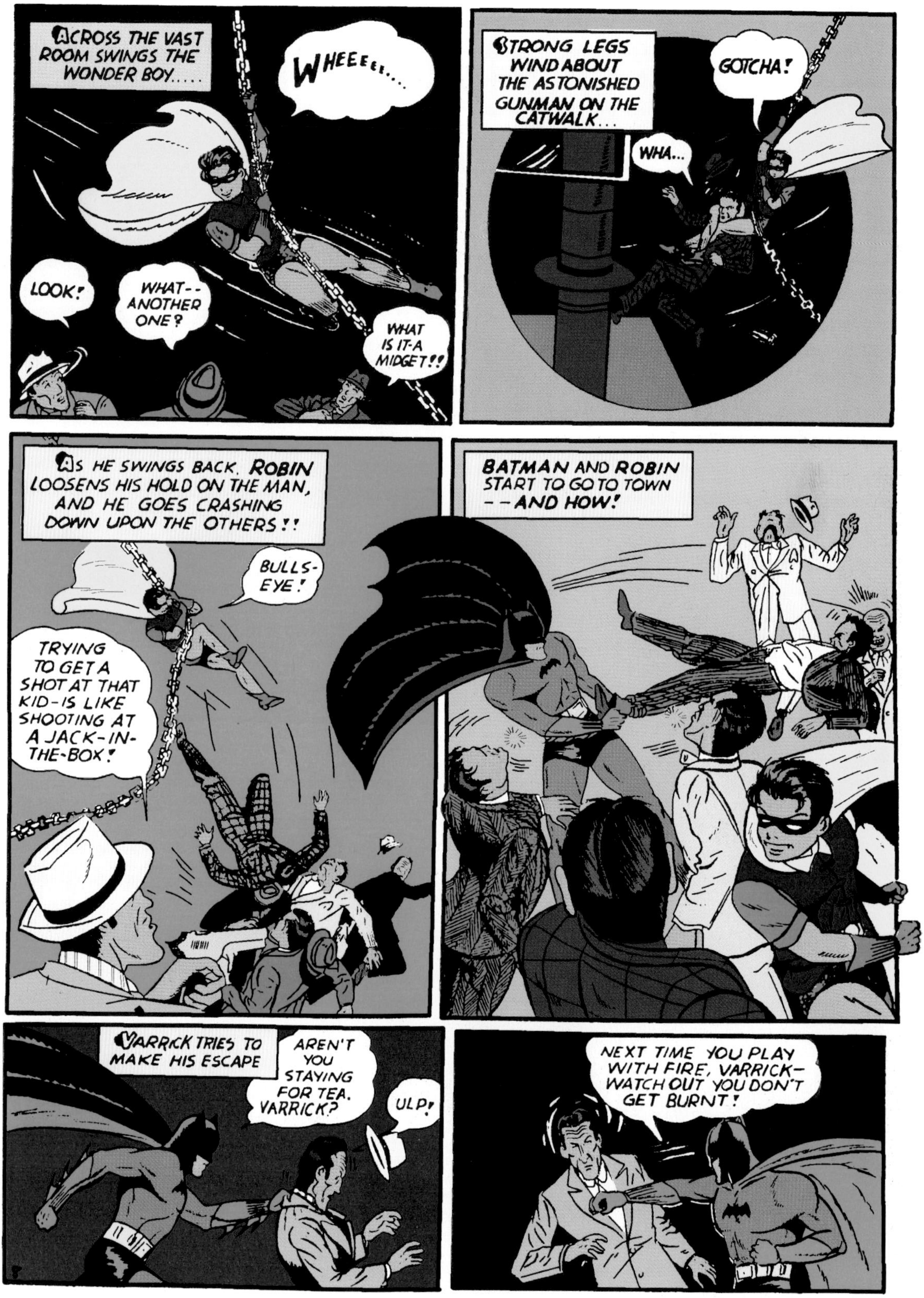
ACROSS THE VAST ROOM SWINGS THE WONDER BOY.....
WHEEEEE....
LOOK!
WHAT--ANOTHER ONE?
WHAT IS IT-A MIDGET!!
STRONG LEGS WIND ABOUT THE ASTONISHED GUNMAN ON THE CATWALK...
GOTCHA!
WHA...
AS HE SWINGS BACK, ROBIN LOOSENS HIS HOLD ON THE MAN, AND HE GOES CRASHING DOWN UPON THE OTHERS!!
BULLS-EYE!
TRYING TO GET A SHOT AT THAT KID-IS LIKE SHOOTING AT A JACK-IN-THE-BOX!
BATMAN AND ROBIN START TO GO TO TOWN --AND HOW!
VARRICK TRIES TO MAKE HIS ESCAPE
AREN'T YOU STAYING FOR TEA, VARRICK?
ULP!
NEXT TIME YOU PLAY WITH FIRE, VARRICK-WATCH OUT YOU DON'T GET BURNT!

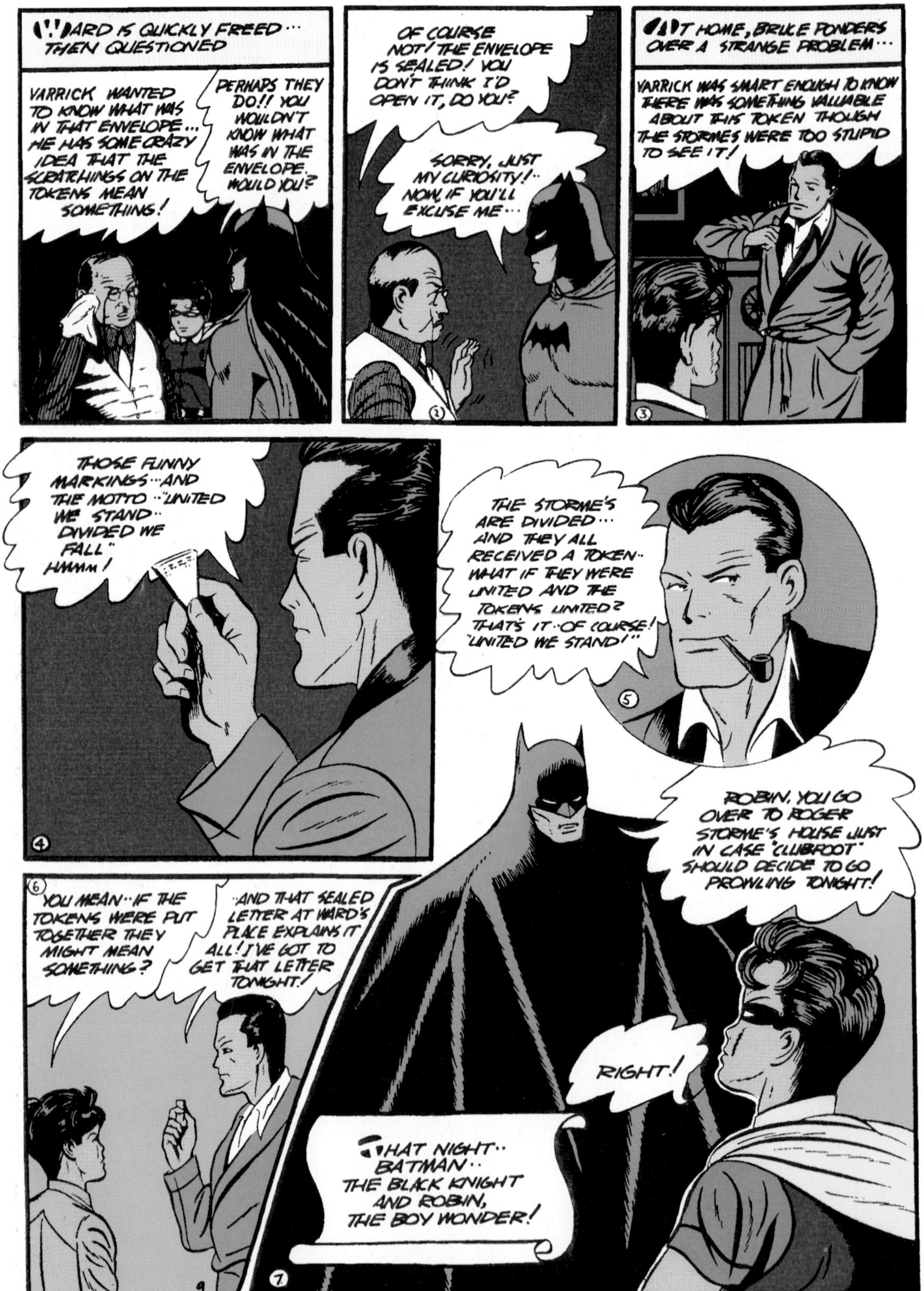
WARD IS QUICKLY FREED... THEN QUESTIONED
VARRICK WANTED TO KNOW WHAT WAS IN THAT ENVELOPE... HE HAS SOME CRAZY IDEA THAT THE SCRATCHINGS ON THE TOKENS MEAN SOMETHING!
PERHAPS THEY DO!! YOU WOULDN'T KNOW WHAT WAS IN THE ENVELOPE, WOULD YOU?
OF COURSE NOT! THE ENVELOPE IS SEALED! YOU DON'T THINK I'D OPEN IT, DO YOU?
SORRY, JUST MY CURIOSITY!.. NOW, IF YOU'LL EXCUSE ME...
AT HOME, BRUCE PONDERS OVER A STRANGE PROBLEM...
VARRICK WAS SMART ENOUGH TO KNOW THERE WAS SOMETHING VALUABLE ABOUT THIS TOKEN THOUGH THE STORMES WERE TOO STUPID TO SEE IT!
THOSE FUNNY MARKINGS..AND THE MOTTO.."UNITED WE STAND.. DIVIDED WE FALL" HMMM!
THE STORME'S ARE DIVIDED... AND THEY ALL RECEIVED A TOKEN.. WHAT IF THEY WERE UNITED AND THE TOKENS UNITED? THAT'S IT..OF COURSE! "UNITED WE STAND!"
YOU MEAN..IF THE TOKENS WERE PUT TOGETHER THEY MIGHT MEAN SOMETHING?
..AND THAT SEALED LETTER AT WARD'S PLACE EXPLAINS IT ALL! I'VE GOT TO GET THAT LETTER TONIGHT!
ROBIN, YOU GO OVER TO ROGER STORME'S HOUSE JUST IN CASE "CLUBFOOT" SHOULD DECIDE TO GO PROWLING TONIGHT!
RIGHT!
THAT NIGHT.. BATMAN.. THE BLACK KNIGHT AND ROBIN, THE BOY WONDER!

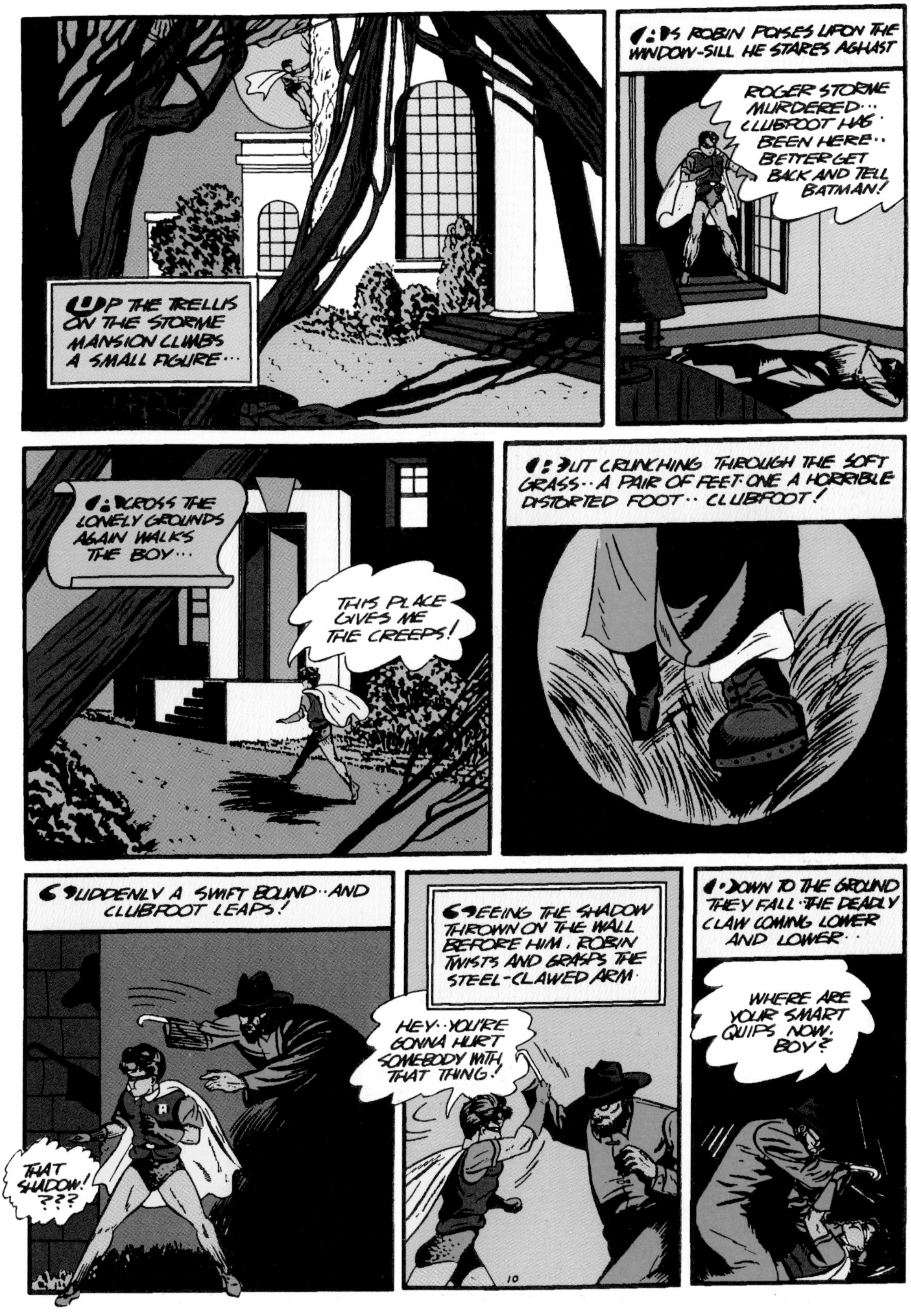
UP THE TRELLIS ON THE STORME MANSION CLIMBS A SMALL FIGURE...
AS ROBIN POISES UPON THE WINDOW-SILL HE STARES AGHAST
ROGER STORME MURDERED... CLUBFOOT HAS BEEN HERE.. BETTER GET BACK AND TELL BATMAN!
ACROSS THE LONELY GROUNDS AGAIN WALKS THE BOY...
THIS PLACE GIVES ME THE CREEPS!
BUT CRUNCHING THROUGH THE SOFT GRASS.. A PAIR OF FEET-ONE A HORRIBLE DISTORTED FOOT.. CLUBFOOT!
SUDDENLY A SWIFT BOUND..AND CLUBFOOT LEAPS!
THAT SHADOW! ???
SEEING THE SHADOW THROWN ON THE WALL BEFORE HIM, ROBIN TWISTS AND GRASPS THE STEEL-CLAWED ARM.
HEY.. YOU'RE GONNA HURT SOMEBODY WITH THAT THING!
DOWN TO THE GROUND THEY FALL-THE DEADLY CLAW COMING LOWER AND LOWER..
WHERE ARE YOUR SMART QUIPS NOW, BOY?
10

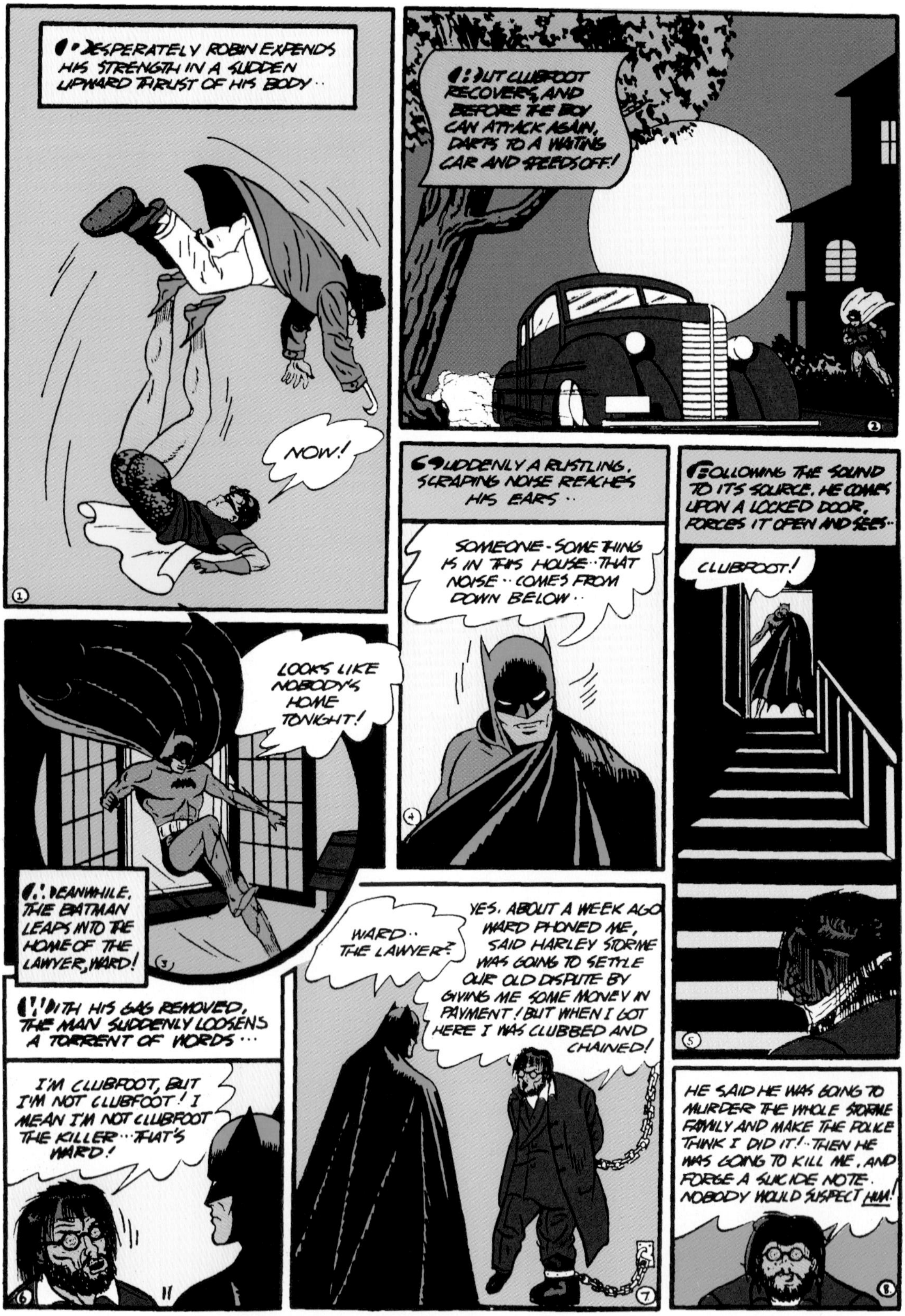
DESPERATELY ROBIN EXPENDS HIS STRENGTH IN A SUDDEN UPWARD THRUST OF HIS BODY..
NOW!
BUT CLUBFOOT RECOVERS, AND BEFORE THE BOY CAN ATTACK AGAIN, DARTS TO A WAITING CAR AND SPEEDS OFF!
MEANWHILE, THE BATMAN LEAPS INTO THE HOME OF THE LAWYER, WARD!
LOOKS LIKE NOBODY'S HOME TONIGHT!
SUDDENLY A RUSTLING, SCRAPING NOISE REACHES HIS EARS..
SOMEONE - SOMETHING IS IN THIS HOUSE..THAT NOISE..COMES FROM DOWN BELOW..
FOLLOWING THE SOUND TO ITS SOURCE, HE COMES UPON A LOCKED DOOR, FORCES IT OPEN AND SEES..
CLUBFOOT!
WITH HIS GAG REMOVED, THE MAN SUDDENLY LOOSENS A TORRENT OF WORDS...
I'M CLUBFOOT, BUT I'M NOT CLUBFOOT! I MEAN I'M NOT CLUBFOOT THE KILLER..THAT'S WARD!
WARD.. THE LAWYER?
YES. ABOUT A WEEK AGO WARD PHONED ME, SAID HARLEY STORME WAS GOING TO SETTLE OUR OLD DISPUTE BY GIVING ME SOME MONEY IN PAYMENT! BUT WHEN I GOT HERE I WAS CLUBBED AND CHAINED!
HE SAID HE WAS GOING TO MURDER THE WHOLE STORME FAMILY AND MAKE THE POLICE THINK I DID IT!..THEN HE WAS GOING TO KILL ME, AND FORGE A SUICIDE NOTE. NOBODY WOULD SUSPECT HIM!

SUDDENLY A MOCKING VOICE·· CLUBFOOT·· THE MURDERER!

CLUBFOOT!

TRUE, AND NO ONE WILL YET! STAND STILL, BATMAN, AND KEEP YOUR HANDS UP!

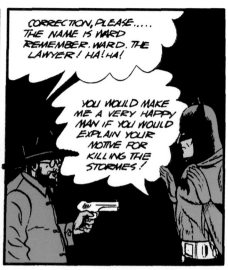

CORRECTION, PLEASE..... THE NAME IS WARD. REMEMBER. WARD. THE LAWYER! HA! HA!

YOU WOULD MAKE ME A VERY HAPPY MAN IF YOU WOULD EXPLAIN YOUR MOTIVE FOR KILLING THE STORMES!

WITH PLEASURE! YOU SEE, IT WAS A GOLDMINE! THAT'S WHAT THE SCRATCHINGS ON THE TOKEN SPELLED OUT WHEN "UNITED!" "DIVIDED" THEY MEANT NOTHING! THIS GOLDMINE WAS LEFT TO HARLEY'S HEIRS!

IF AN HEIR DIED, THE SHARES IN THE MINE WERE TO BE APPORTIONED AGAIN! AND SO ON! IF ALL DIED, THE REMAINING HEIR WOULD RECEIVE ALL OF IT AND SINCE I WAS AN HEIR

SO NATURALLY YOU DECIDED TO KILL THE OTHERS OFF! "CLUBFOOT" BEGGS WOULD BE BLAMED FOR HIS THREAT ON THE FAMILY! YOU WEREN'T A RELATIVE AND NATURALLY WOULDN'T BE EXPECTED TO BE MURDERED

OF COURSE, YOU HAD TO MURDER ALL THE STORMES IN THIRTY DAYS, FOR AT THE END OF THAT TIME THEY WOULD HAVE TO KNOW ABOUT THE MINE!

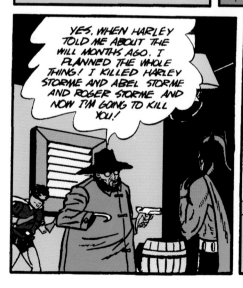

YES, WHEN HARLEY TOLD ME ABOUT THE WILL MONTHS AGO, I PLANNED THE WHOLE THING! I KILLED HARLEY STORME AND ABEL STORME AND ROGER STORME AND NOW I'M GOING TO KILL YOU!

BUT A CREAKING BOARD WARNS THE MURDERER

MURDEROUS SLASH HISSES PAST HIM! ROBIN STEPS BACK

I'LL MAKE SURE THIS TIME!

MISSED AGAIN!

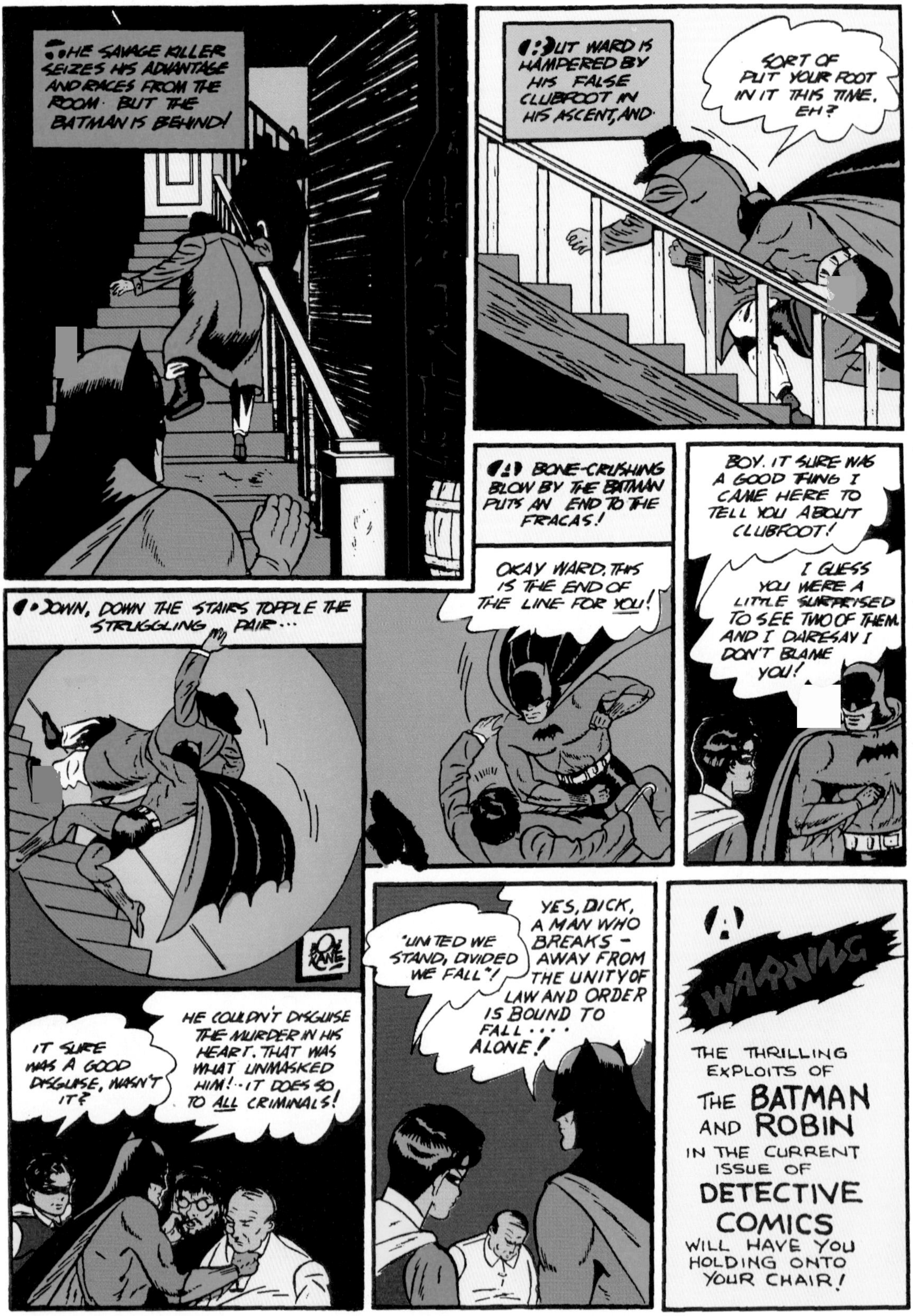
THE SAVAGE KILLER SEIZES HIS ADVANTAGE AND RACES FROM THE ROOM. BUT THE BATMAN IS BEHIND!
BUT WARD IS HAMPERED BY HIS FALSE CLUBFOOT IN HIS ASCENT, AND.
SORT OF PUT YOUR FOOT IN IT THIS TIME, EH?
DOWN, DOWN THE STAIRS TOPPLE THE STRUGGLING PAIR...
A BONE-CRUSHING BLOW BY THE BATMAN PUTS AN END TO THE FRACAS!
OKAY WARD, THIS IS THE END OF THE LINE FOR YOU!
BOY, IT SURE WAS A GOOD THING I CAME HERE TO TELL YOU ABOUT CLUBFOOT!
I GUESS YOU WERE A LITTLE SURPRISED TO SEE TWO OF THEM. AND I DARESAY I DON'T BLAME YOU!
IT SURE WAS A GOOD DISGUISE, WASN'T IT?
HE COULDN'T DISGUISE THE MURDER IN HIS HEART. THAT WAS WHAT UNMASKED HIM! - IT DOES SO TO ALL CRIMINALS!
"UNITED WE STAND, DIVIDED WE FALL"!
YES, DICK, A MAN WHO BREAKS - AWAY FROM THE UNITY OF LAW AND ORDER IS BOUND TO FALL.... ALONE!
A WARNING
THE THRILLING EXPLOITS OF THE BATMAN AND ROBIN IN THE CURRENT ISSUE OF DETECTIVE COMICS WILL HAVE YOU HOLDING ONTO YOUR CHAIR!

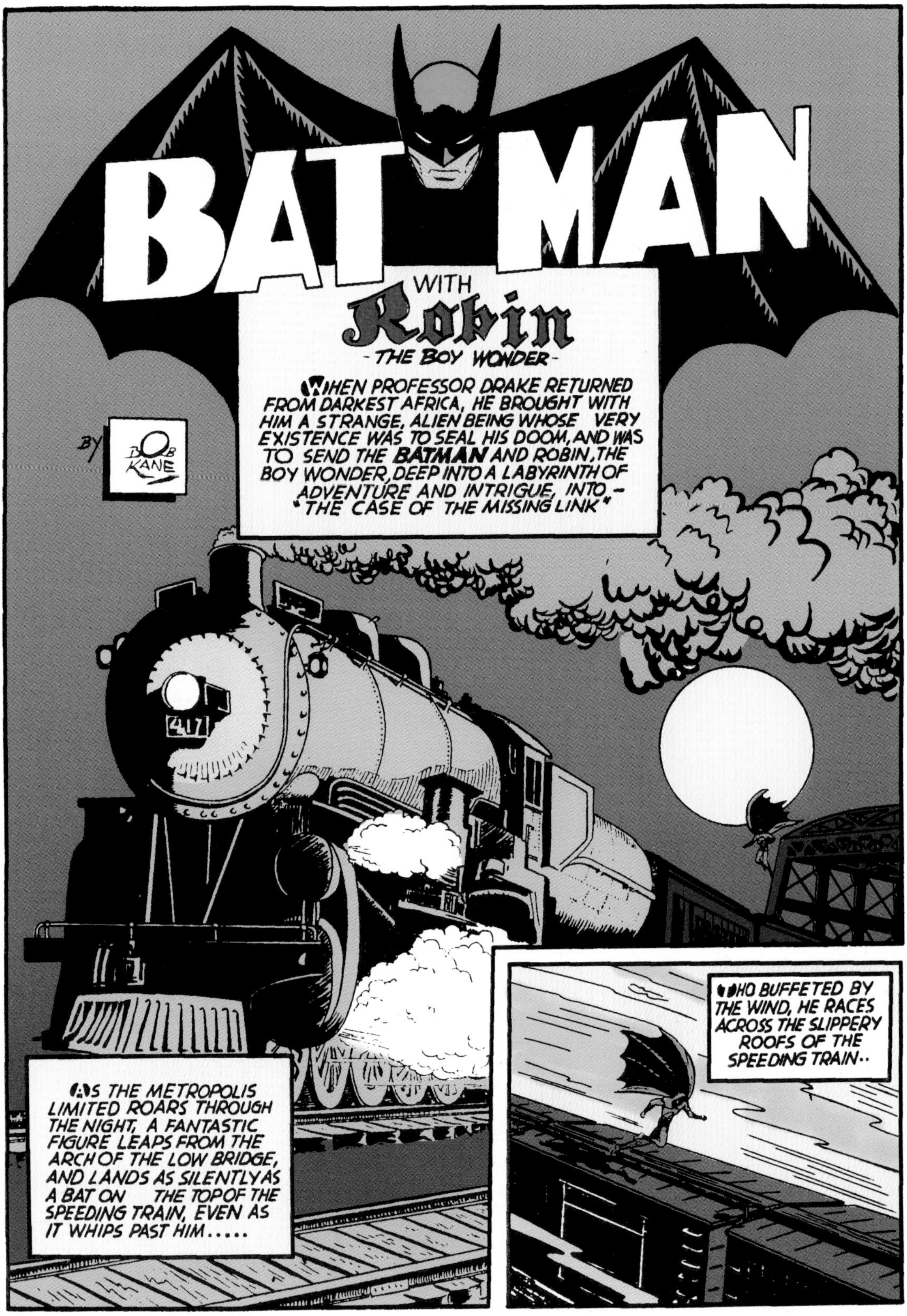
BATMAN
WITH Robin -THE BOY WONDER-
WHEN PROFESSOR DRAKE RETURNED FROM DARKEST AFRICA, HE BROUGHT WITH HIM A STRANGE, ALIEN BEING WHOSE VERY EXISTENCE WAS TO SEAL HIS DOOM, AND WAS TO SEND THE BATMAN AND ROBIN, THE BOY WONDER, DEEP INTO A LABYRINTH OF ADVENTURE AND INTRIGUE, INTO - "THE CASE OF THE MISSING LINK"
BY BOB KANE
417
AS THE METROPOLIS LIMITED ROARS THROUGH THE NIGHT, A FANTASTIC FIGURE LEAPS FROM THE ARCH OF THE LOW BRIDGE, AND LANDS AS SILENTLY AS A BAT ON THE TOP OF THE SPEEDING TRAIN, EVEN AS IT WHIPS PAST HIM.....
WHO BUFFETED BY THE WIND, HE RACES ACROSS THE SLIPPERY ROOFS OF THE SPEEDING TRAIN..

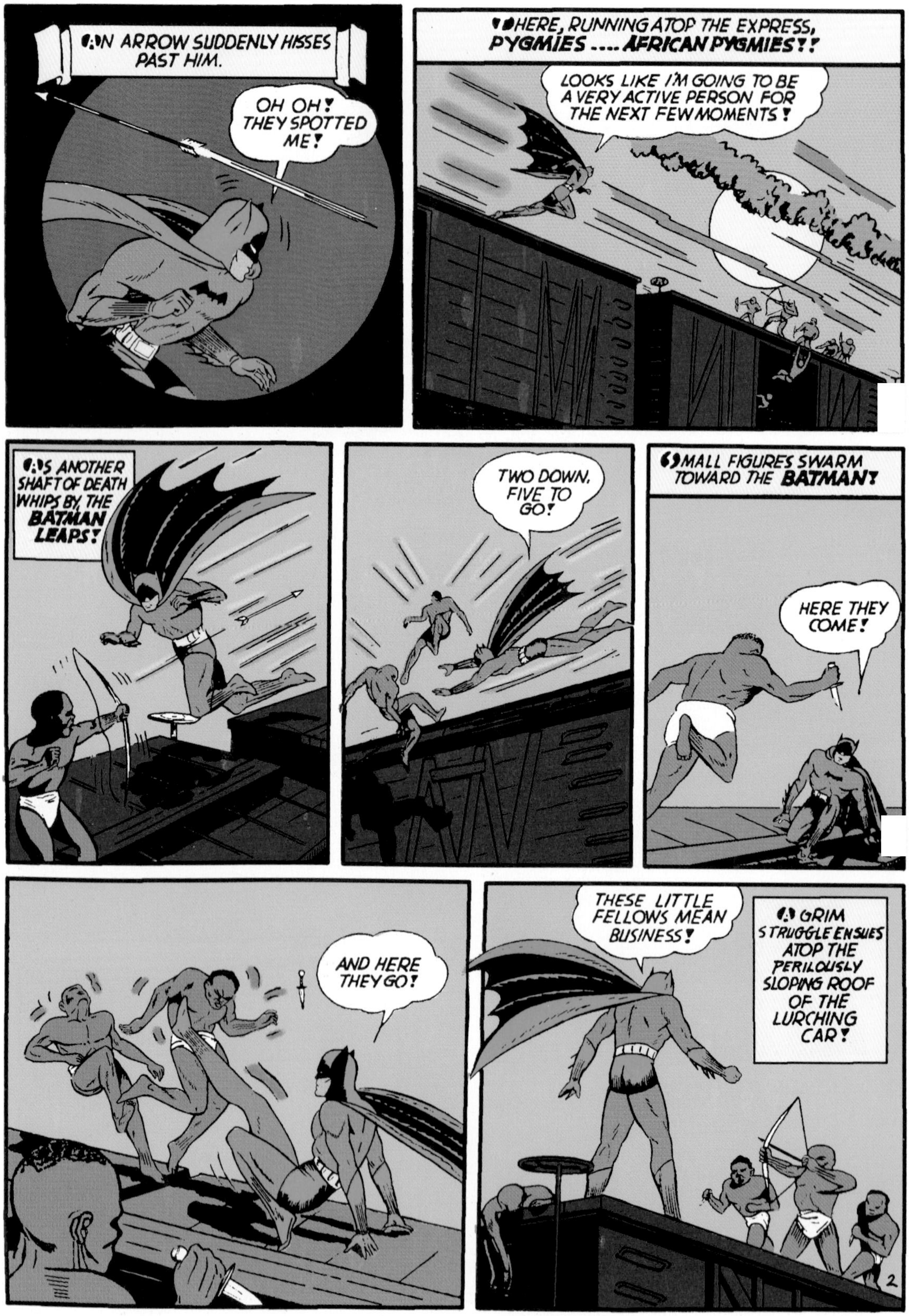
AN ARROW SUDDENLY HISSES PAST HIM.
OH OH! THEY SPOTTED ME!
WHERE, RUNNING ATOP THE EXPRESS, PYGMIES .... AFRICAN PYGMIES!!
LOOKS LIKE I'M GOING TO BE A VERY ACTIVE PERSON FOR THE NEXT FEW MOMENTS!
AS ANOTHER SHAFT OF DEATH WHIPS BY, THE BATMAN LEAPS!
TWO DOWN, FIVE TO GO!
SMALL FIGURES SWARM TOWARD THE BATMAN!
HERE THEY COME!
AND HERE THEY GO!
THESE LITTLE FELLOWS MEAN BUSINESS!
A GRIM STRUGGLE ENSUES ATOP THE PERILOUSLY SLOPING ROOF OF THE LURCHING CAR!
2

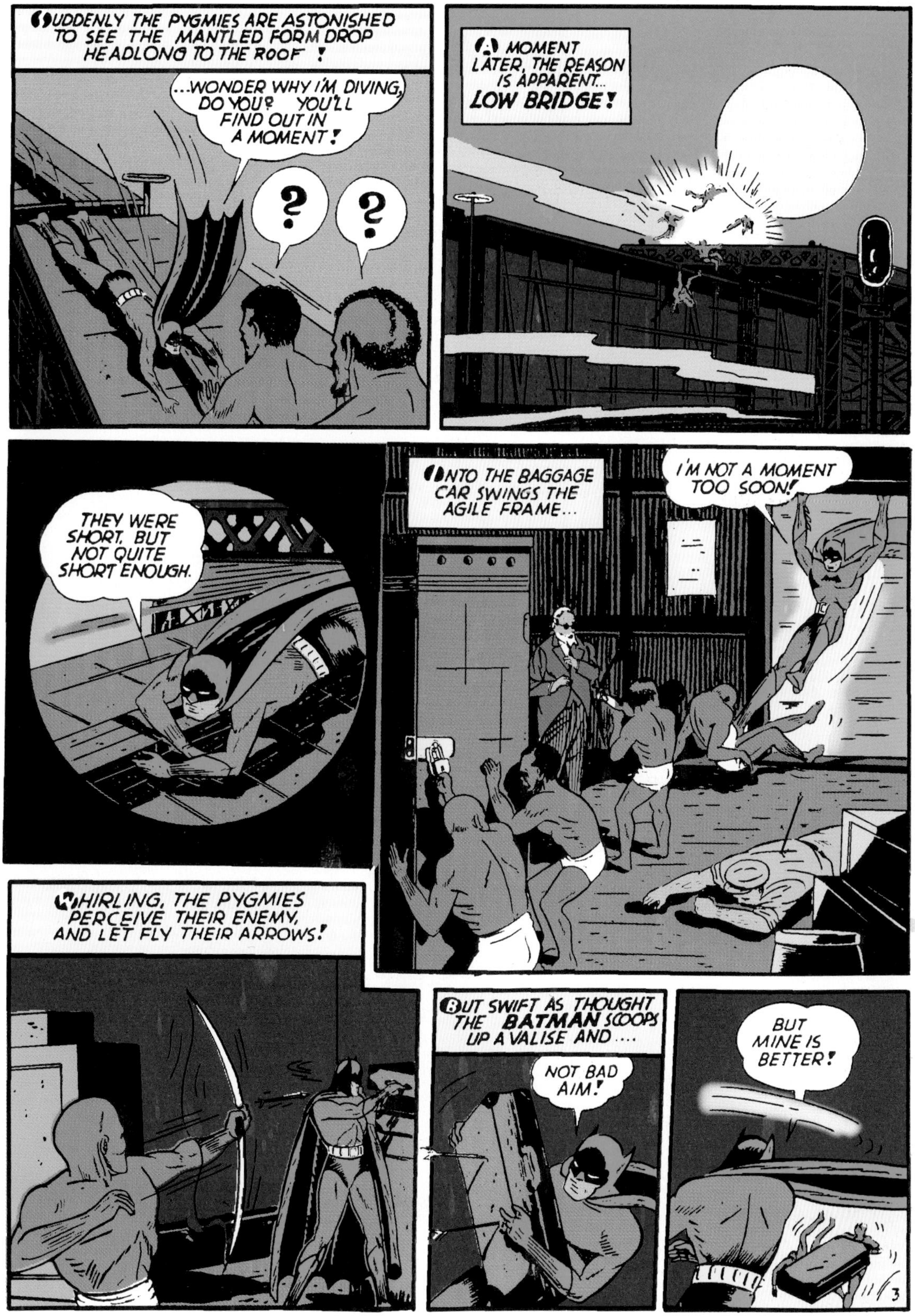
SUDDENLY THE PYGMIES ARE ASTONISHED TO SEE THE MANTLED FORM DROP HEADLONG TO THE ROOF!
...WONDER WHY I'M DIVING, DO YOU? YOU'LL FIND OUT IN A MOMENT!
?
?
A MOMENT LATER, THE REASON IS APPARENT... LOW BRIDGE!
THEY WERE SHORT, BUT NOT QUITE SHORT ENOUGH.
INTO THE BAGGAGE CAR SWINGS THE AGILE FRAME...
I'M NOT A MOMENT TOO SOON!
WHIRLING, THE PYGMIES PERCEIVE THEIR ENEMY, AND LET FLY THEIR ARROWS!
BUT SWIFT AS THOUGHT THE BATMAN SCOOPS UP A VALISE AND....
NOT BAD AIM!
BUT MINE IS BETTER!
3

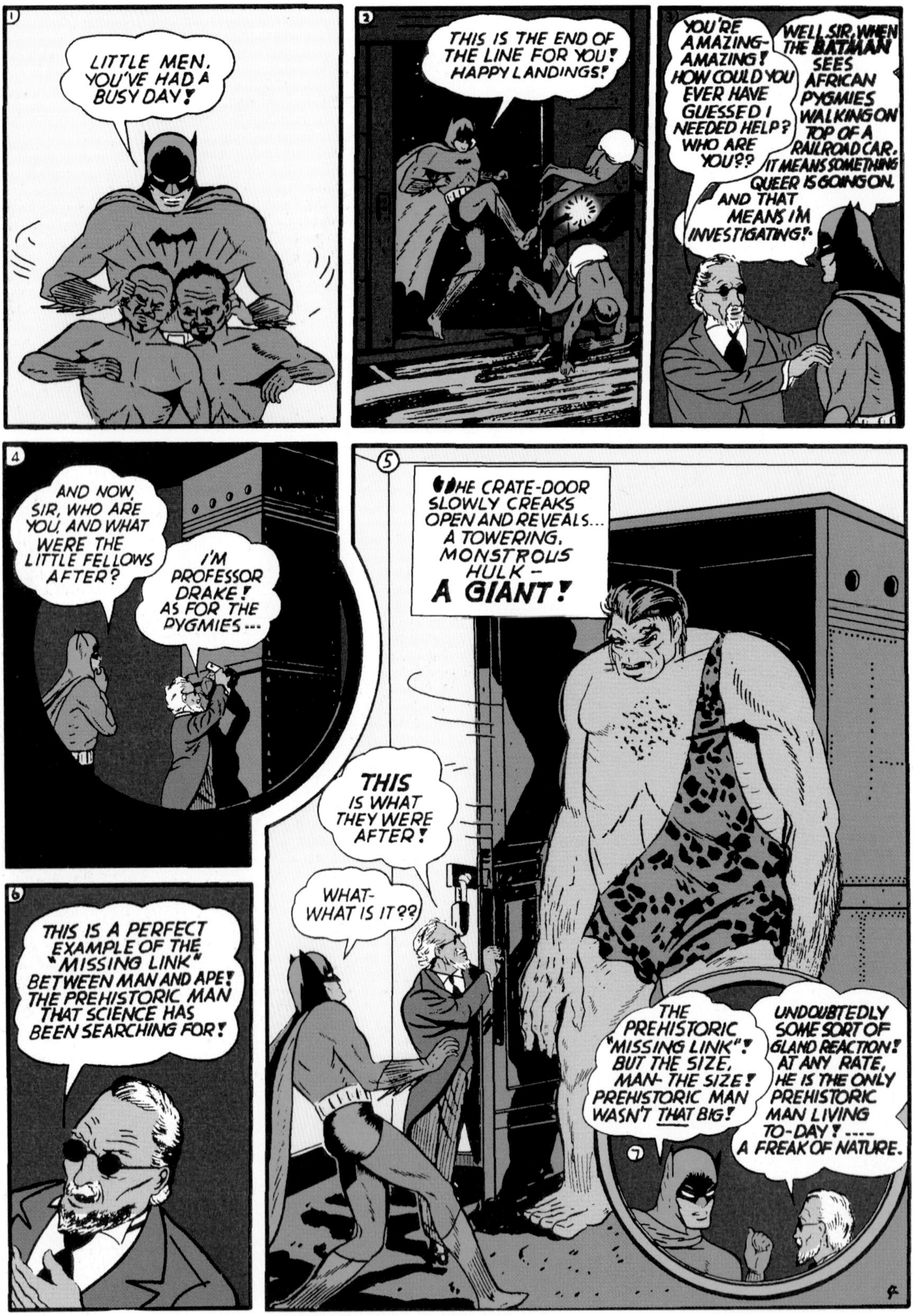
LITTLE MEN, YOU'VE HAD A BUSY DAY!
THIS IS THE END OF THE LINE FOR YOU! HAPPY LANDINGS!
YOU'RE AMAZING- AMAZING! HOW COULD YOU EVER HAVE GUESSED I NEEDED HELP? WHO ARE YOU??
WELL, SIR, WHEN THE BATMAN SEES AFRICAN PYGMIES WALKING ON TOP OF A RAILROAD CAR, IT MEANS SOMETHING QUEER IS GOING ON. AND THAT MEANS I'M INVESTIGATING!
AND NOW, SIR, WHO ARE YOU, AND WHAT WERE THE LITTLE FELLOWS AFTER?
I'M PROFESSOR DRAKE! AS FOR THE PYGMIES---
THE CRATE-DOOR SLOWLY CREAKS OPEN AND REVEALS... A TOWERING, MONSTROUS HULK - A GIANT!
THIS IS WHAT THEY WERE AFTER!
WHAT- WHAT IS IT??
THIS IS A PERFECT EXAMPLE OF THE "MISSING LINK" BETWEEN MAN AND APE! THE PREHISTORIC MAN THAT SCIENCE HAS BEEN SEARCHING FOR!
THE PREHISTORIC "MISSING LINK"! BUT THE SIZE, MAN- THE SIZE! PREHISTORIC MAN WASN'T THAT BIG!
UNDOUBTEDLY SOME SORT OF GLAND REACTION! AT ANY RATE, HE IS THE ONLY PREHISTORIC MAN LIVING TO-DAY! ---- A FREAK OF NATURE.

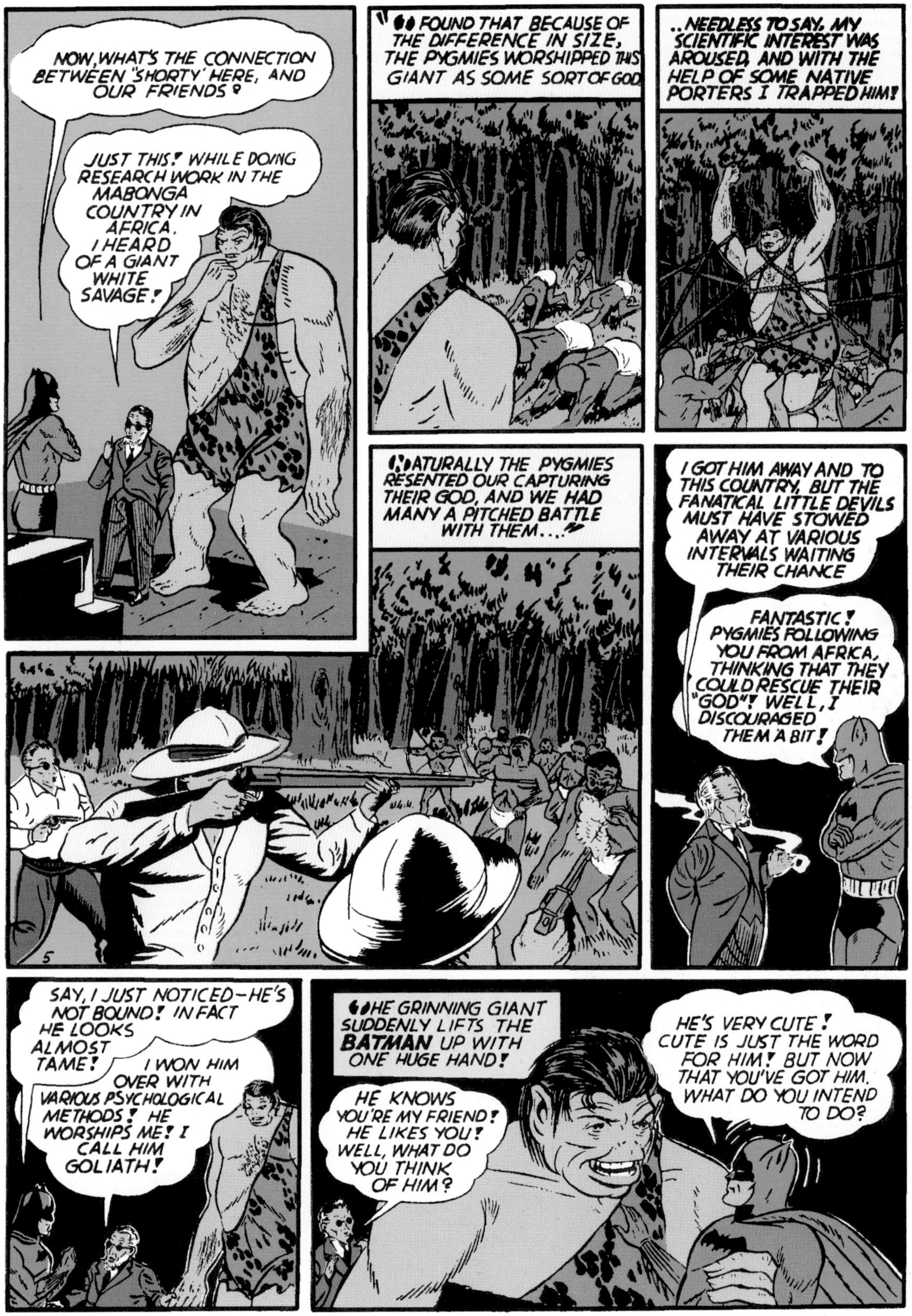
NOW, WHAT'S THE CONNECTION BETWEEN 'SHORTY' HERE, AND OUR FRIENDS?
JUST THIS! WHILE DOING RESEARCH WORK IN THE MABONGA COUNTRY IN AFRICA, I HEARD OF A GIANT WHITE SAVAGE!
"I FOUND THAT BECAUSE OF THE DIFFERENCE IN SIZE, THE PYGMIES WORSHIPPED THIS GIANT AS SOME SORT OF GOD
..NEEDLESS TO SAY, MY SCIENTIFIC INTEREST WAS AROUSED, AND WITH THE HELP OF SOME NATIVE PORTERS I TRAPPED HIM!
"NATURALLY THE PYGMIES RESENTED OUR CAPTURING THEIR GOD, AND WE HAD MANY A PITCHED BATTLE WITH THEM...."
I GOT HIM AWAY AND TO THIS COUNTRY, BUT THE FANATICAL LITTLE DEVILS MUST HAVE STOWED AWAY AT VARIOUS INTERVALS WAITING THEIR CHANCE
FANTASTIC! PYGMIES FOLLOWING YOU FROM AFRICA, THINKING THAT THEY COULD RESCUE THEIR "GOD"! WELL, I DISCOURAGED THEM A BIT!
5
SAY, I JUST NOTICED—HE'S NOT BOUND! IN FACT HE LOOKS ALMOST TAME!
I WON HIM OVER WITH VARIOUS PSYCHOLOGICAL METHODS! HE WORSHIPS ME! I CALL HIM GOLIATH!
"THE GRINNING GIANT SUDDENLY LIFTS THE BATMAN UP WITH ONE HUGE HAND!
HE KNOWS YOU'RE MY FRIEND! HE LIKES YOU! WELL, WHAT DO YOU THINK OF HIM?
HE'S VERY CUTE! CUTE IS JUST THE WORD FOR HIM! BUT NOW THAT YOU'VE GOT HIM, WHAT DO YOU INTEND TO DO?

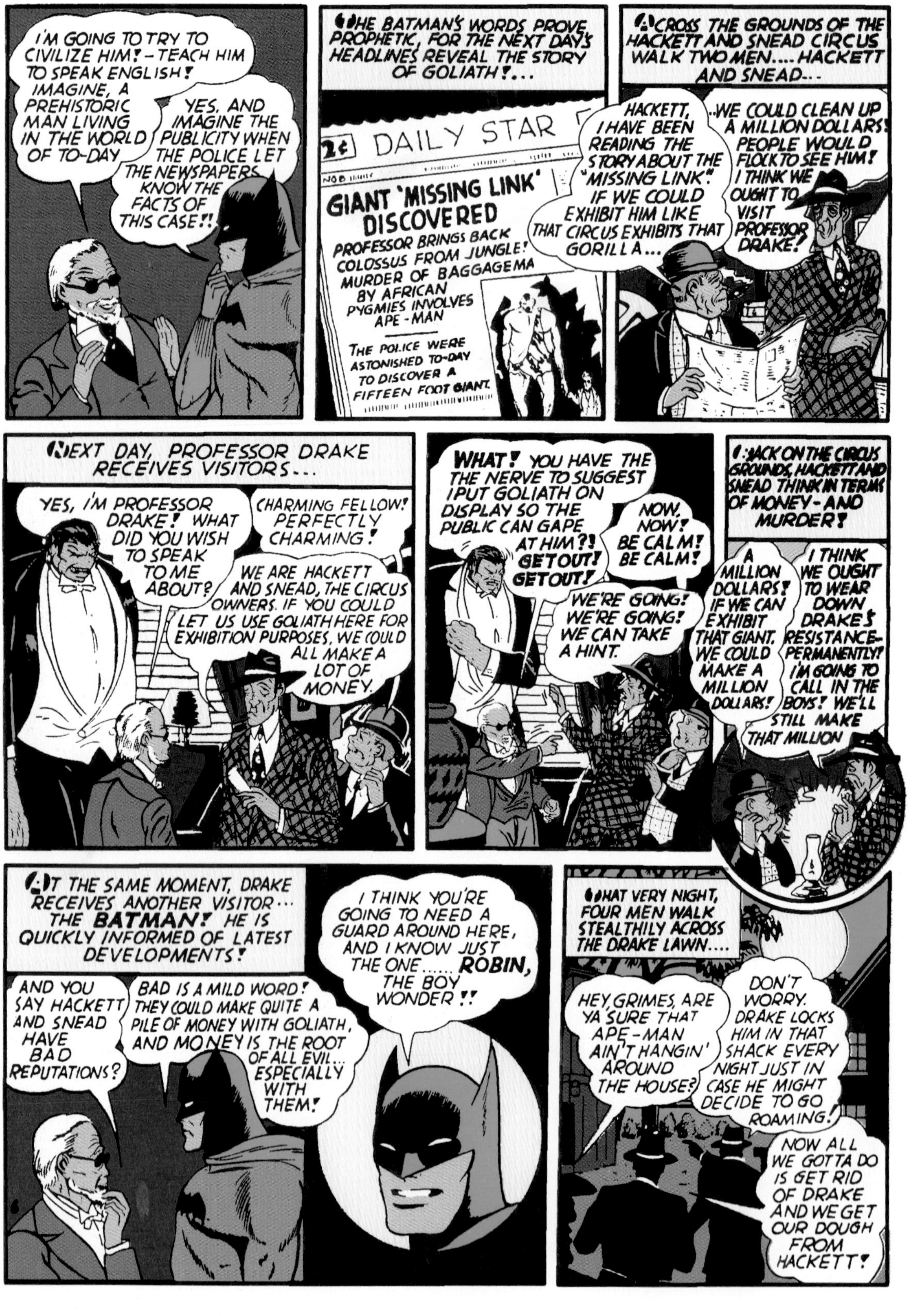
I'M GOING TO TRY TO CIVILIZE HIM! – TEACH HIM TO SPEAK ENGLISH! IMAGINE, A PREHISTORIC MAN LIVING IN THE WORLD OF TO-DAY
YES, AND IMAGINE THE PUBLICITY WHEN THE POLICE LET THE NEWSPAPERS KNOW THE FACTS OF THIS CASE!!
THE BATMAN'S WORDS PROVE PROPHETIC, FOR THE NEXT DAY'S HEADLINES REVEAL THE STORY OF GOLIATH!...
2¢ DAILY STAR
GIANT 'MISSING LINK' DISCOVERED
PROFESSOR BRINGS BACK COLOSSUS FROM JUNGLE! MURDER OF BAGGAGEMA BY AFRICAN PYGMIES INVOLVES APE-MAN
THE POLICE WERE ASTONISHED TO-DAY TO DISCOVER A FIFTEEN FOOT GIANT
ACROSS THE GROUNDS OF THE HACKETT AND SNEAD CIRCUS WALK TWO MEN.... HACKETT AND SNEAD...
HACKETT, I HAVE BEEN READING THE STORY ABOUT THE "MISSING LINK". IF WE COULD EXHIBIT HIM LIKE THAT CIRCUS EXHIBITS THAT GORILLA...
..WE COULD CLEAN UP A MILLION DOLLARS! PEOPLE WOULD FLOCK TO SEE HIM! I THINK WE OUGHT TO VISIT PROFESSOR DRAKE!
NEXT DAY, PROFESSOR DRAKE RECEIVES VISITORS...
YES, I'M PROFESSOR DRAKE! WHAT DID YOU WISH TO SPEAK TO ME ABOUT?
CHARMING FELLOW! PERFECTLY CHARMING!
WE ARE HACKETT AND SNEAD, THE CIRCUS OWNERS. IF YOU COULD LET US USE GOLIATH HERE FOR EXHIBITION PURPOSES, WE COULD ALL MAKE A LOT OF MONEY.
WHAT! YOU HAVE THE THE NERVE TO SUGGEST I PUT GOLIATH ON DISPLAY SO THE PUBLIC CAN GAPE AT HIM?! GET OUT! GET OUT!
NOW, NOW! BE CALM! BE CALM!
WE'RE GOING! WE'RE GOING! WE CAN TAKE A HINT.
BACK ON THE CIRCUS GROUNDS, HACKETT AND SNEAD THINK IN TERMS OF MONEY - AND MURDER!
A MILLION DOLLARS! IF WE CAN EXHIBIT THAT GIANT, WE COULD MAKE A MILLION DOLLARS!
I THINK WE OUGHT TO WEAR DOWN DRAKE'S RESISTANCE-PERMANENTLY! I'M GOING TO CALL IN THE BOYS! WE'LL STILL MAKE THAT MILLION
AT THE SAME MOMENT, DRAKE RECEIVES ANOTHER VISITOR... THE BATMAN! HE IS QUICKLY INFORMED OF LATEST DEVELOPMENTS!
AND YOU SAY HACKETT AND SNEAD HAVE BAD REPUTATIONS?
BAD IS A MILD WORD! THEY COULD MAKE QUITE A PILE OF MONEY WITH GOLIATH, AND MONEY IS THE ROOT OF ALL EVIL... ESPECIALLY WITH THEM!
I THINK YOU'RE GOING TO NEED A GUARD AROUND HERE, AND I KNOW JUST THE ONE...... ROBIN, THE BOY WONDER!!
THAT VERY NIGHT, FOUR MEN WALK STEALTHILY ACROSS THE DRAKE LAWN....
HEY, GRIMES, ARE YA SURE THAT APE-MAN AIN'T HANGIN' AROUND THE HOUSE?
DON'T WORRY. DRAKE LOCKS HIM IN THAT SHACK EVERY NIGHT JUST IN CASE HE MIGHT DECIDE TO GO ROAMING!
NOW ALL WE GOTTA DO IS GET RID OF DRAKE AND WE GET OUR DOUGH FROM HACKETT!

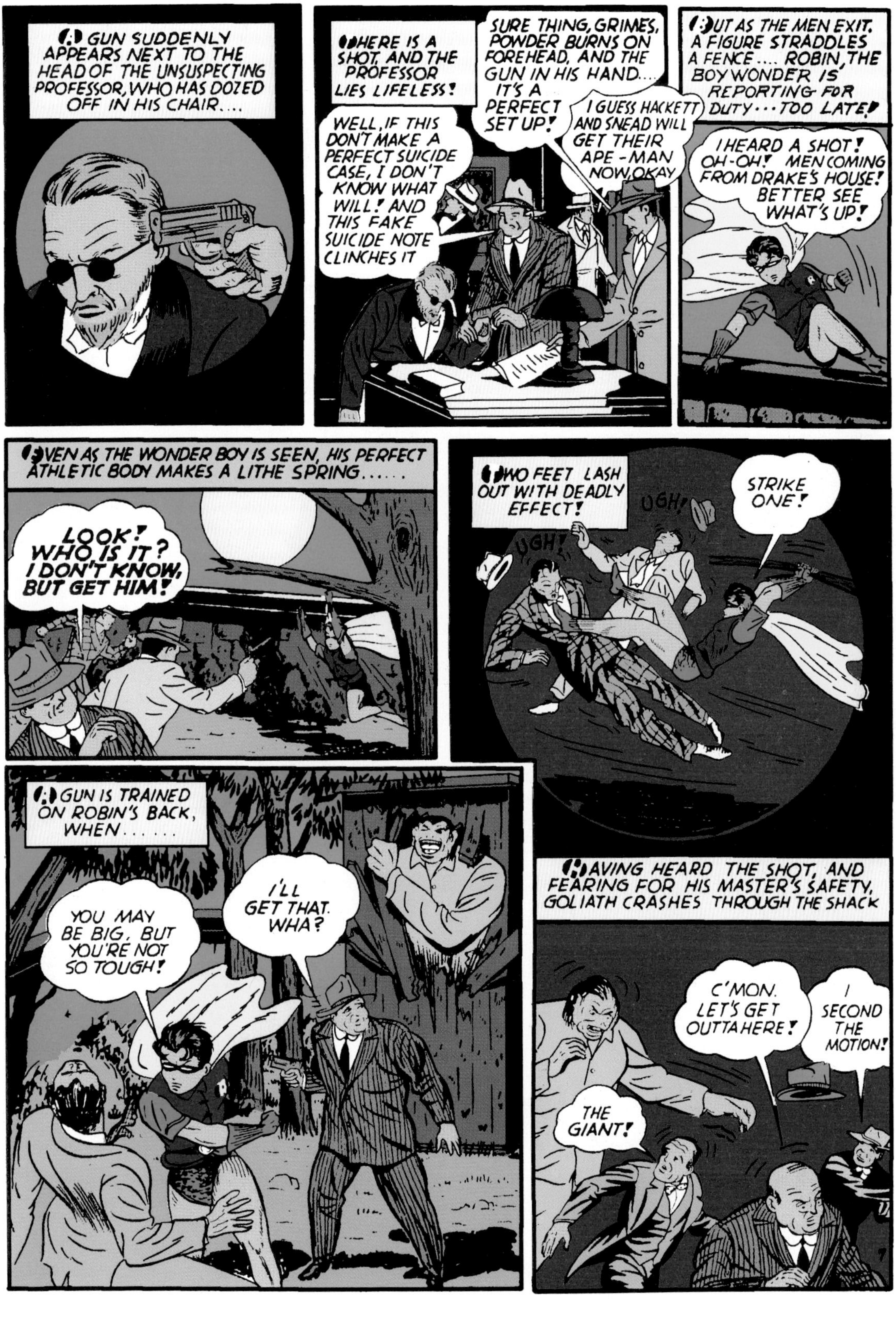
A GUN SUDDENLY APPEARS NEXT TO THE HEAD OF THE UNSUSPECTING PROFESSOR, WHO HAS DOZED OFF IN HIS CHAIR....
THERE IS A SHOT, AND THE PROFESSOR LIES LIFELESS!
WELL, IF THIS DON'T MAKE A PERFECT SUICIDE CASE, I DON'T KNOW WHAT WILL! AND THIS FAKE SUICIDE NOTE CLINCHES IT
SURE THING, GRIMES, POWDER BURNS ON FOREHEAD, AND THE GUN IN HIS HAND.... IT'S A PERFECT SET UP!
I GUESS HACKETT AND SNEAD WILL GET THEIR APE-MAN NOW, OKAY
BUT AS THE MEN EXIT, A FIGURE STRADDLES A FENCE.... ROBIN, THE BOY WONDER IS REPORTING FOR DUTY... TOO LATE!
I HEARD A SHOT! OH-OH! MEN COMING FROM DRAKE'S HOUSE! BETTER SEE WHAT'S UP!
EVEN AS THE WONDER BOY IS SEEN, HIS PERFECT ATHLETIC BODY MAKES A LITHE SPRING......
LOOK! WHO IS IT? I DON'T KNOW, BUT GET HIM!
TWO FEET LASH OUT WITH DEADLY EFFECT!
UGH!
UGH!
STRIKE ONE!
A GUN IS TRAINED ON ROBIN'S BACK, WHEN......
YOU MAY BE BIG, BUT YOU'RE NOT SO TOUGH!
I'LL GET THAT. WHA?
HAVING HEARD THE SHOT, AND FEARING FOR HIS MASTER'S SAFETY, GOLIATH CRASHES THROUGH THE SHACK
C'MON. LET'S GET OUTTA HERE!
I SECOND THE MOTION!
THE GIANT!

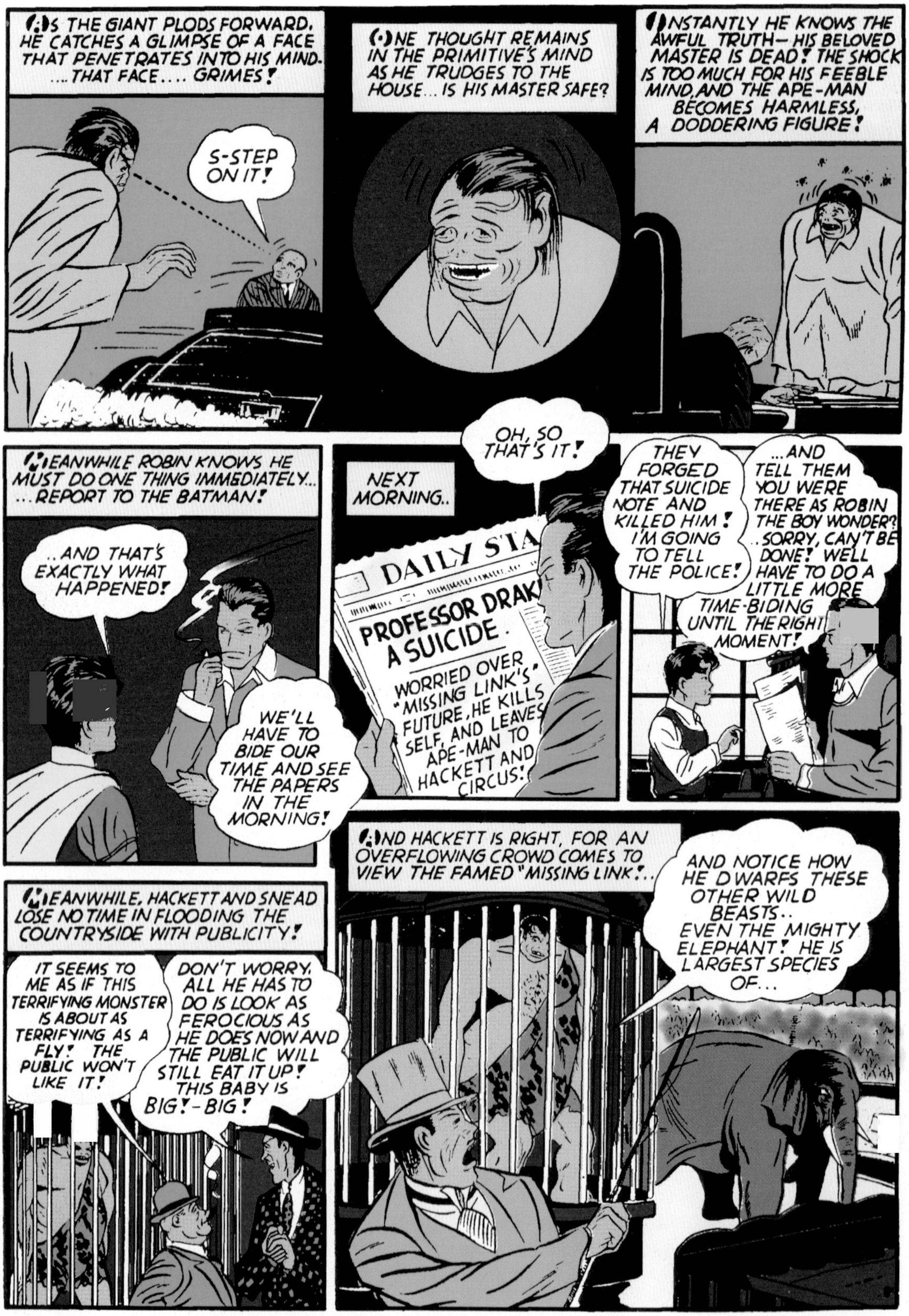
AS THE GIANT PLODS FORWARD. HE CATCHES A GLIMPSE OF A FACE THAT PENETRATES INTO HIS MIND. ....THAT FACE.... GRIMES!
S-STEP ON IT!
ONE THOUGHT REMAINS IN THE PRIMITIVE'S MIND AS HE TRUDGES TO THE HOUSE... IS HIS MASTER SAFE?
INSTANTLY HE KNOWS THE AWFUL TRUTH— HIS BELOVED MASTER IS DEAD! THE SHOCK IS TOO MUCH FOR HIS FEEBLE MIND, AND THE APE-MAN BECOMES HARMLESS, A DODDERING FIGURE!
MEANWHILE ROBIN KNOWS HE MUST DO ONE THING IMMEDIATELY... ...REPORT TO THE BATMAN!
..AND THAT'S EXACTLY WHAT HAPPENED!
WE'LL HAVE TO BIDE OUR TIME AND SEE THE PAPERS IN THE MORNING!
NEXT MORNING..
OH, SO THAT'S IT!
DAILY STA
PROFESSOR DRAK
A SUICIDE
WORRIED OVER "MISSING LINK'S" FUTURE, HE KILLS SELF, AND LEAVES APE-MAN TO HACKETT AND CIRCUS!
THEY FORGED THAT SUICIDE NOTE AND KILLED HIM! I'M GOING TO TELL THE POLICE!
...AND TELL THEM YOU WERE THERE AS ROBIN THE BOY WONDER? ..SORRY, CAN'T BE DONE! WELL HAVE TO DO A LITTLE MORE TIME-BIDING UNTIL THE RIGHT MOMENT!
MEANWHILE, HACKETT AND SNEAD LOSE NO TIME IN FLOODING THE COUNTRYSIDE WITH PUBLICITY!
IT SEEMS TO ME AS IF THIS TERRIFYING MONSTER IS ABOUT AS TERRIFYING AS A FLY! THE PUBLIC WON'T LIKE IT!
DON'T WORRY. ALL HE HAS TO DO IS LOOK AS FEROCIOUS AS HE DOES NOW AND THE PUBLIC WILL STILL EAT IT UP! THIS BABY IS BIG!-BIG!
AND HACKETT IS RIGHT, FOR AN OVERFLOWING CROWD COMES TO VIEW THE FAMED "MISSING LINK"!..
AND NOTICE HOW HE DWARFS THESE OTHER WILD BEASTS.. EVEN THE MIGHTY ELEPHANT! HE IS LARGEST SPECIES OF...

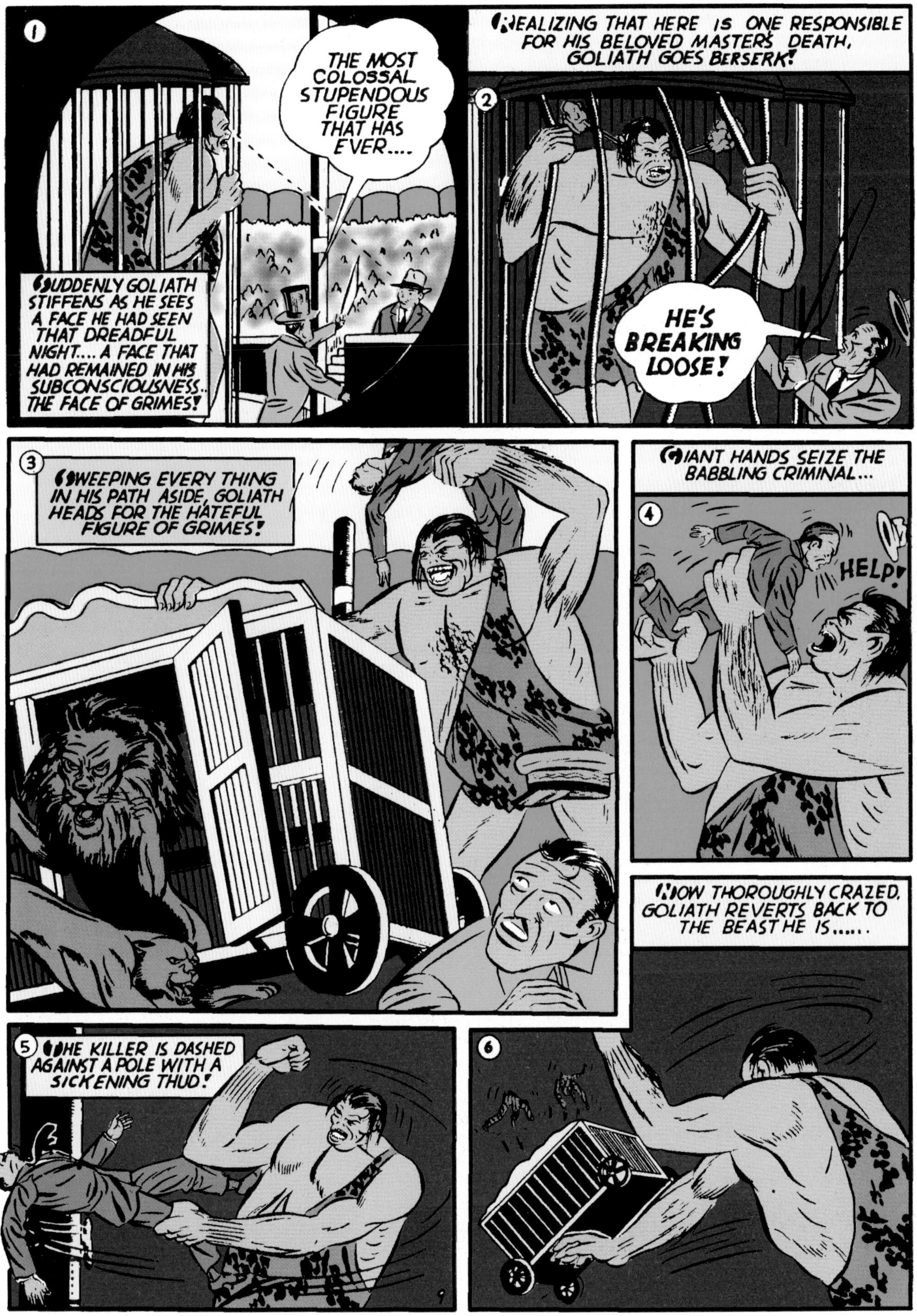
1
THE MOST COLOSSAL STUPENDOUS FIGURE THAT HAS EVER....
SUDDENLY GOLIATH STIFFENS AS HE SEES A FACE HE HAD SEEN THAT DREADFUL NIGHT.... A FACE THAT HAD REMAINED IN HIS SUBCONSCIOUSNESS.. THE FACE OF GRIMES!
REALIZING THAT HERE IS ONE RESPONSIBLE FOR HIS BELOVED MASTER'S DEATH, GOLIATH GOES BERSERK!
2
HE'S BREAKING LOOSE!
3
SWEEPING EVERY THING IN HIS PATH ASIDE, GOLIATH HEADS FOR THE HATEFUL FIGURE OF GRIMES!
GIANT HANDS SEIZE THE BABBLING CRIMINAL...
4
HELP!
NOW THOROUGHLY CRAZED, GOLIATH REVERTS BACK TO THE BEAST HE IS......
5
THE KILLER IS DASHED AGAINST A POLE WITH A SICKENING THUD!
6

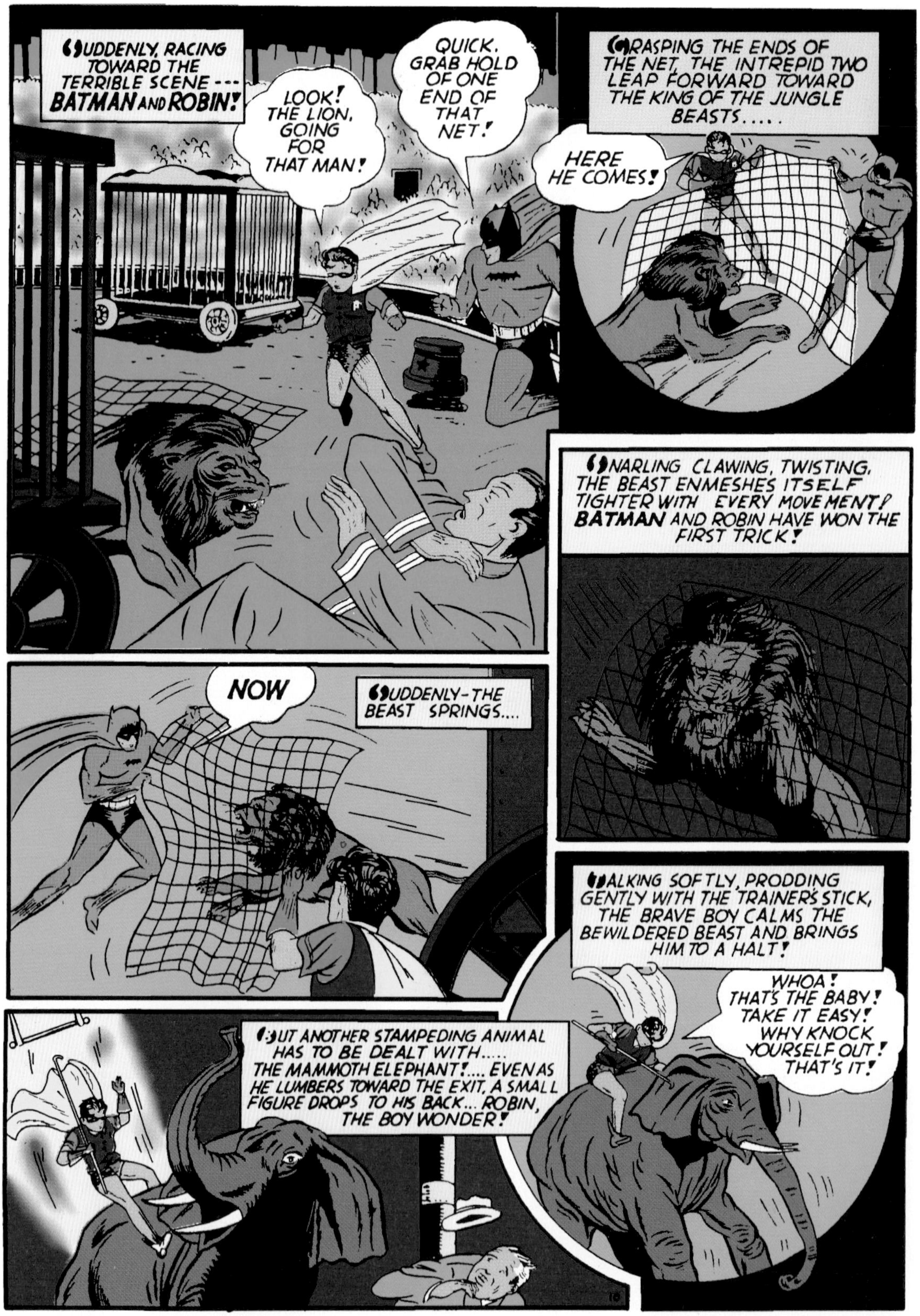
SUDDENLY, RACING TOWARD THE TERRIBLE SCENE --- BATMAN AND ROBIN!
LOOK! THE LION. GOING FOR THAT MAN!
QUICK. GRAB HOLD OF ONE END OF THAT NET!
GRASPING THE ENDS OF THE NET, THE INTREPID TWO LEAP FORWARD TOWARD THE KING OF THE JUNGLE BEASTS.....
HERE HE COMES!
NOW
SUDDENLY-THE BEAST SPRINGS....
SNARLING CLAWING, TWISTING, THE BEAST ENMESHES ITSELF TIGHTER WITH EVERY MOVEMENT! BATMAN AND ROBIN HAVE WON THE FIRST TRICK!
BUT ANOTHER STAMPEDING ANIMAL HAS TO BE DEALT WITH..... THE MAMMOTH ELEPHANT!.... EVEN AS HE LUMBERS TOWARD THE EXIT, A SMALL FIGURE DROPS TO HIS BACK... ROBIN, THE BOY WONDER!
WALKING SOFTLY, PRODDING GENTLY WITH THE TRAINER'S STICK, THE BRAVE BOY CALMS THE BEWILDERED BEAST AND BRINGS HIM TO A HALT!
WHOA! THAT'S THE BABY! TAKE IT EASY! WHY KNOCK YOURSELF OUT! THAT'S IT!

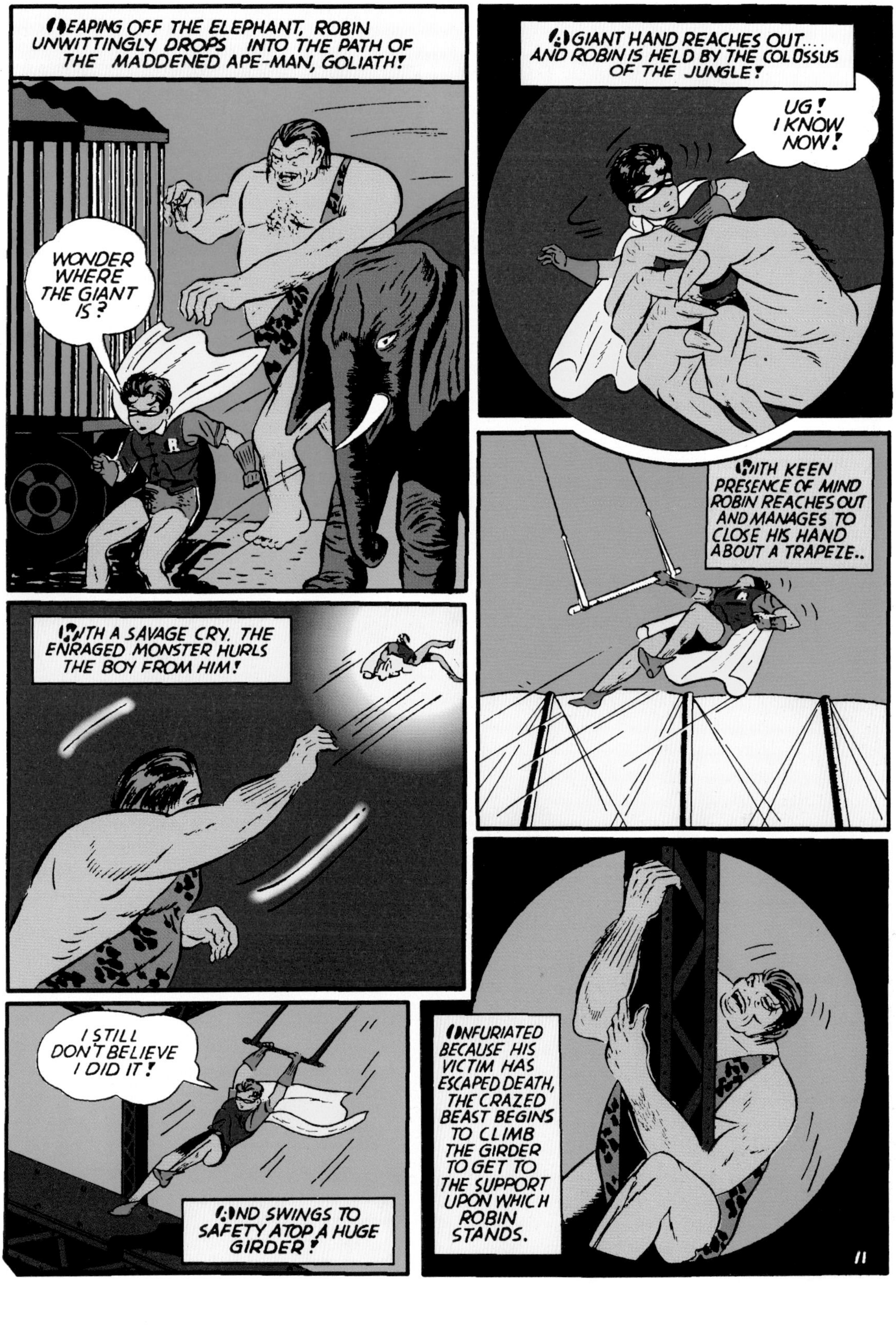
LEAPING OFF THE ELEPHANT, ROBIN UNWITTINGLY DROPS INTO THE PATH OF THE MADDENED APE-MAN, GOLIATH!
WONDER WHERE THE GIANT IS?
A GIANT HAND REACHES OUT.... AND ROBIN IS HELD BY THE COLOSSUS OF THE JUNGLE!
UG! I KNOW NOW!
WITH A SAVAGE CRY, THE ENRAGED MONSTER HURLS THE BOY FROM HIM!
WITH KEEN PRESENCE OF MIND ROBIN REACHES OUT AND MANAGES TO CLOSE HIS HAND ABOUT A TRAPEZE..
I STILL DON'T BELIEVE I DID IT!
AND SWINGS TO SAFETY ATOP A HUGE GIRDER!
INFURIATED BECAUSE HIS VICTIM HAS ESCAPED DEATH, THE CRAZED BEAST BEGINS TO CLIMB THE GIRDER TO GET TO THE SUPPORT UPON WHICH ROBIN STANDS.
11

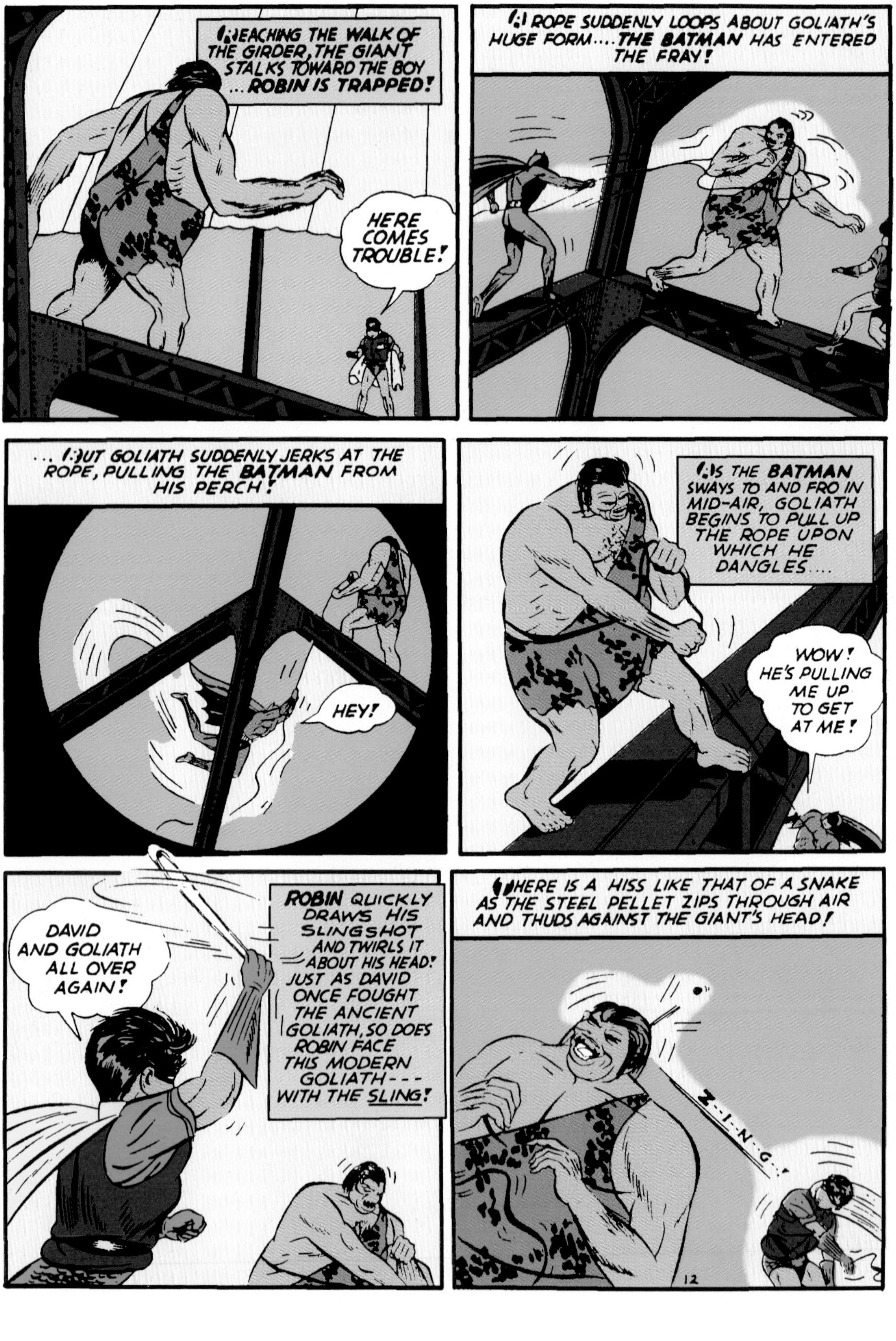
REACHING THE WALK OF THE GIRDER, THE GIANT STALKS TOWARD THE BOY ... ROBIN IS TRAPPED!
HERE COMES TROUBLE!
A ROPE SUDDENLY LOOPS ABOUT GOLIATH'S HUGE FORM.... THE BATMAN HAS ENTERED THE FRAY!
... BUT GOLIATH SUDDENLY JERKS AT THE ROPE, PULLING THE BATMAN FROM HIS PERCH!
HEY!
AS THE BATMAN SWAYS TO AND FRO IN MID-AIR, GOLIATH BEGINS TO PULL UP THE ROPE UPON WHICH HE DANGLES....
WOW! HE'S PULLING ME UP TO GET AT ME!
DAVID AND GOLIATH ALL OVER AGAIN!
ROBIN QUICKLY DRAWS HIS SLINGSHOT AND TWIRLS IT ABOUT HIS HEAD! JUST AS DAVID ONCE FOUGHT THE ANCIENT GOLIATH, SO DOES ROBIN FACE THIS MODERN GOLIATH--- WITH THE SLING!
THERE IS A HISS LIKE THAT OF A SNAKE AS THE STEEL PELLET ZIPS THROUGH AIR AND THUDS AGAINST THE GIANT'S HEAD!
Z-I-N-G!
12

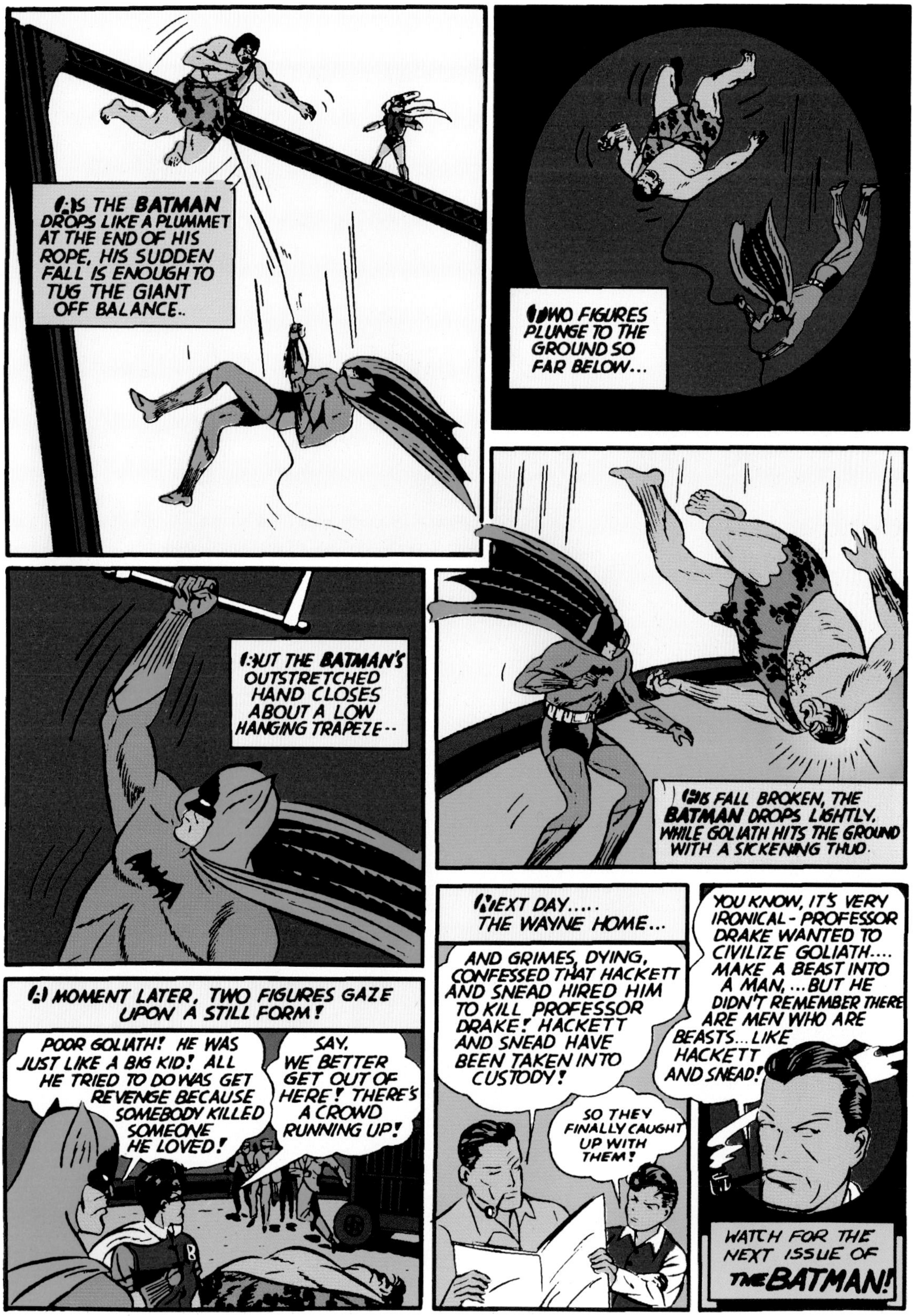
AS THE BATMAN DROPS LIKE A PLUMMET AT THE END OF HIS ROPE, HIS SUDDEN FALL IS ENOUGH TO TUG THE GIANT OFF BALANCE..
TWO FIGURES PLUNGE TO THE GROUND SO FAR BELOW...
BUT THE BATMAN'S OUTSTRETCHED HAND CLOSES ABOUT A LOW HANGING TRAPEZE--
HIS FALL BROKEN, THE BATMAN DROPS LIGHTLY, WHILE GOLIATH HITS THE GROUND WITH A SICKENING THUD.
A MOMENT LATER, TWO FIGURES GAZE UPON A STILL FORM!
POOR GOLIATH! HE WAS JUST LIKE A BIG KID! ALL HE TRIED TO DO WAS GET REVENGE BECAUSE SOMEBODY KILLED SOMEONE HE LOVED!
SAY, WE BETTER GET OUT OF HERE! THERE'S A CROWD RUNNING UP!
NEXT DAY..... THE WAYNE HOME...
AND GRIMES, DYING, CONFESSED THAT HACKETT AND SNEAD HIRED HIM TO KILL PROFESSOR DRAKE! HACKETT AND SNEAD HAVE BEEN TAKEN INTO CUSTODY!
SO THEY FINALLY CAUGHT UP WITH THEM!
YOU KNOW, IT'S VERY IRONICAL - PROFESSOR DRAKE WANTED TO CIVILIZE GOLIATH.... MAKE A BEAST INTO A MAN, ...BUT HE DIDN'T REMEMBER THERE ARE MEN WHO ARE BEASTS... LIKE HACKETT AND SNEAD!
WATCH FOR THE NEXT ISSUE OF THE BATMAN!

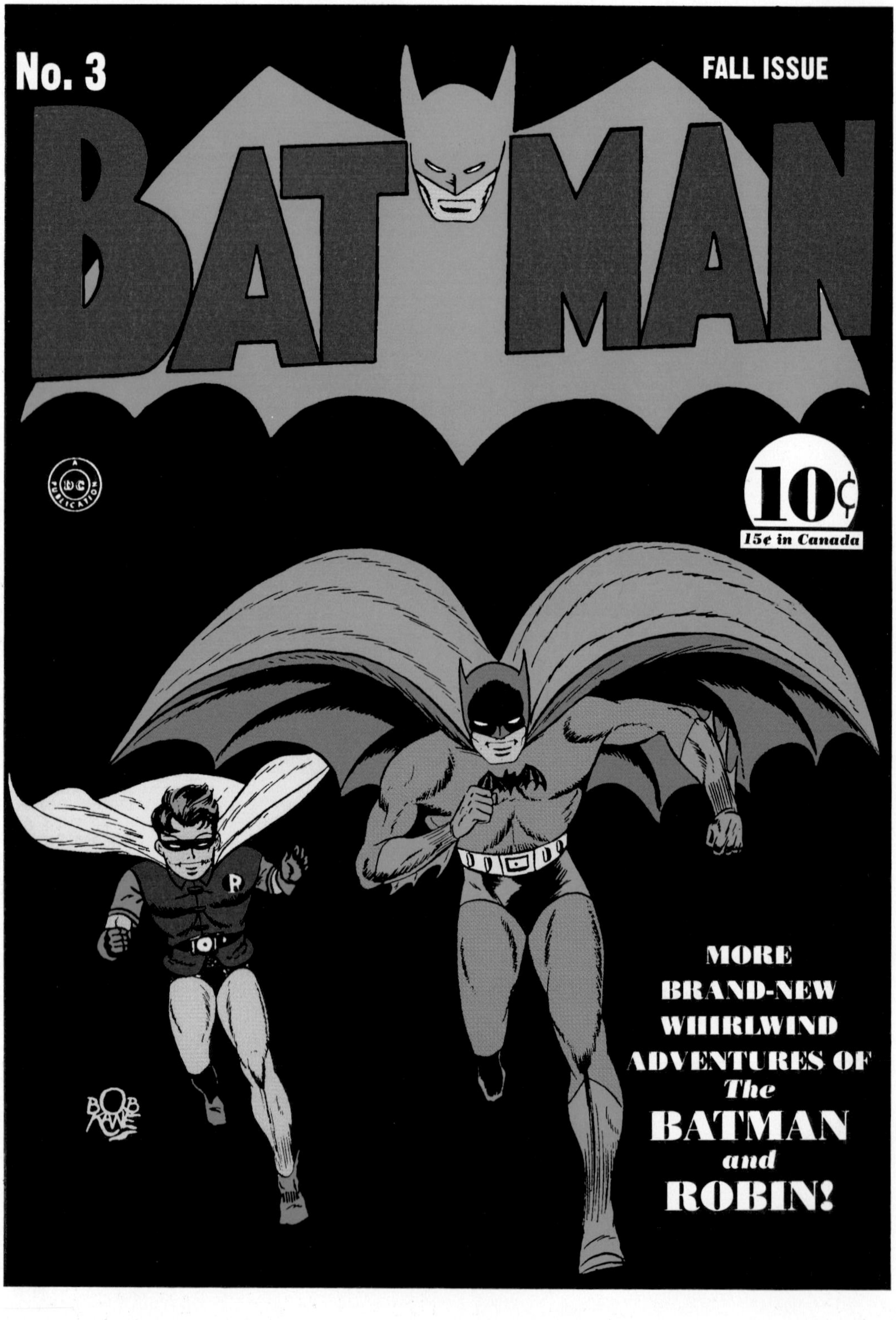
No. 3
FALL ISSUE
BATMAN
10¢
15¢ in Canada
MORE
BRAND-NEW
WHIRLWIND
ADVENTURES OF
The
BATMAN
and
ROBIN!
BOB KANE

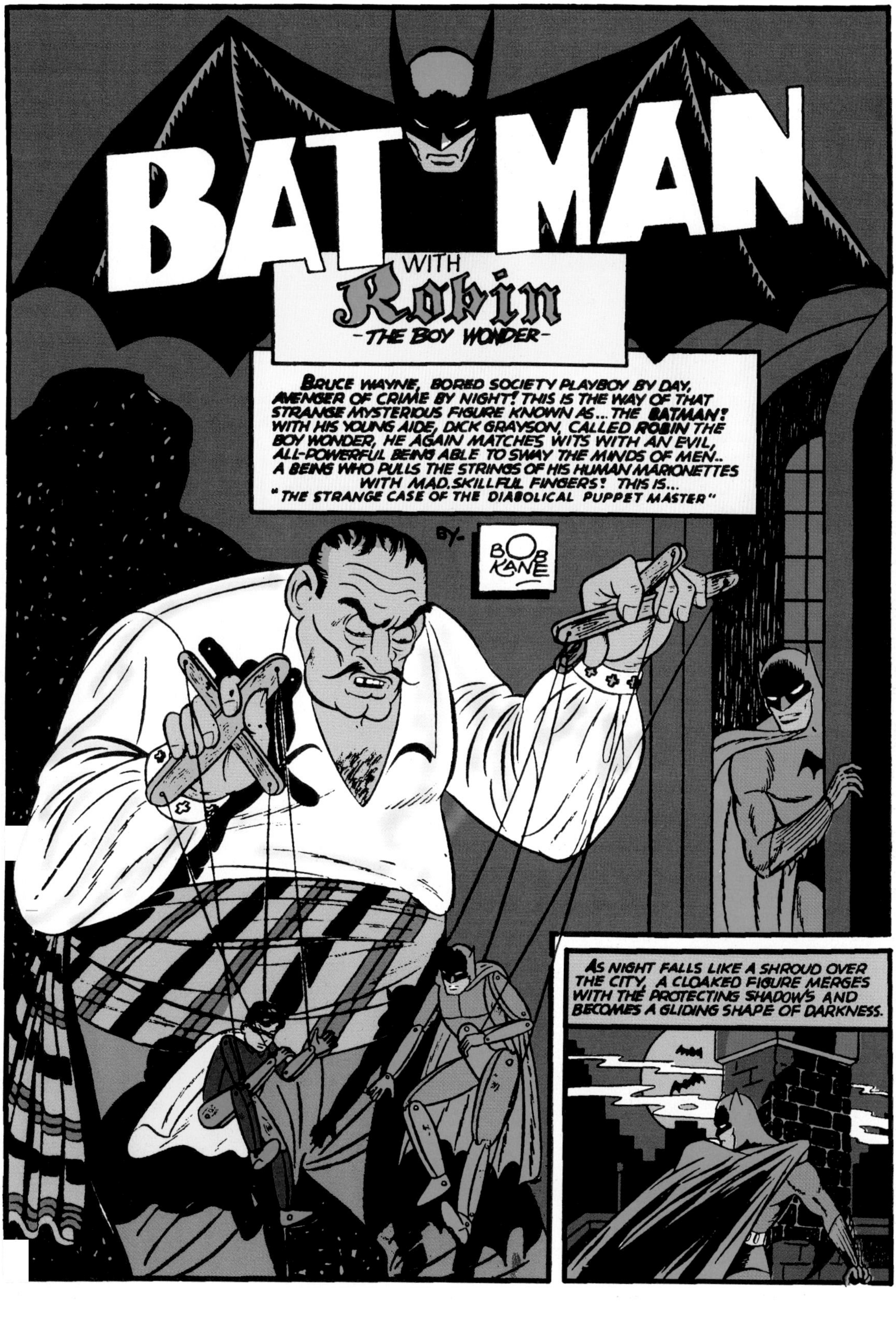
BATMAN
WITH
Robin
-THE BOY WONDER-
BRUCE WAYNE, BORED SOCIETY PLAYBOY BY DAY, AVENGER OF CRIME BY NIGHT! THIS IS THE WAY OF THAT STRANGE MYSTERIOUS FIGURE KNOWN AS... THE BATMAN! WITH HIS YOUNG AIDE, DICK GRAYSON, CALLED ROBIN THE BOY WONDER, HE AGAIN MATCHES WITS WITH AN EVIL, ALL-POWERFUL BEING ABLE TO SWAY THE MINDS OF MEN.. A BEING WHO PULLS THE STRINGS OF HIS HUMAN MARIONETTES WITH MAD, SKILLFUL FINGERS! THIS IS... "THE STRANGE CASE OF THE DIABOLICAL PUPPET MASTER"
BY- BOB KANE
AS NIGHT FALLS LIKE A SHROUD OVER THE CITY, A CLOAKED FIGURE MERGES WITH THE PROTECTING SHADOWS AND BECOMES A GLIDING SHAPE OF DARKNESS.

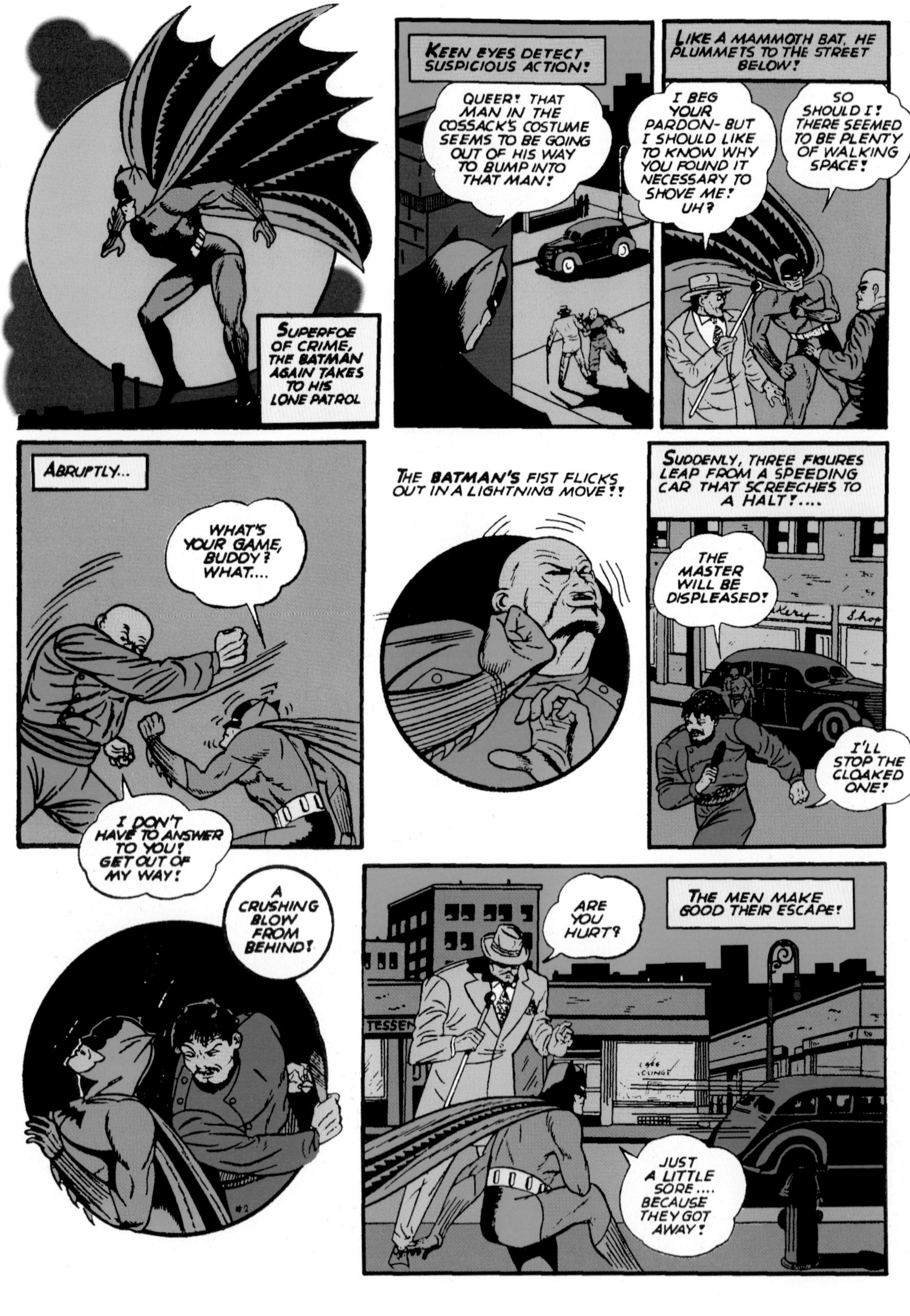
SUPERFOE OF CRIME, THE BATMAN AGAIN TAKES TO HIS LONE PATROL
KEEN EYES DETECT SUSPICIOUS ACTION!
QUEER! THAT MAN IN THE COSSACK'S COSTUME SEEMS TO BE GOING OUT OF HIS WAY TO BUMP INTO THAT MAN!
LIKE A MAMMOTH BAT, HE PLUMMETS TO THE STREET BELOW!
I BEG YOUR PARDON- BUT I SHOULD LIKE TO KNOW WHY YOU FOUND IT NECESSARY TO SHOVE ME! UH?
SO SHOULD I! THERE SEEMED TO BE PLENTY OF WALKING SPACE!
ABRUPTLY...
WHAT'S YOUR GAME, BUDDY? WHAT....
I DON'T HAVE TO ANSWER TO YOU! GET OUT OF MY WAY!
THE BATMAN'S FIST FLICKS OUT IN A LIGHTNING MOVE!!
SUDDENLY, THREE FIGURES LEAP FROM A SPEEDING CAR THAT SCREECHES TO A HALT!....
THE MASTER WILL BE DISPLEASED!
I'LL STOP THE CLOAKED ONE!
A CRUSHING BLOW FROM BEHIND!
ARE YOU HURT?
THE MEN MAKE GOOD THEIR ESCAPE!
JUST A LITTLE SORE.... BECAUSE THEY GOT AWAY!

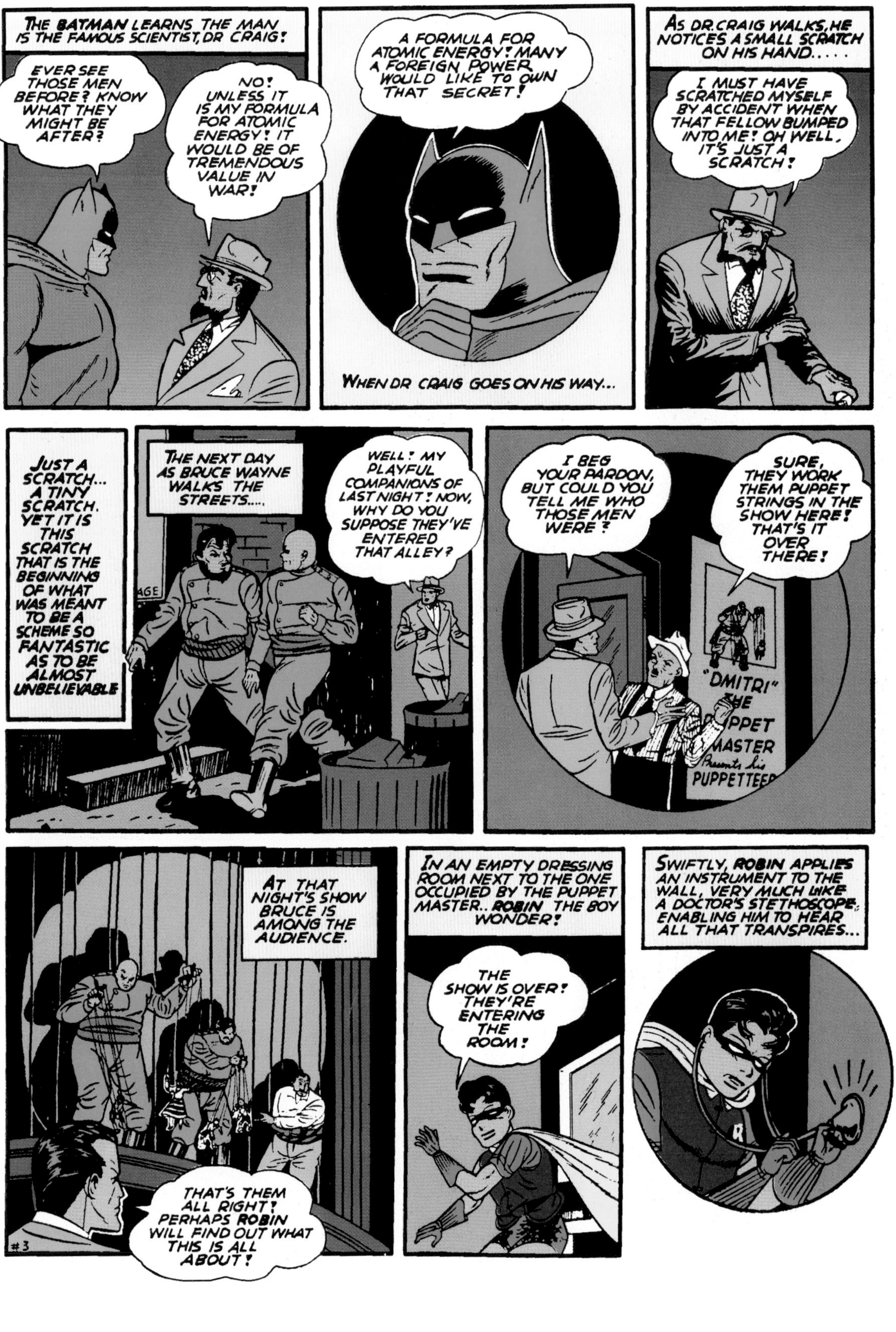
THE BATMAN LEARNS THE MAN IS THE FAMOUS SCIENTIST, DR CRAIG!
EVER SEE THOSE MEN BEFORE? KNOW WHAT THEY MIGHT BE AFTER?
NO! UNLESS IT IS MY FORMULA FOR ATOMIC ENERGY! IT WOULD BE OF TREMENDOUS VALUE IN WAR!
A FORMULA FOR ATOMIC ENERGY! MANY A FOREIGN POWER WOULD LIKE TO OWN THAT SECRET!
WHEN DR CRAIG GOES ON HIS WAY...
AS DR. CRAIG WALKS, HE NOTICES A SMALL SCRATCH ON HIS HAND.....
I MUST HAVE SCRATCHED MYSELF BY ACCIDENT WHEN THAT FELLOW BUMPED INTO ME! OH WELL, IT'S JUST A SCRATCH!
JUST A SCRATCH... A TINY SCRATCH. YET IT IS THIS SCRATCH THAT IS THE BEGINNING OF WHAT WAS MEANT TO BE A SCHEME SO FANTASTIC AS TO BE ALMOST UNBELIEVABLE
THE NEXT DAY AS BRUCE WAYNE WALKS THE STREETS.....
WELL! MY PLAYFUL COMPANIONS OF LAST NIGHT! NOW, WHY DO YOU SUPPOSE THEY'VE ENTERED THAT ALLEY?
I BEG YOUR PARDON, BUT COULD YOU TELL ME WHO THOSE MEN WERE?
SURE, THEY WORK THEM PUPPET STRINGS IN THE SHOW HERE! THAT'S IT OVER THERE!
"DMITRI" THE PUPPET MASTER Presents his PUPPETTEER
AT THAT NIGHT'S SHOW BRUCE IS AMONG THE AUDIENCE.
THAT'S THEM ALL RIGHT! PERHAPS ROBIN WILL FIND OUT WHAT THIS IS ALL ABOUT!
#3
IN AN EMPTY DRESSING ROOM NEXT TO THE ONE OCCUPIED BY THE PUPPET MASTER.. ROBIN THE BOY WONDER!
THE SHOW IS OVER! THEY'RE ENTERING THE ROOM!
SWIFTLY, ROBIN APPLIES AN INSTRUMENT TO THE WALL, VERY MUCH LIKE A DOCTOR'S STETHOSCOPE, ENABLING HIM TO HEAR ALL THAT TRANSPIRES...

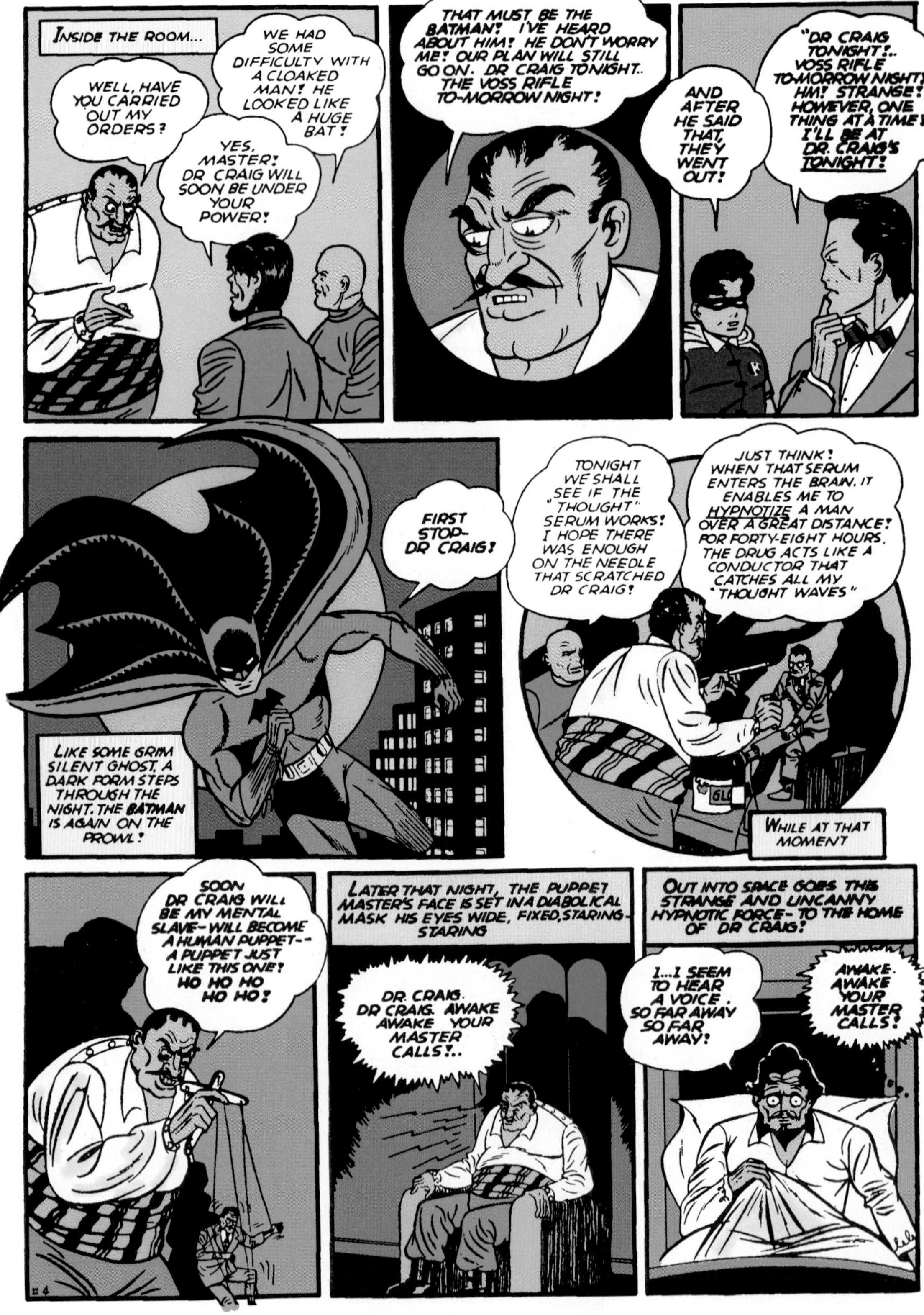
INSIDE THE ROOM...
WELL, HAVE YOU CARRIED OUT MY ORDERS?
WE HAD SOME DIFFICULTY WITH A CLOAKED MAN! HE LOOKED LIKE A HUGE BAT!
YES, MASTER! DR CRAIG WILL SOON BE UNDER YOUR POWER!
THAT MUST BE THE BATMAN! I'VE HEARD ABOUT HIM! HE DON'T WORRY ME! OUR PLAN WILL STILL GO ON. DR CRAIG TONIGHT.. THE VOSS RIFLE TO-MORROW NIGHT!
AND AFTER HE SAID THAT, THEY WENT OUT!
"DR CRAIG TONIGHT!.. VOSS RIFLE TO-MORROW NIGHT!" HM! STRANGE! HOWEVER, ONE THING AT A TIME! I'LL BE AT DR. CRAIG'S TONIGHT!
FIRST STOP- DR CRAIG!
LIKE SOME GRIM SILENT GHOST, A DARK FORM STEPS THROUGH THE NIGHT. THE BATMAN IS AGAIN ON THE PROWL!
WHILE AT THAT MOMENT
TONIGHT WE SHALL SEE IF THE "THOUGHT" SERUM WORKS! I HOPE THERE WAS ENOUGH ON THE NEEDLE THAT SCRATCHED DR CRAIG!
JUST THINK! WHEN THAT SERUM ENTERS THE BRAIN, IT ENABLES ME TO HYPNOTIZE A MAN OVER A GREAT DISTANCE! FOR FORTY-EIGHT HOURS, THE DRUG ACTS LIKE A CONDUCTOR THAT CATCHES ALL MY "THOUGHT WAVES"
SOON DR CRAIG WILL BE MY MENTAL SLAVE- WILL BECOME A HUMAN PUPPET-- A PUPPET JUST LIKE THIS ONE! HO HO HO HO HO!
LATER THAT NIGHT, THE PUPPET MASTER'S FACE IS SET IN A DIABOLICAL MASK HIS EYES WIDE, FIXED, STARING-STARING
DR. CRAIG. DR CRAIG. AWAKE AWAKE YOUR MASTER CALLS!..
OUT INTO SPACE GOES THIS STRANGE AND UNCANNY HYPNOTIC FORCE- TO THE HOME OF DR CRAIG!
I...I SEEM TO HEAR A VOICE. SO FAR AWAY SO FAR AWAY!
AWAKE. AWAKE YOUR MASTER CALLS!

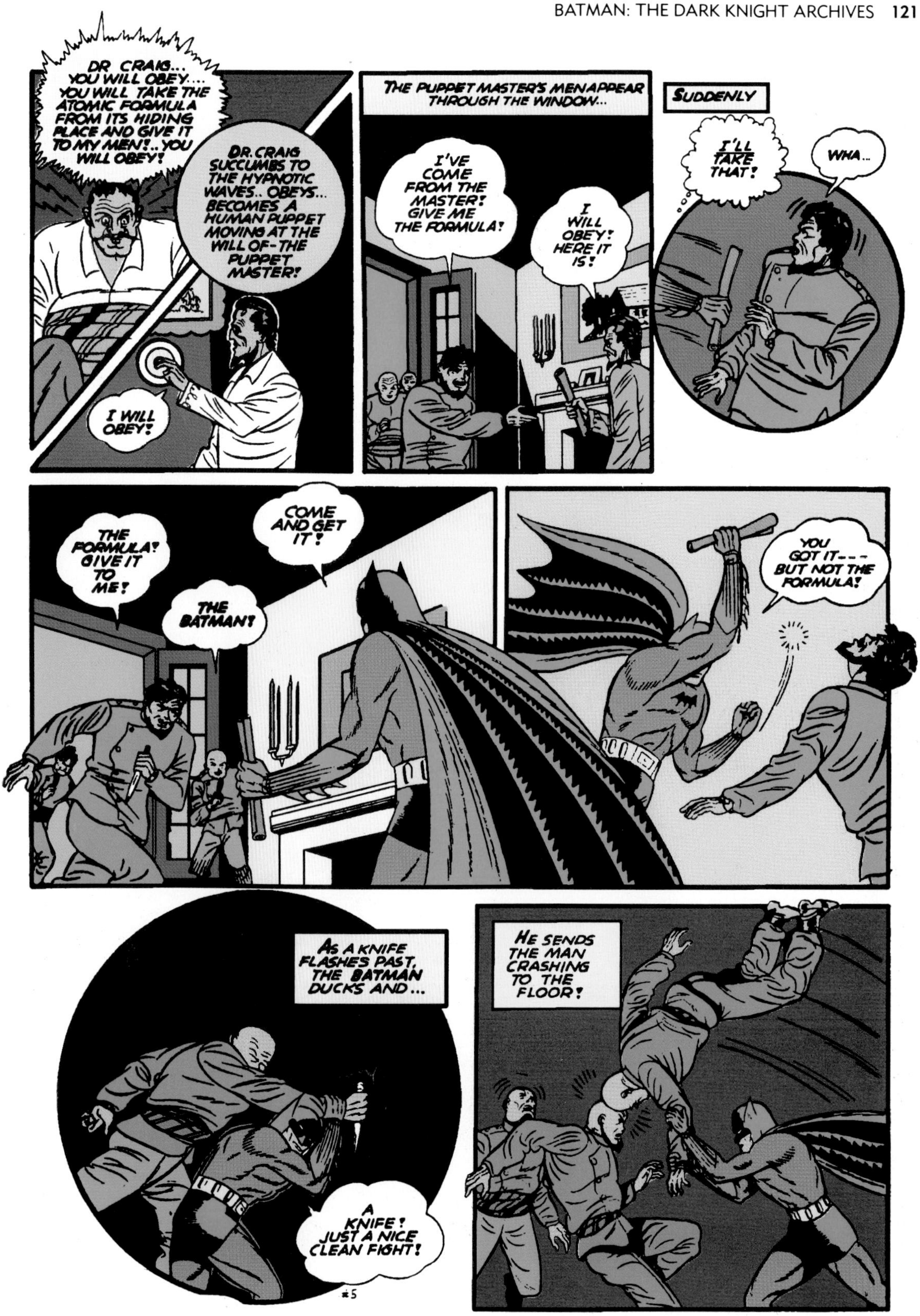
DR. CRAIG... YOU WILL OBEY.... YOU WILL TAKE THE ATOMIC FORMULA FROM ITS HIDING PLACE AND GIVE IT TO MY MEN!..YOU WILL OBEY!
DR. CRAIG SUCCUMBS TO THE HYPNOTIC WAVES.. OBEYS... BECOMES A HUMAN PUPPET MOVING AT THE WILL OF-THE PUPPET MASTER!
I WILL OBEY!
THE PUPPET MASTER'S MEN APPEAR THROUGH THE WINDOW...
I'VE COME FROM THE MASTER! GIVE ME THE FORMULA!
I WILL OBEY! HERE IT IS!
SUDDENLY
I'LL TAKE THAT!
WHA...
THE FORMULA! GIVE IT TO ME!
COME AND GET IT!
THE BATMAN!
YOU GOT IT--- BUT NOT THE FORMULA!
AS A KNIFE FLASHES PAST, THE BATMAN DUCKS AND...
A KNIFE! JUST A NICE CLEAN FIGHT!
HE SENDS THE MAN CRASHING TO THE FLOOR!
#5

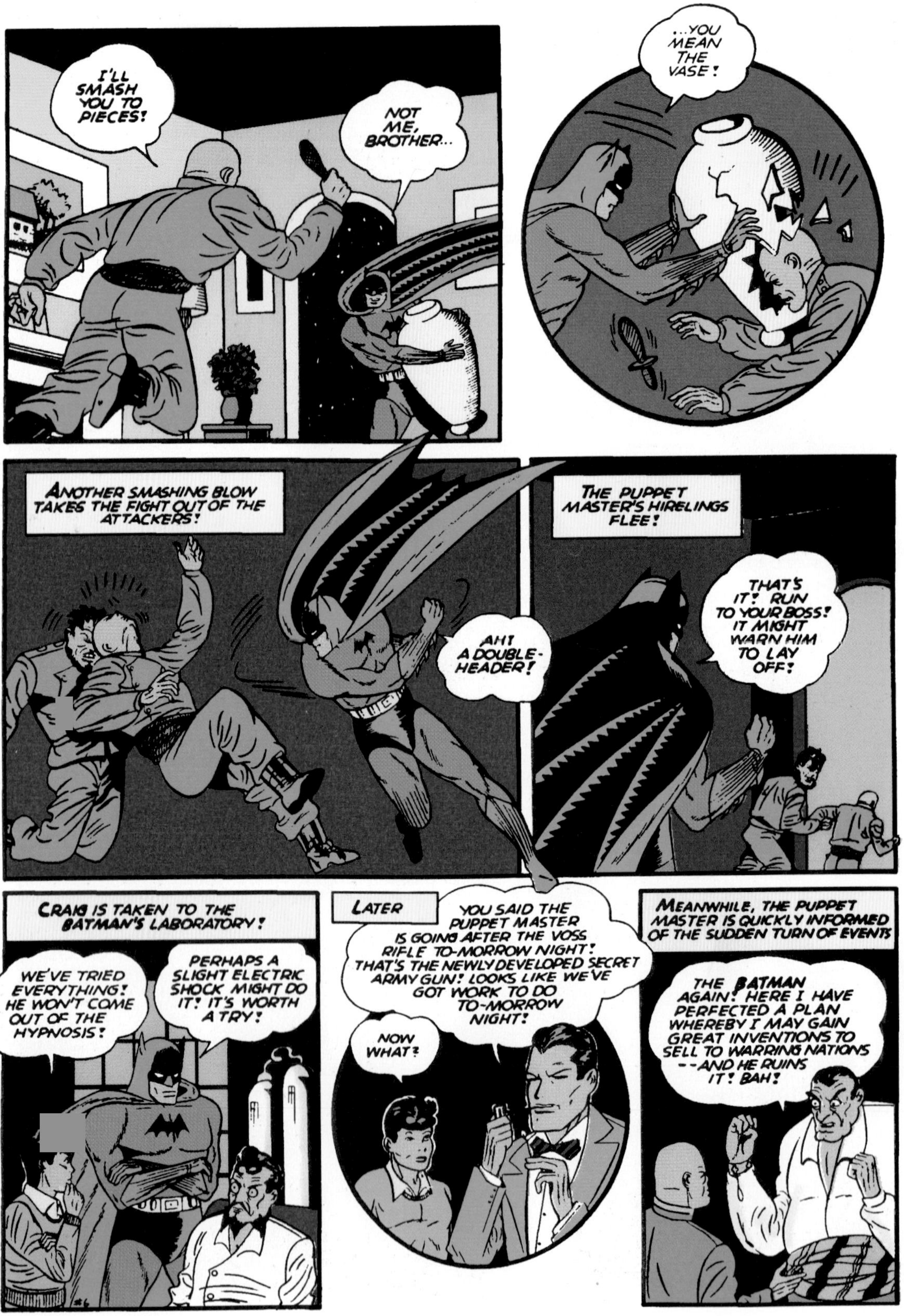
I'LL SMASH YOU TO PIECES!
NOT ME, BROTHER...
...YOU MEAN THE VASE!
ANOTHER SMASHING BLOW TAKES THE FIGHT OUT OF THE ATTACKERS!
AH! A DOUBLE-HEADER!
THE PUPPET MASTER'S HIRELINGS FLEE!
THAT'S IT! RUN TO YOUR BOSS! IT MIGHT WARN HIM TO LAY OFF!
CRAIG IS TAKEN TO THE BATMAN'S LABORATORY!
WE'VE TRIED EVERYTHING! HE WON'T COME OUT OF THE HYPNOSIS!
PERHAPS A SLIGHT ELECTRIC SHOCK MIGHT DO IT! IT'S WORTH A TRY!
LATER
YOU SAID THE PUPPET MASTER IS GOING AFTER THE VOSS RIFLE TO-MORROW NIGHT! THAT'S THE NEWLY DEVELOPED SECRET ARMY GUN! LOOKS LIKE WE'VE GOT WORK TO DO TO-MORROW NIGHT!
NOW WHAT?
MEANWHILE, THE PUPPET MASTER IS QUICKLY INFORMED OF THE SUDDEN TURN OF EVENTS
THE BATMAN AGAIN! HERE I HAVE PERFECTED A PLAN WHEREBY I MAY GAIN GREAT INVENTIONS TO SELL TO WARRING NATIONS --AND HE RUINS IT! BAH!

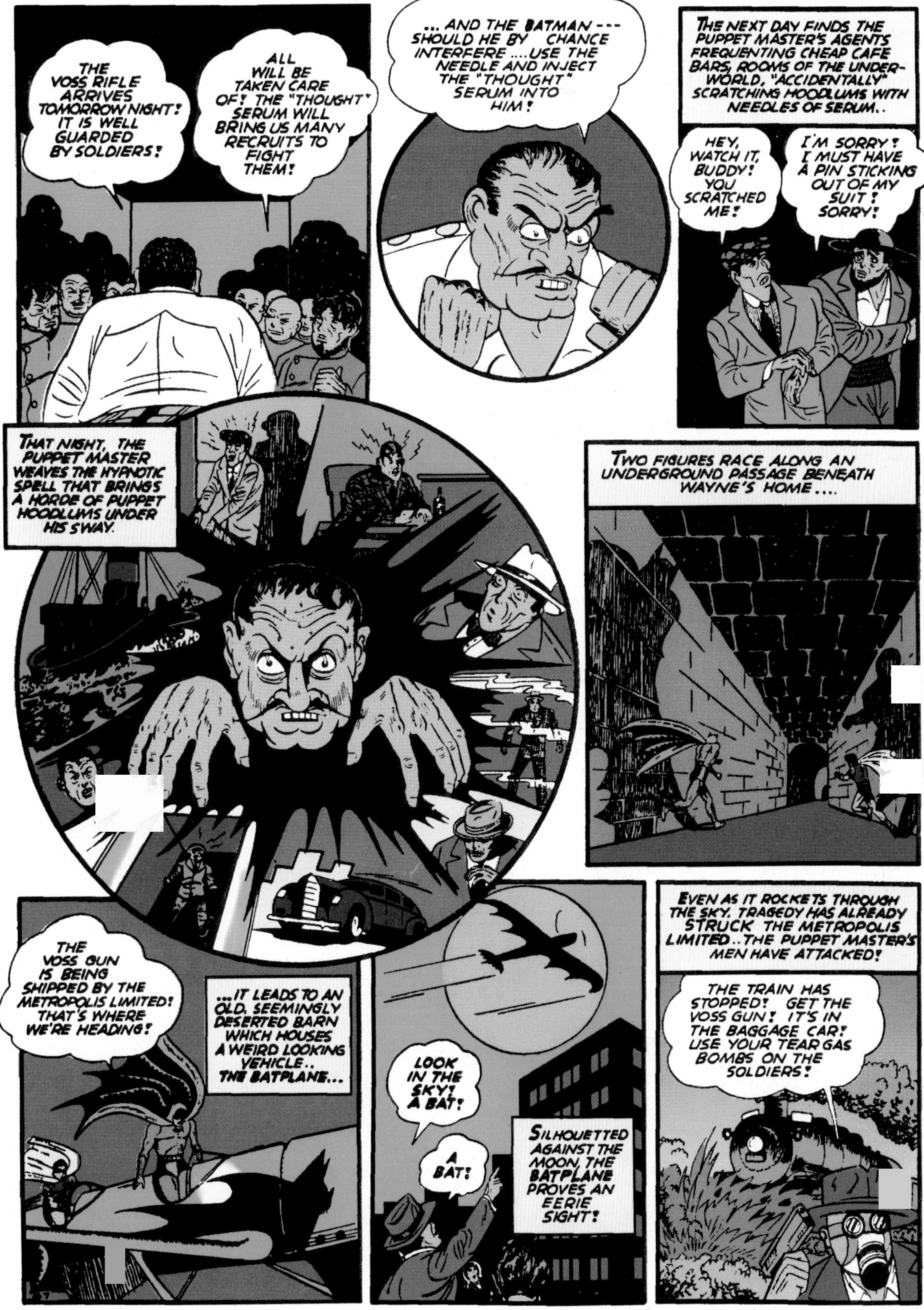
THE VOSS RIFLE ARRIVES TOMORROW NIGHT! IT IS WELL GUARDED BY SOLDIERS!
ALL WILL BE TAKEN CARE OF! THE "THOUGHT" SERUM WILL BRING US MANY RECRUITS TO FIGHT THEM!
...AND THE BATMAN --- SHOULD HE BY CHANCE INTERFERE ....USE THE NEEDLE AND INJECT THE "THOUGHT" SERUM INTO HIM!
THE NEXT DAY FINDS THE PUPPET MASTER'S AGENTS FREQUENTING CHEAP CAFE BARS, ROOMS OF THE UNDER-WORLD, "ACCIDENTALLY" SCRATCHING HOODLUMS WITH NEEDLES OF SERUM..
HEY, WATCH IT, BUDDY! YOU SCRATCHED ME!
I'M SORRY! I MUST HAVE A PIN STICKING OUT OF MY SUIT! SORRY!
THAT NIGHT, THE PUPPET MASTER WEAVES THE HYPNOTIC SPELL THAT BRINGS A HORDE OF PUPPET HOODLUMS UNDER HIS SWAY.
TWO FIGURES RACE ALONG AN UNDERGROUND PASSAGE BENEATH WAYNE'S HOME....
THE VOSS GUN IS BEING SHIPPED BY THE METROPOLIS LIMITED! THAT'S WHERE WE'RE HEADING!
...IT LEADS TO AN OLD, SEEMINGLY DESERTED BARN WHICH HOUSES A WEIRD LOOKING VEHICLE.. THE BATPLANE...
LOOK IN THE SKY! A BAT!
A BAT!
SILHOUETTED AGAINST THE MOON, THE BATPLANE PROVES AN EERIE SIGHT!
EVEN AS IT ROCKETS THROUGH THE SKY, TRAGEDY HAS ALREADY STRUCK THE METROPOLIS LIMITED..THE PUPPET MASTER'S MEN HAVE ATTACKED!
THE TRAIN HAS STOPPED! GET THE VOSS GUN! IT'S IN THE BAGGAGE CAR! USE YOUR TEAR GAS BOMBS ON THE SOLDIERS!

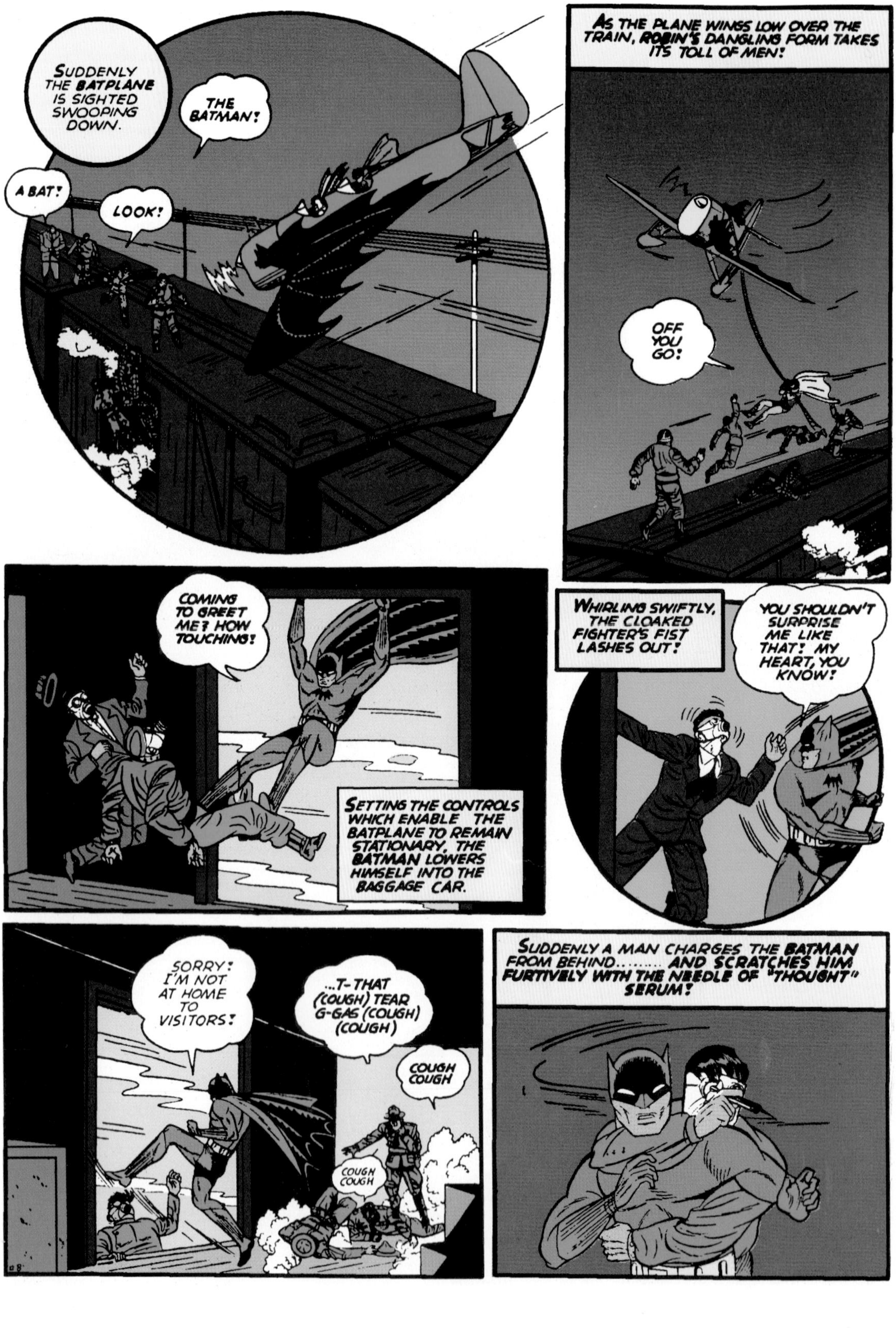
SUDDENLY THE BATPLANE IS SIGHTED SWOOPING DOWN.
THE BATMAN!
A BAT!
LOOK!
AS THE PLANE WINGS LOW OVER THE TRAIN, ROBIN'S DANGLING FORM TAKES ITS TOLL OF MEN!
OFF YOU GO!
COMING TO GREET ME? HOW TOUCHING!
SETTING THE CONTROLS WHICH ENABLE THE BATPLANE TO REMAIN STATIONARY, THE BATMAN LOWERS HIMSELF INTO THE BAGGAGE CAR.
WHIRLING SWIFTLY, THE CLOAKED FIGHTER'S FIST LASHES OUT!
YOU SHOULDN'T SURPRISE ME LIKE THAT! MY HEART, YOU KNOW!
SORRY! I'M NOT AT HOME TO VISITORS!
...T-THAT (COUGH) TEAR G-GAS (COUGH) (COUGH)
COUGH COUGH
COUGH COUGH
SUDDENLY A MAN CHARGES THE BATMAN FROM BEHIND........ AND SCRATCHES HIM FURTIVELY WITH THE NEEDLE OF "THOUGHT" SERUM!

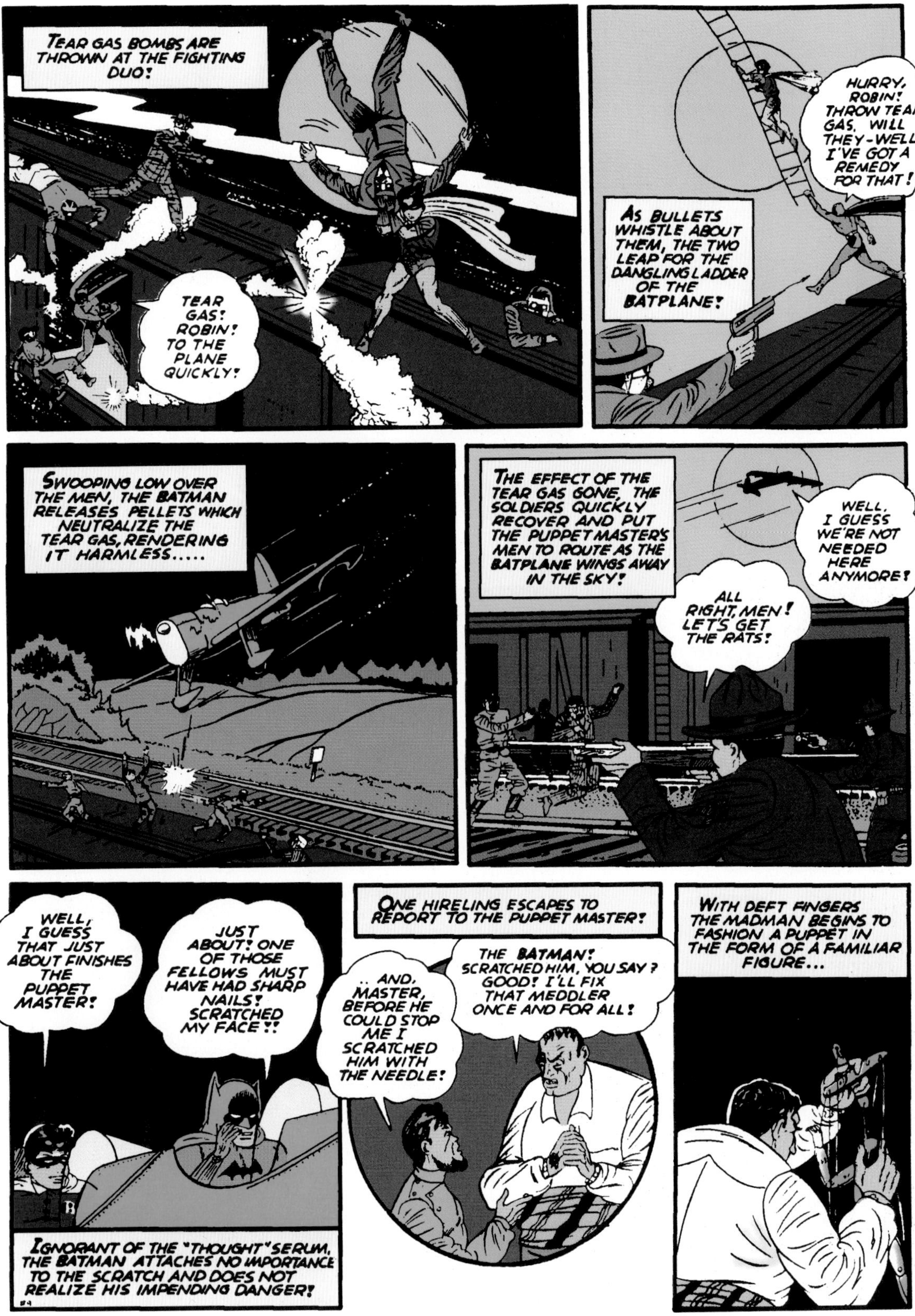
TEAR GAS BOMBS ARE THROWN AT THE FIGHTING DUO!
TEAR GAS! ROBIN! TO THE PLANE QUICKLY!
AS BULLETS WHISTLE ABOUT THEM, THE TWO LEAP FOR THE DANGLING LADDER OF THE BATPLANE!
HURRY, ROBIN! THROW TEAR GAS. WILL THEY-WELL, I'VE GOT A REMEDY FOR THAT!
SWOOPING LOW OVER THE MEN, THE BATMAN RELEASES PELLETS WHICH NEUTRALIZE THE TEAR GAS, RENDERING IT HARMLESS.....
THE EFFECT OF THE TEAR GAS GONE, THE SOLDIERS QUICKLY RECOVER AND PUT THE PUPPET MASTER'S MEN TO ROUTE AS THE BATPLANE WINGS AWAY IN THE SKY!
WELL, I GUESS WE'RE NOT NEEDED HERE ANYMORE!
ALL RIGHT, MEN! LET'S GET THE RATS!
WELL, I GUESS THAT JUST ABOUT FINISHES THE PUPPET MASTER!
JUST ABOUT! ONE OF THOSE FELLOWS MUST HAVE HAD SHARP NAILS! SCRATCHED MY FACE!!
IGNORANT OF THE "THOUGHT" SERUM, THE BATMAN ATTACHES NO IMPORTANCE TO THE SCRATCH AND DOES NOT REALIZE HIS IMPENDING DANGER!
ONE HIRELING ESCAPES TO REPORT TO THE PUPPET MASTER!
.. AND, MASTER, BEFORE HE COULD STOP ME I SCRATCHED HIM WITH THE NEEDLE!
THE BATMAN! SCRATCHED HIM, YOU SAY? GOOD! I'LL FIX THAT MEDDLER ONCE AND FOR ALL!
WITH DEFT FINGERS THE MADMAN BEGINS TO FASHION A PUPPET IN THE FORM OF A FAMILIAR FIGURE...

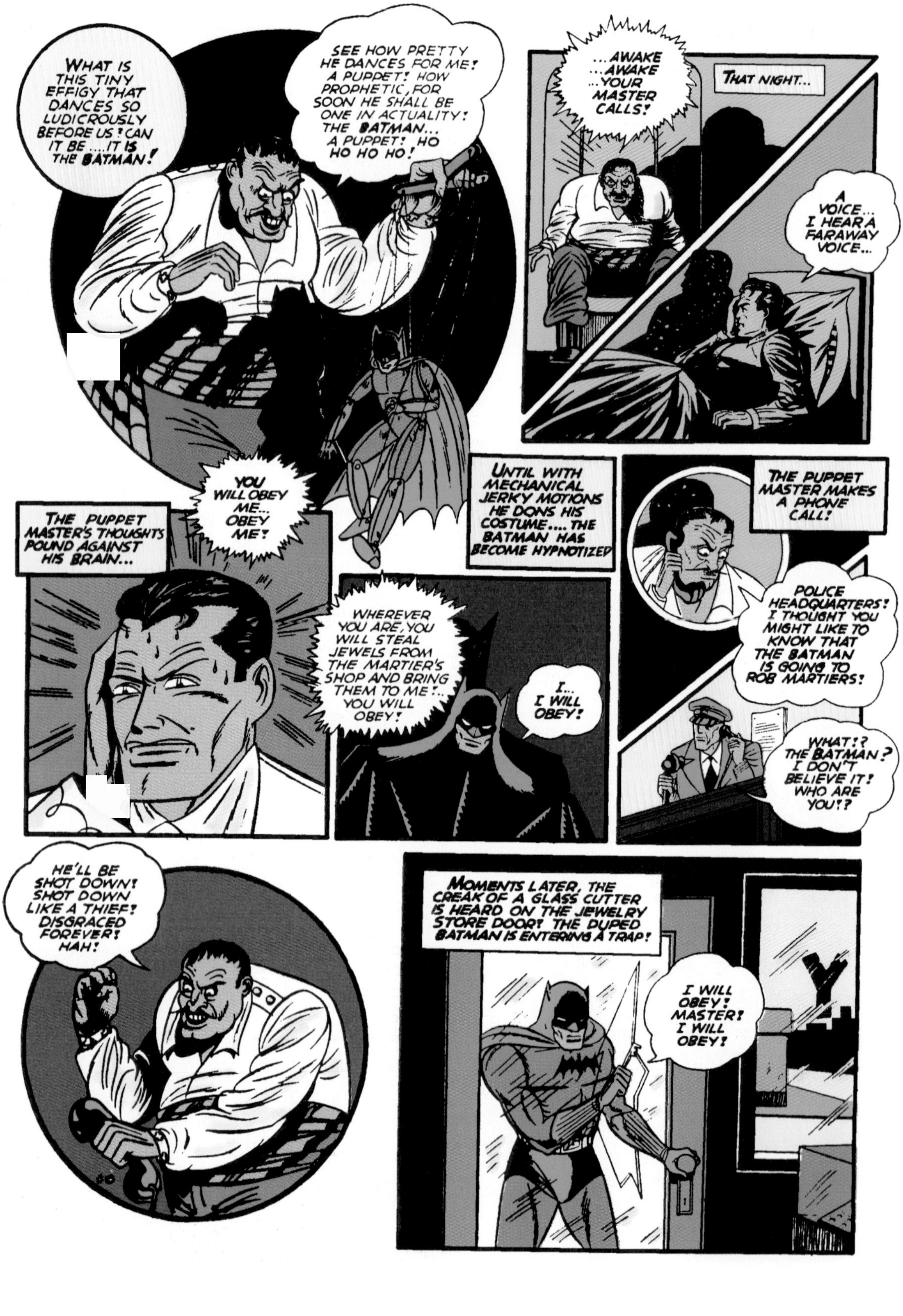
WHAT IS THIS TINY EFFIGY THAT DANCES SO LUDICROUSLY BEFORE US? CAN IT BE ....IT IS THE BATMAN!
SEE HOW PRETTY HE DANCES FOR ME! A PUPPET! HOW PROPHETIC, FOR SOON HE SHALL BE ONE IN ACTUALITY! THE BATMAN... A PUPPET! HO HO HO HO!
...AWAKE ...AWAKE ...YOUR MASTER CALLS!
THAT NIGHT...
A VOICE... I HEAR A FARAWAY VOICE...
THE PUPPET MASTER'S THOUGHTS POUND AGAINST HIS BRAIN...
YOU WILL OBEY ME... OBEY ME!
UNTIL WITH MECHANICAL JERKY MOTIONS HE DONS HIS COSTUME.... THE BATMAN HAS BECOME HYPNOTIZED
WHEREVER YOU ARE, YOU WILL STEAL JEWELS FROM THE MARTIER'S SHOP AND BRING THEM TO ME!.. YOU WILL OBEY!
I... I WILL OBEY!
THE PUPPET MASTER MAKES A PHONE CALL!
POLICE HEADQUARTERS! I THOUGHT YOU MIGHT LIKE TO KNOW THAT THE BATMAN IS GOING TO ROB MARTIERS!
WHAT!? THE BATMAN? I DON'T BELIEVE IT! WHO ARE YOU!?
HE'LL BE SHOT DOWN! SHOT DOWN LIKE A THIEF! DISGRACED FOREVER! HAH!
MOMENTS LATER, THE CREAK OF A GLASS CUTTER IS HEARD ON THE JEWELRY STORE DOOR! THE DUPED BATMAN IS ENTERING A TRAP!
I WILL OBEY! MASTER! I WILL OBEY!

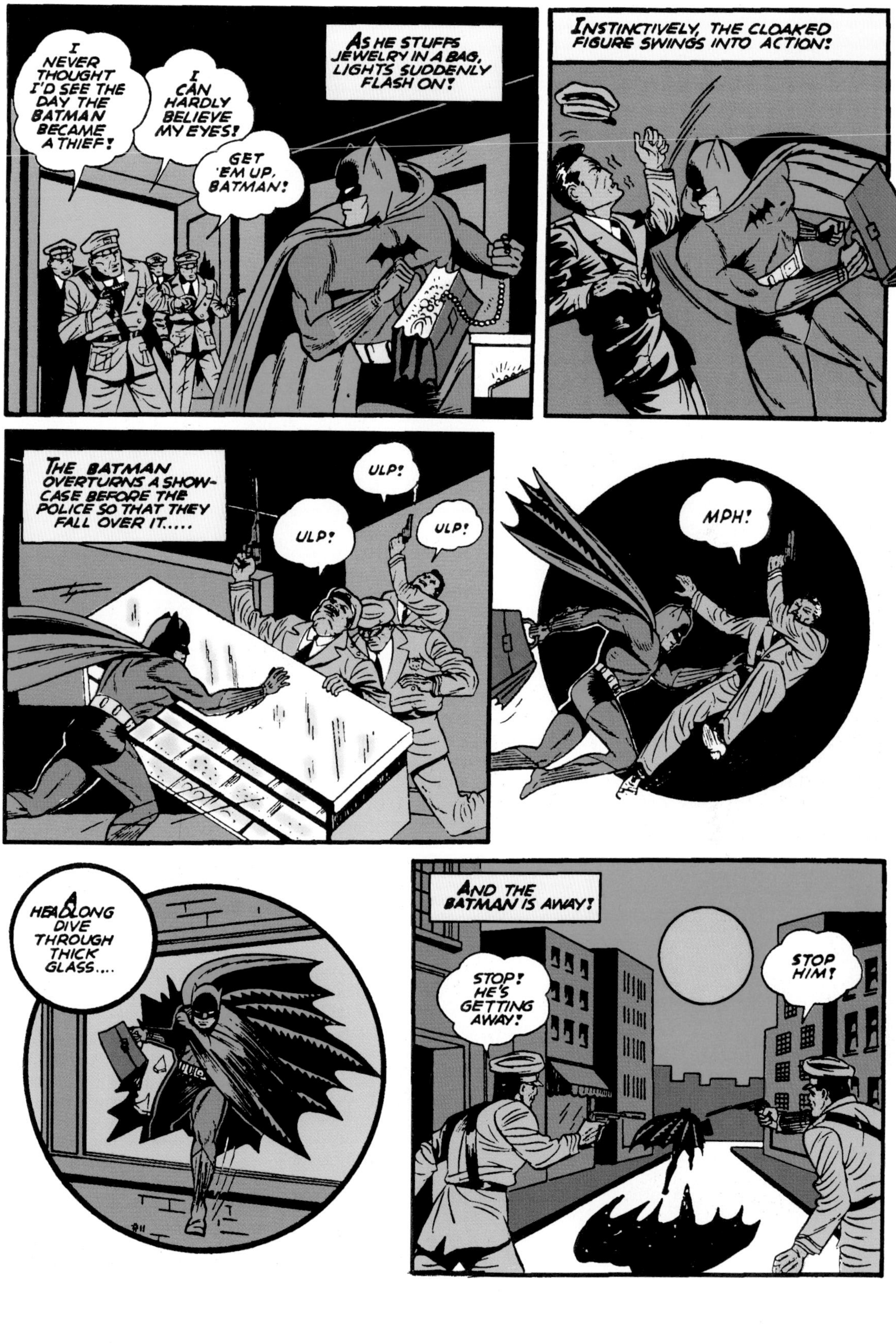
I NEVER THOUGHT I'D SEE THE DAY THE BATMAN BECAME A THIEF!
I CAN HARDLY BELIEVE MY EYES!
GET 'EM UP, BATMAN!
AS HE STUFFS JEWELRY IN A BAG, LIGHTS SUDDENLY FLASH ON!
INSTINCTIVELY, THE CLOAKED FIGURE SWINGS INTO ACTION!
THE BATMAN OVERTURNS A SHOW-CASE BEFORE THE POLICE SO THAT THEY FALL OVER IT.....
ULP!
ULP!
ULP!
MPH!
A HEADLONG DIVE THROUGH THICK GLASS....
AND THE BATMAN IS AWAY!
STOP! HE'S GETTING AWAY!
STOP HIM!

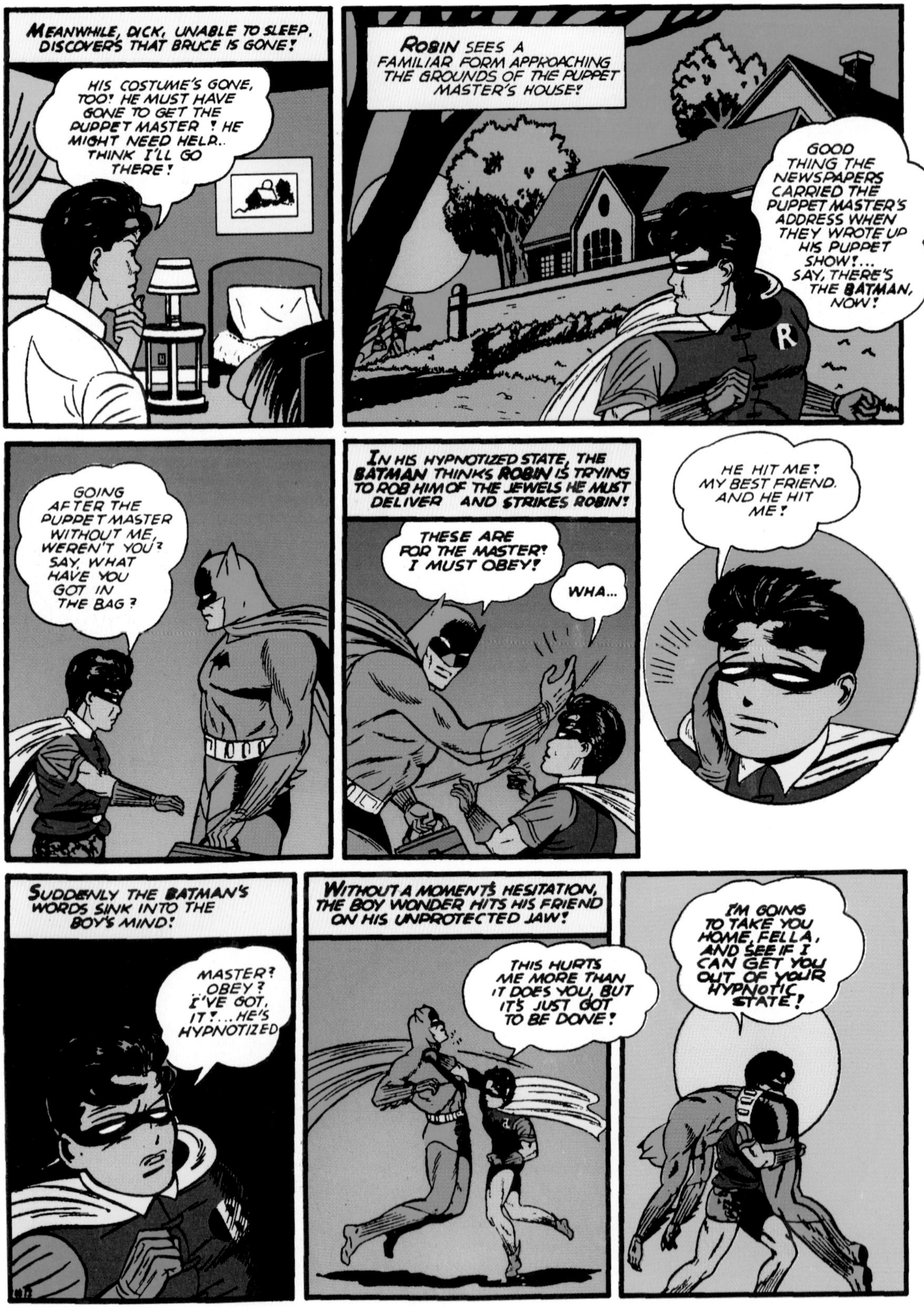
MEANWHILE, DICK, UNABLE TO SLEEP, DISCOVERS THAT BRUCE IS GONE!
HIS COSTUME'S GONE, TOO! HE MUST HAVE GONE TO GET THE PUPPET MASTER ! HE MIGHT NEED HELP.. THINK I'LL GO THERE!
ROBIN SEES A FAMILIAR FORM APPROACHING THE GROUNDS OF THE PUPPET MASTER'S HOUSE!
GOOD THING THE NEWSPAPERS CARRIED THE PUPPET MASTER'S ADDRESS WHEN THEY WROTE UP HIS PUPPET SHOW!... SAY, THERE'S THE BATMAN, NOW!
GOING AFTER THE PUPPET MASTER WITHOUT ME, WEREN'T YOU? SAY, WHAT HAVE YOU GOT IN THE BAG?
IN HIS HYPNOTIZED STATE, THE BATMAN THINKS ROBIN IS TRYING TO ROB HIM OF THE JEWELS HE MUST DELIVER AND STRIKES ROBIN!
THESE ARE FOR THE MASTER! I MUST OBEY!
WHA...
HE HIT ME! MY BEST FRIEND. AND HE HIT ME!
SUDDENLY THE BATMAN'S WORDS SINK INTO THE BOY'S MIND!
MASTER? ..OBEY? I'VE GOT IT!...HE'S HYPNOTIZED
WITHOUT A MOMENT'S HESITATION, THE BOY WONDER HITS HIS FRIEND ON HIS UNPROTECTED JAW!
THIS HURTS ME MORE THAN IT DOES YOU, BUT IT'S JUST GOT TO BE DONE!
I'M GOING TO TAKE YOU HOME, FELLA, AND SEE IF I CAN GET YOU OUT OF YOUR HYPNOTIC STATE!

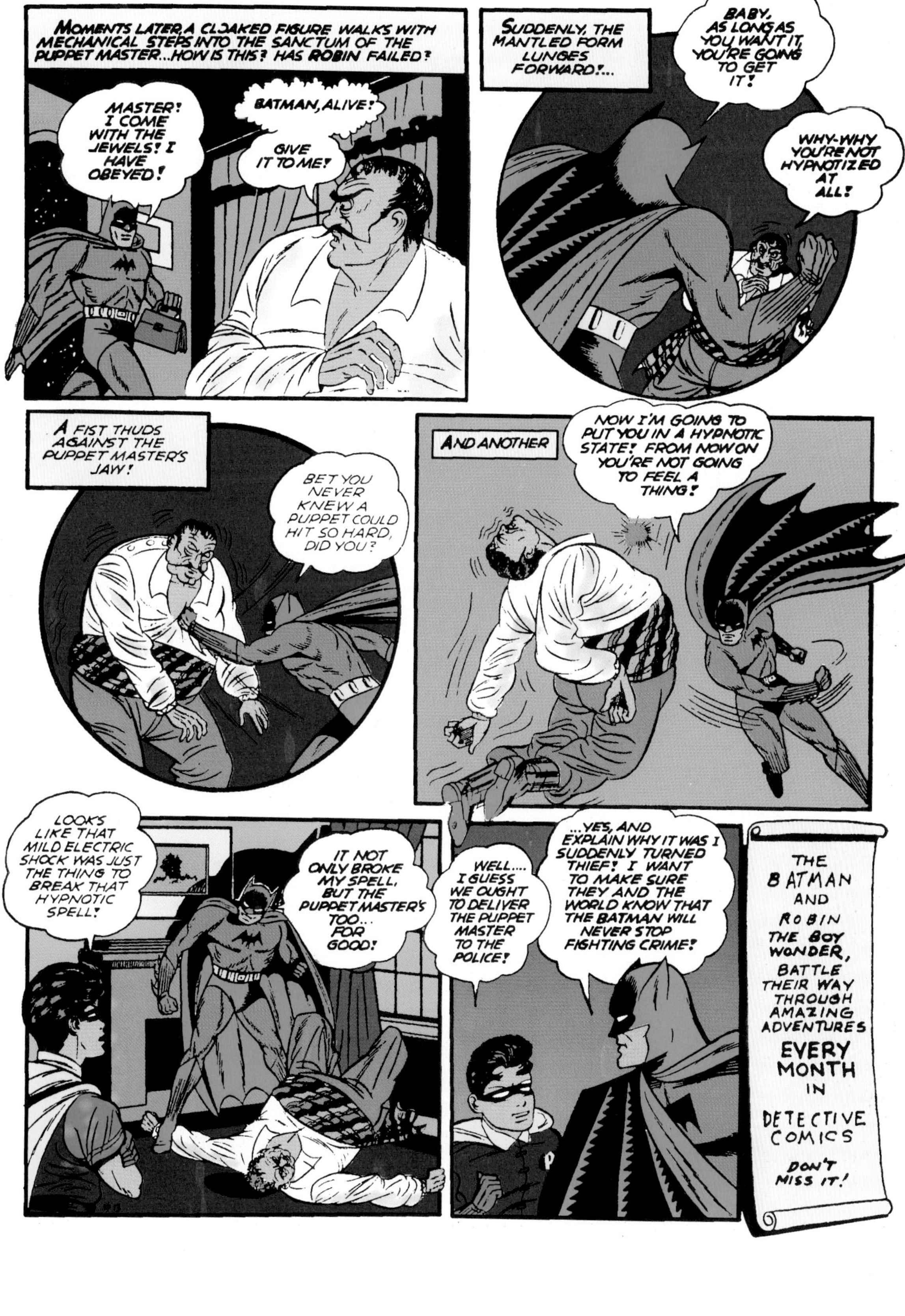
MOMENTS LATER, A CLOAKED FIGURE WALKS WITH MECHANICAL STEPS INTO THE SANCTUM OF THE PUPPET MASTER...HOW IS THIS? HAS ROBIN FAILED?
MASTER! I COME WITH THE JEWELS! I HAVE OBEYED!
BATMAN, ALIVE!
GIVE IT TO ME!
SUDDENLY, THE MANTLED FORM LUNGES FORWARD!...
BABY, AS LONG AS YOU WANT IT, YOU'RE GOING TO GET IT!
WHY-WHY YOU'RE NOT HYPNOTIZED AT ALL!
A FIST THUDS AGAINST THE PUPPET MASTER'S JAW!
BET YOU NEVER KNEW A PUPPET COULD HIT SO HARD, DID YOU?
AND ANOTHER
NOW I'M GOING TO PUT YOU IN A HYPNOTIC STATE! FROM NOW ON YOU'RE NOT GOING TO FEEL A THING!
LOOKS LIKE THAT MILD ELECTRIC SHOCK WAS JUST THE THING TO BREAK THAT HYPNOTIC SPELL!
IT NOT ONLY BROKE MY SPELL, BUT THE PUPPET MASTER'S TOO... FOR GOOD!
WELL.... I GUESS WE OUGHT TO DELIVER THE PUPPET MASTER TO THE POLICE!
...YES, AND EXPLAIN WHY IT WAS I SUDDENLY TURNED THIEF! I WANT TO MAKE SURE THEY AND THE WORLD KNOW THAT THE BATMAN WILL NEVER STOP FIGHTING CRIME!
THE BATMAN AND ROBIN THE BOY WONDER, BATTLE THEIR WAY THROUGH AMAZING ADVENTURES EVERY MONTH IN DETECTIVE COMICS
DON'T MISS IT!

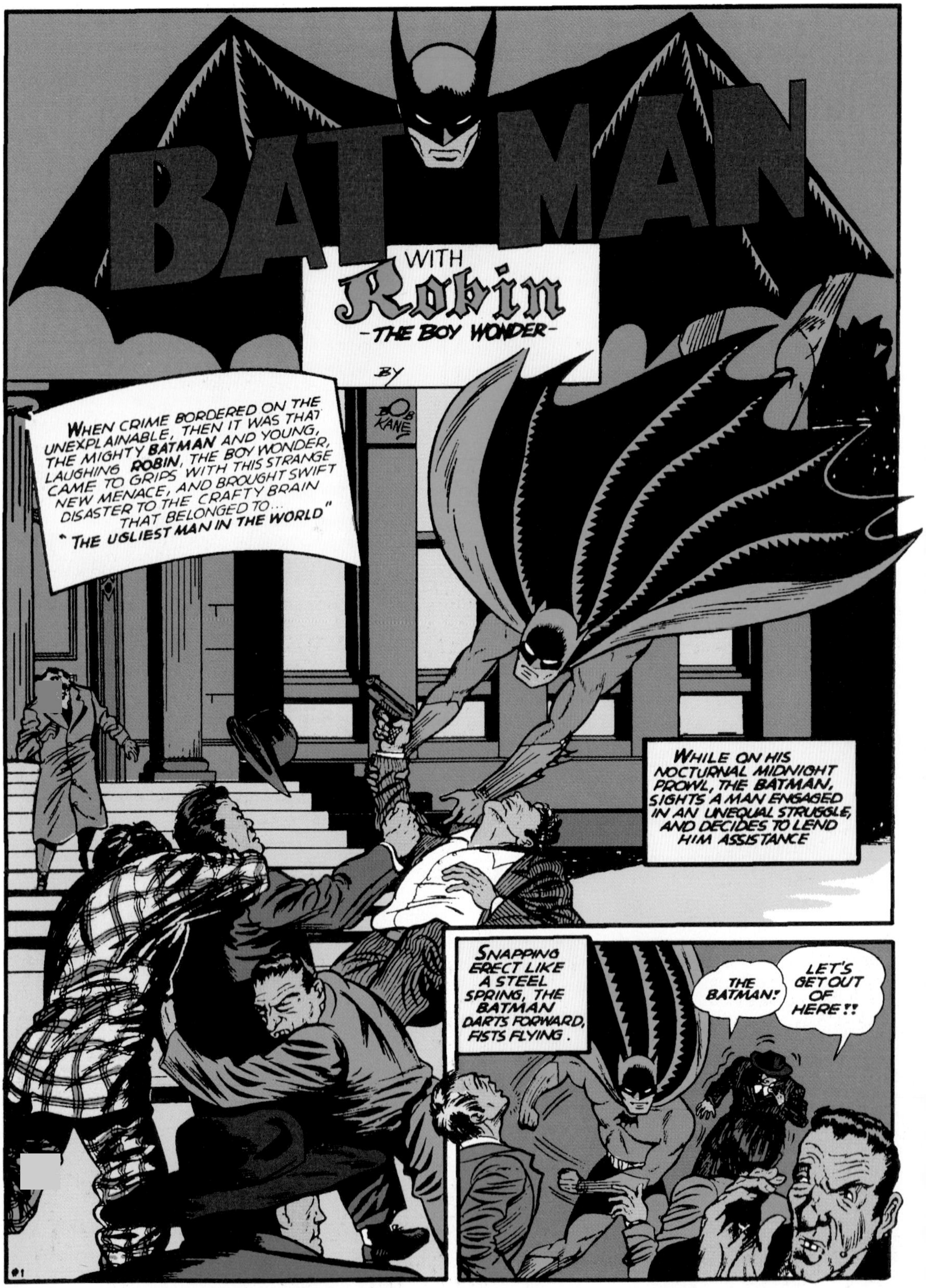
BATMAN
WITH Robin -THE BOY WONDER-
BY BOB KANE
WHEN CRIME BORDERED ON THE UNEXPLAINABLE, THEN IT WAS THAT THE MIGHTY BATMAN AND YOUNG, LAUGHING ROBIN, THE BOY WONDER, CAME TO GRIPS WITH THIS STRANGE NEW MENACE, AND BROUGHT SWIFT DISASTER TO THE CRAFTY BRAIN THAT BELONGED TO... "THE UGLIEST MAN IN THE WORLD"
WHILE ON HIS NOCTURNAL MIDNIGHT PROWL, THE BATMAN, SIGHTS A MAN ENGAGED IN AN UNEQUAL STRUGGLE, AND DECIDES TO LEND HIM ASSISTANCE
SNAPPING ERECT LIKE A STEEL SPRING, THE BATMAN DARTS FORWARD, FISTS FLYING.
THE BATMAN!
LET'S GET OUT OF HERE!!
#1

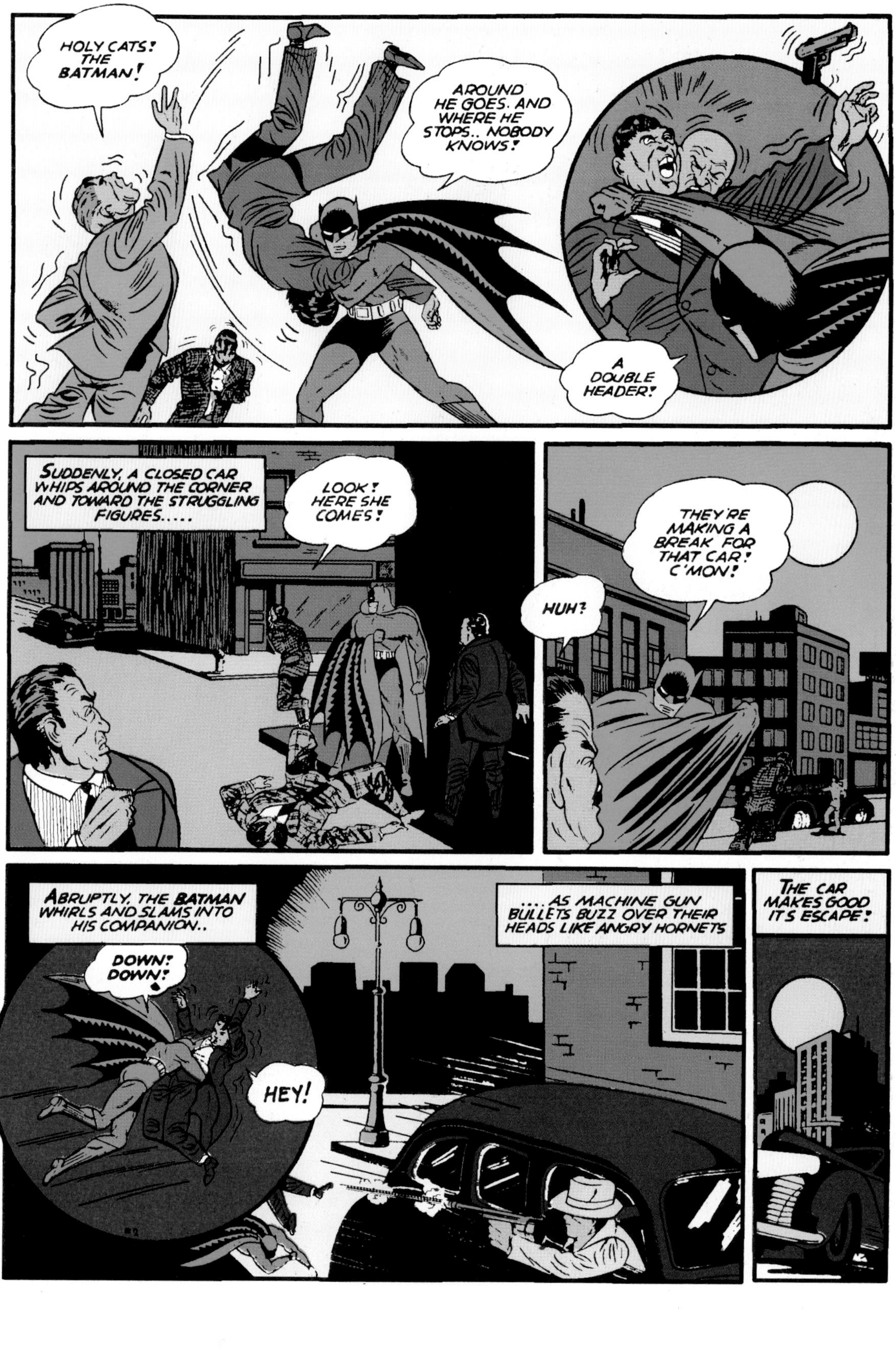
HOLY CATS! THE BATMAN!
AROUND HE GOES. AND WHERE HE STOPS.. NOBODY KNOWS!
A DOUBLE HEADER!
SUDDENLY, A CLOSED CAR WHIPS AROUND THE CORNER AND TOWARD THE STRUGGLING FIGURES.....
LOOK! HERE SHE COMES!
THEY'RE MAKING A BREAK FOR THAT CAR! C'MON!
HUH?
ABRUPTLY, THE BATMAN WHIRLS AND SLAMS INTO HIS COMPANION..
DOWN! DOWN!
HEY!
....AS MACHINE GUN BULLETS BUZZ OVER THEIR HEADS LIKE ANGRY HORNETS
THE CAR MAKES GOOD ITS ESCAPE!

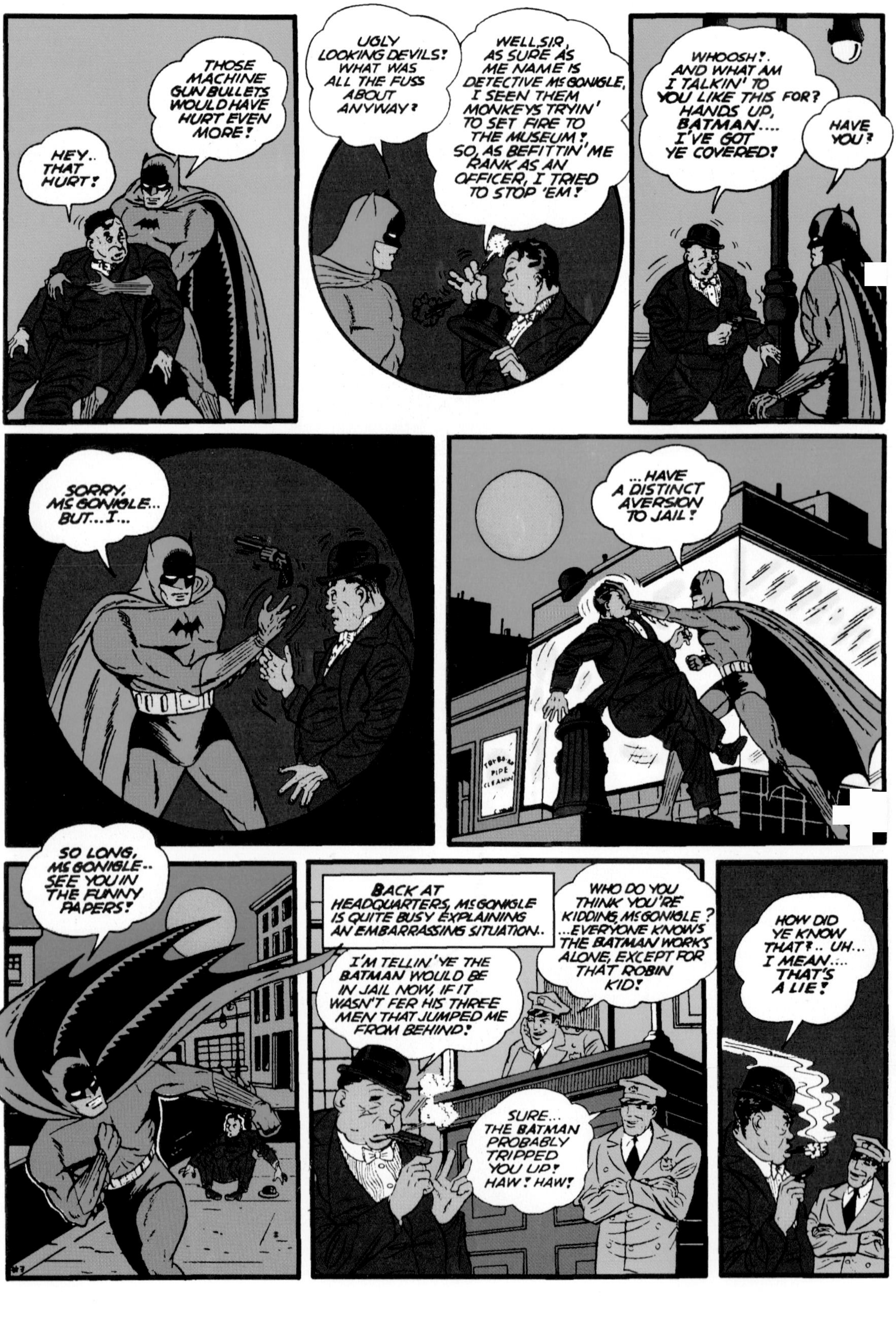
THOSE MACHINE GUN BULLETS WOULD HAVE HURT EVEN MORE!
HEY.. THAT HURT!
UGLY LOOKING DEVILS! WHAT WAS ALL THE FUSS ABOUT ANYWAY?
WELL,SIR, AS SURE AS ME NAME IS DETECTIVE MCGONIGLE, I SEEN THEM MONKEYS TRYIN' TO SET FIRE TO THE MUSEUM! SO, AS BEFITTIN' ME RANK AS AN OFFICER, I TRIED TO STOP 'EM!
WHOOSH!. AND WHAT AM I TALKIN' TO YOU LIKE THIS FOR? HANDS UP, BATMAN.... I'VE GOT YE COVERED!
HAVE YOU?
SORRY, MCGONIGLE... BUT...I...
...HAVE A DISTINCT AVERSION TO JAIL!
SO LONG, MCGONIGLE.. SEE YOU IN THE FUNNY PAPERS!
BACK AT HEADQUARTERS, MCGONIGLE IS QUITE BUSY EXPLAINING AN EMBARRASSING SITUATION..
I'M TELLIN' YE THE BATMAN WOULD BE IN JAIL NOW, IF IT WASN'T FER HIS THREE MEN THAT JUMPED ME FROM BEHIND!
WHO DO YOU THINK YOU'RE KIDDING, MCGONIGLE? ...EVERYONE KNOWS THE BATMAN WORKS ALONE, EXCEPT FOR THAT ROBIN KID!
SURE... THE BATMAN PROBABLY TRIPPED YOU UP! HAW! HAW!
HOW DID YE KNOW THAT?.. UH... I MEAN.... THAT'S A LIE!

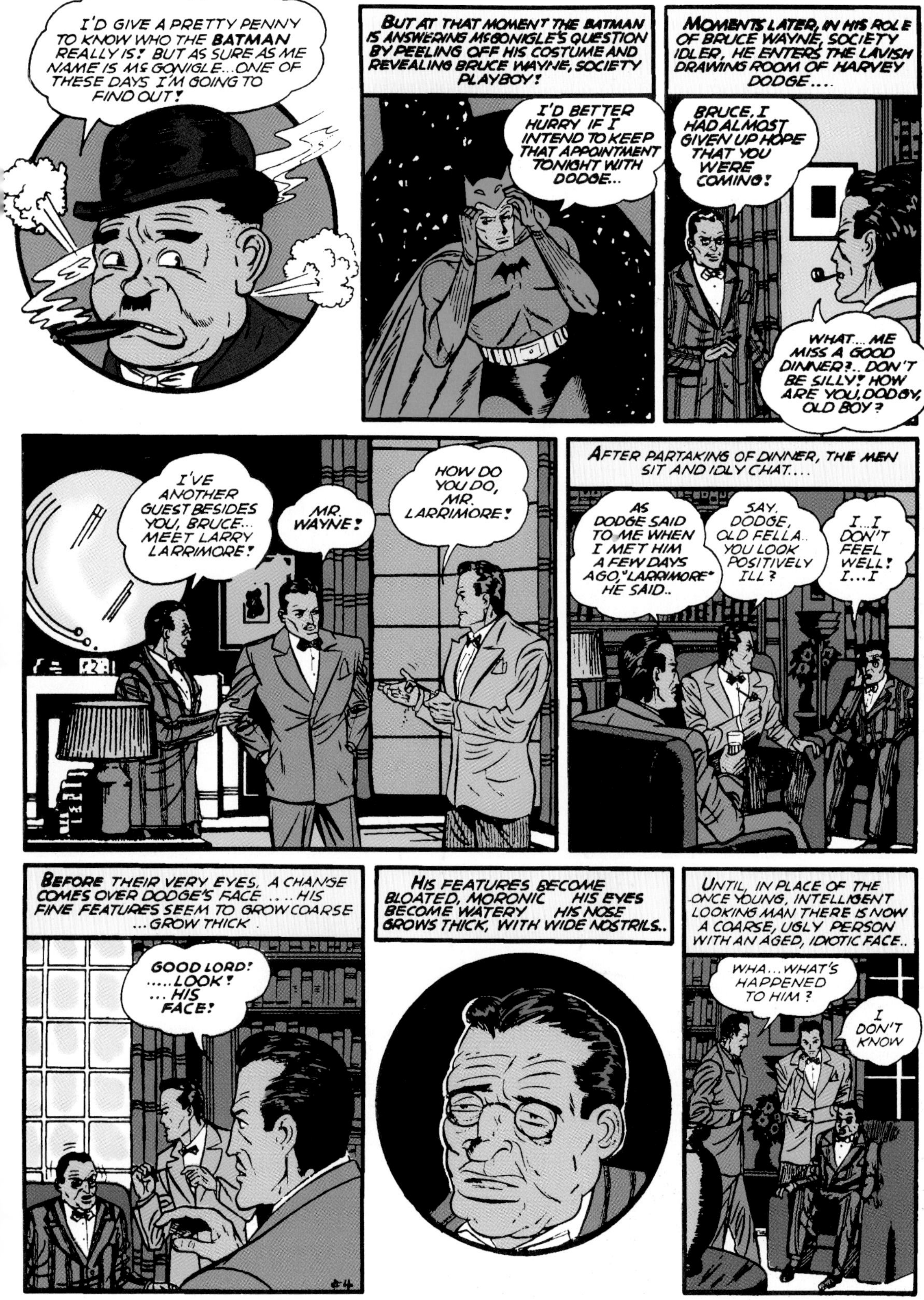
I'D GIVE A PRETTY PENNY TO KNOW WHO THE BATMAN REALLY IS! BUT AS SURE AS ME NAME IS McGONIGLE...ONE OF THESE DAYS I'M GOING TO FIND OUT!
BUT AT THAT MOMENT THE BATMAN IS ANSWERING McGONIGLE'S QUESTION BY PEELING OFF HIS COSTUME AND REVEALING BRUCE WAYNE, SOCIETY PLAYBOY!
I'D BETTER HURRY IF I INTEND TO KEEP THAT APPOINTMENT TONIGHT WITH DODGE...
MOMENTS LATER, IN HIS ROLE OF BRUCE WAYNE, SOCIETY IDLER, HE ENTERS THE LAVISH DRAWING ROOM OF HARVEY DODGE....
BRUCE, I HAD ALMOST GIVEN UP HOPE THAT YOU WERE COMING!
WHAT.... ME MISS A GOOD DINNER?.. DON'T BE SILLY! HOW ARE YOU, DODGY, OLD BOY?
I'VE ANOTHER GUEST BESIDES YOU, BRUCE... MEET LARRY LARRIMORE!
MR. WAYNE!
HOW DO YOU DO, MR. LARRIMORE!
AFTER PARTAKING OF DINNER, THE MEN SIT AND IDLY CHAT....
AS DODGE SAID TO ME WHEN I MET HIM A FEW DAYS AGO, "LARRIMORE" HE SAID..
SAY, DODGE, OLD FELLA.. YOU LOOK POSITIVELY ILL?
I...I DON'T FEEL WELL! I...I
BEFORE THEIR VERY EYES, A CHANGE COMES OVER DODGE'S FACE ....HIS FINE FEATURES SEEM TO GROW COARSE ...GROW THICK
GOOD LORD! .....LOOK! ...HIS FACE!
HIS FEATURES BECOME BLOATED, MORONIC HIS EYES BECOME WATERY HIS NOSE GROWS THICK, WITH WIDE NOSTRILS..
UNTIL, IN PLACE OF THE ONCE YOUNG, INTELLIGENT LOOKING MAN THERE IS NOW A COARSE, UGLY PERSON WITH AN AGED, IDIOTIC FACE..
WHA...WHAT'S HAPPENED TO HIM?
I DON'T KNOW

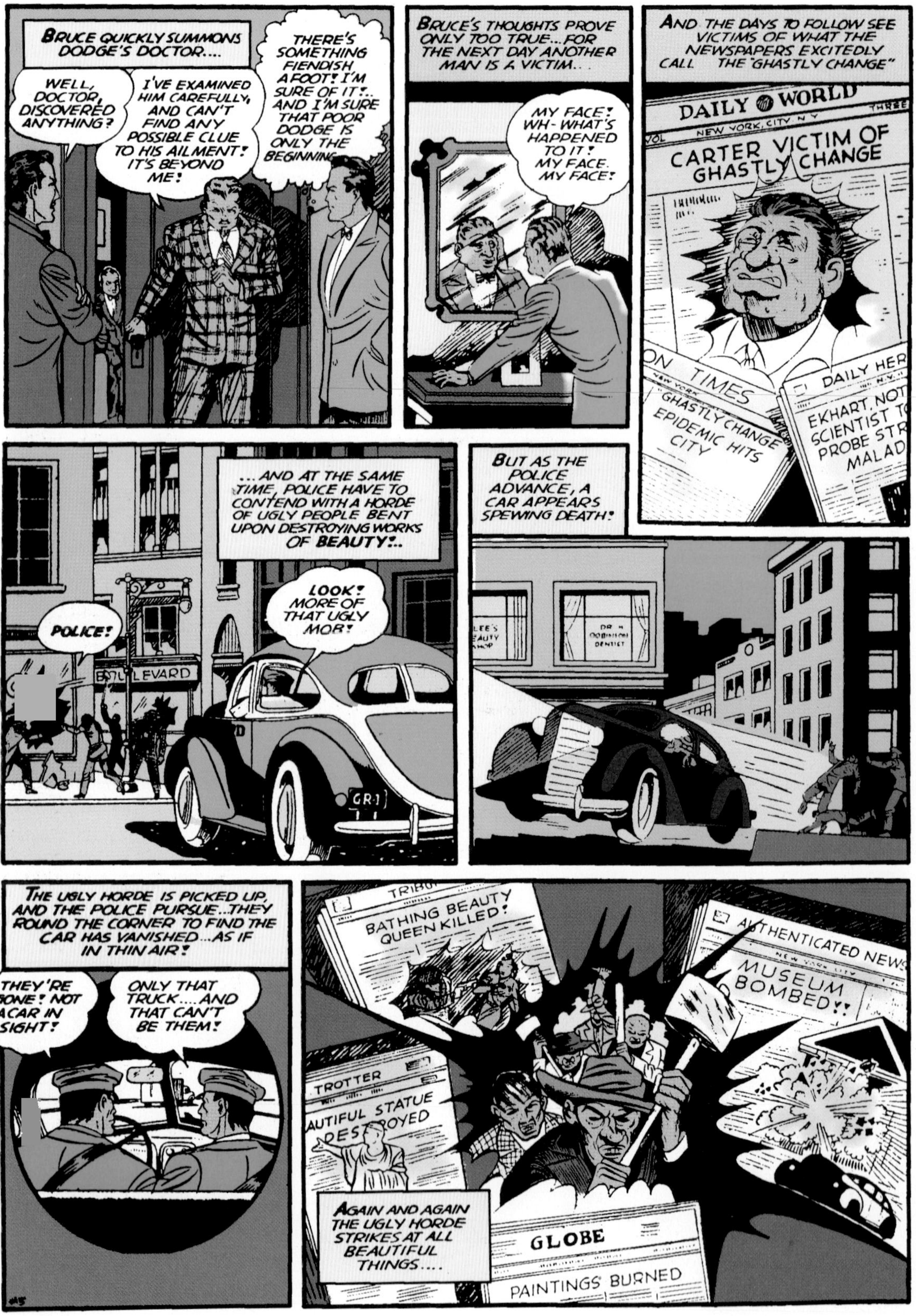
BRUCE QUICKLY SUMMONS DODGE'S DOCTOR....
WELL, DOCTOR, DISCOVERED ANYTHING?
I'VE EXAMINED HIM CAREFULLY, AND CAN'T FIND ANY POSSIBLE CLUE TO HIS AILMENT! IT'S BEYOND ME!
THERE'S SOMETHING FIENDISH AFOOT! I'M SURE OF IT!.. AND I'M SURE THAT POOR DODGE IS ONLY THE BEGINNING
BRUCE'S THOUGHTS PROVE ONLY TOO TRUE...FOR THE NEXT DAY ANOTHER MAN IS A VICTIM...
MY FACE! WH-WHAT'S HAPPENED TO IT! MY FACE. MY FACE!
AND THE DAYS TO FOLLOW SEE VICTIMS OF WHAT THE NEWSPAPERS EXCITEDLY CALL THE "GHASTLY CHANGE"
DAILY WORLD
NEW YORK CITY N Y
CARTER VICTIM OF GHASTLY CHANGE
TIMES
"GHASTLY CHANGE" EPIDEMIC HITS CITY
DAILY HER
EKHART, NOT SCIENTIST T PROBE STR MALAD
...AND AT THE SAME TIME, POLICE HAVE TO CONTEND WITH A HORDE OF UGLY PEOPLE BENT UPON DESTROYING WORKS OF BEAUTY!..
POLICE!
LOOK! MORE OF THAT UGLY MOB!
LEVARD
GR-1
BUT AS THE POLICE ADVANCE, A CAR APPEARS SPEWING DEATH!
DR. ROBINSON DENTIST
THE UGLY HORDE IS PICKED UP, AND THE POLICE PURSUE...THEY ROUND THE CORNER TO FIND THE CAR HAS VANISHED...AS IF IN THIN AIR!
THEY'RE GONE! NOT A CAR IN SIGHT!
ONLY THAT TRUCK....AND THAT CAN'T BE THEM!
BATHING BEAUTY QUEEN KILLED!
AUTHENTICATED NEWS
MUSEUM BOMBED!!
TROTTER
AUTIFUL STATUE DESTROYED
AGAIN AND AGAIN THE UGLY HORDE STRIKES AT ALL BEAUTIFUL THINGS....
GLOBE
PAINTINGS BURNED

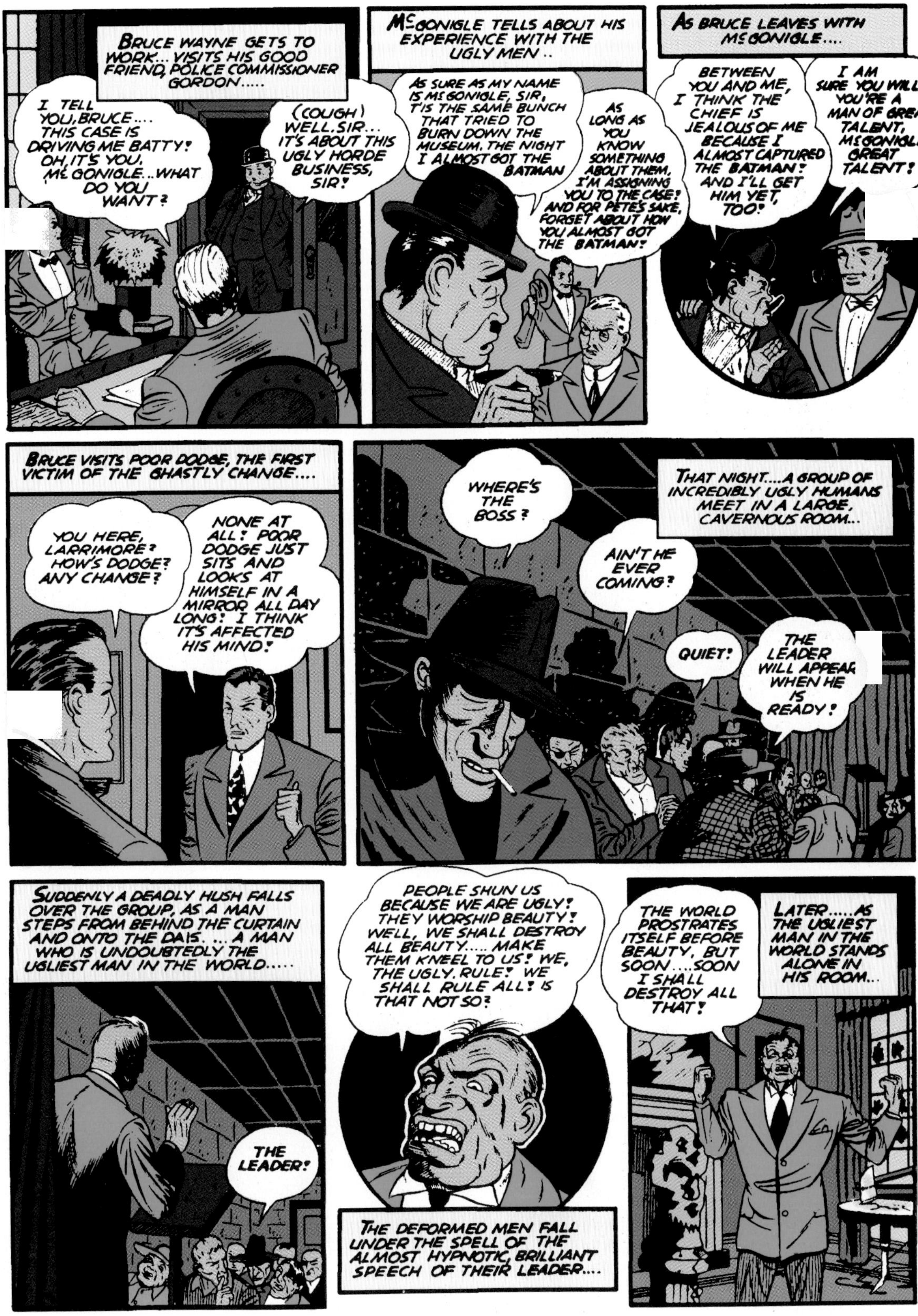
BRUCE WAYNE GETS TO WORK... VISITS HIS GOOD FRIEND, POLICE COMMISSIONER GORDON.....
I TELL YOU, BRUCE.... THIS CASE IS DRIVING ME BATTY! OH, IT'S YOU, MC GONIGLE...WHAT DO YOU WANT?
(COUGH) WELL, SIR... IT'S ABOUT THIS UGLY HORDE BUSINESS, SIR!
MCGONIGLE TELLS ABOUT HIS EXPERIENCE WITH THE UGLY MEN..
AS SURE AS MY NAME IS MCGONIGLE, SIR, T'IS THE SAME BUNCH THAT TRIED TO BURN DOWN THE MUSEUM, THE NIGHT I ALMOST GOT THE BATMAN
AS LONG AS YOU KNOW SOMETHING ABOUT THEM, I'M ASSIGNING YOU TO THE CASE! AND FOR PETE'S SAKE, FORGET ABOUT HOW YOU ALMOST GOT THE BATMAN!
AS BRUCE LEAVES WITH MCGONIGLE....
BETWEEN YOU AND ME, I THINK THE CHIEF IS JEALOUS OF ME BECAUSE I ALMOST CAPTURED THE BATMAN! AND I'LL GET HIM YET, TOO!
I AM SURE YOU WILL! YOU'RE A MAN OF GREAT TALENT, MCGONIGLE.. GREAT TALENT!
BRUCE VISITS POOR DODGE, THE FIRST VICTIM OF THE GHASTLY CHANGE....
YOU HERE, LARRIMORE? HOW'S DODGE? ANY CHANGE?
NONE AT ALL! POOR DODGE JUST SITS AND LOOKS AT HIMSELF IN A MIRROR ALL DAY LONG! I THINK IT'S AFFECTED HIS MIND!
THAT NIGHT....A GROUP OF INCREDIBLY UGLY HUMANS MEET IN A LARGE, CAVERNOUS ROOM...
WHERE'S THE BOSS?
AIN'T HE EVER COMING?
QUIET!
THE LEADER WILL APPEAR WHEN HE IS READY!
SUDDENLY A DEADLY HUSH FALLS OVER THE GROUP, AS A MAN STEPS FROM BEHIND THE CURTAIN AND ONTO THE DAIS. ... A MAN WHO IS UNDOUBTEDLY THE UGLIEST MAN IN THE WORLD.....
THE LEADER!
PEOPLE SHUN US BECAUSE WE ARE UGLY! THEY WORSHIP BEAUTY! WELL, WE SHALL DESTROY ALL BEAUTY..... MAKE THEM KNEEL TO US! WE, THE UGLY, RULE! WE SHALL RULE ALL! IS THAT NOT SO?
THE DEFORMED MEN FALL UNDER THE SPELL OF THE ALMOST HYPNOTIC, BRILLIANT SPEECH OF THEIR LEADER....
LATER.....AS THE UGLIEST MAN IN THE WORLD STANDS ALONE IN HIS ROOM...
THE WORLD PROSTRATES ITSELF BEFORE BEAUTY, BUT SOON....SOON I SHALL DESTROY ALL THAT!

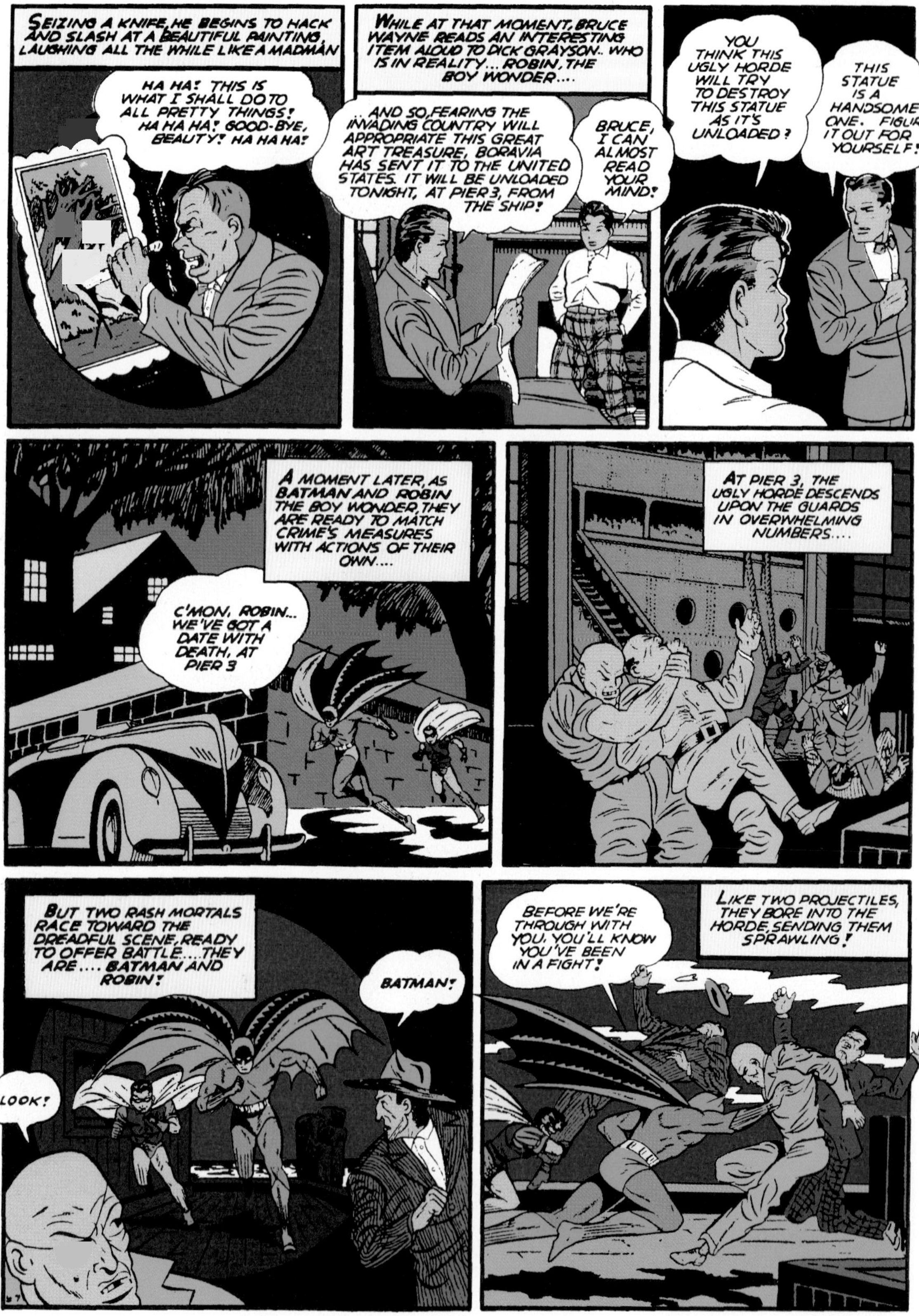
SEIZING A KNIFE, HE BEGINS TO HACK AND SLASH AT A BEAUTIFUL PAINTING, LAUGHING ALL THE WHILE LIKE A MADMAN
HA HA! THIS IS WHAT I SHALL DO TO ALL PRETTY THINGS! HA HA HA! GOOD-BYE, BEAUTY! HA HA HA!
WHILE AT THAT MOMENT, BRUCE WAYNE READS AN INTERESTING ITEM ALOUD TO DICK GRAYSON.. WHO IS IN REALITY... ROBIN, THE BOY WONDER....
...AND SO, FEARING THE INVADING COUNTRY WILL APPROPRIATE THIS GREAT ART TREASURE, BORAVIA HAS SENT IT TO THE UNITED STATES. IT WILL BE UNLOADED TONIGHT, AT PIER 3, FROM THE SHIP!
BRUCE, I CAN ALMOST READ YOUR MIND!
YOU THINK THIS UGLY HORDE WILL TRY TO DESTROY THIS STATUE AS IT'S UNLOADED?
THIS STATUE IS A HANDSOME ONE. FIGURE IT OUT FOR YOURSELF!
A MOMENT LATER, AS BATMAN AND ROBIN THE BOY WONDER, THEY ARE READY TO MATCH CRIME'S MEASURES WITH ACTIONS OF THEIR OWN....
C'MON, ROBIN... WE'VE GOT A DATE WITH DEATH, AT PIER 3
AT PIER 3, THE UGLY HORDE DESCENDS UPON THE GUARDS IN OVERWHELMING NUMBERS....
BUT TWO RASH MORTALS RACE TOWARD THE DREADFUL SCENE, READY TO OFFER BATTLE.... THEY ARE.... BATMAN AND ROBIN!
BATMAN!
LOOK!
LIKE TWO PROJECTILES, THEY BORE INTO THE HORDE, SENDING THEM SPRAWLING!
BEFORE WE'RE THROUGH WITH YOU, YOU'LL KNOW YOU'VE BEEN IN A FIGHT!

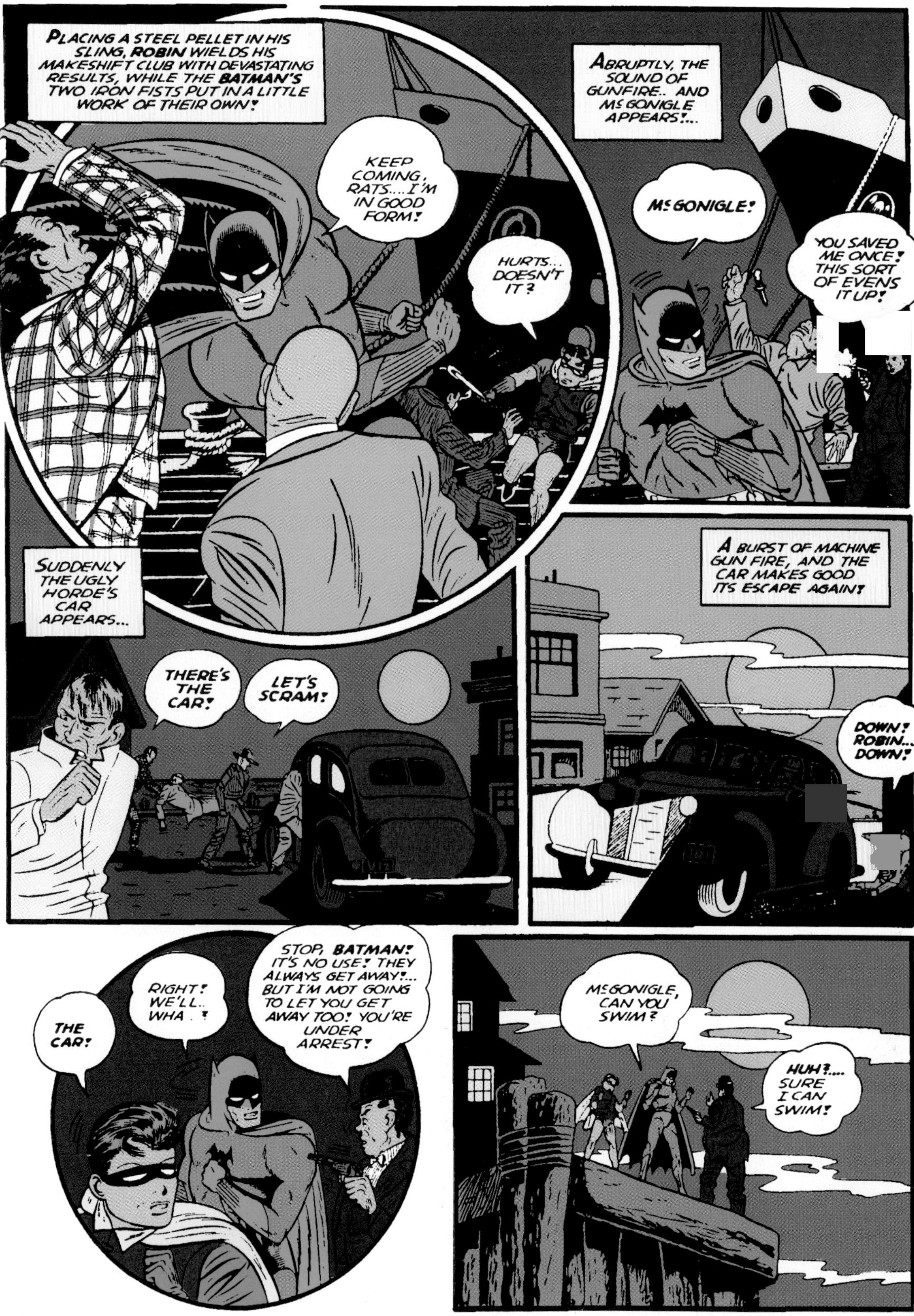
PLACING A STEEL PELLET IN HIS SLING, ROBIN WIELDS HIS MAKESHIFT CLUB WITH DEVASTATING RESULTS, WHILE THE BATMAN'S TWO IRON FISTS PUT IN A LITTLE WORK OF THEIR OWN!
KEEP COMING, RATS.... I'M IN GOOD FORM!
HURTS... DOESN'T IT?
ABRUPTLY, THE SOUND OF GUNFIRE.. AND MCGONIGLE APPEARS!...
MCGONIGLE!
YOU SAVED ME ONCE! THIS SORT OF EVENS IT UP!
SUDDENLY THE UGLY HORDE'S CAR APPEARS...
THERE'S THE CAR!
LET'S SCRAM!
A BURST OF MACHINE GUN FIRE, AND THE CAR MAKES GOOD ITS ESCAPE AGAIN!
DOWN! ROBIN... DOWN!
THE CAR!
RIGHT! WE'LL.. WHA . . ?
STOP, BATMAN! IT'S NO USE! THEY ALWAYS GET AWAY!... BUT I'M NOT GOING TO LET YOU GET AWAY TOO! YOU'RE UNDER ARREST!
MCGONIGLE, CAN YOU SWIM?
HUH?.... SURE I CAN SWIM!

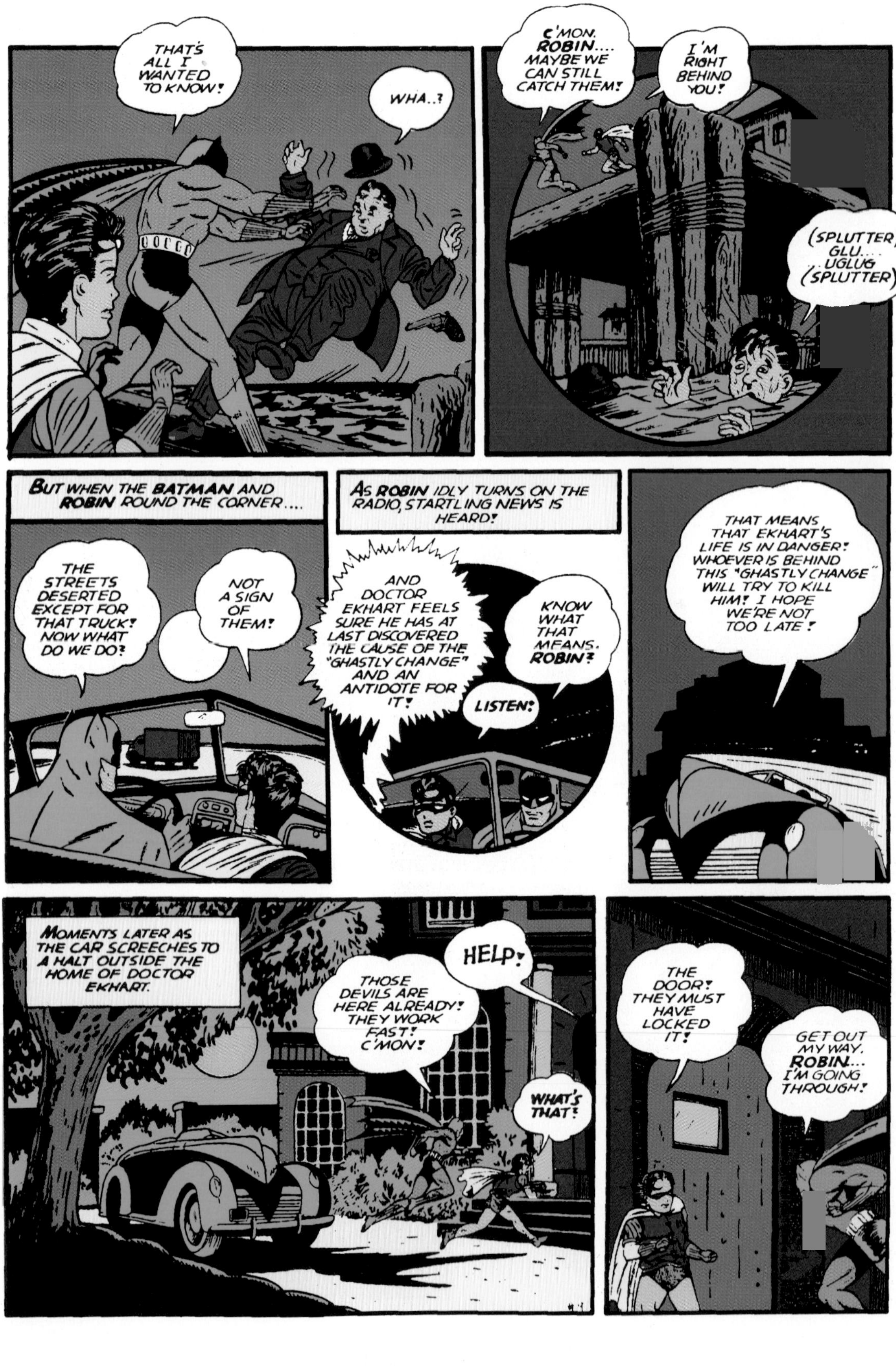

THAT'S ALL I WANTED TO KNOW!
WHA..?
C'MON. ROBIN.... MAYBE WE CAN STILL CATCH THEM!
I'M RIGHT BEHIND YOU!
(SPLUTTER) GLU.... ..UGLUG (SPLUTTER)
BUT WHEN THE BATMAN AND ROBIN ROUND THE CORNER....
THE STREETS DESERTED EXCEPT FOR THAT TRUCK! NOW WHAT DO WE DO?
NOT A SIGN OF THEM!
AS ROBIN IDLY TURNS ON THE RADIO, STARTLING NEWS IS HEARD!
AND DOCTOR EKHART FEELS SURE HE HAS AT LAST DISCOVERED THE CAUSE OF THE "GHASTLY CHANGE" AND AN ANTIDOTE FOR IT!
LISTEN!
KNOW WHAT THAT MEANS, ROBIN?
THAT MEANS THAT EKHART'S LIFE IS IN DANGER! WHOEVER IS BEHIND THIS "GHASTLY CHANGE" WILL TRY TO KILL HIM! I HOPE WE'RE NOT TOO LATE!
MOMENTS LATER AS THE CAR SCREECHES TO A HALT OUTSIDE THE HOME OF DOCTOR EKHART.
HELP!
THOSE DEVILS ARE HERE ALREADY! THEY WORK FAST! C'MON!
WHAT'S THAT?
THE DOOR! THEY MUST HAVE LOCKED IT!
GET OUT MY WAY, ROBIN... I'M GOING THROUGH!

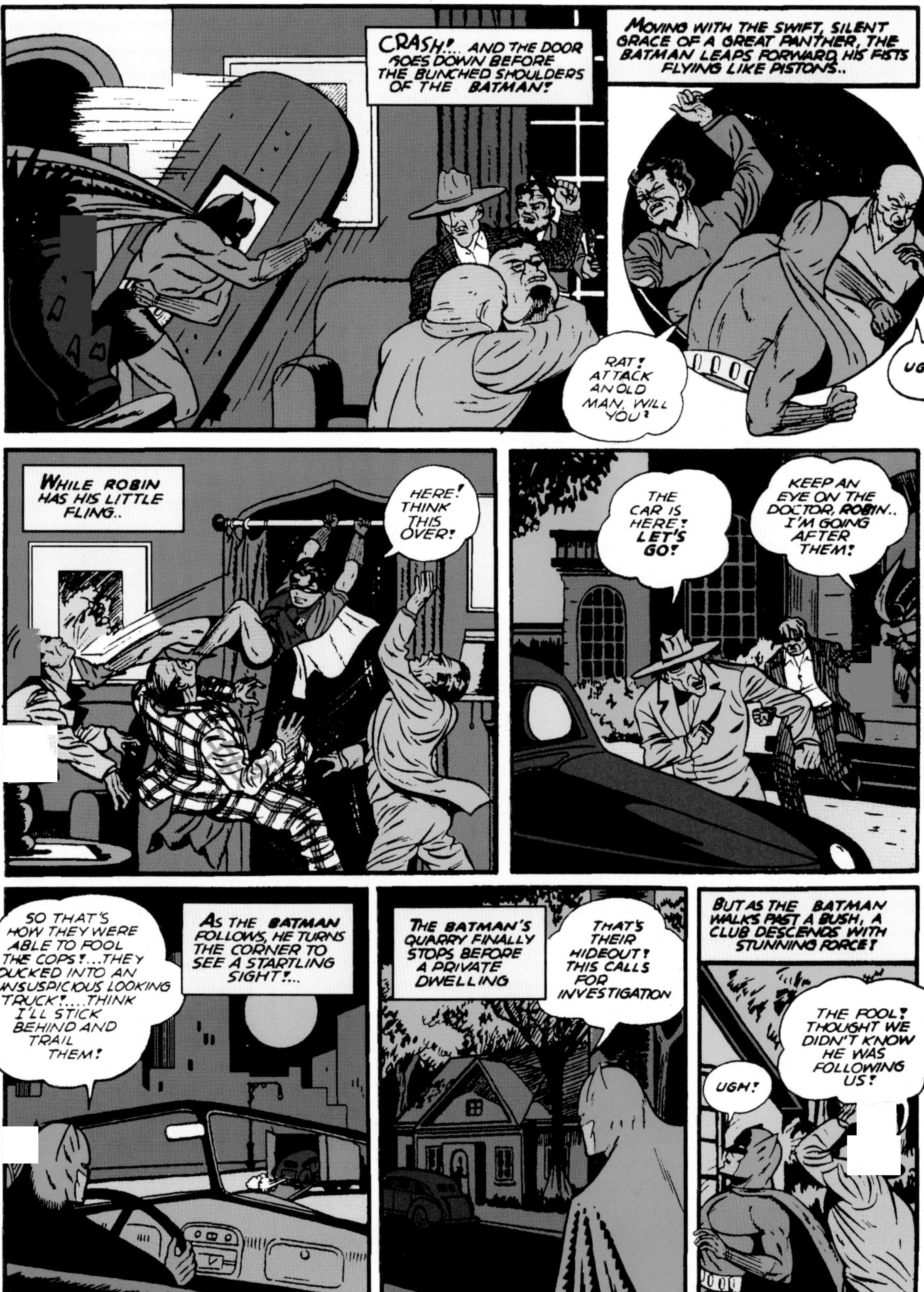
CRASH!... AND THE DOOR GOES DOWN BEFORE THE BUNCHED SHOULDERS OF THE BATMAN!
MOVING WITH THE SWIFT, SILENT GRACE OF A GREAT PANTHER, THE BATMAN LEAPS FORWARD HIS FISTS FLYING LIKE PISTONS..
RAT! ATTACK AN OLD MAN, WILL YOU?
UGH!
WHILE ROBIN HAS HIS LITTLE FLING..
HERE! THINK THIS OVER!
THE CAR IS HERE! LET'S GO!
KEEP AN EYE ON THE DOCTOR, ROBIN.. I'M GOING AFTER THEM!
SO THAT'S HOW THEY WERE ABLE TO FOOL THE COPS!...THEY DUCKED INTO AN UNSUSPICIOUS LOOKING TRUCK!....THINK I'LL STICK BEHIND AND TRAIL THEM!
AS THE BATMAN FOLLOWS, HE TURNS THE CORNER TO SEE A STARTLING SIGHT!...
THE BATMAN'S QUARRY FINALLY STOPS BEFORE A PRIVATE DWELLING
THAT'S THEIR HIDEOUT! THIS CALLS FOR INVESTIGATION
BUT AS THE BATMAN WALKS PAST A BUSH, A CLUB DESCENDS WITH STUNNING FORCE!
THE FOOL! THOUGHT WE DIDN'T KNOW HE WAS FOLLOWING US!
UGH!

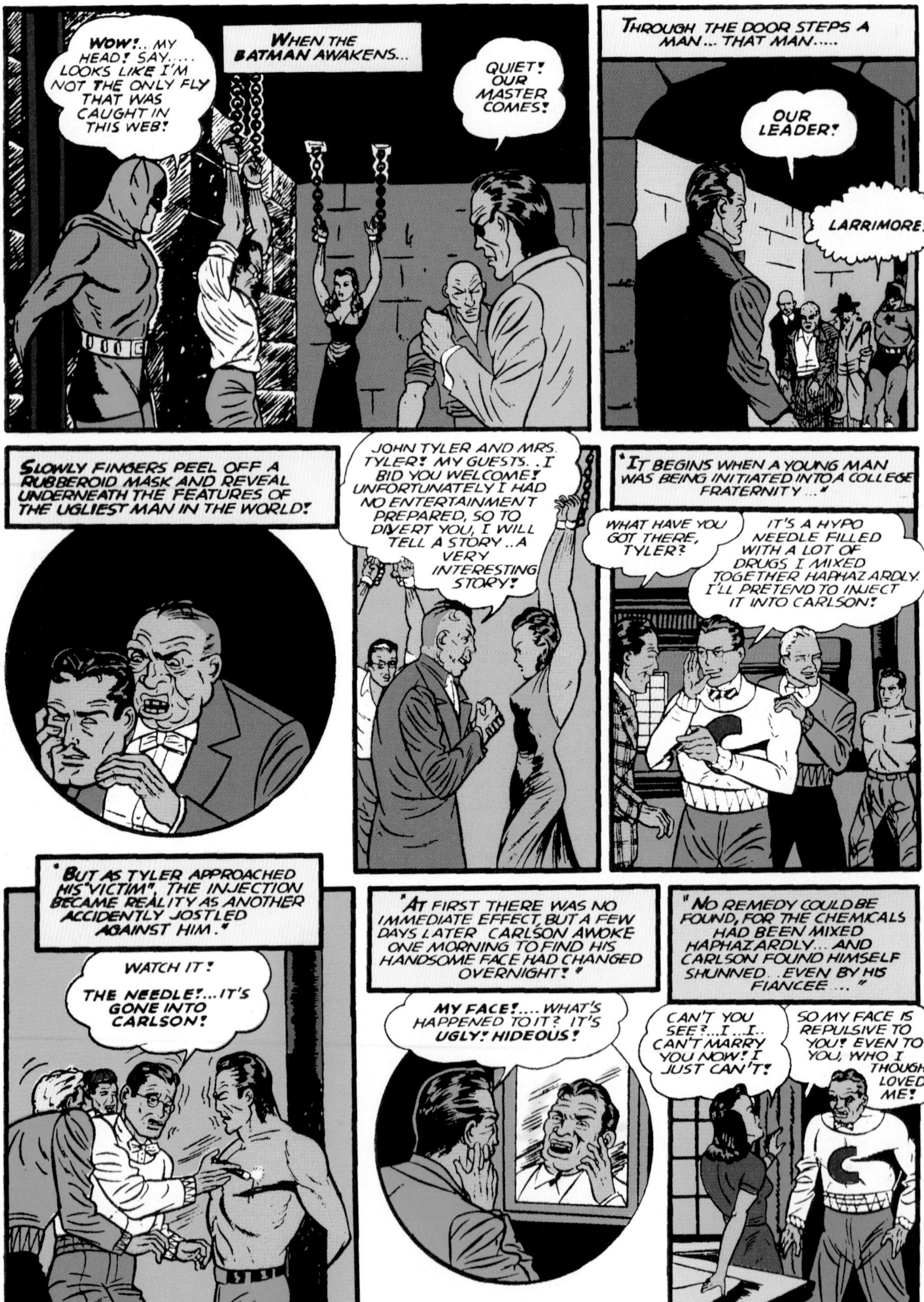
WOW!... MY HEAD! SAY..... LOOKS LIKE I'M NOT THE ONLY FLY THAT WAS CAUGHT IN THIS WEB!
WHEN THE BATMAN AWAKENS...
QUIET! OUR MASTER COMES!
THROUGH THE DOOR STEPS A MAN... THAT MAN.....
OUR LEADER!
LARRIMORE!
SLOWLY FINGERS PEEL OFF A RUBBEROID MASK AND REVEAL UNDERNEATH THE FEATURES OF THE UGLIEST MAN IN THE WORLD!
JOHN TYLER AND MRS. TYLER! MY GUESTS. . I BID YOU WELCOME! UNFORTUNATELY I HAD NO ENTERTAINMENT PREPARED, SO TO DIVERT YOU, I WILL TELL A STORY ..A VERY INTERESTING STORY!
"IT BEGINS WHEN A YOUNG MAN WAS BEING INITIATED INTO A COLLEGE FRATERNITY ..."
WHAT HAVE YOU GOT THERE, TYLER?
IT'S A HYPO NEEDLE FILLED WITH A LOT OF DRUGS I MIXED TOGETHER HAPHAZARDLY. I'LL PRETEND TO INJECT IT INTO CARLSON!
"BUT AS TYLER APPROACHED HIS "VICTIM", THE INJECTION BECAME REALITY AS ANOTHER ACCIDENTLY JOSTLED AGAINST HIM."
WATCH IT! THE NEEDLE!...IT'S GONE INTO CARLSON!
"AT FIRST THERE WAS NO IMMEDIATE EFFECT, BUT A FEW DAYS LATER CARLSON AWOKE ONE MORNING TO FIND HIS HANDSOME FACE HAD CHANGED OVERNIGHT!"
MY FACE!.... WHAT'S HAPPENED TO IT? IT'S UGLY! HIDEOUS!
"NO REMEDY COULD BE FOUND, FOR THE CHEMICALS HAD BEEN MIXED HAPHAZARDLY... AND CARLSON FOUND HIMSELF SHUNNED. .EVEN BY HIS FIANCEE ..."
CAN'T YOU SEE?...I ...I.. CAN'T MARRY YOU NOW! I JUST CAN'T!
SO MY FACE IS REPULSIVE TO YOU! EVEN TO YOU, WHO I THOUGHT LOVED ME!

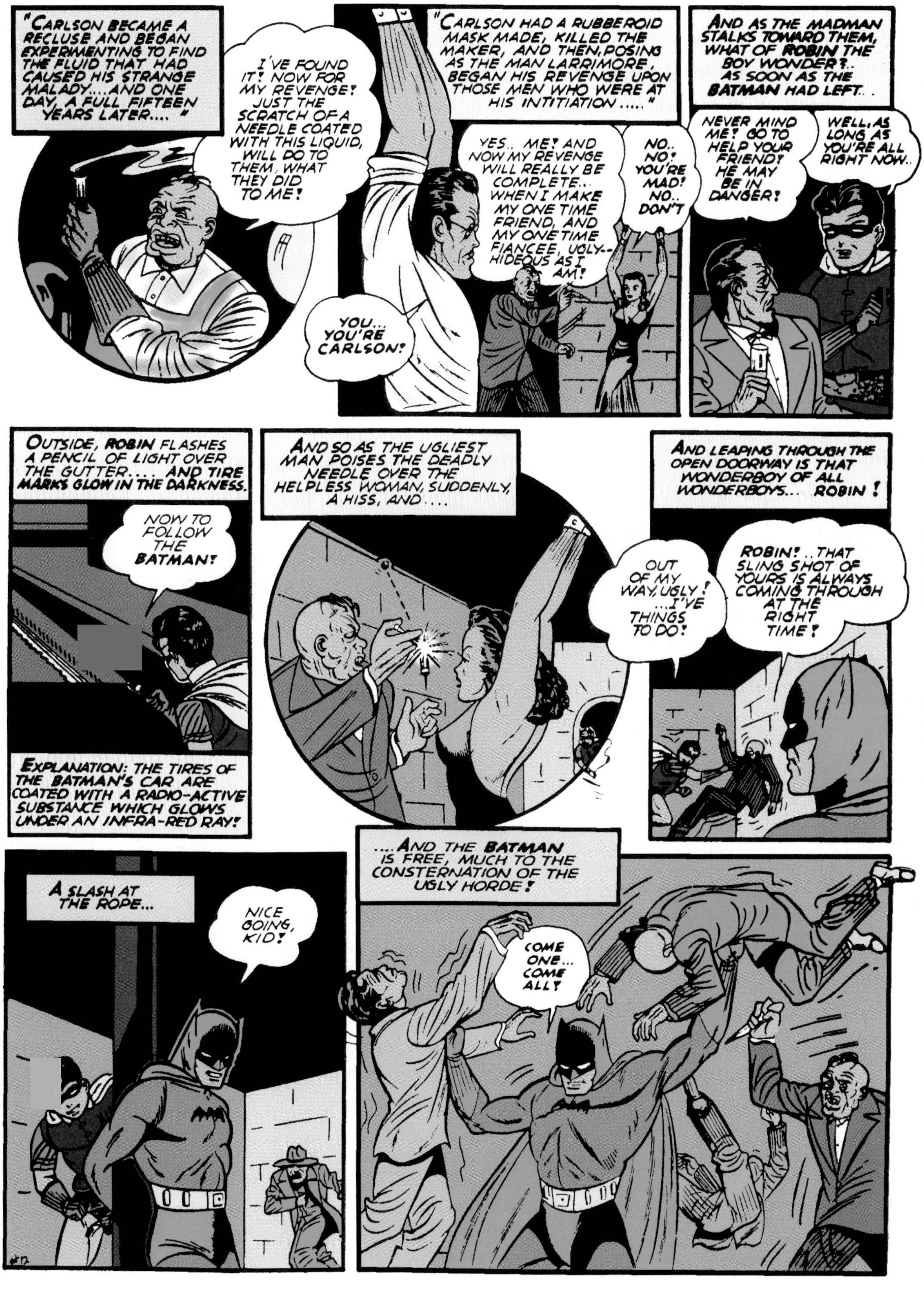
"CARLSON BECAME A RECLUSE AND BEGAN EXPERIMENTING TO FIND THE FLUID THAT HAD CAUSED HIS STRANGE MALADY.... AND ONE DAY, A FULL FIFTEEN YEARS LATER.... "
I'VE FOUND IT! NOW FOR MY REVENGE! JUST THE SCRATCH OF A NEEDLE COATED WITH THIS LIQUID, WILL DO TO THEM, WHAT THEY DID TO ME!
"CARLSON HAD A RUBBEROID MASK MADE, KILLED THE MAKER, AND THEN, POSING AS THE MAN LARRIMORE, BEGAN HIS REVENGE UPON THOSE MEN WHO WERE AT HIS INTITIATION ..... "
YOU... YOU'RE CARLSON!
YES.. ME! AND NOW MY REVENGE WILL REALLY BE COMPLETE.. WHEN I MAKE MY ONE TIME FRIEND, AND MY ONE TIME FIANCEE, UGLY-- HIDEOUS AS I AM!
NO.. NO! YOU'RE MAD! NO.. DON'T
AND AS THE MADMAN STALKS TOWARD THEM, WHAT OF ROBIN THE BOY WONDER?.. AS SOON AS THE BATMAN HAD LEFT..
NEVER MIND ME! GO TO HELP YOUR FRIEND! HE MAY BE IN DANGER!
WELL, AS LONG AS YOU'RE ALL RIGHT NOW..
OUTSIDE, ROBIN FLASHES A PENCIL OF LIGHT OVER THE GUTTER.... AND TIRE MARKS GLOW IN THE DARKNESS.
NOW TO FOLLOW THE BATMAN!
EXPLANATION: THE TIRES OF THE BATMAN'S CAR ARE COATED WITH A RADIO-ACTIVE SUBSTANCE WHICH GLOWS UNDER AN INFRA-RED RAY!
AND SO AS THE UGLIEST MAN POISES THE DEADLY NEEDLE OVER THE HELPLESS WOMAN, SUDDENLY, A HISS, AND....
AND LEAPING THROUGH THE OPEN DOORWAY IS THAT WONDERBOY OF ALL WONDERBOYS... ROBIN!
OUT OF MY WAY, UGLY! ...I'VE THINGS TO DO!
ROBIN! ..THAT SLING SHOT OF YOURS IS ALWAYS COMING THROUGH AT THE RIGHT TIME!
A SLASH AT THE ROPE...
NICE GOING, KID!
....AND THE BATMAN IS FREE, MUCH TO THE CONSTERNATION OF THE UGLY HORDE!
COME ONE... COME ALL!

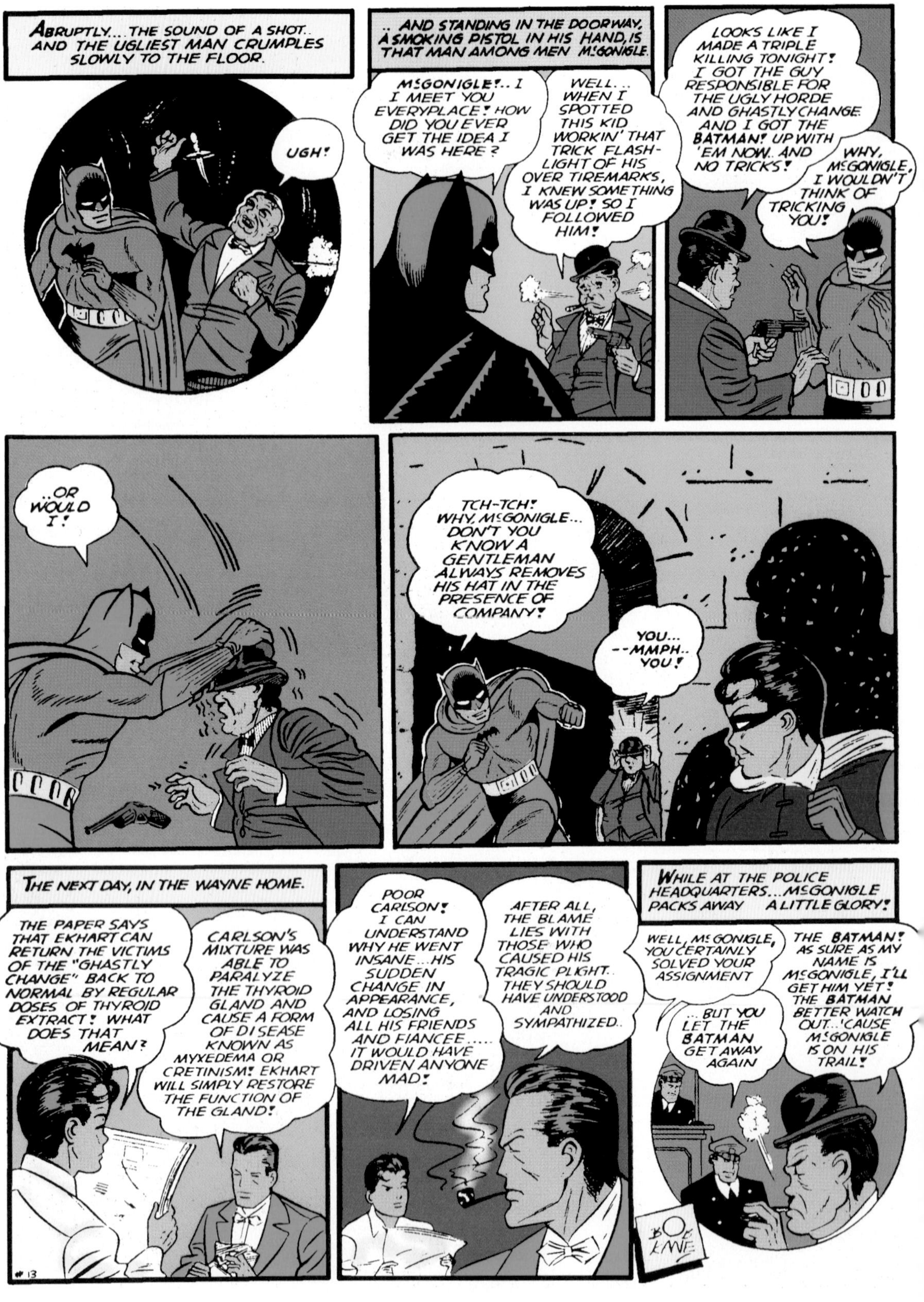
ABRUPTLY.... THE SOUND OF A SHOT.. AND THE UGLIEST MAN CRUMPLES SLOWLY TO THE FLOOR.
UGH!
.. AND STANDING IN THE DOORWAY, A SMOKING PISTOL IN HIS HAND, IS THAT MAN AMONG MEN McGONIGLE.
McGONIGLE!.. I I MEET YOU EVERYPLACE! HOW DID YOU EVER GET THE IDEA I WAS HERE?
WELL... WHEN I SPOTTED THIS KID WORKIN' THAT TRICK FLASH-LIGHT OF HIS OVER TIREMARKS, I KNEW SOMETHING WAS UP! SO I FOLLOWED HIM!
LOOKS LIKE I MADE A TRIPLE KILLING TONIGHT! I GOT THE GUY RESPONSIBLE FOR THE UGLY HORDE AND GHASTLY CHANGE AND I GOT THE BATMAN! UP WITH 'EM NOW.. AND NO TRICKS!
WHY, McGONIGLE, I WOULDN'T THINK OF TRICKING YOU!
..OR WOULD I!
TCH-TCH! WHY, McGONIGLE... DON'T YOU KNOW A GENTLEMAN ALWAYS REMOVES HIS HAT IN THE PRESENCE OF COMPANY!
YOU... --MMPH.. YOU!
THE NEXT DAY, IN THE WAYNE HOME.
THE PAPER SAYS THAT EKHART CAN RETURN THE VICTIMS OF THE "GHASTLY CHANGE" BACK TO NORMAL BY REGULAR DOSES OF THYROID EXTRACT! WHAT DOES THAT MEAN?
CARLSON'S MIXTURE WAS ABLE TO PARALYZE THE THYROID GLAND AND CAUSE A FORM OF DISEASE KNOWN AS MYXEDEMA OR CRETINISM! EKHART WILL SIMPLY RESTORE THE FUNCTION OF THE GLAND!
#13
POOR CARLSON! I CAN UNDERSTAND WHY HE WENT INSANE... HIS SUDDEN CHANGE IN APPEARANCE, AND LOSING ALL HIS FRIENDS AND FIANCEE..... IT WOULD HAVE DRIVEN ANYONE MAD!
AFTER ALL, THE BLAME LIES WITH THOSE WHO CAUSED HIS TRAGIC PLIGHT.. THEY SHOULD HAVE UNDERSTOOD AND SYMPATHIZED..
WHILE AT THE POLICE HEADQUARTERS... McGONIGLE PACKS AWAY A LITTLE GLORY!
WELL, McGONIGLE, YOU CERTAINLY SOLVED YOUR ASSIGNMENT
... BUT YOU LET THE BATMAN GET AWAY AGAIN
THE BATMAN! AS SURE AS MY NAME IS McGONIGLE, I'LL GET HIM YET! THE BATMAN BETTER WATCH OUT... 'CAUSE McGONIGLE IS ON HIS TRAIL!
BOB KANE

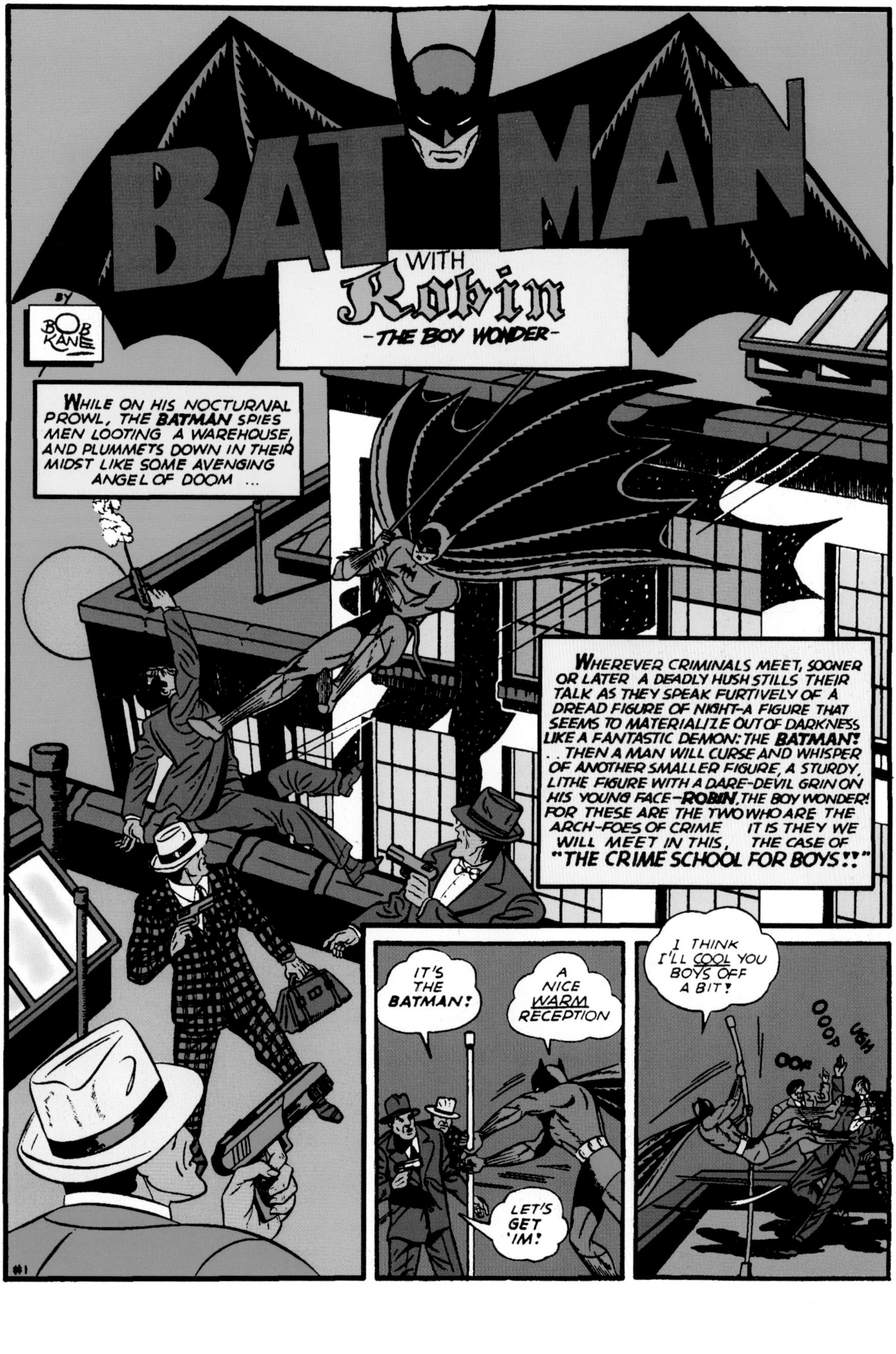
BATMAN
WITH
Robin
-THE BOY WONDER-
BY BOB KANE
WHILE ON HIS NOCTURNAL PROWL, THE BATMAN SPIES MEN LOOTING A WAREHOUSE, AND PLUMMETS DOWN IN THEIR MIDST LIKE SOME AVENGING ANGEL OF DOOM ...
WHEREVER CRIMINALS MEET, SOONER OR LATER A DEADLY HUSH STILLS THEIR TALK AS THEY SPEAK FURTIVELY OF A DREAD FIGURE OF NIGHT-A FIGURE THAT SEEMS TO MATERIALIZE OUT OF DARKNESS LIKE A FANTASTIC DEMON: THE BATMAN! . . THEN A MAN WILL CURSE AND WHISPER OF ANOTHER SMALLER FIGURE, A STURDY, LITHE FIGURE WITH A DARE-DEVIL GRIN ON HIS YOUNG FACE-ROBIN, THE BOY WONDER! FOR THESE ARE THE TWO WHO ARE THE ARCH-FOES OF CRIME IT IS THEY WE WILL MEET IN THIS, THE CASE OF "THE CRIME SCHOOL FOR BOYS!!"
IT'S THE BATMAN!
A NICE WARM RECEPTION
LET'S GET 'IM!
I THINK I'LL COOL YOU BOYS OFF A BIT!
OOOP
UGH
OOF

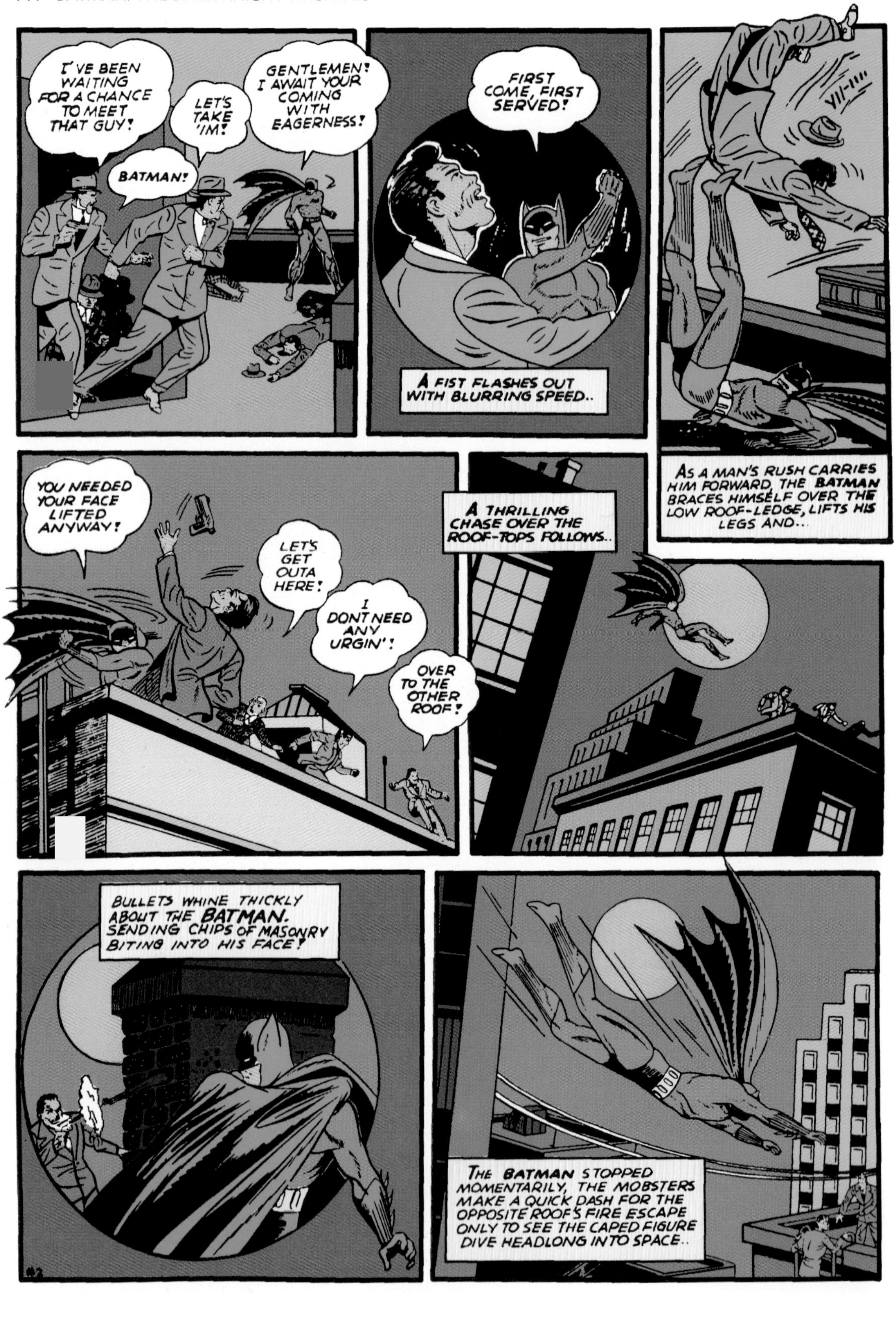
I'VE BEEN WAITING FOR A CHANCE TO MEET THAT GUY!
LET'S TAKE 'IM!
GENTLEMEN! I AWAIT YOUR COMING WITH EAGERNESS!
BATMAN!
FIRST COME, FIRST SERVED!
A FIST FLASHES OUT WITH BLURRING SPEED..
YII-III
AS A MAN'S RUSH CARRIES HIM FORWARD, THE BATMAN BRACES HIMSELF OVER THE LOW ROOF-LEDGE, LIFTS HIS LEGS AND...
YOU NEEDED YOUR FACE LIFTED ANYWAY!
LET'S GET OUTA HERE!
I DONT NEED ANY URGIN'!
OVER TO THE OTHER ROOF!
A THRILLING CHASE OVER THE ROOF-TOPS FOLLOWS..
BULLETS WHINE THICKLY ABOUT THE BATMAN, SENDING CHIPS OF MASONRY BITING INTO HIS FACE!
THE BATMAN STOPPED MOMENTARILY, THE MOBSTERS MAKE A QUICK DASH FOR THE OPPOSITE ROOF'S FIRE ESCAPE ONLY TO SEE THE CAPED FIGURE DIVE HEADLONG INTO SPACE..

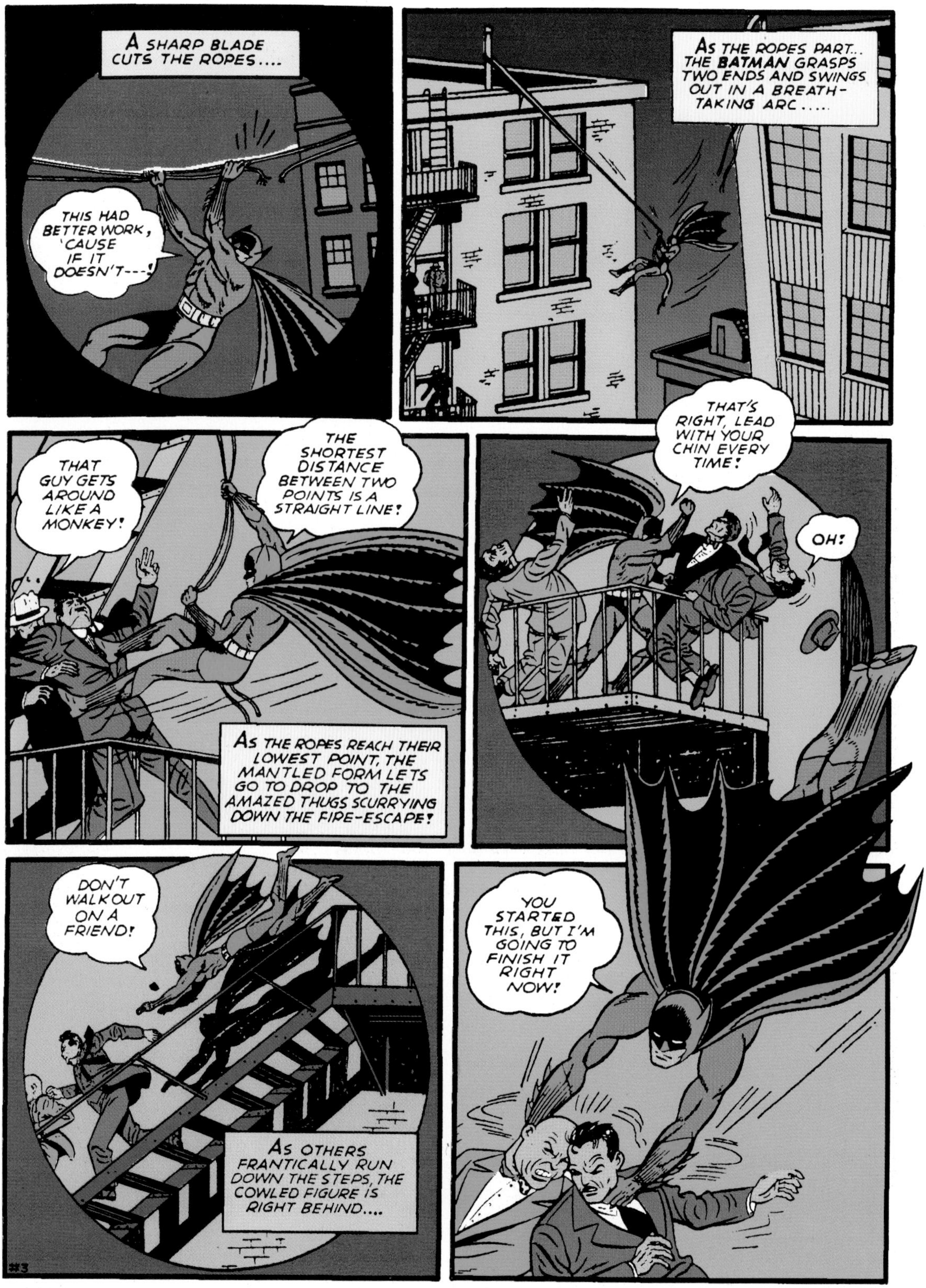
A SHARP BLADE CUTS THE ROPES....
THIS HAD BETTER WORK, 'CAUSE IF IT DOESN'T---!
AS THE ROPES PART... THE BATMAN GRASPS TWO ENDS AND SWINGS OUT IN A BREATH-TAKING ARC....
THAT GUY GETS AROUND LIKE A MONKEY!
THE SHORTEST DISTANCE BETWEEN TWO POINTS IS A STRAIGHT LINE!
AS THE ROPES REACH THEIR LOWEST POINT, THE MANTLED FORM LETS GO TO DROP TO THE AMAZED THUGS SCURRYING DOWN THE FIRE-ESCAPE!
THAT'S RIGHT, LEAD WITH YOUR CHIN EVERY TIME!
OH!
DON'T WALK OUT ON A FRIEND!
AS OTHERS FRANTICALLY RUN DOWN THE STEPS, THE COWLED FIGURE IS RIGHT BEHIND....
#3
YOU STARTED THIS, BUT I'M GOING TO FINISH IT RIGHT NOW!

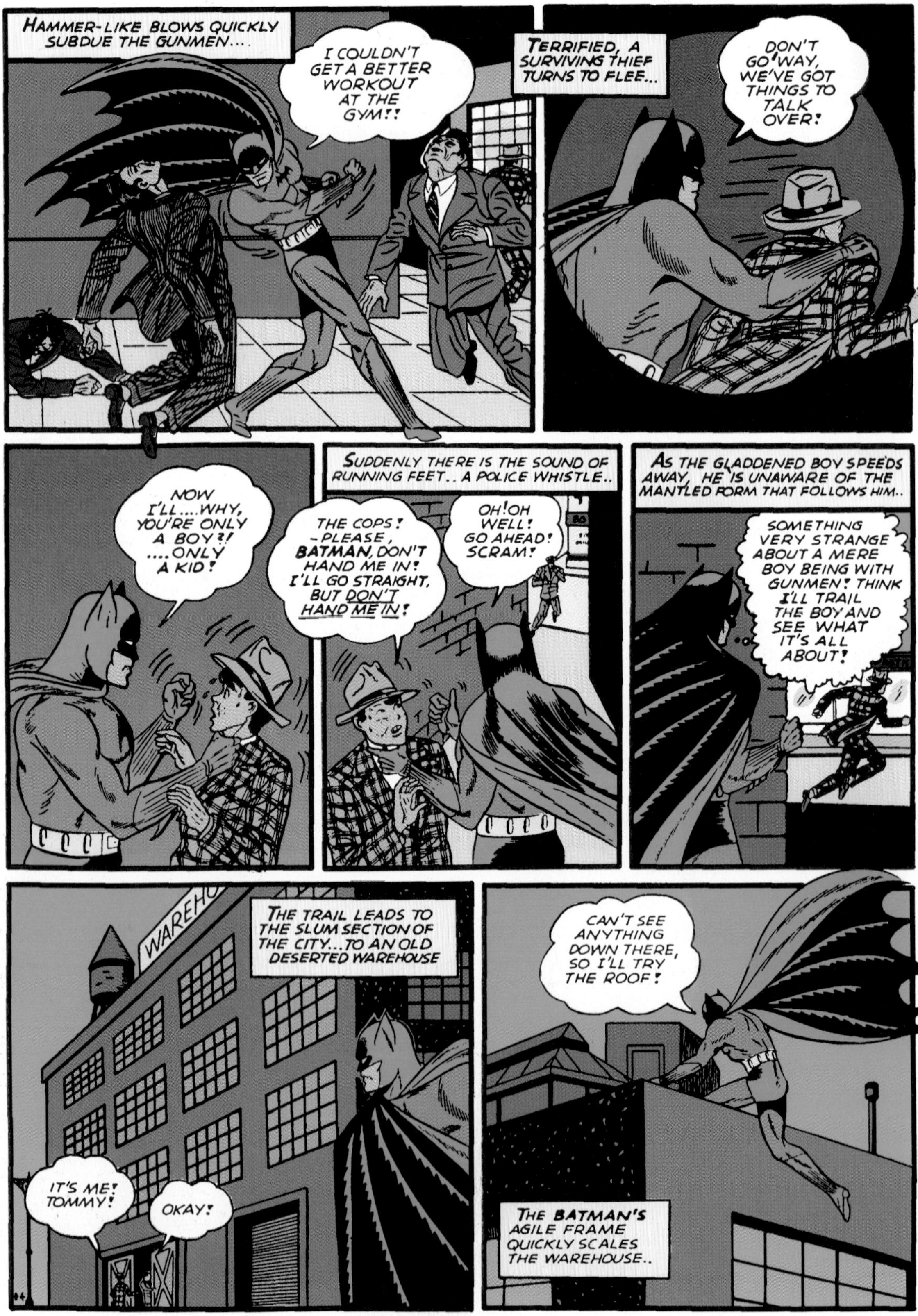
HAMMER-LIKE BLOWS QUICKLY SUBDUE THE GUNMEN....
I COULDN'T GET A BETTER WORKOUT AT THE GYM!!
TERRIFIED, A SURVIVING THIEF TURNS TO FLEE...
DON'T GO 'WAY, WE'VE GOT THINGS TO TALK OVER!
NOW I'LL....WHY, YOU'RE ONLY A BOY?! ....ONLY A KID!
SUDDENLY THERE IS THE SOUND OF RUNNING FEET.. A POLICE WHISTLE..
THE COPS! -PLEASE, BATMAN, DON'T HAND ME IN! I'LL GO STRAIGHT, BUT DON'T HAND ME IN!
OH! OH WELL! GO AHEAD! SCRAM!
AS THE GLADDENED BOY SPEEDS AWAY, HE IS UNAWARE OF THE MANTLED FORM THAT FOLLOWS HIM..
SOMETHING VERY STRANGE ABOUT A MERE BOY BEING WITH GUNMEN! THINK I'LL TRAIL THE BOY AND SEE WHAT IT'S ALL ABOUT!
THE TRAIL LEADS TO THE SLUM SECTION OF THE CITY...TO AN OLD DESERTED WAREHOUSE
WAREHO
IT'S ME! TOMMY!
OKAY!
CAN'T SEE ANYTHING DOWN THERE, SO I'LL TRY THE ROOF!
THE BATMAN'S AGILE FRAME QUICKLY SCALES THE WAREHOUSE..

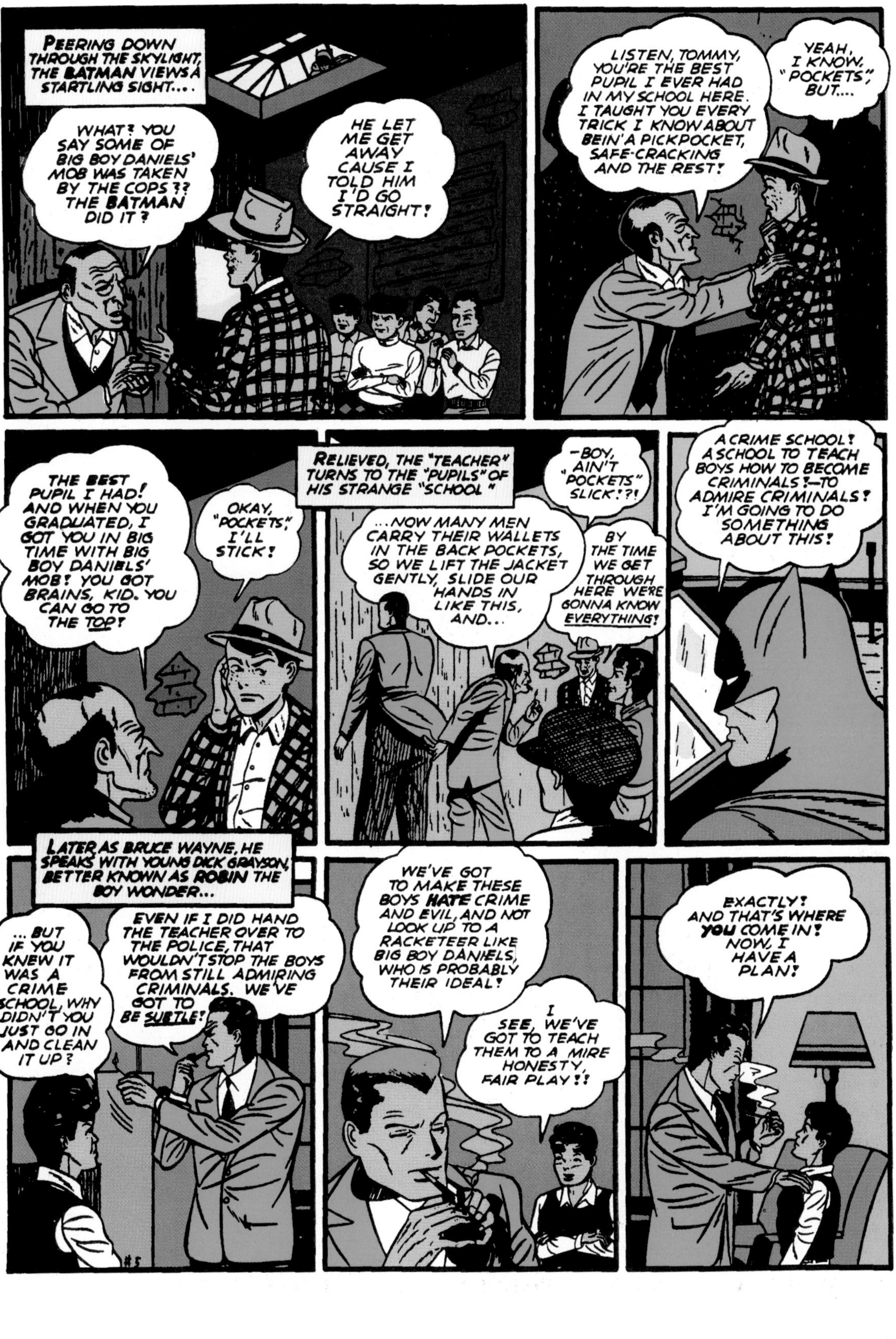
PEERING DOWN THROUGH THE SKYLIGHT, THE BATMAN VIEWS A STARTLING SIGHT....
WHAT? YOU SAY SOME OF BIG BOY DANIELS' MOB WAS TAKEN BY THE COPS?? THE BATMAN DID IT?
HE LET ME GET AWAY CAUSE I TOLD HIM I'D GO STRAIGHT!
LISTEN, TOMMY, YOU'RE THE BEST PUPIL I EVER HAD IN MY SCHOOL HERE. I TAUGHT YOU EVERY TRICK I KNOW ABOUT BEIN' A PICKPOCKET, SAFE-CRACKING AND THE REST!
YEAH, I KNOW, "POCKETS," BUT....
THE BEST PUPIL I HAD! AND WHEN YOU GRADUATED, I GOT YOU IN BIG TIME WITH BIG BOY DANIELS' MOB! YOU GOT BRAINS, KID. YOU CAN GO TO THE TOP!
OKAY, "POCKETS," I'LL STICK!
RELIEVED, THE "TEACHER" TURNS TO THE "PUPILS" OF HIS STRANGE "SCHOOL"
...NOW MANY MEN CARRY THEIR WALLETS IN THE BACK POCKETS, SO WE LIFT THE JACKET GENTLY, SLIDE OUR HANDS IN LIKE THIS, AND...
-BOY, AIN'T "POCKETS" SLICK!?!
BY THE TIME WE GET THROUGH HERE WE'RE GONNA KNOW EVERYTHING!
A CRIME SCHOOL! A SCHOOL TO TEACH BOYS HOW TO BECOME CRIMINALS!—TO ADMIRE CRIMINALS! I'M GOING TO DO SOMETHING ABOUT THIS!
LATER AS BRUCE WAYNE, HE SPEAKS WITH YOUNG DICK GRAYSON, BETTER KNOWN AS ROBIN THE BOY WONDER...
...BUT IF YOU KNEW IT WAS A CRIME SCHOOL, WHY DIDN'T YOU JUST GO IN AND CLEAN IT UP?
EVEN IF I DID HAND THE TEACHER OVER TO THE POLICE, THAT WOULDN'T STOP THE BOYS FROM STILL ADMIRING CRIMINALS. WE'VE GOT TO BE SUBTLE!
WE'VE GOT TO MAKE THESE BOYS HATE CRIME AND EVIL, AND NOT LOOK UP TO A RACKETEER LIKE BIG BOY DANIELS, WHO IS PROBABLY THEIR IDEAL!
I SEE, WE'VE GOT TO TEACH THEM TO A MIRE HONESTY, FAIR PLAY!!
EXACTLY! AND THAT'S WHERE YOU COME IN! NOW, I HAVE A PLAN!

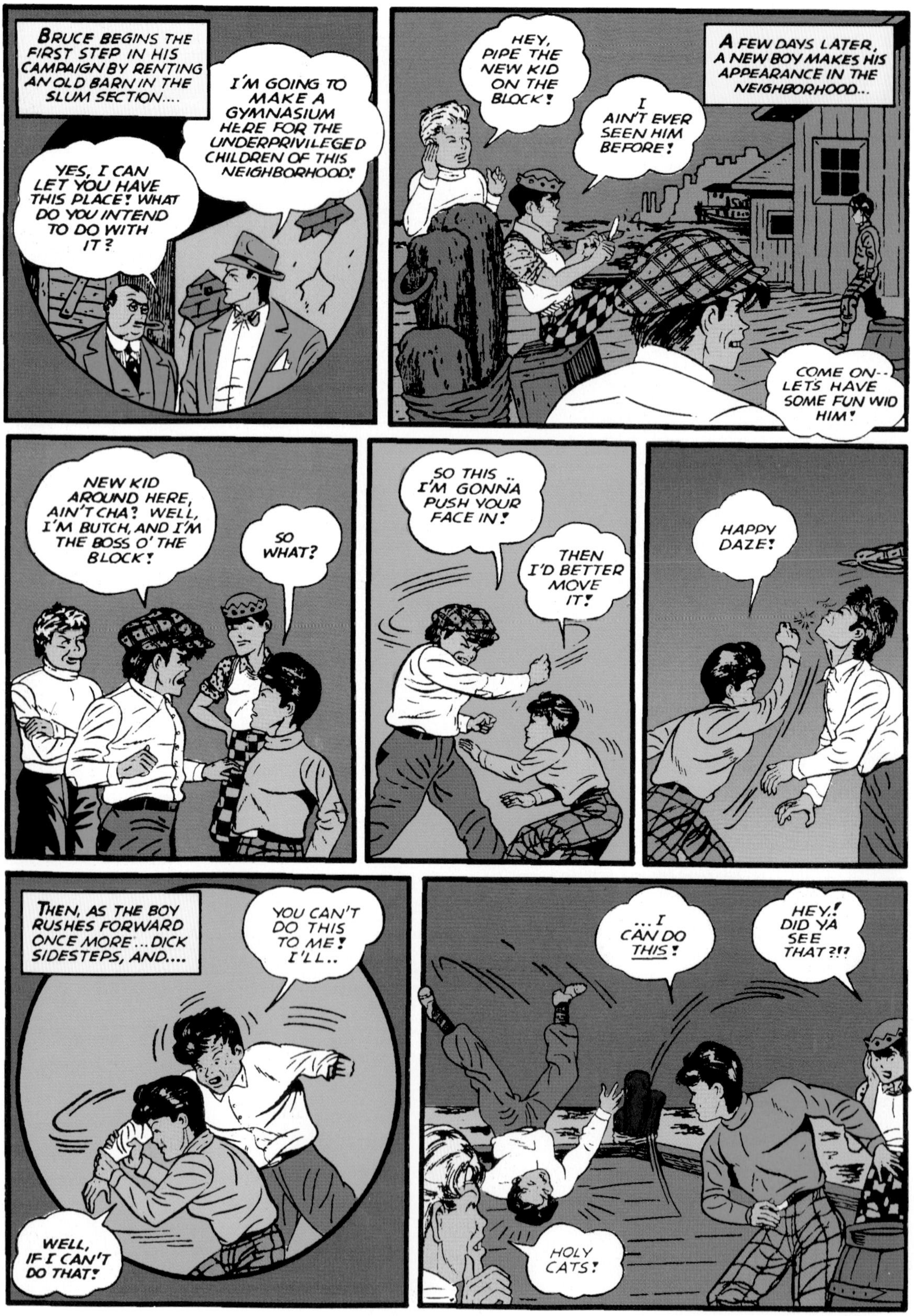
BRUCE BEGINS THE FIRST STEP IN HIS CAMPAIGN BY RENTING AN OLD BARN IN THE SLUM SECTION....
I'M GOING TO MAKE A GYMNASIUM HERE FOR THE UNDERPRIVILEGED CHILDREN OF THIS NEIGHBORHOOD!
YES, I CAN LET YOU HAVE THIS PLACE! WHAT DO YOU INTEND TO DO WITH IT?
A FEW DAYS LATER, A NEW BOY MAKES HIS APPEARANCE IN THE NEIGHBORHOOD...
HEY, PIPE THE NEW KID ON THE BLOCK!
I AIN'T EVER SEEN HIM BEFORE!
COME ON-- LET'S HAVE SOME FUN WID HIM!
NEW KID AROUND HERE, AIN'T CHA? WELL, I'M BUTCH, AND I'M THE BOSS O' THE BLOCK!
SO WHAT?
SO THIS .. I'M GONNA PUSH YOUR FACE IN!
THEN I'D BETTER MOVE IT!
HAPPY DAZE!
THEN, AS THE BOY RUSHES FORWARD ONCE MORE...DICK SIDESTEPS, AND....
YOU CAN'T DO THIS TO ME! I'LL..
WELL, IF I CAN'T DO THAT!
...I CAN DO THIS!
HEY.! DID YA SEE THAT?!?
HOLY CATS!

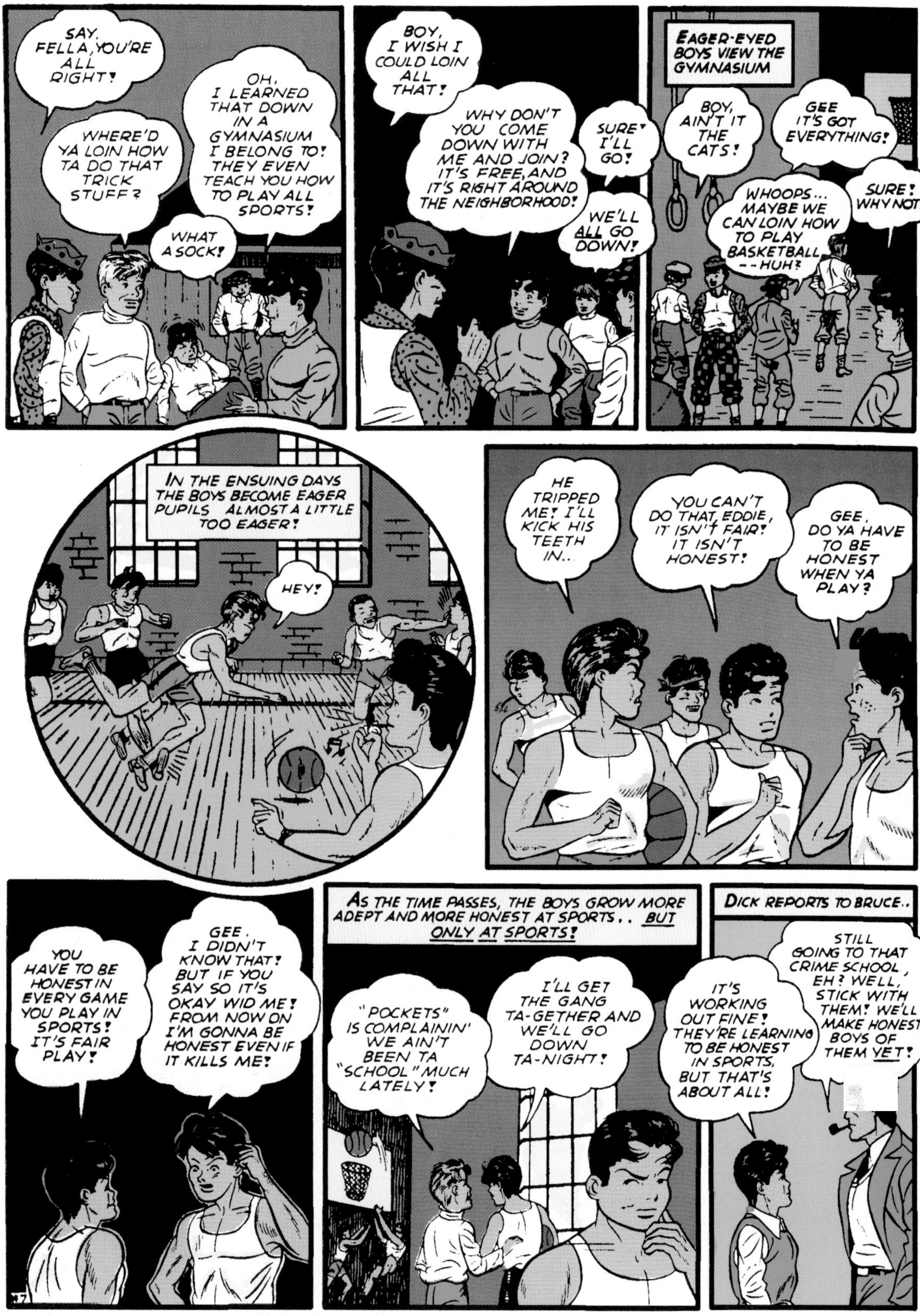
SAY, FELLA, YOU'RE ALL RIGHT!
WHERE'D YA LOIN HOW TA DO THAT TRICK STUFF?
OH, I LEARNED THAT DOWN IN A GYMNASIUM I BELONG TO! THEY EVEN TEACH YOU HOW TO PLAY ALL SPORTS!
WHAT A SOCK!
BOY, I WISH I COULD LOIN ALL THAT!
WHY DON'T YOU COME DOWN WITH ME AND JOIN? IT'S FREE, AND IT'S RIGHT AROUND THE NEIGHBORHOOD!
SURE! I'LL GO!
WE'LL ALL GO DOWN!
EAGER-EYED BOYS VIEW THE GYMNASIUM
BOY, AIN'T IT THE CATS!
GEE IT'S GOT EVERYTHING!
WHOOPS... MAYBE WE CAN LOIN HOW TO PLAY BASKETBALL --HUH?
SURE! WHY NOT!
IN THE ENSUING DAYS THE BOYS BECOME EAGER PUPILS ALMOST A LITTLE TOO EAGER!
HEY!
HE TRIPPED ME! I'LL KICK HIS TEETH IN..
YOU CAN'T DO THAT, EDDIE, IT ISN'T FAIR! IT ISN'T HONEST!
GEE, DO YA HAVE TO BE HONEST WHEN YA PLAY?
YOU HAVE TO BE HONEST IN EVERY GAME YOU PLAY IN SPORTS! IT'S FAIR PLAY!
GEE, I DIDN'T KNOW THAT! BUT IF YOU SAY SO IT'S OKAY WID ME! FROM NOW ON I'M GONNA BE HONEST EVEN IF IT KILLS ME!
AS THE TIME PASSES, THE BOYS GROW MORE ADEPT AND MORE HONEST AT SPORTS.. BUT ONLY AT SPORTS!
"POCKETS" IS COMPLAININ' WE AIN'T BEEN TA "SCHOOL" MUCH LATELY!
I'LL GET THE GANG TA-GETHER AND WE'LL GO DOWN TA-NIGHT!
DICK REPORTS TO BRUCE..
IT'S WORKING OUT FINE! THEY'RE LEARNING TO BE HONEST IN SPORTS, BUT THAT'S ABOUT ALL!
STILL GOING TO THAT CRIME SCHOOL, EH? WELL, STICK WITH THEM! WE'LL MAKE HONEST BOYS OF THEM YET!

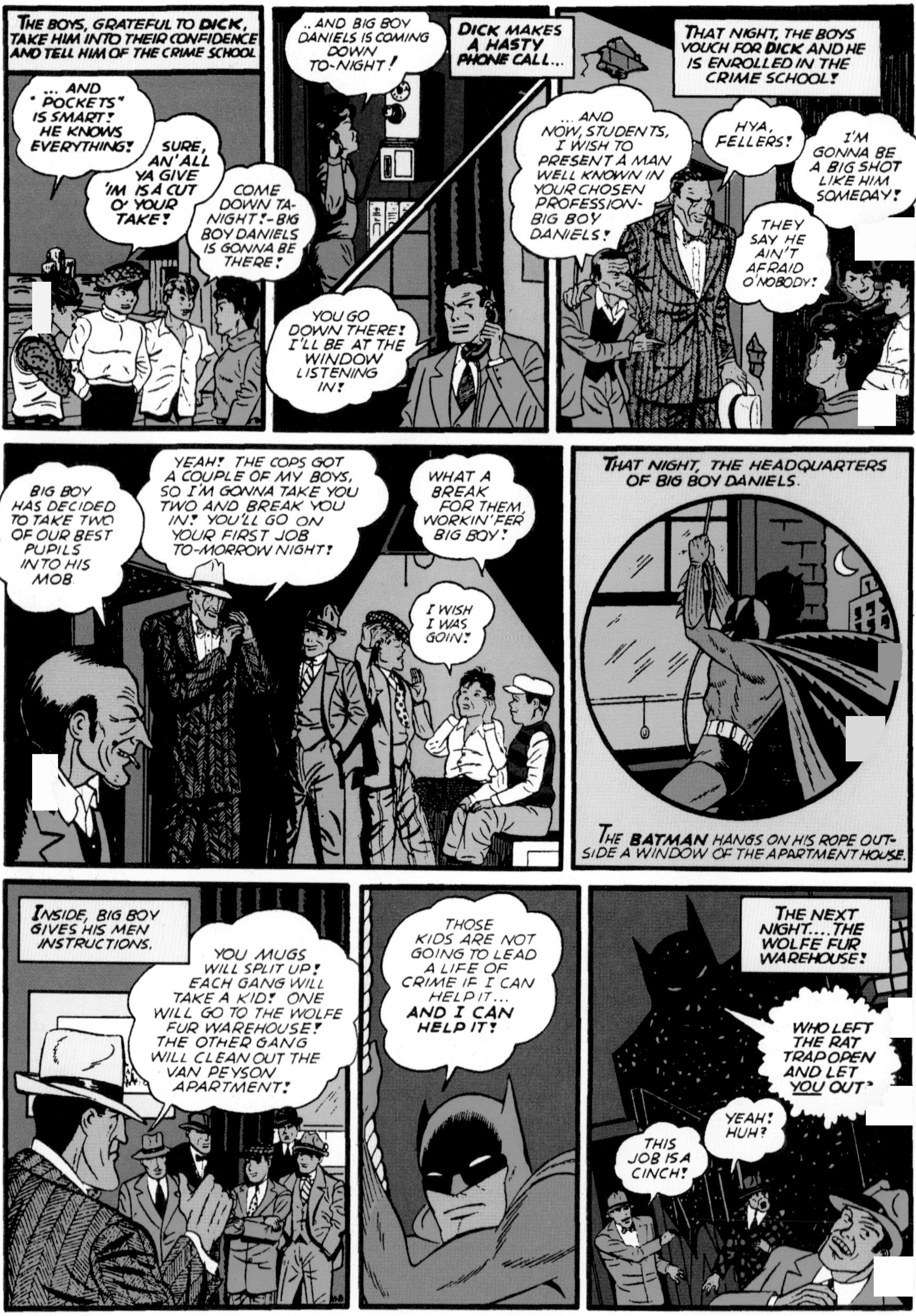
THE BOYS, GRATEFUL TO DICK, TAKE HIM INTO THEIR CONFIDENCE AND TELL HIM OF THE CRIME SCHOOL
... AND "POCKETS" IS SMART! HE KNOWS EVERYTHING!
SURE, AN' ALL YA GIVE 'IM IS A CUT O' YOUR TAKE!
COME DOWN TA-NIGHT!- BIG BOY DANIELS IS GONNA BE THERE!
.. AND BIG BOY DANIELS IS COMING DOWN TO-NIGHT!
DICK MAKES A HASTY PHONE CALL...
YOU GO DOWN THERE! I'LL BE AT THE WINDOW LISTENING IN!
THAT NIGHT, THE BOYS VOUCH FOR DICK AND HE IS ENROLLED IN THE CRIME SCHOOL!
... AND NOW, STUDENTS, I WISH TO PRESENT A MAN WELL KNOWN IN YOUR CHOSEN PROFESSION- BIG BOY DANIELS!
HYA, FELLERS!
I'M GONNA BE A BIG SHOT LIKE HIM SOMEDAY!
THEY SAY HE AIN'T AFRAID O' NOBODY!
BIG BOY HAS DECIDED TO TAKE TWO OF OUR BEST PUPILS INTO HIS MOB
YEAH! THE COPS GOT A COUPLE OF MY BOYS, SO I'M GONNA TAKE YOU TWO AND BREAK YOU IN! YOU'LL GO ON YOUR FIRST JOB TO-MORROW NIGHT!
WHAT A BREAK FOR THEM, WORKIN' FER BIG BOY!
I WISH I WAS GOIN'!
THAT NIGHT, THE HEADQUARTERS OF BIG BOY DANIELS.
THE BATMAN HANGS ON HIS ROPE OUTSIDE A WINDOW OF THE APARTMENT HOUSE.
INSIDE, BIG BOY GIVES HIS MEN INSTRUCTIONS.
YOU MUGS WILL SPLIT UP! EACH GANG WILL TAKE A KID! ONE WILL GO TO THE WOLFE FUR WAREHOUSE! THE OTHER GANG WILL CLEAN OUT THE VAN PEYSON APARTMENT!
THOSE KIDS ARE NOT GOING TO LEAD A LIFE OF CRIME IF I CAN HELP IT... AND I CAN HELP IT!
THE NEXT NIGHT.... THE WOLFE FUR WAREHOUSE!
WHO LEFT THE RAT TRAP OPEN AND LET YOU OUT?
YEAH! HUH?
THIS JOB IS A CINCH!

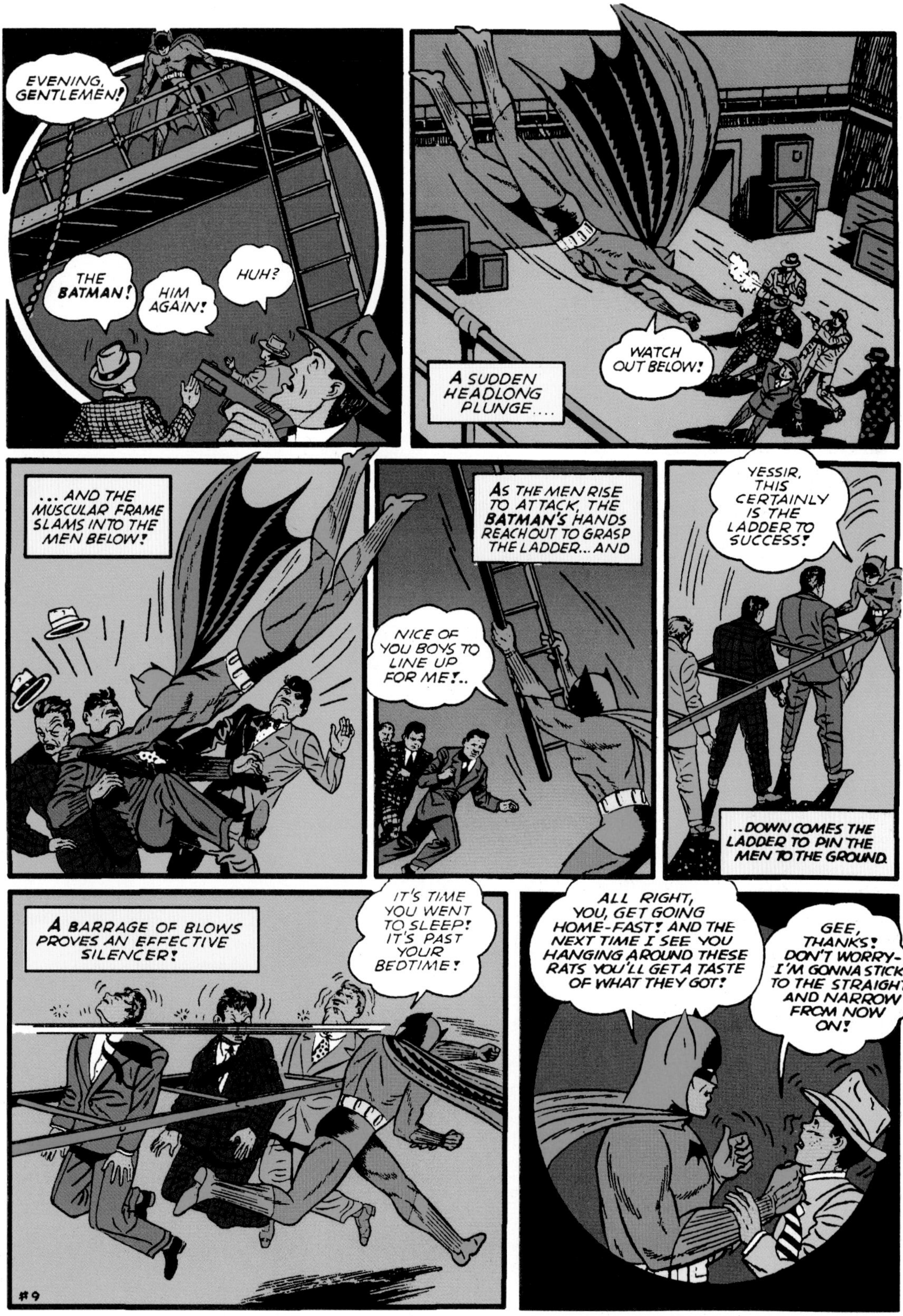
EVENING, GENTLEMEN!
THE BATMAN!
HIM AGAIN!
HUH?
A SUDDEN HEADLONG PLUNGE....
WATCH OUT BELOW!
... AND THE MUSCULAR FRAME SLAMS INTO THE MEN BELOW!
AS THE MEN RISE TO ATTACK, THE BATMAN'S HANDS REACH OUT TO GRASP THE LADDER... AND
NICE OF YOU BOYS TO LINE UP FOR ME!..
YESSIR, THIS CERTAINLY IS THE LADDER TO SUCCESS!
..DOWN COMES THE LADDER TO PIN THE MEN TO THE GROUND.
A BARRAGE OF BLOWS PROVES AN EFFECTIVE SILENCER!
IT'S TIME YOU WENT TO SLEEP! IT'S PAST YOUR BEDTIME!
#9
ALL RIGHT, YOU, GET GOING HOME-FAST! AND THE NEXT TIME I SEE YOU HANGING AROUND THESE RATS YOU'LL GET A TASTE OF WHAT THEY GOT!
GEE, THANKS! DON'T WORRY-- I'M GONNA STICK TO THE STRAIGHT AND NARROW FROM NOW ON!

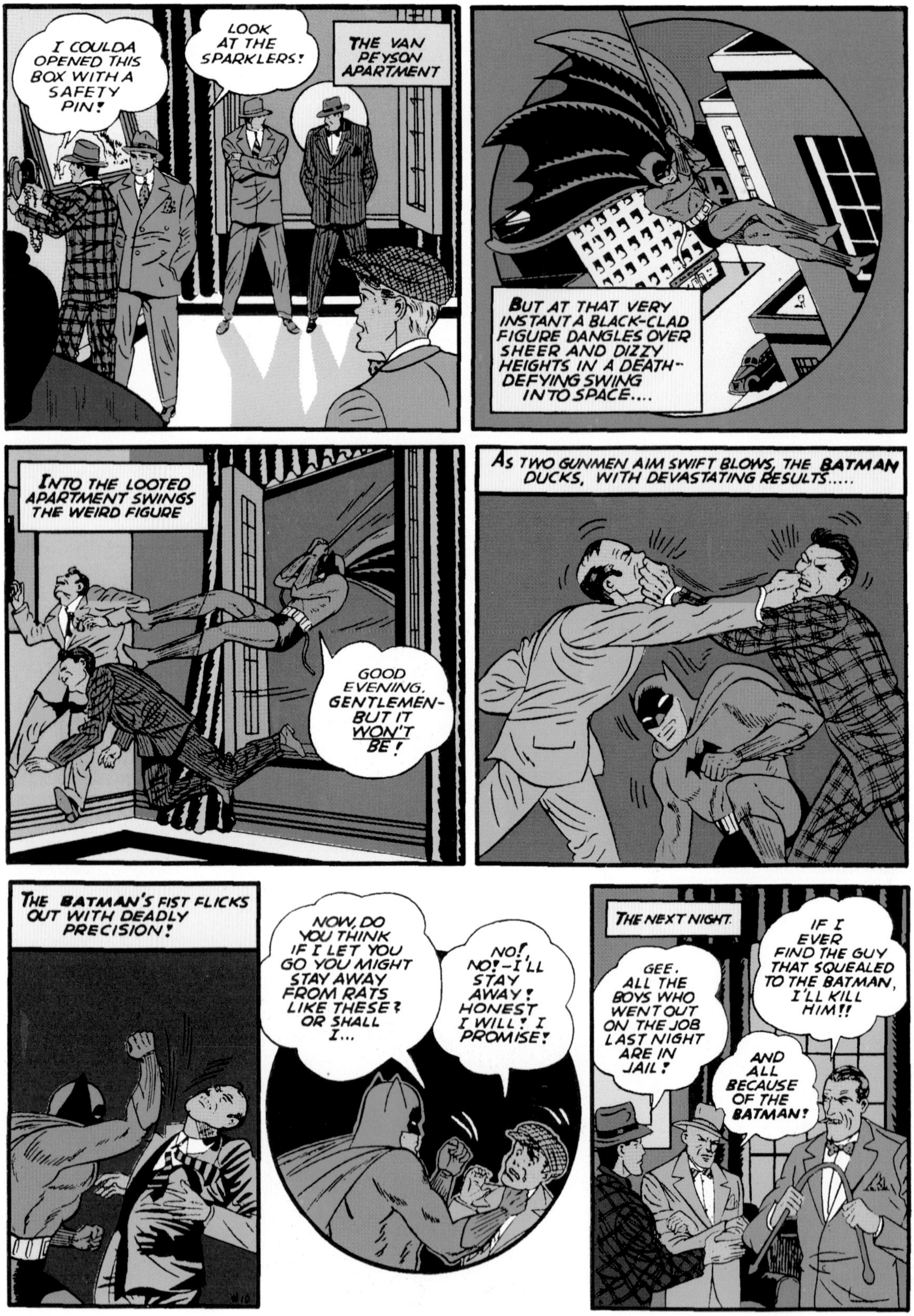
THE VAN PEYSON APARTMENT
I COULDA OPENED THIS BOX WITH A SAFETY PIN!
LOOK AT THE SPARKLERS!
BUT AT THAT VERY INSTANT A BLACK-CLAD FIGURE DANGLES OVER SHEER AND DIZZY HEIGHTS IN A DEATH-DEFYING SWING INTO SPACE....
INTO THE LOOTED APARTMENT SWINGS THE WEIRD FIGURE
GOOD EVENING, GENTLEMEN- BUT IT WON'T BE!
AS TWO GUNMEN AIM SWIFT BLOWS, THE BATMAN DUCKS, WITH DEVASTATING RESULTS.....
THE BATMAN'S FIST FLICKS OUT WITH DEADLY PRECISION!
NOW, DO YOU THINK IF I LET YOU GO YOU MIGHT STAY AWAY FROM RATS LIKE THESE? OR SHALL I...
NO!, NO!-I'LL STAY AWAY! HONEST I WILL! I PROMISE!
THE NEXT NIGHT.
GEE, ALL THE BOYS WHO WENT OUT ON THE JOB LAST NIGHT ARE IN JAIL!
IF I EVER FIND THE GUY THAT SQUEALED TO THE BATMAN, I'LL KILL HIM!!
AND ALL BECAUSE OF THE BATMAN!

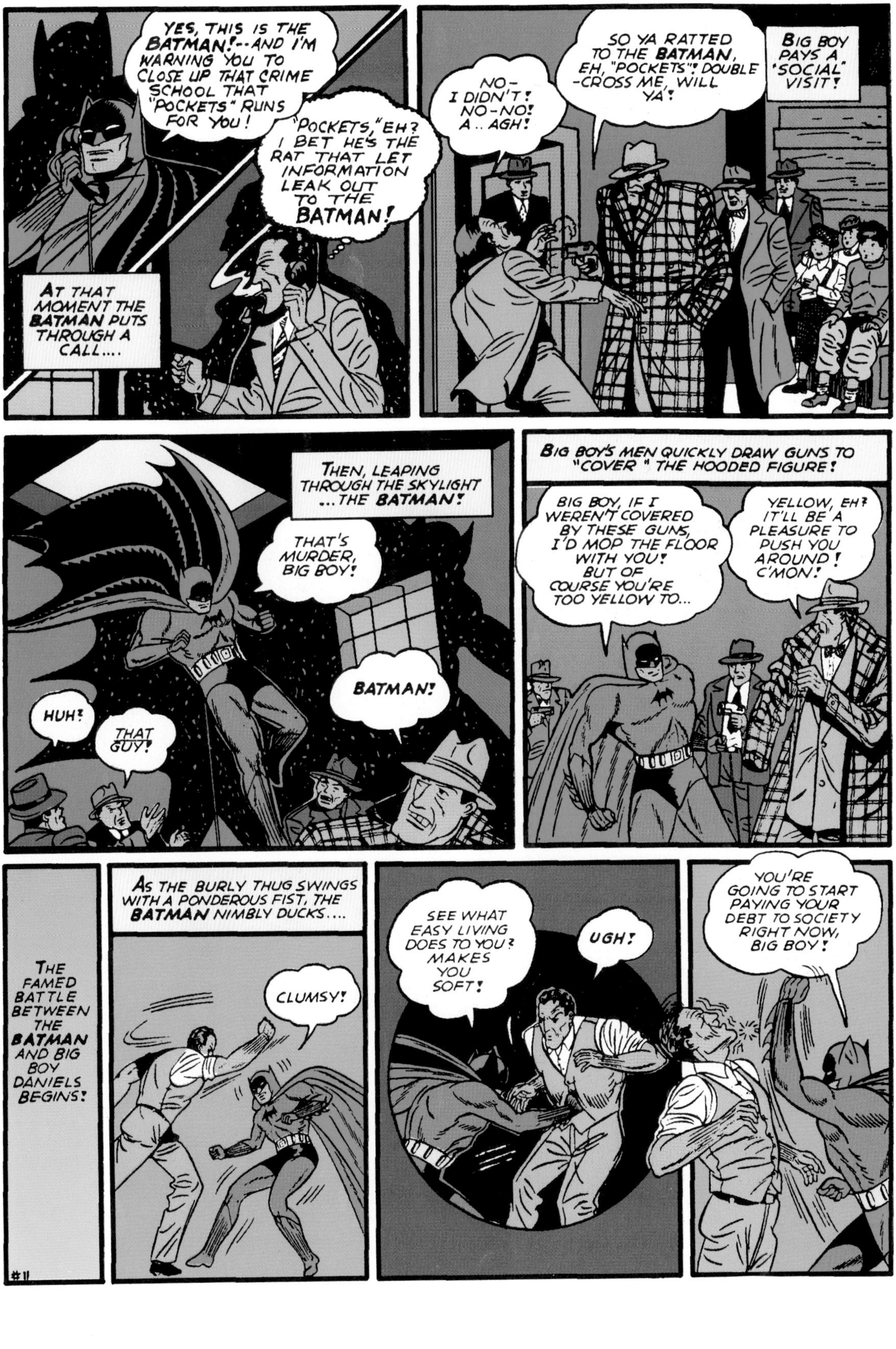
YES, THIS IS THE BATMAN!--AND I'M WARNING YOU TO CLOSE UP THAT CRIME SCHOOL THAT "POCKETS" RUNS FOR YOU!
"POCKETS," EH? I BET HE'S THE RAT THAT LET INFORMATION LEAK OUT TO THE BATMAN!
AT THAT MOMENT THE BATMAN PUTS THROUGH A CALL....
BIG BOY PAYS A "SOCIAL" VISIT!
SO YA RATTED TO THE BATMAN, EH, "POCKETS"? DOUBLE-CROSS ME, WILL YA?
NO-I DIDN'T! NO-NO! A..AGH!
THEN, LEAPING THROUGH THE SKYLIGHT ...THE BATMAN!
THAT'S MURDER, BIG BOY!
HUH?
THAT GUY!
BATMAN!
BIG BOY'S MEN QUICKLY DRAW GUNS TO "COVER" THE HOODED FIGURE!
BIG BOY, IF I WEREN'T COVERED BY THESE GUNS, I'D MOP THE FLOOR WITH YOU! BUT OF COURSE YOU'RE TOO YELLOW TO...
YELLOW, EH? IT'LL BE A PLEASURE TO PUSH YOU AROUND! C'MON!
THE FAMED BATTLE BETWEEN THE BATMAN AND BIG BOY DANIELS BEGINS!
AS THE BURLY THUG SWINGS WITH A PONDEROUS FIST, THE BATMAN NIMBLY DUCKS....
CLUMSY!
SEE WHAT EASY LIVING DOES TO YOU? MAKES YOU SOFT!
UGH!
YOU'RE GOING TO START PAYING YOUR DEBT TO SOCIETY RIGHT NOW, BIG BOY!
#11

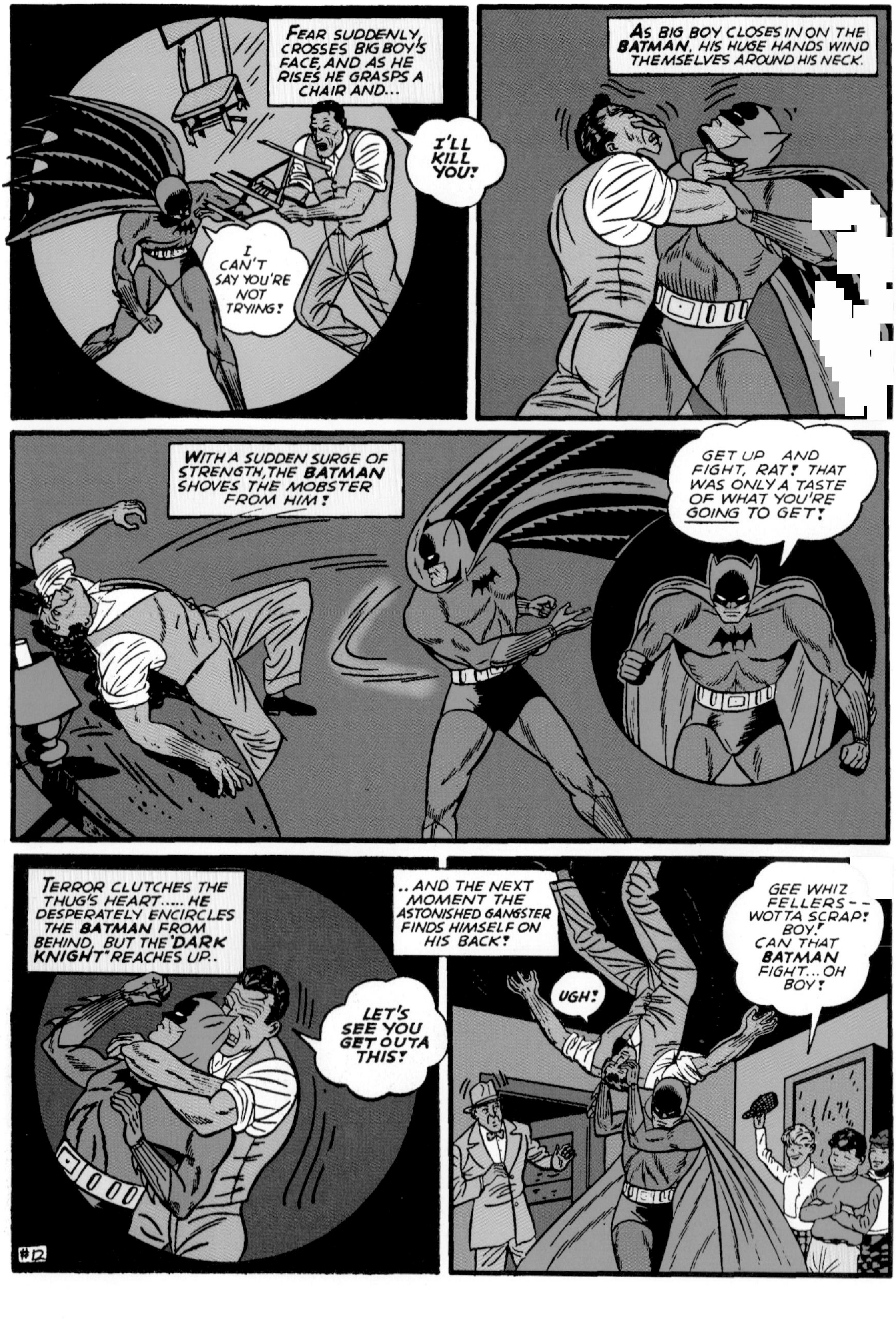
FEAR SUDDENLY CROSSES BIG BOY'S FACE, AND AS HE RISES HE GRASPS A CHAIR AND...
I'LL KILL YOU!
I CAN'T SAY YOU'RE NOT TRYING!
AS BIG BOY CLOSES IN ON THE BATMAN, HIS HUGE HANDS WIND THEMSELVES AROUND HIS NECK.
WITH A SUDDEN SURGE OF STRENGTH, THE BATMAN SHOVES THE MOBSTER FROM HIM!
GET UP AND FIGHT, RAT! THAT WAS ONLY A TASTE OF WHAT YOU'RE GOING TO GET!
TERROR CLUTCHES THE THUG'S HEART..... HE DESPERATELY ENCIRCLES THE BATMAN FROM BEHIND, BUT THE "DARK KNIGHT" REACHES UP..
LET'S SEE YOU GET OUTA THIS!
#12
..AND THE NEXT MOMENT THE ASTONISHED GANGSTER FINDS HIMSELF ON HIS BACK!
UGH!
GEE WHIZ FELLERS-- WOTTA SCRAP! BOY! CAN THAT BATMAN FIGHT... OH BOY!

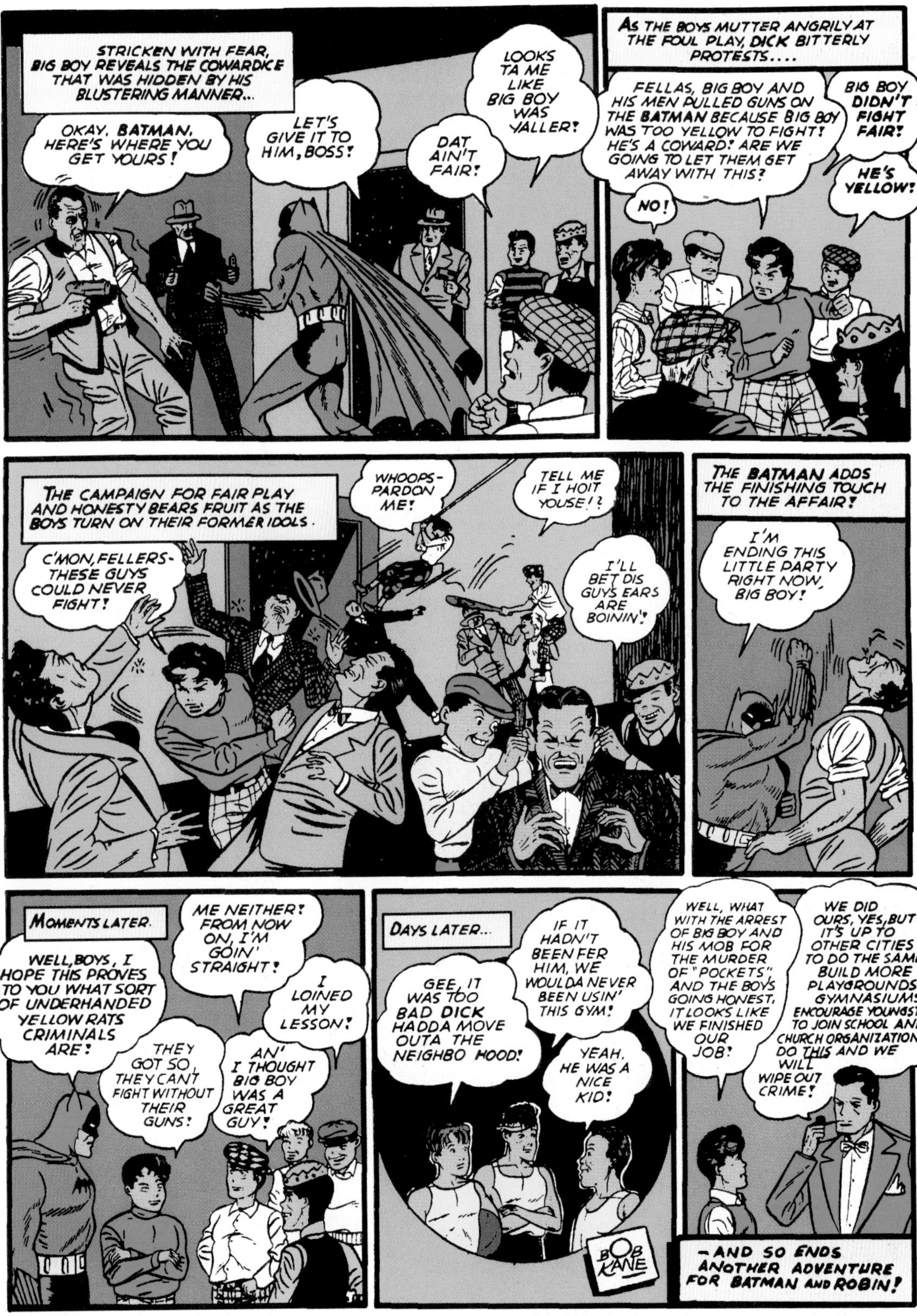
STRICKEN WITH FEAR, BIG BOY REVEALS THE COWARDICE THAT WAS HIDDEN BY HIS BLUSTERING MANNER...
OKAY, BATMAN, HERE'S WHERE YOU GET YOURS!
LET'S GIVE IT TO HIM, BOSS!
LOOKS TA ME LIKE BIG BOY WAS YALLER!
DAT AIN'T FAIR!
AS THE BOYS MUTTER ANGRILY AT THE FOUL PLAY, DICK BITTERLY PROTESTS....
FELLAS, BIG BOY AND HIS MEN PULLED GUNS ON THE BATMAN BECAUSE BIG BOY WAS TOO YELLOW TO FIGHT! HE'S A COWARD! ARE WE GOING TO LET THEM GET AWAY WITH THIS?
BIG BOY DIDN'T FIGHT FAIR!
HE'S YELLOW!
NO!
THE CAMPAIGN FOR FAIR PLAY AND HONESTY BEARS FRUIT AS THE BOYS TURN ON THEIR FORMER IDOLS.
WHOOPS-PARDON ME!
TELL ME IF I HOIT YOUSE!?
C'MON, FELLERS-THESE GUYS COULD NEVER FIGHT!
I'LL BET DIS GUY'S EARS ARE BOININ'!
THE BATMAN ADDS THE FINISHING TOUCH TO THE AFFAIR!
I'M ENDING THIS LITTLE PARTY RIGHT NOW, BIG BOY!
MOMENTS LATER.
WELL, BOYS, I HOPE THIS PROVES TO YOU WHAT SORT OF UNDERHANDED YELLOW RATS CRIMINALS ARE!
ME NEITHER! FROM NOW ON, I'M GOIN' STRAIGHT!
THEY GOT SO, THEY CAN'T FIGHT WITHOUT THEIR GUNS!
I LOINED MY LESSON!
AN' I THOUGHT BIG BOY WAS A GREAT GUY!
DAYS LATER...
GEE, IT WAS TOO BAD DICK HADDA MOVE OUTA THE NEIGHBO HOOD!
IF IT HADN'T BEEN FER HIM, WE WOULDA NEVER BEEN USIN' THIS GYM!
YEAH, HE WAS A NICE KID!
BOB KANE
WELL, WHAT WITH THE ARREST OF BIG BOY AND HIS MOB FOR THE MURDER OF "POCKETS" AND THE BOYS GOING HONEST, IT LOOKS LIKE WE FINISHED OUR JOB!
WE DID OURS, YES, BUT IT'S UP TO OTHER CITIES TO DO THE SAME BUILD MORE PLAYGROUNDS, GYMNASIUMS - ENCOURAGE YOUNGSTERS TO JOIN SCHOOL AND CHURCH ORGANIZATIONS DO THIS AND WE WILL WIPE OUT CRIME!
-AND SO ENDS ANOTHER ADVENTURE FOR BATMAN AND ROBIN!

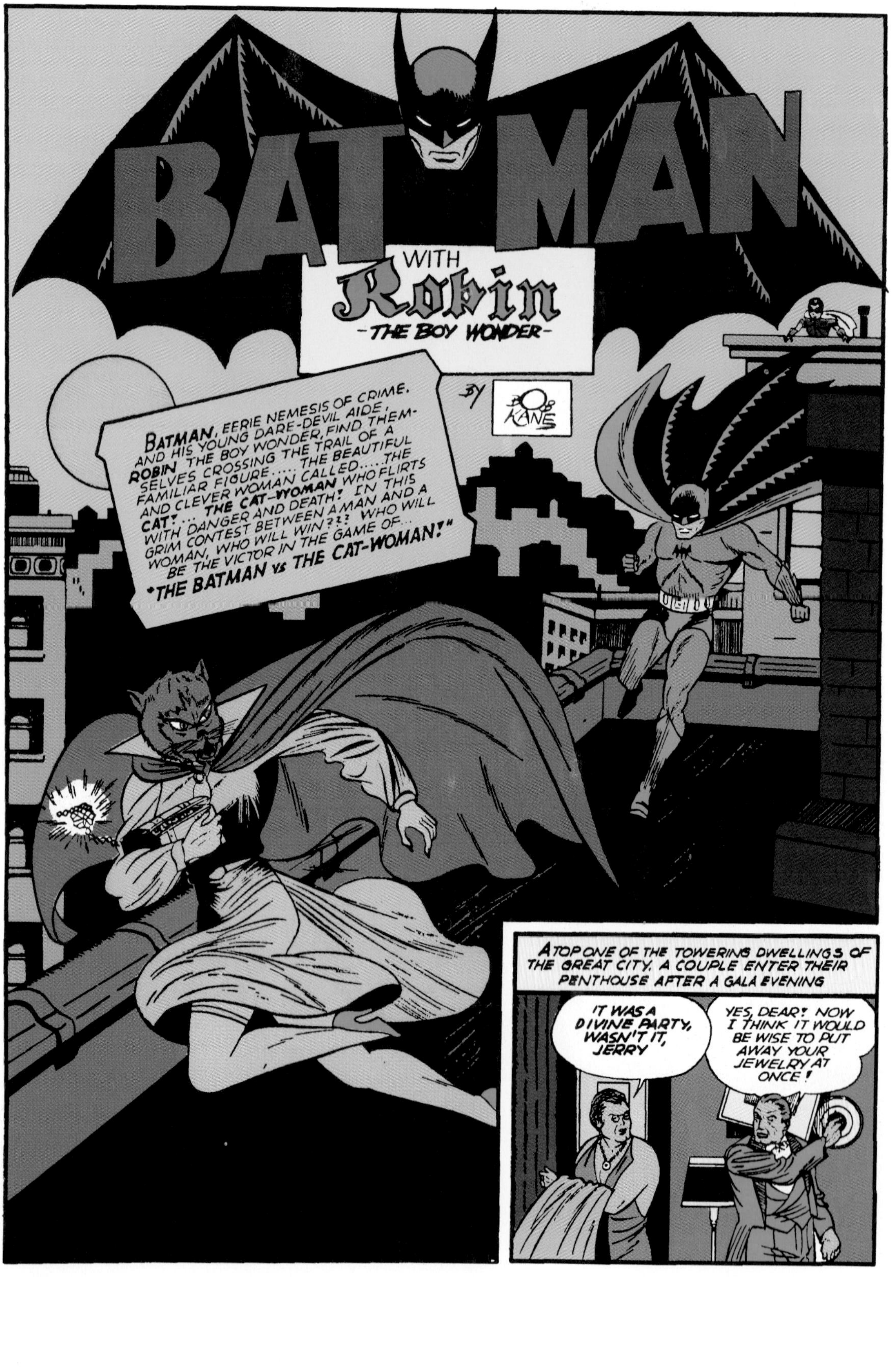
BATMAN
WITH Robin -THE BOY WONDER-
BY BOB KANE
BATMAN, EERIE NEMESIS OF CRIME, AND HIS YOUNG DARE-DEVIL AIDE, ROBIN THE BOY WONDER, FIND THEMSELVES CROSSING THE TRAIL OF A FAMILIAR FIGURE..... THE BEAUTIFUL AND CLEVER WOMAN CALLED.....THE CAT!... THE CAT-WOMAN WHO FLIRTS WITH DANGER AND DEATH! IN THIS GRIM CONTEST BETWEEN A MAN AND A WOMAN, WHO WILL WIN??? WHO WILL BE THE VICTOR IN THE GAME OF...
"THE BATMAN vs THE CAT-WOMAN!"
ATOP ONE OF THE TOWERING DWELLINGS OF THE GREAT CITY, A COUPLE ENTER THEIR PENTHOUSE AFTER A GALA EVENING
IT WAS A DIVINE PARTY, WASN'T IT, JERRY
YES, DEAR! NOW I THINK IT WOULD BE WISE TO PUT AWAY YOUR JEWELRY AT ONCE!

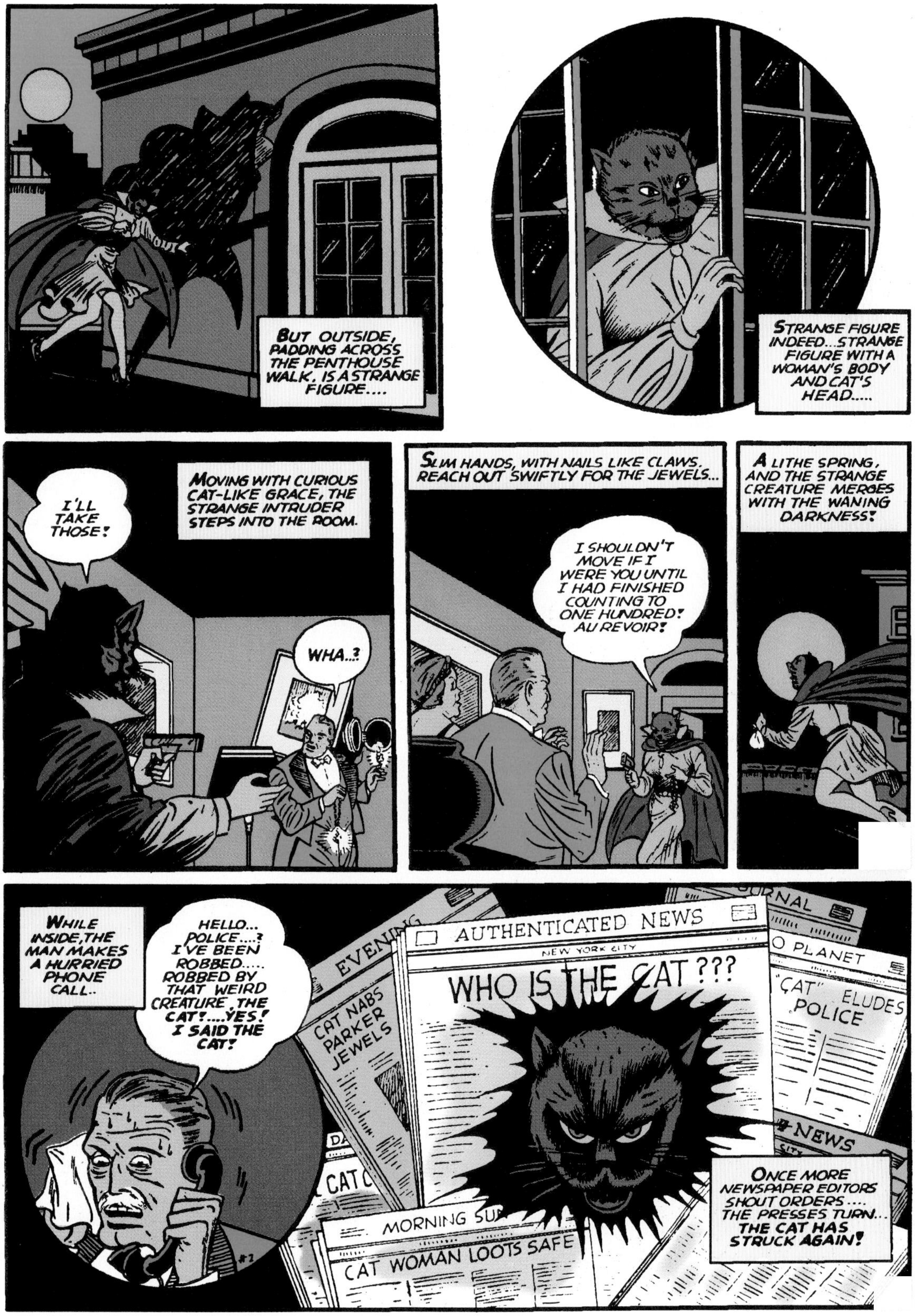
BUT OUTSIDE, PADDING ACROSS THE PENTHOUSE WALK, IS A STRANGE FIGURE....
STRANGE FIGURE INDEED...STRANGE FIGURE WITH A WOMAN'S BODY AND CAT'S HEAD.....
MOVING WITH CURIOUS CAT-LIKE GRACE, THE STRANGE INTRUDER STEPS INTO THE ROOM.
I'LL TAKE THOSE!
WHA..?
SLIM HANDS, WITH NAILS LIKE CLAWS, REACH OUT SWIFTLY FOR THE JEWELS...
I SHOULDN'T MOVE IF I WERE YOU UNTIL I HAD FINISHED COUNTING TO ONE HUNDRED! AU REVOIR!
A LITHE SPRING, AND THE STRANGE CREATURE MERGES WITH THE WANING DARKNESS!
WHILE INSIDE, THE MAN MAKES A HURRIED PHONE CALL..
HELLO... POLICE....? I'VE BEEN ROBBED..... ROBBED BY THAT WEIRD CREATURE, THE CAT!....YES! I SAID THE CAT!
EVENING
CAT NABS PARKER JEWELS
AUTHENTICATED NEWS
NEW YORK CITY
WHO IS THE CAT ???
O PLANET
"CAT" ELUDES POLICE
NEWS
MORNING
CAT WOMAN LOOTS SAFE
ONCE MORE NEWSPAPER EDITORS SHOUT ORDERS.... THE PRESSES TURN... THE CAT HAS STRUCK AGAIN!

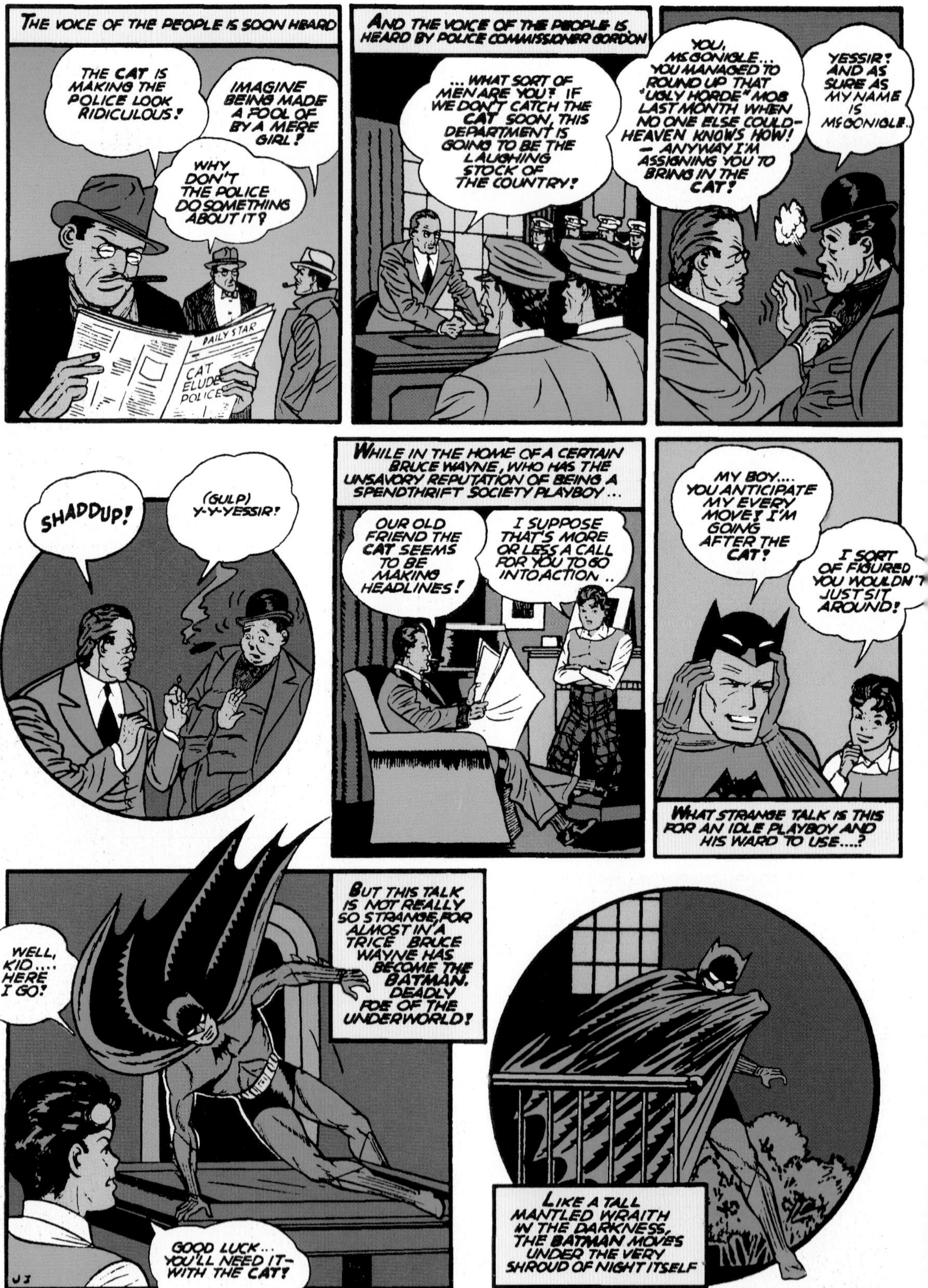
THE VOICE OF THE PEOPLE IS SOON HEARD
THE CAT IS MAKING THE POLICE LOOK RIDICULOUS!
IMAGINE BEING MADE A FOOL OF BY A MERE GIRL!
WHY DON'T THE POLICE DO SOMETHING ABOUT IT?
DAILY STAR
CAT ELUDES POLICE
AND THE VOICE OF THE PEOPLE IS HEARD BY POLICE COMMISSIONER GORDON
... WHAT SORT OF MEN ARE YOU? IF WE DON'T CATCH THE CAT SOON, THIS DEPARTMENT IS GOING TO BE THE LAUGHING STOCK OF THE COUNTRY!
YOU, McGONIGLE... YOU MANAGED TO ROUND UP THAT "UGLY HORDE" MOB LAST MONTH WHEN NO ONE ELSE COULD- HEAVEN KNOWS HOW! — ANYWAY I'M ASSIGNING YOU TO BRING IN THE CAT!
YESSIR! AND AS SURE AS MY NAME IS McGONIGLE..
SHADDUP!
(GULP) Y-Y-YESSIR!
WHILE IN THE HOME OF A CERTAIN BRUCE WAYNE, WHO HAS THE UNSAVORY REPUTATION OF BEING A SPENDTHRIFT SOCIETY PLAYBOY...
OUR OLD FRIEND THE CAT SEEMS TO BE MAKING HEADLINES!
I SUPPOSE THAT'S MORE OR LESS A CALL FOR YOU TO GO INTO ACTION ..
MY BOY.... YOU ANTICIPATE MY EVERY MOVE! I'M GOING AFTER THE CAT!
I SORT OF FIGURED YOU WOULDN'T JUST SIT AROUND!
WHAT STRANGE TALK IS THIS FOR AN IDLE PLAYBOY AND HIS WARD TO USE....?
WELL, KID.... HERE I GO!
BUT THIS TALK IS NOT REALLY SO STRANGE, FOR ALMOST IN A TRICE BRUCE WAYNE HAS BECOME THE BATMAN, DEADLY FOE OF THE UNDERWORLD!
GOOD LUCK... YOU'LL NEED IT- WITH THE CAT!
LIKE A TALL MANTLED WRAITH IN THE DARKNESS, THE BATMAN MOVES UNDER THE VERY SHROUD OF NIGHT ITSELF

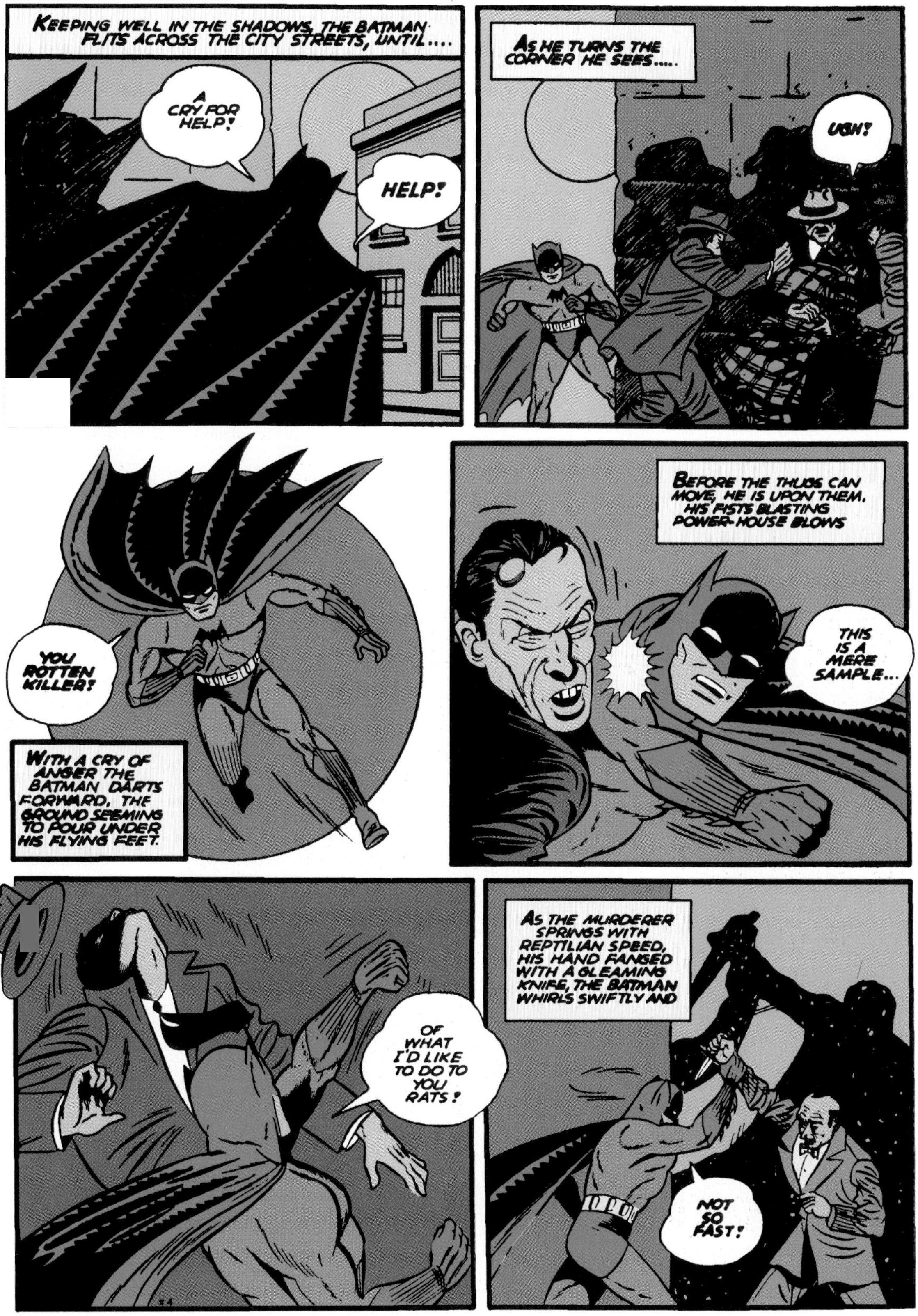
KEEPING WELL IN THE SHADOWS, THE BATMAN FLITS ACROSS THE CITY STREETS, UNTIL....
A CRY FOR HELP!
HELP!
AS HE TURNS THE CORNER HE SEES.....
UGH!
WITH A CRY OF ANGER THE BATMAN DARTS FORWARD, THE GROUND SEEMING TO POUR UNDER HIS FLYING FEET.
YOU ROTTEN KILLER!
BEFORE THE THUGS CAN MOVE, HE IS UPON THEM, HIS FISTS BLASTING POWER-HOUSE BLOWS
THIS IS A MERE SAMPLE...
OF WHAT I'D LIKE TO DO TO YOU RATS!
AS THE MURDERER SPRINGS WITH REPTILIAN SPEED, HIS HAND FANGED WITH A GLEAMING KNIFE, THE BATMAN WHIRLS SWIFTLY AND
NOT SO FAST!

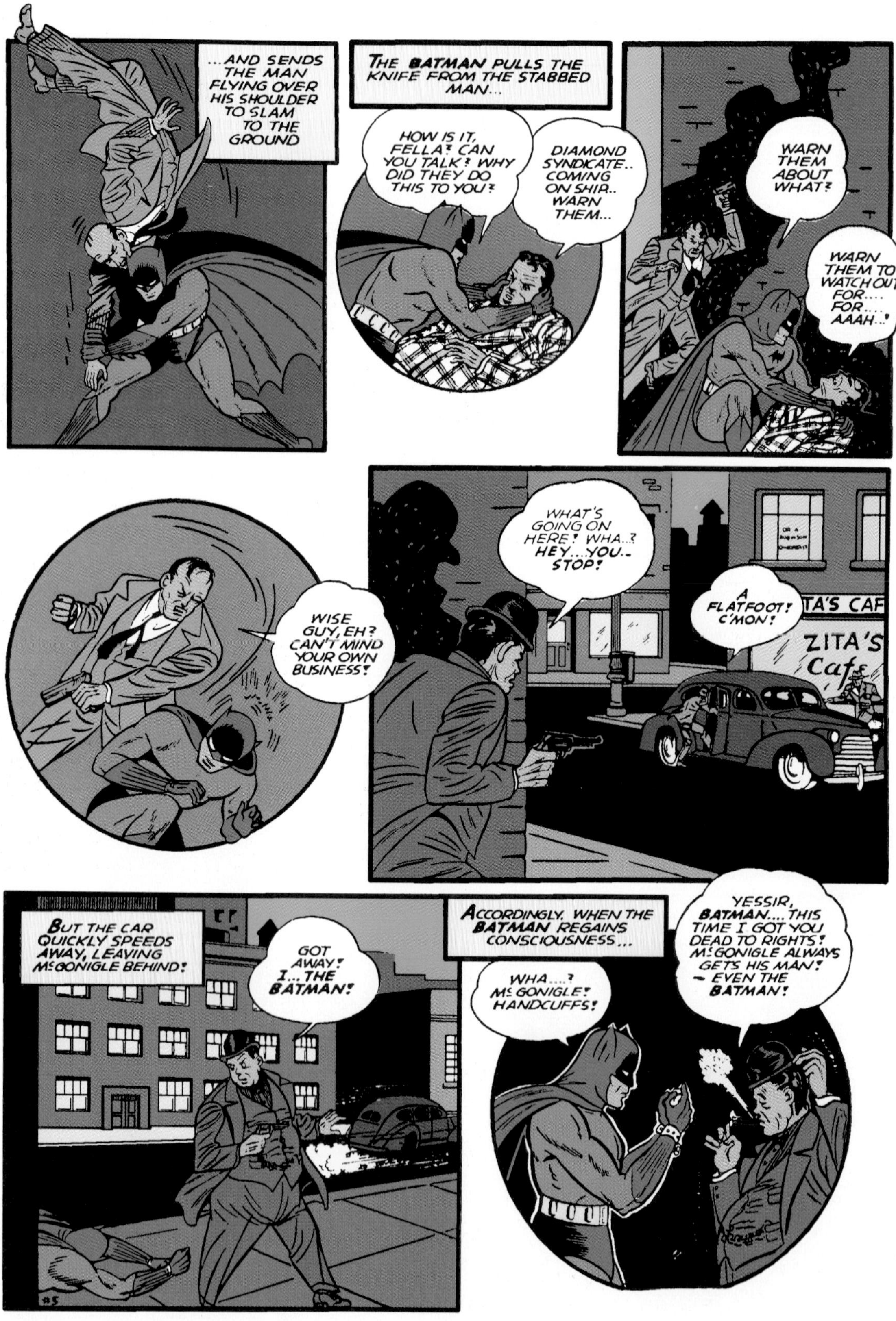
...AND SENDS THE MAN FLYING OVER HIS SHOULDER TO SLAM TO THE GROUND
THE BATMAN PULLS THE KNIFE FROM THE STABBED MAN...
HOW IS IT, FELLA? CAN YOU TALK? WHY DID THEY DO THIS TO YOU?
DIAMOND SYNDICATE.. COMING ON SHIP.. WARN THEM...
WARN THEM ABOUT WHAT?
WARN THEM TO WATCH OUT FOR.... FOR.... AAAH..!
WISE GUY, EH? CAN'T MIND YOUR OWN BUSINESS!
WHAT'S GOING ON HERE! WHA..? HEY....YOU.. STOP!
A FLATFOOT! C'MON!
ZITA'S CAFÉ
BUT THE CAR QUICKLY SPEEDS AWAY, LEAVING MCGONIGLE BEHIND!
GOT AWAY! I...THE BATMAN!
ACCORDINGLY, WHEN THE BATMAN REGAINS CONSCIOUSNESS...
WHA....? MCGONIGLE! HANDCUFFS!
YESSIR, BATMAN.... THIS TIME I GOT YOU DEAD TO RIGHTS! MCGONIGLE ALWAYS GETS HIS MAN! - EVEN THE BATMAN!

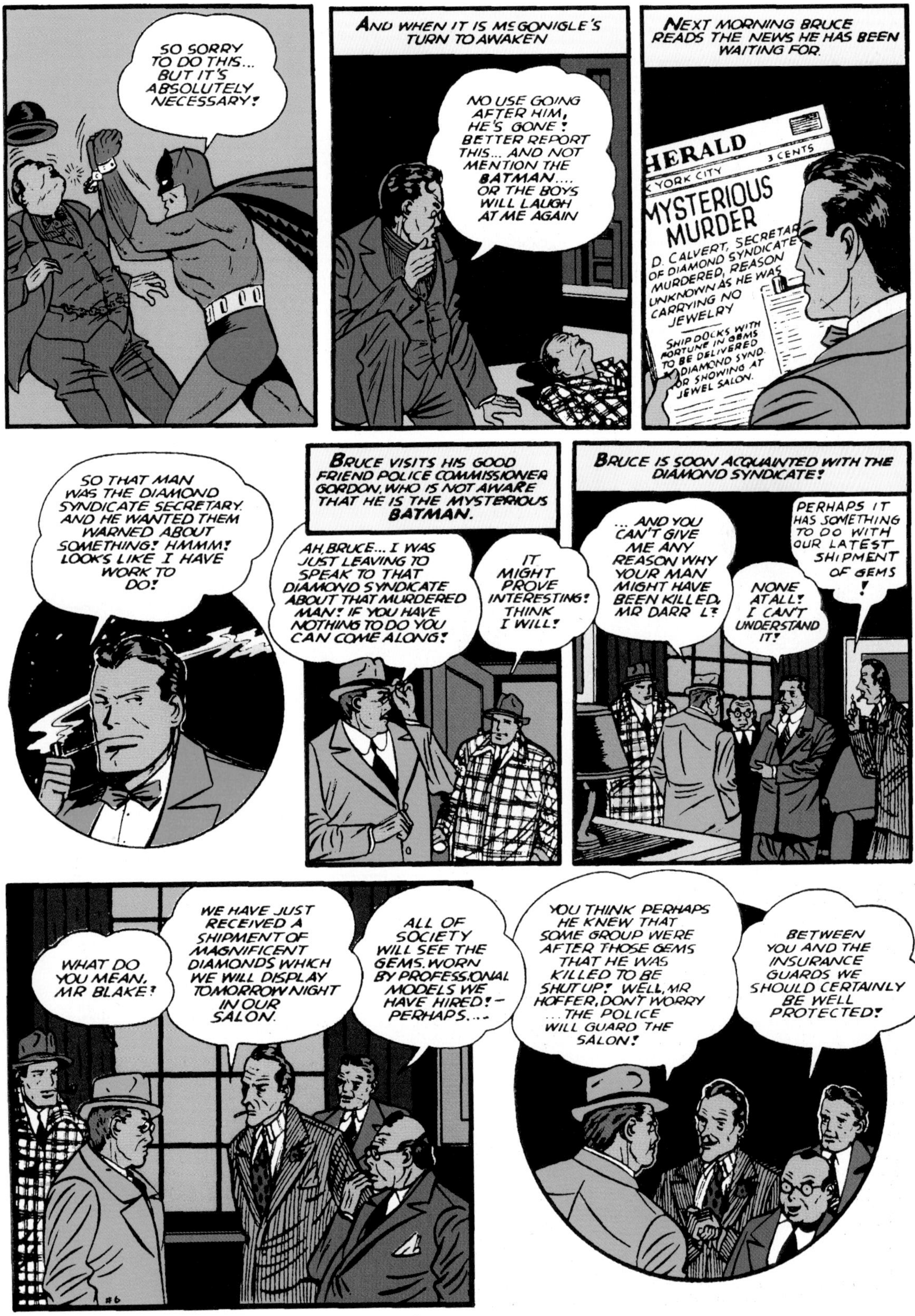
SO SORRY TO DO THIS... BUT IT'S ABSOLUTELY NECESSARY!
AND WHEN IT IS MCGONIGLE'S TURN TO AWAKEN
NO USE GOING AFTER HIM, HE'S GONE! BETTER REPORT THIS... AND NOT MENTION THE BATMAN.... OR THE BOYS WILL LAUGH AT ME AGAIN
NEXT MORNING BRUCE READS THE NEWS HE HAS BEEN WAITING FOR.
HERALD
YORK CITY
3 CENTS
MYSTERIOUS MURDER
D. CALVERT, SECRETAR OF DIAMOND SYNDICATE MURDERED, REASON UNKNOWN AS HE WAS CARRYING NO JEWELRY
SHIP DOCKS WITH FORTUNE IN GEMS TO BE DELIVERED DIAMOND SYND. FOR SHOWING AT JEWEL SALON.
SO THAT MAN WAS THE DIAMOND SYNDICATE SECRETARY. AND HE WANTED THEM WARNED ABOUT SOMETHING! HMMM! LOOKS LIKE I HAVE WORK TO DO!
BRUCE VISITS HIS GOOD FRIEND POLICE COMMISSIONER GORDON, WHO IS NOT AWARE THAT HE IS THE MYSTERIOUS BATMAN.
AH, BRUCE... I WAS JUST LEAVING TO SPEAK TO THAT DIAMOND SYNDICATE ABOUT THAT MURDERED MAN! IF YOU HAVE NOTHING TO DO YOU CAN COME ALONG!
IT MIGHT PROVE INTERESTING! THINK I WILL!
BRUCE IS SOON ACQUAINTED WITH THE DIAMOND SYNDICATE!
... AND YOU CAN'T GIVE ME ANY REASON WHY YOUR MAN MIGHT HAVE BEEN KILLED, MR DARR L?
NONE AT ALL! I CAN'T UNDERSTAND IT!
PERHAPS IT HAS SOMETHING TO DO WITH OUR LATEST SHIPMENT OF GEMS!
WHAT DO YOU MEAN, MR BLAKE?
WE HAVE JUST RECEIVED A SHIPMENT OF MAGNIFICENT DIAMONDS WHICH WE WILL DISPLAY TOMORROW NIGHT IN OUR SALON.
ALL OF SOCIETY WILL SEE THE GEMS, WORN BY PROFESSIONAL MODELS WE HAVE HIRED! — PERHAPS....
YOU THINK PERHAPS HE KNEW THAT SOME GROUP WERE AFTER THOSE GEMS THAT HE WAS KILLED TO BE SHUT UP! WELL, MR HOFFER, DON'T WORRY ... THE POLICE WILL GUARD THE SALON!
BETWEEN YOU AND THE INSURANCE GUARDS WE SHOULD CERTAINLY BE WELL PROTECTED!
#6

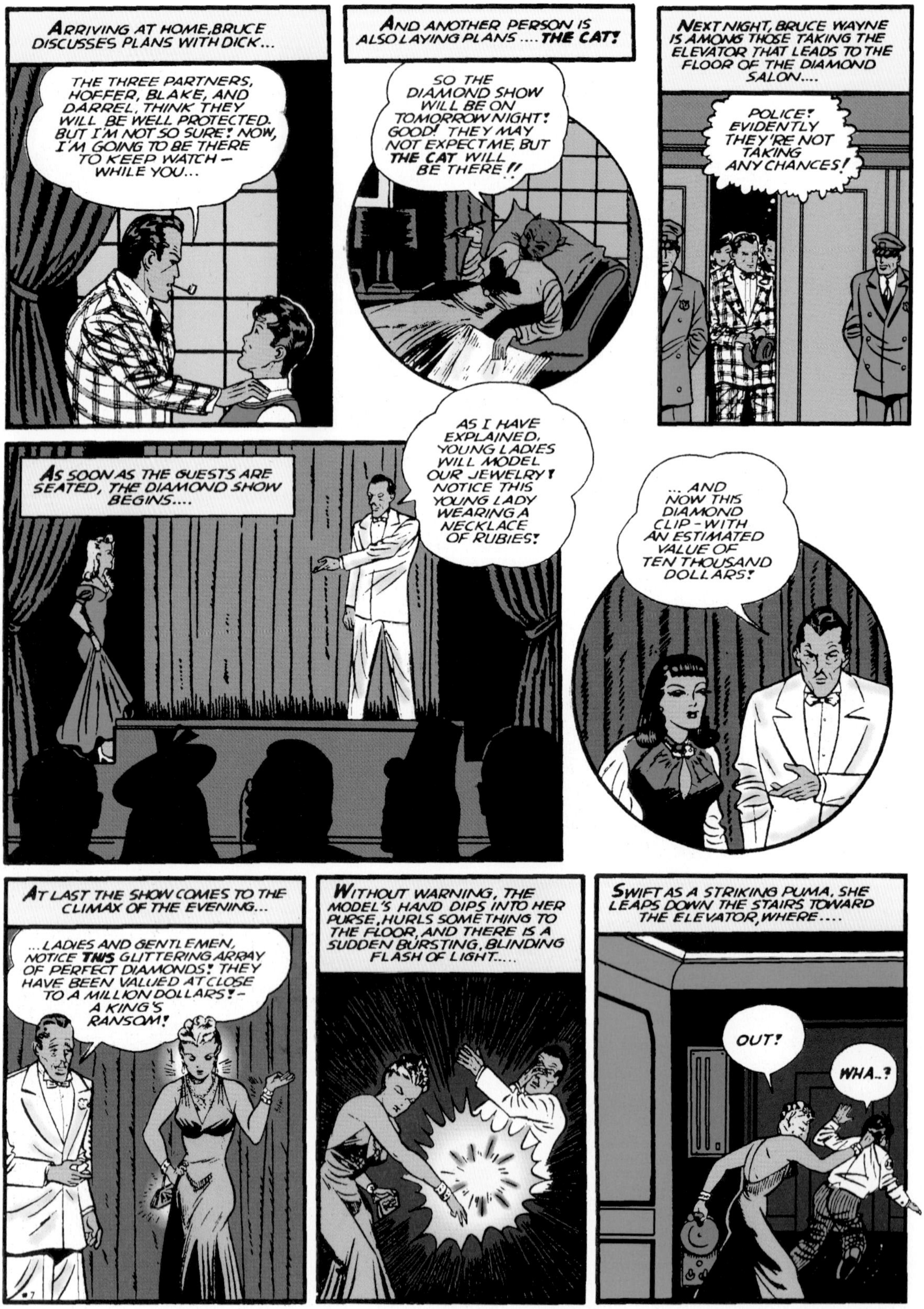
ARRIVING AT HOME, BRUCE DISCUSSES PLANS WITH DICK...
THE THREE PARTNERS, HOFFER, BLAKE, AND DARREL, THINK THEY WILL BE WELL PROTECTED. BUT I'M NOT SO SURE! NOW, I'M GOING TO BE THERE TO KEEP WATCH — WHILE YOU...
AND ANOTHER PERSON IS ALSO LAYING PLANS .... THE CAT!
SO THE DIAMOND SHOW WILL BE ON TOMORROW NIGHT! GOOD! THEY MAY NOT EXPECT ME, BUT THE CAT WILL BE THERE!!
NEXT NIGHT, BRUCE WAYNE IS AMONG THOSE TAKING THE ELEVATOR THAT LEADS TO THE FLOOR OF THE DIAMOND SALON....
POLICE! EVIDENTLY THEY'RE NOT TAKING ANY CHANCES!
AS SOON AS THE GUESTS ARE SEATED, THE DIAMOND SHOW BEGINS....
AS I HAVE EXPLAINED, YOUNG LADIES WILL MODEL OUR JEWELRY! NOTICE THIS YOUNG LADY WEARING A NECKLACE OF RUBIES!
... AND NOW THIS DIAMOND CLIP - WITH AN ESTIMATED VALUE OF TEN THOUSAND DOLLARS!
AT LAST THE SHOW COMES TO THE CLIMAX OF THE EVENING...
... LADIES AND GENTLEMEN, NOTICE THIS GLITTERING ARRAY OF PERFECT DIAMONDS! THEY HAVE BEEN VALUED AT CLOSE TO A MILLION DOLLARS! — A KING'S RANSOM!
WITHOUT WARNING, THE MODEL'S HAND DIPS INTO HER PURSE, HURLS SOMETHING TO THE FLOOR, AND THERE IS A SUDDEN BURSTING, BLINDING FLASH OF LIGHT....
SWIFT AS A STRIKING PUMA, SHE LEAPS DOWN THE STAIRS TOWARD THE ELEVATOR, WHERE....
OUT!
WHA..?

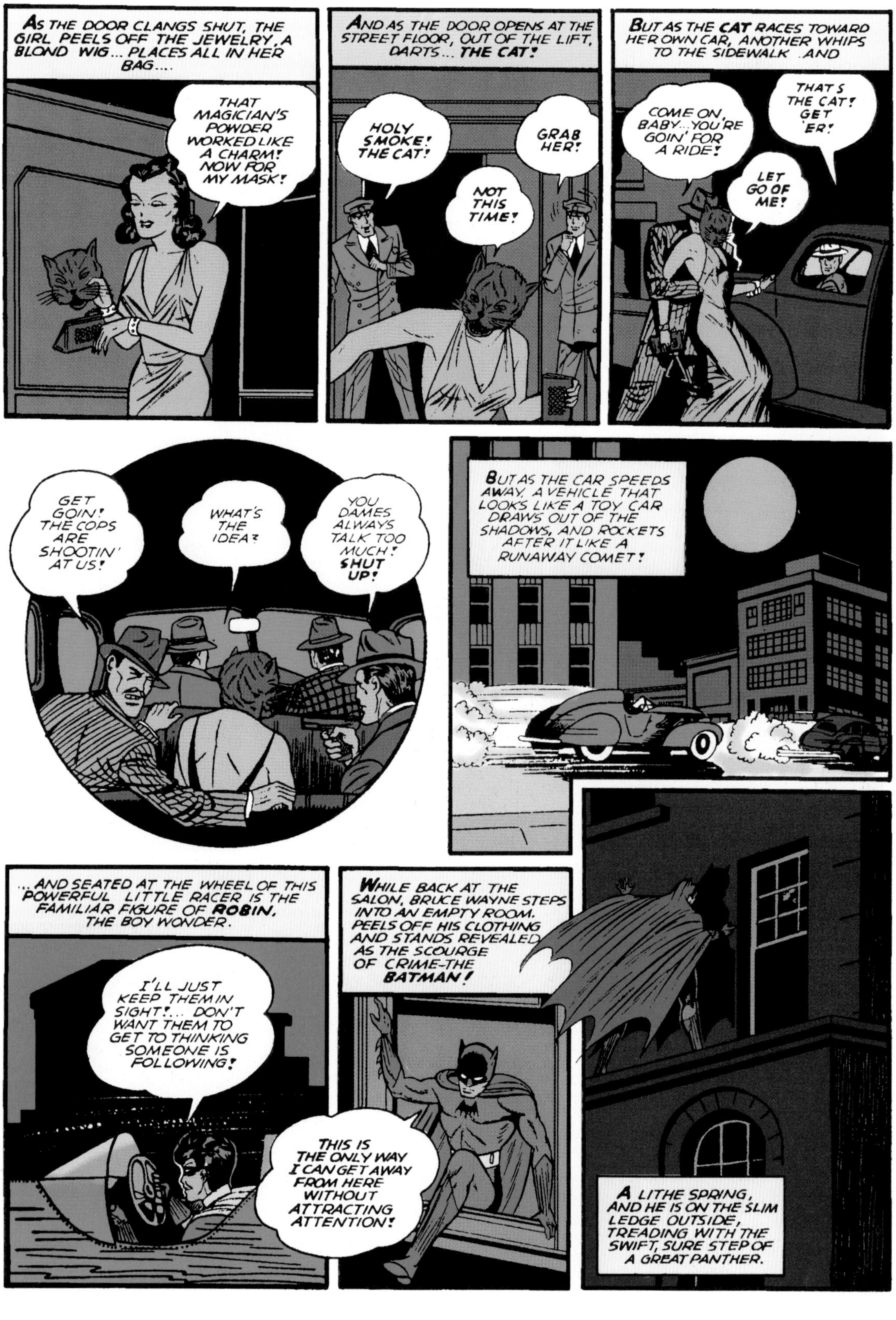
AS THE DOOR CLANGS SHUT, THE GIRL PEELS OFF THE JEWELRY, A BLOND WIG... PLACES ALL IN HER BAG....
THAT MAGICIAN'S POWDER WORKED LIKE A CHARM! NOW FOR MY MASK!
AND AS THE DOOR OPENS AT THE STREET FLOOR, OUT OF THE LIFT, DARTS... THE CAT!
HOLY SMOKE! THE CAT!
GRAB HER!
NOT THIS TIME!
BUT AS THE CAT RACES TOWARD HER OWN CAR, ANOTHER WHIPS TO THE SIDEWALK .AND
COME ON, BABY... YOU'RE GOIN' FOR A RIDE!
THAT'S THE CAT! GET 'ER!
LET GO OF ME!
GET GOIN'! THE COPS ARE SHOOTIN' AT US!
WHAT'S THE IDEA?
YOU DAMES ALWAYS TALK TOO MUCH! SHUT UP!
BUT AS THE CAR SPEEDS AWAY, A VEHICLE THAT LOOKS LIKE A TOY CAR DRAWS OUT OF THE SHADOWS, AND ROCKETS AFTER IT LIKE A RUNAWAY COMET!
...AND SEATED AT THE WHEEL OF THIS POWERFUL LITTLE RACER IS THE FAMILIAR FIGURE OF ROBIN, THE BOY WONDER.
I'LL JUST KEEP THEM IN SIGHT!... DON'T WANT THEM TO GET TO THINKING SOMEONE IS FOLLOWING!
WHILE BACK AT THE SALON, BRUCE WAYNE STEPS INTO AN EMPTY ROOM, PEELS OFF HIS CLOTHING AND STANDS REVEALED AS THE SCOURGE OF CRIME-THE BATMAN!
THIS IS THE ONLY WAY I CAN GET AWAY FROM HERE WITHOUT ATTRACTING ATTENTION!
A LITHE SPRING, AND HE IS ON THE SLIM LEDGE OUTSIDE, TREADING WITH THE SWIFT, SURE STEP OF A GREAT PANTHER.

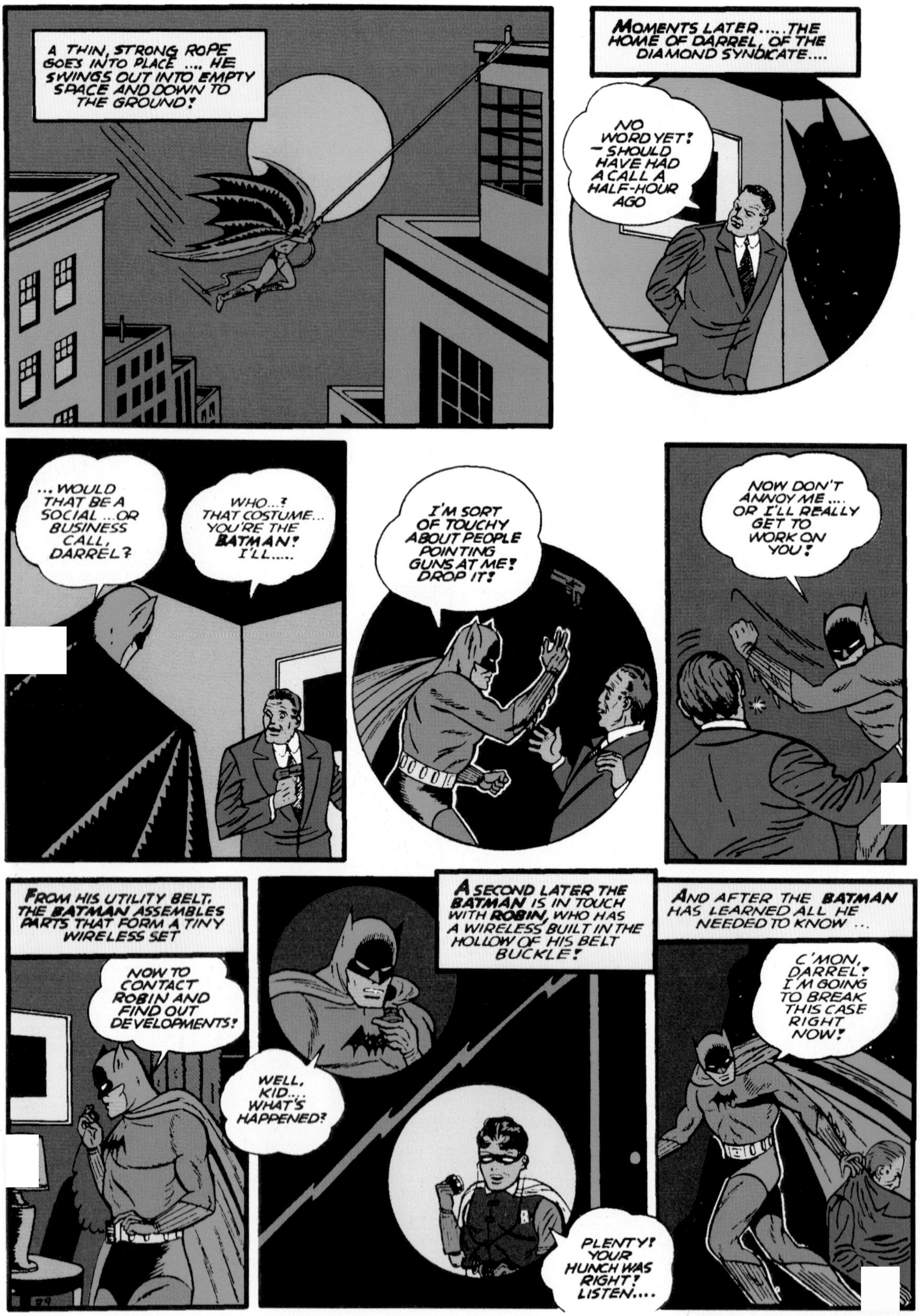
A THIN, STRONG ROPE GOES INTO PLACE .... HE SWINGS OUT INTO EMPTY SPACE AND DOWN TO THE GROUND!
MOMENTS LATER..... THE HOME OF DARREL, OF THE DIAMOND SYNDICATE....
NO WORD YET! — SHOULD HAVE HAD A CALL A HALF-HOUR AGO
...WOULD THAT BE A SOCIAL ...OR BUSINESS CALL, DARREL?
WHO...? THAT COSTUME... YOU'RE THE BATMAN! I'LL.....
I'M SORT OF TOUCHY ABOUT PEOPLE POINTING GUNS AT ME! DROP IT!
NOW DON'T ANNOY ME .... OR I'LL REALLY GET TO WORK ON YOU!
FROM HIS UTILITY BELT, THE BATMAN ASSEMBLES PARTS THAT FORM A TINY WIRELESS SET
NOW TO CONTACT ROBIN AND FIND OUT DEVELOPMENTS!
A SECOND LATER THE BATMAN IS IN TOUCH WITH ROBIN, WHO HAS A WIRELESS BUILT IN THE HOLLOW OF HIS BELT BUCKLE!
WELL, KID... WHAT'S HAPPENED?
PLENTY! YOUR HUNCH WAS RIGHT! LISTEN....
AND AFTER THE BATMAN HAS LEARNED ALL HE NEEDED TO KNOW ...
C'MON, DARREL! I'M GOING TO BREAK THIS CASE RIGHT NOW!

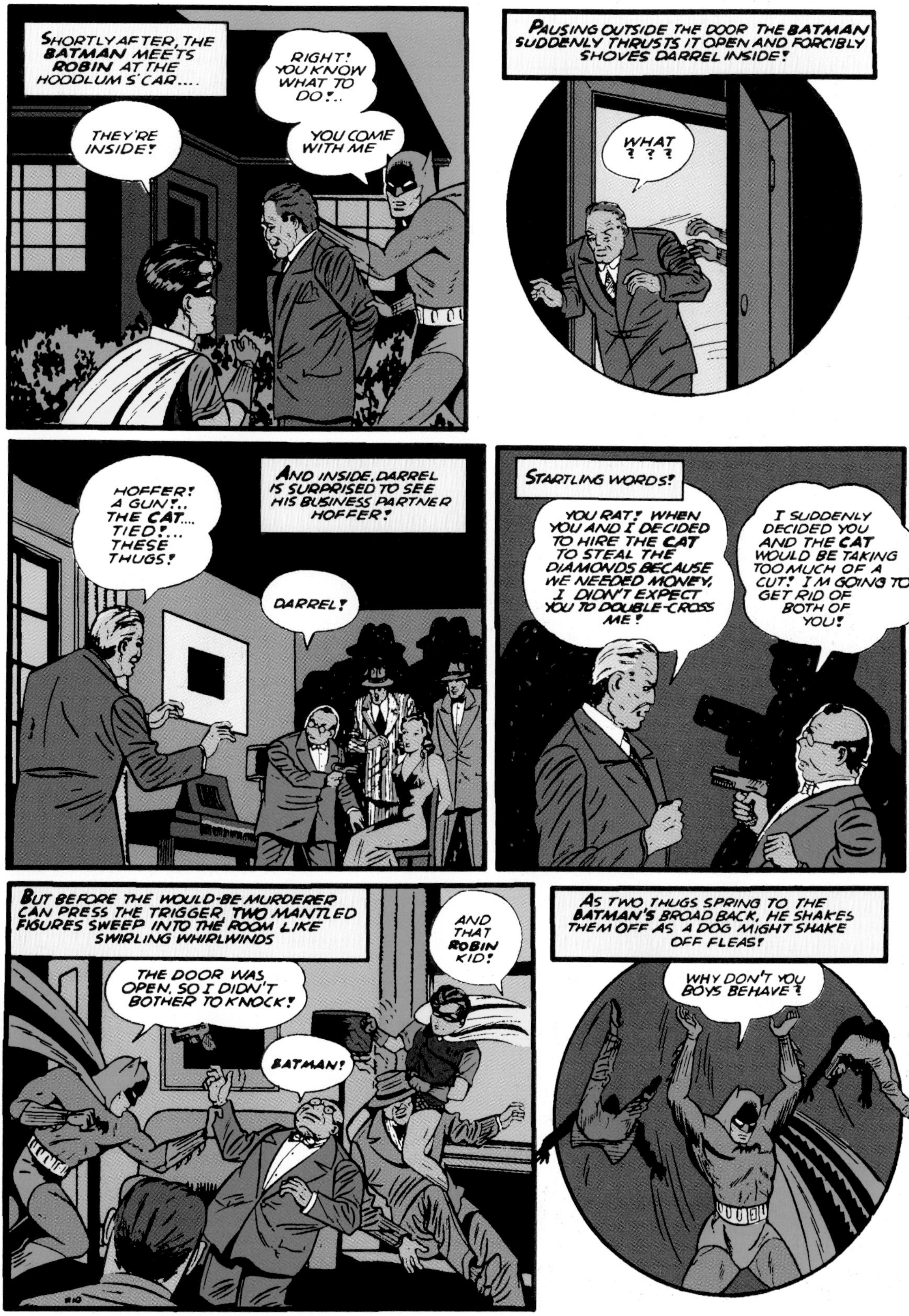
SHORTLY AFTER, THE BATMAN MEETS ROBIN AT THE HOODLUM'S CAR....
THEY'RE INSIDE!
RIGHT! YOU KNOW WHAT TO DO!..
YOU COME WITH ME
PAUSING OUTSIDE THE DOOR THE BATMAN SUDDENLY THRUSTS IT OPEN AND FORCIBLY SHOVES DARREL INSIDE!
WHAT ? ? ?
AND INSIDE, DARREL IS SURPRISED TO SEE HIS BUSINESS PARTNER HOFFER!
HOFFER! A GUN!.. THE CAT.... TIED!... THESE THUGS!
DARREL!
STARTLING WORDS!
YOU RAT! WHEN YOU AND I DECIDED TO HIRE THE CAT TO STEAL THE DIAMONDS BECAUSE WE NEEDED MONEY, I DIDN'T EXPECT YOU TO DOUBLE-CROSS ME!
I SUDDENLY DECIDED YOU AND THE CAT WOULD BE TAKING TOO MUCH OF A CUT! I'M GOING TO GET RID OF BOTH OF YOU!
BUT BEFORE THE WOULD-BE MURDERER CAN PRESS THE TRIGGER, TWO MANTLED FIGURES SWEEP INTO THE ROOM LIKE SWIRLING WHIRLWINDS
THE DOOR WAS OPEN, SO I DIDN'T BOTHER TO KNOCK!
BATMAN!
AND THAT ROBIN KID!
AS TWO THUGS SPRING TO THE BATMAN'S BROAD BACK, HE SHAKES THEM OFF AS A DOG MIGHT SHAKE OFF FLEAS!
WHY DON'T YOU BOYS BEHAVE?

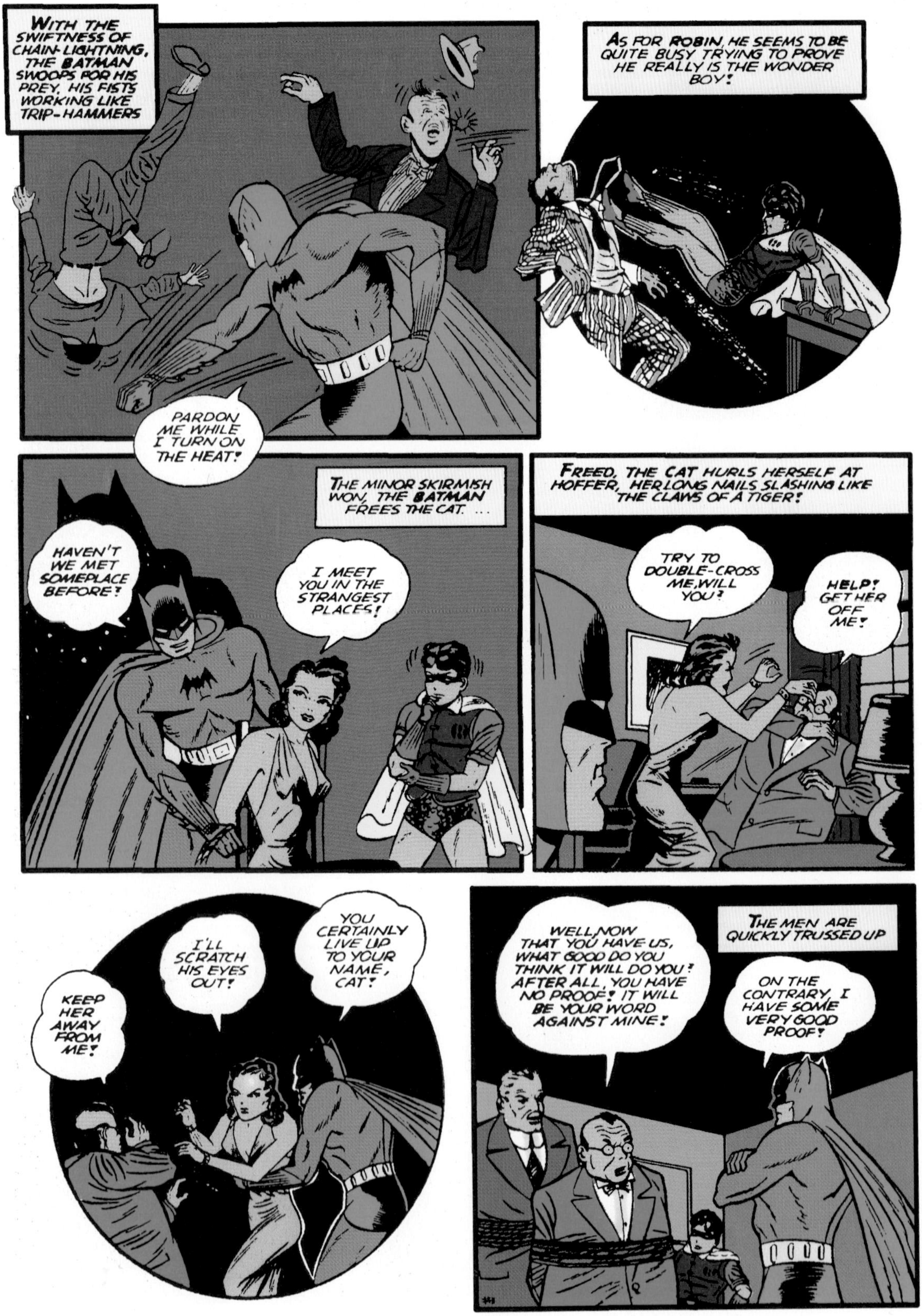
WITH THE SWIFTNESS OF CHAIN-LIGHTNING, THE BATMAN SWOOPS FOR HIS PREY, HIS FISTS WORKING LIKE TRIP-HAMMERS
PARDON ME WHILE I TURN ON THE HEAT!
AS FOR ROBIN, HE SEEMS TO BE QUITE BUSY TRYING TO PROVE HE REALLY IS THE WONDER BOY!
THE MINOR SKIRMISH WON, THE BATMAN FREES THE CAT. ...
HAVEN'T WE MET SOMEPLACE BEFORE?
I MEET YOU IN THE STRANGEST PLACES!
FREED, THE CAT HURLS HERSELF AT HOFFER, HER LONG NAILS SLASHING LIKE THE CLAWS OF A TIGER!
TRY TO DOUBLE-CROSS ME, WILL YOU?
HELP! GET HER OFF ME!
KEEP HER AWAY FROM ME!
I'LL SCRATCH HIS EYES OUT!
YOU CERTAINLY LIVE UP TO YOUR NAME, CAT!
THE MEN ARE QUICKLY TRUSSED UP
WELL, NOW THAT YOU HAVE US, WHAT GOOD DO YOU THINK IT WILL DO YOU? AFTER ALL, YOU HAVE NO PROOF! IT WILL BE YOUR WORD AGAINST MINE!
ON THE CONTRARY, I HAVE SOME VERY GOOD PROOF!

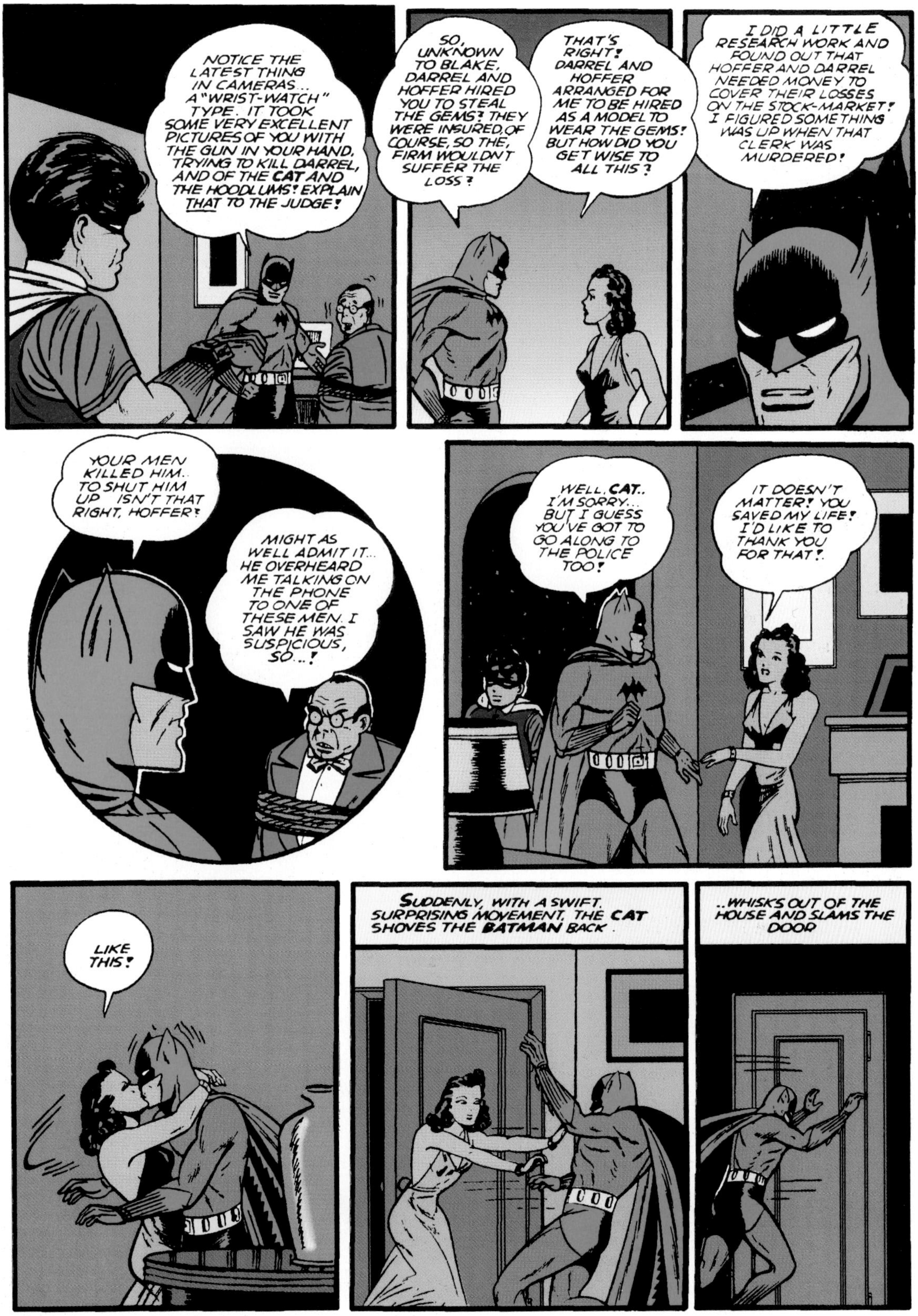
NOTICE THE LATEST THING IN CAMERAS... A "WRIST-WATCH" TYPE. IT TOOK SOME VERY EXCELLENT PICTURES OF YOU WITH THE GUN IN YOUR HAND, TRYING TO KILL DARREL, AND OF THE CAT AND THE HOODLUMS! EXPLAIN THAT TO THE JUDGE!
SO, UNKNOWN TO BLAKE, DARREL AND HOFFER HIRED YOU TO STEAL THE GEMS? THEY WERE INSURED, OF COURSE, SO THE FIRM WOULDN'T SUFFER THE LOSS?
THAT'S RIGHT! DARREL AND HOFFER ARRANGED FOR ME TO BE HIRED AS A MODEL TO WEAR THE GEMS! BUT HOW DID YOU GET WISE TO ALL THIS?
I DID A LITTLE RESEARCH WORK AND FOUND OUT THAT HOFFER AND DARREL NEEDED MONEY TO COVER THEIR LOSSES ON THE STOCK-MARKET! I FIGURED SOMETHING WAS UP WHEN THAT CLERK WAS MURDERED!
YOUR MEN KILLED HIM.. TO SHUT HIM UP ISN'T THAT RIGHT, HOFFER?
MIGHT AS WELL ADMIT IT... HE OVERHEARD ME TALKING ON THE PHONE TO ONE OF THESE MEN. I SAW HE WAS SUSPICIOUS, SO...!
WELL, CAT.. I'M SORRY... BUT I GUESS YOU'VE GOT TO GO ALONG TO THE POLICE TOO!
IT DOESN'T MATTER! YOU SAVED MY LIFE! I'D LIKE TO THANK YOU FOR THAT!
LIKE THIS!
SUDDENLY, WITH A SWIFT, SURPRISING MOVEMENT, THE CAT SHOVES THE BATMAN BACK.
..WHISKS OUT OF THE HOUSE AND SLAMS THE DOOR

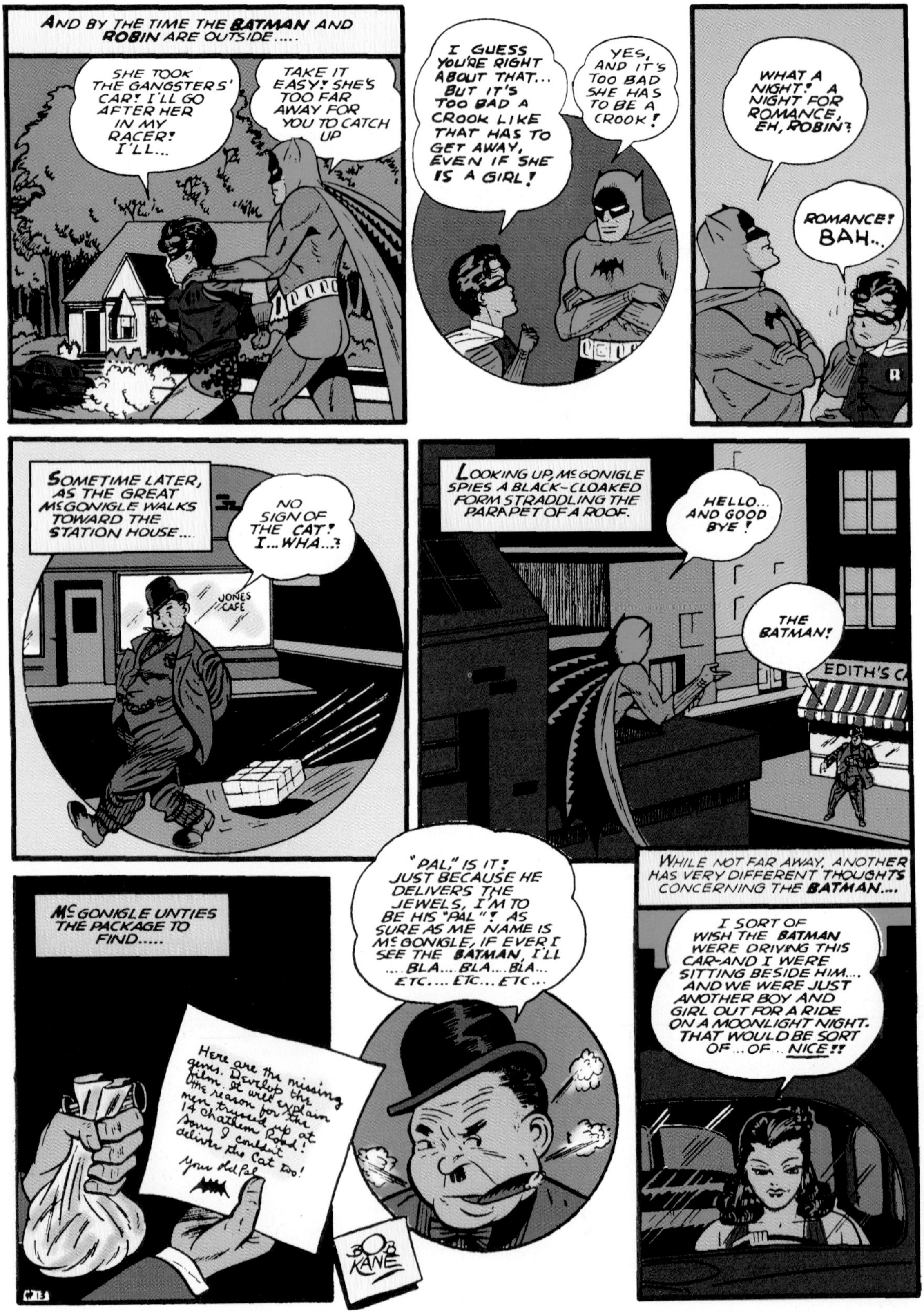
AND BY THE TIME THE BATMAN AND ROBIN ARE OUTSIDE.....
SHE TOOK THE GANGSTERS' CAR! I'LL GO AFTER HER IN MY RACER! I'LL...
TAKE IT EASY! SHE'S TOO FAR AWAY FOR YOU TO CATCH UP
I GUESS YOU'RE RIGHT ABOUT THAT... BUT IT'S TOO BAD A CROOK LIKE THAT HAS TO GET AWAY, EVEN IF SHE IS A GIRL!
YES, AND IT'S TOO BAD SHE HAS TO BE A CROOK!
WHAT A NIGHT! A NIGHT FOR ROMANCE, EH, ROBIN?
ROMANCE! BAH...
SOMETIME LATER, AS THE GREAT McGONIGLE WALKS TOWARD THE STATION HOUSE....
NO SIGN OF THE CAT! I...WHA...?
JONES CAFE
LOOKING UP, McGONIGLE SPIES A BLACK-CLOAKED FORM STRADDLING THE PARAPET OF A ROOF.
HELLO... AND GOOD BYE!
THE BATMAN!
EDITH'S CA
McGONIGLE UNTIES THE PACKAGE TO FIND.....
Here are the missing gems. Develop the film. It will explain the reason for the men trussed up at 14 Chatham Road! Sorry I couldn't deliver the Cat too! Your old Pal
"PAL," IS IT! JUST BECAUSE HE DELIVERS THE JEWELS, I'M TO BE HIS "PAL"! AS SURE AS ME NAME IS McGONIGLE, IF EVER I SEE THE BATMAN, I'LL ....BLA....BLA....BLA... ETC.... ETC... ETC...
BOB KANE
WHILE NOT FAR AWAY, ANOTHER HAS VERY DIFFERENT THOUGHTS CONCERNING THE BATMAN....
I SORT OF WISH THE BATMAN WERE DRIVING THIS CAR-AND I WERE SITTING BESIDE HIM.... AND WE WERE JUST ANOTHER BOY AND GIRL OUT FOR A RIDE ON A MOONLIGHT NIGHT. THAT WOULD BE SORT OF ... OF... NICE!!

The BATMAN

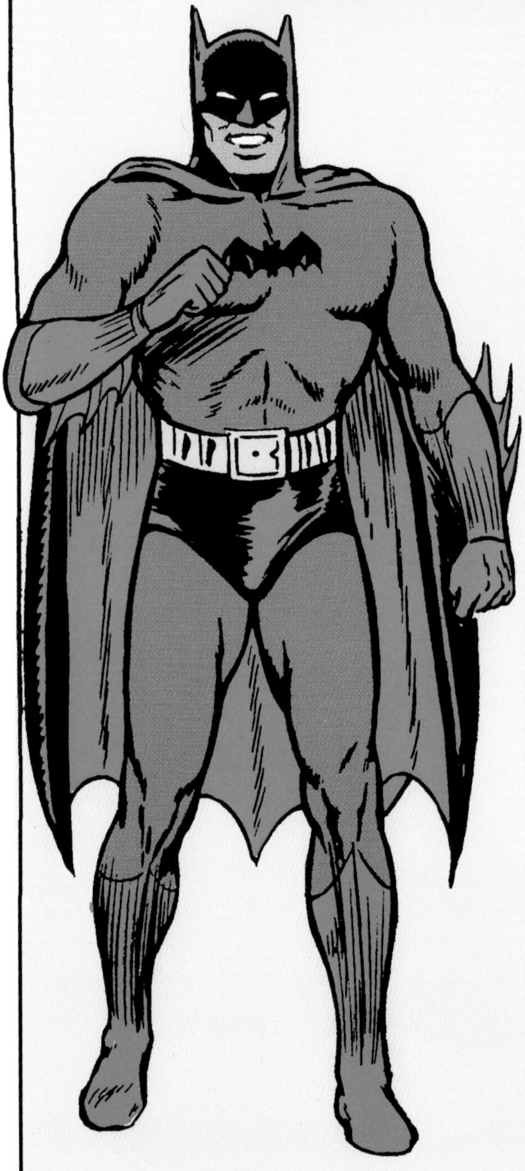

SAYS:

HELLO, Readers! Now that you've read all these new adventures of mine and Robin's, I'd like to talk right AT you for a minute or so.

I think Robin and I make it pretty clear that WE HATE CRIME AND CRIMINALS! There's nothing we like better than to crack down on the distasteful denizens of the underworld. Why? Because we're proud of being AMERICANS—and we know there's no place in this great country of ours for lawbreakers!

That phrase, "CRIME DOESN'T PAY," has been used over and over again to the point where I hesitate to repeat it. But remember this: IT'S JUST AS TRUE NOW AS IT EVER WAS—AND THAT'S PLENTY TRUE!

Sure, it may seem that lawbreakers DO get away with breaking the law. Some may get away with it longer than others. But in the end, every crook gets what's coming to him—and that means plenty of trouble with the law!

Robin and I hope that our adventures may help to "put over" that fact. We'd like to feel that our efforts may help every youngster to grow up into an honest, useful citizen.

It depends on YOU and YOU and YOU. You've got to govern your own lives so that they can be worthwhile, fruitful lives—not lives wasted in prison, or even thrown away altogether before the ready guns of the law-enforcement agents who duty it is to guard those of us who are honest from those of us who are not. And not only must you guide your OWN life in the proper channels—you must also strive to be a good influence on the lives of others.

If you do all this, if you are definitely on the side of Law and Order, then Robin and I salute you and are glad to number you among our friends!

....and what the BATMAN says goes DOUBLE for me!

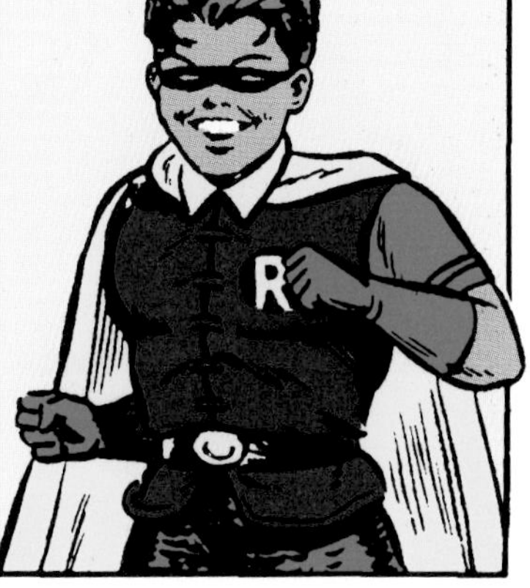
R

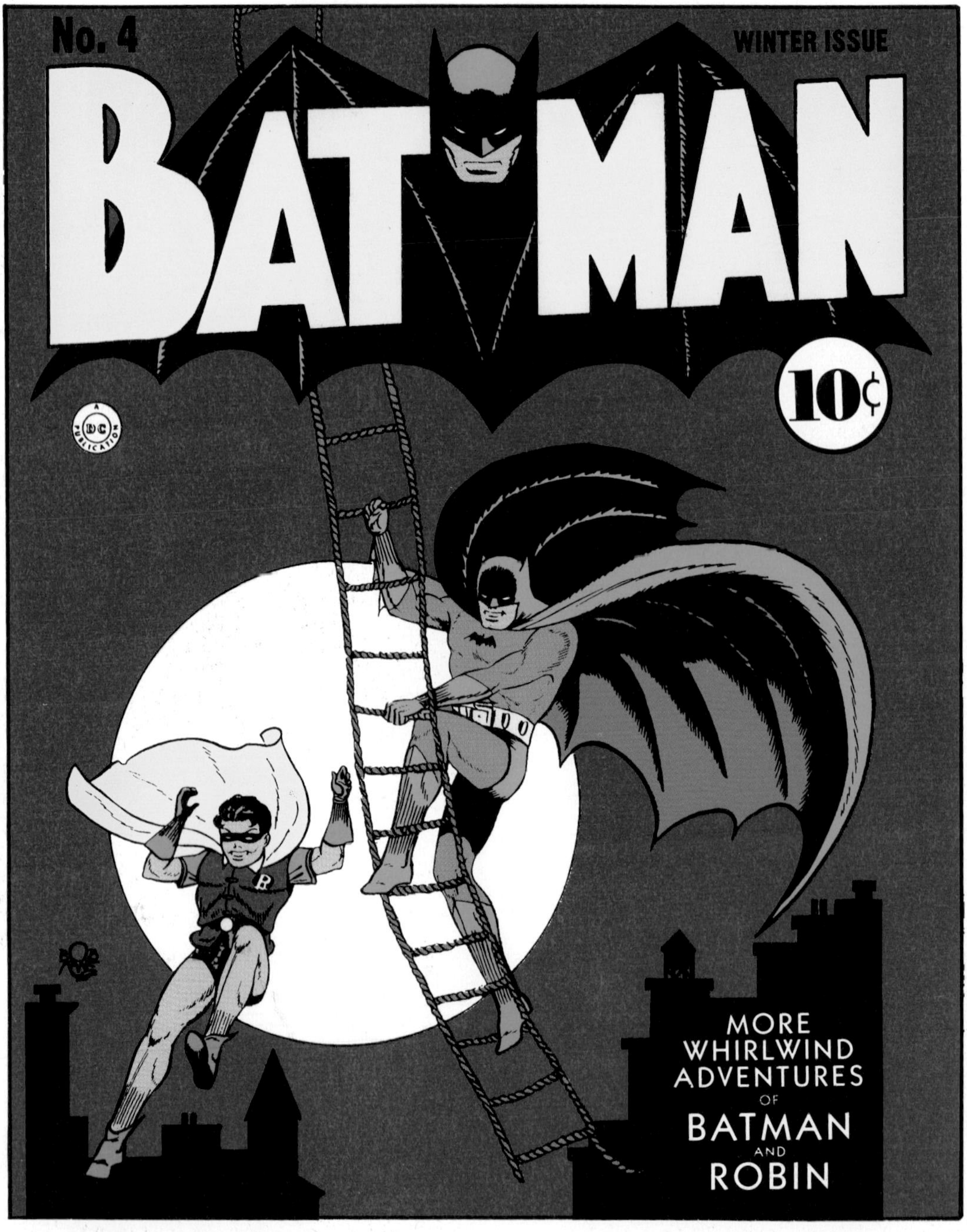
No. 4
WINTER ISSUE
BATMAN
10¢
A DC PUBLICATION
MORE
WHIRLWIND
ADVENTURES
OF
BATMAN
AND
ROBIN

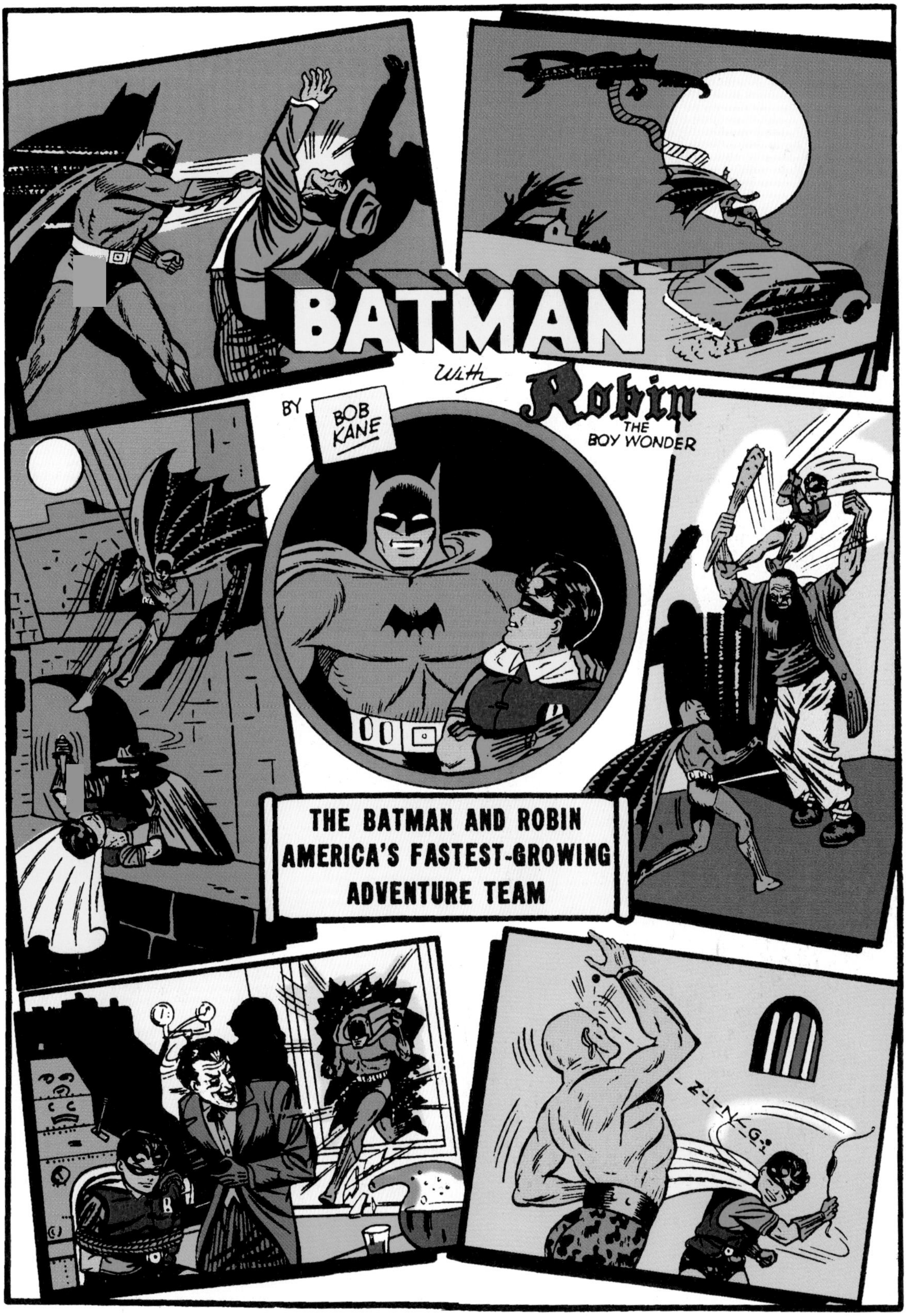
BATMAN
with
Robin
THE BOY WONDER
BY
BOB KANE
THE BATMAN AND ROBIN
AMERICA'S FASTEST-GROWING
ADVENTURE TEAM
Z-I-N-G-!

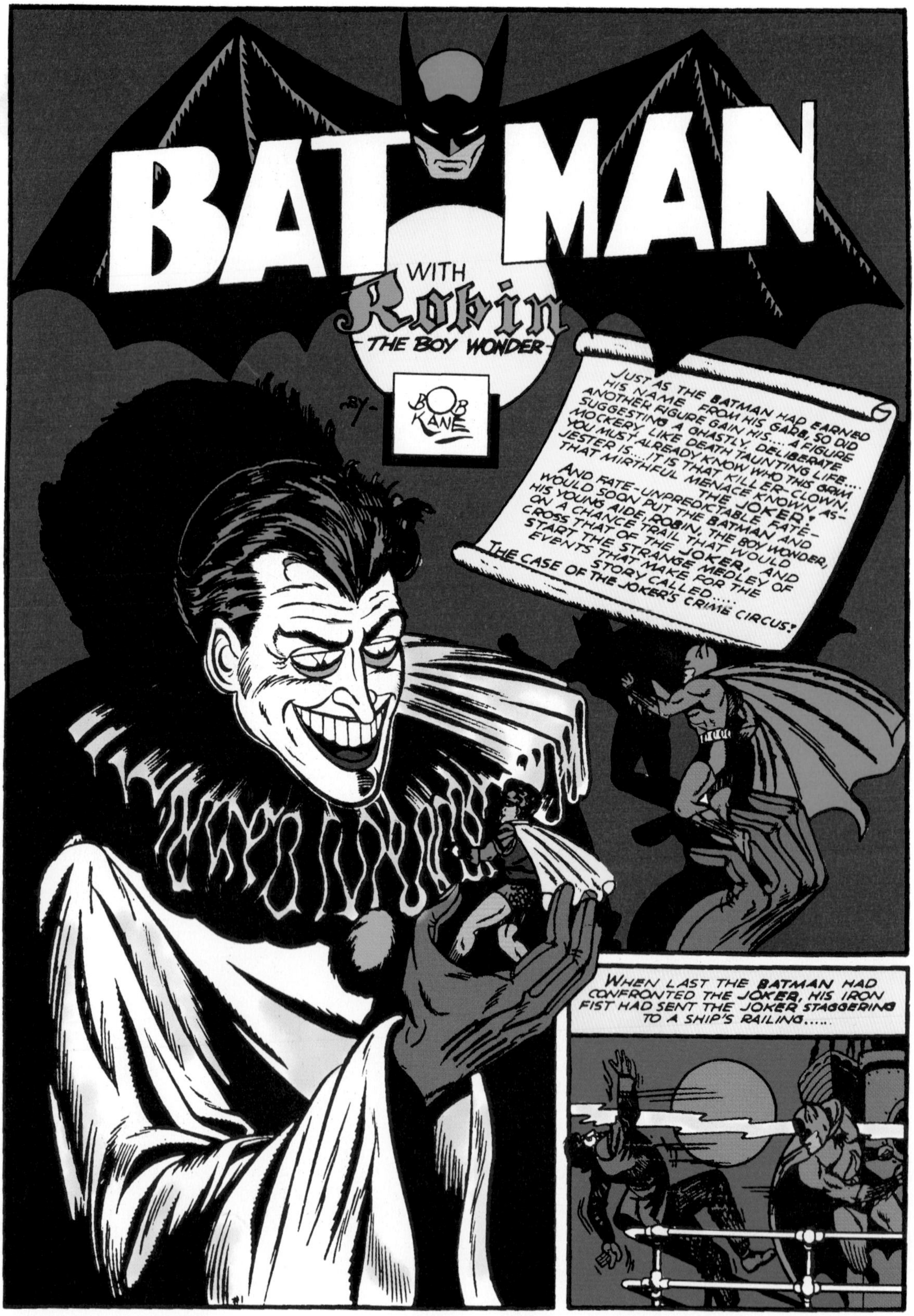
BATMAN
WITH Robin -THE BOY WONDER-
-BY- BOB KANE
JUST AS THE BATMAN HAD EARNED HIS NAME FROM HIS GARB, SO DID ANOTHER FIGURE GAIN HIS.... A FIGURE SUGGESTING A GHASTLY, DELIBERATE MOCKERY LIKE DEATH TAUNTING LIFE.... YOU MUST ALREADY KNOW WHO THIS GRIM JESTER IS....IT IS THAT KILLER-CLOWN, THAT MIRTHFUL MENACE KNOWN AS- THE JOKER!
AND FATE-UNPREDICTABLE FATE-WOULD SOON PUT THE BATMAN AND HIS YOUNG AIDE, ROBIN, THE BOY WONDER, ON A CHANCE TRAIL THAT WOULD CROSS THAT OF THE JOKER! AND START THE STRANGE MEDLEY OF EVENTS THAT MAKE FOR THE STORY CALLED.....
THE CASE OF THE JOKER'S CRIME CIRCUS!
WHEN LAST THE BATMAN HAD CONFRONTED THE JOKER, HIS IRON FIST HAD SENT THE JOKER STAGGERING TO A SHIP'S RAILING.....

.....THE JOKER PLUMMETED DOWN TO HIT THE WATERS AND REMAIN BELOW......

I WONDER IF THIS IS REALLY THE END OF THE JOKER AT LAST?

.....AS THE LIGHTS OF THE SHIP TWINKLE LIKE FIREFLIES IN THE DISTANCE, A FIGURE RISES TO THE SURFACE OF THE WATER... IT IS THE JOKER!

.....HOURS LATER, A YACHT MAKES OUT HIS BOBBING FORM...

MAN AHEAD, SIR- LOOKS LIKE HE'S CLINGING TO A BIT OF DRIFTWOOD!

GIVE THE NECESSARY ORDER TO PICK HIM UP!

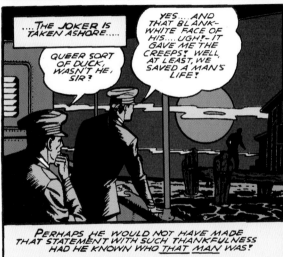

.....THE JOKER IS TAKEN ASHORE.....

QUEER SORT OF DUCK, WASN'T HE, SIR?

YES.....AND THAT BLANK-WHITE FACE OF HIS.....UGH!- IT GAVE ME THE CREEPS! WELL, AT LEAST, WE SAVED A MAN'S LIFE!

PERHAPS HE WOULD NOT HAVE MADE THAT STATEMENT WITH SUCH THANKFULNESS HAD HE KNOWN WHO _THAT MAN_ WAS!

UNOBSERVED, HE STEALS TO THE EDGE OF TOWN TO A SEEMINGLY DESERTED, GLOOMY OLD MANSION DUBBED BY THE PEOPLE AS "HAUNTED".....

BUT THE STRANGE-LOOKING MANSION IS NOT REALLY "HAUNTED" AND DESERTED..... IN REALITY, IT IS THE HIDDEN SANCTUM OF THE JOKER...

.....THEN, THE JOKER LAUGHS. A WILD, JEERING LAUGH THAT MAKES THE VERY SILENCE OF THE ROOM CRAWL WITH MENACE.

I'M ALIVE! HA HA! I'M ALIVE! HA HA HA HA!

THE CLEVEREST AND THE MOST DANGEROUS CRIMINAL IN THE ANNALS OF CRIME WAS STILL AT LIBERTY!

THE BATMAN THINKS I'M DEAD. HE'LL KNOW DIFFERENTLY WHEN WE MEET AGAIN! .....AND WE SHALL MEET AGAIN!

THE TIME WAS CLOSE WHEN NEW FACTORS WOULD BRING ABOUT AN ACTUAL DUEL BETWEEN THE BATMAN AND THE JOKER!

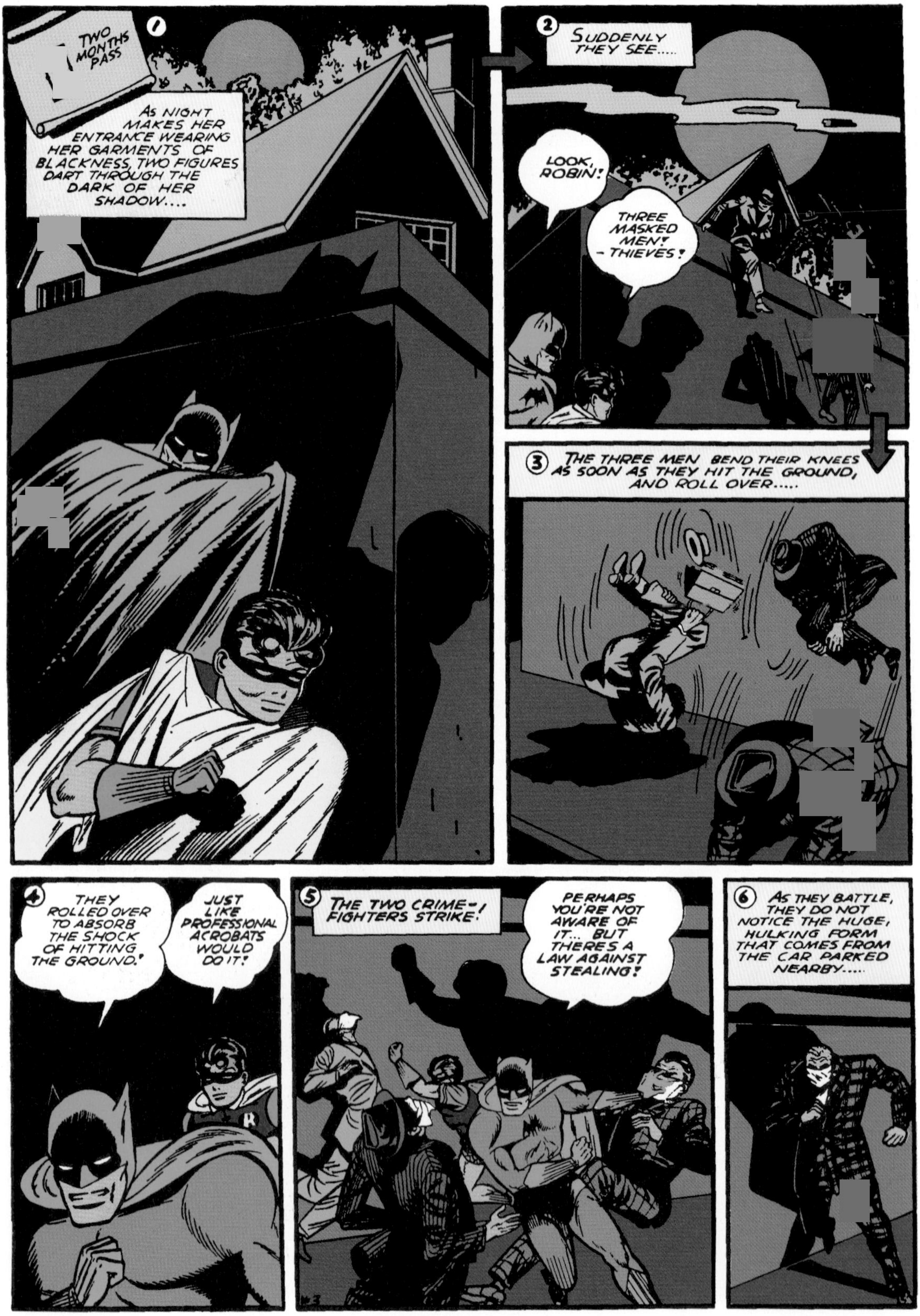
TWO MONTHS PASS
AS NIGHT MAKES HER ENTRANCE WEARING HER GARMENTS OF BLACKNESS, TWO FIGURES DART THROUGH THE DARK OF HER SHADOW....
SUDDENLY THEY SEE.....
LOOK, ROBIN!
THREE MASKED MEN! - THIEVES!
THE THREE MEN BEND THEIR KNEES AS SOON AS THEY HIT THE GROUND, AND ROLL OVER.....
THEY ROLLED OVER TO ABSORB THE SHOCK OF HITTING THE GROUND.
JUST LIKE PROFESSIONAL ACROBATS WOULD DO IT!
THE TWO CRIME-FIGHTERS STRIKE!
PERHAPS YOU'RE NOT AWARE OF IT... BUT THERE'S A LAW AGAINST STEALING!
AS THEY BATTLE, THEY DO NOT NOTICE THE HUGE, HULKING FORM THAT COMES FROM THE CAR PARKED NEARBY.....

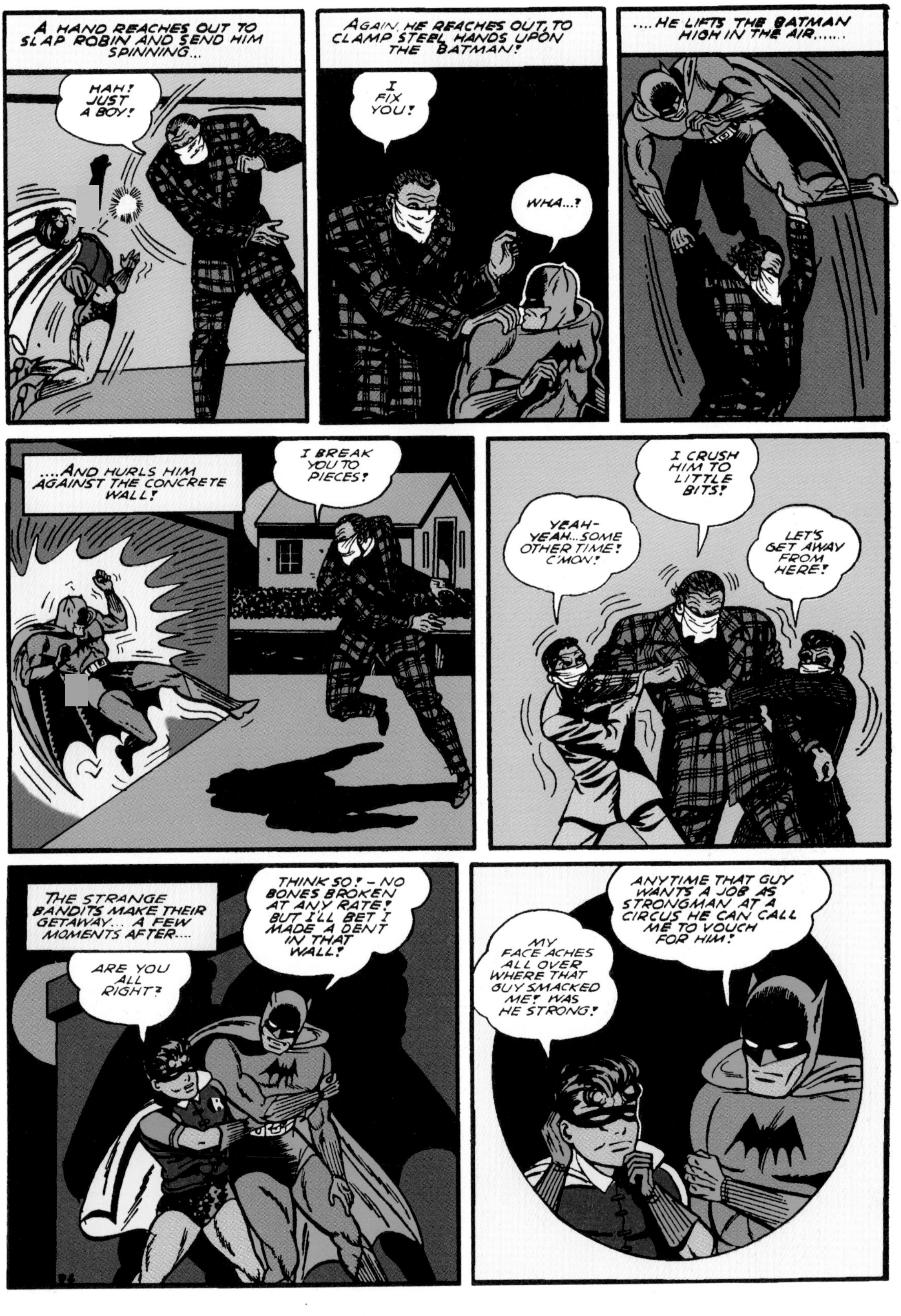
A HAND REACHES OUT TO SLAP ROBIN AND SEND HIM SPINNING...
HAH! JUST A BOY!
AGAIN, HE REACHES OUT, TO CLAMP STEEL HANDS UPON THE BATMAN!
I FIX YOU!
WHA...?
....HE LIFTS THE BATMAN HIGH IN THE AIR.......
....AND HURLS HIM AGAINST THE CONCRETE WALL!
I BREAK YOU TO PIECES!
I CRUSH HIM TO LITTLE BITS!
YEAH-YEAH...SOME OTHER TIME! C'MON!
LET'S GET AWAY FROM HERE!
THE STRANGE BANDITS MAKE THEIR GETAWAY... A FEW MOMENTS AFTER....
ARE YOU ALL RIGHT?
THINK SO! - NO BONES BROKEN AT ANY RATE! BUT I'LL BET I MADE A DENT IN THAT WALL!
ANYTIME THAT GUY WANTS A JOB AS STRONGMAN AT A CIRCUS HE CAN CALL ME TO VOUCH FOR HIM!
MY FACE ACHES ALL OVER WHERE THAT GUY SMACKED ME! WAS HE STRONG!

A WEEK LATER, ANOTHER RICH HOME IS ROBBED..

GOTHAM CITY GAZETTE

VAN PLATT HOM ROBBED......

FIFTH RICH HOME LOOTED IN LATEST ROBBERY EPIDEMIC

THOSE MYSTERIOUS BURGLARS, WHO HAVE BEEN STRIKING AT THE SOCIETY RICH THIS PAST MONTH, BRAZENLY ENTERED THE VAN PLATT MANSION LAST NIGHT, AND......

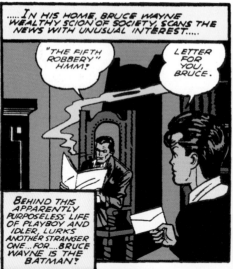

.....IN HIS HOME, BRUCE WAYNE WEALTHY SCION OF SOCIETY SCANS THE NEWS WITH UNUSUAL INTEREST.....

"THE FIFTH ROBBERY" HMM!

LETTER FOR YOU, BRUCE.

BEHIND THIS APPARENTLY PURPOSELESS LIFE OF PLAYBOY AND IDLER, LURKS ANOTHER STRANGER ONE...FOR....BRUCE WAYNE IS THE BATMAN!

THE LETTER.....

You are cordially invited to attend a ball to be given this Saturday at eight thirty o'clock... and to C.R.Darcey—

ACCORDINGLY.....THAT SATURDAY NIGHT.....

AH, BRUCE— GLAD YOU COULD COME!

WILD HORSES COULDN'T KEEP ME AWAY, DARCEY.

BRUCE SEEMS TO GO OUT OF HIS WAY TO PROVE HE IS THE NO.1. CANDIDATE FOR THE "IDLE RICH, BORED WITH LIFE —CLUB."...

THERE'S BRUCE, YAWNING AS USUAL! JUST LOOK AT HIM!

HE HAS NO MORE BRAINS IN HIS HEAD THAN THE HEAD OF HIS WALKING STICK HAS!

...SUDDENLY, THERE IS A ROLL ON THE DRUMS, AND DARCEY ADDRESSES HIS GUESTS..

FRIENDS—NOW I HAVE A TREAT IN STORE FOR YOU! THE BALL ROOM WILL BE CLEARED AND YOU WILL BE GIVEN SEATS SO THAT YOU MAY WATCH A CIRCUS!

....A MINIATURE CIRCUS SHOW IS PUT ON IN THE BALLROOM... ACROBATS PERFORM

A STRONG MAN BENDS IRON BARS AND LIFTS TREMENDOUS WEIGHTS...

AJAX...THE STRONGEST, MIGHTIEST MAN IN THE WORLD!

REPLETE WITH ACROBATS, STRONG MAN, TRAPEZE ARTISTS, CLOWN, THE CIRCUS IS A HOWLING SUCCESS.....

HA HA!
HA HA!
HA HA!

ODD, HOW THAT CLOWN REMINDS ME OF SOMEONE!

THAT NIGHT, WHEN THEIR ENGAGEMENT ENDS, THE CIRCUS TROUPE TOILS UP THE LONELY ROAD THAT LEADS TO THE "HAUNTED HOUSE".....

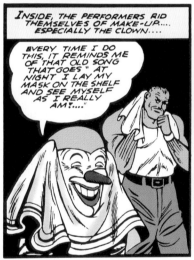

INSIDE, THE PERFORMERS RID THEMSELVES OF MAKE-UP.... ESPECIALLY THE CLOWN....

EVERY TIME I DO THIS, IT REMINDS ME OF THAT OLD SONG THAT GOES "AT NIGHT I LAY MY MASK ON THE SHELF AND SEE MYSELF AS I REALLY AM?...."

.....BE A PUNCHINELLO... LAUGH, CLOWN, LAUGH! HA HA HA HA!

UNDER THE HUMOROUS MAKE-UP IS THE REAL CLOWN...THE KILLER-CLOWN....THE JOKER!.....

.....AND EXACTLY THREE DAYS LATER....

BRUCE! BRUCE! THE DARCEYS-THE PEOPLE WHOSE PARTY YOU WENT TO-THEY'VE BEEN ROBBED!

WH-AT? THAT MAKES THE SIXTH RICH FAMILY ROBBED THIS MONTH!

BRUCE INVESTIGATES, AND AT THE END OF THE DAY ANNOUNCES HIS FINDINGS AND SUSPICIONS TO DICK....

...YOU MEAN TO SAY YOU'VE FOUND OUT THAT EVERY RICH HOME THAT HAS BEEN ROBBED HAS HAD THIS CIRCUS PLAY AN ENGAGEMENT AT THEIR HOUSE?

YES.....AND REMEMBER WHEN WE HAD THAT RUN-IN THE OTHER NIGHT?.. THE CROOKS HOPPED AROUND LIKE PROFESSIONAL ACROBATS!

.... AND ONE WAS STRONG LIKE THE STRONG MAN OF A CIRCUS! NOW, WHAT'S TO PREVENT THIS CROOKED CIRCUS FROM PLAYING A RICH HOME AND "CASING" IT FOR A FUTURE ROBBERY? LOGICAL, ISN'T IT?

GOSH! THE SOCIETY COLUMN SAYS "THE MORGANBILTS' PARTY TONIGHT WILL FEATURE THE MINIATURE CIRCUS THAT IS THE CURRENT RAGE OF SOCIETY!"

WE CAN'T TELL WHEN THEY'LL STRIKE, SO WE'VE GOT TO PREVENT A FUTURE CRIME! DICK, WE'RE STEPPING OUT... TONIGHT!

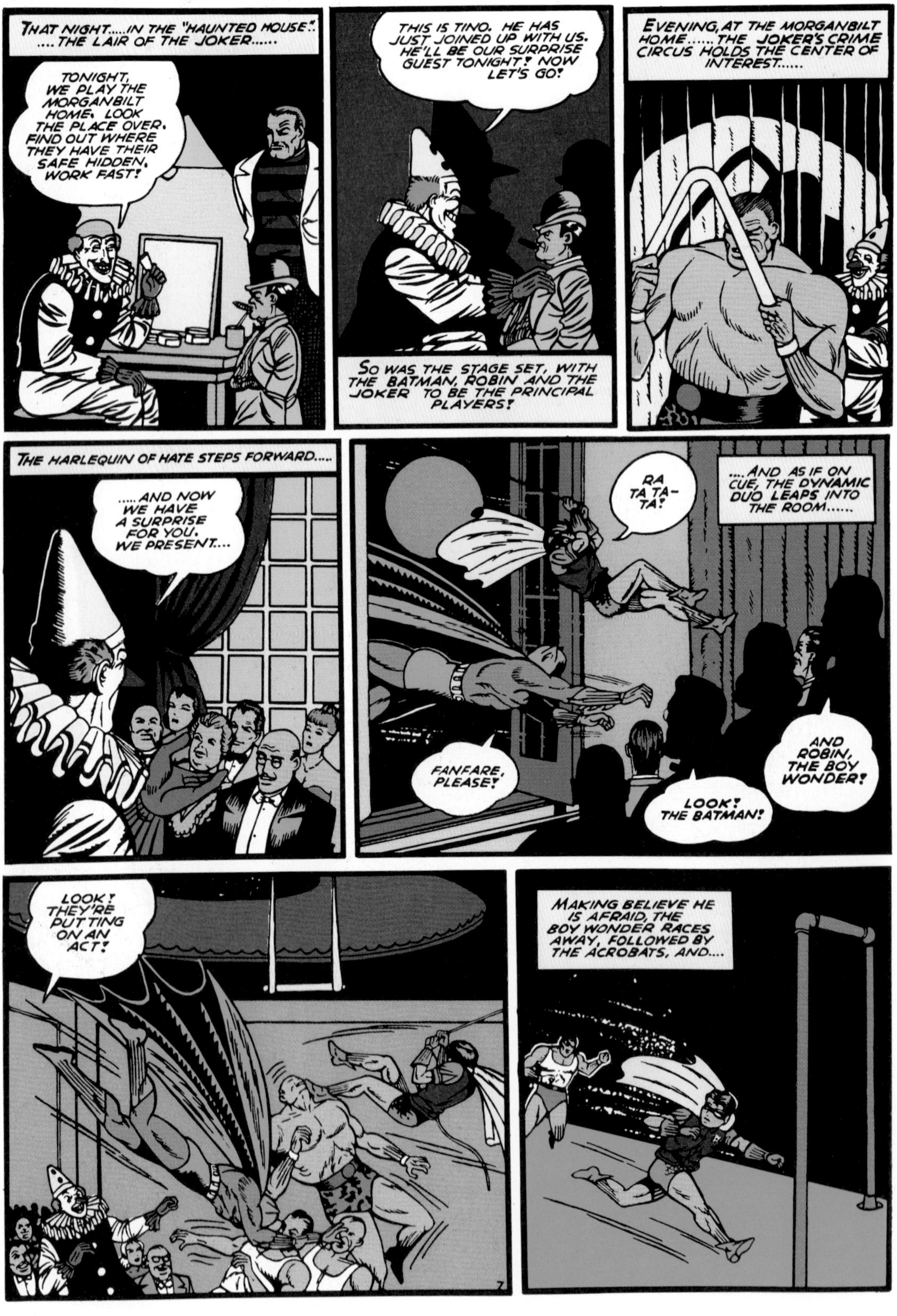
THAT NIGHT.....IN THE "HAUNTED HOUSE".. ....THE LAIR OF THE JOKER......
TONIGHT, WE PLAY THE MORGANBILT HOME. LOOK THE PLACE OVER. FIND OUT WHERE THEY HAVE THEIR SAFE HIDDEN. WORK FAST!
THIS IS TINO. HE HAS JUST JOINED UP WITH US. HE'LL BE OUR SURPRISE GUEST TONIGHT! NOW LET'S GO!
SO WAS THE STAGE SET, WITH THE BATMAN, ROBIN AND THE JOKER TO BE THE PRINCIPAL PLAYERS!
EVENING, AT THE MORGANBILT HOME......THE JOKER'S CRIME CIRCUS HOLDS THE CENTER OF INTEREST......
THE HARLEQUIN OF HATE STEPS FORWARD.....
.....AND NOW WE HAVE A SURPRISE FOR YOU. WE PRESENT....
RA TA TA-TA!
....AND AS IF ON CUE, THE DYNAMIC DUO LEAPS INTO THE ROOM......
FANFARE, PLEASE!
LOOK! THE BATMAN!
AND ROBIN, THE BOY WONDER!
LOOK! THEY'RE PUTTING ON AN ACT!
MAKING BELIEVE HE IS AFRAID, THE BOY WONDER RACES AWAY, FOLLOWED BY THE ACROBATS, AND....

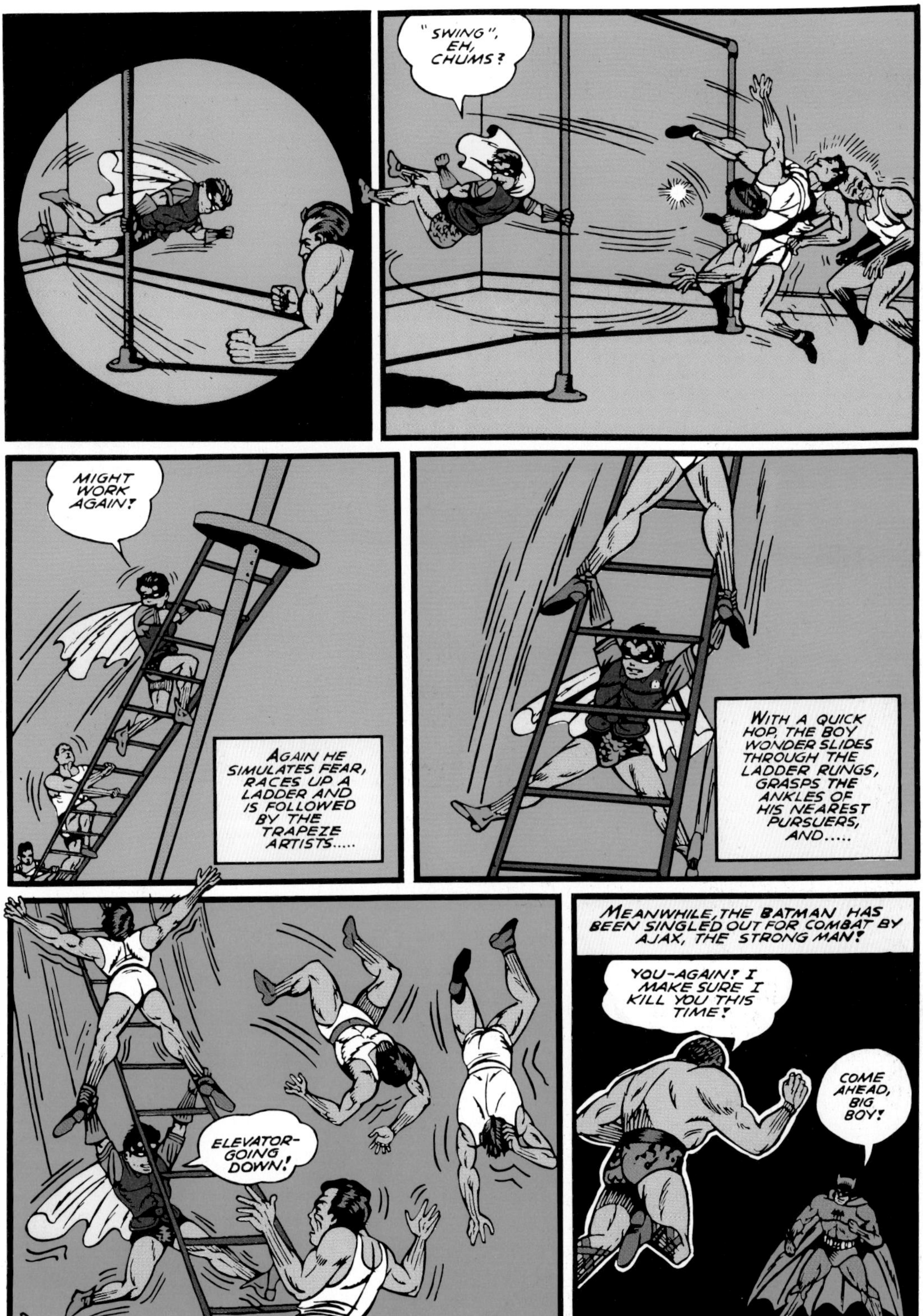
"SWING", EH, CHUMS?
MIGHT WORK AGAIN!
AGAIN HE SIMULATES FEAR, RACES UP A LADDER AND IS FOLLOWED BY THE TRAPEZE ARTISTS.....
WITH A QUICK HOP, THE BOY WONDER SLIDES THROUGH THE LADDER RUNGS, GRASPS THE ANKLES OF HIS NEAREST PURSUERS, AND.....
ELEVATOR-GOING DOWN!
8
MEANWHILE, THE BATMAN HAS BEEN SINGLED OUT FOR COMBAT BY AJAX, THE STRONG MAN!
YOU-AGAIN! I MAKE SURE I KILL YOU THIS TIME!
COME AHEAD, BIG BOY!

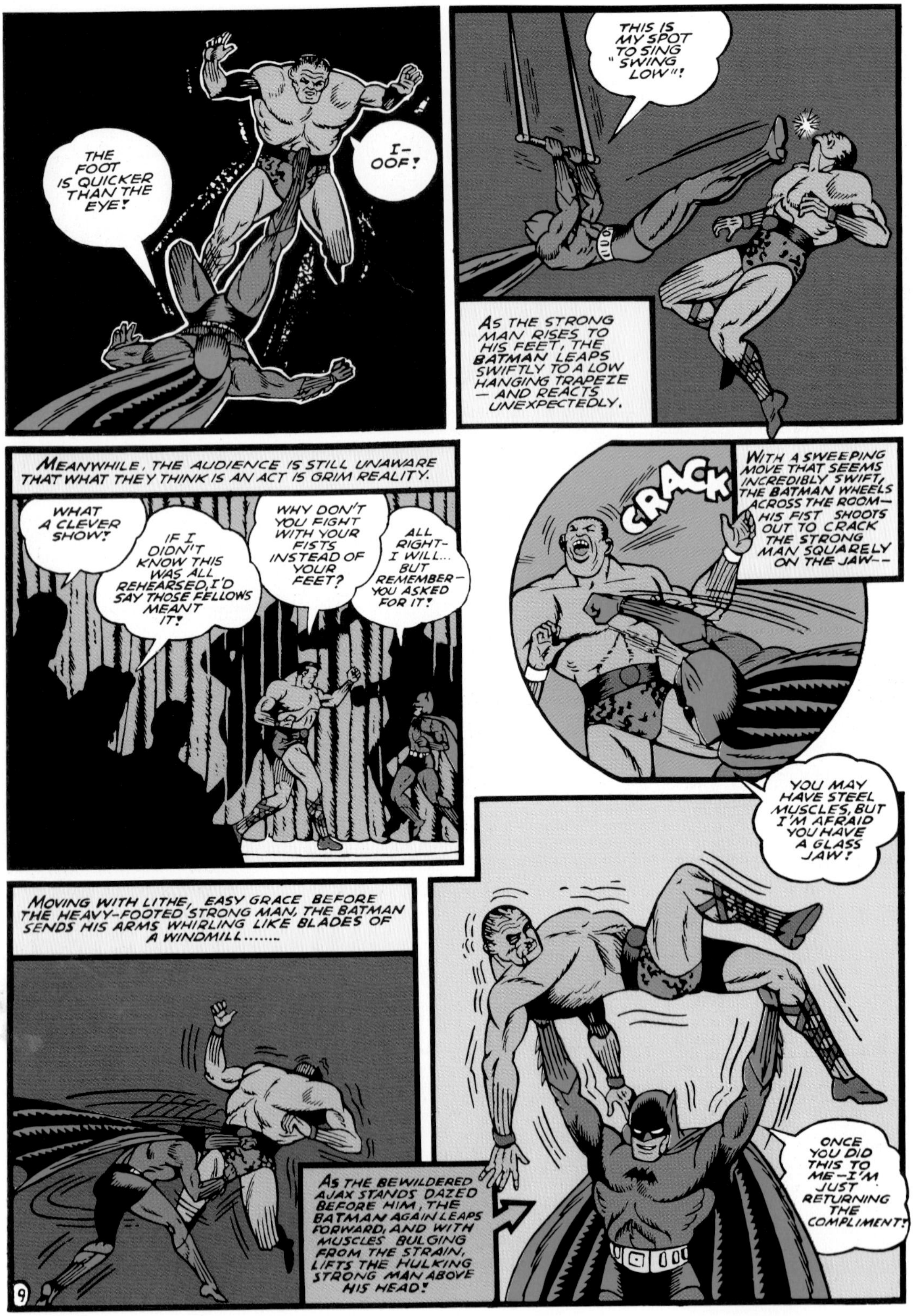
THE FOOT IS QUICKER THAN THE EYE!
I-OOF!
THIS IS MY SPOT TO SING "SWING LOW"!
AS THE STRONG MAN RISES TO HIS FEET, THE BATMAN LEAPS SWIFTLY TO A LOW HANGING TRAPEZE — AND REACTS UNEXPECTEDLY.
MEANWHILE, THE AUDIENCE IS STILL UNAWARE THAT WHAT THEY THINK IS AN ACT IS GRIM REALITY.
WHAT A CLEVER SHOW!
IF I DIDN'T KNOW THIS WAS ALL REHEARSED, I'D SAY THOSE FELLOWS MEANT IT!
WHY DON'T YOU FIGHT WITH YOUR FISTS INSTEAD OF YOUR FEET?
ALL RIGHT- I WILL... BUT REMEMBER- YOU ASKED FOR IT!
WITH A SWEEPING MOVE THAT SEEMS INCREDIBLY SWIFT, THE BATMAN WHEELS ACROSS THE ROOM— HIS FIST SHOOTS OUT TO CRACK THE STRONG MAN SQUARELY ON THE JAW--
CRACK
YOU MAY HAVE STEEL MUSCLES, BUT I'M AFRAID YOU HAVE A GLASS JAW!
MOVING WITH LITHE, EASY GRACE BEFORE THE HEAVY-FOOTED STRONG MAN, THE BATMAN SENDS HIS ARMS WHIRLING LIKE BLADES OF A WINDMILL.......
AS THE BEWILDERED AJAX STANDS DAZED BEFORE HIM, THE BATMAN AGAIN LEAPS FORWARD, AND WITH MUSCLES BULGING FROM THE STRAIN, LIFTS THE HULKING STRONG MAN ABOVE HIS HEAD!
ONCE YOU DID THIS TO ME—I'M JUST RETURNING THE COMPLIMENT!
9

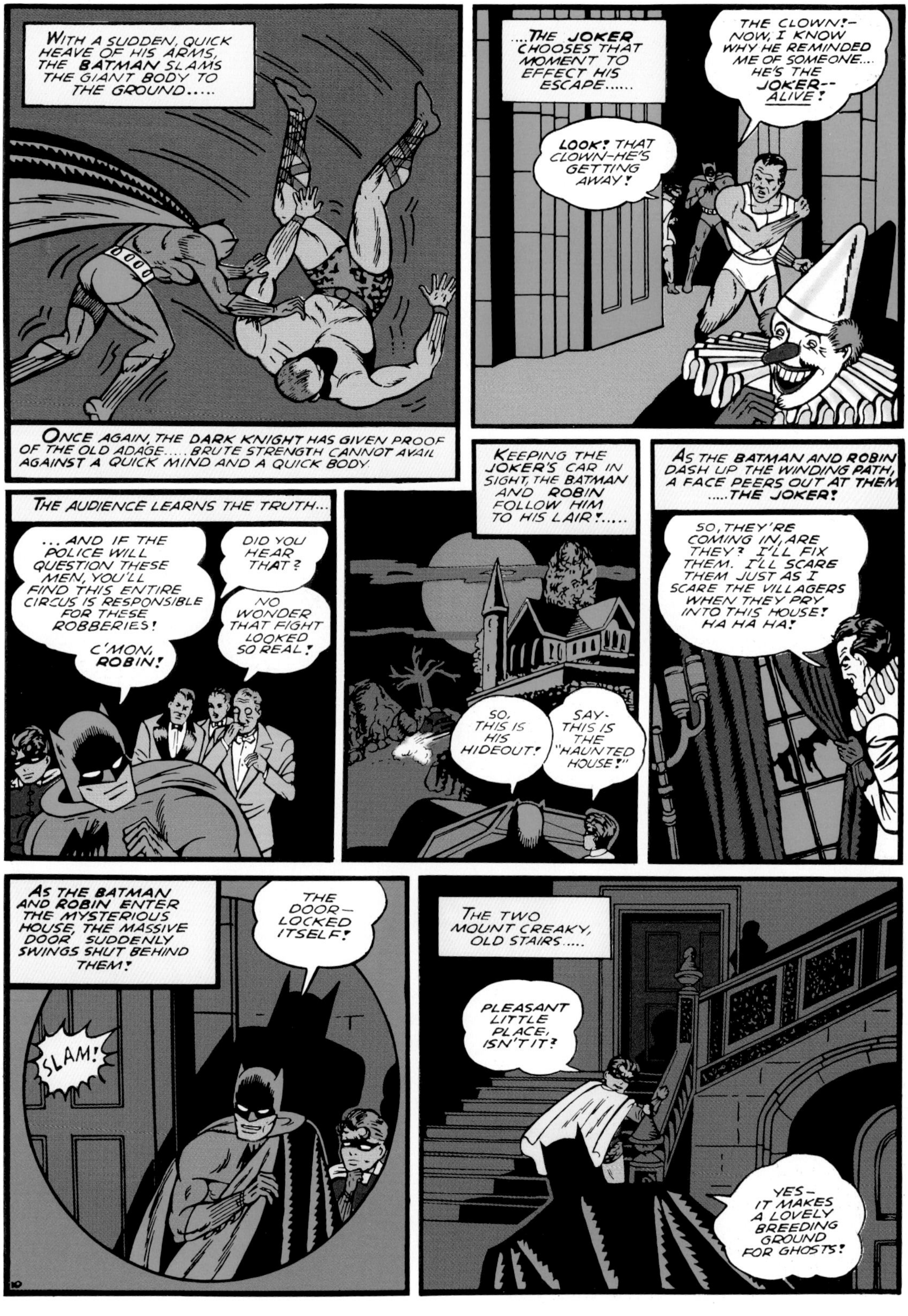
WITH A SUDDEN, QUICK HEAVE OF HIS ARMS, THE BATMAN SLAMS THE GIANT BODY TO THE GROUND.....
ONCE AGAIN, THE DARK KNIGHT HAS GIVEN PROOF OF THE OLD ADAGE..... BRUTE STRENGTH CANNOT AVAIL AGAINST A QUICK MIND AND A QUICK BODY.
....THE JOKER CHOOSES THAT MOMENT TO EFFECT HIS ESCAPE......
LOOK! THAT CLOWN-HE'S GETTING AWAY!
THE CLOWN!-- NOW, I KNOW WHY HE REMINDED ME OF SOMEONE... HE'S THE JOKER-- ALIVE!
THE AUDIENCE LEARNS THE TRUTH...
... AND IF THE POLICE WILL QUESTION THESE MEN, YOU'LL FIND THIS ENTIRE CIRCUS IS RESPONSIBLE FOR THESE ROBBERIES!
DID YOU HEAR THAT?
NO WONDER THAT FIGHT LOOKED SO REAL!
C'MON, ROBIN!
KEEPING THE JOKER'S CAR IN SIGHT, THE BATMAN AND ROBIN FOLLOW HIM TO HIS LAIR!.....
SO, THIS IS HIS HIDEOUT!
SAY- THIS IS THE "HAUNTED HOUSE!"
AS THE BATMAN AND ROBIN DASH UP THE WINDING PATH, A FACE PEERS OUT AT THEM .....THE JOKER!
SO, THEY'RE COMING IN, ARE THEY? I'LL FIX THEM. I'LL SCARE THEM JUST AS I SCARE THE VILLAGERS WHEN THEY PRY INTO THIS HOUSE! HA HA HA!
AS THE BATMAN AND ROBIN ENTER THE MYSTERIOUS HOUSE, THE MASSIVE DOOR SUDDENLY SWINGS SHUT BEHIND THEM!
THE DOOR-- LOCKED ITSELF!
SLAM!
THE TWO MOUNT CREAKY, OLD STAIRS.....
PLEASANT LITTLE PLACE, ISN'T IT?
YES-- IT MAKES A LOVELY BREEDING GROUND FOR GHOSTS!

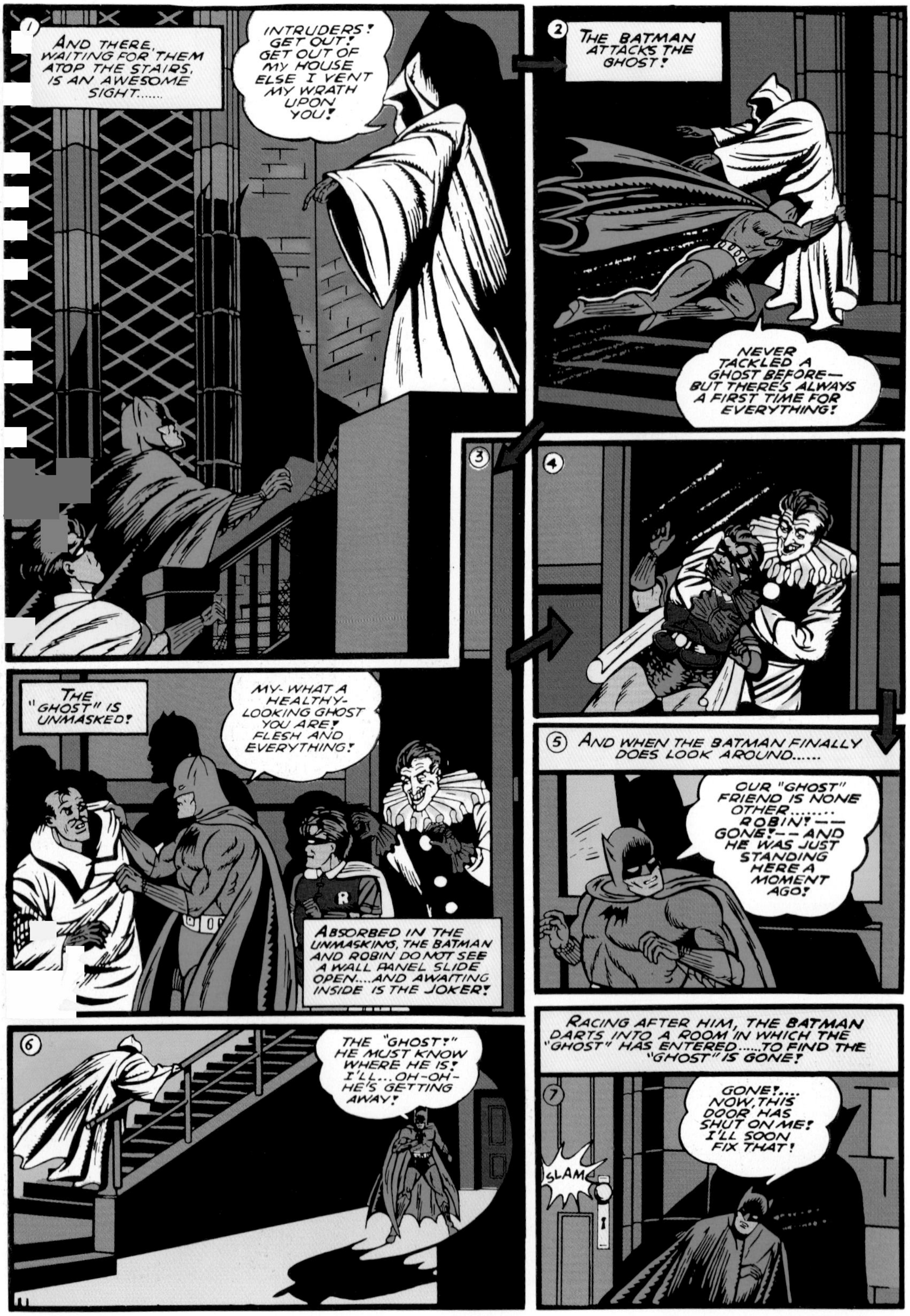
AND THERE, WAITING FOR THEM ATOP THE STAIRS, IS AN AWESOME SIGHT......
INTRUDERS! GET OUT! GET OUT OF MY HOUSE ELSE I VENT MY WRATH UPON YOU!
THE BATMAN ATTACKS THE GHOST!
NEVER TACKLED A GHOST BEFORE— BUT THERE'S ALWAYS A FIRST TIME FOR EVERYTHING!
THE "GHOST" IS UNMASKED!
MY- WHAT A HEALTHY-LOOKING GHOST YOU ARE! FLESH AND EVERYTHING!
ABSORBED IN THE UNMASKING, THE BATMAN AND ROBIN DO NOT SEE A WALL PANEL SLIDE OPEN....AND AWAITING INSIDE IS THE JOKER!
AND WHEN THE BATMAN FINALLY DOES LOOK AROUND......
OUR "GHOST" FRIEND IS NONE OTHER........ ROBIN! —— GONE! -- AND HE WAS JUST STANDING HERE A MOMENT AGO!
THE "GHOST!" HE MUST KNOW WHERE HE IS! I'LL...OH-OH- HE'S GETTING AWAY!
RACING AFTER HIM, THE BATMAN DARTS INTO A ROOM IN WHICH THE "GHOST" HAS ENTERED......TO FIND THE "GHOST" IS GONE!
GONE!.... NOW, THIS DOOR HAS SHUT ON ME! I'LL SOON FIX THAT!
SLAM

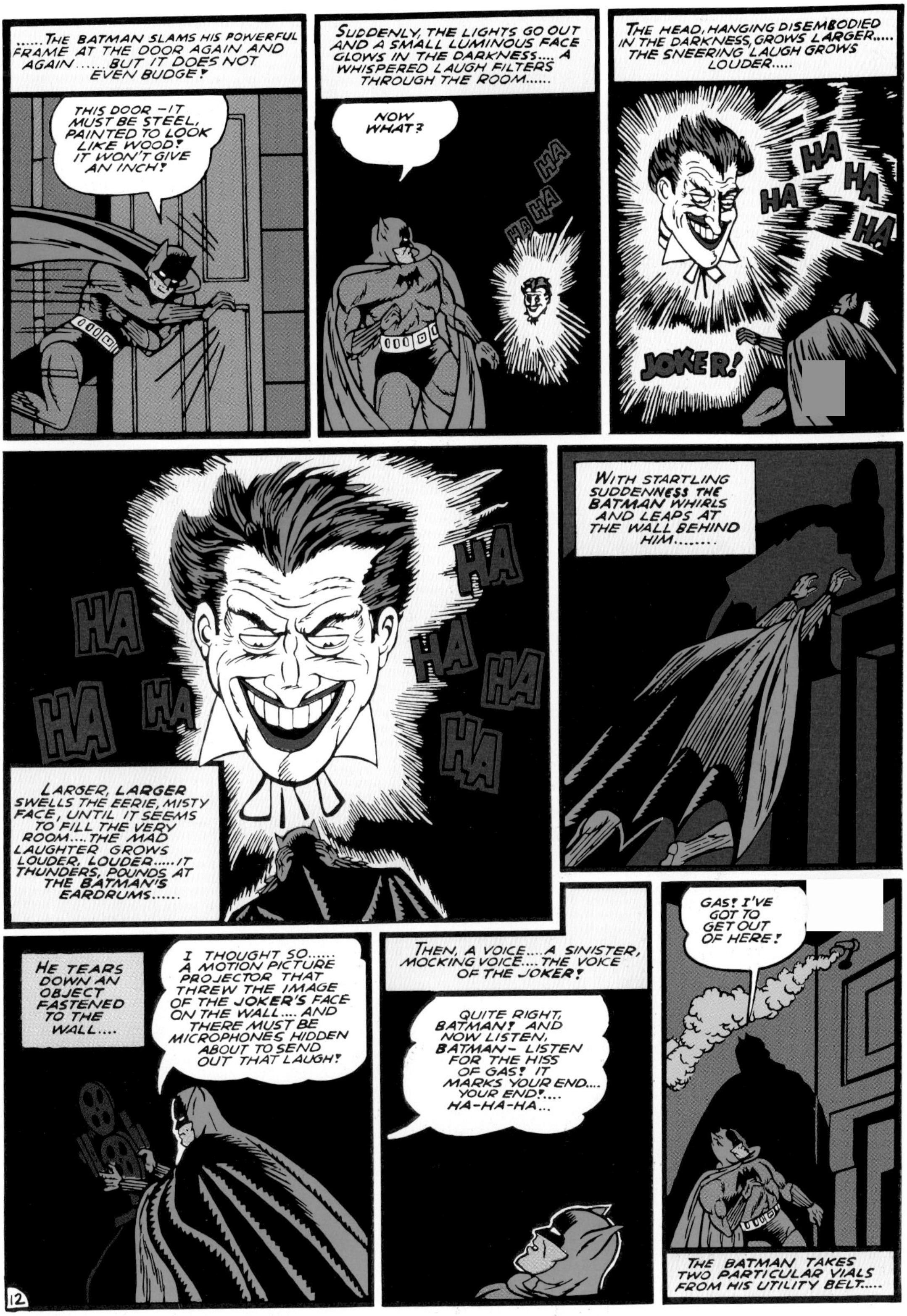
......THE BATMAN SLAMS HIS POWERFUL FRAME AT THE DOOR AGAIN AND AGAIN...... BUT IT DOES NOT EVEN BUDGE!
THIS DOOR -IT MUST BE STEEL, PAINTED TO LOOK LIKE WOOD! IT WON'T GIVE AN INCH!
SUDDENLY, THE LIGHTS GO OUT AND A SMALL LUMINOUS FACE GLOWS IN THE DARKNESS.... A WHISPERED LAUGH FILTERS THROUGH THE ROOM......
NOW WHAT?
HA HA HA HA
THE HEAD, HANGING DISEMBODIED IN THE DARKNESS, GROWS LARGER..... THE SNEERING LAUGH GROWS LOUDER.....
HA HA HA HA HA
JOKER!
HA HA HA HA HA HA HA HA
LARGER, LARGER SWELLS THE EERIE, MISTY FACE, UNTIL IT SEEMS TO FILL THE VERY ROOM.... THE MAD LAUGHTER GROWS LOUDER, LOUDER..... IT THUNDERS, POUNDS AT THE BATMAN'S EARDRUMS......
WITH STARTLING SUDDENNESS THE BATMAN WHIRLS AND LEAPS AT THE WALL BEHIND HIM........
HE TEARS DOWN AN OBJECT FASTENED TO THE WALL....
I THOUGHT SO...... A MOTION PICTURE PROJECTOR THAT THREW THE IMAGE OF THE JOKER'S FACE ON THE WALL.... AND THERE MUST BE MICROPHONES HIDDEN ABOUT TO SEND OUT THAT LAUGH!
THEN, A VOICE.... A SINISTER, MOCKING VOICE.... THE VOICE OF THE JOKER!
QUITE RIGHT, BATMAN! AND NOW LISTEN, BATMAN- LISTEN FOR THE HISS OF GAS! IT MARKS YOUR END.... YOUR END!.... HA-HA-HA...
GAS! I'VE GOT TO GET OUT OF HERE!
THE BATMAN TAKES TWO PARTICULAR VIALS FROM HIS UTILITY BELT.....
12

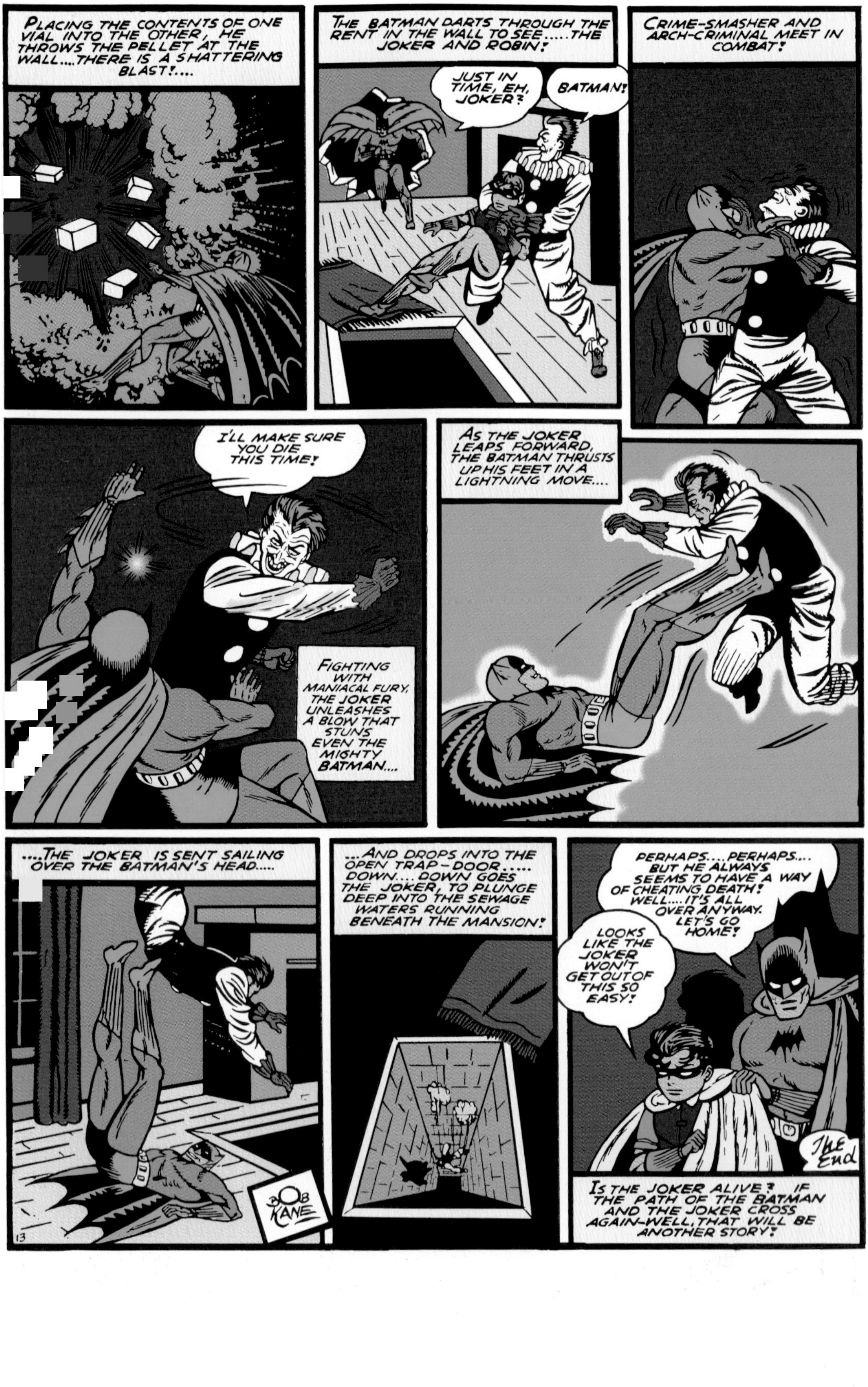
PLACING THE CONTENTS OF ONE VIAL INTO THE OTHER, HE THROWS THE PELLET AT THE WALL....THERE IS A SHATTERING BLAST!....
THE BATMAN DARTS THROUGH THE RENT IN THE WALL TO SEE.....THE JOKER AND ROBIN!
JUST IN TIME, EH, JOKER?
BATMAN!
CRIME-SMASHER AND ARCH-CRIMINAL MEET IN COMBAT!
I'LL MAKE SURE YOU DIE THIS TIME!
FIGHTING WITH MANIACAL FURY, THE JOKER UNLEASHES A BLOW THAT STUNS EVEN THE MIGHTY BATMAN....
AS THE JOKER LEAPS FORWARD, THE BATMAN THRUSTS UP HIS FEET IN A LIGHTNING MOVE....
....THE JOKER IS SENT SAILING OVER THE BATMAN'S HEAD.....
BOB KANE
13
...AND DROPS INTO THE OPEN TRAP-DOOR..... DOWN.... DOWN GOES THE JOKER, TO PLUNGE DEEP INTO THE SEWAGE WATERS RUNNING BENEATH THE MANSION!
LOOKS LIKE THE JOKER WON'T GET OUT OF THIS SO EASY!
PERHAPS....PERHAPS.... BUT HE ALWAYS SEEMS TO HAVE A WAY OF CHEATING DEATH! WELL....IT'S ALL OVER ANYWAY. LET'S GO HOME!
THE End
IS THE JOKER ALIVE? IF THE PATH OF THE BATMAN AND THE JOKER CROSS AGAIN-WELL, THAT WILL BE ANOTHER STORY!

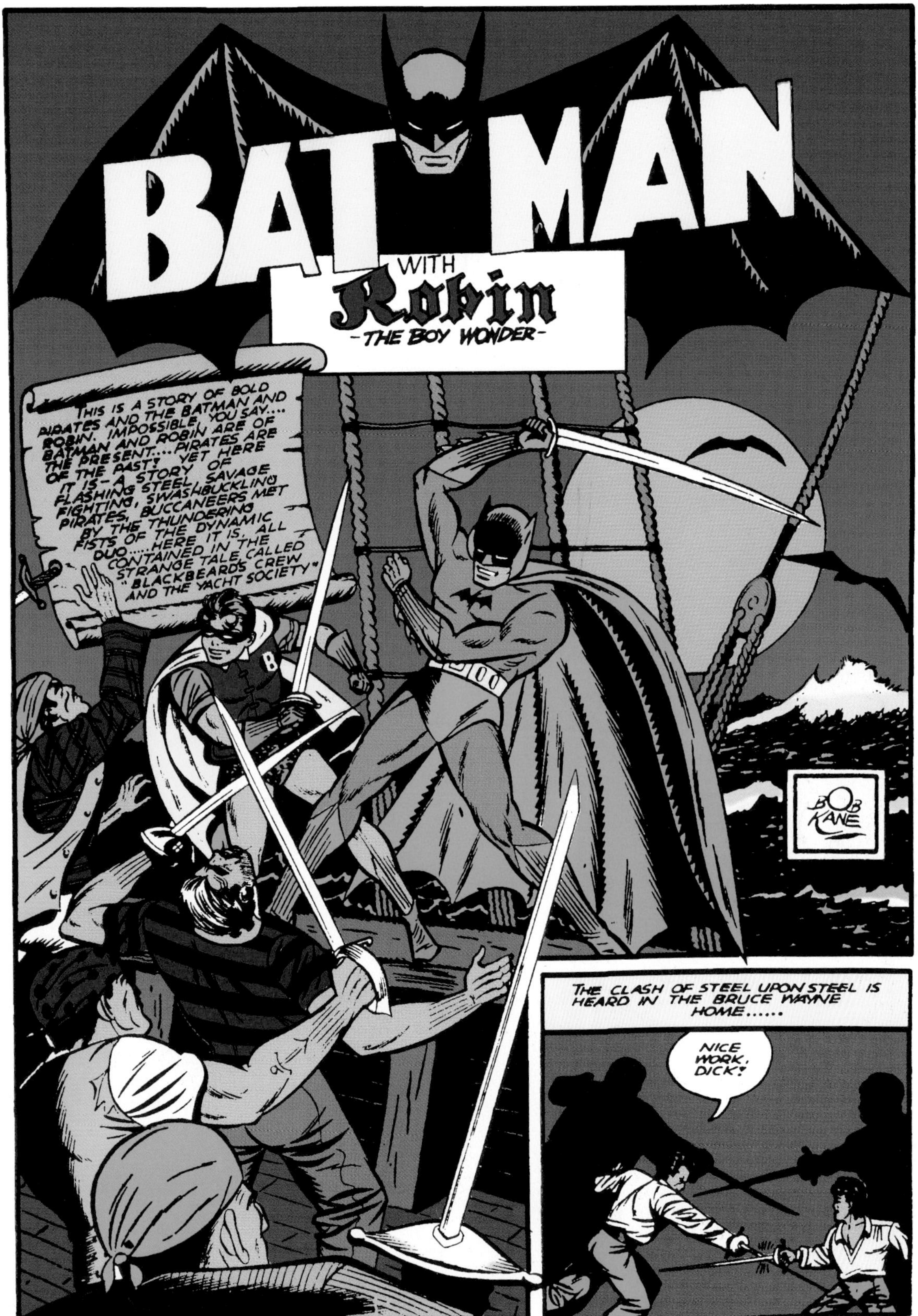
BATMAN
WITH
Robin
-THE BOY WONDER-
THIS IS A STORY OF BOLD PIRATES AND THE BATMAN AND ROBIN. IMPOSSIBLE, YOU SAY.... BATMAN AND ROBIN ARE OF THE PRESENT.... PIRATES ARE OF THE PAST! YET HERE IT IS—A STORY OF FLASHING STEEL, SAVAGE FIGHTING, SWASHBUCKLING PIRATES, BUCCANEERS MET BY THE THUNDERING FISTS OF THE DYNAMIC DUO.... HERE IT IS, ALL CONTAINED IN THE STRANGE TALE CALLED "BLACKBEARD'S CREW AND THE YACHT SOCIETY"
BOB KANE
THE CLASH OF STEEL UPON STEEL IS HEARD IN THE BRUCE WAYNE HOME......
NICE WORK, DICK!

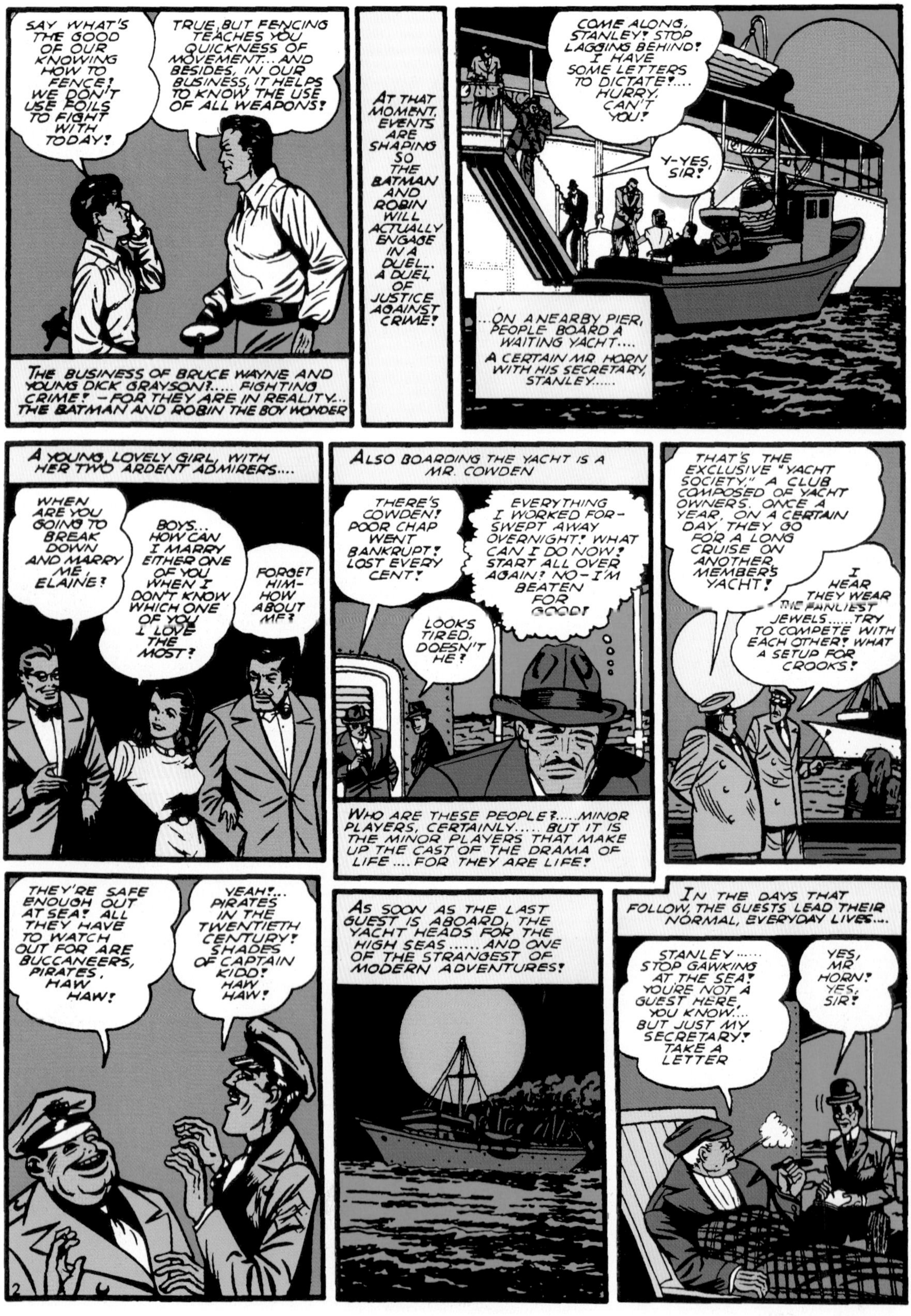
SAY WHAT'S THE GOOD OF OUR KNOWING HOW TO FENCE? WE DON'T USE FOILS TO FIGHT WITH TODAY!
TRUE, BUT FENCING TEACHES YOU QUICKNESS OF MOVEMENT... AND BESIDES, IN OUR BUSINESS, IT HELPS TO KNOW THE USE OF ALL WEAPONS!
THE BUSINESS OF BRUCE WAYNE AND YOUNG DICK GRAYSON?..... FIGHTING CRIME! —FOR THEY ARE IN REALITY... THE BATMAN AND ROBIN THE BOY WONDER
AT THAT MOMENT, EVENTS ARE SHAPING SO THE BATMAN AND ROBIN WILL ACTUALLY ENGAGE IN A DUEL.. A DUEL OF JUSTICE AGAINST CRIME!
...ON A NEARBY PIER, PEOPLE BOARD A WAITING YACHT....
A CERTAIN MR HORN WITH HIS SECRETARY, STANLEY.....
COME ALONG, STANLEY! STOP LAGGING BEHIND! I HAVE SOME LETTERS TO DICTATE!.... HURRY, CAN'T YOU!
Y-YES, SIR!
A YOUNG, LOVELY GIRL, WITH HER TWO ARDENT ADMIRERS....
WHEN ARE YOU GOING TO BREAK DOWN AND MARRY ME, ELAINE?
BOYS... HOW CAN I MARRY EITHER ONE OF YOU WHEN I DON'T KNOW WHICH ONE OF YOU I LOVE THE MOST?
FORGET HIM-HOW ABOUT ME?
ALSO BOARDING THE YACHT IS A MR. COWDEN
THERE'S COWDEN! POOR CHAP WENT BANKRUPT! LOST EVERY CENT!
LOOKS TIRED, DOESN'T HE?
EVERYTHING I WORKED FOR-SWEPT AWAY OVERNIGHT! WHAT CAN I DO NOW? START ALL OVER AGAIN? NO-I'M BEATEN FOR GOOD!
WHO ARE THESE PEOPLE?.....MINOR PLAYERS, CERTAINLY..... BUT IT IS THE MINOR PLAYERS THAT MAKE UP THE CAST OF THE DRAMA OF LIFE.... FOR THEY ARE LIFE!
THAT'S THE EXCLUSIVE "YACHT SOCIETY," A CLUB COMPOSED OF YACHT OWNERS. ONCE A YEAR, ON A CERTAIN DAY, THEY GO FOR A LONG CRUISE ON ANOTHER MEMBER'S YACHT!
I HEAR THEY WEAR THE FANCIEST JEWELS......TRY TO COMPETE WITH EACH OTHER! WHAT A SETUP FOR CROOKS!
THEY'RE SAFE ENOUGH OUT AT SEA! ALL THEY HAVE TO WATCH OUT FOR ARE BUCCANEERS, PIRATES, HAW HAW!
YEAH!... PIRATES IN THE TWENTIETH CENTURY! SHADES OF CAPTAIN KIDD! HAW HAW!
AS SOON AS THE LAST GUEST IS ABOARD, THE YACHT HEADS FOR THE HIGH SEAS...... AND ONE OF THE STRANGEST OF MODERN ADVENTURES!
IN THE DAYS THAT FOLLOW, THE GUESTS LEAD THEIR NORMAL, EVERYDAY LIVES....
STANLEY..... STOP GAWKING AT THE SEA! YOU'RE NOT A GUEST HERE, YOU KNOW... BUT JUST MY SECRETARY! TAKE A LETTER
YES, MR HORN! YES, SIR!

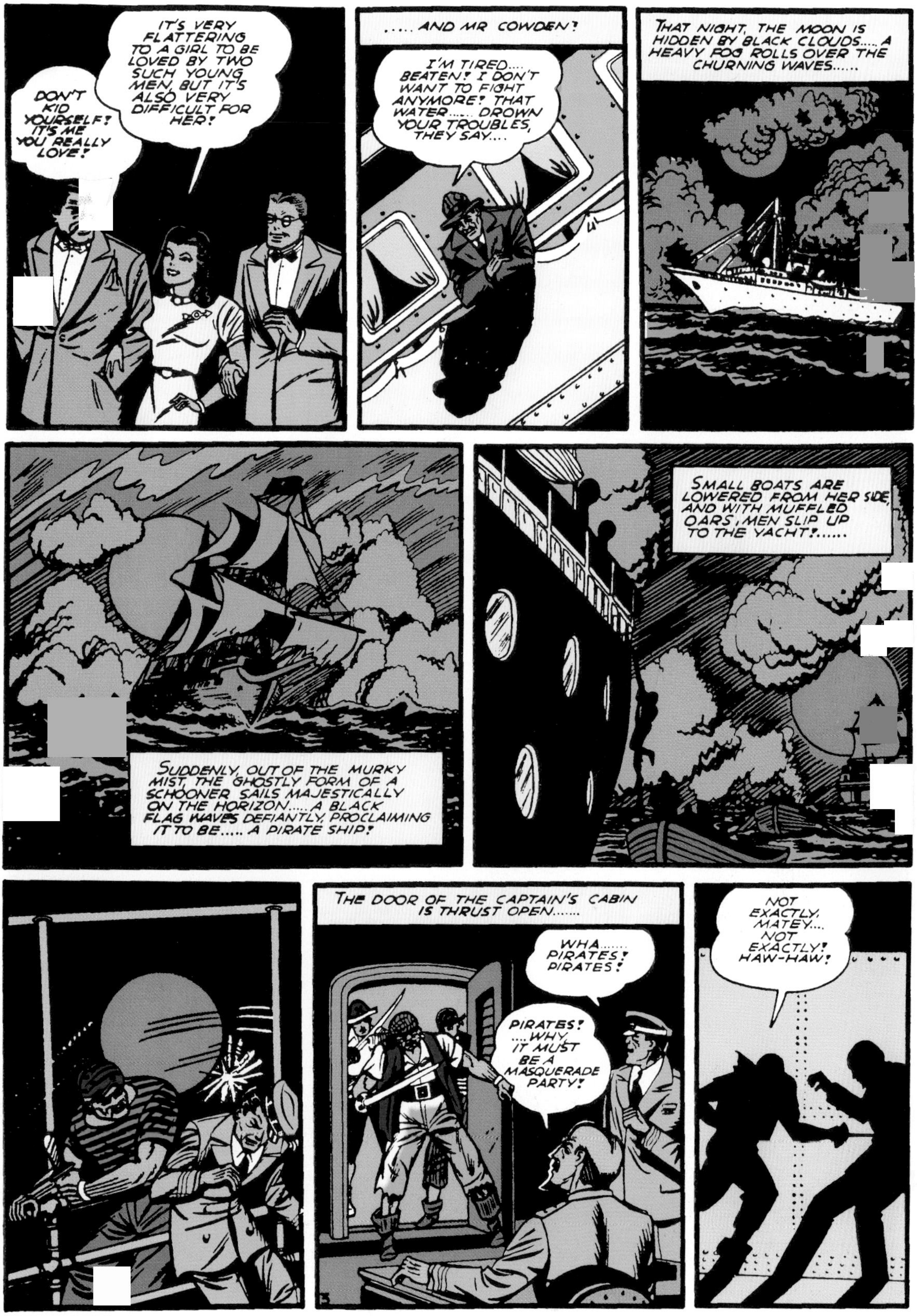
IT'S VERY FLATTERING TO A GIRL TO BE LOVED BY TWO SUCH YOUNG MEN, BUT IT'S ALSO VERY DIFFICULT FOR HER!
DON'T KID YOURSELF! IT'S ME YOU REALLY LOVE!
.....AND MR COWDEN?
I'M TIRED.... BEATEN! I DON'T WANT TO FIGHT ANYMORE! THAT WATER...... DROWN YOUR TROUBLES, THEY SAY....
THAT NIGHT, THE MOON IS HIDDEN BY BLACK CLOUDS..... A HEAVY FOG ROLLS OVER THE CHURNING WAVES......
SUDDENLY, OUT OF THE MURKY MIST, THE GHOSTLY FORM OF A SCHOONER SAILS MAJESTICALLY ON THE HORIZON..... A BLACK FLAG WAVES DEFIANTLY, PROCLAIMING IT TO BE..... A PIRATE SHIP!
SMALL BOATS ARE LOWERED FROM HER SIDE, AND WITH MUFFLED OARS, MEN SLIP UP TO THE YACHT!......
THE DOOR OF THE CAPTAIN'S CABIN IS THRUST OPEN.......
WHA...... PIRATES! PIRATES!
PIRATES! ....WHY, IT MUST BE A MASQUERADE PARTY!
NOT EXACTLY, MATEY.... NOT EXACTLY! HAW-HAW!

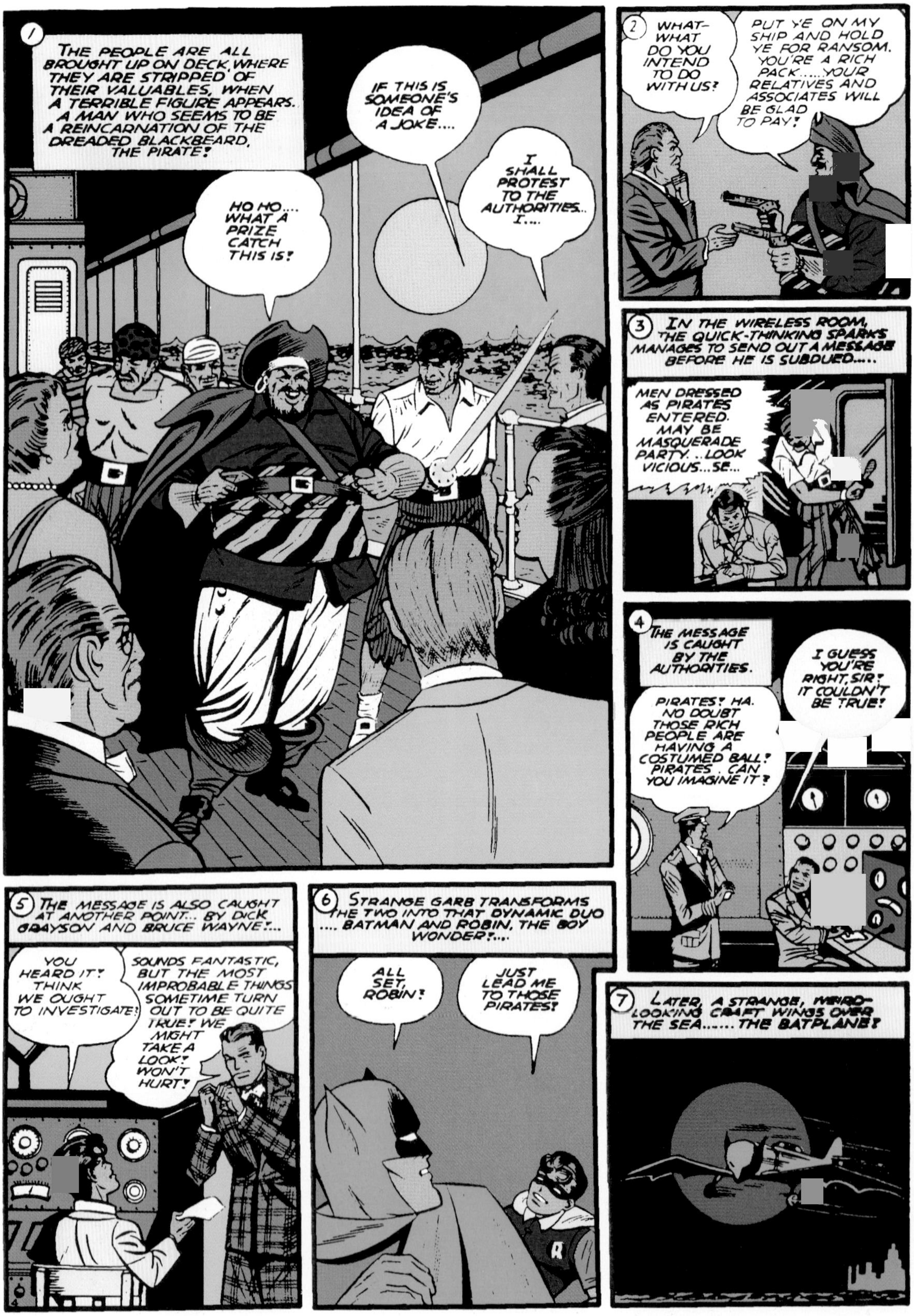
1
THE PEOPLE ARE ALL BROUGHT UP ON DECK, WHERE THEY ARE STRIPPED OF THEIR VALUABLES, WHEN A TERRIBLE FIGURE APPEARS. A MAN WHO SEEMS TO BE A REINCARNATION OF THE DREADED BLACKBEARD, THE PIRATE!
HO HO.... WHAT A PRIZE CATCH THIS IS!
IF THIS IS SOMEONE'S IDEA OF A JOKE....
I SHALL PROTEST TO THE AUTHORITIES... I....
2
WHAT-WHAT DO YOU INTEND TO DO WITH US?
PUT YE ON MY SHIP AND HOLD YE FOR RANSOM. YOU'RE A RICH PACK.....YOUR RELATIVES AND ASSOCIATES WILL BE GLAD TO PAY!
3
IN THE WIRELESS ROOM, THE QUICK-THINKING SPARKS MANAGES TO SEND OUT A MESSAGE BEFORE HE IS SUBDUED.....
MEN DRESSED AS PIRATES ENTERED. MAY BE MASQUERADE PARTY...LOOK VICIOUS...SE...
4
THE MESSAGE IS CAUGHT BY THE AUTHORITIES.
PIRATES? HA. NO DOUBT THOSE RICH PEOPLE ARE HAVING A COSTUMED BALL! PIRATES. CAN YOU IMAGINE IT?
I GUESS YOU'RE RIGHT, SIR! IT COULDN'T BE TRUE!
5
THE MESSAGE IS ALSO CAUGHT AT ANOTHER POINT... BY DICK GRAYSON AND BRUCE WAYNE!...
YOU HEARD IT! THINK WE OUGHT TO INVESTIGATE!
SOUNDS FANTASTIC, BUT THE MOST IMPROBABLE THINGS SOMETIME TURN OUT TO BE QUITE TRUE! WE MIGHT TAKE A LOOK! WON'T HURT!
6
STRANGE GARB TRANSFORMS THE TWO INTO THAT DYNAMIC DUO .... BATMAN AND ROBIN, THE BOY WONDER!....
ALL SET, ROBIN!
JUST LEAD ME TO THOSE PIRATES!
7
LATER, A STRANGE, WEIRD-LOOKING CRAFT WINGS OVER THE SEA...... THE BATPLANE!

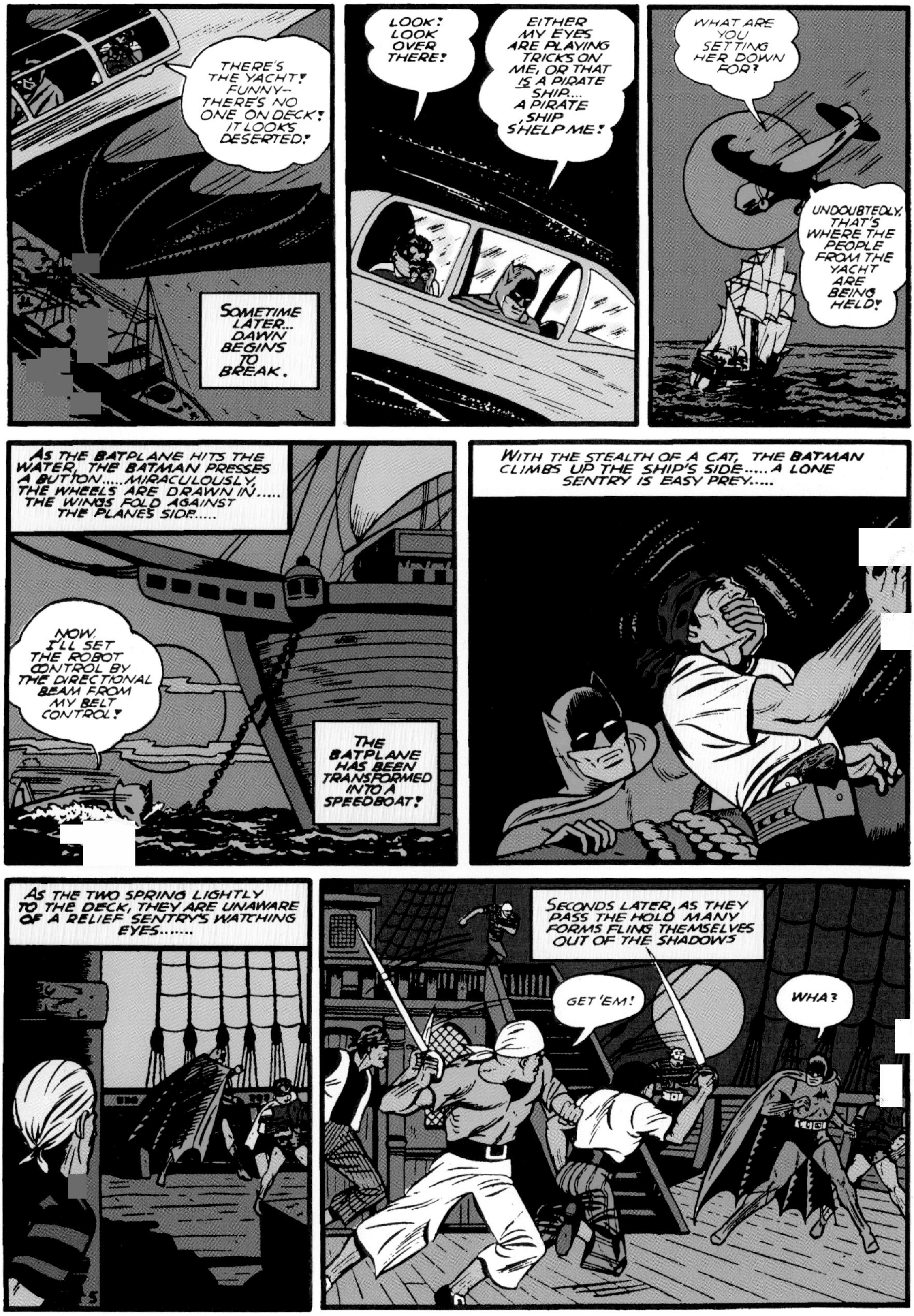
SOMETIME LATER... DAWN BEGINS TO BREAK.
THERE'S THE YACHT! FUNNY-- THERE'S NO ONE ON DECK! IT LOOKS DESERTED!
LOOK! LOOK OVER THERE!
EITHER MY EYES ARE PLAYING TRICKS ON ME, OR THAT IS A PIRATE SHIP.... A PIRATE SHIP, S'HELP ME!
WHAT ARE YOU SETTING HER DOWN FOR?
UNDOUBTEDLY, THAT'S WHERE THE PEOPLE FROM THE YACHT ARE BEING HELD!
AS THE BATPLANE HITS THE WATER, THE BATMAN PRESSES A BUTTON.....MIRACULOUSLY, THE WHEELS ARE DRAWN IN..... THE WINGS FOLD AGAINST THE PLANE'S SIDE.....
NOW, I'LL SET THE ROBOT CONTROL BY THE DIRECTIONAL BEAM FROM MY BELT CONTROL!
THE BATPLANE HAS BEEN TRANSFORMED INTO A SPEEDBOAT!
WITH THE STEALTH OF A CAT, THE BATMAN CLIMBS UP THE SHIP'S SIDE..... A LONE SENTRY IS EASY PREY.....
AS THE TWO SPRING LIGHTLY TO THE DECK, THEY ARE UNAWARE OF A RELIEF SENTRY'S WATCHING EYES.......
SECONDS LATER, AS THEY PASS THE HOLD MANY FORMS FLING THEMSELVES OUT OF THE SHADOWS
GET 'EM!
WHA?

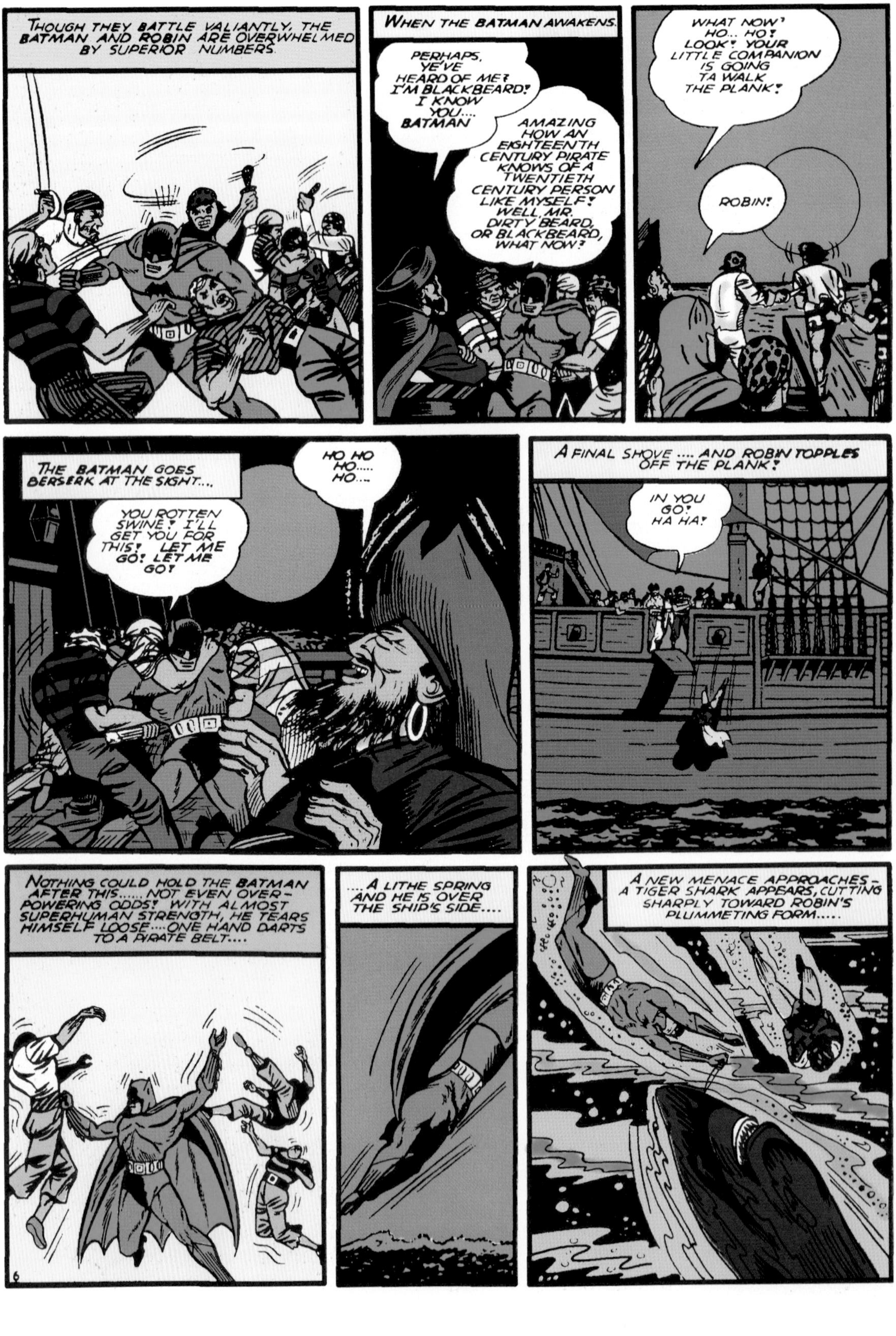
THOUGH THEY BATTLE VALIANTLY, THE BATMAN AND ROBIN ARE OVERWHELMED BY SUPERIOR NUMBERS.
WHEN THE BATMAN AWAKENS.
PERHAPS, YE'VE HEARD OF ME? I'M BLACKBEARD! I KNOW YOU.... BATMAN
AMAZING HOW AN EIGHTEENTH CENTURY PIRATE KNOWS OF A TWENTIETH CENTURY PERSON LIKE MYSELF! WELL, MR. DIRTY BEARD, OR BLACKBEARD, WHAT NOW?
WHAT NOW? HO... HO! LOOK! YOUR LITTLE COMPANION IS GOING TA WALK THE PLANK!
ROBIN!
THE BATMAN GOES BERSERK AT THE SIGHT....
HO HO HO..... HO....
YOU ROTTEN SWINE! I'LL GET YOU FOR THIS! LET ME GO! LET ME GO!
A FINAL SHOVE .... AND ROBIN TOPPLES OFF THE PLANK!
IN YOU GO! HA HA!
NOTHING COULD HOLD THE BATMAN AFTER THIS..... NOT EVEN OVER-POWERING ODDS! WITH ALMOST SUPERHUMAN STRENGTH, HE TEARS HIMSELF LOOSE....ONE HAND DARTS TO A PIRATE BELT....
....A LITHE SPRING AND HE IS OVER THE SHIP'S SIDE....
A NEW MENACE APPROACHES - A TIGER SHARK APPEARS, CUTTING SHARPLY TOWARD ROBIN'S PLUMMETING FORM.....
6

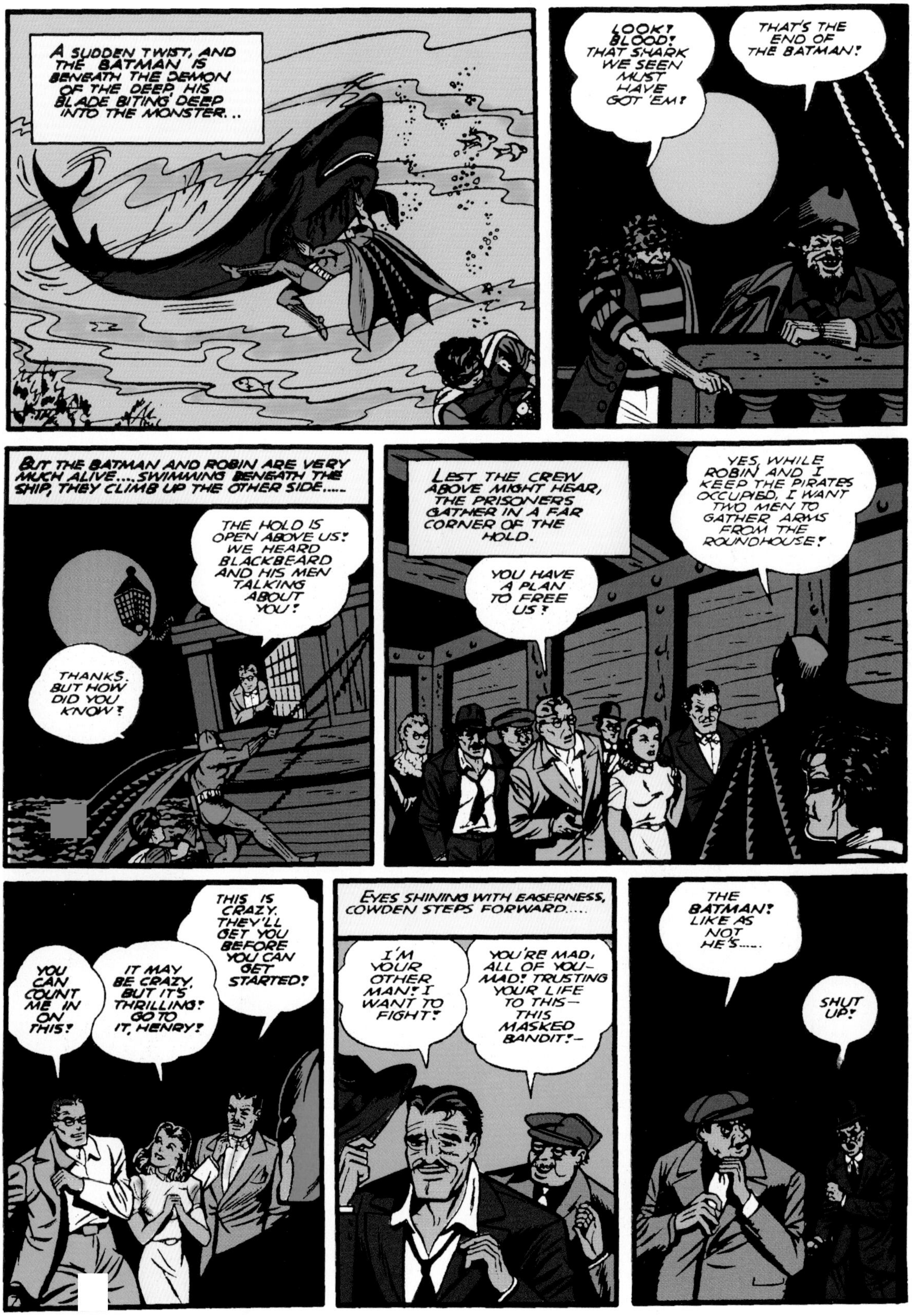
A SUDDEN TWIST, AND THE BATMAN IS BENEATH THE DEMON OF THE DEEP, HIS BLADE BITING DEEP INTO THE MONSTER...
LOOK! BLOOD! THAT SHARK WE SEEN MUST HAVE GOT 'EM!
THAT'S THE END OF THE BATMAN!
BUT THE BATMAN AND ROBIN ARE VERY MUCH ALIVE....SWIMMING BENEATH THE SHIP, THEY CLIMB UP THE OTHER SIDE.....
THE HOLD IS OPEN ABOVE US! WE HEARD BLACKBEARD AND HIS MEN TALKING ABOUT YOU!
THANKS. BUT HOW DID YOU KNOW?
LEST THE CREW ABOVE MIGHT HEAR, THE PRISONERS GATHER IN A FAR CORNER OF THE HOLD.
YOU HAVE A PLAN TO FREE US?
YES, WHILE ROBIN AND I KEEP THE PIRATES OCCUPIED, I WANT TWO MEN TO GATHER ARMS FROM THE ROUNDHOUSE!
THIS IS CRAZY. THEY'LL GET YOU BEFORE YOU CAN GET STARTED!
YOU CAN COUNT ME IN ON THIS!
IT MAY BE CRAZY, BUT IT'S THRILLING! GO TO IT, HENRY!
EYES SHINING WITH EAGERNESS, COWDEN STEPS FORWARD.....
I'M YOUR OTHER MAN! I WANT TO FIGHT!
YOU'RE MAD, ALL OF YOU-MAD! TRUSTING YOUR LIFE TO THIS— THIS MASKED BANDIT!—
THE BATMAN! LIKE AS NOT HE'S.....
SHUT UP!

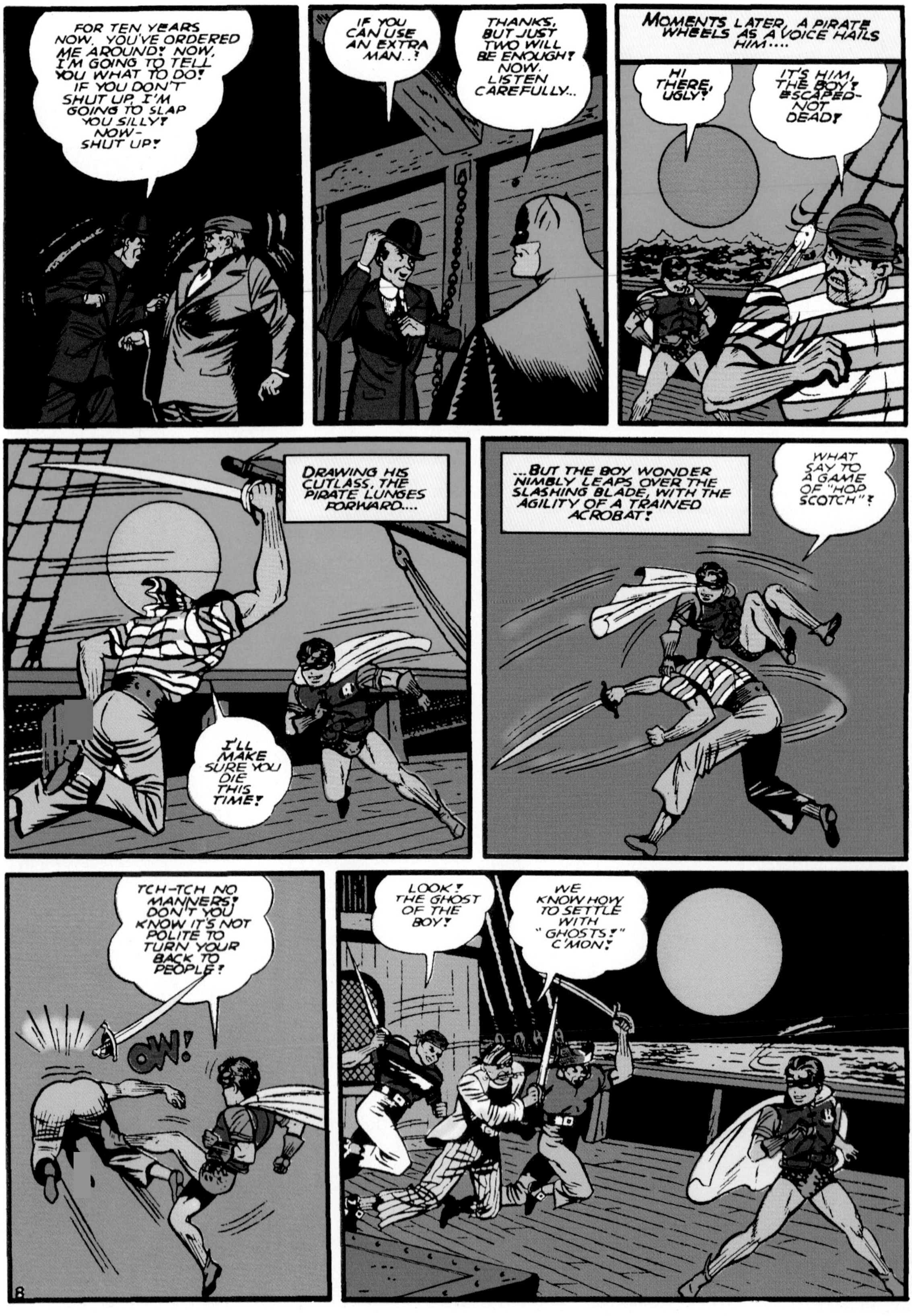
FOR TEN YEARS NOW, YOU'VE ORDERED ME AROUND! NOW, I'M GOING TO TELL YOU WHAT TO DO! IF YOU DON'T SHUT UP, I'M GOING TO SLAP YOU SILLY! NOW- SHUT UP!
IF YOU CAN USE AN EXTRA MAN..?
THANKS, BUT JUST TWO WILL BE ENOUGH! NOW, LISTEN CAREFULLY...
MOMENTS LATER, A PIRATE WHEELS AS A VOICE HAILS HIM....
HI THERE, UGLY!
IT'S HIM, THE BOY! ESCAPED-NOT DEAD!
DRAWING HIS CUTLASS, THE PIRATE LUNGES FORWARD....
I'LL MAKE SURE YOU DIE THIS TIME!
...BUT THE BOY WONDER NIMBLY LEAPS OVER THE SLASHING BLADE, WITH THE AGILITY OF A TRAINED ACROBAT!
WHAT SAY TO A GAME OF "HOP SCOTCH"?
TCH-TCH NO MANNERS! DON'T YOU KNOW IT'S NOT POLITE TO TURN YOUR BACK TO PEOPLE?
OW!
8
LOOK! THE GHOST OF THE BOY!
WE KNOW HOW TO SETTLE WITH "GHOSTS!" C'MON!

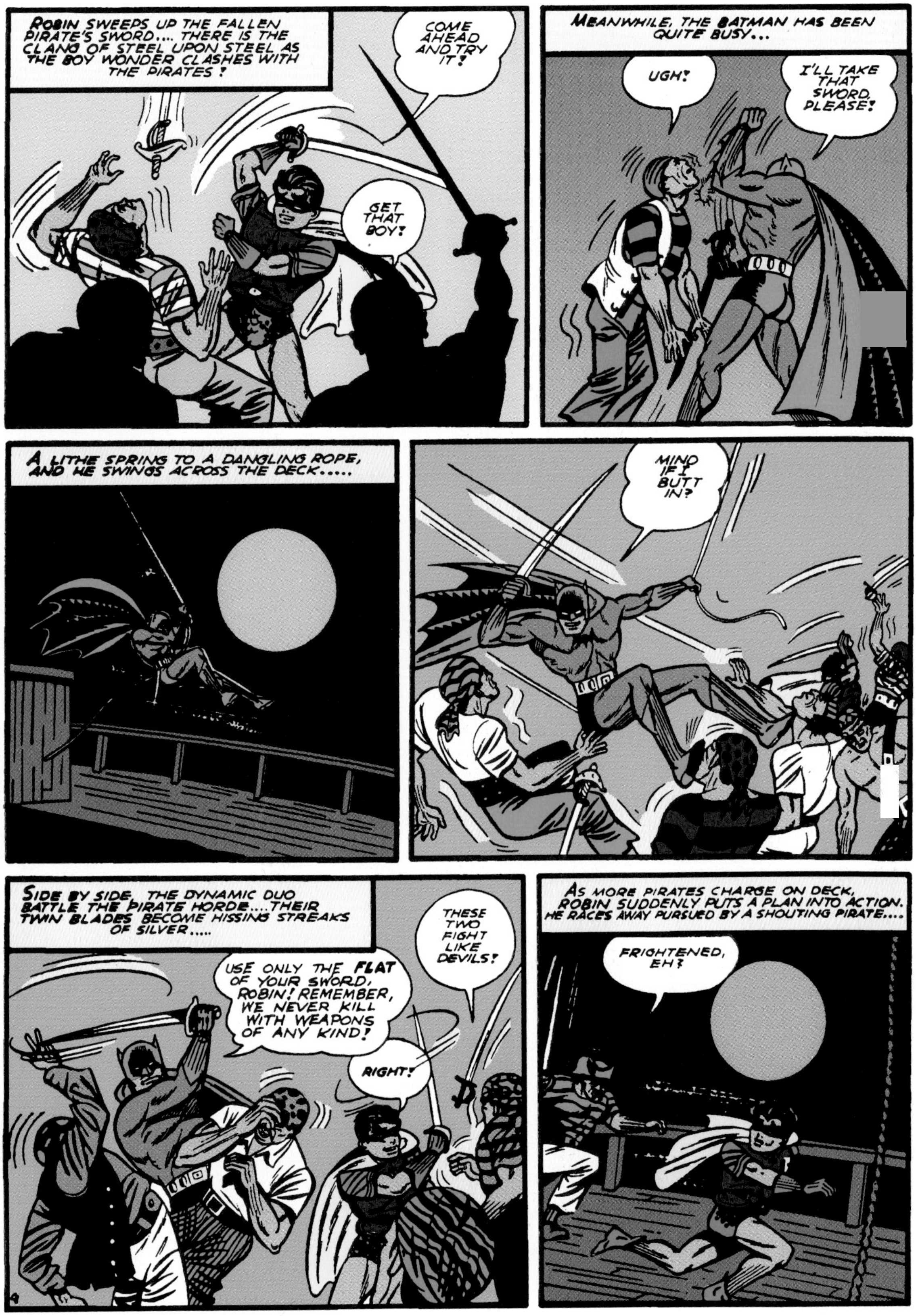
ROBIN SWEEPS UP THE FALLEN PIRATE'S SWORD.... THERE IS THE CLANG OF STEEL UPON STEEL AS THE BOY WONDER CLASHES WITH THE PIRATES!
COME AHEAD AND TRY IT!
GET THAT BOY!
MEANWHILE, THE BATMAN HAS BEEN QUITE BUSY...
UGH!
I'LL TAKE THAT SWORD, PLEASE!
A LITHE SPRING TO A DANGLING ROPE, AND HE SWINGS ACROSS THE DECK.....
MIND IF I BUTT IN?
SIDE BY SIDE, THE DYNAMIC DUO BATTLE THE PIRATE HORDE....THEIR TWIN BLADES BECOME HISSING STREAKS OF SILVER.....
THESE TWO FIGHT LIKE DEVILS!
USE ONLY THE FLAT OF YOUR SWORD, ROBIN! REMEMBER, WE NEVER KILL WITH WEAPONS OF ANY KIND!
RIGHT!
AS MORE PIRATES CHARGE ON DECK, ROBIN SUDDENLY PUTS A PLAN INTO ACTION. HE RACES AWAY PURSUED BY A SHOUTING PIRATE....
FRIGHTENED, EH?

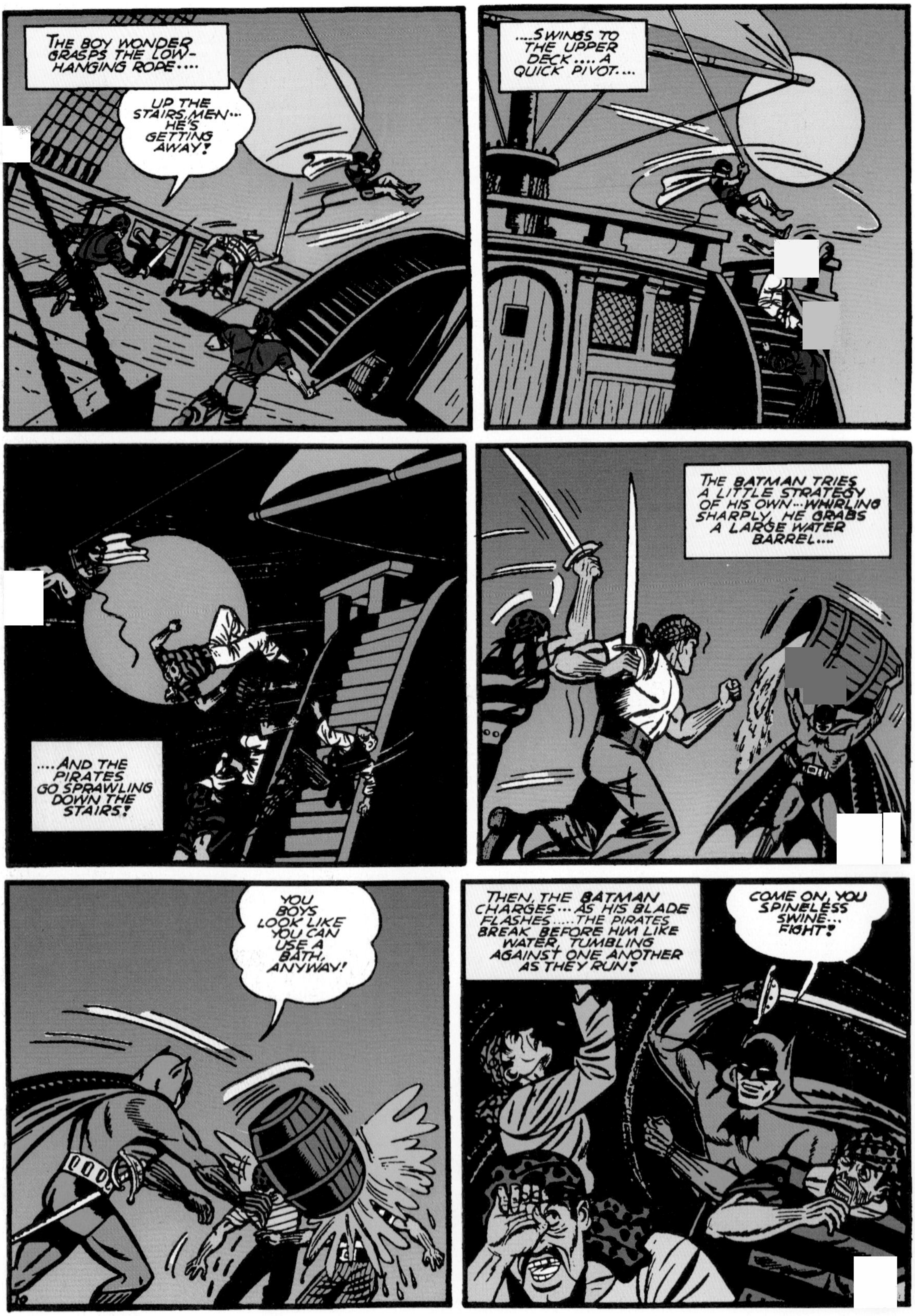
THE BOY WONDER GRASPS THE LOW-HANGING ROPE....
UP THE STAIRS, MEN... HE'S GETTING AWAY!
...SWINGS TO THE UPPER DECK.... A QUICK PIVOT....
....AND THE PIRATES GO SPRAWLING DOWN THE STAIRS!
THE BATMAN TRIES A LITTLE STRATEGY OF HIS OWN...WHIRLING SHARPLY, HE GRABS A LARGE WATER BARREL....
YOU BOYS LOOK LIKE YOU CAN USE A BATH, ANYWAY!
THEN, THE BATMAN CHARGES... AS HIS BLADE FLASHES.....THE PIRATES BREAK BEFORE HIM LIKE WATER, TUMBLING AGAINST ONE ANOTHER AS THEY RUN!
COME ON, YOU SPINELESS SWINE... FIGHT!

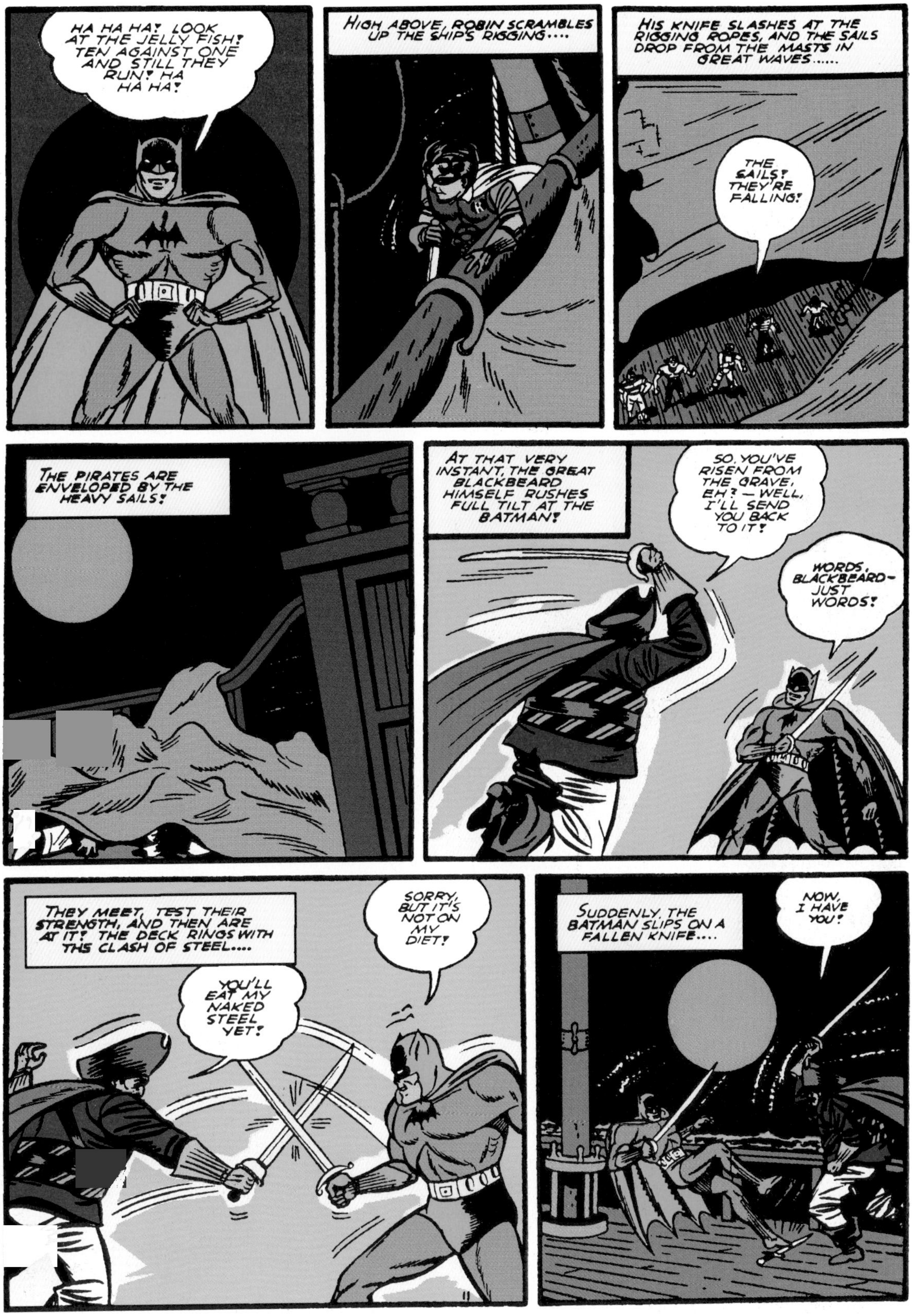
HA HA HA! LOOK AT THE JELLY FISH! TEN AGAINST ONE AND STILL THEY RUN! HA HA HA!
HIGH ABOVE, ROBIN SCRAMBLES UP THE SHIP'S RIGGING....
HIS KNIFE SLASHES AT THE RIGGING ROPES, AND THE SAILS DROP FROM THE MASTS IN GREAT WAVES......
THE SAILS! THEY'RE FALLING!
THE PIRATES ARE ENVELOPED BY THE HEAVY SAILS!
AT THAT VERY INSTANT, THE GREAT BLACKBEARD HIMSELF RUSHES FULL TILT AT THE BATMAN!
SO, YOU'VE RISEN FROM THE GRAVE, EH? — WELL, I'LL SEND YOU BACK TO IT!
WORDS, BLACKBEARD — JUST WORDS!
THEY MEET, TEST THEIR STRENGTH, AND THEN ARE AT IT! THE DECK RINGS WITH THE CLASH OF STEEL....
YOU'LL EAT MY NAKED STEEL YET!
SORRY, BUT IT'S NOT ON MY DIET!
SUDDENLY, THE BATMAN SLIPS ON A FALLEN KNIFE....
NOW, I HAVE YOU!

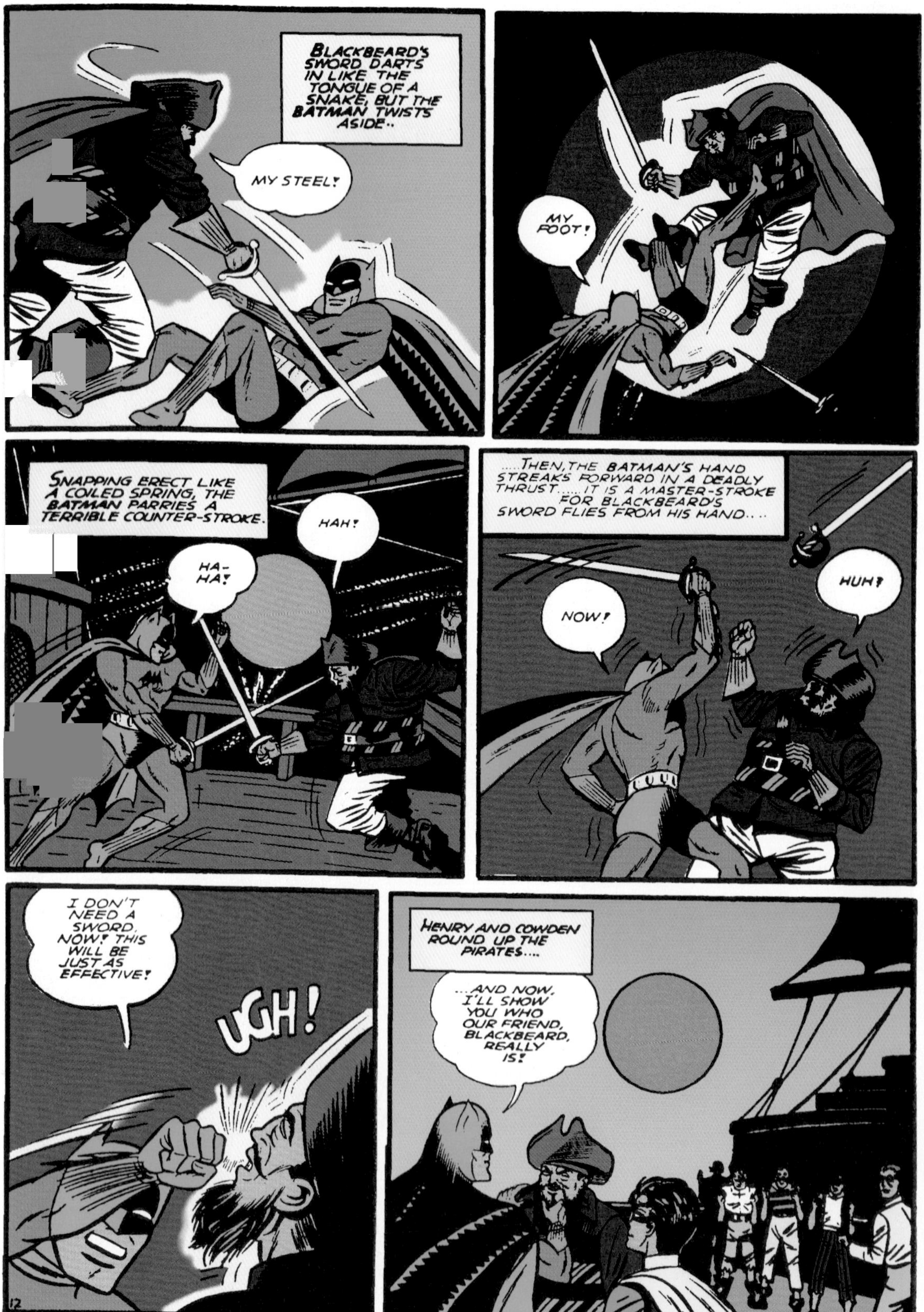
BLACKBEARD'S SWORD DARTS IN LIKE THE TONGUE OF A SNAKE, BUT THE BATMAN TWISTS ASIDE..
MY STEEL!
MY FOOT!
SNAPPING ERECT LIKE A COILED SPRING, THE BATMAN PARRIES A TERRIBLE COUNTER-STROKE.
HA-HA!
HAH!
....THEN, THE BATMAN'S HAND STREAKS FORWARD IN A DEADLY THRUST..... IT IS A MASTER-STROKE FOR BLACKBEARD'S SWORD FLIES FROM HIS HAND....
NOW!
HUH?
I DON'T NEED A SWORD NOW! THIS WILL BE JUST AS EFFECTIVE!
UGH!
12
HENRY AND COWDEN ROUND UP THE PIRATES....
...AND NOW, I'LL SHOW YOU WHO OUR FRIEND, BLACKBEARD, REALLY IS!

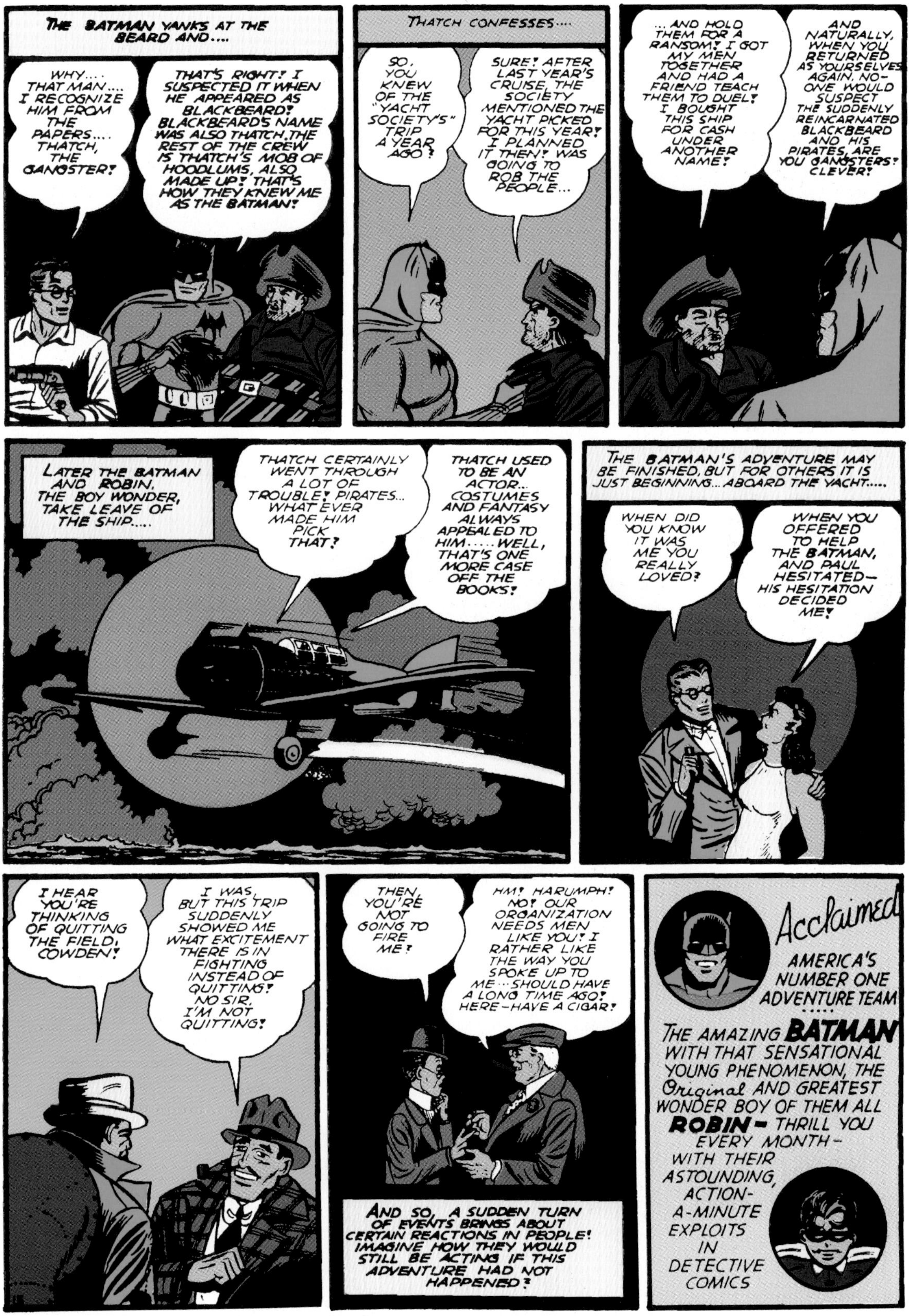
THE BATMAN YANKS AT THE BEARD AND....
WHY.... THAT MAN.... I RECOGNIZE HIM FROM THE PAPERS.... THATCH, THE GANGSTER!
THAT'S RIGHT! I SUSPECTED IT WHEN HE APPEARED AS BLACKBEARD! BLACKBEARD'S NAME WAS ALSO THATCH. THE REST OF THE CREW IS THATCH'S MOB OF HOODLUMS, ALSO MADE UP! THAT'S HOW THEY KNEW ME AS THE BATMAN!
THATCH CONFESSES....
SO, YOU KNEW OF THE "YACHT SOCIETY'S" TRIP A YEAR AGO?
SURE! AFTER LAST YEAR'S CRUISE, THE SOCIETY MENTIONED THE YACHT PICKED FOR THIS YEAR! I PLANNED IT THEN! WAS GOING TO ROB THE PEOPLE...
...AND HOLD THEM FOR A RANSOM! I GOT MY MEN TOGETHER AND HAD A FRIEND TEACH THEM TO DUEL! I BOUGHT THIS SHIP FOR CASH UNDER ANOTHER NAME!
AND NATURALLY, WHEN YOU RETURNED AS YOURSELVES AGAIN, NO-ONE WOULD SUSPECT THE SUDDENLY REINCARNATED BLACKBEARD AND HIS PIRATES, ARE YOU GANGSTERS! CLEVER!
LATER THE BATMAN AND ROBIN, THE BOY WONDER, TAKE LEAVE OF THE SHIP....
THATCH CERTAINLY WENT THROUGH A LOT OF TROUBLE! PIRATES... WHAT EVER MADE HIM PICK THAT?
THATCH USED TO BE AN ACTOR.. COSTUMES AND FANTASY ALWAYS APPEALED TO HIM......WELL, THAT'S ONE MORE CASE OFF THE BOOKS!
THE BATMAN'S ADVENTURE MAY BE FINISHED, BUT FOR OTHERS IT IS JUST BEGINNING... ABOARD THE YACHT....
WHEN DID YOU KNOW IT WAS ME YOU REALLY LOVED?
WHEN YOU OFFERED TO HELP THE BATMAN, AND PAUL HESITATED— HIS HESITATION DECIDED ME!
I HEAR YOU'RE THINKING OF QUITTING THE FIELD, COWDEN!
I WAS, BUT THIS TRIP SUDDENLY SHOWED ME WHAT EXCITEMENT THERE IS IN FIGHTING INSTEAD OF QUITTING! NO SIR, I'M NOT QUITTING!
THEN, YOU'RE NOT GOING TO FIRE ME?
HM! HARUMPH! NO! OUR ORGANIZATION NEEDS MEN LIKE YOU! I RATHER LIKE THE WAY YOU SPOKE UP TO ME...SHOULD HAVE A LONG TIME AGO! HERE—HAVE A CIGAR!
AND SO, A SUDDEN TURN OF EVENTS BRINGS ABOUT CERTAIN REACTIONS IN PEOPLE! IMAGINE HOW THEY WOULD STILL BE ACTING IF THIS ADVENTURE HAD NOT HAPPENED?
Acclaimed
AMERICA'S NUMBER ONE ADVENTURE TEAM
....
THE AMAZING BATMAN WITH THAT SENSATIONAL YOUNG PHENOMENON, THE Original AND GREATEST WONDER BOY OF THEM ALL ROBIN— THRILL YOU EVERY MONTH— WITH THEIR ASTOUNDING, ACTION-A-MINUTE EXPLOITS IN DETECTIVE COMICS

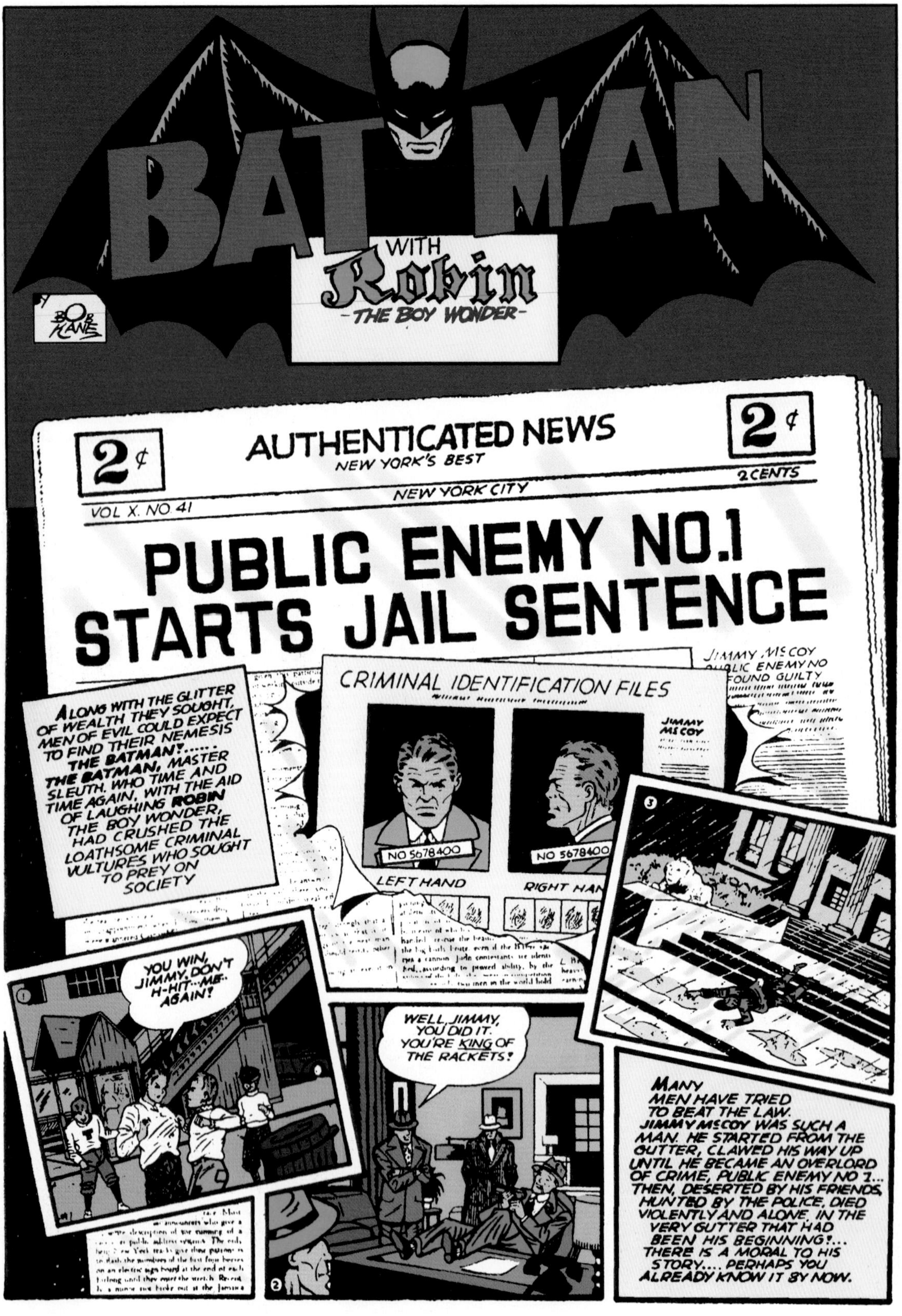
BATMAN
WITH
Robin
-THE BOY WONDER-
BY BOB KANE
AUTHENTICATED NEWS
NEW YORK'S BEST
2¢
2¢
2 CENTS
NEW YORK CITY
VOL X. NO. 41
PUBLIC ENEMY NO.1 STARTS JAIL SENTENCE
JIMMY McCOY PUBLIC ENEMY NO FOUND GUILTY
CRIMINAL IDENTIFICATION FILES
JIMMY McCOY
NO 5678400
NO 5678400
LEFT HAND
RIGHT HAN
ALONG WITH THE GLITTER OF WEALTH THEY SOUGHT, MEN OF EVIL COULD EXPECT TO FIND THEIR NEMESIS THE BATMAN!..... THE BATMAN, MASTER SLEUTH, WHO TIME AND TIME AGAIN, WITH THE AID OF LAUGHING ROBIN THE BOY WONDER, HAD CRUSHED THE LOATHSOME CRIMINAL VULTURES WHO SOUGHT TO PREY ON SOCIETY
YOU WIN, JIMMY, DON'T H-HIT- ME- AGAIN!
WELL, JIMMY, YOU DID IT. YOU'RE KING OF THE RACKETS!
MANY MEN HAVE TRIED TO BEAT THE LAW. JIMMY McCOY WAS SUCH A MAN. HE STARTED FROM THE GUTTER, CLAWED HIS WAY UP UNTIL HE BECAME AN OVERLORD OF CRIME, PUBLIC ENEMY NO 1... THEN, DESERTED BY HIS FRIENDS, HUNTED BY THE POLICE, DIED VIOLENTLY AND ALONE, IN THE VERY GUTTER THAT HAD BEEN HIS BEGINNING!... THERE IS A MORAL TO HIS STORY.... PERHAPS YOU ALREADY KNOW IT BY NOW.

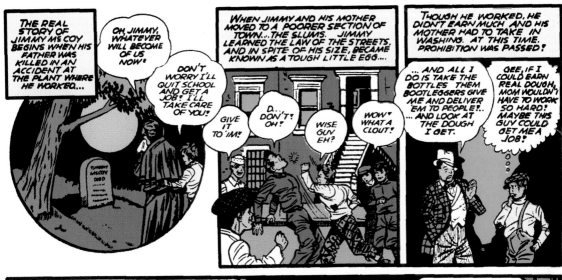

THE REAL STORY OF JIMMY McCOY BEGINS WHEN HIS FATHER WAS KILLED IN AN ACCIDENT AT THE PLANT WHERE HE WORKED...

OH, JIMMY, WHATEVER WILL BECOME OF US NOW!

DON'T WORRY! I'LL QUIT SCHOOL AND GET A JOB! I'LL TAKE CARE OF YOU!

WHEN JIMMY AND HIS MOTHER MOVED TO A POORER SECTION OF TOWN...THE SLUMS. JIMMY LEARNED THE LAW OF THE STREETS, AND IN SPITE OF HIS SIZE, BECAME KNOWN AS A TOUGH LITTLE EGG....

GIVE IT TO 'IM!

D...DON'T! OH!

WISE GUY EH?

WOW! WHAT A CLOUT!

THOUGH HE WORKED, HE DIDN'T EARN MUCH, AND HIS MOTHER HAD TO TAKE IN WASHING. AT THIS TIME, PROHIBITION WAS PASSED!

... AND ALL I DO IS TAKE THE BOTTLES THEM BOOTLEGGERS GIVE ME AND DELIVER 'EM TO PEOPLE!.. ... AND LOOK AT THE DOUGH I GET!

GEE, IF I COULD EARN REAL DOUGH, MOM WOULDN'T HAVE TO WORK SO HARD! MAYBE THIS GUY COULD GET ME A JOB!

IT WASN'T LONG BEFORE JIMMY WAS DELIVERING BOOTLEG LIQUOR! HE TOLD HIS MOTHER HE HAD A GOOD JOB IN AN OFFICE.. AND SHE....GULLIBLE SOUL.....BELIEVED HIM!

HERE'S THE STUFF FOR MR. COURTNEY!

OKAY! HE TOLD ME TO TELL YOU TO BRING SOME MORE FOR THE PARTY HE'S THROWING TOMORROW NIGHT!

THEN, ONE DAY, JIMMY WAS CAUGHT AND TRIED BEFORE A JUSTICE..

BUT HE WAS ALWAYS SUCH A GOOD BOY!

NEVER THE-LESS, IT IS THE DUTY OF THIS COURT TO SENTENCE YOU TO THE BOY'S REFORMATORY TILL YOU REACH THE AGE OF EIGHTEEN.

THAT'S A YEAR AND A HALF!

UPON HEARING THE SENTENCE, HIS MOTHER GAVE A HEART-RENDING SHRIEK AND TOPPLED TO THE FLOOR! THE SHOCK WAS TOO MUCH, AND SHE DIED WITH HER SON'S NAME ON HER LIPS!

MOM.. MOM!

JIMMY... AHHHH!

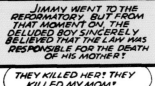

JIMMY WENT TO THE REFORMATORY, BUT FROM THAT MOMENT ON, THE DELUDED BOY SINCERELY BELIEVED THAT THE LAW WAS RESPONSIBLE FOR THE DEATH OF HIS MOTHER!

THEY KILLED HER! THEY KILLED MY MOM!

WHEN HE WAS RELEASED, JIMMY SECURED ANOTHER JOB DELIVERING BOOTLEG LIQUOR, BUT HE WAS SOON CAUGHT AGAIN!

... AND SINCE YOU ARE TOO OLD TO BE SENT TO THE BOYS' REFORMATORY, I MUST SENTENCE YOU TO ONE YEAR AT THE STATE PENITENTIARY!

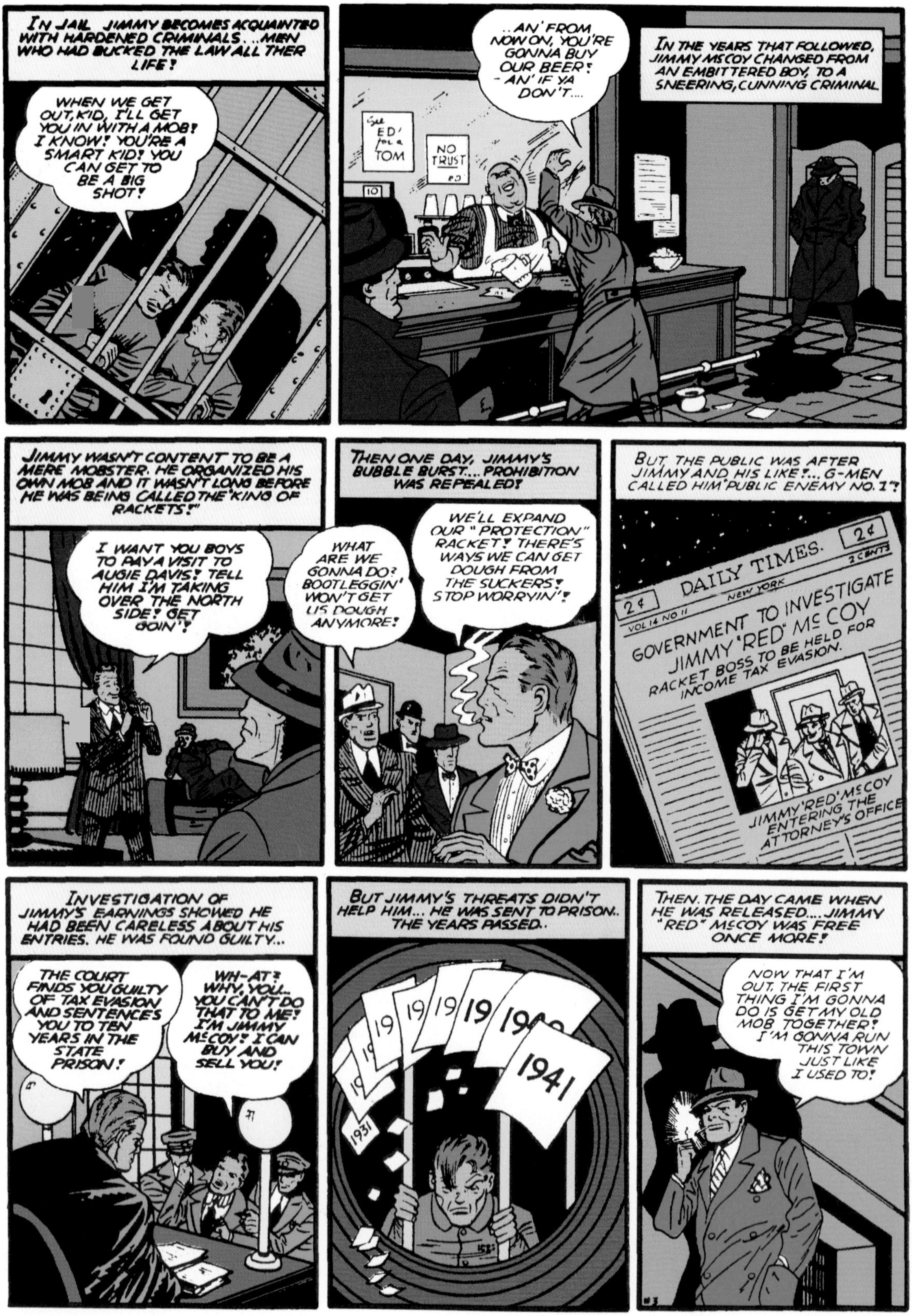
IN JAIL JIMMY BECOMES ACQUAINTED WITH HARDENED CRIMINALS... MEN WHO HAD BUCKED THE LAW ALL THER LIFE!
WHEN WE GET OUT, KID, I'LL GET YOU IN WITH A MOB! I KNOW! YOU'RE A SMART KID! YOU CAN GET TO BE A BIG SHOT!
...AN' FROM NOW ON, YOU'RE GONNA BUY OUR BEER! - AN' IF YA DON'T....
ED' for a TOM
NO TRUST
10
IN THE YEARS THAT FOLLOWED, JIMMY MCCOY CHANGED FROM AN EMBITTERED BOY, TO A SNEERING, CUNNING CRIMINAL
JIMMY WASN'T CONTENT TO BE A MERE MOBSTER. HE ORGANIZED HIS OWN MOB AND IT WASN'T LONG BEFORE HE WAS BEING CALLED THE "KING OF RACKETS!"
I WANT YOU BOYS TO PAY A VISIT TO AUGIE DAVIS! TELL HIM I'M TAKING OVER THE NORTH SIDE! GET GOIN'!
THEN ONE DAY, JIMMY'S BUBBLE BURST.... PROHIBITION WAS REPEALED!
WHAT ARE WE GONNA DO? BOOTLEGGIN' WON'T GET US DOUGH ANYMORE!
WE'LL EXPAND OUR "PROTECTION" RACKET! THERE'S WAYS WE CAN GET DOUGH FROM THE SUCKERS! STOP WORRYIN'!
BUT THE PUBLIC WAS AFTER JIMMY AND HIS LIKE!... G-MEN CALLED HIM "PUBLIC ENEMY NO. 1"!
DAILY TIMES.
2¢
2 CENTS
NEW YORK
VOL 14 NO 11
GOVERNMENT TO INVESTIGATE JIMMY "RED" McCOY
RACKET BOSS TO BE HELD FOR INCOME TAX EVASION.
JIMMY "RED" McCOY ENTERING THE ATTORNEY'S OFFICE
INVESTIGATION OF JIMMY'S EARNINGS SHOWED HE HAD BEEN CARELESS ABOUT HIS ENTRIES. HE WAS FOUND GUILTY...
THE COURT FINDS YOU GUILTY OF TAX EVASION AND SENTENCES YOU TO TEN YEARS IN THE STATE PRISON!
WH-AT? WHY, YOU... YOU CAN'T DO THAT TO ME! I'M JIMMY McCOY! I CAN BUY AND SELL YOU!
BUT JIMMY'S THREATS DIDN'T HELP HIM... HE WAS SENT TO PRISON.. THE YEARS PASSED..
1931
1941
THEN, THE DAY CAME WHEN HE WAS RELEASED.... JIMMY "RED" McCOY WAS FREE ONCE MORE!
NOW THAT I'M OUT, THE FIRST THING I'M GONNA DO IS GET MY OLD MOB TOGETHER! I'M GONNA RUN THIS TOWN JUST LIKE I USED TO!

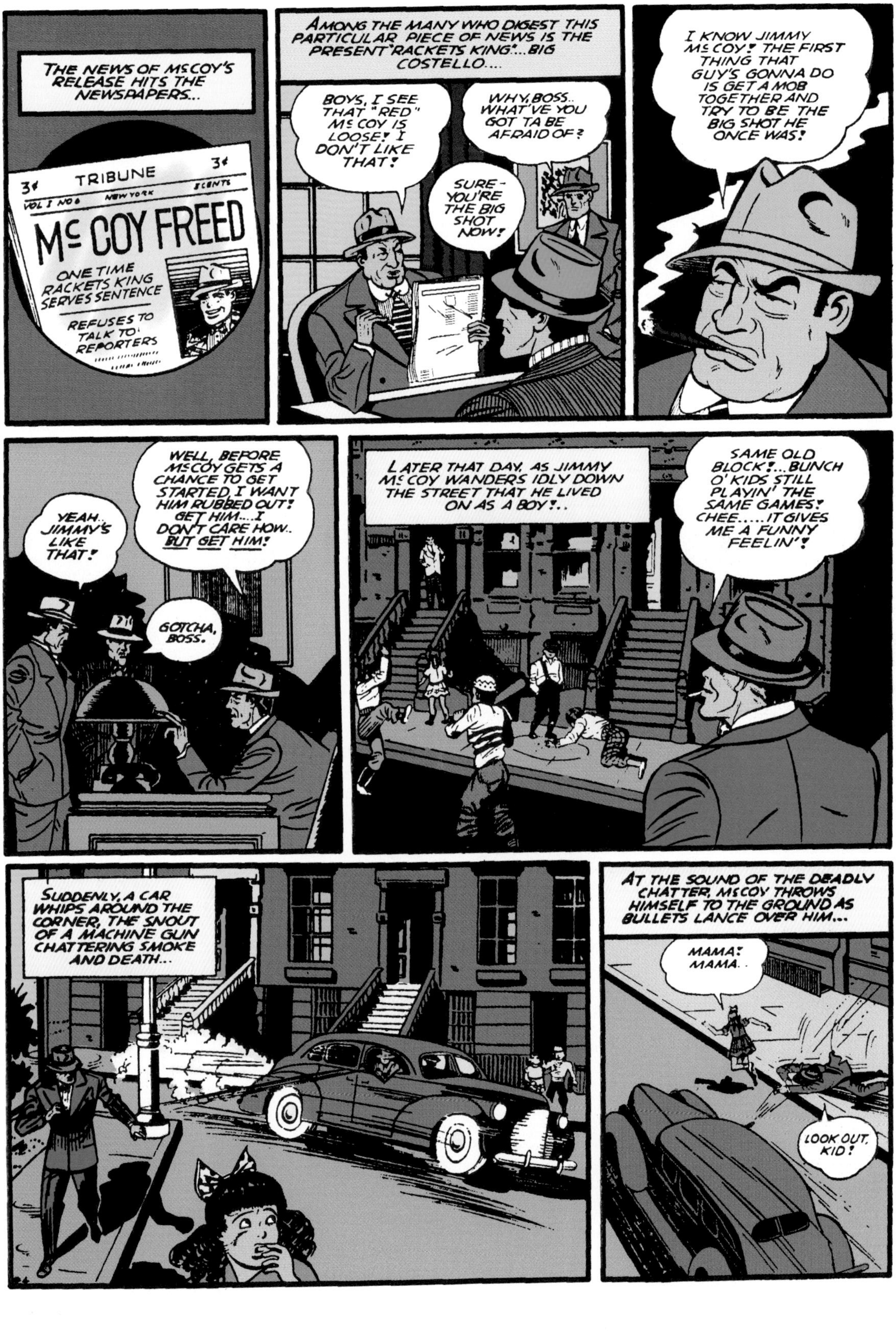
THE NEWS OF McCOY'S RELEASE HITS THE NEWSPAPERS...
3¢ TRIBUNE 3¢
VOL I NO 6 NEW YORK 3 CENTS
McCOY FREED
ONE TIME RACKETS KING SERVES SENTENCE
REFUSES TO TALK TO REPORTERS
AMONG THE MANY WHO DIGEST THIS PARTICULAR PIECE OF NEWS IS THE PRESENT "RACKETS KING"... BIG COSTELLO....
BOYS, I SEE THAT "RED" McCOY IS LOOSE! I DON'T LIKE THAT!
WHY, BOSS.. WHAT'VE YOU GOT TA BE AFRAID OF?
SURE - YOU'RE THE BIG SHOT NOW!
I KNOW JIMMY McCOY! THE FIRST THING THAT GUY'S GONNA DO IS GET A MOB TOGETHER AND TRY TO BE THE BIG SHOT HE ONCE WAS!
YEAH.. JIMMY'S LIKE THAT!
WELL, BEFORE McCOY GETS A CHANCE TO GET STARTED, I WANT HIM RUBBED OUT! GET HIM....I DON'T CARE HOW.. BUT GET HIM!
GOTCHA, BOSS.
LATER THAT DAY, AS JIMMY McCOY WANDERS IDLY DOWN THE STREET THAT HE LIVED ON AS A BOY!..
SAME OLD BLOCK!... BUNCH O' KIDS STILL PLAYIN' THE SAME GAMES! CHEE..... IT GIVES ME A FUNNY FEELIN'!
SUDDENLY, A CAR WHIPS AROUND THE CORNER, THE SNOUT OF A MACHINE GUN CHATTERING SMOKE AND DEATH...
AT THE SOUND OF THE DEADLY CHATTER, McCOY THROWS HIMSELF TO THE GROUND AS BULLETS LANCE OVER HIM...
MAMA! MAMA..
LOOK OUT, KID!

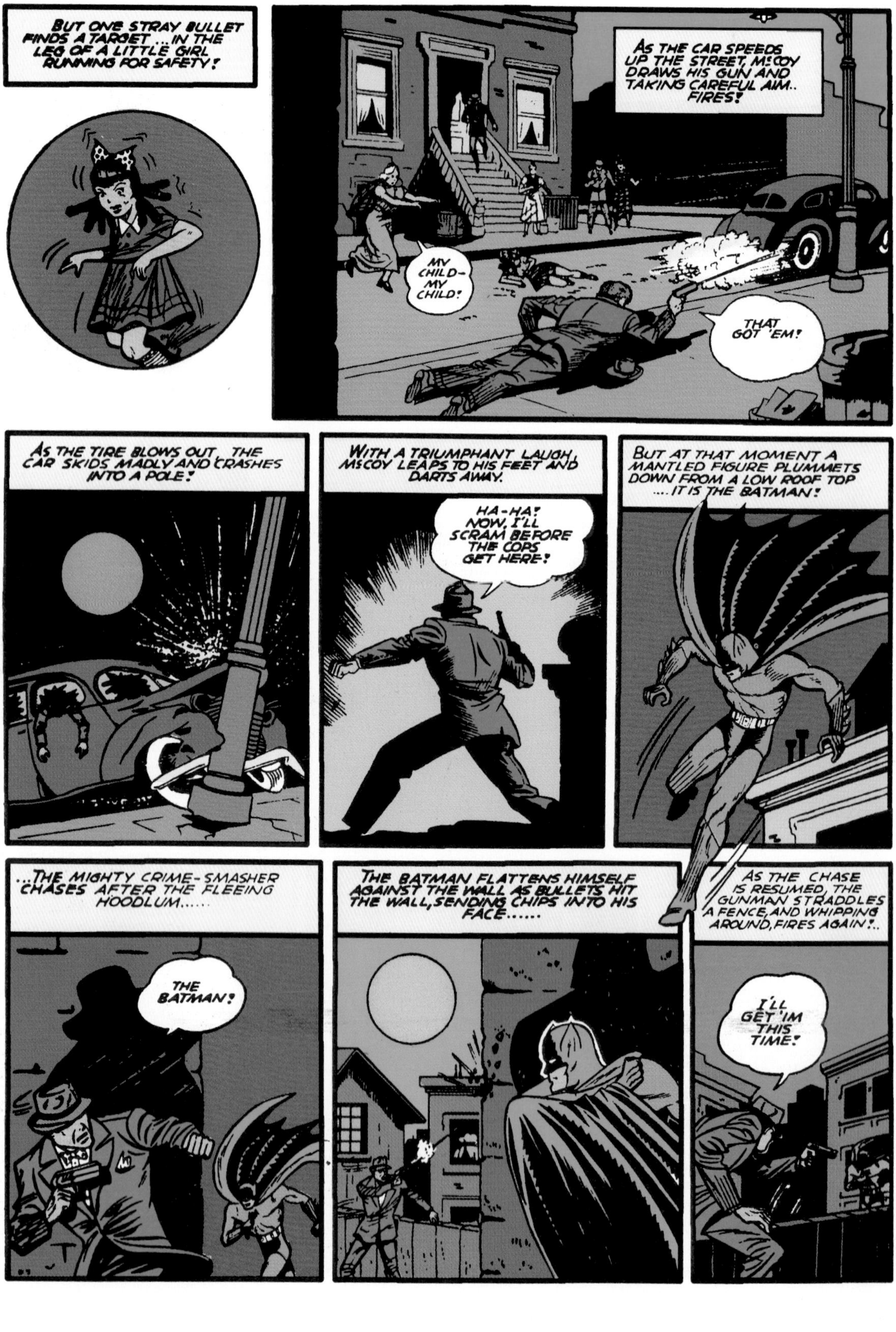
BUT ONE STRAY BULLET FINDS A TARGET ... IN THE LEG OF A LITTLE GIRL RUNNING FOR SAFETY!
AS THE CAR SPEEDS UP THE STREET, McCOY DRAWS HIS GUN AND TAKING CAREFUL AIM.. FIRES!
MY CHILD-MY CHILD!
THAT GOT 'EM!
AS THE TIRE BLOWS OUT, THE CAR SKIDS MADLY AND CRASHES INTO A POLE!
WITH A TRIUMPHANT LAUGH, McCOY LEAPS TO HIS FEET AND DARTS AWAY.
HA-HA! NOW, I'LL SCRAM BEFORE THE COPS GET HERE!
BUT AT THAT MOMENT A MANTLED FIGURE PLUMMETS DOWN FROM A LOW ROOF TOP ....IT IS THE BATMAN!
...THE MIGHTY CRIME-SMASHER CHASES AFTER THE FLEEING HOODLUM.....
THE BATMAN!
THE BATMAN FLATTENS HIMSELF AGAINST THE WALL AS BULLETS HIT THE WALL, SENDING CHIPS INTO HIS FACE......
AS THE CHASE IS RESUMED, THE GUNMAN STRADDLES A FENCE, AND WHIPPING AROUND, FIRES AGAIN!..
I'LL GET 'IM THIS TIME!

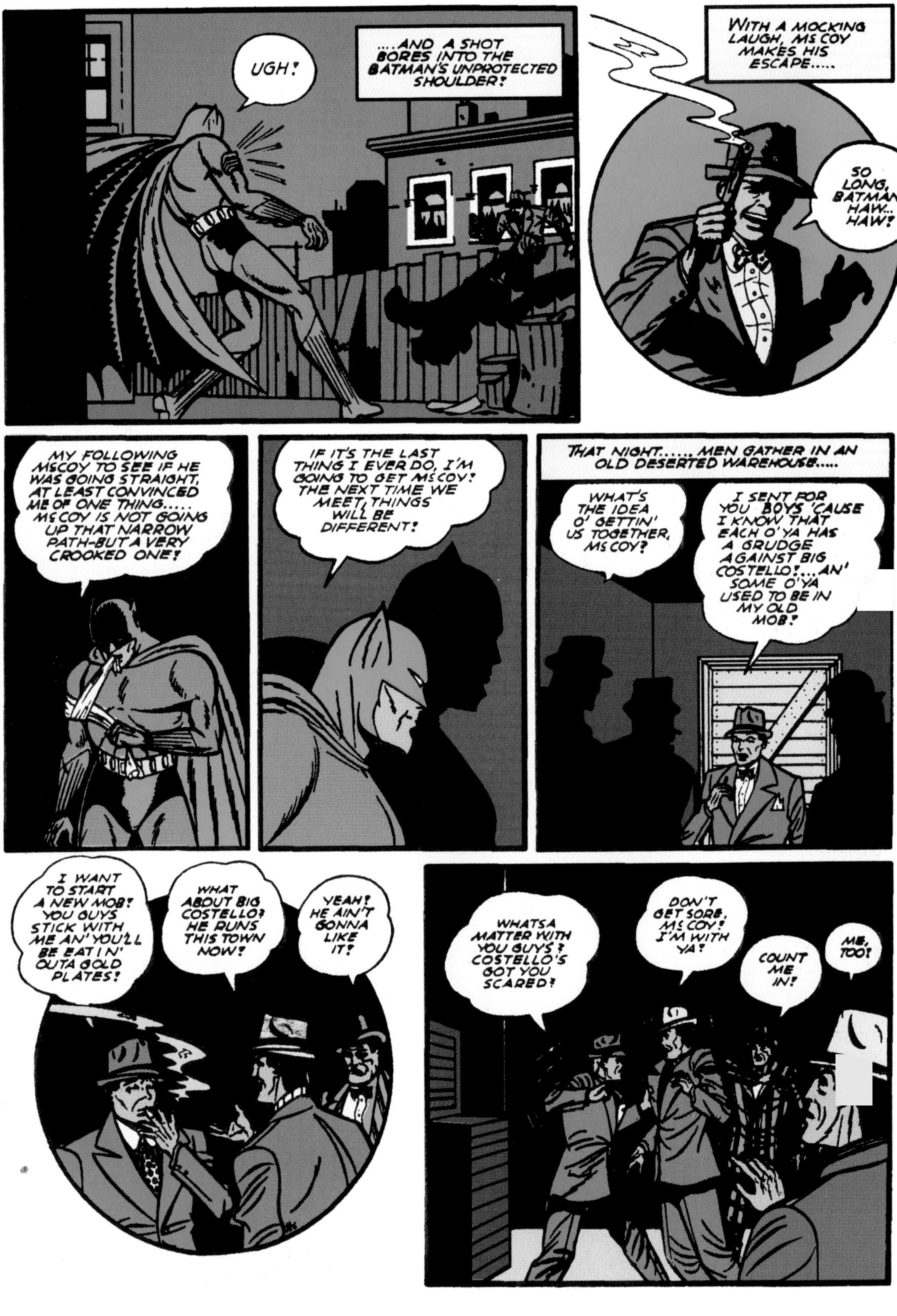
....AND A SHOT BORES INTO THE BATMAN'S UNPROTECTED SHOULDER!
UGH!
WITH A MOCKING LAUGH, MCCOY MAKES HIS ESCAPE.....
SO LONG, BATMAN! HAW... HAW!
MY FOLLOWING MCCOY TO SEE IF HE WAS GOING STRAIGHT, AT LEAST CONVINCED ME OF ONE THING..... MCCOY IS NOT GOING UP THAT NARROW PATH-BUT A VERY CROOKED ONE!
IF IT'S THE LAST THING I EVER DO, I'M GOING TO GET MCCOY! THE NEXT TIME WE MEET, THINGS WILL BE DIFFERENT!
THAT NIGHT...... MEN GATHER IN AN OLD DESERTED WAREHOUSE.....
WHAT'S THE IDEA O' GETTIN' US TOGETHER, MCCOY?
I SENT FOR YOU BOYS 'CAUSE I KNOW THAT EACH O'YA HAS A GRUDGE AGAINST BIG COSTELLO!...AN' SOME O'YA USED TO BE IN MY OLD MOB!
I WANT TO START A NEW MOB! YOU GUYS STICK WITH ME AN' YOU'LL BE EATIN' OUTA GOLD PLATES!
WHAT ABOUT BIG COSTELLO? HE RUNS THIS TOWN NOW!
YEAH! HE AIN'T GONNA LIKE IT!
WHATSA MATTER WITH YOU GUYS? COSTELLO'S GOT YOU SCARED?
DON'T GET SORE, MCCOY! I'M WITH YA!
COUNT ME IN!
ME, TOO!

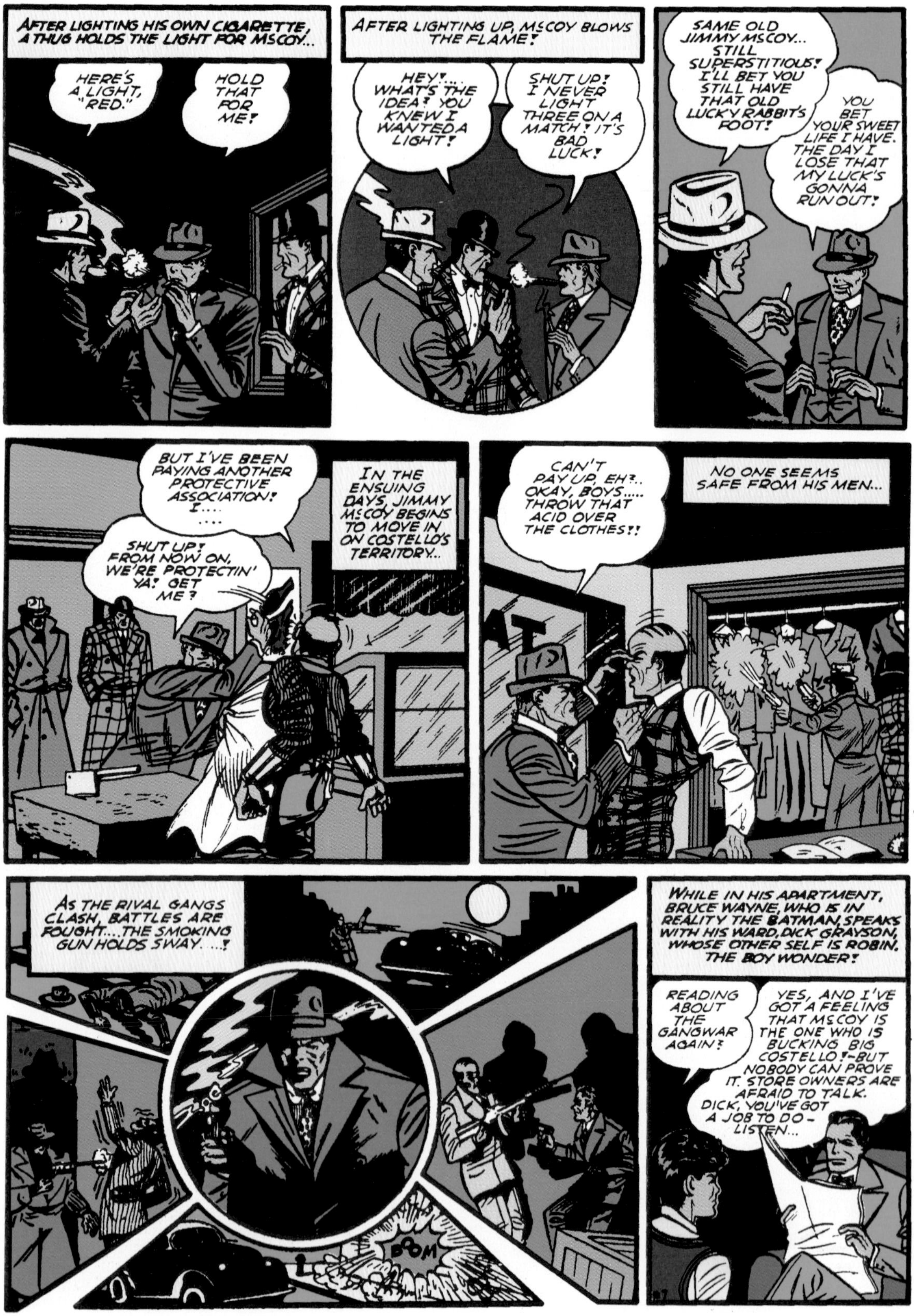
AFTER LIGHTING HIS OWN CIGARETTE, A THUG HOLDS THE LIGHT FOR McCOY...
HERE'S A LIGHT, "RED."
HOLD THAT FOR ME!
AFTER LIGHTING UP, McCOY BLOWS THE FLAME!
HEY!... WHAT'S THE IDEA? YOU KNEW I WANTED A LIGHT!
SHUT UP! I NEVER LIGHT THREE ON A MATCH! IT'S BAD LUCK!
SAME OLD JIMMY McCOY... STILL SUPERSTITIOUS! I'LL BET YOU STILL HAVE THAT OLD LUCKY RABBIT'S FOOT!
YOU BET YOUR SWEET LIFE I HAVE. THE DAY I LOSE THAT MY LUCK'S GONNA RUN OUT!
IN THE ENSUING DAYS, JIMMY McCOY BEGINS TO MOVE IN ON COSTELLO'S TERRITORY..
BUT I'VE BEEN PAYING ANOTHER PROTECTIVE ASSOCIATION! I.... ....
SHUT UP! FROM NOW ON, WE'RE PROTECTIN' YA! GET ME?
CAN'T PAY UP, EH?.. OKAY, BOYS..... THROW THAT ACID OVER THE CLOTHES!!
NO ONE SEEMS SAFE FROM HIS MEN...
AS THE RIVAL GANGS CLASH, BATTLES ARE FOUGHT....THE SMOKING GUN HOLDS SWAY....!
BOOM
WHILE IN HIS APARTMENT, BRUCE WAYNE, WHO IS IN REALITY THE BATMAN, SPEAKS WITH HIS WARD, DICK GRAYSON, WHOSE OTHER SELF IS ROBIN, THE BOY WONDER!
READING ABOUT THE GANGWAR AGAIN?
YES, AND I'VE GOT A FEELING THAT McCOY IS THE ONE WHO IS BUCKING BIG COSTELLO!-BUT NOBODY CAN PROVE IT. STORE OWNERS ARE AFRAID TO TALK. DICK, YOU'VE GOT A JOB TO DO- LISTEN...

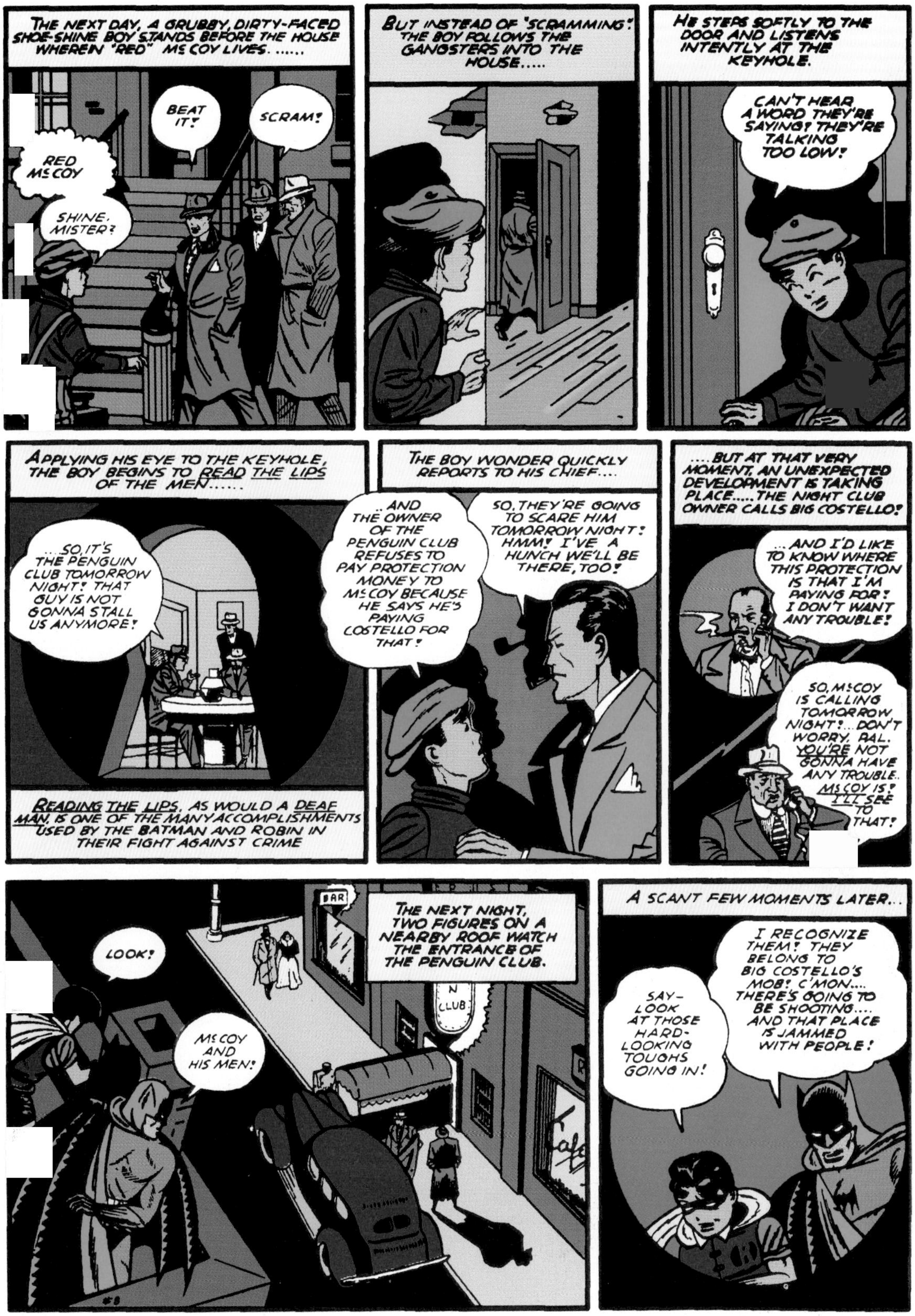
THE NEXT DAY, A GRUBBY, DIRTY-FACED SHOE-SHINE BOY STANDS BEFORE THE HOUSE WHEREIN "RED" McCOY LIVES......
RED McCOY
SHINE, MISTER?
BEAT IT!
SCRAM!
BUT INSTEAD OF "SCRAMMING" THE BOY FOLLOWS THE GANGSTERS INTO THE HOUSE.....
HE STEPS SOFTLY TO THE DOOR AND LISTENS INTENTLY AT THE KEYHOLE.
CAN'T HEAR A WORD THEY'RE SAYING! THEY'RE TALKING TOO LOW!
APPLYING HIS EYE TO THE KEYHOLE, THE BOY BEGINS TO READ THE LIPS OF THE MEN......
...SO, IT'S THE PENGUIN CLUB TOMORROW NIGHT! THAT GUY IS NOT GONNA STALL US ANYMORE!
READING THE LIPS, AS WOULD A DEAF MAN, IS ONE OF THE MANY ACCOMPLISHMENTS USED BY THE BATMAN AND ROBIN IN THEIR FIGHT AGAINST CRIME
THE BOY WONDER QUICKLY REPORTS TO HIS CHIEF....
..AND THE OWNER OF THE PENGUIN CLUB REFUSES TO PAY PROTECTION MONEY TO McCOY BECAUSE HE SAYS HE'S PAYING COSTELLO FOR THAT!
SO, THEY'RE GOING TO SCARE HIM TOMORROW NIGHT! HMM! I'VE A HUNCH WE'LL BE THERE, TOO!
....BUT AT THAT VERY MOMENT, AN UNEXPECTED DEVELOPMENT IS TAKING PLACE.....THE NIGHT CLUB OWNER CALLS BIG COSTELLO!
...AND I'D LIKE TO KNOW WHERE THIS PROTECTION IS THAT I'M PAYING FOR! I DON'T WANT ANY TROUBLE!
SO, McCOY IS CALLING TOMORROW NIGHT!...DON'T WORRY, PAL, YOU'RE NOT GONNA HAVE ANY TROUBLE.. McCOY IS! I'LL SEE TO THAT!
THE NEXT NIGHT, TWO FIGURES ON A NEARBY ROOF WATCH THE ENTRANCE OF THE PENGUIN CLUB.
LOOK!
McCOY AND HIS MEN!
BAR
N CLUB
A SCANT FEW MOMENTS LATER...
SAY- LOOK AT THOSE HARD-LOOKING TOUGHS GOING IN!
I RECOGNIZE THEM! THEY BELONG TO BIG COSTELLO'S MOB! C'MON.... THERE'S GOING TO BE SHOOTING.... AND THAT PLACE IS JAMMED WITH PEOPLE!

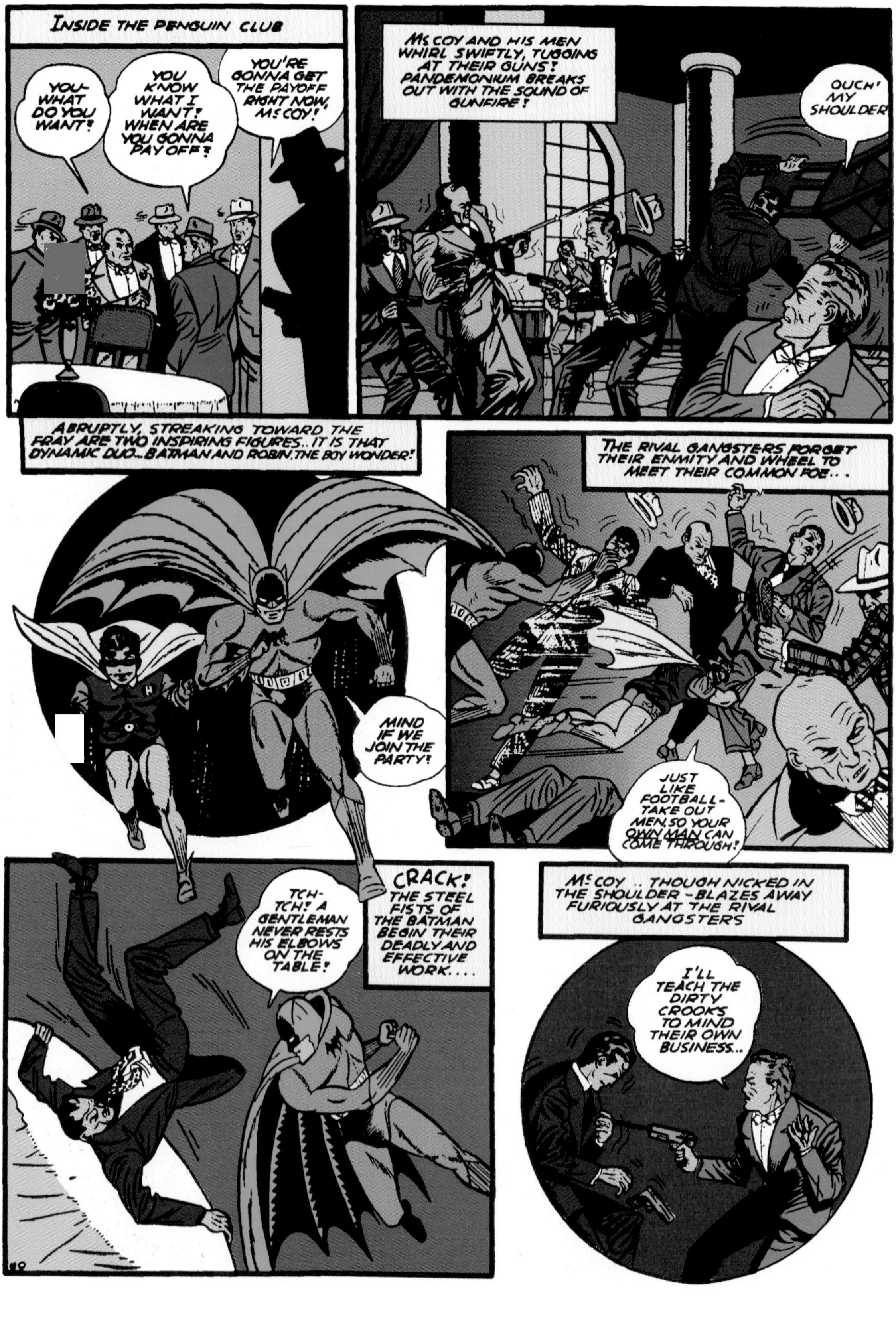
INSIDE THE PENGUIN CLUB
YOU- WHAT DO YOU WANT?
YOU KNOW WHAT I WANT? WHEN ARE YOU GONNA PAY OFF?
YOU'RE GONNA GET THE PAYOFF RIGHT NOW, McCOY!
McCOY AND HIS MEN WHIRL SWIFTLY, TUGGING AT THEIR GUNS! PANDEMONIUM BREAKS OUT WITH THE SOUND OF GUNFIRE!
OUCH! MY SHOULDER!
ABRUPTLY, STREAKING TOWARD THE FRAY ARE TWO INSPIRING FIGURES.. IT IS THAT DYNAMIC DUO...BATMAN AND ROBIN,THE BOY WONDER!
MIND IF WE JOIN THE PARTY?
THE RIVAL GANGSTERS FORGET THEIR ENMITY AND WHEEL TO MEET THEIR COMMON FOE...
JUST LIKE FOOTBALL- TAKE OUT MEN,SO YOUR OWN MAN CAN COME THROUGH!
TCH-TCH! A GENTLEMAN NEVER RESTS HIS ELBOWS ON THE TABLE!
CRACK!
THE STEEL FISTS OF THE BATMAN BEGIN THEIR DEADLY AND EFFECTIVE WORK....
McCOY .. THOUGH NICKED IN THE SHOULDER - BLAZES AWAY FURIOUSLY AT THE RIVAL GANGSTERS
I'LL TEACH THE DIRTY CROOKS TO MIND THEIR OWN BUSINESS..

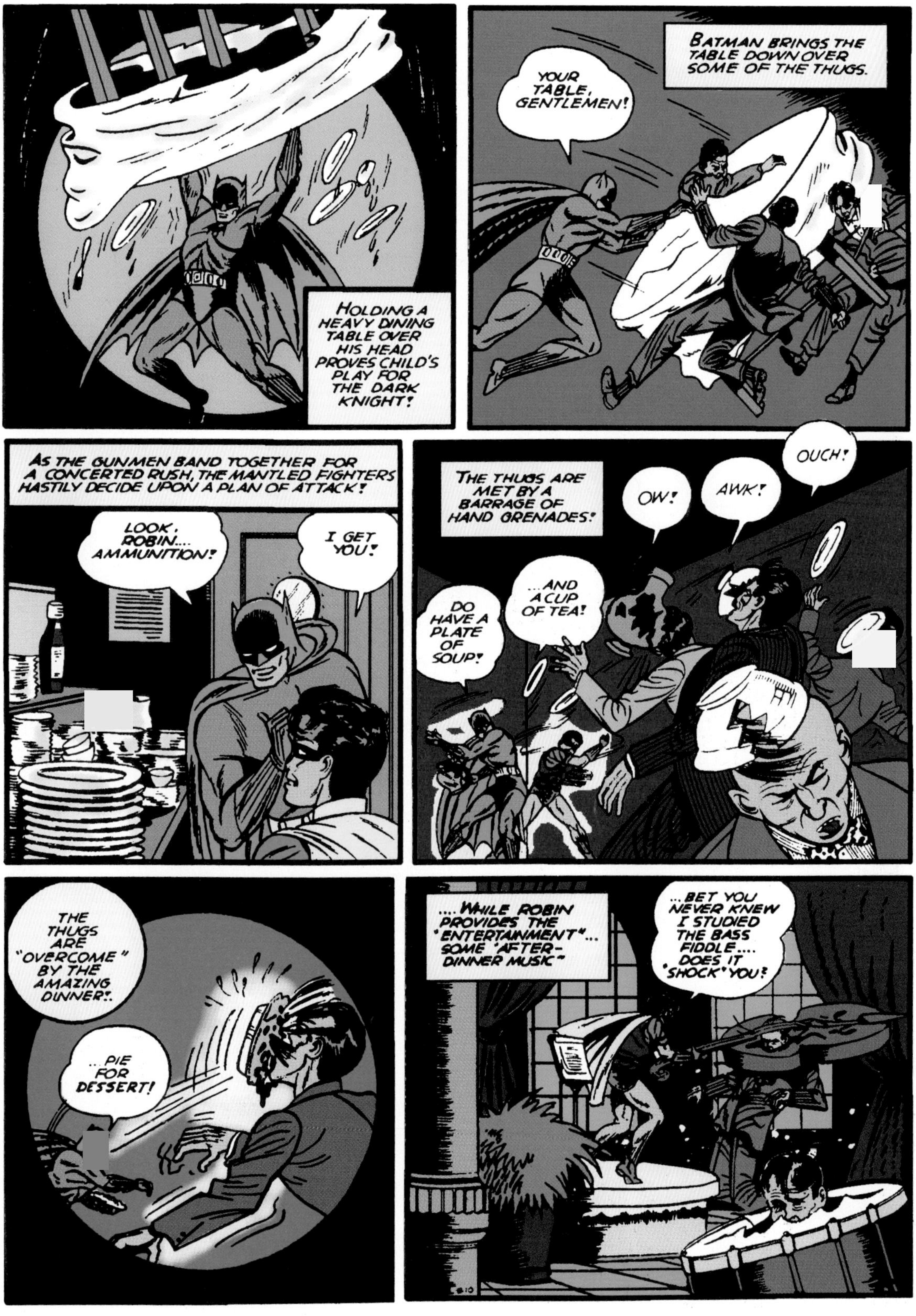
HOLDING A HEAVY DINING TABLE OVER HIS HEAD PROVES CHILD'S PLAY FOR THE DARK KNIGHT!
BATMAN BRINGS THE TABLE DOWN OVER SOME OF THE THUGS.
YOUR TABLE, GENTLEMEN!
AS THE GUNMEN BAND TOGETHER FOR A CONCERTED RUSH, THE MANTLED FIGHTERS HASTILY DECIDE UPON A PLAN OF ATTACK!
LOOK, ROBIN.... AMMUNITION!
I GET YOU!
THE THUGS ARE MET BY A BARRAGE OF HAND GRENADES!
OW!
AWK!
OUCH!
DO HAVE A PLATE OF SOUP!
...AND A CUP OF TEA!
THE THUGS ARE "OVERCOME" BY THE AMAZING DINNER!.
...PIE FOR DESSERT!
....WHILE ROBIN PROVIDES THE "ENTERTAINMENT"... SOME "AFTER-DINNER MUSIC"
...BET YOU NEVER KNEW I STUDIED THE BASS FIDDLE.... DOES IT "SHOCK" YOU?

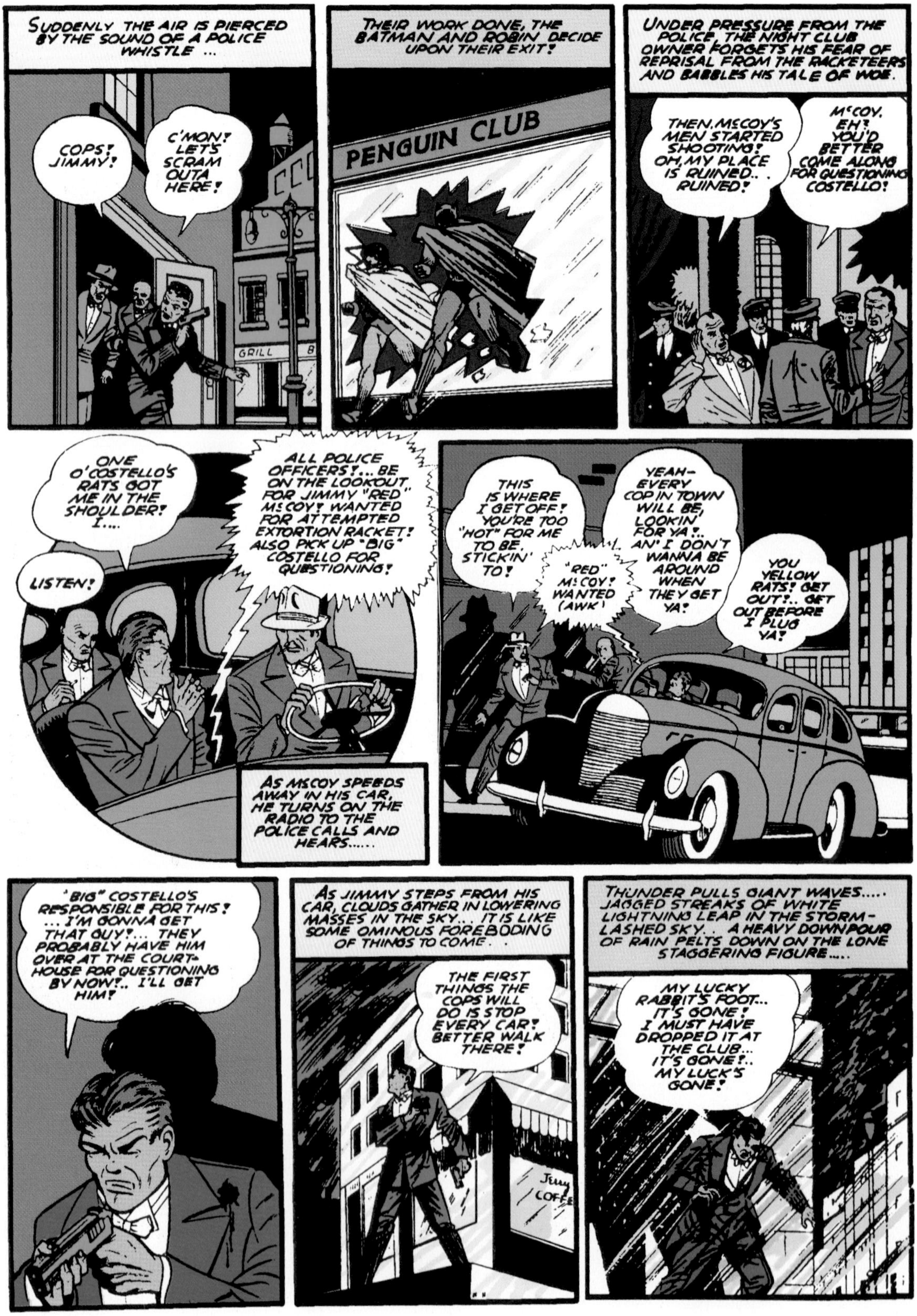
SUDDENLY THE AIR IS PIERCED BY THE SOUND OF A POLICE WHISTLE ...
COPS! JIMMY!
C'MON! LET'S SCRAM OUTA HERE!
GRILL
THEIR WORK DONE, THE BATMAN AND ROBIN DECIDE UPON THEIR EXIT!
PENGUIN CLUB
UNDER PRESSURE FROM THE POLICE, THE NIGHT CLUB OWNER FORGETS HIS FEAR OF REPRISAL FROM THE RACKETEERS AND BABBLES HIS TALE OF WOE.
THEN, McCOY'S MEN STARTED SHOOTING! OH, MY PLACE IS RUINED.. . RUINED!
McCOY, EH? YOU'D BETTER COME ALONG FOR QUESTIONING COSTELLO!
ONE O'COSTELLO'S RATS GOT ME IN THE SHOULDER! I....
LISTEN!
ALL POLICE OFFICERS!... BE ON THE LOOKOUT FOR JIMMY "RED" McCOY! WANTED FOR ATTEMPTED EXTORTION RACKET! ALSO PICK UP "BIG" COSTELLO FOR QUESTIONING!
AS McCOY SPEEDS AWAY IN HIS CAR, HE TURNS ON THE RADIO TO THE POLICE CALLS AND HEARS.....
THIS IS WHERE I GET OFF! YOU'RE TOO "HOT" FOR ME TO BE STICKIN' TO!
"RED" McCOY! WANTED (AWK)
YEAH- EVERY COP IN TOWN WILL BE LOOKIN' FOR YA!.. AN' I DON'T WANNA BE AROUND WHEN THEY GET YA!
YOU YELLOW RATS! GET OUT!.. GET OUT BEFORE I PLUG YA!
"BIG" COSTELLO'S RESPONSIBLE FOR THIS! ... I'M GONNA GET THAT GUY!... THEY PROBABLY HAVE HIM OVER AT THE COURT-HOUSE FOR QUESTIONING BY NOW!.. I'LL GET HIM!
AS JIMMY STEPS FROM HIS CAR, CLOUDS GATHER IN LOWERING MASSES IN THE SKY... IT IS LIKE SOME OMINOUS FOREBODING OF THINGS TO COME. .
THE FIRST THINGS THE COPS WILL DO IS STOP EVERY CAR! BETTER WALK THERE!
THUNDER PULLS GIANT WAVES..... JAGGED STREAKS OF WHITE LIGHTNING LEAP IN THE STORM-LASHED SKY.. A HEAVY DOWNPOUR OF RAIN PELTS DOWN ON THE LONE STAGGERING FIGURE.....
MY LUCKY RABBIT'S FOOT... IT'S GONE! I MUST HAVE DROPPED IT AT THE CLUB... IT'S GONE!.. MY LUCK'S GONE!

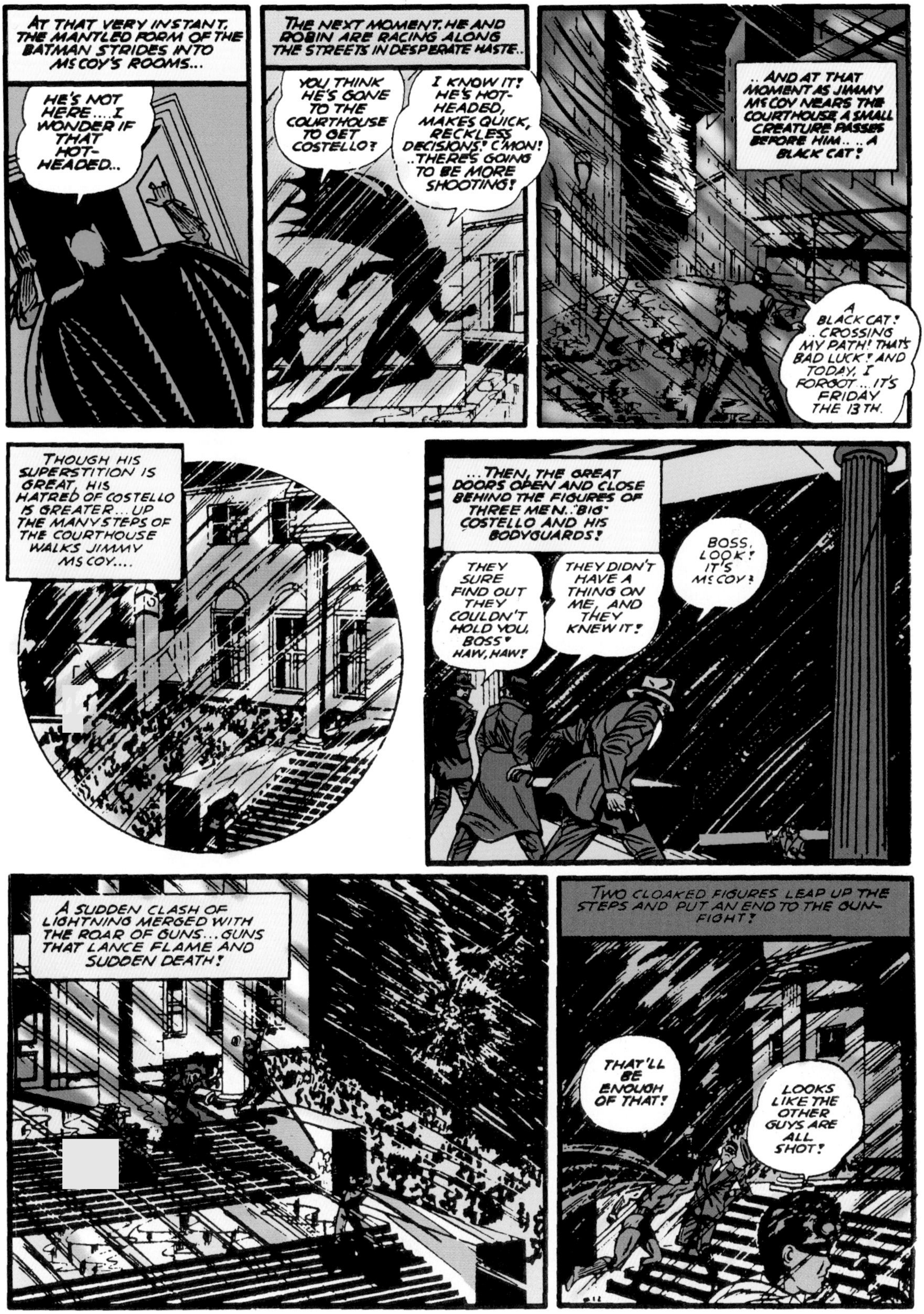
AT THAT VERY INSTANT, THE MANTLED FORM OF THE BATMAN STRIDES INTO McCOY'S ROOMS...
HE'S NOT HERE....I WONDER IF THAT HOT-HEADED...
THE NEXT MOMENT, HE AND ROBIN ARE RACING ALONG THE STREETS IN DESPERATE HASTE..
YOU THINK HE'S GONE TO THE COURTHOUSE TO GET COSTELLO?
I KNOW IT! HE'S HOT-HEADED, MAKES QUICK, RECKLESS DECISIONS! C'MON! ..THERE'S GOING TO BE MORE SHOOTING!
..AND AT THAT MOMENT AS JIMMY McCOY NEARS THE COURTHOUSE, A SMALL CREATURE PASSES BEFORE HIM....A BLACK CAT!
A BLACK CAT! ..CROSSING MY PATH! THAT'S BAD LUCK! AND TODAY, I FORGOT...IT'S FRIDAY THE 13TH.
THOUGH HIS SUPERSTITION IS GREAT, HIS HATRED OF COSTELLO IS GREATER...UP THE MANY STEPS OF THE COURTHOUSE WALKS JIMMY McCOY....
...THEN, THE GREAT DOORS OPEN AND CLOSE BEHIND THE FIGURES OF THREE MEN..."BIG" COSTELLO AND HIS BODYGUARDS!
THEY SURE FIND OUT THEY COULDN'T HOLD YOU, BOSS! HAW, HAW!
THEY DIDN'T HAVE A THING ON ME, AND THEY KNEW IT!
BOSS, LOOK! IT'S McCOY!
A SUDDEN CLASH OF LIGHTNING MERGED WITH THE ROAR OF GUNS...GUNS THAT LANCE FLAME AND SUDDEN DEATH!
TWO CLOAKED FIGURES LEAP UP THE STEPS AND PUT AN END TO THE GUN-FIGHT!
THAT'LL BE ENOUGH OF THAT!
LOOKS LIKE THE OTHER GUYS ARE ALL SHOT!

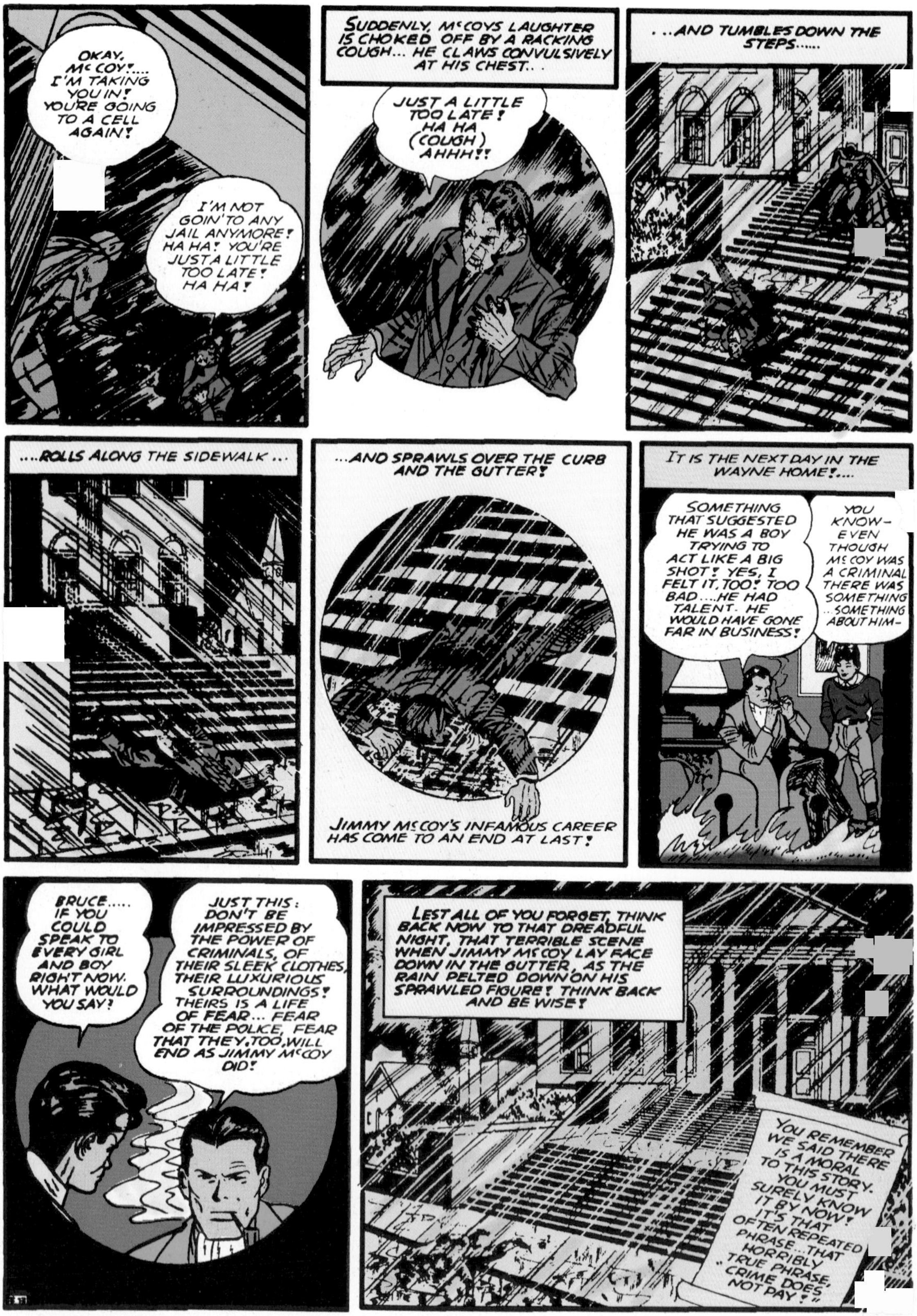
OKAY, MᶜCOY!.... I'M TAKING YOU IN! YOU'RE GOING TO A CELL AGAIN!
I'M NOT GOIN' TO ANY JAIL ANYMORE! HA HA! YOU'RE JUST A LITTLE TOO LATE! HA HA!
SUDDENLY, MᶜCOYS LAUGHTER IS CHOKED OFF BY A RACKING COUGH... HE CLAWS CONVULSIVELY AT HIS CHEST..
JUST A LITTLE TOO LATE! HA HA (COUGH) AHHH!!
...AND TUMBLES DOWN THE STEPS......
....ROLLS ALONG THE SIDEWALK ...
...AND SPRAWLS OVER THE CURB AND THE GUTTER!
JIMMY MᶜCOY'S INFAMOUS CAREER HAS COME TO AN END AT LAST!
IT IS THE NEXT DAY IN THE WAYNE HOME!....
YOU KNOW- EVEN THOUGH MᶜCOY WAS A CRIMINAL THERE WAS SOMETHING ...SOMETHING ABOUT HIM-
SOMETHING THAT SUGGESTED HE WAS A BOY TRYING TO ACT LIKE A BIG SHOT! YES, I FELT IT, TOO! TOO BAD....HE HAD TALENT. HE WOULD HAVE GONE FAR IN BUSINESS!
BRUCE..... IF YOU COULD SPEAK TO EVERY GIRL AND BOY RIGHT NOW. WHAT WOULD YOU SAY?
JUST THIS: DON'T BE IMPRESSED BY THE POWER OF CRIMINALS, OF THEIR SLEEK CLOTHES, THEIR LUXURIOUS SURROUNDINGS! THEIRS IS A LIFE OF FEAR... FEAR OF THE POLICE, FEAR THAT THEY, TOO, WILL END AS JIMMY MᶜCOY DID!
LEST ALL OF YOU FORGET, THINK BACK NOW TO THAT DREADFUL NIGHT, THAT TERRIBLE SCENE WHEN JIMMY MᶜCOY LAY FACE DOWN IN THE GUTTER, AS THE RAIN PELTED DOWN ON HIS SPRAWLED FIGURE! THINK BACK AND BE WISE!
YOU REMEMBER WE SAID THERE IS A MORAL TO THIS STORY. YOU MUST SURELY KNOW IT BY NOW! IT'S THAT OFTEN REPEATED PHRASE...THAT HORRIBLY TRUE PHRASE, "CRIME DOES NOT PAY!"

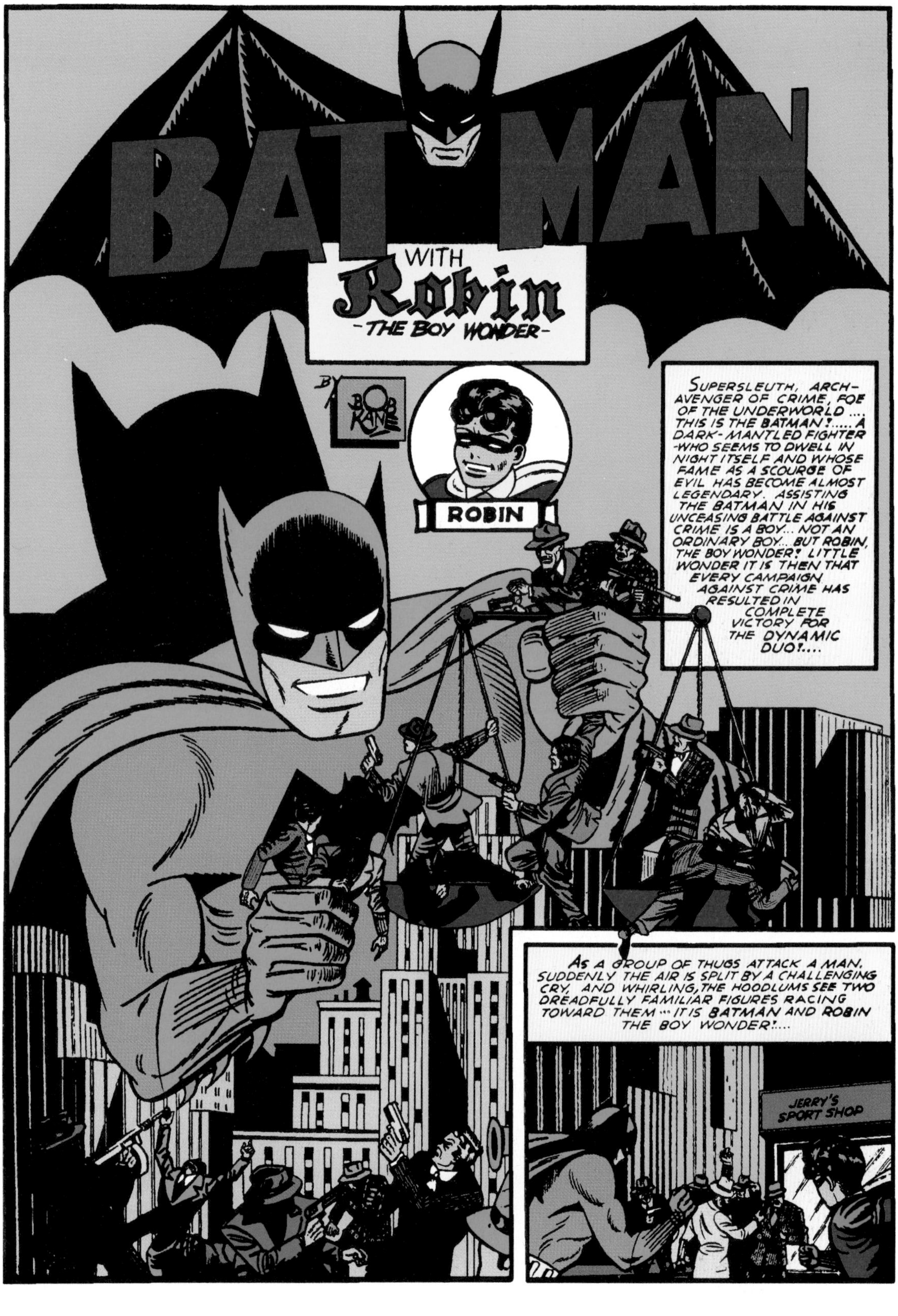
BATMAN
WITH
Robin
-THE BOY WONDER-
BY BOB KANE
ROBIN
SUPERSLEUTH, ARCH-AVENGER OF CRIME, FOE OF THE UNDERWORLD .... THIS IS THE BATMAN!..... A DARK-MANTLED FIGHTER -WHO SEEMS TO DWELL IN NIGHT ITSELF AND WHOSE FAME AS A SCOURGE OF EVIL HAS BECOME ALMOST LEGENDARY. ASSISTING THE BATMAN IN HIS UNCEASING BATTLE AGAINST CRIME IS A BOY... NOT AN ORDINARY BOY... BUT ROBIN, THE BOY WONDER! LITTLE WONDER IT IS THEN THAT EVERY CAMPAIGN AGAINST CRIME HAS RESULTED IN COMPLETE VICTORY FOR THE DYNAMIC DUO!....
AS A GROUP OF THUGS ATTACK A MAN, SUDDENLY THE AIR IS SPLIT BY A CHALLENGING CRY, AND WHIRLING, THE HOODLUMS SEE TWO DREADFULLY FAMILIAR FIGURES RACING TOWARD THEM ... IT IS BATMAN AND ROBIN THE BOY WONDER!...
JERRY'S SPORT SHOP

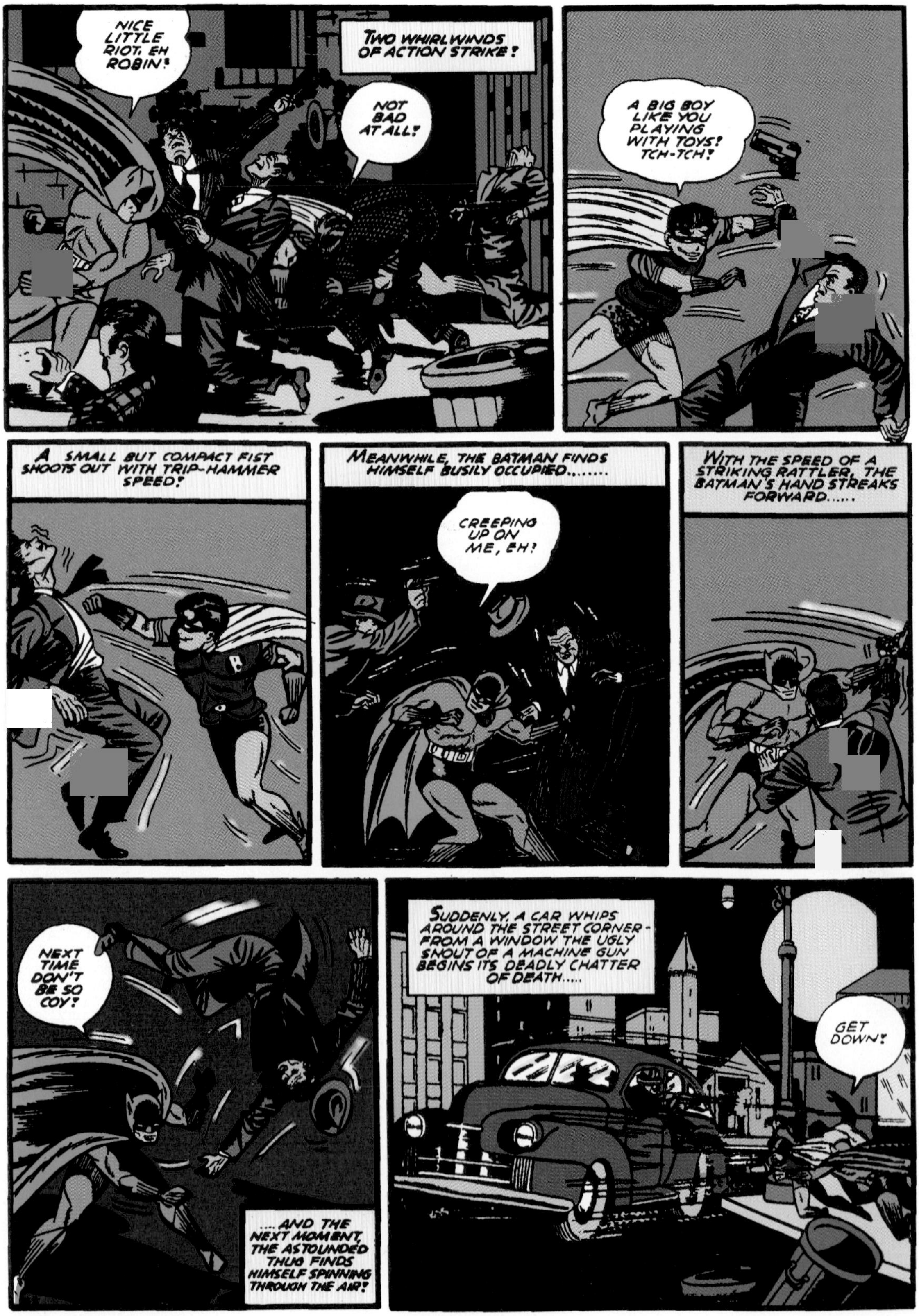
NICE LITTLE RIOT, EH ROBIN!
TWO WHIRLWINDS OF ACTION STRIKE!
NOT BAD AT ALL!
A BIG BOY LIKE YOU PLAYING WITH TOYS! TCH-TCH!
A SMALL BUT COMPACT FIST SHOOTS OUT WITH TRIP-HAMMER SPEED!
MEANWHILE, THE BATMAN FINDS HIMSELF BUSILY OCCUPIED........
CREEPING UP ON ME, EH?
WITH THE SPEED OF A STRIKING RATTLER, THE BATMAN'S HAND STREAKS FORWARD......
NEXT TIME DON'T BE SO COY!
....AND THE NEXT MOMENT, THE ASTOUNDED THUG FINDS HIMSELF SPINNING THROUGH THE AIR!
SUDDENLY, A CAR WHIPS AROUND THE STREET CORNER - FROM A WINDOW THE UGLY SNOUT OF A MACHINE GUN BEGINS ITS DEADLY CHATTER OF DEATH.....
GET DOWN!

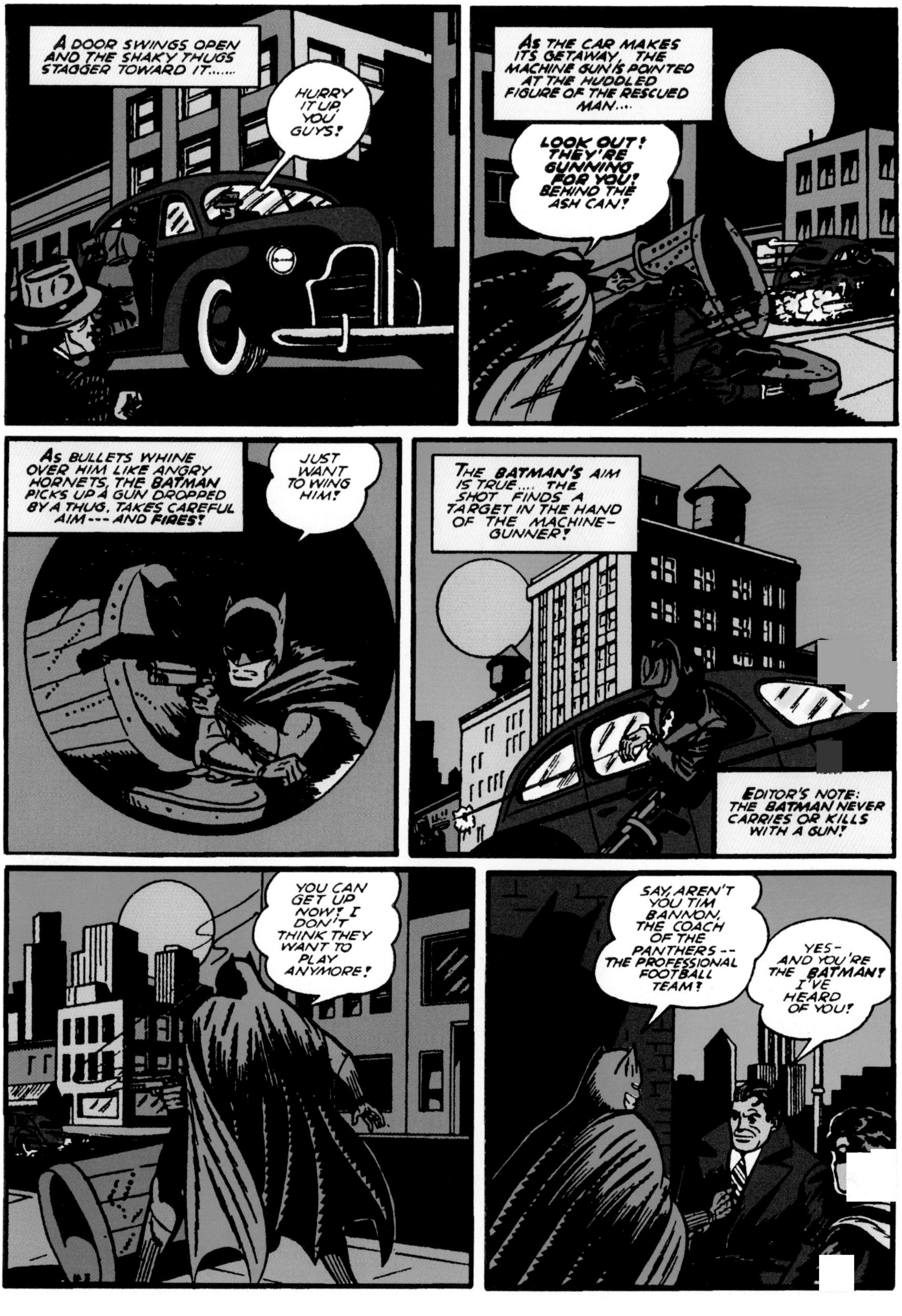
A DOOR SWINGS OPEN AND THE SHAKY THUGS STAGGER TOWARD IT......
HURRY IT UP, YOU GUYS!
AS THE CAR MAKES ITS GETAWAY, THE MACHINE GUN IS POINTED AT THE HUDDLED FIGURE OF THE RESCUED MAN....
LOOK OUT! THEY'RE GUNNING FOR YOU! BEHIND THE ASH CAN!
AS BULLETS WHINE OVER HIM LIKE ANGRY HORNETS, THE BATMAN PICKS UP A GUN DROPPED BY A THUG, TAKES CAREFUL AIM --- AND FIRES!
JUST WANT TO WING HIM!
THE BATMAN'S AIM IS TRUE.... THE SHOT FINDS A TARGET IN THE HAND OF THE MACHINE-GUNNER!
EDITOR'S NOTE: THE BATMAN NEVER CARRIES OR KILLS WITH A GUN!
YOU CAN GET UP NOW! I DON'T THINK THEY WANT TO PLAY ANYMORE!
SAY, AREN'T YOU TIM BANNON, THE COACH OF THE PANTHERS -- THE PROFESSIONAL FOOTBALL TEAM?
YES- AND YOU'RE THE BATMAN! I'VE HEARD OF YOU!

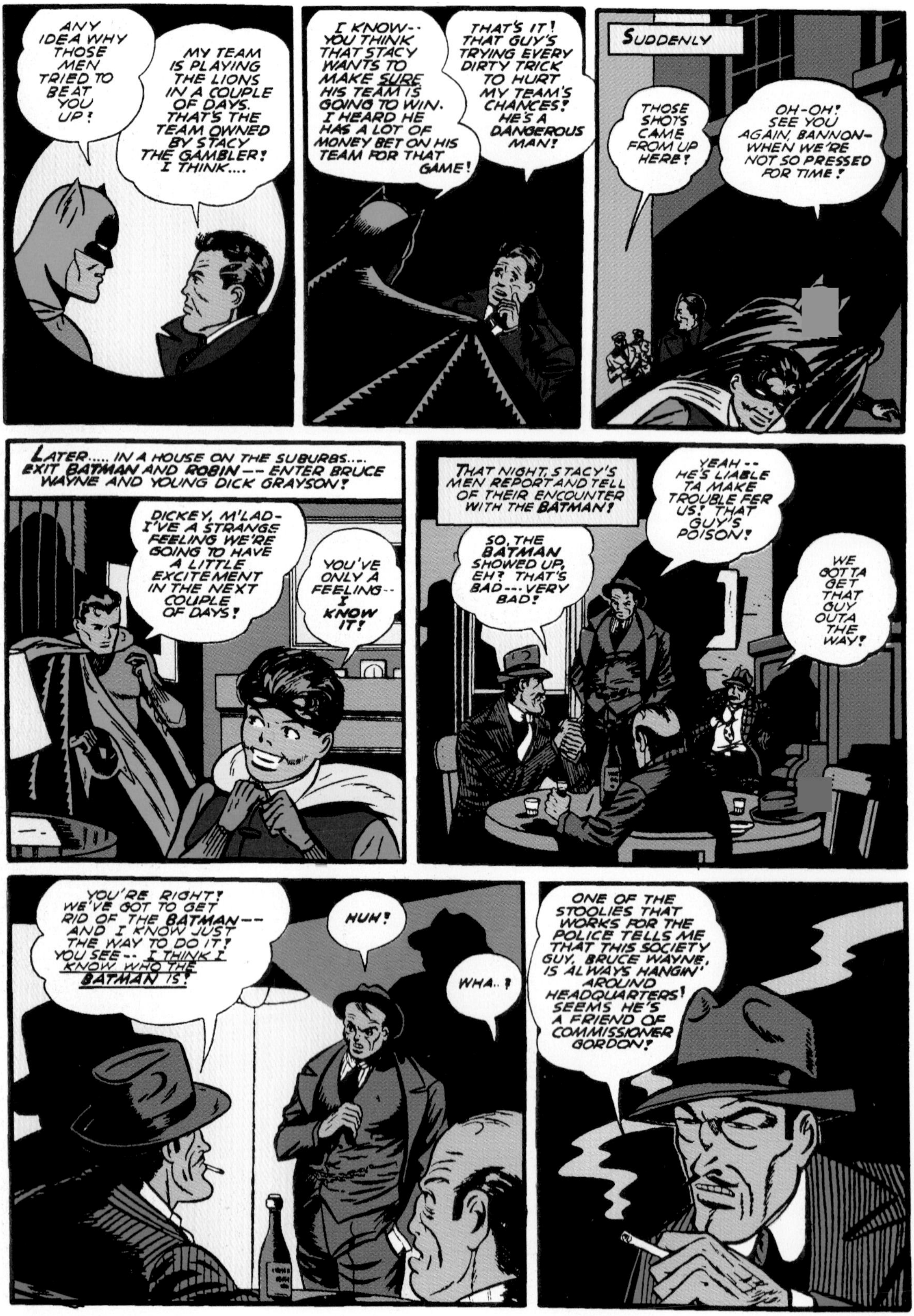
ANY IDEA WHY THOSE MEN TRIED TO BEAT YOU UP?
MY TEAM IS PLAYING THE LIONS IN A COUPLE OF DAYS. THAT'S THE TEAM OWNED BY STACY THE GAMBLER! I THINK....
I KNOW-- YOU THINK THAT STACY WANTS TO MAKE SURE HIS TEAM IS GOING TO WIN. I HEARD HE HAS A LOT OF MONEY BET ON HIS TEAM FOR THAT GAME!
THAT'S IT! THAT GUY'S TRYING EVERY DIRTY TRICK TO HURT MY TEAM'S CHANCES! HE'S A DANGEROUS MAN!
SUDDENLY
THOSE SHOTS CAME FROM UP HERE!
OH-OH! SEE YOU AGAIN, BANNON- WHEN WE'RE NOT SO PRESSED FOR TIME!
LATER..... IN A HOUSE ON THE SUBURBS.... EXIT BATMAN AND ROBIN -- ENTER BRUCE WAYNE AND YOUNG DICK GRAYSON!
DICKEY, M'LAD- I'VE A STRANGE FEELING WE'RE GOING TO HAVE A LITTLE EXCITEMENT IN THE NEXT COUPLE OF DAYS!
YOU'VE ONLY A FEELING-- I KNOW IT!
THAT NIGHT, STACY'S MEN REPORT AND TELL OF THEIR ENCOUNTER WITH THE BATMAN!
SO, THE BATMAN SHOWED UP, EH? THAT'S BAD--- VERY BAD!
YEAH -- HE'S LIABLE TA MAKE TROUBLE FER US! THAT GUY'S POISON!
WE GOTTA GET THAT GUY OUTA THE WAY!
YOU'RE RIGHT! WE'VE GOT TO GET RID OF THE BATMAN -- AND I KNOW JUST THE WAY TO DO IT! YOU SEE-- I THINK I KNOW WHO THE BATMAN IS!
HUH!
WHA..?
ONE OF THE STOOLIES THAT WORKS FOR THE POLICE TELLS ME THAT THIS SOCIETY GUY, BRUCE WAYNE, IS ALWAYS HANGIN' AROUND HEADQUARTERS! SEEMS HE'S A FRIEND OF COMMISSIONER GORDON!

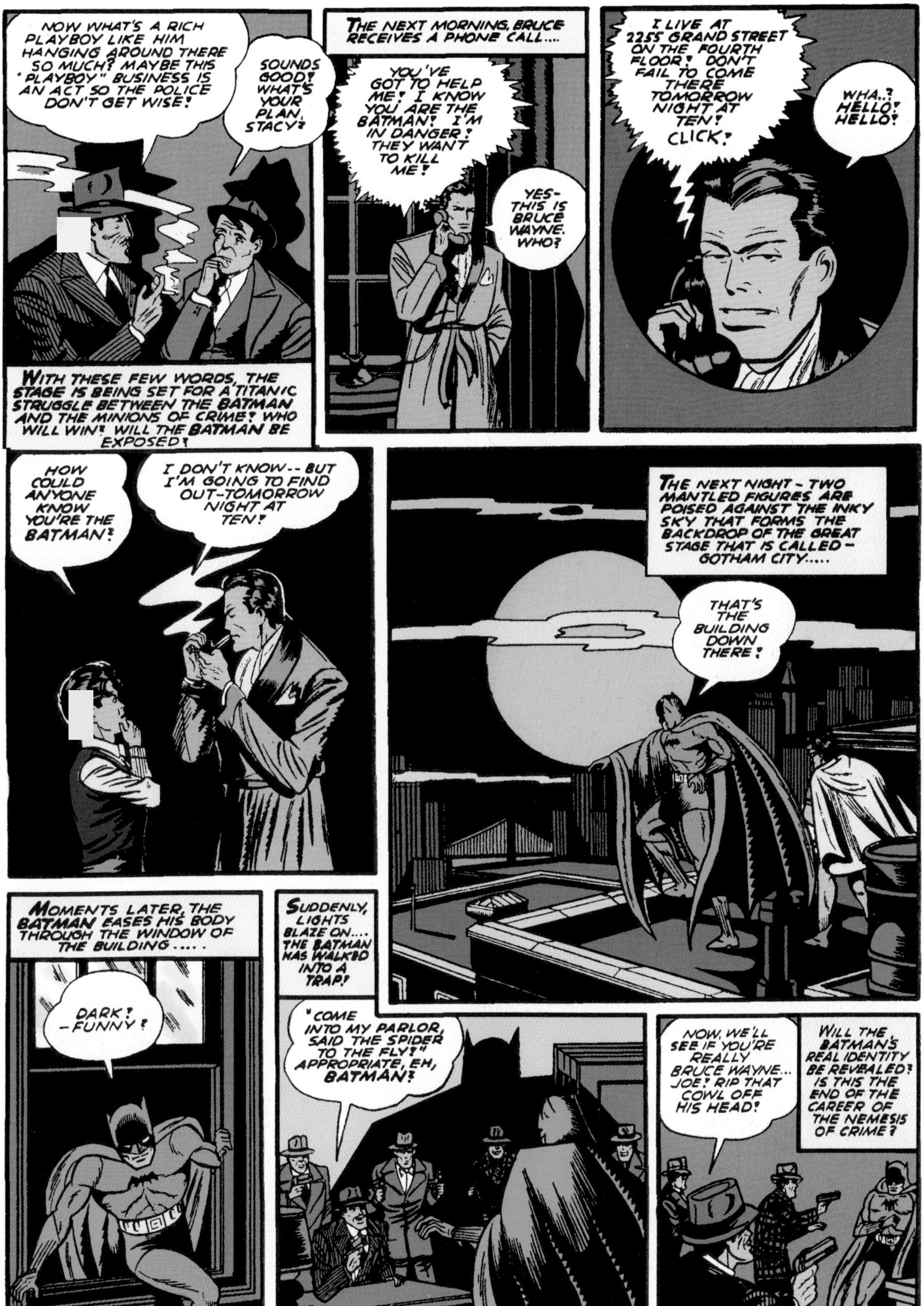
NOW WHAT'S A RICH PLAYBOY LIKE HIM HANGING AROUND THERE SO MUCH? MAYBE THIS "PLAYBOY" BUSINESS IS AN ACT SO THE POLICE DON'T GET WISE!
SOUNDS GOOD! WHAT'S YOUR PLAN, STACY?
WITH THESE FEW WORDS, THE STAGE IS BEING SET FOR A TITANIC STRUGGLE BETWEEN THE BATMAN AND THE MINIONS OF CRIME! WHO WILL WIN? WILL THE BATMAN BE EXPOSED?
THE NEXT MORNING, BRUCE RECEIVES A PHONE CALL....
YOU'VE GOT TO HELP ME! I KNOW YOU ARE THE BATMAN! I'M IN DANGER! THEY WANT TO KILL ME!
YES-THIS IS BRUCE WAYNE. WHO?
I LIVE AT 2255 GRAND STREET ON THE FOURTH FLOOR! DON'T FAIL TO COME THERE TOMORROW NIGHT AT TEN! CLICK!
WHA..? HELLO! HELLO!
HOW COULD ANYONE KNOW YOU'RE THE BATMAN?
I DON'T KNOW-- BUT I'M GOING TO FIND OUT-TOMORROW NIGHT AT TEN!
THE NEXT NIGHT - TWO MANTLED FIGURES ARE POISED AGAINST THE INKY SKY THAT FORMS THE BACKDROP OF THE GREAT STAGE THAT IS CALLED - GOTHAM CITY.....
THAT'S THE BUILDING DOWN THERE!
MOMENTS LATER, THE BATMAN EASES HIS BODY THROUGH THE WINDOW OF THE BUILDING.....
DARK! -FUNNY!
SUDDENLY, LIGHTS BLAZE ON.... THE BATMAN HAS WALKED INTO A TRAP!
"COME INTO MY PARLOR, SAID THE SPIDER TO THE FLY!" APPROPRIATE, EH, BATMAN?
NOW, WE'LL SEE IF YOU'RE REALLY BRUCE WAYNE... JOE! RIP THAT COWL OFF HIS HEAD!
WILL THE BATMAN'S REAL IDENTITY BE REVEALED? IS THIS THE END OF THE CAREER OF THE NEMESIS OF CRIME?

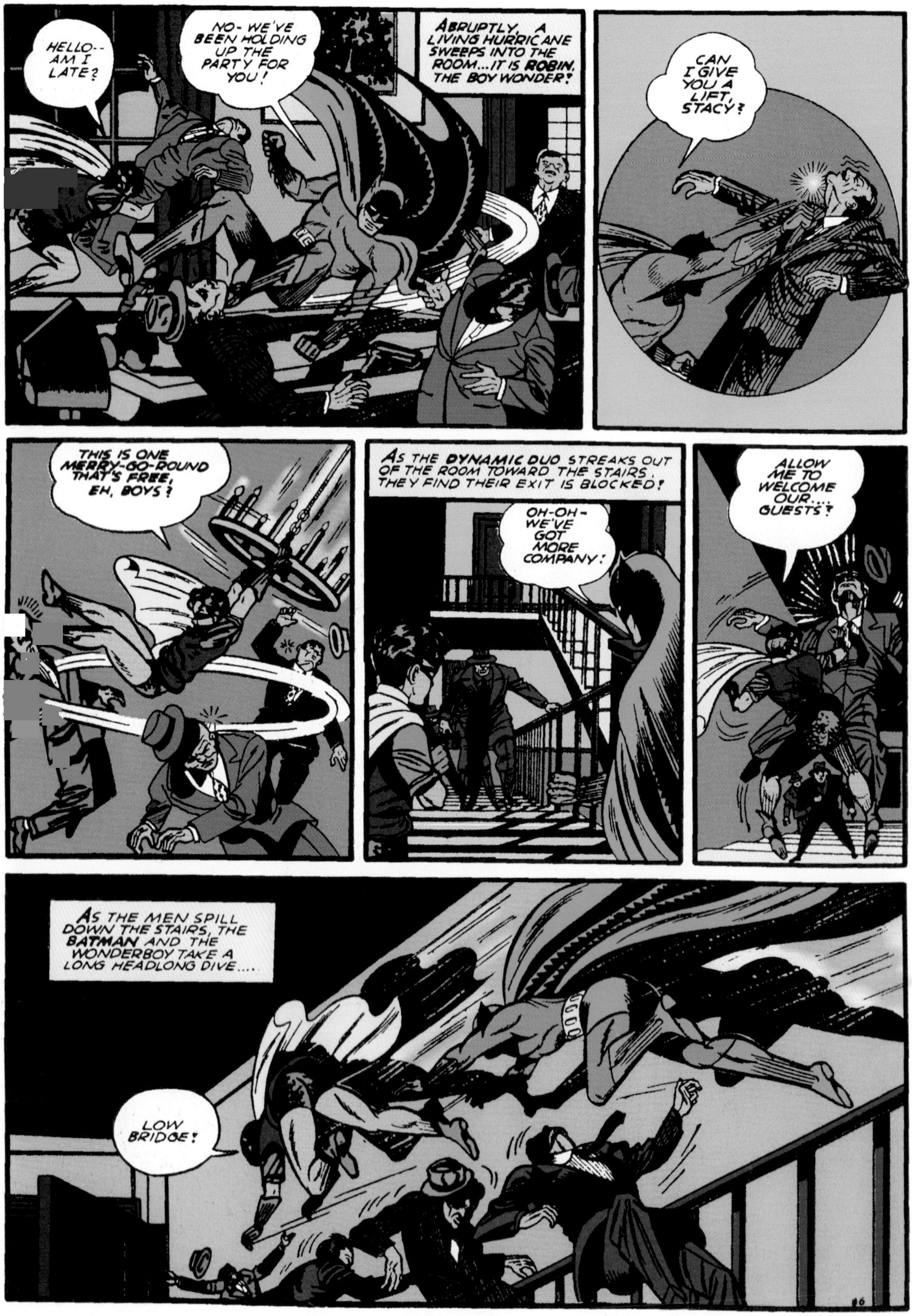
HELLO-- AM I LATE?
NO- WE'VE BEEN HOLDING UP THE PARTY FOR YOU!
ABRUPTLY, A LIVING HURRICANE SWEEPS INTO THE ROOM...IT IS ROBIN, THE BOY WONDER!
CAN I GIVE YOU A LIFT, STACY?
THIS IS ONE MERRY-GO-ROUND THAT'S FREE, EH, BOYS?
AS THE DYNAMIC DUO STREAKS OUT OF THE ROOM TOWARD THE STAIRS, THEY FIND THEIR EXIT IS BLOCKED!
OH-OH- WE'VE GOT MORE COMPANY!
ALLOW ME TO WELCOME OUR.... GUESTS!
AS THE MEN SPILL DOWN THE STAIRS, THE BATMAN AND THE WONDERBOY TAKE A LONG HEADLONG DIVE....
LOW BRIDGE!

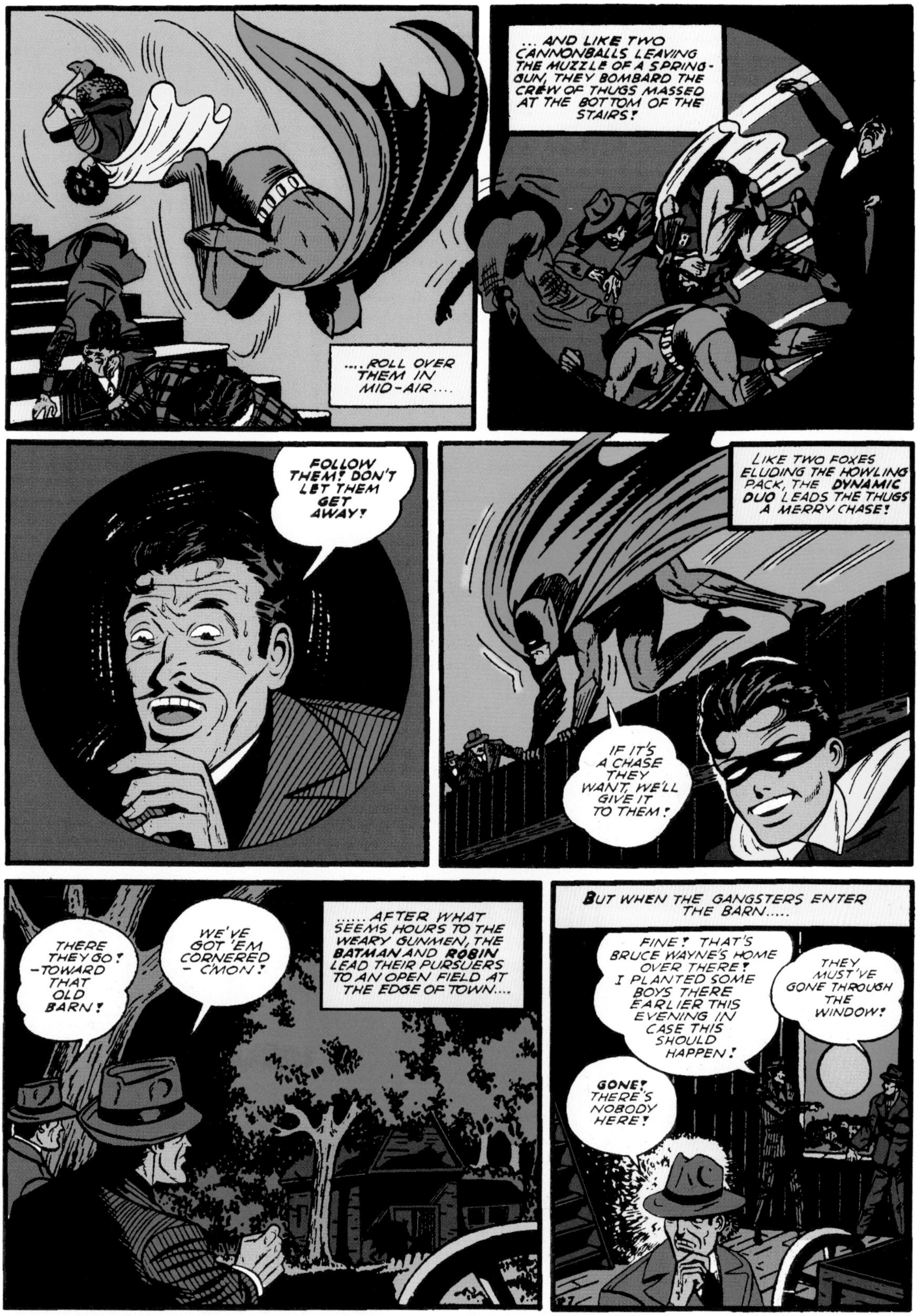
....ROLL OVER THEM IN MID-AIR....
... AND LIKE TWO CANNONBALLS LEAVING THE MUZZLE OF A SPRING-GUN, THEY BOMBARD THE CREW OF THUGS MASSED AT THE BOTTOM OF THE STAIRS!
FOLLOW THEM! DON'T LET THEM GET AWAY!
LIKE TWO FOXES ELUDING THE HOWLING PACK, THE DYNAMIC DUO LEADS THE THUGS A MERRY CHASE!
IF IT'S A CHASE THEY WANT, WE'LL GIVE IT TO THEM!
THERE THEY GO! -TOWARD THAT OLD BARN!
WE'VE GOT 'EM CORNERED - C'MON!
...... AFTER WHAT SEEMS HOURS TO THE WEARY GUNMEN, THE BATMAN AND ROBIN LEAD THEIR PURSUERS TO AN OPEN FIELD AT THE EDGE OF TOWN....
BUT WHEN THE GANGSTERS ENTER THE BARN.....
FINE! THAT'S BRUCE WAYNE'S HOME OVER THERE! I PLANTED SOME BOYS THERE EARLIER THIS EVENING IN CASE THIS SHOULD HAPPEN!
THEY MUST'VE GONE THROUGH THE WINDOW!
GONE! THERE'S NOBODY HERE!

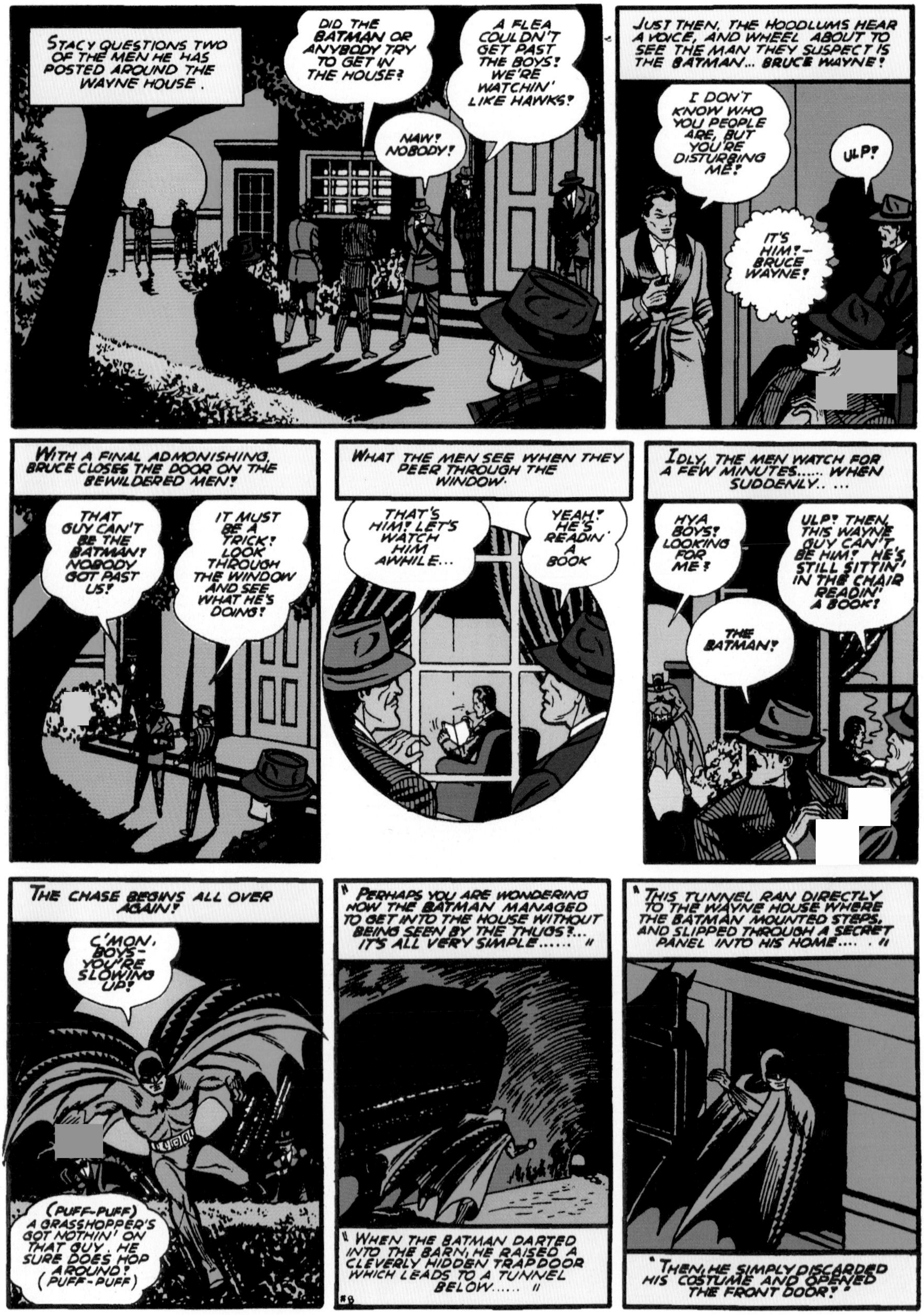
STACY QUESTIONS TWO OF THE MEN HE HAS POSTED AROUND THE WAYNE HOUSE.
DID THE BATMAN OR ANYBODY TRY TO GET IN THE HOUSE?
NAW! NOBODY!
A FLEA COULDN'T GET PAST THE BOYS! WE'RE WATCHIN' LIKE HAWKS!
JUST THEN, THE HOODLUMS HEAR A VOICE, AND WHEEL ABOUT TO SEE THE MAN THEY SUSPECT IS THE BATMAN... BRUCE WAYNE!
I DON'T KNOW WHO YOU PEOPLE ARE, BUT YOU'RE DISTURBING ME!
ULP!
IT'S HIM!-- BRUCE WAYNE!
WITH A FINAL ADMONISHING, BRUCE CLOSES THE DOOR ON THE BEWILDERED MEN!
THAT GUY CAN'T BE THE BATMAN! NOBODY GOT PAST US!
IT MUST BE A TRICK! LOOK THROUGH THE WINDOW AND SEE WHAT HE'S DOING!
WHAT THE MEN SEE WHEN THEY PEER THROUGH THE WINDOW.
THAT'S HIM! LET'S WATCH HIM AWHILE...
YEAH! HE'S READIN' A BOOK
IDLY, THE MEN WATCH FOR A FEW MINUTES...... WHEN SUDDENLY.. ...
HYA BOYS! LOOKING FOR ME?
ULP! THEN, THIS WAYNE GUY CAN'T BE HIM! HE'S STILL SITTIN' IN THE CHAIR READIN' A BOOK!
THE BATMAN!
THE CHASE BEGINS ALL OVER AGAIN!
C'MON, BOYS-- YOU'RE SLOWING UP!
(PUFF-PUFF) A GRASSHOPPER'S GOT NOTHIN' ON THAT GUY. HE SURE DOES HOP AROUND! (PUFF-PUFF)
"PERHAPS YOU ARE WONDERING HOW THE BATMAN MANAGED TO GET INTO THE HOUSE WITHOUT BEING SEEN BY THE THUGS?... IT'S ALL VERY SIMPLE...... "
"WHEN THE BATMAN DARTED INTO THE BARN, HE RAISED A CLEVERLY HIDDEN TRAPDOOR WHICH LEADS TO A TUNNEL BELOW...... "
#8
"THIS TUNNEL RAN DIRECTLY TO THE WAYNE HOUSE WHERE THE BATMAN MOUNTED STEPS, AND SLIPPED THROUGH A SECRET PANEL INTO HIS HOME.... . "
"THEN, HE SIMPLY DISCARDED HIS COSTUME AND OPENED THE FRONT DOOR!"

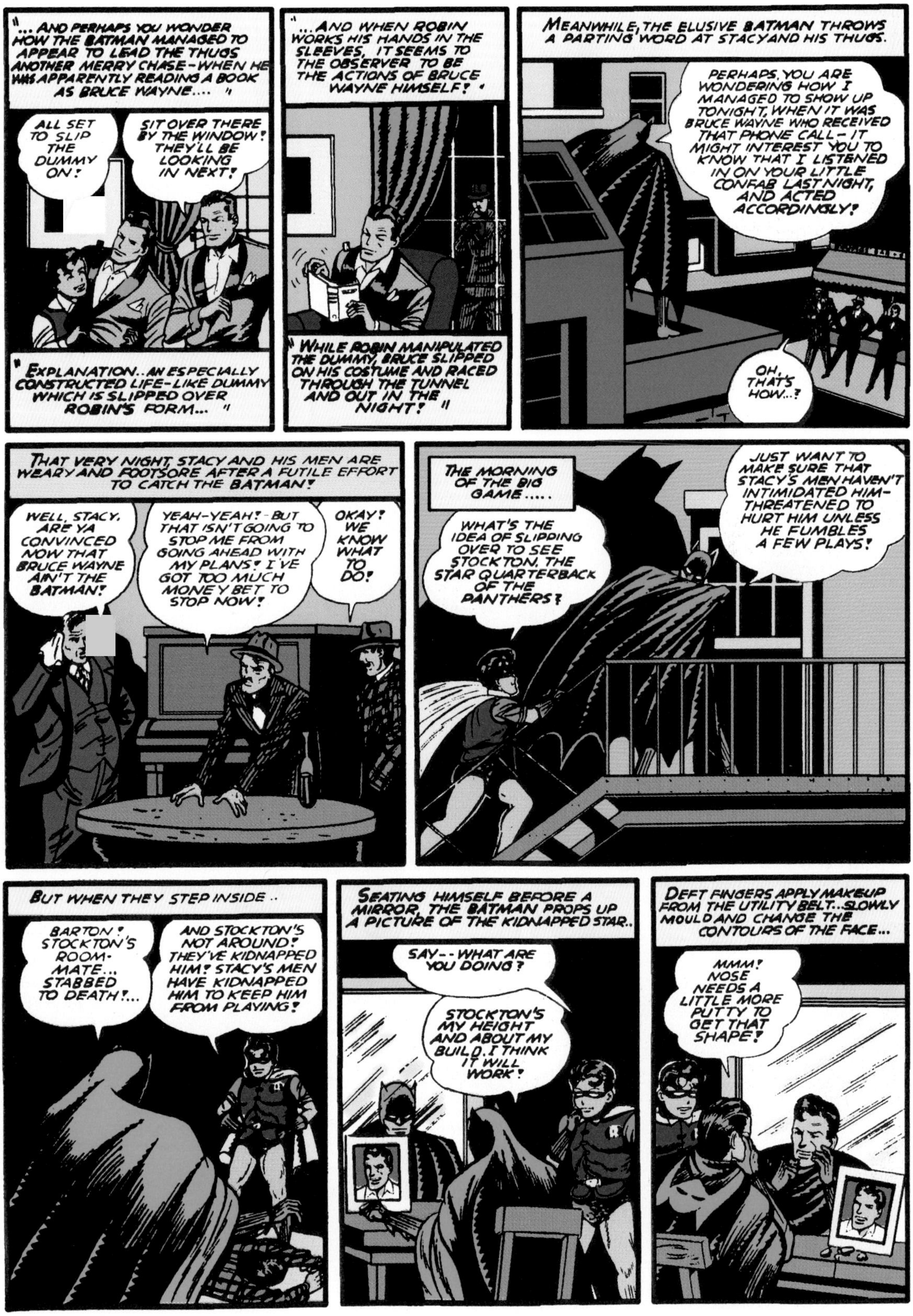
"...AND PERHAPS YOU WONDER HOW THE BATMAN MANAGED TO APPEAR TO LEAD THE THUGS ANOTHER MERRY CHASE-WHEN HE WAS APPARENTLY READING A BOOK AS BRUCE WAYNE.... "
ALL SET TO SLIP THE DUMMY ON!
SIT OVER THERE BY THE WINDOW! THEY'LL BE LOOKING IN NEXT!
" EXPLANATION..AN ESPECIALLY CONSTRUCTED LIFE-LIKE DUMMY WHICH IS SLIPPED OVER ROBIN'S FORM... "
"...AND WHEN ROBIN WORKS HIS HANDS IN THE SLEEVES, IT SEEMS TO THE OBSERVER TO BE THE ACTIONS OF BRUCE WAYNE HIMSELF! "
" WHILE ROBIN MANIPULATED THE DUMMY, BRUCE SLIPPED ON HIS COSTUME AND RACED THROUGH THE TUNNEL AND OUT IN THE NIGHT! "
MEANWHILE, THE ELUSIVE BATMAN THROWS A PARTING WORD AT STACY AND HIS THUGS.
PERHAPS, YOU ARE WONDERING HOW I MANAGED TO SHOW UP TONIGHT, WHEN IT WAS BRUCE WAYNE WHO RECEIVED THAT PHONE CALL - IT MIGHT INTEREST YOU TO KNOW THAT I LISTENED IN ON YOUR LITTLE CONFAB LAST NIGHT, AND ACTED ACCORDINGLY!
OH, THAT'S HOW...?
THAT VERY NIGHT, STACY AND HIS MEN ARE WEARY AND FOOTSORE AFTER A FUTILE EFFORT TO CATCH THE BATMAN!
WELL, STACY, ARE YA CONVINCED NOW THAT BRUCE WAYNE AIN'T THE BATMAN!
YEAH-YEAH! - BUT THAT ISN'T GOING TO STOP ME FROM GOING AHEAD WITH MY PLANS! I'VE GOT TOO MUCH MONEY BET TO STOP NOW!
OKAY! WE KNOW WHAT TO DO!
THE MORNING OF THE BIG GAME.....
WHAT'S THE IDEA OF SLIPPING OVER TO SEE STOCKTON, THE STAR QUARTERBACK OF THE PANTHERS?
JUST WANT TO MAKE SURE THAT STACY'S MEN HAVEN'T INTIMIDATED HIM-THREATENED TO HURT HIM UNLESS HE FUMBLES A FEW PLAYS!
BUT WHEN THEY STEP INSIDE ..
BARTON! STOCKTON'S ROOM-MATE... STABBED TO DEATH!...
AND STOCKTON'S NOT AROUND! THEY'VE KIDNAPPED HIM! STACY'S MEN HAVE KIDNAPPED HIM TO KEEP HIM FROM PLAYING!
SEATING HIMSELF BEFORE A MIRROR, THE BATMAN PROPS UP A PICTURE OF THE KIDNAPPED STAR..
SAY--WHAT ARE YOU DOING?
STOCKTON'S MY HEIGHT AND ABOUT MY BUILD. I THINK IT WILL WORK!
DEFT FINGERS APPLY MAKEUP FROM THE UTILITY BELT...SLOWLY MOULD AND CHANGE THE CONTOURS OF THE FACE...
MMM! NOSE NEEDS A LITTLE MORE PUTTY TO GET THAT SHAPE!

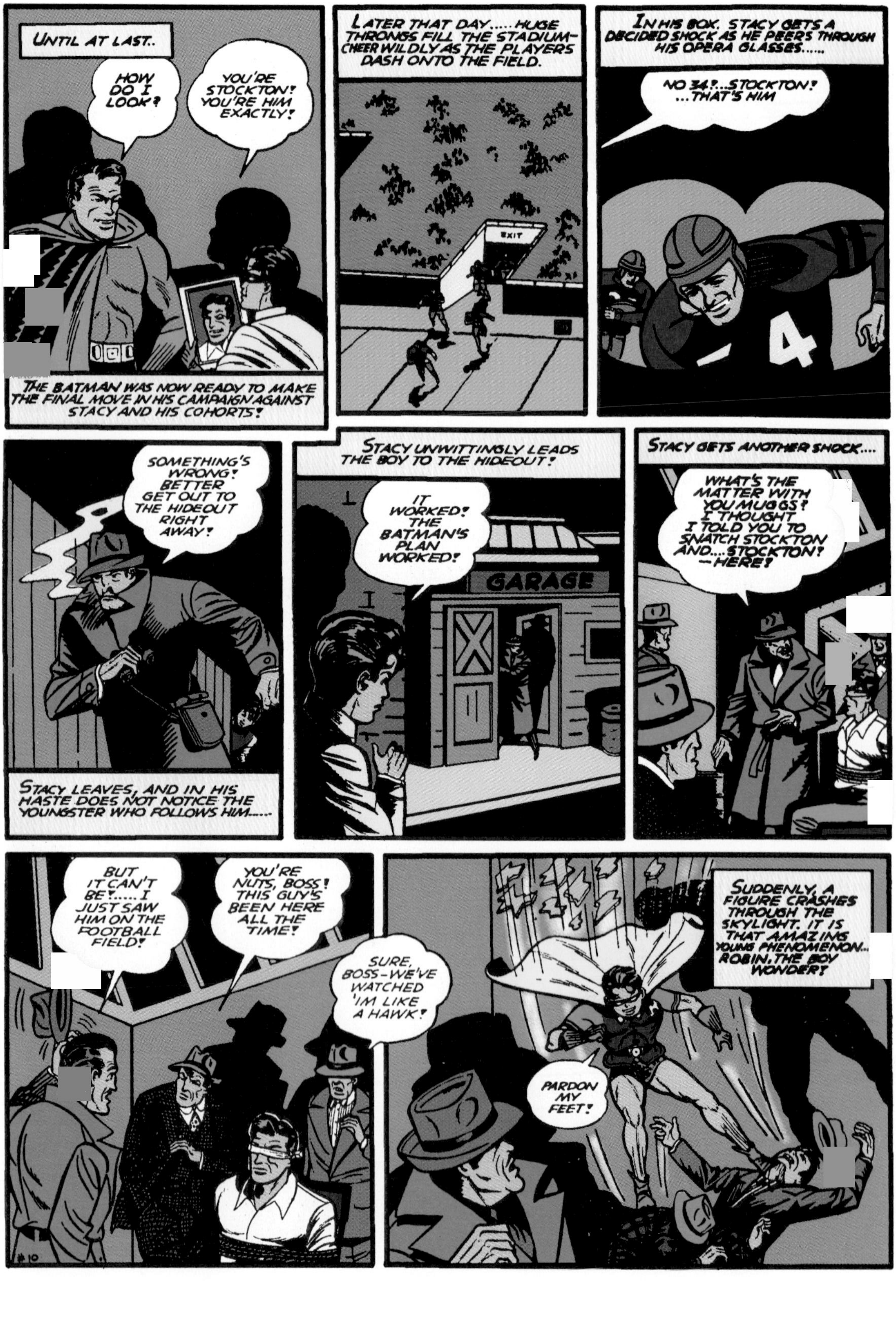
UNTIL AT LAST..
HOW DO I LOOK?
YOU'RE STOCKTON! YOU'RE HIM EXACTLY!
THE BATMAN WAS NOW READY TO MAKE THE FINAL MOVE IN HIS CAMPAIGN AGAINST STACY AND HIS COHORTS!
LATER THAT DAY..... HUGE THRONGS FILL THE STADIUM- CHEER WILDLY AS THE PLAYERS DASH ONTO THE FIELD.
EXIT
IN HIS BOX, STACY GETS A DECIDED SHOCK AS HE PEERS THROUGH HIS OPERA GLASSES......
NO 34?...STOCKTON? ...THAT'S HIM
SOMETHING'S WRONG! BETTER GET OUT TO THE HIDEOUT RIGHT AWAY!
STACY LEAVES, AND IN HIS HASTE DOES NOT NOTICE THE YOUNGSTER WHO FOLLOWS HIM.....
STACY UNWITTINGLY LEADS THE BOY TO THE HIDEOUT!
IT WORKED! THE BATMAN'S PLAN WORKED!
GARAGE
STACY GETS ANOTHER SHOCK....
WHAT'S THE MATTER WITH YOU MUGGS? I THOUGHT I TOLD YOU TO SNATCH STOCKTON AND....STOCKTON? —HERE?
BUT IT CAN'T BE?.....I JUST SAW HIM ON THE FOOTBALL FIELD!
YOU'RE NUTS, BOSS! THIS GUY'S BEEN HERE ALL THE TIME!
SURE, BOSS-WE'VE WATCHED 'IM LIKE A HAWK!
SUDDENLY, A FIGURE CRASHES THROUGH THE SKYLIGHT. IT IS THAT AMAZING YOUNG PHENOMENON... ROBIN, THE BOY WONDER!
PARDON MY FEET!

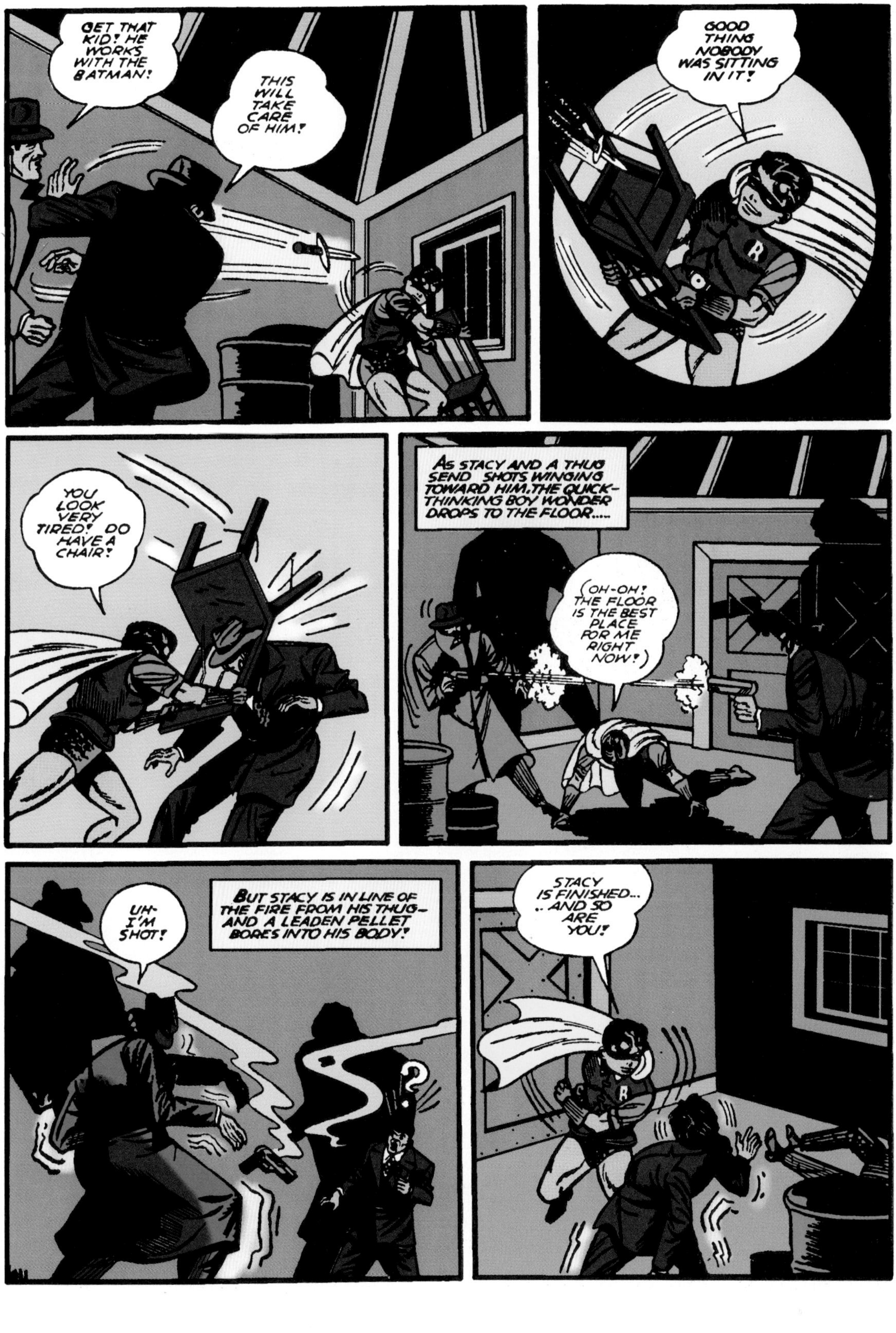
GET THAT KID! HE WORKS WITH THE BATMAN!
THIS WILL TAKE CARE OF HIM!
GOOD THING NOBODY WAS SITTING IN IT!
YOU LOOK VERY TIRED! DO HAVE A CHAIR!
AS STACY AND A THUG SEND SHOTS WINGING TOWARD HIM. THE QUICK-THINKING BOY WONDER DROPS TO THE FLOOR.....
(OH-OH! THE FLOOR IS THE BEST PLACE FOR ME RIGHT NOW!)
UH-I'M SHOT!
BUT STACY IS IN LINE OF THE FIRE FROM HIS THUG-AND A LEADEN PELLET BORES INTO HIS BODY!
STACY IS FINISHED... ..AND SO ARE YOU!

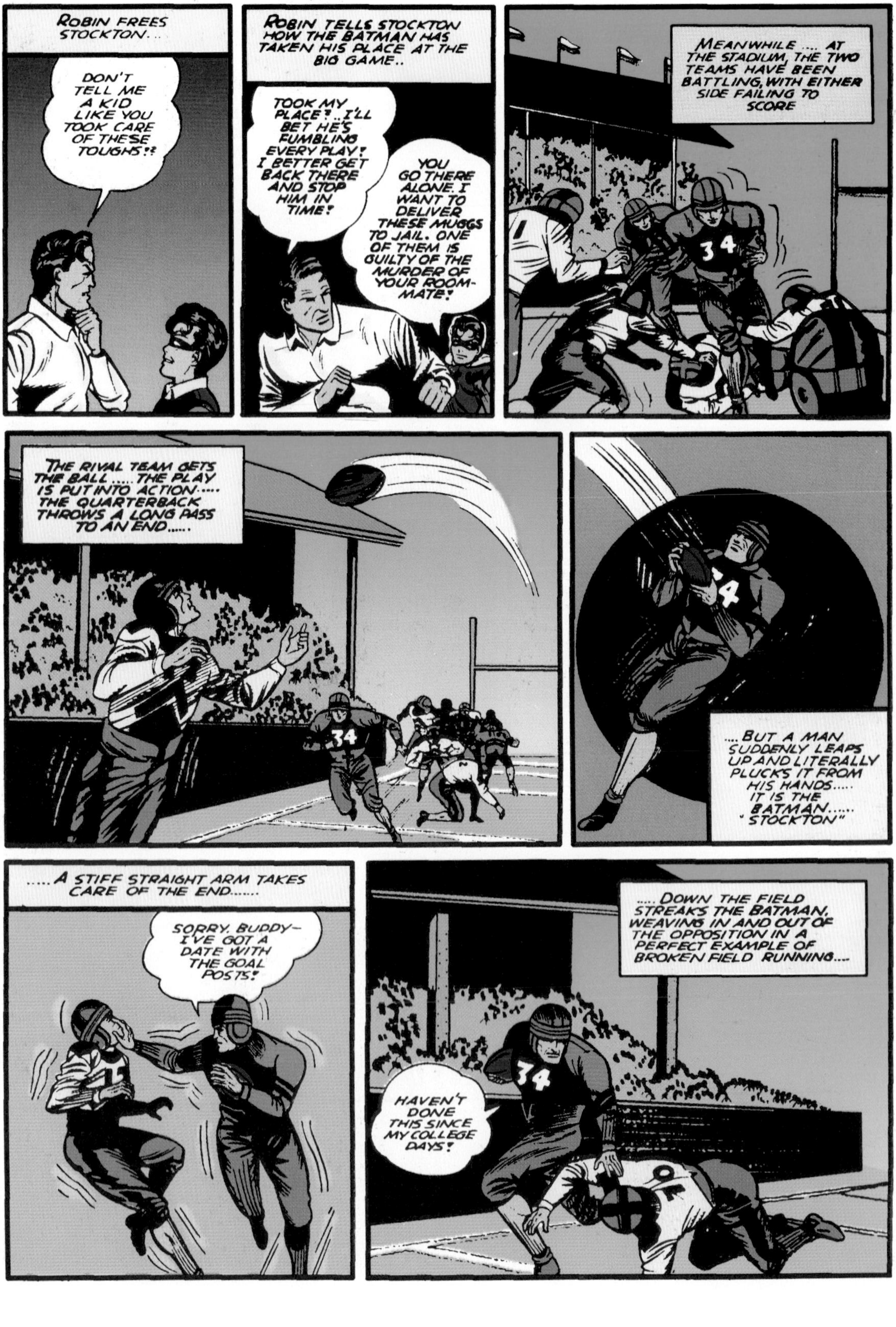
ROBIN FREES STOCKTON...
DON'T TELL ME A KID LIKE YOU TOOK CARE OF THESE TOUGHS?!
ROBIN TELLS STOCKTON HOW THE BATMAN HAS TAKEN HIS PLACE AT THE BIG GAME..
TOOK MY PLACE?..I'LL BET HE'S FUMBLING EVERY PLAY! I BETTER GET BACK THERE AND STOP HIM IN TIME!
YOU GO THERE ALONE. I WANT TO DELIVER THESE MUGGS TO JAIL. ONE OF THEM IS GUILTY OF THE MURDER OF YOUR ROOM-MATE!
MEANWHILE .... AT THE STADIUM, THE TWO TEAMS HAVE BEEN BATTLING, WITH EITHER SIDE FAILING TO SCORE
THE RIVAL TEAM GETS THE BALL .....THE PLAY IS PUT INTO ACTION..... THE QUARTERBACK THROWS A LONG PASS TO AN END.....
....BUT A MAN SUDDENLY LEAPS UP AND LITERALLY PLUCKS IT FROM HIS HANDS..... IT IS THE BATMAN...... "STOCKTON"
.....A STIFF STRAIGHT ARM TAKES CARE OF THE END.......
SORRY, BUDDY— I'VE GOT A DATE WITH THE GOAL POSTS!
.....DOWN THE FIELD STREAKS THE BATMAN, WEAVING IN AND OUT OF THE OPPOSITION IN A PERFECT EXAMPLE OF BROKEN FIELD RUNNING....
HAVEN'T DONE THIS SINCE MY COLLEGE DAYS!

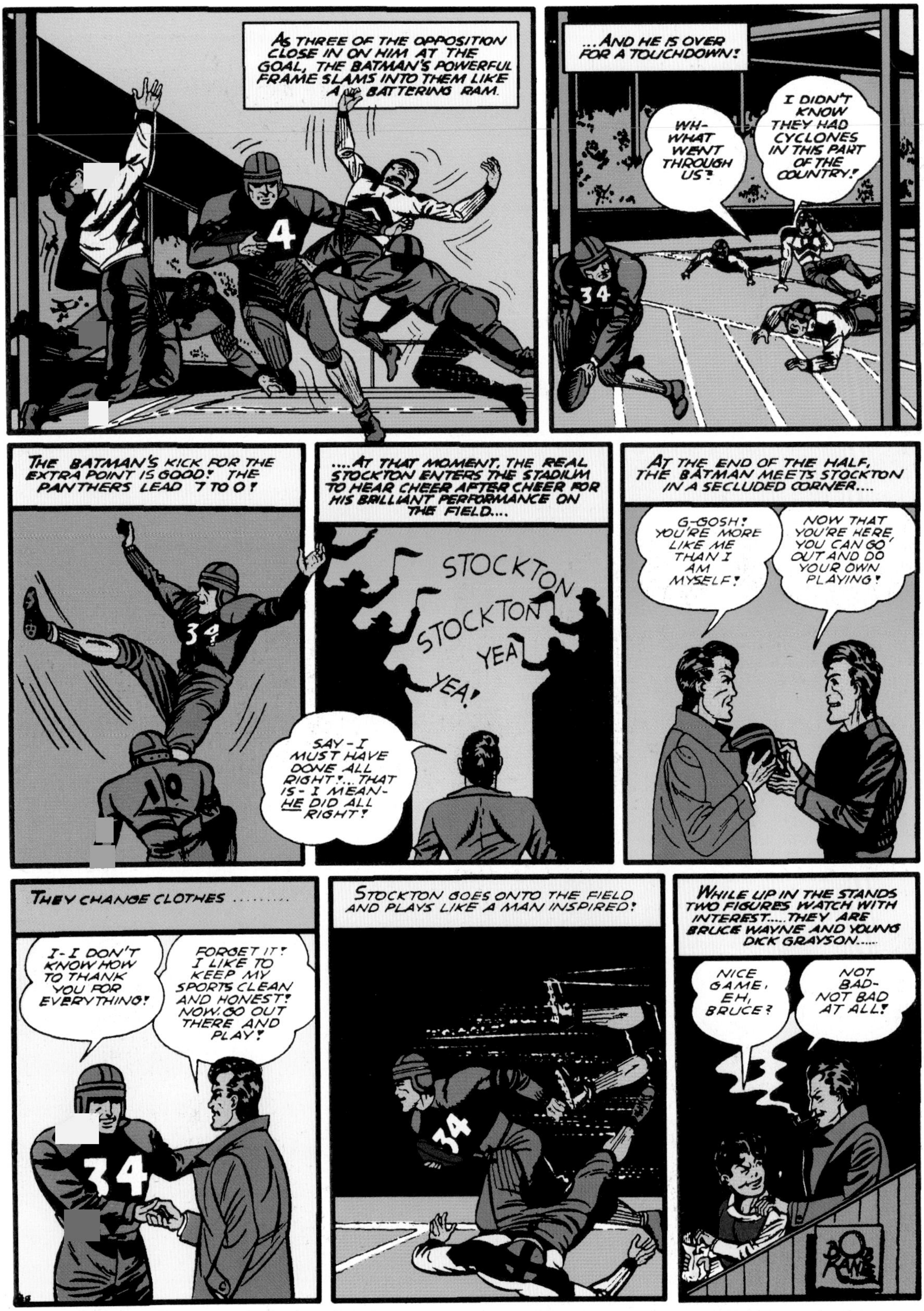
AS THREE OF THE OPPOSITION CLOSE IN ON HIM AT THE GOAL, THE BATMAN'S POWERFUL FRAME SLAMS INTO THEM LIKE A BATTERING RAM.
4
...AND HE IS OVER FOR A TOUCHDOWN!
WH-WHAT WENT THROUGH US?
I DIDN'T KNOW THEY HAD CYCLONES IN THIS PART OF THE COUNTRY!
34
THE BATMAN'S KICK FOR THE EXTRA POINT IS GOOD! THE PANTHERS LEAD 7 TO 0!
34
10
....AT THAT MOMENT, THE REAL STOCKTON ENTERS THE STADIUM TO HEAR CHEER AFTER CHEER FOR HIS BRILLIANT PERFORMANCE ON THE FIELD....
STOCKTON
STOCKTON
YEA
YEA!
SAY - I MUST HAVE DONE ALL RIGHT!... THAT IS - I MEAN - HE DID ALL RIGHT!
AT THE END OF THE HALF, THE BATMAN MEETS STOCKTON IN A SECLUDED CORNER....
G-GOSH! YOU'RE MORE LIKE ME THAN I AM MYSELF!
NOW THAT YOU'RE HERE, YOU CAN GO OUT AND DO YOUR OWN PLAYING!
THEY CHANGE CLOTHES ....
I-I DON'T KNOW HOW TO THANK YOU FOR EVERYTHING!
FORGET IT! I LIKE TO KEEP MY SPORTS CLEAN AND HONEST! NOW, GO OUT THERE AND PLAY!
34
STOCKTON GOES ONTO THE FIELD AND PLAYS LIKE A MAN INSPIRED!
34
WHILE UP IN THE STANDS TWO FIGURES WATCH WITH INTEREST.....THEY ARE BRUCE WAYNE AND YOUNG DICK GRAYSON.....
NICE GAME, EH, BRUCE?
NOT BAD-NOT BAD AT ALL!
BOB KANE

WHITNEY ELLSWORTH

Whitney Ellsworth was born November 27, 1908. In late 1934, he became associated with Major Malcolm Wheeler-Nicholson's National Allied Publishing, a precursor of DC Comics. He wrote and drew stories, pencilled and inked covers, and served as co-editor of Nicholson's titles as of mid-1936. In 1940, he was made editorial director for all DC titles.

In addition, he wrote some of *The Adventures of Superman* radio shows and a number of the *Superman* newspaper continuities, among other things. Beginning in 1940, and for about six years, Ellsworth drew rough dummy cover layouts for DC's top titles, including *Batman*.

Serving as consultant on the first season of *The Adventures of Superman* television program, he subsequently became producer, story editor, legal advisor and business manager for the balance of the series, co-writing a number of episodes as well. Ellsworth wrote the *Batman and Robin* newspaper strip continuities from 1966–1970, departing DC in 1971. He died September 7, 1980.

BILL FINGER

William Finger met cartoonist Bob Kane at a party in 1938. They subsequently collaborated on several adventure strips, with Finger writing Batman's first two adventures in *Detective Comics*.

Although chronically and notoriously tardy with submissions, Finger simultaneously was a gifted and prodigious writer, turning out thousands of pages of work in his lifetime. For DC, he worked on numerous characters, including Batman, Green Lantern, Johnny Quick, Superman, Superboy, Challengers of the Unknown and Lois Lane. He scripted a number of the 1940s daily and Sunday *Batman and Robin* newspaper strip continuities and wrote for Quality Comics *(Plastic Man)*, Fawcett Publications and Timely *(Captain America Comics* and *All Winners Comics)*.

He wrote for the *77 Sunset Strip, The Roaring Twenties* and *Hawaiian Eye* TV shows during the late 1950s and early 1960s and worked on two episodes of the *Batman* TV series (#45: "The Clock King's Crazy Crimes," and #46: "The King Gets Crowned"). He died in Manhattan on January 24, 1974.

GARDNER FOX

Gardner Fox was born in 1911. A young lawyer, he began writing for DC Comics in 1937. Throughout his career in comics, he generally worked for DC, with some scripting for Columbia, ME, Avon, E.C., Warren, Skywald and Marvel. A few of his most memorable creations include Flash, Adam Strange, Dr. Fate and Hawkman.

He is considered by some to be the most prolific writer in the history of comic books, having written at least 4,250 stories by his own count. Fox also wrote over 100 novels and many short stories for various pulp magazines. An author of breadth as well as depth, he wrote science fiction, westerns, mysteries, horror and funny animal comics in addition to super-heroes.

Fox was the first writer to handle a Batman story after Bill Finger. His initial script for the Gotham Guardian appeared in *Detective Comics #29*, only the third adventure of Batman.

He died December 24, 1986.

BOB KANE

In 1936, Bob Kane pencilled and inked his first comic book work, Hiram Hick. By 1938, he was selling short, humorous fillers to DC Comics, including Jest a Second, Oscar the Gumshoe and Ginger Snap.

Kane and writer Bill Finger collaborated on Batman, with the first story appearing in *Detective Comics #27* (May 1939). In the earliest years of Batman, Kane was pencilling and doing significant amounts of inking, but in 1943, he discontinued comic books to concentrate on pencilling the daily *Batman and Robin* newspaper strip. After the strip's 1946 cancellation, he returned to comics with the help of several assistants, until departing in 1968.

He developed the anthropomorphic Batman and Robin par-ody *Courageous Cat and Minute Mouse* (1960). Another animated show of his, *Cool McCool*, premiered in 1966.

The popularity of the *Batman* television series brought Kane and his art to the forefront in 1966. Kane has had a number of one-man art shows in galleries and museums nationwide and released a series of five limited-edition lithographs in 1978 with another group in 1989. He served as a consultant on the immensely successful 1989 movie *Batman*.

SHELDON MOLDOFF

Shelly Moldoff began illustrating filler pages for DC Comics in the late 1930s. He was the first artist to assist Bob Kane on Batman *(Detective Comics #30–35)*, inking backgrounds and lettering.

During the early 1940s, Moldoff worked on Hawkman, Black Pirate, Clip Carson and others in addition to drawing covers for *Flash* and *Green Lantern*.

He worked for Quality, Fawcett, Pines, E.C., ACG and Marvel, returning to DC in the 1950s with *Mr. District Attorney, House of Mystery* and many others. In 1953, Moldoff became Kane's regular ghost, pencilling Batman stories and covers until 1967. He illustrated the initial ten weeks of the *Batman and Robin* newspaper strip in 1966.

He was a member of the National Cartoonists Society and did over 300 storyboards for animated TV shows, including *Courageous Cat and Minute Mouse, Cool McCool*, and *Professor Whizdom*. In recent years, he has written and illustrated advertising comics for Red Lobster, Shoney's and Big Boy restaurants, among others.

JERRY ROBINSON

Jerry Robinson was 17, studying creative writing at Columbia University, when he began working on Batman late in 1939. Initially lettering and inking backgrounds, within three years he was completely pencilling, lettering, inking and even coloring some Batman stories and covers.

Robinson's credits include comic book work on Vigilante, The Black Terror, Lassie, and Bat Masterson, among others. He created and illustrated various syndicated newspaper features and has taught and lectured on graphic journalism.

Robinson is the only past president of both the National Cartoonists Society and the Association of American Editorial Cartoonists. He has written several books and illustrated over 30 others.

He maintains a full schedule with a syndicated political cartoon, *Life With Robinson*, and as President and Editorial Director of Cartoonists & Writers Syndicate. He serves on the Board of Directors of the International Museum of Cartoon Art in Boca Raton, Florida, and has curated major museum and gallery exhibitions of cartoon art in the U.S., Europe and the Far East.

GEORGE ROUSSOS

George Roussos attended the Pratt Institute, later studying with illustrator Frank Riley. Roussos's career in the comic book field spans over a half century, and his contributions are too numerous to describe here in detail. Some highlights:

His first comic book work appeared in 1940 on Batman, where he began lettering and inking backgrounds. Roussos later pencilled, inked and colored Airwave, as well as inking Johnny Quick, Star Spangled Kid, Vigilante, Gang Busters and other DC characters and titles.

From the late 1940s and into the 1950s, he worked freelance for a number of other comic book publishers, including Harvey, Hillman, Avon, Ziff-Davis, Fiction House, Timely, Prize and Pines. In 1963, he began inking stories for Marvel, including X-Men, Avengers, Fantastic Four, Captain America, Ghost Rider and many others. He left DC around 1970 to work full-time for Marvel. He soon became cover colorist, working with Stan Lee. Roussos still colors for Marvel today. He has also worked on syndicated newspaper strips and in advertising.

BIOGRAPHICAL MATERIAL RESEARCHED AND WRITTEN BY JOE DESRIS.